CBT: Science Into Practice

Series Editor
Nikolaos Kazantzis, Cognitive Behavior Therapy Research Unit,
Melbourne, Australia

This series addresses topics that reflect current thinking in the field of cognitive behavior therapy, the most widely accepted form of therapy across mental health disciplines. Despite the consensus that CBT is an effective treatment modality, much of the existing clinical literature focuses on single facets, such as specific disorders or populations. Mostly it does not take into account the latest evidence for transdiagnostic change mechanisms and processes. This series provides guidance on how the latest evidence can be translated into practice. Volumes focus on enhancing flexibility in both the selection and delivery of techniques tailored to individual clients. Each provides clinical insights enhanced by case studies and vignettes to ensure relevance for the practicing professional.

Marcella L. Woud

Editor

Interpretational Processing Biases in Emotional Psychopathology

From Experimental Investigation to
Clinical Practice

 Springer

Editor
Marcella L. Woud
Mental Health Research and Treatment Center
Faculty of Psychology, Ruhr-University Bochum
Bochum, Germany

ISSN 2946-5427   ISSN 2946-5419   (electronic)
CBT: Science Into Practice
ISBN 978-3-031-23652-5   ISBN 978-3-031-23650-1   (eBook)
https://doi.org/10.1007/978-3-031-23650-1

© The Editor(s) (if applicable) and The Author(s), under exclusive license to Springer Nature Switzerland AG 2023
This work is subject to copyright. All rights are solely and exclusively licensed by the Publisher, whether the whole or part of the material is concerned, specifically the rights of translation, reprinting, reuse of illustrations, recitation, broadcasting, reproduction on microfilms or in any other physical way, and transmission or information storage and retrieval, electronic adaptation, computer software, or by similar or dissimilar methodology now known or hereafter developed.
The use of general descriptive names, registered names, trademarks, service marks, etc. in this publication does not imply, even in the absence of a specific statement, that such names are exempt from the relevant protective laws and regulations and therefore free for general use.
The publisher, the authors, and the editors are safe to assume that the advice and information in this book are believed to be true and accurate at the date of publication. Neither the publisher nor the authors or the editors give a warranty, expressed or implied, with respect to the material contained herein or for any errors or omissions that may have been made. The publisher remains neutral with regard to jurisdictional claims in published maps and institutional affiliations.

This Springer imprint is published by the registered company Springer Nature Switzerland AG
The registered company address is: Gewerbestrasse 11, 6330 Cham, Switzerland

For Sophie, Mathilda, and Simon.
My everlasting positive bias.

Foreword

I am delighted that the book *Interpretational Processing Biases in Emotional Psychopathology* is being published in the "Cognitive Behavior Therapy: Science into Practice" book series. The field of cognitive behavior therapy (CBT) has evolved at an exponential rate adopting research methodologies and producing an evidence base for practice that is far beyond what was previously conceived as possible. Each book within the series consists of chapters that synthesize innovative research findings together with practice-focused case material, examples of client-therapist dialogue, and practical guidance for the clinician. Therefore, this book series bridges the gap that exists between science and practice.

Within this volume, you will find an introductory chapter from Dr. Emily A. Holmes (Uppsala University, Sweden) (Chap. 1) that contextualizes the book's contributions in the context of the need for greater research on the mechanisms of psychopathology.

Then, in Part I, the book features *Scientific Innovations on Mechanisms of Psychopathology* that includes a compelling account of how basic research can ultimately lead to the development of an evidence-based treatment manual (Chap. 2), followed by expert contributions outlining fresh insights into methods of assessment (Chap. 3), cognitive predictors serving as risk factors of emotional psychopathology (Chap. 4), and interactions between interpretational and other cognitive biases, such as attention, memory, and cognitive control (Chap. 5). Included are chapters outlining different interventions and mechanisms, including imagery-focused techniques (Chap. 6), the role of fear conditioning (Chap. 7), the role of genetics (Chap. 8), neural correlates (Chap. 9), pharmacology (Chap. 10), and interpretation training (Chap. 11). Equally important, though, is this book's emphasis on clinical practice.

In Part II, the book features *Clinical Guidance for Interpretational Bias Modification Across Different Emotional Disorders*, beginning with a brief history of cognitive reappraisal (Chap. 12) from Dr. Stefan G. Hofmann (Philipps-University Marburg, Germany and Boston University, USA) and the editor Dr. Marcella L. Woud (Ruhr-University Bochum, Germany). A series of clinically focused chapters are then presented outlining the implementation of the science from Part I, in psychological assessment and therapy for posttraumatic stress disorder (Chap. 13), depression (Chap. 14), obsessive-compulsive disorder (Chap. 15), social anxiety disorder (Chap. 16), and panic disorder (Chap. 17). I applaud all the contributors to this volume for their excellent work.

This book is edited by Dr. Marcella L. Woud, one of the foremost researchers bridging experimental investigation and clinical translation for posttraumatic stress disorder and panic disorder. She started publishing in high-quality journals from an early developmental stage in her career and now has over 70 scholarly articles, with a particular focus on cognitive appraisals in trauma experience, from experimental lab studies to RCTs, as well as important reviews and meta-analyses on interpretational processing biases in emotional psychopathology. Additionally, Dr. Woud has recently published in many of the world's leading scholarly journals, including, but not limited to *Biological Psychiatry*, *Clinical Psychology Review*, *Journal of Anxiety Disorders*, *Neuropsychopharmacology*, *Psychotherapy*, and *Psychosomatics*, as well as leading practice journals, such as *Cognitive and Behavioral Practice*, and serves as an associate editor of *Cognitive Therapy and Research*. Dr. Woud's work has broad appeal, and she has been a recipient of multiple awards, including the Association for Psychological Science's "Rising Star" Award that is presented in recognition "...of the innovative work that has already advanced the field, signaling great potential for continued contributions to psychological science." With such a background to draw on, Dr. Woud is eminently qualified to offer this book, and she has produced a book with a rich synthesis of evidence to guide practice.

The practice of CBT is complex and requires a tailored approach. Every technique has a specific target but may be used for multiple purposes simultaneously in support of the client's therapeutic goals. The purpose of Dr. Woud's book is to elucidate the ways in which interpretational biases can be a focus of intervention for CBT therapists at all stages of professional development, from those undertaking training to master clinicians. Dr. Woud has succeeded admirably in this regard.

Melbourne, Australia   Nikolaos Kazantzis

Preface

Ambiguity is ubiquitous in our everyday life, and as human beings, we have to interpret this ambiguity in order to make sense of what is happening around us. Interpretational processing is thus a meaning-making-process, and arguably one of the central processes through which we construct our idiosyncratic reality. Imagine, for example, that you are at a party and enter the kitchen to get yourself a drink. As soon as you enter the kitchen, the people standing in the kitchen turn and look at you. This is a highly ambiguous situation because it can be interpreted in many different ways, e.g., as a sign that you are welcome to join or as a sign that you are disturbing their conversation. The way that you interpret this situation will depend on many factors, for example, how anxious you are in general and your past experiences with such situations. Your interpretation will then, in turn, influence not only how you feel and what you do next, but potentially also your subsequent memory and evaluation of the party as a whole.

In the absence of psychopathology, people may sometimes interpret situations in a positive or benign manner, and sometimes in a negative or threatening manner, and there is most likely some kind of balance between these different kinds of interpretations. Further, even if a certain situation is interpreted negatively, this may not have a huge impact. If, however, psychopathology is present, the situation is different. That is, individuals with, e.g., elevated levels of anxiety or depression have a tendency to generate more negative and fewer positive interpretations in response to ambiguous situations. This is called an *interpretation bias*. Importantly, such interpretational processing biases are not isolated, purely cognitive phenomena, but are linked to a set of bias-congruent behavioral, emotional, and physiological responses. Further, interpretation biases should not be thought of as just epiphenomena or simple mood-dependent correlates: According to the many cognitive theories in the context of emotional psychopathology, including early theorizing by Beck, interpretation biases are considered proximal, transdiagnostic factors that play a causal role in the onset and maintenance of emotional psychopathology. This assumption is indeed supported by a large body of research, and it is expected that evidence for a causal role of interpretation biases will continue to accumulate over the coming years, in parallel with a refined and more fine-grained understanding of their underlying processes. Given their prominent role in theories of emotional psycho-pathology, and increasing evidence for their importance, it is thus not a surprise that interpretation biases are a primary and core target in many cognitive and behavioral treatments for anxiety disorders and depression.

The strong theoretical and empirical foundation for the importance of interpreta-tional processing biases, in combination with their status as a vital therapeutic tar-get, provided the motivation for the present book. In line with this combination of both theoretical and practical importance, the book is thus intended for both researchers and clinicians. In this book, *Interpretational Processing Biases in Emotional Psychopathology*, part of the *Cognitive Behavior Therapy: Science into Practice* series, international experts with extensive experience in both research on interpretational processing biases and their treatment in clinical practice were brought together. I still find it very exciting that so many experts agreed to my invi-tation – and all of them provided excellent, unique, contributions that represent clear advances in our knowledge of interpretation biases in emotional psychopa-thology, from both a scientific and clinical perspective. This fusion of science and clinical practice is central to the aims of the book, which are twofold: To provide an overview of the current state of basic and clinical research in the context of interpre-tational processing biases, and to provide an overview and concrete illustrations of contemporary, evidence-based techniques to tackle interpretational processing biases in therapy. Ultimately, both research and clinical practice can inspire and learn from each other, and further fueling and fostering this interaction is a long-term aim of this book.

The introduction chapter by Emily A. Holmes sets the stage for reading this book, presenting some fresh and inspiring ideas as to how we can move ourselves forward in the context of interpretational processing biases in emotional psychopa-thology via the interplay of scientific research and clinical practice (Chap. 2). The first part of the book then focuses on providing an update on the present state of our scientific knowledge. It begins with a chapter by Barbara Cludius and Thomas Ehring (Chap. 2), in which a conceptual and stepwise framework for translational research is presented. The framework's steps are outlined, including the relevant research questions and corresponding methods per step, starting from basic research, to experimental psychopathology and through to clinical trials. Since translational research comes with a number of challenges, I expect that this overview, especially in combination with the hands-on recommendations provided by the authors, will be of great value to all researchers in the context of translational psychology as well as in the broader context of clinical research. Next, Felix Würtz and Alvaro Sanchez-Lopez present an overview of measures to assess interpretational processing biases (Chap. 3), including consideration of this measurement across different processing levels (e.g., automatic vs. controlled). Each measure is described briefly, including the processing level targeted, using examples from disorders in which the corre-sponding measure has been applied. If available, the measure's psychometric prop-erties are also discussed. This chapter, therefore, provides a very helpful and practical guideline for all those whose research focuses on assessing interpretation biases. The next chapter, by Reuma Gadassi Polack, Anna Leah Davis, and Jutta

Joormann, includes a state-of-the-art examination of the central mechanisms by which interpretation biases are linked to emotional disorders as well as the mechanisms that attenuate this relationship (Chap. 4). Emotion regulation is presented as one of the central mediators linking interpretation biases to emotional disorders, and moderators that are discussed include age, gender, and symptom severity levels. Accordingly, this chapter sets an excellent stage to further zoom in on the mechanisms underpinning interpretational processing biases, a focus that is further continued by the chapter of Jonas Everaert, Sarah Struyf, and Ernst H.W. Koster (Chap. 5). This chapter starts by presenting a brief review of existing theoretical models describing the potential interaction between interpretation biases and other cognitive biases. After that, empirical research addressing the potential interaction between interpretation biases and biases in attention, memory, and cognitive control is summarized. This compelling overview is followed by the chapter of Simon E. Blackwell, which includes an excellent discussion of the role of mental imagery in the context of interpretational processing biases (Chap. 6). Specifically, this chapter explores the relationships between mental imagery and interpretational processing biases, particularly focusing on how imagery can enhance such biases, and also presents an overview of computerized training methods illustrating how mental imagery can be used to change interpretation biases. Sara Scheveneels and Yannick Boddez then provide an innovative perspective on how biased interpretational processing might mediate biased behavior in fear conditioning tasks (Chap. 7), postulating that stimuli might become ambiguous as a result of fear conditioning procedures, and this, in combination with a tendency to interpret these ambiguous stimuli as threatening, might be related with phenomena such as "return of fear" or "fear generalization," especially in anxiety-prone individuals. Their chapter also includes a model in which interpretation biases are described as a latent cognitive process that may mediate the relationship between, e.g., an individual's learning history and biased behaviors in fear conditioning tasks. The book then turns to a more biological perspective on interpretational processing biases, with John Vincent and Elaine Fox providing a fascinating overview of the role of genetics in interpretation biases (Chap. 8). Their overview starts with a summary of twin studies and molecular genetic research highlighting genetic and environmental influences on interpretation biases, including the shared genetic architecture with depression and anxiety. Further, an integrated theory, the CogBIAS Hypothesis, is presented, bringing together the research discussed in the chapter and presenting some first, longitudinal research results conducted in the context of the CogBIAS Hypothesis. Continuing the line of biological perspectives on interpretation biases, Ya-Chung Feng and Colette R. Hirsch review studies examining the relationship between interpretation biases and event-related potentials (ERPs), with a special focus on research on the N-400 amplitude, including summaries of studies testing both subclinical and clinical samples (Chap. 9). In addition, this chapter discusses methodological issues in material development when assessing ERPs and also provides brief guidelines for material development procedures. As such, this chapter combines both in-depth and hands-on information about assessing neuronal correlates in the context of interpretation biases. Next, Marieke A.G. Martens and Catherine

J. Harmer present an outstanding overview of how antidepressant treatments can change emotional processing biases, including those relating to interpretational processing (Chap. 10). Furthermore, the chapter explains how antidepressant treatments may interact with social and emotional experiences, which in turn may then produce the observed antidepressant effects. In addition, ideas are presented as to how these results can be used to inform, e.g., both treatment choice and development, further highlighting the cutting-edge nature of this type of research. This first part of this book ends with a chapter written by Elske Salemink, Vera Bouwman, Lynn Mobach, and me, providing an overview of computerized training procedures to modify interpretation biases, Cognitive Bias Modification of Interpretations (CBM-I) (Chap. 11). Specifically, the chapter provides an overview of the different training paradigms that have been developed and used over the past years, across various forms of psychopathology. The chapter also summarizes the present evidence on mediators and moderators of the training's effects and offers ideas as to how the training's effects could be strengthened.

The second part of the book includes five case studies. The main focus of these case studies is to illustrate how interpretational processing biases are manifested and treated in the different disorders presented. That is, concrete examples of the patients' biased cognitions, beliefs, and appraisals are described, as well as how these were treated using various evidence-based techniques. The authors of the case studies were also asked to write about the particular challenges they encountered during treatment and how these challenges were resolved. A hint of the patients' main cognitive bias is already given by the chapters' title, and I hope that the summaries presented below will be a good appetizer and further increase your curiosity for the second part of the book.

This second part starts off with an introductory chapter written by Stefan G. Hofmann and me (Chap. 12). The chapter begins with a brief summary of the historical background of the development of Cognitive Behavioral Therapy (CBT), followed by a description of key principles of CBT-based interventions as well as an overview of specific techniques targeting biased interpretational processes (e.g., cognitive restructuring, behavioral experiments, exposure, imagery-based techniques). In the next chapter, the first case study is presented by Ulrich Schnyder and describes the treatment of "John," who developed a posttraumatic stress disorder (PTSD) after his fiancée's unexpected death (Chap. 13). Central techniques in this treatment were Socratic dialogue and cognitive restructuring in order to work on John's guilt-related cognitions and emotions, i.e., to achieve a more realistic view regarding his responsibility in the events that had led to his fiancée's passing away. Importantly for this case, the sessions including the "self-invented" exposure were crucial in leading to the final reduction in John's symptoms, and this was also an important learning moment for the therapist. The second case study is written by Michelle L. Moulds and describes "Naomi," a patient suffering from depression and symptoms of anxiety (Chap. 14). Naomi experienced a range of dysfunctional appraisals which centered around themes of, e.g., her incompetence and inability to cope at work, her beliefs that she should be able to cope with her psychological difficulties on her own, and that she should always be responsible for others. Cognitive challenging was applied to address these appraisals; however, this seemed only partially helpful in the context of Naomi's tendency to ruminate. Hence, the therapy shifted from a content to a process focus, and this provided a more fruitful and effective approach. Christine Purdon presents the next case study, "Sundeep," who suffered from moderate-to-severe obsessive-compulsive disorder (OCD) (Chap. 15). Sundeep presented with frequent obsessional concerns about, e.g., contamination and concomitant checking and reassurance-seeking, as well as avoidance enacted to neutralize the harm represented in his obsessions and reduce his distress. The treatment targeted the appraisals of the obsessions and the need to execute the compulsion as well as Sundeep's (rigid) core beliefs for living. The techniques applied included both cognitive and behavioral strategies, such as, e.g., Socratic dialogue, the continuum method, behavioral experiments, and exposure with response prevention. Among others, key components of this successful treatment were addressing the appraisal of the obsessions rather than their content, and targeting Sundeep's unwillingness to trust his own judgment and his deference to the OCD "voice". The fourth case study is written by Katharine E. Daniel and Bethany A. Teachman (Chap. 16). It describes the case of "Gi" and the treatment of his social anxiety disorder. Key cognitions and biased interpretations that were maintaining Gi's anxiety included a judgment that others frequently reject him, the belief that expressing his own needs meant that he would then be unreasonably burdening others, and interpreting his abilities in most social situations as very incompetent. His therapy included exposure therapy centered around violating Gi's dysfunctional cognitions and beliefs of social situations. Psychoeducation, in combination with Socratic questioning, was also applied, helping Gi label many of his thoughts as "mind reading," and the evidence for and against such negative cognitions was explored. Further, role play was used to practice the skills that were learned via the various cognitive techniques. Gi made great progress during treatment, and the applied techniques helped him to shift his thinking style successfully, which ultimately improved his quality of life and his social relationships. Eni S. Becker presents the last case study, the case of "Susan," who was diagnosed with panic disorder and mild agoraphobia (Chap. 17). Susan exhibited some of the typical panic-related misinterpretations, such as misinterpreting bodily symptoms as signs of imminent danger. However, there were also some underlying dysfunctional beliefs that maintained the disorder and challenged treatment. In order to change Susan's catastrophic interpretations, exposure was chosen as the main intervention, specifically interoceptive exposure, in combination with cognitive restructuring. The agoraphobia was targeted with in vivo exposure, with limited effects in the beginning due to ingrained safety behaviors. By the end of the treatment, however, Susan had experienced significant improvements – the panic attacks and agoraphobic behaviors had vanished and she was able to enjoy life again.

Via the book's two parts, the first spanning theory and research, and the second presenting concrete demonstrations of treatment, this collection of chapters provides a demonstration and realization of the series' title, *CBT: Science into Practice*. Further, it provides not only a state-of-the-art overview of our current knowledge in relation to interpretation processing biases, but also a rich source of inspiration for further thought, research, and clinical innovation.

I am indebted to all of the contributing authors who provided their unique and invaluable insights into the research and treatment of interpretational processing biases in emotional psychopathology. The strength of this book is entirely the result of the knowledge, experience, and skills expressed in their work, and I am convinced that this collected expertise provides both an important marker for the current state of the field, and a springboard for the important work still to be done. I am also very grateful to the series' editor Nikolaos Kazantzis and Sharon Panulla from Springer who offered me this wonderful opportunity to edit this book.

Bochum, Germany   Marcella L. Woud

Contents

Contributors

Eni S. Becker Behavioural Science Institute, Radboud University Nijmegen, Nijmegen, The Netherlands

Simon E. Blackwell Mental Health Research and Treatment Center, Faculty of Psychology, Ruhr-University Bochum, Bochum, Germany

Yannick Boddez Department of Experimental Clinical and Health Psychology, Ghent University, Ghent, Belgium

Vera Bouwman Department of Clinical Psychology, Faculty of Social and Behavioural Sciences, Utrecht University, Utrecht, The Netherlands

Barbara Cludius Department of Psychology, LMU Munich, Munich, Germany

Katharine E. Daniel Department of Psychology, University of Virginia, Charlottesville, VA, USA

Anna Leah Davis Department of Psychology, Yale University, New Haven, CT, USA

Thomas Ehring Department of Psychology, LMU Munich, Munich, Germany

Jonas Everaert Department of Medical and Clinical Psychology, Tilburg School of Social and Behavioral Sciences, Tilburg University, Tilburg, The Netherlands

Ya-Chun Feng Institute of Education, National Sun Yat-sen University, Kaohsiung City, Taiwan

Elaine Fox Faculty of Health and Medical Sciences, The University of Adelaide, Adelaide, SA, Australia

Catherine J. Harmer Wellcome Centre for Integrative Neuroimaging, Department of Psychiatry, University of Oxford, Oxford, UK

Colette R. Hirsch Institute of Psychiatry, Psychology & Neuroscience, King's College London, London, UK

Stefan G. Hofmann Department of Clinical Translational Psychology, Faculty of Psychology, Philipps-University Marburg, Marburg, Germany

Emily A. Holmes Department of Psychology, Uppsala University, Uppsala, Sweden

Jutta Joormann Department of Psychology, Yale University, New Haven, CT, USA

Ernst H. W. Koster Department of Experimental Clinical and Health Psychology, Faculty of Psychology and Educational Sciences, Ghent University, Ghent, Belgium

Marieke A. G. Martens Wellcome Centre for Integrative Neuroimaging, Department of Psychiatry, University of Oxford, Oxford, UK

Lynn Mobach Department of Clinical Psychology, Faculty of Social and Behavioural Sciences, Utrecht University, Utrecht, The Netherlands

Michelle L. Moulds School of Psychology, UNSW Sydney, The University of New South Wales, Sydney, NSW, Australia

Reuma Gadassi Polack Departments of Psychology and Psychiatry, Yale University, New Haven, CT, USA

Christine Purdon Department of Psychology, University of Waterloo, Waterloo, ON, Canada

Elske Salemink Department of Clinical Psychology, Faculty of Social and Behavioural Sciences, Utrecht University, Utrecht, The Netherlands

Alvaro Sanchez-Lopez Department of Personality, Evaluation and Clinical Psychology, Faculty of Psychology, Complutense University of Madrid, Madrid, Spain

Sara Scheveneels Center for the Psychology of Learning and Experimental Psychopathology, KU Leuven, Leuven, Belgium

Ulrich Schnyder University of Zurich, Zurich, Switzerland

Sarah Struyf Department of Experimental Clinical and Health Psychology, Faculty of Psychology and Educational Sciences, Ghent University, Ghent, Belgium

Bethany A. Teachman Department of Psychology, University of Virginia, Charlottesville, VA, USA

John Vincent Department Institute of Psychiatry, Psychology and Neuroscience, Kings College London, London, UK

Marcella L. Woud Mental Health Research and Treatment Center, Faculty of Psychology, Ruhr-University Bochum, Bochum, Germany

Felix Würtz Mental Health Research and Treatment Center, Faculty of Psychology, Ruhr-University Bochum, Bochum, Germany

Chapter 1
Introduction: Imagining Science Reaching Practice and Moving Forward – Transforming Psychological Treatments via Mental Health Science

Emily A. Holmes

Welcome, and thank you for starting here at the beginning. I imagine that when you open this book, you will find yourself skipping through this introduction and racing to get to the exciting series of chapters ahead. So as that is the case, I will try to keep this short and explain why this book is needed. This book will help us better imagine science reaching practice and in doing so move us forward toward achieving that goal.

1.1 Up for Interpretation

This book, edited by Marcella Woud, deals with *Interpretational Processing Biases in Emotional Psychopathology*. The noun "interpretation" means "the particular way in which something is understood or explained" (Oxford English Dictionary). The same source describes "bias" as "a strong feeling in favour of or against one group of people, or one side in an argument, often not based on fair judgement." One can see how combining these two concepts presents a dangerous mixture – including the capacity of a potentially negative interpretation and a negative bias for generating powerful negative emotions. A dysfunctional bias in the particular way in which something is understood or explained can fuel emotional psychopathology. Yet, by appreciating that biases are modifiable, the reverse is also true.

As clinician scientists, better delineating dysfunctional biases in interpretation opens up the cause for hope as biases could be readdressed. Implicit to the definition of interpretation is that there is more than one way in which something can be

E. A. Holmes (✉)
Department of Psychology, Uppsala University, Uppsala, Sweden
e-mail: emily.holmes@psyk.uu.se

© The Author(s), under exclusive license to Springer Nature Switzerland AG 2023   1
M. L. Woud (ed.), *Interpretational Processing Biases in Emotional Psychopathology*,
CBT: Science Into Practice, https://doi.org/10.1007/978-3-031-23650-1_1

understood or explained, and thus the job is to illuminate such other ways. Doing so could help create change and advance treatment. Biases can be shifted, the particular way in which something is understood or explained can be altered, more "fairer judgement" found, and alternative feelings experienced.

1.2 There Are Many Ways to Crack a Nut

The other introduction in this book, that is, the introduction to case examples in Part II by Woud and Hofmann (see Chap. 12), takes us as time travelers through the history of changing dysfunctional interpretations in cognitive behavioral therapy (CBT). They elegantly encapsulate the basic principles of CBT "in a nutshell." To continue on this nuciferous theme, it can also be said that "There are many ways to crack a nut." That means that once we have the kernel of the problem established (e.g., a particular dysfunctional interpretational bias), there can be numerous ways by which to change it. From a mechanistic perspective, a bias could be altered at many levels, from cognitive and behavioral techniques familiar to CBT therapists to pharmacological agents, to forms of computerized cognitive bias modification (CBM) – and many more. We could imagine other tools from the molecular to the social. Mechanisms can operate at all levels. This book spans just this and brings diverse methods together with a common aim of bias change.

1.3 What and Why Is Mental Health Science?

Mental Health Science is fundamentally about working on asking the right questions. Questions that could make a difference to mental health. Science needs to ask questions that matter and that push the dial. The field of improving treatments needs the dial pushed rather dramatically due to the slow rate of progress over the last few decades compared to other areas of health science. We stand inspired by the progress made in the areas of for example cancer or vaccine development.

In 2014, we put out "a call for mental-health science" to improve psychological treatments (Holmes et al., 2014), arguing that clinicians and neuroscientists must work together to understand and improve psychological treatments. The three steps proposed were to (1) uncover the mechanisms of existing psychological treatments, (2) optimize psychological treatments and generate new ones, and (3) forge links between clinical and laboratory researchers. The elegant collection of chapters in this book is doing just this for the field of dysfunctional interpretations and emotional psychopathology.

We have used the term mental health sciences "to reflect the many different disciplines, including, but not limited to, psychology, psychiatry, clinical medicine, behavioral and social sciences, and neuroscience, that will need to work together in a multidisciplinary fashion together with people with lived experience of mental health issues … to address these research priorities" (Holmes et al., 2020). Again, this book is doing just this and also bringing people around the same table, or at least into the same volume on your bookshelf – exactly what we need. For our patients with emotional psychopathology, it is shifting the problem that matters, not the discipline of the researcher, and we need all heads together for progress under one umbrella. Here, in this book, you will find not only behavioral approaches that are critical but also, for example, pharmacology (Chap. 10 by Martens and Harmer) and genetics (Chap. 8 by Vincent and Fox).

Applying mental health science to psychological treatments is arguably in its infancy, given the scale of the problem we need to address. The scale of the problem ahead is a vast and global one – as illustrated by the COVID-19 pandemic and the war in Ukraine just to start with at the time of writing. Here, some of the big questions to get us started on the voyage (Holmes et al., 2018), questions which as you will see are seized and explored within this book as you turn from chapter to chapter. The first question *why* burns fuel in many chapters (e.g., Chap. 4 by Gadassi Polack, Davis, and Joormann; Chap. 5 by Everaert, Struyf, and Koster; Chap. 7 by Scheveneels and Boddez). And the questions that follow help us imagine goals for where we must be heading – for treatments that 1 day become scalable globally.

- Why do existing treatments work? that is, making the case for mechanisms of psychological treatments.
- Where can psychological treatments be deployed? that is, research to improve mental health worldwide.
- With what? The potential for synergistic treatment effects: using and developing cross-modal treatment approaches.
- When in life? Psychological science, prevention, and early intervention: getting it right from the start.
- Technology: Can we transform the availability and efficacy of psychological treatment through new technologies?
- Who should we treat for what and with what? Embracing the complexity of mental disorders from personalized models to universal approaches.

1.4 Taking a Line for a Walk

The job for mental health science that lies ahead is huge, given the scale of mental health needs globally. In the big picture of how to proceed with science, how do we see the wood for the trees? Even a tree in itself can be rather complicated. And – being unable to resist the pun here (or in Cognitive Bias Modification method speak, the near homophone at play), perhaps we could explore one example – the Woud for the trees … a treetop view of one line of enquiry. I take great pleasure in having discussed interpretational processing biases in emotional psychopathology with Marcella Woud for some years (science conversations always seem to take many years). The starting point for our discussion was a curiosity about the type of mental imagery that intrudes to mind after aversive experiences (intrusive memories, as, for example, can occur after trauma). After being in a forest fire (traumatic event), a survivor could be haunted by vivid mental images of a burning branch crashing down dangerously close to where they were – seeing in their image a flash of red flames and the motion of branch falling. Intrusive memories such as this can drive emotional psychopathology, such as post-traumatic stress disorder (PTSD) symptoms. Note, since intrusive images are transdiagnostic symptoms, they can also depend on their content, fuel symptoms of not only PTSD but also depression, anxiety disorders, and so forth. Intrusive images comprise a very interesting treatment target in their own right (see Chap. 6 by Blackwell).

The key idea in this particular Woudian line of enquiry we are exploring is that intrusive memories are a mental phenomenon that in themselves can be interpreted in different ways. The particular way in which someone understands or explains having intrusive images can vary from "this flash of memory is my brain keeping me safe so I can swiftly avoid danger in another fire" to "this image is a sign I am going mad" or "this image means I will never get over this". The interpretation – here an explicit appraisal about what having intrusive memories means – can be manipulated in an interpretation training procedure.

Beginning in the laboratory, the first job was to see if shifting the bias via a computerized reappraisal training had the hypothesized impact on ameliorating intrusive memories (Woud et al., 2012, 2013). These experiments showed promise – it was possible to modify dysfunctional appraisals and reduce analogue trauma symptoms with non-clinical participants. Of note, the content of the computerized reappraisal training was designed based on adaptive/maladaptive appraisals from people who had experienced real trauma. A longitudinal study of firefighters in Australia had allowed us to isolate those appraisals most associated with poorer long-term outcomes in terms of emotional psychopathology and thus focused our attention on which a subset of interpretations about intrusive memories change (e.g., Bryant & Guthrie, 2007). This illustrates how mental health science seeks to continuously move between lab and clinic (see Chap. 2 by Cludius and Ehring) and vice versa.

Continuing to take this line of enquiry for a walk, Woud next worked with colleagues in Germany to journey from the lab to the clinic by investigating the same form of computerized reappraisal training with inpatients with PTSD (Woud et al., 2018). Using a proof-of-principle double-blind randomized controlled trial, Woud et al. (2021) compared cognitive bias modification for appraisals to a sham training with 80 PTSD patients in an inpatient clinic.

The training schedule in both arms comprised eight sessions over 2 weeks, as an adjunct to the standard treatment program. Patients who received the active training had a greater reduction in dysfunctional appraisals and also improvements in PTSD symptoms. The reductions in dysfunctional appraisals were associated with improvements in PTSD symptoms. To paint a picture, the idea is that a patient learns to interpret having their intrusive memories in a more benign way, "this flash of memory is my brain keeping me safe so I can swiftly avoid danger in another fire," shifting the bias away from dysfunctional and distressing interpretations that intrusions are a sign they are damaged and cannot recover. Doing so starts to help them with the distress associated with intrusive memories and critically the number of times intrusions reoccurs. Overall, this improvement in appraisal bias yields downstream effects for emotional psychopathology. And the idea of this approach is that this occurs without having to discuss the trauma in detail (as in trauma-focused CBT) since that can be aversive for some patients. As said, there are many ways to crack a nut and seeking to develop gentler treatments and treatments that could be readily scalable is clearly a valuable goal for mental health science to aim for.

1.5   Imagining Science Reaching Practice—It Can

This book helps us moving forward, updating us about the present scientific and clinical knowledge in the context of interpretation biases in emotional psychopathology. It brings to life how science can reach practice, illustrated not only by the science chapters but also by the five case examples which bring this into relief. As such, it seems clear to me that this book can inspire innovative and exciting developments in both clinical research and practice. It will be a handy reference on your office shelf or packed in your travel bag on a journey. In the face of complexity, simplicity, a clear focus, and interdisciplinary collaborations can help – and mental health science is no exception. With clear examples, encouraging lines of research enquiry, and a resounding scientific curiosity – the future is rosy, and this book is one that will help to keep up the rosy future. Interpretations will always be critical to our mental life and critical for improving mental well-being. Onwards. And enjoy reading.

References

Bryant, R. A., & Guthrie, R. M. (2007). Maladaptive self-appraisals before trauma exposure predict post traumatic stress disorder. *Journal of Consulting and Clinical Psychology, 75,* 812–815. https://doi.org/10.1037/0022-006x.75.5.812

Holmes, E. A., Craske, M. G., & Graybiel, A. M. (2014). A call for mental-health science. Clinicians and neuroscientists must work together to understand and improve psychological treatments. *Nature, 511*(7509), 287–289. https://doi.org/10.1038/511287a

Holmes, E. A., Ghaderi, A., Harmer, C., Ramchandani, P. G., Cuijpers, P., Morrison, A. P., Roiser, J. P., Bockting, C. L. H., O'Connor, R. C., Shafran, R., Moulds, M. L., & Craske, M. G. (2018). The Lancet Psychiatry Commission on psychological treatments research in tomorrow's science. *Lancet Psychiatry, 5*(3), 237–286. https://doi.org/10.1016/S2215-0366(17)30513-8

Holmes, E. A., O'Connor, R. C., Perry, V. H., Tracey, I., Wessely, S., Arseneault, L., Ballard, C., Christensen, H., Cohen Silver, R., Everall, I., Ford, T., John, A., Kabir, T., King, K., Madan, I., Michie, S., Przybylski, A. K., Shafran, R., Sweeney, A., Worthman, C. M., Yardley, L., Cowan, K., Cope, C., Hotopf, M., & Bullmore, E. (2020). Multidisciplinary research priorities for the COVID-19 pandemic: A call for action for mental health science. *The Lancet Psychiatry, 7*(6), 547–560. https://doi.org/10.1016/S2215-0366(20)30168-1

Woud, M. L., Holmes, E. A., Postma, P., Dalgleish, T., & Mackintosh, B. (2012). Ameliorating intrusive memories of distressing experiences using computerized reappraisal training. *Emotion, 12*(4), 778–784. https://doi.org/10.1037/a0024992

Woud, M. L., Postma, P., Holmes, E. A., & Mackintosh, B. (2013). Reducing analogue trauma symptoms by computerized reappraisal training – Considering a cognitive prophylaxis? *Journal of Behavior Therapy and Experimental Psychiatry, 44*(3), 312–315. https://doi.org/10.1016/j. jbtep.2013.01.003

Woud, M. L., Blackwell, S. E., Cwik, J. C., Margraf, J., Holmes, E. A., Steudte-Schmiedgen, S., & Kessler, H. (2018). Augmenting inpatient treatment for post-traumatic stress disorder with a computerized cognitive bias modification procedure targeting appraisals (CBM-App): Protocol for a randomized controlled trial. *BMJ Open, 8*(6), e019964. https://doi.org/10.1136/ bmjopen-2017-019964

Woud, M. L., Blackwell, S. E., Shkreli, L., Würtz, F., Cwik, J. C., Margraf, J., Holmes, E. A., Steudte-Schmiedgen, S., Herpertz, S., & Kessler, H. (2021). The effects of modifying dysfunctional appraisals in posttraumatic stress disorder using a form of cognitive bias modification: Results of a randomized controlled trial in an inpatient setting. *Psychotherapy and Psychosomatics, 90*(6), 386–402. https://doi.org/10.1159/000514166

Emily A. Holmes is a clinical psychologist with a PhD in cognitive neuroscience. She is a professor at the Department of Psychology, Uppsala University. She is also affiliated with the Karolinska Institutet, Sweden. She has championed the field of mental health science. She has a particular interest in mental imagery and has demonstrated that mental imagery has a more powerful impact on emotion than does verbal cognition. Prof. Holmes has published more than 240 peer-reviewed articles and several treatment manuals. Adopting an interdisciplinary approach, her translational research findings from experimental studies inform the development of innovative interventions.

Part I
Scientific Innovations on Mechanisms of Psychopathology

Chapter 2
The Challenge of Translational Research: How Do We Get from Basic Research Findings to Evidence-Based Interventions?

Barbara Cludius and Thomas Ehring

2.1 Introduction

In the past decades, clinical psychological science has led to the development of efficacious evidence-based psychological treatments for the vast majority of mental disorders. In particular, cognitive-behavioral therapy (CBT) has proven to be highly efficacious and effective (e.g., Santoft et al., 2019). However, across disorders about half of the patients do not fully benefit from CBT (i.e., show no symptom remission, e.g., Santoft et al., 2019; Springer et al., 2018). In addition, about one-third (Wojnarowski et al., 2019) to half (Ali et al., 2017) of those who do benefit experience a relapse within the following years. Therefore, it remains of paramount importance to further improve existing psychological treatments and develop new efficacious interventions for mental disorders.

Of the different possible routes to developing and improving psychological treatments, translational research appears especially promising as it transfers insights from basic research into clinical application. At the same time, researchers aiming to go down this route will soon realize that it is very challenging and that there are numerous obstacles along the way. This chapter aims to highlight challenges related to translational research in clinical psychology and makes some recommendations what (aspiring) scientist–practitioners may want to pay attention to when embarking on the adventure of translational research. We will start by outlining a conceptual framework of translational research in clinical psychology, spanning from basic research to clinical trials. In addition, the chapter will provide suggestions on methodological considerations related to specific steps in the translational chain as well as some overarching topics related to translational clinical psychological research.

B. Cludius (✉) · T. Ehring
Department of Psychology, LMU Munich, Munich, Germany
e-mail: Barbara.cludius@psy.lmu.de; Thomas.Ehring@psy.lmu.de

© The Author(s), under exclusive license to Springer Nature Switzerland AG 2023

M. L. Woud (ed.), *Interpretational Processing Biases in Emotional Psychopathology*,
CBT: Science Into Practice, https://doi.org/10.1007/978-3-031-23650-1_2

One useful example for translational research is the development of cognitive bias modification (CBM), as it is based on numerous findings on the role of cognitive biases in psychopathology. CBM uses computerized trainings with the aim to directly manipulate and reduce (disorder-specific) cognitive biases. Targeted cognitive biases can include, for example, attentional biases, approach-avoidance biases, or interpretation biases. CBM aiming to change interpretation biases (CBM-I) can, for example, use an ambiguous scenario task, in which patients are trained to repeatedly and systematically resolve ambiguous disorder-relevant situations in a positive and functional manner. Examples from the CBM literature will therefore guide us through the chapter to illustrate the various steps (for more information on CBM, see Hertel & Mathews, 2011; Jones & Sharpe, 2017; Kuckertz & Amir, 2017; and for an overview of how to manipulate interpretation biases, see Chap. 11 by Salemink et al.). However, the main ideas presented in this chapter are of relevance for translational research in clinical psychology more generally. The selection of recommendations and promising areas of research will inevitably be highly selective, non-exhaustive, and possibly also biased by our own experience and research interests. They should therefore not be regarded as a manual for translational research but rather as an opportunity to reflect on potentially important methodological and strategic issues.

2.2 A Conceptual Framework of Translational Research in Clinical Psychology

One challenge related to translational research is that it requires a combination of different research designs, methods, variables, tasks, and expertise along the translational chain. It repeatedly confronts researchers with the need to make decisions about when it is time to move from basic research designs to treatment development and ultimately clinical trial research, as well as methodological and design choices that are appropriate for the current research question at hand. We believe that for these decisions, a general roadmap on translational research can be helpful. Therefore, we have recently proposed a conceptual framework on translational research (Ehring et al., 2022), which is based on general concepts of translational research in clinical psychology and psychiatry (Fulford et al., 2014) as well as on earlier suggestions related to experimental research in clinical psychology (e.g., Clark, 2004; Kindt, 2018; Van Den Hout et al., 2017; Vervliet & Raes, 2013; Waters et al., 2017). It involves several steps from basic research to clinical trials that are typically followed in a sequential order (see Fig. 2.1). Thus, research in one step depends on the outcomes of the research of the previous step. However, the interrelations are more complex in such that results from subsequent steps can also inform continued research on previous steps (see also Waters et al., 2017, and Sect. 2.3.3.3). In our conceptual framework, we propose that at each step, only certain questions can be answered and specific methods are needed do so (for an overview,

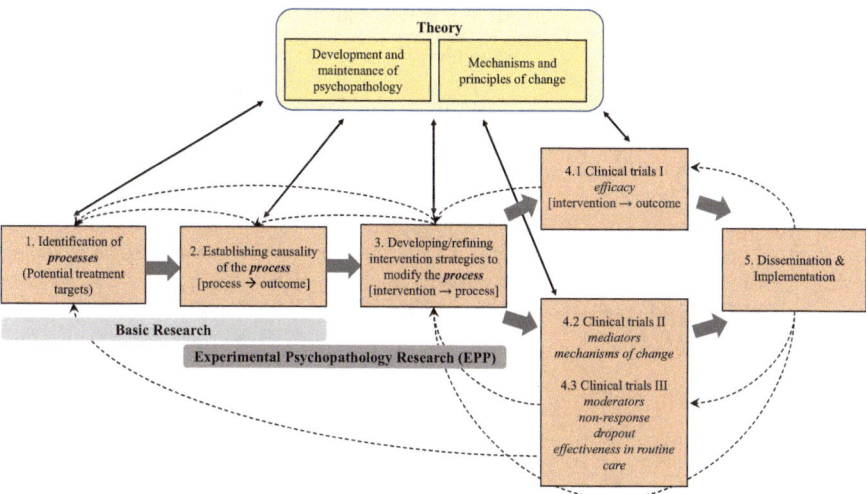

Fig. 2.1 Conceptual framework for translational research in clinical psychology. *Note*. The figure shows a conceptual model for translational research, which involves a number of sequential steps, whereby each subsequent step is based on the results of the earlier ones. Within [the parentheses] in Steps 2, 3, and 4.1, we name the manipulated variable a followed by the dependent variable. The dotted arrows symbolize that later steps also influence earlier steps. (This is a modified version of a figure by Ehring et al. (2022), available at https://psyarxiv.com/7cvh6, under a CC-BY4.0 license)

see Table 2.1). Another important aspect highlighted by the framework is the need for all research steps to be guided by clear theoretical models, detailing both assumptions regarding the role of certain processes in the development and maintenance of clinical phenomena as well as proposing key mechanisms of change. Decisions regarding the inclusion of specific processes, outcomes, and interventions in the studies should always be clearly based on and driven by theory.

2.2.1   Step 1. Identification of Processes

The first step uses basic research designs to identify processes that can serve as potential treatment targets. Numerous possible processes have been suggested in theoretical models and identified in empirical research (see, e.g., Research Domain Criteria, RDOC; National Institute of Mental Health, 2022). Some examples of processes include interpretation biases, emotion regulation, or arousal. Processes for this type of research are typically selected based on theory, but exploratory findings and/or clinical observations can provide critical additional information (Clark, 2004). Designs that can be used to assess whether a certain process is associated with symptomatology are correlational designs or designs in which a process is compared between a clinical and one or several (non-)clinical groups. For example,

Table 2.1 Overview of Steps 1–4 of the translational chain

Step	Question	Example	Study design and sample
Step 1	Which processes are related to psychopathology and can serve as potential treatment target?	Is a negative interpretation bias in relation to ambiguous, bodily-related information associated with panic symptoms?	Correlational or longitudinal designs including patients compared to healthy controls, or community samples.
Step 2	Does changing the process also change psychopathology (e.g., symptoms of a mental disorder)?	Does inducing negative interpretations in relation to bodily sensations lead to (an increase in) panic symptoms? Does reducing negative interpretations in relation to bodily sensations lead to a *reduction in panic symptoms*?	Experimental designs including healthy, subclinical, or clinical participants, depending on the research question (for details, see Sect. 2.3.2.2).
Step 3	Which intervention works best to modify the *process*?	Does a cognitive bias modification training for interpretation biases (CBM-I; e.g., ambiguous scenario training) lead to more benign *interpretations in relation to bodily sensations*? How can the training be refined to optimize the effect in inducing more benign *interpretation in relation to bodily sensations*?	Experimental analogue designs including healthy or subclinical populations, and "therapy experiments" (experimental studies comparing different versions of an intervention) including (sub-)clinical samples, with the *process* serving as the dependent variable and the comparison of different *procedures to modify this process* serving as the independent variable.
Step 4.1	Can this specific intervention also modify the associated *psychopathology* (e.g., symptoms of a certain mental disorder)? (Examples for related questions include: How does this intervention change the symptoms? For whom does it work best? Why do certain groups not benefit from this intervention?)	Does a cognitive bias modification training (e.g., ambiguous scenario training) lead to a reduction in *panic symptoms*?	Clinical trials (e.g., randomized-controlled trials), including patients.

Note. In the examples provided in this table, the symptoms are panic symptoms, the related process is the misinterpretation of bodily sensations, and the intervention is a cognitive bias modification training (e.g., an ambiguous scenario training)

interpretation biases in relation to ambiguous, bodily sensations as measured by the Brief Body Sensations Interpretation Questionnaire (Clark et al., 1997) were found to be elevated in individuals with clinical and subclinical panic disorder, whereas the control group did not show such a bias (Richards et al., 2001).

To test whether a process precedes the onset or exacerbation of symptomatology, longitudinal studies are then necessary. For example, Woud et al. (2014) found that a panic-related interpretation bias predicted the onset of panic disorder 1.5 years later. Of note, longitudinal studies are still in essence correlational. They can only give an indication whether a process may serve as a risk or maintaining factor for psychopathology, but they cannot be used to test causality, as it cannot be ruled out that a third variable may be responsible for the observed correlation (e.g., Van Den Hout et al., 2017).

2.2.2 Step 2. Establishing Causality of the Process

Once a process has reliably been shown to be associated with psychopathology, the next step is to test whether the process plays a causal role in leading to the development of or change in psychopathology (for a conceptual paper on causal risk factors, see Kraemer et al., 1997). Toward this aim, *Experimental Psychopathology (EPP) Research* is used (for reviews, see Waters et al., 2017; Van Den Hout et al., 2017; Ouimet & Ferguson, 2019). EPP research aims to elucidate *whether, how, when,* and *why* a psychological process results in some feature or symptom of psychopathology, using an experimental approach. To this end, the putative causal process (e.g., a negative interpretation bias in relation to ambiguous, bodily sensations) is manipulated, and the effect of this manipulation on psychopathology (e.g., increased heart rate, panic-related cognitions) is examined. Thus, in EPP research, the psychological process serves as the independent variable and is experimentally manipulated, to then test its effect on psychopathology, which, in turn, serves as the dependent variable.

2.2.3 Step 3. Developing/Refining Intervention Strategies to Modify the Process

Once it has been shown that a psychological process is causally linked to the development, maintenance, or modulation of psychopathology in an experimental design (EPP) research, this process can be regarded as a promising treatment target. Thus, in the next step, intervention strategies to modify this process need to be developed and refined. The development of intervention strategies is usually based on theories of mechanisms and principles of change as well as clinical expertise. Now, the *psychological process* serves as the dependent variable, and the interventions (vs.

control conditions) are the independent variable that is experimentally manipulated to study its effects on the process. This crucial step within the translational chain often requires systematic research efforts and an iterative process to optimize intervention strategies and best ways of delivery (Clark, 2004; Waters et al., 2017). During such a process, experimental analogue studies in non-clinical or subclinical populations (Waters et al., 2017) as well as "therapy experiments"[1] in (sub-)clinical samples (Clark, 2004) are combined to develop and refine intervention strategies. Relevant research questions in the context of CBM-I, for example, could be which dose of the intervention (e.g., number of training trials, length and spacing of the training), rationale (e.g., explicit vs. implicit; induction of outcome expectations), or setting (e.g., face-to-face, online, app-based) is optimal. Of note, this step requires a clear distinction between the psychopathological *process* (e.g., attentional bias toward threat) that is the target of the intervention and thus serves as the dependent variable, versus the *procedure* used to modify this process (e.g., attention bias modification training), which serves as the independent variable in this design (see MacLeod & Grafton, 2016, for a detailed discussion of this issue).

2.2.4 Step 4. Clinical Trials

Based on results regarding how a certain process can be modified best (Step 3), theoretical ideas on mechanisms of change, and clinical expertise, new interventions are developed or existing interventions are optimized (Step 4). In this fourth step, clinical trial methodology is used to test the intervention's efficacy (Step 4.1). To do so, different research designs can be used, which have different advantages and disadvantages. *Randomized controlled trials* (RCTs) are regarded as the gold standard in this phase of research (Guidi et al., 2018). In RCTs, the effect of an intervention on psychopathological outcomes is investigated using an experimental design. However, there is also an increasing interest in alternative designs (for more information, see Sect. 2.3.3.1).

As stated in the introduction of this chapter, even though the efficacy of CBT treatments is good, there is still considerable room for improvement. Thus, it is also important to assess which processes *mediate* treatment effects and could even be regarded as *mechanisms of change* (Kazdin, 2007). Once mechanisms of change are identified, they can specifically be targeted in treatment, which can help to optimize treatments further (Step 4.2, for more information, see Sect. 2.3.3.2). Additionally, it is important to identify moderators for treatment effects (Kazdin, 2007). Moderators give an indication as to which treatment works best for, for example, a specific group of patients. Further, to enhance acceptability and efficacy of treatments, we also need to understand how *treatment non-response* can be predicted

---

[1] Clark (2004) defines therapy experiments as experimental studies comparing different versions of an intervention.

(Springer et al., 2018) and what predictors of *dropout* are (Swift & Greenberg, 2012) (Step 4.3). A final very crucial aspect in clinical trial research is testing the effectiveness of interventions. By implementing such effectiveness trials, it can be tested whether treatments that have been shown to be efficacious in controlled clinical trial research (which, e.g., relies on well-trained therapists with high adherence to treatment manuals and typically includes selective patient populations) can be transferred into routine clinical settings and show similar results under less controlled circumstances (including, e.g., non-selective patient populations and therapists with typical training, supervision, and case load).

2.2.5   Step 5. Implementation and Dissemination

Interventions that have been shown to be efficacious and effective in Step 4 then need to be disseminated to a large number of clinicians and implemented in clinical practice. Describing this step is beyond the scope of this chapter. For an overview of how to optimize systematic research for this process, see, e.g., a review by Lilienfeld et al. (2013).

2.3   Doing Translational Research: Challenges, Recommendations, and Perspectives

Based on the general framework introduced in Sect. 2.2, we will now discuss some challenges of translational research and make recommendations for researchers using this approach. Whereas some issues are specifically related to certain steps (e.g., Sect. 2.3.3.1), others have been found to be relevant across various steps (e.g., Sect. 2.3.1.3).

2.3.1   Issues Related to Basic Research (Steps 1 and 2)

The first steps in the translational process focus on identifying processes that are risk or maintaining factors of psychopathology and can therefore serve as promising treatment targets for interventions (Steps 1 and 2). It is conceivable that only a minority of processes investigated at this step will lead to sufficiently promising results to be identified as novel treatment targets, and only a subgroup of these will then ultimately lead to efficacious novel interventions. So, how can we increase the chances to pick-up a target process that will indeed help to improve treatments? We will argue later that one important strategy is to carry out systematic pre-clinical research in Steps 2 and 3 before leaping from the identification of target processes to the development and testing of treatment protocols in clinical samples (see also Blackwell & Woud, 2022, for an excellent recent discussion on this issue). However, even after successful systematic pre-clinical research, we are still confronted with the question which processes (i.e., processes that have been shown to be related to psychopathology in Step 1) appear most promising to be further explored as possible treatment targets. We suggest that two aspects are especially important: focus on processes with a sound theoretical basis (Sect. 2.3.1.1) and prioritize processes showing stable and replicable effects (Sect. 2.3.1.2).

2.3.1.1   Focus on Theory

Many of the currently available evidence-based treatments have not been developed based on basic research findings but are rather based on clinical experience (see Ehring et al., 2022). As a result, there are several evidence-based interventions that clearly work, but it is unclear how exactly they work as they lack a clear theoretical model detailing the active ingredients, target processes, and causal links between processes and symptomatology. However, it can be expected that the *translational* route to novel treatments only works if the studies across all steps in the translational chain are based on a clear theory that is guiding the process. Even though basic research in clinical psychology is usually theory driven, it has recently been suggested that psychological theories often lack the precision and falsifiability needed for this purpose (e.g., Eronen & Bringmann, 2021; Robinaugh et al., 2021). When selecting a promising theory for translational research, there may be key aspects to look out for. First, theories usually have high explanatory power when they are hard to vary, in that changing a specific detail would affect the whole theory (see also Deutsch, 2011), making them very specific and therefore highly falsifiable. Easy-to-vary theories are, on the other hand, underspecified, can easily accommodate unexpected empirical findings, and are therefore very difficult (if not impossible) to falsify, which ultimately reduces explanatory power. Making theories harder to vary can, for example, be achieved by formalizing theories. Formal theories use very precise (mathematical) language (e.g., Robinaugh et al., 2021). Second, theories should entail constructs that are very clearly defined to enable the use of reliable and valid measurements (Eronen & Bringmann, 2021). Thus, increasing the chances of finding good treatment effects may start right here at the beginning: invest time and effort into formulating and testing theories with high explanatory power.

2.3.1.2   Focus on Stable and Replicable Effects

A second key recommendation for early steps in the translational chain is to put a strong emphasis on the stability and replicability of effects. In other words, only those processes should be considered as potential treatment targets for the later steps that show a stable and substantial relationship with psychopathology. This is important to emphasize as the replicability crisis in psychological science has also

Table 2.2 Examples of aspects that can influence the stability and replicability of research results

Aspect	Example on how an aspect can influence the stability and replicability of results
Is the study adequately powered?	Many studies in psychological research have been found to be underpowered (see Sect. 2.3.1.3).
Is there an indication of publication bias or questionable research practices?	There is evidence for publication biases and questionable research practices in clinical psychological research, leading to false positive findings. A possible solution could be to focus on research findings that are based on pre-registrations and principles of open science (Shrout & Rodgers, 2018).
Is the measure suitable to assess a certain process?	There is little consensus on which tasks are well suited to test certain aspects of interpretation biases (Everaert et al., 2017).
Is the measure suitable to assess the process in specific populations?	One study has shown that the AX-CPT (an indirect measure of attentional control) showed significantly better re-test reliability in patients with schizophrenia compared to the healthy control group (Cooper et al., 2017).
Is the measure reliable?	Especially the reliability of indirect tasks is often found to be low (see Sect. 2.3.1.4).
Is the underlying theory correct?	In the emotional dot probe task (a measure of attentional biases), it was found that difference scores, which are based on the theory that attentional biases, are stable over time, yielded low reliability scores. However, scores that treated attentional processes as dynamic led to higher reliability scores (Rodebaugh et al., 2016).

been found to apply to the field of clinical psychology (Tackett et al., 2019). A complete discussion of issues related to the stability and replicability of research findings in psychology is clearly beyond the scope of this chapter (see Table 2.2 for some examples). However, to give at least some examples, we will review two of these aspects more closely in the following paragraphs.

2.3.1.3   Statistical Power

Pre-study power calculations to estimate the necessary sample size to find an effect is highly important when planning a study. However, a large number of studies in psychological research have been found to be under-powered (Shrout & Rodgers, 2018). As the effect size estimations depend on the quality of previously studied research, the quality and power of published psychological studies in general should increase. To do so, researchers have proposed several options, for example, setting Type I error rates for multiple testing, preregistering the objectives, hypotheses, designs, materials, and planned analysis of studies, providing detailed power analyses, publishing null findings as long as the study design and power levels justify this, using Bayesian analysis to provide probabilities for both the null and alternative hypotheses (Szucs & Ioannidis, 2017; Shrout & Rodgers, 2018).

2.3.1.4 Reliability of the Task

Another often overlooked challenge to establish stable findings is related to measurement issues. For example, achieving adequate reliability of tasks such as those used in experimental clinical psychology, including research into cognitive biases, has been notoriously challenging. However, achieving adequate reliability is a prerequisite for obtaining consistent results (across populations, time points, etc.).

Indeed, in a meta-analysis on interpretation biases in depression, it has been found that the measurement method had a significant effect on the results. Specifically, whereas studies using direct measures (i.e., self-report measures) found significant effect sizes, studies using indirect measures (i.e., measures that use behavioral responses such as reaction times) showed non-significant effects (Everaert et al., 2017). Worryingly, the reliability of measures assessing cognitive biases (including interpretation biases) as well as tasks assessing psychological constructs of relevance to psychopathology in general is rarely reported. Additionally, when it has been reported, it has often found to be low, especially for indirect measures (e.g., Parsons et al., 2019; Rodebaugh et al., 2016). Two recent meta-analyses have evaluated tasks that assess cognitive biases (Gonsalves et al., 2019; Würtz et al., 2022), and optimally more clinical researchers will conduct such analyses in the future.

In sum, to be able to identify processes that are causally linked to psychopathology and that can potentially serve as treatment targets, we need to be able to find replicable and stable results. We have outlined two examples of specific issues that need to be considered (statistical power, reliability of measures), and more examples are shown in Table 2.2. Taking these different factors into consideration, researchers should critically ask themselves whether they can be confident enough that a certain process is related to psychopathology in a stable and replicable way. If the answer is no, it appears rather unlikely that translating this process into an effective intervention will be successful.

2.3.1.5 Focus on Transdiagnostic Processes and Clinical Areas with Need for Improvement

Basic research in clinical psychology can serve very different aims, and the aim to better understand a certain psychopathological process can be regarded as an interesting endeavor per se. However, *if* our aim is to ultimately improve clinical practice, we may want to add another, more strategic perspective to our question regarding which processes as potential treatment targets we should look out for. In the last decades, research in clinical psychology has mainly been disorder-focused. This has without any doubt led to highly effective interventions. Recently, however, researchers have increasingly highlighted that it may not be the best strategy to further improve disorder-focused psychological interventions and that a focus on *transdiagnostic processes* may be more promising (Dalgleish et al., 2020). Transdiagnostic processes are defined as processes that play a role in several disorders, and they serve as a risk factor and/or maintain a disorder. From a translational perspective, transdiagnostic processes appear thus particularly well suited to be studied in basic research and to be translated into clinical trial research (for a recent review of the promises and challenges of transdiagnostic approaches, see Dalgleish et al., 2020). RDoC (National Institute of Mental Health, 2022) may be a useful framework for this. Additionally, when thinking strategically, it may be important to consider processes in areas with substantial need for improvement in terms of both treatment efficacy and effectiveness. For example, developing yet another treatment for specific phobias may be less promising with regard to the clinical benefit compared to developing novel or improved treatments for highly comorbid, chronic, or complex cases, treatment non-responders, or currently under-studied and/or under-served groups.

2.3.2 Issues Related to Experimental Psychopathology Research (EPP; Step 2) and the Development and Refinement of Intervention Strategies (Step 3)

2.3.2.1 Steps 2 and 3 Should Not Be Skipped

Even if a specific process has been identified, namely, a process that is derived from a sound theory which shows stable associations with psychopathology, we still cannot be sure that this process will indeed be a useful target for clinical interventions. (Have we already mentioned that conducting translational research is hard?) There are two crucial additional questions that need to be addressed, using specialized research designs and methodology:

1. Is the process *causally* involved in the development and/or maintenance of psychopathology? (Step 2)
2. Are there interventions that can alter this *process* in a reliable and effective way? (Step 3)

Although these two key questions appear commonsense at first sight, when looking at the published literature in clinical psychology, it becomes apparent that the vast majority of studies currently focus on either Step 1 (i.e., correlational research identifying processes related to psychopathology) or Step 4.1 (i.e., studies testing the effect of novel interventions targeting processes identified in Step 1 on psychopathological outcomes; see, e.g., Waters et al., 2017). This means that once a process has been found to be associated with psychopathology, researchers often take the leap and develop clinical interventions that are assumed to target this process, and these interventions are then tested in (large randomized) clinical trials. From a translational perspective, however, this is not the optimal strategy. Incorporating "Step 2 studies" in the translational process is of great importance because we expect treatments to be most effective if the process has a *causal effect* on the development and/or maintenance of psychopathology. Whereas Step 1 uses correlational designs and cannot test causality, Step 4.1 tests the causal relationship between an intervention and psychopathology, but not the causal effect of manipulating the process on psychopathological outcomes. Experimental Psychopathology research in Step 2 is thus needed to establish this causal relationship between the process and the psychopathological outcome of interest.

However, even if we have established causality of a process, we do not know for sure whether this process is indeed malleable by psychological or pharmacological interventions. Results of Step 2 studies merely give us an indication *that* we should target a certain process in treatment, but it cannot answer *how* this process can be targeted best. Again, writing a clinical manual and running RCTs based on evidence from Steps 1 and 2 may not be an ideal strategy (Blackwell & Woud, 2022). Instead, studies using Step 3 methodologies are needed to give us an indication about which intervention procedure should be used to modify a process in order to become a potential treatment target in the future.

The first and most important recommendation therefore is not to skip Steps 2 and 3 but to invest time and effort into conducting research to establish causality and optimize treatment interventions before leaping into clinical trials research. However, the experimental research designs needed to do so come with some challenges, two of which we are turning to in the following paragraphs.

2.3.2.2 Choosing the Right Sample in Experimental Psychopathology Research

First, choosing the right sample to test causality can be challenging. Importantly, the decision which population is optimal and should be recruited in EPP studies heavily depends on the research question that is addressed (Van Den Hout et al., 2017). Following a classification by Forsyth and Zvolensky (2001), *Type-I EPP research* addresses the question whether the induction of a psychological process leads to the emergence of a symptom (e.g., the induction of a negative interpretation bias in relation to bodily sensations leads to increased panic symptoms). This question can only be addressed appropriately by using a healthy sample that does not show the tested symptoms, to then be able to test whether the induced process is indeed sufficient for the symptom to occur. Applying such a research design gives a first indication of whether the induced process could serve as a risk factor for the development of a mental disorder. (As a side note, it is sometimes stated as a limitation that non-clinical samples are frequently used in EPP research. However, when using this research design and testing whether a factor is a risk factor, non-clinical samples are not a limitation but are actually needed.) For ethical and practical reasons, such studies of course need to focus on dependent variables that reflect transient symptoms of low severity.

Type-II EPP research, on the other hand, investigates whether the elimination or reduction of the psychological process also reduces or eliminates the symptom. For example, does the reduction of a negative interpretation bias in relation to bodily sensations lead to a reduction in panic symptoms? As we assess the reduction of symptoms, we can only include individuals who currently suffer from these symptoms (i.e., subclinical or clinical groups). Such a research design also gives an indication about possible treatment effects. It should be noted, however, that subclinical groups may not be ideal for studying treatment effects (also see Sect. 2.3.2.3) as they can only give an indication whether a treatment should then be studied in a clinical sample. However, as the recruitment of subclinical groups is less time consuming and expensive than that of patients, such studies are nevertheless a good starting point when testing the effects of a potential new intervention (Van Den Hout et al., 2017).

Although the distinction between Type I and Type II EPP research has been a part of the literature for more than 20 years, EPP studies have not always followed this guidance in a systematic way. However, if the sample does not show an adequate fit with the research question, the conclusions that can be drawn from the corresponding study are limited.

2.3.2.3   External Validity in Step 2 and Step 3 Research

EPP research studies (Step 2 and 3 studies) are necessarily reductionistic in that they study the effects of manipulating a process on psychopathology or different interventions on a target process using a highly controlled experimental design. As described above, some research questions require testing healthy or sub-clinical samples instead of clinical populations. Additionally, in almost all Step 2 and 3 studies, only reduced versions of the interventions are used (e.g., single components of an intervention, low intensity or duration, short-time interval between intervention and outcome; Scheveneels et al., 2016; Van Den Hout et al., 2017). Importantly, this is not a limitation of the study designs but rather an important pre-requisite for research at this stage. Nevertheless, the conclusions we can draw from these studies depend on the external validity of the experimental model (Vervliet & Raes, 2013; Scheveneels et al., 2016). Recently, Vervliet and Raes (2013) have suggested criteria for the external validity of EPP research that can be taken into consideration when planning and evaluating EPP studies (for an overview, see Table 2.3). In most published EPP studies, authors mainly refer to the face validity of their paradigm when reflecting on the external validity of their findings (and then frequently highlight this as a key limitation, which is often not justified when the research question demands non-clinical samples and reductionistic set-ups). Logically, however, face validity is neither necessary nor sufficient for the validity of an experimental model (for a detailed discussion, see Scheveneels et al., 2016) and may therefore be hugely overestimated as a criterion. Instead, a focus on predictive, construct, and diagnostic validity appears useful, although such concepts are far from trivial to be implemented in specific studies. Whereas an exhaustive discussion of this important issue is beyond the scope of this chapter, we can nevertheless add another recommendation to our list: When planning studies at Step 2 and/or 3, we recommend to make one's criteria explicit, namely, why one assumes that the implemented reductionist setting is externally valid given the clinical phenomena and/or interventions of interest.

Table 2.3 Criteria to assess external validity as suggested by Vervliet and Raes (2013) with fear conditioning as an example for exposure therapy for specific phobia (Scheveneels et al., 2016)

Criterion	Definition	Example
Face validity	Phenomenological similarity between the treatment model and the treatment itself.	The repeated exposure to a fear-eliciting stimulus leads to a decrease in outcome variables that are indicative of fear and anxiety (e.g., elevated heartbeat, avoidance) in both extinction training and exposure-based treatments.
Predictive validity	Changes in the treatment model predict changes in the outcome after clinical treatment.	In both fear extinction training and exposure-based treatments it has been shown that administering D-cycloserine enhances the treatment's effect.
Construct validity	The mechanisms that are responsible for behavioral changes in the treatment model are the same as those that are responsible for the behavioral changes in the clinical treatment.	Extinction effects are attributed to inhibitory learning (i.e., a new association between the fear-conditioned stimulus and no-threat is learned). Approaches that facilitate inhibitory learning (e.g., maximizing expectancy violation) optimize exposure therapy.
Diagnostic validity	Processes/behaviors differ between patients and healthy groups.	Patients with anxiety disorders differ from healthy individuals regarding their pattern of fear reactions in the model, especially during periods of safety.

2.3.3   Considerations Related to Clinical Trials (Step 4)

In translational research, clinical trials should be conducted after having identified a process as a treatment target (Step 1); after having established that the process is causally linked to psychopathology (Step 2); and after having developed, evaluated, and possibly optimized interventions that modify the process (Step 3). Subsequently, it can be tested whether a certain intervention also changes psychopathological outcomes (Step 4). In the following paragraphs, we will discuss some methodological considerations related to clinical trials in the translational chain.

2.3.3.1   Bridging Designs

RCTs are often regarded as the gold standard in research testing the efficacy of clinical interventions. However, RCTs also have some disadvantages (e.g., stringent inclusion criteria limit external validity; Möller, 2011). An alternative are single-case designs, examining the effect of an intervention on defined outcomes variables over time (Kazdin, 2019). Instead of using a control group, researchers draw causal inferences about the effects of a certain treatment from the comparison of different time frames during continuous assessments (e.g., several assessments before treatment, assessments after each session, and after the treatment has been completed). An important subtype is the multiple-baseline design that starts with a baseline phase including repeated assessments of one or several psychological processes and symptoms (e.g., interpretation biases, panic attacks). Importantly, participants are randomized to different lengths of these baseline intervals. Changes during the baseline phase will then be compared to changes during the intervention phase. If the changes in the intervention phase are stronger, this would indicate that the intervention is responsible for the observed changes. Advantages of the single-case designs are the small number of participants that need to be included and the possibility to integrate the design into routine clinical practice (as no randomization to treatment vs. control condition is necessary), which, in turn, leads to much shorter and less costly studies that nevertheless provide an indication of whether or not a certain treatment may be helpful. Single-case designs can also help in elucidating the schedule of an intervention, therefore optimizing an intervention, and give an indication about which measures should be used to assess changes. Taken together, single-case designs can work as a bridge between basic and EPP research, on the one hand, and more sophisticated but also higher-risk research designs, such as RCTs, on the other hand (Kazdin, 2019). One example from the context of CBM research is a single-case series that assessed the impact of several sessions of CBM-I promoting positive mental imagery in participants with a current major depressive episode. Seven participants were tested on a daily base, before and during an intervention phase (1 week each), once after the intervention, and at two-week follow-up. Four of the seven participants showed improvements in interpretation bias, mood and/or mental health (depressive symptoms and general mental health as measured by the Symptom-Checklist-90-Revised; Blackwell & Holmes, 2010).

In addition to single-case designs, adaptive rolling designs, which test multiple treatment options simultaneously and use Bayesian statistics to remove or add treatment arms while the study is ongoing, have become more prominent in disciplines within somatic medicine. Adaptive rolling designs are used with the aim to first identify and optimize promising, novel treatments before running confirmatory trials (The Adaptive Platform Trials Coalition, 2019). An adapted version for clinical trials testing psychological interventions (the *leapfrog design*) has recently been proposed (Blackwell et al., 2019).

2.3.3.2 Research Assessing Mediators and Mechanisms of Change

To be able to improve psychological interventions, it is not only necessary to understand *whether* treatments work, but especially *why, how, and for whom* they work (Kazdin, 2007; Lemmens et al., 2016). This can be done by studying mediators as well as mechanisms of change related to the (specific) interventions. A mediator is an intervening variable that (statistically) accounts for the relationship between an independent variable (e.g., a certain treatment) and a dependent variable (e.g., change in symptoms of a mental disorder). The mechanism of change is more specific than a mediator. It explains how the change came about and what is responsible for the observed effects on the studied symptoms. Table 2.4 gives an overview of criteria that need to be met to establish a mechanism of change (Kazdin, 2007). As

Table 2.4 Criteria for mechanisms of change (or mediator for statistical analyses) according to Kazdin (2007)

Strong association	There needs to be a strong association between the mediator and the intervention as well as the mediator and the therapeutic change.
Specificity	The mediator accounts for the therapeutic change, whereas other plausible constructs do not.
Consistency	The relationship between the mediator, the intervention, and the therapeutic change can be replicated across studies, samples, and conditions.
Experimental manipulation	Experimentally manipulating the mechanism of change shows a change in the outcome (see Step 2 of our framework).
Timeline	The mediator precedes the outcome.
Gradient	A dose–response relationship between mediator and outcome can be found.
Plausibility and coherence	A plausible and theoretically coherent explanation for a mechanism of change can be found.

can be seen from the criteria, RCTs are not sufficient to assess mechanisms of change (e.g., the design is not suitable to test whether a change in a possible mechanism precedes a change in the therapeutic outcome). Several authors have pointed out that establishing a process as a mechanism of change in psychotherapy is highly complicated because it may need interdisciplinary research efforts (Kazdin, 2007) and because ultimately not just one mechanism but the interplay between numerous mechanisms may account for the change in the therapeutic outcome (e.g., Lemmens et al., 2016). However, next to experimental study designs already discussed in Step 2 (i.e., testing the possible mechanism of change's effect on a therapeutic outcome) and Step 3 (i.e., testing the effect of a clinical intervention on the possible mechanism of change), some specific recommendations for treatment studies have been made to further our understanding of mechanisms of change.

Kazdin (2007), for example, proposes that even if the focus of a treatment study is on the efficacy of the intervention, measures for mechanisms of change should be included. Ideally, measures for several possible mechanisms should be assessed simultaneously, and the possible mechanisms of change as well as the therapeutic outcome should be assessed on several occasions throughout the treatment (to establish that a change in the mechanism(s) precedes a change in the outcome). For example, both the putative mechanism of change and the outcome could be assessed on a weekly basis throughout the treatment study.

2.3.3.3 Back Translation

When a certain treatment has been found to be efficacious in clinical trials (Step 4.1) and some results on possible mediators, moderators, and predictors of response have been found (Steps 4.2 and 4.3), new research questions can arise. This can make it necessary to move back to earlier steps in the translational chain to, for example, study possible mechanisms of change using experimental designs (Steps 2 and 3) or to systematically test how the intervention techniques can be adapted for subgroups of patients who do not sufficiently benefit from the current treatment (Steps 1–3). This process has been called *back translation* (e.g., Kindt, 2018).

One example of a psychological treatment that has improved substantially because of back translation is exposure in vivo for anxiety disorders. Its original version was already very strongly based on basic research in clinical psychology, namely, early learning theory. Through a long series of basic research (Steps 2 and 3) and clinical trials (Step 4, including research on mediators, predictors for treatment outcome, etc.), possible mechanisms of change were then identified and further investigated in basic research (Steps 2 and 3). This research has shown that instead of erasing the threat-association of the stimulus (e.g., height = danger), an additional, non-threat association with the same stimulus is learned (e.g., height = no danger; Craske et al., 2008). Based on these findings, the mediating role of processes related to learning and retrieving the non-threat association with the stimulus has been tested in various settings and has revealed some promising results for treatment success (for an overview, see Weisman & Rodebaugh, 2018).

2.3.3.4 Studying Personalized Treatments and Focusing on Add-On Interventions

Again, we conclude this section by reflecting on some strategic issues, specifically the question which type of interventions are most promising to focus on when aiming at improving clinical practice using translational research. We would like to briefly highlight two alternatives to disorder-specific interventions that we think are particularly promising for translational research.

As suggested above, there are many arguments for taking a transdiagnostic perspective that is focused on identifying key processes cutting across different clinical phenomena. Those processes are first examined with regard to their stable association with psychopathology (Step 1), causal role in the development and/or maintenance of psychopathology (Step 2), and interventions that are effective in modifying this process (Step 3). The resulting intervention will most likely neither be an intervention lending itself to be used as a stand-alone treatment nor an intervention to be offered to all individuals falling within a certain diagnostic category. Instead, such an intervention will most likely be efficacious and clinically useful for individuals for whom the targeted transdiagnostic process is relevant. Such transdiagnostic interventions may then be part of personalized treatments (rather than disorder-focused treatment) that are tailored toward an individual patient and are based on a case formulation and treatment planning for that individual person. Current developments that are relevant for such an approach are attempts to focus on person-specific, dynamic assessment to guide case formulation (Fisher & Boswell, 2016), as well as the development of transdiagnostic modular treatments that lend themselves to personalized intervention delivery. Modular treatments are defined as treatments that consists of several units, which are independent from each other but can interact with each other. Within each unit, one specific process is targeted and changed (Chorpita et al., 2005); for a recent example, see the HARMONIC trial (Black et al., 2018).

Of note, although the focus on personalized modular treatments appears promising, it remains to be shown whether they indeed lead to more efficacious treatments since these treatment approaches are still in their infancy. In the meantime, a more pragmatic strategy may consist in evaluating novel process-focused interventions as add-on interventions to existing and well-established evidence-based treatments. This appears especially promising in cases where add-on interventions are designed to directly target potential mechanisms of change, namely, mechanisms of change that CBT interventions only target indirectly. For example, CBM-I has been recognized as a promising add-on intervention to CBT as the latter mostly relies on explicit instructions and verbal dialogue to change dysfunctional cognitions. Cognitive restructuring is a CBT intervention that trains patients to explicitly modify their maladaptive appraisals of, for example, previous situations in order to target patients' interpretation biases. It is thus assumed that cognitive restructuring facilitates strategic control over dysfunctional interpretations. In contrast to CBT, CBM-I uses a bottom-up approach, during which patients train to repeatedly and systematically resolve ambiguous, disorder-relevant situations in a positive and functional manner. Such training is then supposed to modify patients' interpretation biases in a more implicit and less direct manner (Beard, 2011). Thus, CBM-I may be suited to directly target certain aspects of interpretation biases (e.g., the more automatic aspects) and/or create synergistic effects with the rather controlled techniques patients learn to apply via CBT. Furthermore, CBM-I is mostly delivered as a computerized training, which makes it easy to implement in addition to CBT (or other treatments). In this context, Beard et al. (2019), for example, developed a transdiagnostic CBM-I intervention which is based on the Word Sentence Association Paradigm (Beard & Amir, 2009) and trains participants to endorse benign and reject negative interpretations of ambiguous sentences. The CBM-I-intervention lasted 10 minutes and was administered as a daily add-on intervention to a CBT-based partial hospital treatment for psychiatric patients. Its effects were compared to a control group that engaged in a neutral control task which used words that were unrelated to the emotional interpretation of the ambiguous sentences. Results showed a stronger shift toward benign interpretations in the CBM-I group compared to the control group. Further, exploratory analyses showed small augmentative effects on anxiety but not depression symptoms (Beard et al., 2019).

2.4 Conclusion

When scientists embark on the journey of conducting research to improve clinical treatments, they can take as an inspiration how some of the most effective psychological interventions came to be. One example is exposure therapy for anxiety disorders, which stems from basic research on learning principles, and has been developed and further improved over decades using joint efforts in translational research (Weisman & Rodebaugh, 2018). This example shows that translational research offers a great opportunity to develop and improve effective psychological treatments. However, as outlined in this chapter, translating basic research findings into developing and testing psychological treatments is a difficult endeavor and needs a thorough theoretical foundation and well-conducted (series of) studies. At each step of the translational chain, specific challenges arise when planning studies, some of which can be tackled by the individual researcher, and some of which need to be overcome by the field of clinical psychology. Thus, we believe that it is warranted that clinical psychology as a field more explicitly discusses and develops strategies to improve translation. Nevertheless, we believe that each individual scientist can already make a huge contribution to translational research, and we hope that this chapter may help in doing so (for a related discussion about the interplay of scientific research and clinical practice, see Chap. 1 by Holmes). Our framework of translational research is supposed to offer a guide to determine at which step in the translational chain the research question lies, and, consequently, which methods should be used when conducting a study at that step. Furthermore, we hope that we could outline some of the key challenges related to (each step of) translational research, as well as offering some motivating recommendations that can be followed to overcome those challenges.

References

Ali, S., Rhodes, L., Moreea, O., McMillan, D., Gilbody, S., Leach, C., Lucock, M., Lutz, W., & Delgadillo, J. (2017). How durable is the effect of low intensity CBT for depression and anxiety? Remission and relapse in a longitudinal cohort study. *Behaviour Research and Therapy, 94*, 1–8. https://doi.org/10.1016/j.brat.2017.04.006

Beard, C. (2011). Cognitive bias modification for anxiety: Current evidence and future directions. *Expert Review of Neurotherapeutics, 11*, 299–311. https://doi.org/10.1586/ern.10.194

Beard, C., & Amir, N. (2009). Interpretation in social anxiety: When meaning precedes ambiguity. *Cognitive Therapy and Research, 33*, 406–415. https://doi.org/10.1007/s10608-009-9235-0

Beard, C., Rifkin, L. S., Silverman, A. L., & Björgvinsson, T. (2019). Translating CBM-I into real-world settings: Augmenting a CBT-based psychiatric hospital program. *Behavior Therapy, 50*, 515–530. https://doi.org/10.1016/j.beth.2018.09.002

Black, M., Hitchcock, C., Bevan, A., Leary, C. O., Clarke, J., Elliott, R., Watson, P., LaFortune, L., Rae, S., Gilbody, S., Kuyken, W., Johnston, D., Newby, J. M., & Dalgleish, T. (2018). The HARMONIC trial: study protocol for a randomised controlled feasibility trial of Shaping Healthy Minds—a modular transdiagnostic intervention for mood, stressor-related and anxiety disorders in adults. *BMJ Open, 8*, e024546. https://doi.org/10.1136/bmjopen-2018-024546

Blackwell, S. E., & Holmes, E. A. (2010). Modifying interpretation and imagination in clinical depression: A single case series using cognitive bias modification. *Applied Cognitive Psychology, 24*, 338–350. https://doi.org/10.1002/acp.1680

Blackwell, S. E., & Woud, M. L. (2022). Making the leap: From experimental psychopathology to clinical trials. *Journal of Experimental Psychopathology, 13*, 204380872210800. https://doi.org/10.1177/20438087221080075

Blackwell, S. E., Woud, M. L., Margraf, J., & Schönbrodt, F. D. (2019). Introducing the leapfrog design: A simple Bayesian adaptive rolling trial design for accelerated treatment development and optimization. *Clinical Psychological Science, 7*, 1222–1243. https://doi. org/10.1177/2167702619858071

Chorpita, B. F., Daleiden, E. L., & Weisz, J. R. (2005). Modularity in the design and application of therapeutic interventions. *Applied and Preventive Psychology, 11*, 141–156. https://doi. org/10.1016/j.appsy.2005.05.002

Clark, D. M. (2004). Developing new treatments: On the interplay between theories, experimental science and clinical innovation. *Behaviour Research and Therapy, 42*, 1089–1104. https://doi. org/10.1016/j.brat.2004.05.002

Clark, D. M., Salkovskis, P. M., Öst, L.-G., Breitholtz, E., Koehler, K. A., Westling, B. E., Jeavons, A., & Gelder, M. (1997). Misinterpretation of body sensations in panic disorder. *Journal of Consulting and Clinical Psychology, 65*(2), 203–213. https://doi. org/10.1037/0022-006X.65.2.2033

Cooper, S. R., Gonthier, C., Barch, D. M., & Braver, T. S. (2017). The role of psychometrics in individual differences research in cognition: A case study of the AX-CPT. *Frontiers in Psychology, 8*, 1482. https://doi.org/10.3389/fpsyg.2017.01482

Craske, M. G., Kircanski, K., Zelikowsky, M., Mystkowski, J., Chowdhury, N., & Baker, A. (2008). Optimizing inhibitory learning during exposure therapy. *Behaviour Research and Therapy, 46*, 5–27. https://doi.org/10.1016/j.brat.2007.10.003

Dalgleish, T., Black, M., Johnston, D., & Bevan, A. (2020). Transdiagnostic approaches to mental health problems: Current status and future directions. *Journal of Consulting and Clinical Psychology, 88*(3), 179–195. https://doi.org/10.1037/ccp0000482

Deutsch, D. (2011). *The beginning of infinity: Explanations that transform the world*. Penguin.

Ehring, T., Limburg, K., Kunze, A. E., Wittekind, C. E., Werner, G. G., Wolkenstein, L., Guzey, B., & Cludius, B. (2022). (When and how) does basic research in clinical psychology lead to more effective psychological treatment for mental disorders? *Clinical Psychology Review, 95*, 102163. https://doi.org/10.1016/j.cpr.2022.102163

Eronen, M. I., & Bringmann, L. F. (2021). The theory crisis in psychology: How to move forward. *Perspectives on Psychological Science, 16*, 779–788. https://doi. org/10.1177/1745691620970586

Everaert, J., Podina, I. R., & Koster, E. H. W. (2017). A comprehensive meta-analysis of interpretation biases in depression. *Clinical Psychology Review, 58*, 33–48. https://doi.org/10.1016/j. cpr.2017.09.005

Fisher, A. J., & Boswell, J. F. (2016). Enhancing the personalization of psychotherapy with dynamic assessment and modeling. *Assessment, 23*, 496–506. https://doi. org/10.1177/1073191116638735

Forsyth, J. P., & Zvolensky, M. J. (2001). Experimental psychopathology, clinical science, and practice: An irrelevant or indispensable alliance? *Applied and Preventive Psychology, 10*, 243–264. https://doi.org/10.1016/S0962-1849(01)80002-0

Fulford, K. W. M., Bortolotti, L., & Broome, M. (2014). Taking the long view: An emerging framework for translational psychiatric science. *World Psychiatry, 13*, 110–117. https://doi. org/10.1002/wps.20139

Gonsalves, M., Whittles, R. L., Weisberg, R. B., & Beard, C. (2019). A systematic review of the word sentence association paradigm (WSAP). *Journal of Behavior Therapy and Experimental Psychiatry, 64*, 133–148. https://doi.org/10.1016/j.jbtep.2019.04.003

Guidi, J., Brakemeier, E.-L., Bockting, C. L. H., Cosci, F., Cuijpers, P., Jarrett, R. B., Linden, M., Marks, I., Peretti, C. S., Rafanelli, C., Rief, W., Schneider, S., Schnyder, U., Sensky, T., Tomba, E., Vazquez, C., Vieta, E., Zipfel, S., Wright, J. H., & Fava, G. A. (2018). Methodological recommendations for trials of psychological interventions. *Psychotherapy and Psychosomatics, 87*, 276–284. https://doi.org/10.1159/000490574

Hertel, P. T., & Mathews, A. (2011). Cognitive bias modification: Past perspectives, current findings, and future applications. *Perspectives on Psychological Science, 6*, 521–536. https://doi. org/10.1177/1745691611421205

Jones, E. B., & Sharpe, L. (2017). Cognitive bias modification: A review of meta-analyses. *Journal of Affective Disorders, 223*, 175–183. https://doi.org/10.1016/j.jad.2017.07.034

Kazdin, A. E. (2007). Mediators and mechanisms of change in psychotherapy research. *Annual Review of Clinical Psychology, 3*, 1–27. https://doi.org/10.1146/annurev.clinpsy.3.022806.091432

Kazdin, A. E. (2019). Single-case experimental designs. Evaluating interventions in research and clinical practice. *Behaviour Research and Therapy, 117*, 3–17. https://doi.org/10.1016/j.brat.2018.11.015

Kindt, M. (2018). The surprising subtleties of changing fear memory: A challenge for translational science. *Philosophical Transactions of the Royal Society B. Biological Science, 373*, 20170033. https://doi.org/10.1098/rstb.2017.0033

Kraemer, H. C., Kazdin, A. E., Offord, D. R., Kessler, R. C., Jensen, P. S., & Kupfer, D. J. (1997). Coming to terms with the terms of risk. *Archives of General Psychiatry, 54*, 337–343. https://doi.org/10.1001/archpsyc.1997.01830160065009

Kuckertz, J. M., & Amir, N. (2017). Cognitive bias modification. In S. G. Hofmann & G. J. G. Asmundson (Eds.), *The science of cognitive behavioral therapy* (pp. 463–491). Elsevier Academic Press. https://doi.org/10.1016/B978-0-12-803457-6.00019-2

Lemmens, L. H. J. M., Müller, V. N. L. S., Arntz, A., & Huibers, M. J. H. (2016). Mechanisms of change in psychotherapy for depression: An empirical update and evaluation of research aimed at identifying psychological mediators. *Clinical Psychology Review, 50*, 95–107. https://doi.org/10.1016/j.cpr.2016.09.004

Lilienfeld, S. O., Ritschel, L. A., Lynn, S. J., Cautin, R. L., & Latzman, R. D. (2013). Why many clinical psychologists are resistant to evidence-based practice: Root causes and constructive remedies. *Clinical Psychology Review, 33*, 883–900. https://doi.org/10.1016/j.cpr.2012.09.008

MacLeod, C., & Grafton, B. (2016). Anxiety-linked attentional bias and its modification: Illustrating the importance of distinguishing processes and procedures in experimental psychopathology research. *Behaviour Research and Therapy, 86*, 68–86. https://doi.org/10.1016/j.brat.2016.07.005

Möller, H.-J. (2011). Effectiveness studies: Advantages and disadvantages. *Dialogues in Clinical Neuroscience, 13*, 199–207. https://doi.org/10.31887/DCNS.2011.13.2/hmoeller

National Institute of Mental Health. (2022). Research Domain Criteria (RDoC). https://www.nimh.nih.gov/research-priorities/rdoc/index.shtml. Accessed 5 June 2020.

Ouimet, A. J., & Ferguson, R. J. (2019). Innovations and advances in cognitive behavioral therapy: Insights from experimental psychopathology. *Journal of Experimental Psychopathology, 10*, 204380871987496. https://doi.org/10.1177/2043808719874966

Parsons, S., Kruijt, A.-W., & Fox, E. (2019). Psychological science needs a standard practice of reporting the reliability of cognitive-behavioral measurements. *Advanced Methods and Practices in Psychological Science, 2*(4), 378–395. https://doi.org/10.1177/2515245919879695

Richards, J. C., Austin, D. W., & Alvarenga, M. E. (2001). Interpretation of ambiguous interoceptive stimuli in panic disorder and nonclinical panic. *Cognitive Therapy and Research, 25*, 235–246. https://doi.org/10.1023/A:1010783427196

Robinaugh, D. J., Haslbeck, J. M. B., Ryan, O., Fried, E. I., & Waldorp, L. J. (2021). Invisible hands and fine calipers: A call to use formal theory as a toolkit for theory construction. *Perspectives on Psychological Science, 16*, 725–743. https://doi.org/10.1177/1745691620974697

Rodebaugh, T. L., Scullin, R. B., Langer, J. K., Dixon, D. J., Huppert, J. D., Bernstein, A., Zvielli, A., & Lenze, E. J. (2016). Unreliability as a threat to understanding psychopathology: The cautionary tale of attentional bias. *Journal of Abnormal Psychology, 125*(6), 840–851. https://doi.org/10.1037/abn0000184

Santoft, F., Axelsson, E., Öst, L.-G., Hedman-Lagerlöf, M., Fust, J., & Hedman-Lagerlöf, E. (2019). Cognitive behaviour therapy for depression in primary care: Systematic review and meta-analysis. *Psychological Medicine, 49*, 1266–1274. https://doi.org/10.1017/S0033291718004208

Scheveneels, S., Boddez, Y., Vervliet, B., & Hermans, D. (2016). The validity of laboratory-based treatment research: Bridging the gap between fear extinction and exposure treatment. *Behaviour Research and Therapy, 86*, 87–94. https://doi.org/10.1016/j.brat.2016.08.015

Shrout, P. E., & Rodgers, J. L. (2018). Psychology, science, and knowledge construction: Broadening perspectives from the replication crisis. *Annual Review of Psychology, 69*, 487–510. https://doi.org/10.1146/annurev-psych-122216-011845

Springer, K. S., Levy, H. C., & Tolin, D. F. (2018). Remission in CBT for adult anxiety disorders: A meta-analysis. *Clinical Psychology Review, 61*, 1–8. https://doi.org/10.1016/j.cpr.2018.03.002

Swift, J. K., & Greenberg, R. P. (2012). Premature discontinuation in adult psychotherapy: A meta-analysis. *Journal of Consulting and Clinical Psychology, 80*, 547–559. https://doi.org/10.1037/a0028226

Szucs, D., & Ioannidis, J. P. A. (2017). Empirical assessment of published effect sizes and power in the recent cognitive neuroscience and psychology literature. *PLoS Biology, 15*, e2000797. https://doi.org/10.1371/journal.pbio.2000797

Tackett, J. L., Brandes, C. M., King, K. M., & Markon, K. E. (2019). Psychology's replication crisis and clinical psychological science. *Annual Review of Clinical Psychology, 15*, 579–604. https://doi.org/10.1146/annurev-clinpsy-050718-095710

The Adaptive Platform Trials Coalition. (2019). Adaptive platform trials: Definition, design, conduct and reporting considerations. *Nature Reviews Drug Discovery, 18*, 797–807. https://doi.org/10.1038/s41573-019-0034-3

Van Den Hout, M. A., Engelhard, I. M., & McNally, R. J. (2017). Thoughts on experimental psychopathology. *Psychopathology Review, a4*(2), 141–154. https://doi.org/10.5127/pr.045115

Vervliet, B., & Raes, F. (2013). Criteria of validity in experimental psychopathology: Application to models of anxiety and depression. *Psychological Medicine, 43*, 2241–2244. https://doi.org/10.1017/S0033291712002267

Waters, A. M., LeBeau, R. T., & Craske, M. G. (2017). Experimental psychopathology and clinical psychology: An integrative model to guide clinical science and practice. *Psychopathology Review, a4*(2), 112–128. https://doi.org/10.5127/pr.038015

Weisman, J. S., & Rodebaugh, T. L. (2018). Exposure therapy augmentation: A review and extension of techniques informed by an inhibitory learning approach. *Clinical Psychology Review, 59*, 41–51. https://doi.org/10.1016/j.cpr.2017.10.010

Wojnarowski, C., Firth, N., Finegan, M., & Delgadillo, J. (2019). Predictors of depression relapse and recurrence after cognitive behavioural therapy: A systematic review and meta-analysis. *Behavioural and Cognitive Psychotherapy, 47*, 514–529. https://doi.org/10.1017/S1352465819000080

Woud, M. L., Zhang, X. C., Becker, E. S., McNally, R. J., & Margraf, J. (2014). Don't panic: Interpretation bias is predictive of new onsets of panic disorder. *Journal of Anxiety Disorders, 28*, 83–87. https://doi.org/10.1016/j.janxdis.2013.11.008

Würtz, F., Zahler, L., Blackwell, S. E., Margraf, J., Bagheri, M., & Woud, M. L. (2022). Scrambled but valid? The scrambled sentences task as a measure of interpretation biases in psychopathology: A systematic review and meta-analysis. *Clinical Psychology Review, 93*, 102–133.

Barbara Cludius is a postdoctoral researcher at the Chair for Clinical Psychology and Psychological Treatment at the Ludwig-Maximilians-University in Munich. She primarily investigates maladaptive processes related to obsessive–compulsive disorder as well as transdiagnostic processes, in particular emotion regulation and perfectionism. Several of her research projects have been founded by the German Research Foundation (Deutsche Forschungsgemeinschaft, DFG). In her research, she combines both basic research and psychotherapy research and strives to conduct this research with a translational perspective in mind. Barbara Cludius is a licensed cognitive-behavioral psychotherapist.

Thomas Ehring is a full professor of Clinical Psychology and Psychological Treatment at LMU Munich. He held earlier appointments at King's College London (UK), University of Amsterdam (NL), and University of Münster (Germany). His research mainly focuses on the etiology and treatment of posttraumatic stress disorder, the role of transdiagnostic processes (especially repetitive negative thinking; emotional regulation) in psychopathology, and translational research developing novel and/or improved interventions based on basic experimental research. Thomas Ehring is also a registered cognitive-behavioral therapy (CBT) therapist, supervisor, and head of an outpatient psychological treatment centre.

Chapter 3
Assessing Interpretation Biases in Emotional Psychopathology: An Overview

Felix Würtz and Alvaro Sanchez-Lopez

We are frequently confronted with ambiguous situations or events in everyday life – for example, when a friend does not reply to a message or when you approach a group of people, and they stop talking. To adequately respond to these situations, we need to make sense of the ambiguity by attending to the information, comparing this information to previously encountered situations, and then forming an interpretation. The processing of, and the preparation of suitable reactions to, ambiguous situations is thus a highly complex function involving a multitude of factors (e.g., attentional or memory processes; Everaert & Koster, 2020). Given such complexity, interpretations are not always accurate, and individuals tend to show preferential tendencies to interpret ambiguous information that they encounter in either a more positive or negative manner. The tendency to interpret ambiguous information in a negative manner is referred to as a negative interpretation bias (Hirsch et al., 2016) and is argued to be strongly linked to symptoms of emotional psychopathology (for an overview of mediators and moderators of interpretation biases, see Chap. 4 by Gadassi Polack et al.; and for an overview of associated cognitive biases of interpretation biases, see Chap. 5 by Everaert et al.). To illustrate, prominent cognitive theories of psychological disorders postulate that negative interpretation biases play a strong role in maintaining symptoms (e.g., Beck & Bredemeier, 2016; Clark, 1986; Ehlers & Clark, 2000; for a review, see Mathews & MacLeod, 2005), with empirical evidence providing consistent support for a strong link between interpretation biases and both anxiety and depressive symptoms (e.g., Chen et al., 2020; Everaert et al.,

F. Würtz (✉)
Mental Health Research and Treatment Center, Faculty of Psychology,
Ruhr-University Bochum, Bochum, Germany

A. Sanchez-Lopez
Department of Personality, Evaluation and Clinical Psychology, Faculty of Psychology,
Complutense University of Madrid, Madrid, Spain

© The Author(s), under exclusive license to Springer Nature Switzerland AG 2023
M. L. Woud (ed.), *Interpretational Processing Biases in Emotional Psychopathology*,
CBT: Science Into Practice, https://doi.org/10.1007/978-3-031-23650-1_3

2017). Additionally, there is evidence that negative interpretation biases predict the development of both anxiety and affective disorders as well as somatoform disorder (e.g., Rude et al., 2003; Woud et al., 2014, 2016). Overall, a large body of evidence has convincingly established that negative interpretation biases are a transdiagnostic phenomenon that confers risk for and occurs in multiple forms of emotional psychopathology, while healthy controls typically show more benign or positive biases (Hirsch et al., 2016). However, across disorders, interpretation biases differ. For example, while social anxiety disorder is characterized by negative interpretations of ambiguous social cues (e.g., Chen et al., 2020), panic disorder is characterized by catastrophizing misinterpretations of bodily symptoms (e.g., Hermans et al., 2010; Teachman et al., 2007). As such, when aiming to identify and assess negative interpretation biases, sufficiently fine-grained measures are required. Indeed, a variety of measures such as questionnaires and behavioral tasks have been developed to assess negative interpretation biases. Commonly, these measures present ambiguous information and assess participants' tendencies to react to this information in either a disorder-congruent or incongruent manner.

In addition to assessing disorder-specific interpretation biases, measures also vary in the type of processing level they tap into, such as the level of automaticity at which a bias occurs (Teachman et al., 2012). That is, interpretations can either occur immediately and automatically (i.e., online interpretations) or during later reflective or elaborative stages (i.e., offline interpretations). Critically, each type of bias offers valuable information about the interpretational style of an individual. For example, an individual might automatically interpret the way in which another person is looking at them in a negative manner, that is, they might construe their grin as a sign that the other person is making fun of them. However, upon reflection, an individual might then shift toward a more benign interpretation, that is, the person is grinning because of a good joke they made. Each type of interpretation bias (i.e., online vs. offline) requires a different type of assessment method. While directly asking individuals about their interpretation of an ambiguous situation enables the assessment of more controlled or deliberate interpretations, such an approach would not have the capacity to adequately capture more spontaneous or automatic interpretations (cf. Hirsch et al., 2016). Consequently, it is necessary to have access to a broader range of measures to enable the assessment of interpretation biases at different processing levels (i.e., automatic processing vs. strategic processing). This, in turn, provides the advantage that results obtained using one interpretation bias measure can be cross-validated using a different measure, and via such an approach it can be ensured that interpretation biases are not solely an artifact of a single tool (Munafò & Davey Smith, 2018).

In this chapter, we provide an overview of available measures used to assess interpretation biases, at both controlled and automatic levels (for an overview of how to manipulate interpretation biases, see Chap. 11 by Salemink et al.). For illustrative purposes, we will follow the classification introduced by Hirsch et al. (2016), whereby interpretation bias measures are classified as either offline (i.e., assessment permits participants to reflect on the ambiguous material) or as online (i.e., assessment does not permit deliberate reflection on the ambiguous material and instead aims to capture participants' automatic first reaction). However, it should be noted that additional classification systems exist, for example, classifying measurement procedures as either direct or indirect, which are based on whether participants are directly asked for their interpretations, or whether the interpretation is derived indirectly from responses to an ambiguous stimulus (see Everaert et al., 2017).

In the following sections, we present and discuss a selection of measures commonly used to assess interpretation biases, using the offline versus online classification system to structure this presentation. This will include a discussion of the different advantages and caveats of each measure (see Table 3.1). A full systematic review and extensive report of all existing offline and online measures is beyond the scope of this chapter (for overviews, see Hirsch et al., 2016; Schoth & Liossi, 2017). In our overview, we aim to (1) describe how each measure is operationalized to assess a specific interpretation bias, (2) summarize available research on the measure's utility in different emotional disorders, including the measure's reliability and validity indices, and (3) briefly discuss means on how to bridge the conceptualization of interpretation biases in basic research and clinical practice.

3.1 Offline Interpretation Bias Assessments

In the context of emotional psychopathology, there are numerous measures to assess offline interpretation biases, with self-report measures being the most commonly used method. In the following sections, we provide an overview of some of these measures.

3.1.1 The Starting Point: The Cognitive Bias Questionnaire

A large number of measures designed to assess offline interpretation biases has been developed over the past few decades, with the 1980s being the primary starting point of this work. Most of these seminal self-report measures were focused on assessing negative interpretation biases in relation to anxiety and depression (e.g., Butler & Mathews, 1983; Krantz & Hammen, 1979; McNally & Foa, 1987). As an example, a widely used offline measure in the context of depression is the Cognitive Bias Questionnaire (CBQ; Krantz & Hammen, 1979). This measure comprises the presentation of hypothetical problematic, daily life situations, for example, "A person is depicted as a member of an organization who was encouraged by friends to run for the presidency of the organization. She (he) eventually lost." Participants are instructed to put themselves into the described situation and imagine how they would think and feel in that situation. Next, participants are asked to read four interpretations and to select the one that is most closely aligned with their own interpretation of the situation, for example, "When you first heard you'd lost, you immediately:" (1) "feel bad and imagine I've lost by a landslide" (depressive-distorted);

Table 3.1 Summary of interpretation bias measures described in this chapter sorted on a continuum from offline to online measures

Offline	Bias measure	Outcome	Advantages	Disadvantages
→	Questionnaires	Level of agreement with and selection of presented interpretations/explanations of the ambiguous scenario. Estimated likelihood/plausibility of presented interpretations/explanations of ambiguous situations. Rank order of the presented interpretations/explanations of the ambiguous scenario. Imagined pleasantness of presented ambiguous scenarios.	Economic application. Established psychometric properties. Large validation samples. High face validity. Available for most disorder domains. Simple scoring and straightforward data interpretation.	Requires active evaluation of presented interpretation/explanations. Response – and demand effects. Potentially non-idiosyncratic. Inability to assess immediate and automatic interpretations.
	Scenario completion tasks	Disorder-congruency of generated scenario endings.	Economic application. Scenarios can be completed idiosyncratically. High face validity. Straightforward data interpretation.	Requires complex standardization of coding. Response – and demand effects. Inability to assess immediate and automatic interpretations.
	Scrambled Sentences Task (SST)	Ratio between correctly generated disorder-congruent versus all correctly generated sentences.	Limits conscious evaluation of presented material. Available across several disorder domains. Straightforward data interpretation.	Allows a certain level of conscious evaluation of the presented material. Cognitively demanding. Potentially non-idiosyncratic. Limited validation data across several disorder domains. Language characteristics may affect the generation of optimal stimuli.

Method	Measure	Advantages	Disadvantages
Word Sentence Association Paradigm (WSAP)	Endorsement of disorder-congruent vs. incongruent sentence-word combinations. Reaction times to disorder-congruent vs. incongruent sentence-word-combinations.	Capable of assessing reflective and automatic interpretations. Available across several disorder domains. Rich context through the presentation of ambiguous scenarios. Reaction times to disorder-congruent and incongruent targets can be assessed separately, allowing investigation of both positive and negative interpretation biases.	Cognitively demanding. Potentially non-idiosyncratic. Limited validation data across several disorder domains. Analyses of reaction times depend on endorsement rates – potentially limited number of trials for reaction-time analyses.
Lexical decision tasks (LDT) with short scenarios as context stimuli	Reaction times to disorder-congruent or incongruent sentence endings.	Limits conscious evaluation of presented material. Rich context through the presentation of ambiguous scenarios. Reaction times to disorder-congruent and incongruent targets can be assessed separately, allowing investigation of both positive and negative interpretation biases.	Cognitively demanding. Potentially non-idiosyncratic. Limited validation data across several disorder domains. Complex interpretation of reaction times because of comparisons of various trial types.
Lexical decision tasks (LDT) with single-word primes as context stimuli	Reaction times to disorder-congruent or incongruent target words.	Limits conscious evaluation of presented material. One-word stimuli can be easily generated for several disorder domains. Reaction times to disorder-congruent and incongruent targets can be assessed separately, allowing investigation of both positive and negative interpretation biases.	Cognitively demanding. Potentially non-idiosyncratic. Limited validation data across several disorder domains. Non-complex, one-word stimuli. Complex interpretation of reaction times because of comparisons of various trial types.

Online →

(2) "shrug it off as unimportant" (non-depressive distorted); (3) "feel sad and wonder what the total counts were" (depressive-non-distorted); (4) "shrug it off, feeling I tried as hard as I could" (non-depressive-non-distorted)." All problematic situations (the original CBQ includes six of such situations) are designed to trigger responses that represent depression-relevant cognitive distortions, as described by Beck, and thus participants' score index their tendency to select depressive-relevant interpretations. Accordingly, a greater tendency to select depression-relevant responses implies a greater depressive interpretation bias. Results from studies using the CBQ have shown that both dysphoric and clinically depressed individuals are more likely to choose depression-relevant responses compared to non-depressed individuals, supporting the hypothesis that negative interpretation biases are associated with depression (Carver et al., 1985; Krantz & Hammen, 1979; Miller & Norman, 1986). The CBQ has shown good reliability and convergent validity (e.g., Frost & MacInnis, 1983; Krantz & Hammen, 1979), with the selection of depression-relevant interpretations to the problematic situations showing significant positive correlations with other cognitive markers of depressive cognitions, for example, a higher number of depressive verbal behaviors reflecting spontaneous, negative self-statements assessed when asking participants to describe themselves (Frost & MacInnis, 1983).

3.1.2   Rank-Order Questionnaires

Alternative measures to the CBQ were developed during the end of the past century. Unlike measures such as the CBQ, many of these newer measures involved presenting ambiguous rather than problematic scenarios, requiring participants to interpret these ambiguous scenarios. To do so, each scenario is followed by multiple interpretations, and participants are asked to rank-order these interpretations, in terms of the likelihood of each interpretation popping into the participants' mind if they were in a similar situation. For instance, in the Interpretation Questionnaire (IQ) developed by Amir et al. (1998), ambiguous social scenarios (e.g., "Someone you are interested in dating says hello to you") are presented, followed by three potential interpretations of the scenario (i.e., "S/he wants to get to know you," positive interpretation; "S/he says hello to everyone," neutral interpretation; "S/he feels sorry for you," negative interpretation). Participants are asked to rank-order the three interpretations in terms of the likelihood of each presented interpretation popping into the participants' mind if they were in the described situation. The most likely interpretation, that is, the interpretation that is ranked first, is given the highest rating, a score of 3, the second most likely interpretation receives a score of 2, and the least likely interpretation is given a score of 1. The sum of these scores then provides an index of the likelihood to infer negative interpretations in socially relevant, ambiguous situations. Using the IQ, it has been shown that individuals with social anxiety disorder, but not those with obsessive–compulsive disorder or those without an anxiety disorder, tend to rank-order negative interpretations for ambiguous social scenarios as more likely (Amir et al., 1998). Moreover, higher tendencies to preferentially rank-order negative interpretations using the IQ have been found to mediate the effect of social anxiety on state anxiety in response to a momentary social stressor (Beard & Amir, 2010), indicating that the relationship between symptoms of social anxiety and state anxiety can be explained via socially relevant interpretation biases. The IQ has been found to produce relatively high-reliability indices (Amir et al., 1998).

In parallel, variations of rank-order methods were developed for other emotional disorders, such as obsessive–compulsive disorder and panic disorder. Given the type of interpretation biases relevant to each of the corresponding disorders, however, different types of stimuli were required. As an example, the Body Sensations Interpretation Questionnaire (BSIQ; Clark et al., 1997; and see McNally & Foa, 1987) assesses the misinterpretation of bodily sensations in the context of panic disorder. Hence, the BSIQ includes descriptions of ambiguous, bodily related responses and sensations, such as "You notice your heart is beating quickly and pounding. Why?" Participants are asked to rank-order possible explanations, comprising positive ("because you are feeling excited"), neutral ("because you have been physically active"), and panic-related ("because there is something wrong with your heart") interpretations of the presented ambiguous, bodily related responses and sensations. Scores of 3, 2, or 1 are assigned to each interpretation, depending on whether the panic-related interpretation is ranked in the first, second, or third place, and an overall interpretation score is then calculated, representing the mean ratings for panic-related interpretations. Using this measure, it has been shown that patients with panic disorder rank the panic-related interpretations as more probable compared to controls (e.g., Teachman et al., 2007) and patients with other anxiety disorders who had not experienced panic attacks (generalized anxiety disorder, social anxiety disorder; Clark et al., 1997). It is worth noting, however, that other studies have found similar higher rankings for panic-related interpretations for patients with both panic disorder and social anxiety disorder, as compared to healthy controls (e.g., Rosmarin et al., 2009). Further, other studies using rank-order measures have shown that panic-related interpretation biases were evident in both clinical and subclinical groups, but differed from controls (Richards et al., 2001). The BSIQ has satisfactory reliability (Clark et al., 1997; Keogh et al., 2004) and research supports its effectiveness to discriminate between individuals with panic disorder and other anxiety problems (e.g., Clark et al., 1997; but see also Rosmarin et al., 2009).

3.1.3   Imagery-Based Assessments: The Ambiguous Scenarios Test

While the previously described measures mostly instructed participants to imagine themselves in the described situation, they did not explicitly use imagery as a processing mode itself. That is, these measures did not instruct participants to use mental imagery when working through the task's crucial elements. It has been theorized that imagery may prompt a stronger emotional response, and thus may trigger interpretation biases more easily (for an overview of the role of imagery in biased interpretational processing, see Chap. 6 by Blackwell), leading to the development of various imagery-based measures. One example is the Ambiguous Scenarios Test to assess depression-related interpretation biases (AST-D, Berna et al., 2011). The AST comprises ambiguous, scenarios (e.g., "It's New Year's Eve. You think about the year ahead of you."), and participants are asked to form a mental image of the presented scenario. Specifically, participants are instructed to imagine themselves in the described situation and by doing so mentally solve the ambiguity. Participants are then prompted to rate how pleasant their self-generated imagery was, using a 11-point Likert scale, ranging from "extremely unpleasant" to "extremely pleasant." The mean score of this rating provides an index of participants' interpretational style, with lower pleasantness ratings indicating a stronger negative interpretation bias.

Research supports the AST's utility to detect individual differences in depression-relevant interpretation biases (e.g., Berna et al., 2011; Rohrbacher & Reinecke, 2014). Furthermore, the AST has also been successfully applied in other areas of emotional psychopathology, for example, in generalized anxiety disorder or social phobia (see Schoth & Liossi, 2017), and it has been adapted to measure negative interpretation biases in youth (e.g., Sfärlea et al., 2020). Moreover, studies have shown that the AST is a sensitive measure with the capacity to detect changes in interpretation biases with treatment. For instance, Nieto and Vazquez (2021) found that following a cognitive intervention designed to modify negative interpretation biases in depression change in negative interpretation bias, assessed using the AST, accounted for transfers of the intervention in reducing depressive symptoms and dysfunctional attitudes. The AST has shown both good internal consistency (Berna et al., 2011) and convergent validity (Rohrbacher & Reinecke, 2014).

3.1.4 Generation of Multiple Interpretations: The Interpretation Bias Questionnaire

In contrast to measures that present participants with pre-defined interpretations with the instruction to, for example, rate these interpretations or select the most plausible one, the AST and other (contemporary) offline measures have been developed to prompt self-generated solutions to ambiguous scenarios, that is, participants are prompted to self-generate their own idiosyncratic interpretations of the presented ambiguity. This includes the use of open-ended questionnaires, such as the Interpretation Bias Questionnaire (IBQ, Wisco & Nolen-Hoeksema, 2010). In the IBQ as used by Wisco and Nolen-Hoeksama, for example, participants are presented with scenarios describing ambiguous, social situations (e.g., "You call a good friend of yours and leave a message suggesting getting together later in the week. A few days pass, and you haven't heard from them. Why haven't they returned your call?"). Next, participants are asked to write down all possible explanations/ interpretations that come to their mind (interpretation generation). After generating multiple possible interpretations, they then select the interpretation that they consider as the "most likely" explanation of the situation (interpretation selection). In a further step, participants may be also asked to rate the positivity and negativity of their self-generated interpretation, as is required in the AST (see Schoth & Liossi, 2017, for an overview of the variations in these methods). The IBQ requires trained independent coders to rate the negativity and positivity of all interpretations generated by the participant. By doing so, this procedure permits the computation of separate indices of a negative interpretation generation bias (computed by subtracting the sum of all positivity ratings from the sum of all negativity ratings for all interpretations generated across the scenarios) and a negative interpretation selection bias (computed by subtracting the sum of all positivity ratings from the sum of all negativity ratings of the interpretations that were selected as the most likely explanation across the scenarios' descriptions).

Using these indices, it has been shown that depressed, compared to non-depressed, individuals show greater negative biases both in interpretation generation as well as in interpretation selection (Wisco & Nolen-Hoeksema, 2010) and that higher negative interpretation generation and selection biases are related to higher individual levels of both depression (e.g., Normansell & Wisco, 2017; Wisco & Nolen-Hoeksema, 2011) and anxiety symptoms (e.g., O'Connor et al., 2021). Further, this approach has demonstrated good reliability (e.g., coders' interrater reliability for ratings of the responses, in Wisco & Nolen-Hoeksema, 2010), and split-half reliability (O'Connor et al., 2021), as well as positive correlations with other online interpretation bias measures, such as those described below (i.e., the Scrambled Sentence Task and the Word-Sentence Association Paradigm; O'Connor et al., 2021).

3.1.5 Questionnaires Prompting the Completion of Open-Ended Sentences

Sentence completion tasks follow the same logic as the IBQ assessment described earlier. Such completion tasks were initially developed in the context of depression (see, for instance, Barton et al., 2005; Barton & Morley, 1999), but have since been adapted and applied in other contexts of emotional psychopathology, for example, in the context of anxiety (e.g., Huppert et al., 2007). Using this measure, participants are, for example, presented with short sentence stems comprising agent–verb combinations (e.g., "I think ...") or simple nouns (e.g., "The world ...") and are then asked to complete these stems by providing a suitable ending, that is, an interpretation. Participants are allowed to use as many words as they like, and independent coders will then code how many negative, positive, or neutral interpretations were generated. As such, separate indices are derived, reflecting the total number of negative and positive interpretations generated. Such sentence completion tasks have demonstrated validity, by showing that clinically depressed patients generated more negative and fewer positive interpretations compared to healthy controls, as well as high reliability in terms of inter-rater agreement (Barton et al., 2005).

More elaborate versions of open-ended tasks have been developed in other contexts, for example, social anxiety (Hertel et al., 2008) or posttraumatic stress symptoms (Woud et al., 2019, 2021). Such tasks include open-ended scenarios which end abruptly, requiring participants to complete the scenario by writing down the first spontaneous ending that comes to their mind. For instance, open-ended scenarios have been developed to measure appraisal biases in the context of post-traumatic stress symptoms. Using ambiguous, open-ended trauma-related scenarios (e.g., "Since the event happened, I know how I will react in difficult situations. I will react ..."), Woud et al. (2019) found that stronger dysfunctional appraisals were predictive of current posttraumatic stress symptoms. Additionally, Woud et al. (2021) found that changes in dysfunctional appraisals assessed via open-ended scenarios mediated reductions in trauma symptoms, and that, overall, the scenario task showed good psychometric properties, further highlighting the validity of this type of measure.

3.2   Online Interpretation Bias Assessments

Overall, offline assessments as described in the previous section are easy to apply, for example, via paper-and-pencil tasks, and yield reliable indices of interpretation biases. Furthermore, the stimuli used in these measures, especially those that include detailed descriptions of anxious- or depression-relevant (daily-life) situations, are salient cues for many participants, indicating the measures' ecological validity. Nonetheless, offline tasks are characterized by several limitations, partly because they rely on self-report. Specifically, most of these tasks require active and conscious evaluation of the presented ambiguous material in order to infer interpretation biases, and this operationalization is prone to be affected by both response and demand effects. That is, the participant can reflect on how they may want to respond, or they may have expectancies on how they should respond, which in turn compromises the validity of the obtained measure. Further, the need to engage in controlled processing poses the limitation that initial, automatic aspects of interpretation biases cannot be captured (Hirsch et al., 2016).

To overcome some of the abovementioned limitations, online interpretation bias measures have been developed. Online measures rely on behavioral responses to infer the participant's interpretation of the presented material (e.g., their reaction time to categorize stimuli) and thus have the capacity to capture more automatic aspects of interpretation biases. A selection of some of the most commonly used online measures is presented in the following sections.

3.2.1 Making Sense of Scrambled Information: The Scrambled Sentences Task

The Scrambled Sentences Task (SST) was first applied by Wenzlaff and Bates (1998) with the aim to assess interpretation biases in individuals remitted from depression. The focus on remitted depression was motivated by the theoretical notion that negative interpretation biases in depression persist in the state of remission and could potentially confer vulnerability to recurrence, yet are suppressed and thus not consciously available (Beck, 1976). As suppressing these negative interpretations was expected to be an effortful process, it was hypothesized that a lapse of this suppression, for example, by challenging the individual's cognitive capacity via an additional cognitive task (e.g., memorizing a number while performing the SST), would serve to reveal negative interpretations that would otherwise be obscured by controlled processes. Based on this conceptualization, the SST is designed as follows: On each trial, participants are provided with a list of six words with instructions to form grammatically correct sentences from the words provided. However, participants are instructed that one word needs to be omitted to create a correct sentence. The sentences are designed such that depending on which word is omitted, the sentence either has a disorder-congruent or incongruent meaning (e.g., scrambled sentence: "dismal bright future looks very my"; positive solution: "my future looks very bright"; negative solution: "my future looks very dismal"). Simultaneously, participants are required to memorize a six-digit number and to respond within a specific time limit (~8–12 s per set of words) to further reduce the use of deliberate responding. A bias score is derived from the SST by calculating the proportion of negatively formed sentences over completed sentences, resulting in a total score ranging between 0 and 1. This bias score represents the strength of an interpretation bias, with higher scores reflecting a stronger negative bias. While the original task was designed as a paper and pencil task, with participants writing the corresponding numbers above the words, more recent studies used computerized versions of the SST, in which participants sort the words by clicking on them (Blanco et al., 2021; Brockmeyer et al., 2018).

The SST bias score has been shown to be associated with symptoms of depression, such that a stronger negative interpretation bias on the SST has been found to be associated with more severe symptoms of depression (Lee et al., 2016; Lin et al., 2020; Phillips et al., 2012). Further, the SST has been adapted to assess interpretation biases in other areas of psychopathology, with evidence for similar associations between the SST bias score and symptoms of interest, including generalized anxiety disorder and worry (Hirsch et al., 2018, 2020), social anxiety (e.g., de Voogd et al., 2017), anxiety sensitivity in the context of panic (Zahler et al., 2020), and female sexual dysfunction (Zahler et al., 2021). Further, patients show a more negative interpretation bias when compared to healthy control participants in the context of anorexia nervosa (Brockmeyer et al., 2018), psychosis (Savulich et al., 2017), and depression (including remitted depressed individuals; Rude et al., 2010). Overall, the usefulness of the SST has been shown in various participant populations including children (Sfärlea et al., 2020), adolescents (de Voogd et al., 2017), and older adults (Murphy et al., 2015). This measure also demonstrates good psychometric properties, indicated by consistent associations between the bias score and symptoms and good reliability (Würtz et al., 2022). While the SST is designed to overcome some of the disadvantages of purely offline measures, there is an ongoing discussion as to whether the SST is in fact an on- or offline measure of interpretation biases, as the task still allows some active evaluation of the stimuli (O'Connor et al., 2021; for a review and meta-analysis, see Würtz et al., 2022).

3.2.2   Word or Non-Word?: Lexical Decision Tasks

A prominent example of a reaction time-based measure of interpretation bias includes lexical decision tasks. In these tasks, participants are primed with a "context" stimulus, that is, ambiguous or disorder-related words or sentences, and are asked to make a decision on a target word that is presented following the context stimulus, for example, deciding whether the target word is a word or non-word. However, only reaction times to existing words are analyzed. That is, the time taken to categorize disorder-related versus disorder-unrelated target words serves as the measure of interest. The investigation of reaction times in research on interpretation biases follows the general logic of the priming literature (cf. Fischler, 1977). That is, reaction times are considered a measure of the associative strength between a provided context and a target, with faster reaction times indicating a stronger association between context and target. In other words, faster reaction times are considered to be indicative of a stronger conceptual link between disorder-relevant contexts and target stimuli, thus reflecting a stronger disorder-related interpretation bias. While there are different approaches to assessing interpretation biases via lexical decision tasks, most paradigms share a common setup and operationalization. Specifically, participants are presented with a context stimulus and need to decide whether a subsequently presented target stimulus is an existing word or non-word, or whether it grammatically fits with the context stimulus. Three versions of this setup will be described next. The first set-up uses briefly presented semantic primes as context stimuli and participants need to decide whether the subsequently presented word is a word or non-word (e.g., Hermans et al., 2010); the second set-up uses disorder-related scenarios as context stimuli with words and non-words as targets (e.g., Calvo et al., 1994; Hirsch & Mathews, 1997); and the third set-up is an adaptation of the second set-up, yet participants are instructed to decide whether the target stimulus is either a grammatically correct or incorrect ending of the provided context stimulus (e.g., Moser et al., 2008).

The basic set-up of a lexical decision task using semantic primes as context stimuli is as follows: First, participants are presented briefly with a prime (e.g., for ~200 ms), consisting of either a disorder-irrelevant or a disorder-relevant word (e.g., in the context of panic disorder: "flower" vs. "heartbeat"). This is followed by the presentation of a target word, consisting of either a disorder-relevant (e.g., "infarct") or neutral word (e.g., "sun"), or a non-word (e.g., "krish"). Participants are then required to categorize the target word into its corresponding category. Specifically, participants are instructed to categorize the target word into the categories "existing word" or "non-word" as fast as possible, while making as few mistakes as possible. In the most basic application, an interpretation bias score is derived by subtracting the reaction times with which participants react to the disorder-relevant targets following the disorder-relevant primes from reaction times to the disorder-relevant targets following disorder-irrelevant primes (e.g., Zahler et al., 2021).

The second set-up uses more complex context stimuli, such as ambiguous and incomplete disorder-relevant scenarios (e.g., in the context of social anxiety: "You are standing in the front of the class and the audience is…"). After reading the scenario, participants are presented with either a target word that resolves the ambiguity in a positive (e.g., "excited") or negative (e.g., "bored") manner, or a target word that does not resolve the scenario's ambiguity (e.g., a non-word, "utsri"). As with the basic semantic priming paradigms, participants are instructed to categorize the target words as words or non-words as quickly as possible, and reaction times then allow the computation of two different indices. Specifically, reaction times to categorize positive targets allow computing an index for a positive interpretation bias, whereas reaction times to categorize negative targets allow to compute an index of a negative interpretation bias. Faster reaction times are interpreted as reflecting a stronger bias toward the respective valence. A third set-up involves the application of grammatically correct (e.g., using the previous example: "bored" vs. "excited") versus incorrect (e.g., "bore") scenario endings as target words, instead of words versus non-words. When applying this variant, participants are instructed to decide whether the ending is grammatically correct or incorrect. However, the computation of the bias indices and the interpretation of these indices stay the same.

Lexical decision tasks comprising either simple primes or more complex contextual stimuli are frequently applied to assess interpretation biases, in various disorders. Using lexical decision tasks, disorder-related interpretation biases have been found to be associated with panic disorder (e.g., Hermans et al., 2010; Schneider & Schulte, 2007), depression and social phobia (Moser et al., 2012), worry (e.g., Feng et al., 2019), and eating disorders (e.g., Misener & Libben, 2017). For example, Hermans et al. (2010) found that patients with panic disorder were faster to react to panic-related target words following panic-related primes compared to trials containing either neutral target words or neutral primes. Further, using ambiguous sentences as context stimuli, Feng et al. (2019) found that participants with an elevated dispositional tendency to worry reacted equally fast to positive and negative target words resolving the ambiguity, whereas participants with a lower dispositional tendency to worry reacted faster to positive than to negative target words. These results suggest that participants with a low tendency to worry exhibit a positive interpretation bias while this is not found in participants with high dispositional worry. Overall, these studies provide evidence for the validity of lexical decision tasks in the context of emotional psychopathology, as well as their applicability in different participant populations including both diagnosed (e.g., Moser et al., 2012) and subclinical participants (Feng et al., 2019). However, there is currently a lack of evidence on the reliability of lexical decision tasks, leaving the investigation of their psychometric properties a subject for future research.

3.2.3   Related or Unrelated?: The Word-Sentence Association Paradigm (WSAP)

Initially developed by Beard and Amir (2009), the WSAP combines decision-based and reaction time-based assessments of interpretation biases. To illustrate, participants are presented with disorder-congruent or incongruent words (e.g., congruent with social anxiety: "embarrassing," incongruent: "funny"), followed by a short ambiguous disorder-related sentence (e.g., "After delivering a speech, the crowd bursts in laughter"). Participants are instructed to indicate as fast as possible whether or not the word was related to the sentence, and both the decision and the reaction time are recorded. This allows the computation of two possible indices for interpretation biases: (1) a positive interpretation bias index based on endorsing disorder-incongruent or rejecting disorder-congruent words, or (2) a negative interpretation bias index based on endorsing disorder-congruent or rejecting disorder-incongruent words. While the endorsement rate of positive and negative words directly translates to a positive or negative interpretation bias, respectively, interpreting reaction times follows the same logic as for the lexical decision tasks. That is, faster reaction times to endorse negative words or slower reaction times to reject negative words are indicative of a stronger negative interpretation bias, whereas faster reaction times to endorse positive words or reject negative words are indicative of a stronger positive interpretation bias.

The WSAP was initially applied to assess interpretation biases in the context of social anxiety (Beard & Amir, 2008, 2009). In this context, it has been shown that participants with social anxiety endorse more threatening and fewer benign words on the WSAP, compared to non-anxious controls, and are also faster to endorse negative compared to positive words (Beard & Amir, 2009), indicating the postulated negative interpretation bias. More recently, the WSAP has been adopted and applied in various other disorders, and generally, its bias indices have been shown to be associated with symptoms of the respective disorder, for example, eating disorders/body dissatisfaction (Martinelli et al., 2014), depression (e.g., Hindash & Amir, 2012), and obsessive–compulsive disorder (e.g., Kuckertz et al., 2013). Further, the WSAP has been applied in both (in-)patient (e.g., Beard et al., 2019) and sub-clinical samples (e.g., Cowden Hindash & Rottenberg, 2017) including children and adolescents (e.g., Sherman & Ehrenreich-May, 2018). While some studies included interpretation bias indices derived from both the endorsement rates and reaction times with both indices being correlated with symptoms of the target disorder (e.g., Sherman & Ehrenreich-May, 2018), it is worth noting that most studies only assessed endorsement rates (e.g., Amir et al., 2015). Accordingly, there is rich evidence for the applicability and sound psychometric properties of the endorsement rates, yet the evidence is limited for the associated reaction times (for a review, see Gonsalves et al., 2019), thus warranting further research.

3.3   Here and Back Again, Basic Research, and Clinical Application

As presented above, research on interpretation biases has provided several measures, and these measures produced important insights into pathogenesis and maintenance of various mental disorders in the context of emotional psychopathology. Due to their capacity to capture different aspects of interpretation biases, these measures may also provide clinical utility, that is, may have the potential to be used in clinically applied contexts. For example, they may be employed in routine care to track how interpretation biases change during treatment, whether biases differ in strength e.g., pre- to post-treatment, and by doing so inform mechanism-based treatment decisions. Further, administering interpretation biases measures in applied contexts may aid the identification of measures that maintain validity outside the controlled settings of the laboratory or strictly supervised clinical trials. This, in turn, could aid in bridging basic research with clinical practice (for a discussion about moving experimental psychopathology research into clinical practice, see Blackwell & Woud, 2022). However, due to partly unclear psychometric properties, in particular for online reaction time-based measures, interpretation bias measures are not yet suitable as clinical instruments, neither for treatment decisions nor individualized diagnostics.

Another potential way of bridging basic research and clinical practice could be realized by implementing the other direction, that is, the use of the clinical conceptualization of interpretation biases when assessing such biases in basic research. To illustrate, identifying and discussing interpretation biases with patients have a long-standing tradition in cognitive therapy (e.g., Beck, 1976, and for a recent overview, see Woud, 2022), for example, through behavioral experiments (for an overview of therapeutic techniques to change interpretation biases, see also Chap. 12 by Woud & Hofmann). During behavioral experiments, patients are confronted with disorder-related situations that are supposed to help patients to identify their (biased) interpretations and, as a next step, test whether these interpretations correspond to reality and are plausible. Such an explicit approach therefore may provide a tool to assess interpretation biases in a concrete and ecologically valid manner that corresponds to patients' actual and idiosyncratic interpretations. To provide an example, a suitable behavioral experiment in the context of panic disorder is the Straw-Breathing-Task (Taylor & Rachman, 1994). During this behavioral experiment, participants breathe through a narrow straw to provoke panic-relevant symptoms such as palpitations or breathlessness. Since these symptoms are merely unpleasant, yet harmless, patients' evaluations of these symptoms can be used to infer their specific and real-life (mis) interpretations of bodily symptoms (cf. Zahler et al., 2020). The inclusion of such an interpretation bias conceptualization in basic research, that is close to patients' natural, idiosyncratic biases, could be a valuable addition to the rather abstract measures presented in this chapter, in order to index patients' interpretational processing styles in a more holistic and ecologically valid manner. This is of particular interest given the evidence that the effects of potential interventions developed within the framework of experimental psychopathology to reduce interpretation biases (e.g., cognitive bias modification techniques) so far only showed limited and inconsistent transfer to symptoms (for a review of meta-analyses, see Jones & Sharpe, 2017; and for an overview of how to manipulate interpretation biases, see Chap. 11 by Salemink et al.). Ultimately, exchanging methods to assess and conceptualize interpretation biases between basic research and clinical practice has the potential of increasing transferability between the two, potentially leading to both a refinement of our measures and an improvement of our interventions.

3.4 Summary and Outlook

In conclusion, there are several commonly applied offline and online measures in research targeting interpretation biases. The measures' application has provided substantial evidence that interpretation biases are strongly associated with symptoms of emotional psychopathology and may also predict their onset. Given the considerable contributions made by interpretation bias measures in improving our understanding of mental disorders, it seems very important to start including them in clinical practice, for example, to foster mechanism-informed treatment decisions. This, however, is currently limited by a lack of research on the psychometric properties of these measures, in particular for online measures using reaction times as bias indices. Ultimately, the inclusion of interpretation bias measures in clinical practice, as well as the inclusion of the biases' clinical conceptualization in basic research, serves to enable more fine-grained research on basic mechanisms and to develop innovative treatments of emotional psychopathology.

Acknowledgments We are very grateful to Dr. Laura Dondzilo for her assistance and comments on earlier versions of the chapter. Felix Würtz is supported by a doctoral scholarship from the Studienstiftung des deutschen Volkes. Alvaro Sanchez-Lopez has been supported by a grant of the Program of Attraction of Talent, Modality I, of the Community of Madrid (reference 2017-T1/SOC-5359), and a grant of the Spanish Ministry of Science and Innovation, Program "Generation of Knowledge" ref. PGC2018-095723-A-I00, and is currently supported by a grant of the Spanish Ministry of Science and Innovation, Program "Generation of Knowledge" ref. PID2021-127480NB-I00.

References

Amir, N., Foa, E. B., & Coles, M. E. (1998). Negative interpretation bias in social phobia. *Behaviour Research and Therapy, 36*(10), 945–957. https://doi.org/10.1016/S0005-7967(98)00060-6
Amir, N., Kuckertz, J. M., Najmi, S., & Conley, S. L. (2015). Preliminary evidence for the enhancement of self-conducted exposures for OCD using cognitive bias modification. *Cognitive Therapy and Research, 39*(4), 424–440. https://doi.org/10.1007/s10608-015-9675-7
Barton, S., & Morley, S. (1999). Specificity of reference patterns in depressive thinking: Agency and object roles in self-representation. *Journal of Abnormal Psychology, 108*(4), 655–661. https://doi.org/10.1037/0021-843X.108.4.655

Barton, S., Morley, S., Bloxham, G., Kitson, C., & Platts, S. (2005). Sentence completion test for depression (SCD): An idiographic measure of depressive thinking. *British Journal of Clinical Psychology, 44*(1), 29–46. https://doi.org/10.1348/014466504X19794

Beard, C., & Amir, N. (2008). A multi-session interpretation modification program: Changes in interpretation and social anxiety symptoms. *Behaviour Research and Therapy, 46*(10), 1135–1141. https://doi.org/10.1016/j.brat.2008.05.012

Beard, C., & Amir, N. (2009). Interpretation in social anxiety: When meaning precedes ambiguity. *Cognitive Therapy and Research, 33*(4), 406–415. https://doi.org/10.1007/s10608-009-9235-0

Beard, C., & Amir, N. (2010). Negative interpretation bias mediates the effect of social anxiety on state anxiety. *Cognitive Therapy and Research, 34*(3), 292–296. https://doi.org/10.1007/s10608-009-9258-6

Beard, C., Peckham, A. D., Griffin, M. L., Weiss, R. D., Taghian, N., & McHugh, R. K. (2019). Associations among interpretation bias, craving, and abstinence self-efficacy in adults with substance use disorders. *Drug and Alcohol Dependence, 205*, 107644. https://doi.org/10.1016/j.drugalcdep.2019.107644

Beck, A. T. (1976). *Cognitive therapy and the emotional disorders* (p. 356). International Universities Press.

Beck, A. T., & Bredemeier, K. (2016). A unified model of depression: Integrating clinical, cognitive, biological, and evolutionary perspectives. *Clinical Psychological Science, 4*(4), 596–619. https://doi.org/10.1177/2167702616628523

Berna, C., Lang, T. J., Goodwin, G. M., & Holmes, E. A. (2011). Developing a measure of interpretation bias for depressed mood: An ambiguous scenarios test. *Personality and Individual Differences, 51*(3), 349–354. https://doi.org/10.1016/j.paid.2011.04.005

Blackwell, S. E., & Woud, M. L. (2022). Making the leap: From experimental psychopathology to clinical trials. *Journal of Experimental Psychopathology, 13*(1), 204380872210800. https://doi.org/10.1177/20438087221080075

Blanco, I., Boemo, T., & Sanchez-Lopez, A. (2021). An online assessment to evaluate the role of cognitive biases and emotion regulation strategies for mental health during the COVID-19 lockdown of 2020: Structural equation modeling study. *JMIR Mental Health, 8*(11), e30961. https://doi.org/10.2196/30961

Brockmeyer, T., Anderle, A., Schmidt, H., Febry, S., Wünsch-Leiteritz, W., Leiteritz, A., & Friederich, H.-C. (2018). Body image related negative interpretation bias in anorexia nervosa. *Behaviour Research and Therapy, 104*, 69–73. https://doi.org/10.1016/j.brat.2018.03.003

Butler, G., & Mathews, A. (1983). Cognitive processes in anxiety. *Advances in Behaviour Research and Therapy, 5*(1), 51–62. https://doi.org/10.1016/0146-6402(83)90015-2

Calvo, M. G., Eysenck, M. W., & Estevez, A. (1994). Ego-threat interpretive bias in test anxiety: On-line inferences. *Cognition & Emotion, 8*(2), 127–146. https://doi.org/10.1080/02699939408408932

Carver, C. S., Ganellen, R. J., & Behar-Mitrani, V. (1985). Depression and cognitive style: Comparisons between measures. *Journal of Personality and Social Psychology, 49*(3), 722–728. https://doi.org/10.1037/0022-3514.49.3.722

Chen, J., Short, M., & Kemps, E. (2020). Interpretation bias in social anxiety: A systematic review and meta-analysis. *Journal of Affective Disorders, 276*, 1119–1130. https://doi.org/10.1016/j.jad.2020.07.121

Clark, D. M. (1986). A cognitive approach to panic. *Behaviour Research and Therapy, 24*(4), 461–470. https://doi.org/10.1016/0005-7967(86)90011-2

Clark, D. M., Salkovskis, P. M., Öst, L.-G., Breitholtz, E., Koehler, K. A., Westling, B. E., Jeavons, A., & Gelder, M. (1997). Misinterpretation of body sensations in panic disorder. *Journal of Consulting and Clinical Psychology, 65*(2), 203–213. https://doi.org/10.1037/0022-006X.65.2.203

Cowden Hindash, A. H., & Rottenberg, J. (2017). Turning quickly on myself: Automatic interpretation biases in dysphoria are self-referent. *Cognition and Emotion, 31*(2), 395–402. https://doi.org/10.1080/02699931.2015.1105792

de Voogd, E. L., de Hullu, E., Heyes, S. B., Blackwell, S. E., Wiers, R. W., & Salemink, E. (2017). Imagine the bright side of life: A randomized controlled trial of two types of interpretation bias modification procedure targeting adolescent anxiety and depression. *PLoS One, 12*(7). https://doi.org/10.1371/journal.pone.0181147

Ehlers, A., & Clark, D. M. (2000). A cognitive model of posttraumatic stress disorder. *Behaviour Research and Therapy, 38*(4), 319–345. https://doi.org/10.1016/S0005-7967(99)00123-0

Everaert, J., & Koster, E. H. W. (2020). The interplay among attention, interpretation, and memory biases in depression: Revisiting the combined cognitive bias hypothesis. In *Cognitive biases in health and psychiatric disorders: Neurophysiological foundations* (pp. 193–213). Elsevier Academic Press. https://doi.org/10.1016/B978-0-12-816660-4.00009-X

Everaert, J., Podina, I. R., & Koster, E. H. W. (2017). A comprehensive meta-analysis of interpretation biases in depression. *Clinical Psychology Review, 58*, 33–48. https://doi.org/10.1016/j.cpr.2017.09.005

Feng, Y.-C., Krahé, C., Sumich, A., Meeten, F., Lau, J. Y. F., & Hirsch, C. R. (2019). Using event-related potential and behavioural evidence to understand interpretation bias in relation to worry. *Biological Psychology, 148*, 107746. https://doi.org/10.1016/j.biopsycho.2019.107746

Fischler, I. (1977). Semantic facilitation without association in a lexical decision task. *Memory & Cognition, 5*(3), 335–339. https://doi.org/10.3758/BF03197580

Frost, R. O., & MacInnis, D. J. (1983). The cognitive bias questionnaire: Further evidence. *Journal of Personality Assessment, 47*(2), 173–177. https://doi.org/10.1207/s15327752jpa4702_12

Gonsalves, M., Whittles, R. L., Weisberg, R. B., & Beard, C. (2019). A systematic review of the word sentence association paradigm (WSAP). *Journal of Behavior Therapy and Experimental Psychiatry, 64*, 133–148. https://doi.org/10.1016/j.jbtep.2019.04.003

Hermans, D., De Cort, K., Noortman, D., Vansteenwegen, D., Beckers, T., Spruyt, A., & Schruers, K. (2010). Priming associations between bodily sensations and catastrophic misinterpretations: Specific for panic disorder? *Behaviour Research and Therapy, 48*(9), 900–908. https://doi.org/10.1016/j.brat.2010.05.015

Hertel, P. T., Brozovich, F., Joormann, J., & Gotlib, I. H. (2008). Biases in interpretation and memory in generalized social phobia. *Journal of Abnormal Psychology, 117*(2), 278–288. https://doi.org/10.1037/0021-843X.117.2.278

Hindash, A. H. C., & Amir, N. (2012). Negative interpretation bias in individuals with depressive symptoms. *Cognitive Therapy and Research, 36*(5), 502–511. https://doi.org/10.1007/s10608-011-9397-4

Hirsch, C. R., & Mathews, A. (1997). Interpretative inferences when reading about emotional events. *Behaviour Research and Therapy, 35*(12), 1123–1132. https://doi.org/10.1016/S0005-7967(97)00069-7

Hirsch, C. R., Meeten, F., Krahé, C., & Reeder, C. (2016). Resolving ambiguity in emotional disorders: The nature and role of interpretation biases. *Annual Review of Clinical Psychology, 12*(1), 281–305. https://doi.org/10.1146/annurev-clinpsy-021815-093436

Hirsch, C. R., Krahé, C., Whyte, J., Loizou, S., Bridge, L., Norton, S., & Mathews, A. (2018). Interpretation training to target repetitive negative thinking in generalized anxiety disorder and depression. *Journal of Consulting and Clinical Psychology, 86*(12), 1017–1030. https://doi.org/10.1037/ccp0000310

Hirsch, C. R., Krahé, C., Whyte, J., Bridge, L., Loizou, S., Norton, S., & Mathews, A. (2020). Effects of modifying interpretation bias on transdiagnostic repetitive negative thinking. *Journal of Consulting and Clinical Psychology, 88*(3), 226–239. https://doi.org/10.1037/ccp0000455

Huppert, J. D., Pasupuleti, R. V., Foa, E. B., & Mathews, A. (2007). Interpretation biases in social anxiety: Response generation, response selection, and self-appraisals. *Behaviour Research and Therapy, 45*(7), 1505–1515. https://doi.org/10.1016/j.brat.2007.01.006

Jones, E. B., & Sharpe, L. (2017). Cognitive bias modification: A review of meta-analyses. *Journal of Affective Disorders, 223*, 175–183. https://doi.org/10.1016/j.jad.2017.07.034

Keogh, E., Hamid, R., Hamid, S., & Ellery, D. (2004). Investigating the effect of anxiety sensitivity, gender and negative interpretative bias on the perception of chest pain. *Pain, 111*(1), 209–217. https://doi.org/10.1016/j.pain.2004.06.017

Krantz, S., & Hammen, C. L. (1979). Assessment of cognitive bias in depression. *Journal of Abnormal Psychology, 88*(6), 611–619. https://doi.org/10.1037/0021-843X.88.6.611

Kuckertz, J. M., Amir, N., Tobin, A. C., & Najmi, S. (2013). Interpretation of ambiguity in individuals with obsessive-compulsive symptoms. *Cognitive Therapy and Research, 37*(2), 232–241. https://doi.org/10.1007/s10608-012-9478-z

Lee, J. S., Mathews, A., Shergill, S., & Yiend, J. (2016). Magnitude of negative interpretation bias depends on severity of depression. *Behaviour Research and Therapy, 83*, 26–34. https://doi.org/10.1016/j.brat.2016.05.007

Lin, X.-X., Si, S.-W., Gao, R.-R., Sun, Y.-B., Wang, Y.-Z., Wang, N., Luo, F., & Wang, J.-Y. (2020). Does approach-avoidance behavior in response to ambiguous cues reflect depressive interpretation bias? Related but distinct. *Cognitive Therapy and Research, 44*(6), 1091–1105. https://doi.org/10.1007/s10608-020-10133-0

Martinelli, M. K., Holzinger, J. B., & Chasson, G. S. (2014). Validation of an interpretation bias assessment for body dissatisfaction. *Body Image, 11*(4), 557–561. https://doi.org/10.1016/j.bodyim.2014.08.010

Mathews, A., & MacLeod, C. (2005). Cognitive vulnerability to emotional disorders. *Annual Review of Clinical Psychology, 1*(1), 167–195. https://doi.org/10.1146/annurev.clinpsy.1.102803.143916

McNally, R. J., & Foa, E. B. (1987). Cognition and agoraphobia: Bias in the interpretation of threat. *Cognitive Therapy and Research, 11*(5), 567–581. https://doi.org/10.1007/BF01183859

Miller, I. W., & Norman, W. H. (1986). Persistence of depressive cognitions within a subgroup of depressed inpatients. *Cognitive Therapy and Research, 10*(2), 211–224. https://doi.org/10.1007/BF01173726

Misener, K., & Libben, M. (2017). Risk for eating disorders modulates interpretation bias in a semantic priming task. *Body Image, 21*, 103–106. https://doi.org/10.1016/j.bodyim.2017.03.004

Moser, J. S., Hajcak, G., Huppert, J. D., Foa, E. B., & Simons, R. F. (2008). Interpretation bias in social anxiety as detected by event-related brain potentials. *Emotion, 8*(5), 693–700. https://doi.org/10.1037/a0013173

Moser, J. S., Huppert, J. D., Foa, E. B., & Simons, R. F. (2012). Interpretation of ambiguous social scenarios in social phobia and depression: Evidence from event-related brain potentials. *Biological Psychology, 89*(2), 387–397. https://doi.org/10.1016/j.biopsycho.2011.12.001

Munafò, M. R., & Davey Smith, G. (2018). Robust research needs many lines of evidence. *Nature, 553*(7689), 399–401. https://doi.org/10.1038/d41586-018-01023-3

Murphy, S. E., O'Donoghue, M. C., Drazich, E. H. S., Blackwell, S. E., Nobre, A. C., & Holmes, E. A. (2015). Imagining a brighter future: The effect of positive imagery training on mood, prospective mental imagery and emotional bias in older adults. *Psychiatry Research, 230*(1), 36–43. https://doi.org/10.1016/j.psychres.2015.07.059

Nieto, I., & Vazquez, C. (2021). Disentangling the mediating role of modifying interpretation bias on emotional distress using a novel cognitive bias modification program. *Journal of Anxiety Disorders, 83*, 102459. https://doi.org/10.1016/j.janxdis.2021.102459

Normansell, K. M., & Wisco, B. E. (2017). Negative interpretation bias as a mechanism of the relationship between rejection sensitivity and depressive symptoms. *Cognition and Emotion, 31*(5), 950–962. https://doi.org/10.1080/02699931.2016.1185395

O'Connor, C. E., Everaert, J., & Fitzgerald, A. (2021). Interpreting ambiguous emotional information: Convergence among interpretation bias measures and unique relations with depression severity. *Journal of Clinical Psychology, 77*(11), 2529–2544. https://doi.org/10.1002/jclp.23186

Phillips, W. J., Hine, D. W., & Bhullar, N. (2012). A latent profile analysis of implicit and explicit cognitions associated with depression. *Cognitive Therapy and Research, 36*(5), 458–473. https://doi.org/10.1007/s10608-011-9381-z

Richards, J. C., Austin, D. W., & Alvarenga, M. E. (2001). Interpretation of ambiguous interoceptive stimuli in panic disorder and nonclinical panic. *Cognitive Therapy and Research, 25*(3), 235–246. https://doi.org/10.1023/A:1010783427196

Rohrbacher, H., & Reinecke, A. (2014). Measuring change in depression-related interpretation bias: Development and validation of a parallel ambiguous scenarios test. *Cognitive Behaviour Therapy, 43*(3), 239–250. https://doi.org/10.1080/16506073.2014.919605

Rosmarin, D. H., Bourque, L. M., Antony, M. M., & McCabe, R. E. (2009). Interpretation bias in panic disorder: Self-referential or global? *Cognitive Therapy and Research, 33*(6), 624–632. https://doi.org/10.1007/s10608-009-9249-7

Rude, S. S., Valdez, C. R., Odom, S., & Ebrahimi, A. (2003). Negative cognitive biases predict subsequent depression. *Cognitive Therapy and Research, 15*, 415–429. https://doi.org/10.1023/A:1025472413805

Rude, S. S., Durham-Fowler, J. A., Baum, E. S., Rooney, S. B., & Maestas, K. L. (2010). Self-report and cognitive processing measures of depressive thinking predict subsequent major depressive disorder. *Cognitive Therapy and Research, 34*(2), 107–115. https://doi.org/10.1007/s10608-009-9237-y

Savulich, G., Shergill, S. S., & Yiend, J. (2017). Interpretation biases in clinical paranoia. *Clinical Psychological Science, 5*(6), 985–1000. https://doi.org/10.1177/2167702617718180

Schneider, R., & Schulte, D. (2007). Panic patients reveal idiographic associations between anxiety symptoms and catastrophes in a semantic priming task. *Behaviour Research and Therapy, 45*(2), 211–223. https://doi.org/10.1016/j.brat.2006.02.007

Schoth, D. E., & Liossi, C. (2017). A systematic review of experimental paradigms for exploring biased interpretation of ambiguous information with emotional and neutral associations. *Frontiers in Psychology, 8.* https://doi.org/10.3389/fpsyg.2017.00171

Sfärlea, A., Buhl, C., Loechner, J., Neumüller, J., Asperud Thomsen, L., Starman, K., Salemink, E., Schulte-Körne, G., & Platt, B. (2020). 'I am a total…loser'—The role of interpretation biases in youth depression. *Journal of Abnormal Child Psychology, 48*(10), 1337–1350. https://doi.org/10.1007/s10802-020-00670-3

Sherman, J. A., & Ehrenreich-May, J. (2018). Ethnicity's role in the relationship between anxiety and negative interpretation bias among clinically anxious youth: A pilot study. *Child Psychiatry & Human Development, 49*, 396–408. https://doi.org/10.1007/s10578-017-0760-x

Taylor, S., & Rachman, S. (1994). Klein's suffocation theory of panic. *Archives of General Psychiatry, 51*(6), 505. https://doi.org/10.1001/archpsyc.1994.03950060069011

Teachman, B. A., Smith-Janik, S. B., & Saporito, J. (2007). Information processing biases and panic disorder: Relationships among cognitive and symptom measures. *Behaviour Research and Therapy, 45*(8), 1791–1811. https://doi.org/10.1016/j.brat.2007.01.009

Teachman, B. A., Joormann, J., Steinman, S. A., & Gotlib, I. H. (2012). Automaticity in anxiety disorders and major depressive disorder. *Clinical Psychology Review, 32*(6), 575–603. https://doi.org/10.1016/j.cpr.2012.06.004

Wenzlaff, R. M., & Bates, D. E. (1998). Unmasking a cognitive vulnerability to depression: How lapses in mental control reveal depressive thinking. *Journal of Personality and Social Psychology, 75*(6), 1559–1571. https://doi.org/10.1037/0022-3514.75.6.1559

Wisco, B. E., & Nolen-Hoeksema, S. (2010). Interpretation bias and depressive symptoms: The role of self-relevance. *Behaviour Research and Therapy, 48*(11), 1113–1122. https://doi.org/10.1016/j.brat.2010.08.004

Wisco, B. E., & Nolen-Hoeksema, S. (2011). Effect of visual perspective on memory and interpretation in dysphoria. *Behaviour Research and Therapy, 49*(6–7), 406–412. https://doi.org/10.1016/j.brat.2011.03.012

Woud, M. L. (2022). Interpretational biases in emotional psychopathology. *Cognitive and Behavioral Practice, 29*(3), 520–523.

Woud, M. L., Zhang, X. C., Becker, E. S., McNally, R. J., & Margraf, J. (2014). Don't panic: Interpretation bias is predictive of new onsets of panic disorder. *Journal of Anxiety Disorders, 28*(1), 83–87. https://doi.org/10.1016/j.janxdis.2013.11.008

Woud, M. L., Zhang, X. C., Becker, E. S., Zlomuzica, A., & Margraf, J. (2016). Catastrophizing misinterpretations predict somatoform-related symptoms and new onsets of somatoform disorders. *Journal of Psychosomatic Research, 81*, 31–37. https://doi.org/10.1016/j.jpsychores.2015.12.005

Woud, M. L., Cwik, J. C., de Kleine, R. A., Blackwell, S. E., Würtz, F., & Margraf, J. (2019). Assessing trauma-related appraisals by means of a scenario-based approach. *Cognitive Therapy and Research, 43*(1), 185–198. https://doi.org/10.1007/s10608-018-9956-z

Woud, M. L., Blackwell, S. E., Shkreli, L., Würtz, F., Cwik, J. C., Margraf, J., Holmes, E. A., Steudte-Schmiedgen, S., Herpertz, S., & Kessler, H. (2021). The effects of modifying dysfunctional appraisals in posttraumatic stress disorder using a form of cognitive bias modification: Results of a randomized controlled trial in an inpatient setting. *Psychotherapy and Psychosomatics, 90*(6), 386–402. https://doi.org/10.1159/000514166

Würtz, F., Zahler, L., Blackwell, S. E., Margraf, J., Bagheri, M., & Woud, M. L. (2022). Scrambled but valid? The scrambled sentences task as a measure of interpretation biases in psychopathology: A systematic review and meta-analysis. *Clinical Psychology Review, 93*, 102133. https://doi.org/10.1016/j.cpr.2022.102133

Zahler, L., Sommer, K., Reinecke, A., Wilhelm, F. H., Margraf, J., & Woud, M. L. (2020). Cognitive vulnerability in the context of panic: Assessment of panic-related associations and interpretations in individuals with varying levels of anxiety sensitivity. *Cognitive Therapy and Research, 44*(4), 858–873. https://doi.org/10.1007/s10608-020-10103-6

Zahler, L., Meyers, M., Woud, M. L., Blackwell, S. E., Margraf, J., & Velten, J. (2021). Using three indirect measures to assess the role of sexuality-related associations and interpretations for women's sexual desire: An internet-based experimental study. *Archives of Sexual Behavior, 50*(6), 2471–2484. https://doi.org/10.1007/s10508-020-01897-3

Felix Würtz is a Ph.D. candidate in clinical psychology in the Translational Research in Anxiety, Cognition & Emotion (TRACE) Lab at Ruhr-University Bochum, supervised by Prof. Marcella L. Woud and Prof. Jürgen Margraf. He graduated from Ruhr-University Bochum with a M.Sc. in clinical psychology in 2018. In his master's thesis, he investigated potential mechanisms of the effects of imagery-based interventions on depression under the supervision of Dr. Simon E. Blackwell. His current research focus is on the assessment and modification of interpretational- and appraisal processes in psychopathology.

Alvaro Sanchez-Lopez is a Professor at the Department of Personality, Evaluation, and Clinical Psychology of Complutense University of Madrid. He received his Doctoral Degree in 2011 and has previously stayed at the University of Miami and Ghent University, among others. His research is focused on gaining a better understanding of the neural, cognitive, and behavioral mechanisms underlying emotion regulation dysfunctions conferring risk for the onset of depression and anxiety disorders. To this end, he integrates a multitude of measures, including cognitive tasks, psychophysiological measures of stress reactivity and regulation, eye tracking, experience sampling, and neuromodulation techniques. In 2021, he was the recipient of the Early Career Award of the Stress, Trauma, Anxiety, and Resilience Society, which acknowledges the best under-40 years researcher in the study of stress and anxiety.

Chapter 4
Moderators and Mediators of the Interpretation Bias–Emotional Disorders Link

Reuma Gadassi Polack, Anna Leah Davis, and Jutta Joormann

Ambiguity is part of the human experience. Our knowledge is always partial, which means we must process situations in which we do not have all the information. The process of interpretation leads to the resolution of this ambiguity. For example, you invited a friend to watch a movie and did not hear back from them. Because there is no clear yes or no, the situation cannot be called positive or negative definitively. In these types of situations, we use contextual cues to help us interpret the ambiguous situation. That context can include recent interactions with this friend (e.g., you had a heated argument the day before) or previous knowledge about them (e.g., they check their phone only in the evening). Situations are interpreted in either a context-congruent or context-incongruent manner. The majority of people have a preference for context-congruent meanings (Blanchette & Richards, 2010). Context-congruent here means that the explanation chosen is the one that fits best with the information the individual has, the situation itself, and the emotions the individual is experiencing at the time. If your friend has not replied to your invitation after a day, but you are aware that they have been busy with work, a context-congruent interpretation is that they were too busy to reply. This is an example of a positive context-congruent interpretation. However, cognitive distortions can affect the process of interpretation and result in an increased tendency to interpret a situation positively (positive interpretation bias) or negatively (negative interpretation bias). Biases often override contextual cues, and "push" the interpretation in a specific direction (for an overview of the role of interpretation biases in the etiology of emotional psychopathology, see Chap. 12 by Woud & Hofmann). Because this chapter will focus on the

R. Gadassi Polack (✉)
Departments of Psychology and Psychiatry, Yale University, New Haven, CT, USA
e-mail: reuma.gadassipolack@yale.edu

A. L. Davis · J. Joormann
Department of Psychology, Yale University, New Haven, CT, USA

© The Author(s), under exclusive license to Springer Nature Switzerland AG 2023
M. L. Woud (ed.), *Interpretational Processing Biases in Emotional Psychopathology*,
CBT: Science Into Practice, https://doi.org/10.1007/978-3-031-23650-1_4

role of interpretation biases in emotional disorders, which typically refers to a negative bias, we use the term interpretation bias to indicate specifically negative interpretation bias, unless a further specification would be useful (e.g., due to the specific task assessing interpretation biases).

4.1 Interpretation Bias as a Predictor, Mediator, and Outcome of Emotional Disorders

Cognitive models suggest that the way in which we interpret situations may be a risk factor for the development and maintenance of emotional disorders (Beck, 1976; Beck & Clark, 1988; Clark, 1999). Specifically, the tendency to interpret ambiguous stimuli in a negative fashion is hypothesized to predict and precipitate depression and anxiety (e.g., Woud et al., 2014, 2016), since the perception of situations as negative is likely to elevate negative mood. However, interpretation biases may also be an *outcome* of emotional disorders. Indeed, there is vast literature showing that emotional disorders impact interpretation (Hirsch et al., 2016; Mathews & MacLeod, 2005). Due to the dearth of literature that allows us to clearly indicate the direction of the association between interpretation biases and emotional disorder symptoms, this chapter examines the relationship between interpretation bias and emotional disorders, without differentiating between the role of predictor and outcome. We will also briefly review results suggesting that interpretation bias can be a mechanism that mediates the association between other factors relevant to emotion psychopathology (e.g., attention) on depression and anxiety symptoms (for an overview of associated cognitive biases of interpretation biases, see Chap. 5 by Everaert et al.).

4.2 Significance of Mediators and Moderators

A large body of research supports the role of interpretation bias in emotional disorders (Hirsch et al., 2016). An important next step in examining the role of interpretation bias in the etiology and maintenance of emotional disorders is looking at mediators and moderators of the relationship between interpretation bias and symptoms. In short, it can be argued that *mediators* help us understand *how* one factor influences the other (e.g., how does interpretation bias influence symptoms?), whereas *moderators* help us understand for *whom* or under what conditions the relationship between two factors differs in magnitude (e.g., is the association between interpretation bias and symptoms stronger for women vs. men?).

Why is it important to understand how and for whom interpretation bias impacts emotional disorder symptoms? Understanding how, or the mechanism of action, is important because it could help us design interventions that target not only interpretation bias but also its mediator (e.g., emotion regulation). For example, if we learn that interpretation bias exerts its effect on emotional disorders' symptoms through emotion regulation, clinicians could, in cases in which interpretation bias is difficult to change or challenge, focus on the mediating mechanism, thus mitigating the interpretation bias' adverse effect on the client's symptoms indirectly.

The importance of moderators is twofold. First, if we knew for whom the relationship between interpretation bias and symptoms is stronger, this may also help us to understand who is at a higher risk of developing a disorder because of such biases. This information could improve prevention and intervention efforts, for example, by helping us design a more personalized treatment. Second, whereas traditional models of psychopathology emphasized the maladaptive role of having more negative and less positive interpretations, recent evidence of psychopathology calls for a more nuanced understanding. Specifically, it is argued that the valence of an interpretation is not inherently adaptive or maladaptive (Everaert, 2021). There are situations in which negative interpretations can facilitate behavioral change in an adaptive way. To illustrate, if my interpretation of a situation is thinking I hurt someone's feelings when I gave them feedback on their performance, it may cause me to be gentler in the future. Moreover, it has become increasingly evident that the ability to flexibly revise interpretations is more important than the level of bias (Everaert, 2021). Examining moderators is therefore another way of looking at the interpretation bias–emotional disorders link in a more nuanced manner, as it can help us determine for whom and under what conditions interpretation biases have adverse outcomes.

4.3 Mediators of the Relationship Between Interpretation Bias and Emotional Disorders

In this section, we will examine processes that may underlie the interpretation bias–emotional disorders link, namely mediating variables. The main mechanism of action proposed to mediate the effect of interpretation biases on depression and anxiety symptoms is emotion regulation (Fig. 4.1).

Emotion regulation is defined as the process (or processes) that influence the frequency, intensity, duration, and expression of emotional experiences (Gross,

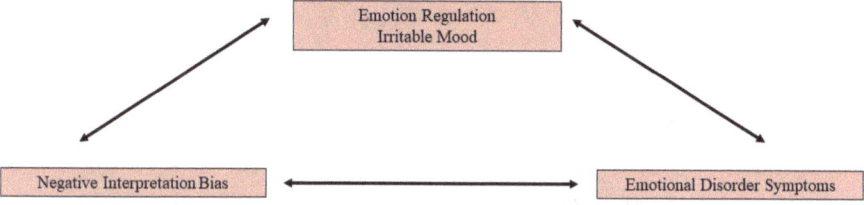

Fig. 4.1 Mediators of the interpretation bias–emotional disorders link

2014). Indeed, interpretation biases are likely to trigger increases in negative mood. Since individuals with emotional disorders have difficulty regulating their emotions (e.g., using more maladaptive emotion regulation strategies in response to negative mood; Cisler & Olatunji, 2012; Joormann & Gotlib, 2010), their response to the increase in negative mood is likely to exacerbate their mood leading to increases in symptom level. Several studies examining different emotion regulation strategies as a mediator of the interpretation bias–emotional disorder link found support for this hypothesis. In this part of this chapter, we will provide an overview of the examined strategies and evidence supporting their mediating role in the interpretation bias–emotional disorders' link.

4.3.1   Positive Reappraisal

Positive reappraisal is one of the most widely researched emotion regulation strategies. It involves altering the meaning of an emotion-eliciting event to reduce its negative impact (Jamieson et al., 2012). The use of positive reappraisal is considered adaptive as it typically leads to reductions in negative mood and amelioration of symptoms of anxiety and depression (Min et al., 2013; Ford et al., 2019). Arguably, positive reappraisal is the effortful attempt to reverse negative interpretations of situations, and thus it may counteract the impact of a negative interpretation bias.

Indeed, in a cross-sectional study of 112 university students who were pre-screened for depression, Everaert et al. (2017) showed that habitual use of positive reappraisal to regulate negative mood mediated the association between interpretation bias (measured using a computerized version of the Scrambled Sentence Test; SST, Wenzlaff & Bates, 1998) and depressive symptoms. Interestingly, although habitual use of positive reappraisal appears to be related to interpretation biases, another study showed that it is unrelated to the ability to modify these biases, that is, to the flexibility of interpretation. In a set of two online studies (total $N = 544$), Everaert et al. (2020) used a novel task that simultaneously examines interpretation biases and their flexibility (Bias Against Disconfirmatory Evidence; BADE, Everaert et al., 2018). These studies found that positive reappraisal was related to a positive interpretation bias of social situations, but it was not related to flexibility and did not mediate the association between flexibility and symptoms of depression and social anxiety. However, the mediation of the positive interpretation bias and symptoms of depression and social anxiety by positive reappraisal was not examined.

4.3.2   Rumination

Rumination is defined as dwelling on the causes and consequences of negative affect repetitively and passively (Nolen-Hoeksema et al., 2008). Rumination is considered a maladaptive response to negative emotion and was shown to be a robust risk factor for the onset and maintenance of many emotional disorders (Nolen-Hoeksema, 2000). Rumination has two main components, brooding and reflective pondering (Treynor et al., 2003). Brooding, the passive and maladaptive form of rumination, is often contrasted with reflective pondering, the more active and potentially adaptive ruminative subtype. In the context of interpretation bias, the repetitive nature of rumination (and particularly of the brooding component) can be argued to enhance the negative side of the interpretation, thus enhancing negativity bias and dampening positivity bias. Indeed, much of the research on the role of rumination and its subcomponents supports its mediating role in the interpretation bias–emotional disorders link.

In a set of two cross-sectional studies of young adults (total N = 199), Wisco et al. (2014) showed that rumination mediated the association between interpretation bias and depressive symptoms using the Interpretation Bias Questionnaire (IBQ; Wisco & Nolen-Hoeksema, 2010). The IBQ presents participants with ambiguous vignettes (e.g., "Your significant other leaves you a voicemail saying 'Hi, it's me. Give me a call.' What does he/she want to talk to you about?") to which they are asked to first generate interpretations and then select the most likely interpretation. Similarly, Everaert et al. (2017) showed that habitual use of brooding mediated the association between interpretation bias (measured using the SST) and depressive symptoms. More recently, a cross-sectional study of 80 participants who completed an online version of the SST to assess interpretation bias found that the use of rumination also mediated the association between interpretation bias in anxiety (Blanco et al., 2021).

In a study that examined interpretation bias as an outcome of anxiety, Badra et al. (2017) looked at the mediating role of rumination using a longitudinal design and a sample of 51 undergraduates. Interpretation biases were assessed using the Interpretation and Judgmental Questionnaire (IJQ; Voncken et al., 2003) and an experimental interpretation bias task. Badra et al. (2017) found that participants who had high levels of social anxiety showed a stronger interpretation bias in the experimental task, not seen in the low social anxiety group. Group differences (low vs. high in social anxiety) in interpretation bias were mediated by rumination (Badra et al., 2017). An important caveat to note, however, is that this study included exploratory analyses looking at the role of depressive symptoms and found that depressive symptoms were an even stronger mediator than rumination. This highlights the need for considering the comorbidity of anxiety and depression in interpretation bias research, and for better understanding of the mediating processes that may or may not overlap across disorders.

So far, only one study examined the mediation of the interpretation bias-depressive symptoms link using a longitudinal design (Wisco & Harp, 2021). Interpretation bias was assessed using the Ambiguous Scenarios Test relevant to Depressed Mood – II (AST-D-II; Berna et al., 2011). This study examined the mediation model in two ways: once, using the baseline assessment of 714 undergraduates, running a cross-sectional model that then indeed supported the mediation (Wisco & Harp, 2021). However, when the longitudinal data was used, on a sub-sample of 278 undergraduates, interpretation bias did not longitudinally mediate the association between rumination and depressive symptoms. Instead, Wisco and Harp (2021) found that interpretation bias mediated the relationship between rumination and depressive symptoms.

In line with Wisco and Harp (2021)'s findings that interpretation bias may act as a mediator between risk factors for emotional disorders and emotional disorder symptoms, there are also other, in fact, earlier studies that examined the role of interpretation biases as a mediator. For example, one study examined interpretation bias as mediating the link between rejection sensitivity and depressive symptoms (Normansell & Wisco, 2017). Rejection sensitivity is an expectation of rejection that involves being hypervigilant to signs of rejection and overreacting to any indication that it may occur (Normansell & Wisco, 2017). Normansell and Wisco (2017) used an undergraduate sample ($N = 89$) to assess the relationship between interpretation bias (measured by the Interpretation Bias Questionnaire; Wisco & Nolen-Hoeksema, 2010), rejection sensitivity (measured by the Rejection Sensitivity Questionnaire; Downey & Feldman, 1996), and depression (measured by the Beck Depression Inventory-II; Beck et al., 1996b). This study showed that interpretation bias mediated the rejection sensitivity–depression relationship. In a longitudinal study testing an undergraduate sample ($N = 160$), Normansell and Wisco (2017) used the Ambiguous Scenarios Test relevant to Depressed Mood – II (Berna et al., 2011) and showed that interpretation bias was a significant mediator of the depression–rejection sensitivity relationship over a 12-week period. Further longitudinal studies are needed to shed light on the nature of the associations between interpretation bias, depression and anxiety symptoms, and other risk factors for emotional disorders.

4.3.3 Dampening

Emotion regulation strategies that focus on negative mood (e.g., positive reappraisal, rumination) have received a lot of attention within the field of interpretation bias and emotional disorders. However, the regulation (and dysregulation) of positive affect is also central to emotional disorders, and in particular to depression. Indeed, anhedonia, or difficulties experiencing and sustaining positive emotion, is a cardinal symptom of depression (APA, 2013). Although traditionally the dysregulation of positive affect was considered a unique feature of depression, it is now recognized that anxiety disorders, particularly social anxiety and generalized anxiety disorder, are often accompanied by dysregulated positive affect (Everaert et al., 2020; Hofmann et al., 2012). A highly relevant emotion regulation strategy focusing on positive affect is dampening. Dampening is defined as a repetitive style of thought in response to positive effect that serves to reduce its intensity and duration by focusing on the negative aspects of the event that lead to the positive affective state (Feldman et al., 2008). Dampening is considered maladaptive, as studies found that it is related to increases in depressive symptoms (e.g., Raes et al., 2012). In the context of interpretation bias, it is likely that dampening acts much like rumination, to increase the salience of negative aspects (Gadassi Polack et al., 2021).

Indeed, in the cross-sectional study of young adults mentioned above, Wisco et al. (2014) showed that dampening contributed to the mediation of the association between interpretation bias and depressive symptoms. The effect of dampening was significant above and beyond the effect of rumination, though its mediating effect was weaker in size. Similarly, dampening was found to be the only emotion regulation strategy (vs. rumination and positive reappraisal) that mediated the effect of inflexibility in revising interpretations biases on depression and social anxiety symptoms (Everaert et al., 2020).

Additional support for the mediation of the interpretation bias–emotional disorders linked by emotion regulation comes from a cross-sectional study of children and adolescents (9–14; Sfärlea et al., 2021). This study (Sfärlea et al., 2021), which compared youth suffering from depression, youth at increased familial risk for depression, and typically developing youth, assessed interpretation bias using a computerized version of the SST (Wenzlaff & Bates, 1998), and a wide range of both adaptive and maladaptive emotion regulation strategies using a self-report questionnaire ("Fragebogen zur Erhebung der Emotionsregulation bei Kindern und Jugendlichen"; FEEL-KJ; Grob & Smolenski, 2005). This study showed that both adaptive and maladaptive emotion regulation strategies mediated the interpretation bias-depressive symptoms link (Sfärlea et al., 2021).

4.3.4   Irritable Mood

Although most of the studies examining the mediation of the interpretation bias–emotional disorders link focused on emotion regulation strategies, there has been some research on general affective components as mediators. For example, a recent study examined the role of irritability as a mediator of the interpretation bias–emotional disorders relationship (Marks et al., 2021). Irritability is broadly defined as excessive reactivity to negative emotional stimuli (Bettencourt et al., 2006; Leibenluft & Stoddard, 2013). In children, depression is often characterized by irritable (and not sad) mood (APA, 2013). In adults, irritability is a common concomitant of depression. However, irritability does not appear in every case of depression and is not considered as one of its symptoms (Verhoeven et al., 2011). Irritability in depression has been tied to more severe depression, more anxiety, and higher suicidality risk (Verhoeven et al., 2011). Importantly, in recent years, irritability has been recognized to be a transdiagnostic vulnerability factor, cutting across internalizing and externalizing disorders (Beauchaine & Tackett, 2020).

In a recent study, Marks et al. (2021) investigated the mediating role of irritability on the interpretation bias–emotional disorders link in two samples – one recruited from an online panel and one sample of undergraduate students. Both samples completed the Word Sentence Association Paradigm – Hostile version (WSAP-H; Dillon et al., 2016) to measure interpretation bias. In the original WSAP (Cowden Hindash

& Rottenberg, 2017), participants judge the association between words (e.g., "embarrassing", "funny") and ambiguous sentences (e.g., "People laugh after something you said.") that are presented separately and for short durations (e.g., 500 ms). The time participants take to endorse or reject a word–sentence pair is recorded and used to infer interpretation biases. For example, participants who take less time to endorse negative (vs. positive) word–sentence pairs are considered to have negative interpretation bias. In the WSAP-H, the sentences included social situations (e.g., "A friend declines your invitation to dinner.") and were combined with neutral (e.g., "busy") or hostile (e.g., "rude") words. Marks et al. (2021) found that for depression, irritable mood mediated the relationship between hostile interpretation bias and depressive symptoms in both samples (Marks et al., 2021). This study also looked at anxiety, but while anxiety was a predictor of hostile interpretation bias, the association between interpretation bias and anxiety was only mediated by irritable mood in the undergraduate sample. Some differences existed between samples, with the online sample having more severe anxiety symptoms and higher irritability, which could potentially explain the different outcome. This lack of similarity between samples indicates that this is an area in need of further research.

4.4 Moderators of the Interpretation Bias and Emotional Disorders' Relationship

In this section, we examine moderators of the interpretation bias–emotional disorder symptoms link. We review moderators related to the population (i.e., the perceiver/participant) first, and then moderators related to the measurement (e.g., stimuli used). Figure 4.2 gives an overview of the moderators examined.

4.4.1 Population Characteristics

4.4.1.1 Age

Research on psychopathology, and particularly research pertaining to risk factors, has increasingly focused on the role of the developmental context in emotional disorders (Sroufe, 2009). As interpretation biases are considered a risk factor for the development of emotional disorders, it is important to examine when, over development, they begins to exert their malevolent influence. Indeed, studies examining interpretation biases in child and adolescent psychopathology have often examined age-related differences. In a meta-analysis encompassing 77 studies ($N = 11,507$, mean age = 11.19) on interpretation bias in anxious youth, Stuijfzand et al. (2018) found that the association between interpretation bias and anxiety increased with age in a linear manner. One explanation for the increase in the association between interpretation bias and anxiety is that at younger ages, interpretation bias is related

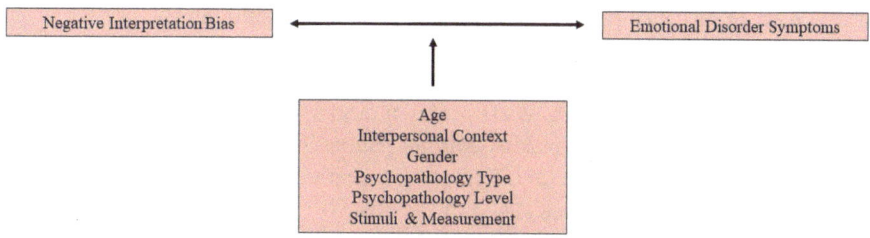

Fig. 4.2 Moderators of the interpretation bias–emotional disorders association

to other cognitive developmental processes (vs. at older ages), such as abstract thinking and reasoning (Dumontheil, 2014). Based on findings that interpretation biases are more prevalent in younger (vs. older) youths, it has been suggested that interpretation bias may be normative at a younger age but in the course of typical development should decline in prevalence (Weems et al., 2001). Therefore, if interpretation biases are still evident at later developmental stages, it is more likely that they are indicative of psychopathology (Cannon & Weems, 2010). Future studies examining the interplay between basic cognitive processes (e.g., abstract reasoning) and interpretation bias are necessary to better understand these developmental changes (Stuijfzand et al., 2018).

Development does not end in young adulthood; rather, it is a lifelong process (Sroufe, 2009). However, studies on interpretation bias in adults are largely based on young adults, without examining whether interpretation biases change over the lifespan (Tadic et al., 2018). In a study of younger (18–30) and older (60+) adults with or without comorbid anxiety and depression ($N = 125$; Tadic et al., 2018), participants completed an interpretation bias task. The task included asking participants to read ambiguous sentences with social or physical themes and to imagine themselves within the scenario. Then, participants were asked to rate the pleasantness of their emotions as they were imagining the scenario, and then judge new but unambiguous sentences' similarity to the sentences they read (recognition phase). Results showed that older (vs. younger) adults rated ambiguous and unambiguous sentences more positively in both control and depression/anxiety groups, suggesting a general positive interpretation bias in older adults regardless of diagnostic status. Moreover, analysis of the task's recognition phase showed that older (vs. younger) adults were better at distinguishing between probes (i.e., the original ambiguous sentences) and distractors to neutral interpretations, whereas younger (vs. older) adults had a greater tendency to endorse threat-related sentences. These age-related differences may explain findings from epidemiological studies that show that the prevalence of anxiety and depression is lower in older (vs. younger) adults (Kessler et al., 2005). In other words, it is possible that younger (vs. older) adults' increased bias is the reason for the higher rates of emotional disorders in younger (vs. older) adults.

Another important understanding that comes from the developmental perspective is that different developmental periods are characterized by different goals and challenges (e.g., during adolescence, independence from family needs to be achieved). Different developmental goals (or themes) may influence the content areas an age group is most reactive to. To illustrate, during the transition to parenthood, young adults, particularly expecting mothers, are likely to react more to infant-related (vs. non-infant-related) stimuli (Elmadih et al., 2016). Most research on interpretation bias is based on interpreting scenarios or other ambiguous stimuli. As we elaborate below, the relevance of the stimuli to the disorder's content area increases the likelihood of activation of the bias (e.g., individuals with social anxiety are more biased when interpreting social vs. non-social stimuli; Stuijfzand et al., 2018). Future research should examine whether certain stimuli are more or less relevant during different developmental periods, potentially shedding more light on psychopathology in a specific age group.

4.4.1.2   Interpersonal Context

Most of the literature on interpretation bias defines it as a within-person, cognitive process. However, the way in which we interpret ambiguous stimuli can be influenced or learned from the way people close to us interpret or react to these stimuli. Most of the studies on the interpersonal context of interpretational processing come from the developmental literature and examine the way parents' interpretations may be associated with their children's interpretations. For example, the process of social referencing, in which we look at other people for information regarding how to respond, has been extensively studied in infants and young children, and to a lesser degree in adolescents (Morris et al., 2007). The process of social referencing has been suggested as a potential factor underlying the development of anxiety disorders (Aktar et al., 2022). In the context of interpretation bias, it has been shown that interpretation biases of children of depressed parents are associated with their parents' biases (Sfärlea et al., 2019) and that daughters of mothers with a history of depression have a more negative interpretation bias compared to daughters of mothers without depression (Dearing & Gotlib, 2009). Similarly, children of patients with panic disorders showed an increase in anxious interpretations after priming, whereas children of parents with animal phobia and children of parents without an anxiety disorder did not display such an increase (Schneider et al., 2002).

Pertaining moderating factors, it has been suggested that the way in which parents respond to their children's emotions may buffer the adverse impact of interpretation bias on children's mental health (Viana et al., 2016). In a study of 44 clinically anxious children (aged 8–12) and their mothers, Viana et al. (2016) examined whether maternal responses to their child's anxiety moderated the association between child interpretation bias and anxiety symptoms. Interpretation bias was assessed using the Children's Negative Cognitive Error Questionnaire (CNCEQ; Leitenberg et al., 1986) and a computerized interpretation task (Word-Sentence Association Paradigm; Beard et al., 2011). Interestingly, this study found that for children of mothers high on minimization response (e.g., telling the child not to make a big deal of a situation) or punitive responses (e.g., sending the child to their room to cool off), the association between interpretation bias and child anxiety symptoms was not significant. However, if mothers were low in punitive and minimizing responses, the link between interpretation bias–child anxiety was significant. These results suggest that parents' reactions can send a message of not taking one's own interpretation to heart, thus helping the child to be less influenced by their own interpretation biases. These results are in line with parent-based interventions that aim at reducing parental behaviors that accommodate child anxiety (e.g., Lebowitz et al., 2014). As the interpersonal context continues to influence our reactions through the lifespan, future studies are needed to locate additional behaviors and interpersonal contexts (e.g., romantic partners and peer groups) that may attenuate the impact of interpretation bias on emotional disorders.

4.4.1.3 Gender

Another important moderator is the participants' gender. Gender is an important factor when considering emotional disorders, as studies consistently show that women are more frequently diagnosed with depression and anxiety disorders compared to men (APA, 2013). However, meta-analytic investigations that examined sex as a moderator did not reveal a significant effect of gender on interpretation bias in emotional disorders (Nieto et al., 2020; Stuijfzand et al., 2018), suggesting that this mechanism cuts across gender. In contrast, a meta-analysis on Cognitive Bias Modification for Interpretation (CBM-I) interventions revealed that women benefited more than men from bias modification (i.e., showed improvement in mood; Menne-Lothmann et al., 2014). Because this meta-analysis also found that women were more likely to be offered imagery-based treatment components, it is possible that they benefited more from intervention because they used imagery more. More research on gender, and particularly research that goes beyond sex as assigned in birth and dichotomous gender definitions, is highly needed.

4.4.1.4 Psychopathology Type

Interpretation biases are considered to play a role in the development and maintenance of multiple emotional disorders (e.g., social anxiety, depression; Everaert et al., 2018); indeed, some consider them a transdiagnostic risk factor. Moreover, because of the high comorbidity rates between depression and anxiety disorders, as well as among different anxiety disorders (e.g., GAD and social anxiety), studies often include samples that are at least partly comorbid (e.g., Badra et al., 2017; Tadic et al., 2018; Yu et al., 2019). Research suggests that the disorder a person suffers from may also moderate the type and magnitude of interpretation bias.

To better understand the moderating role of disorder type on interpretation bias, Yu et al. (2019) conducted a cross-sectional study of adolescents, separated into high ($N = 25$) and low ($N = 29$) socially anxious groups. Results showed that depressive symptoms were associated with lower levels of positive interpretations (measured by the Adolescents' Interpretation Bias Questionnaire; AIBQ; Miers et al., 2008) in both groups. Importantly, increased negative interpretations of social situations were found only for youths with high levels of social anxiety (Yu et al., 2019). Interestingly, findings from a meta-analysis show that comorbidity with other psychiatric disorders did not moderate interpretation biases in anxious youths, suggesting that social anxiety symptoms are robustly related to interpretation bias (Stuijfzand et al., 2018). Conversely, studies on adult samples suggest that differences in interpretation bias between those with low and high social anxiety are mediated by depressive symptoms (Badra et al., 2017), although other studies found that differences in interpretation bias between those with low and high anxiety remain significant even after controlling for levels of depressive symptoms (e.g., Kanai et al., 2010; Wilson & Rapee, 2005). Additional studies comparing the different roles of anxiety and depression, as well as systematic examination regarding the possible differential role of interpretation bias in anxiety and depression are needed.

Similar findings regarding the moderating role of disorder type come from literature on Cognitive Bias Modification for Interpretation bias (CBM-I). For example, a meta-analysis examining the effect of CBM-I found that CBM-I is robustly related to improvement in individuals with anxiety disorders, whereas the effect of CBM-I was inconsistent in patients with depression or those who had comorbid depression (Fodor et al., 2020). One possible explanation for the differential effect of CBM-I on individuals with anxiety vs. depression is that interpretation bias plays a more central role in the maintenance of anxiety (vs. depression). Alternatively, it is possible that depressive symptoms (e.g., anhedonia) decrease patients' ability to comply with treatment, and that is why CBM-I has worse results for individuals with depression (for an overview of how to manipulate interpretation biases, see Chap. 11 by Salemink et al.).

4.4.1.5 Psychopathology Severity

Studies also examined interpretation bias in populations with different psychopathology severity levels; some focused on patients or individuals with clinically diagnosed disorders, whereas others focused on sub-clinical, general population or student samples and assessed symptomatology dimensionally; another group examined individuals at high risk for developing the disorder (e.g., Dearing & Gotlib, 2009; Wisco & Harp, 2021; Zahler et al., 2020). Although one might assume that interpretation biases are more pronounced in diagnosed populations, meta-analyses that examined symptom severity as a moderator show that this is not the case (Chen et al., 2020; Everaert et al., 2017; Stuijfzand et al., 2018; Würtz et al., 2022). This suggests that interpretation bias is an important target for intervention, regardless of psychopathology severity level, making it a good candidate for prevention interventions.

4.4.2 Methodological Factors

4.4.2.1 Stimuli

The main factor that attenuates the association between interpretation bias and emotional disorder symptoms is the to-be-interpreted stimuli. In other words, in addition to considering *who* is interpreting and how that contributes to the effect of the interpretation bias, we need to consider *what* is interpreted, or the characteristics of the stimuli.

4.4.2.2 Self-Relevance of the Stimuli

An important characteristic to be considered is the degree to which the interpreted stimuli is related to the perceiver's self, or its self-relevance (for a related discussion, see also Chap. 9 by Fen & Hirsch). Theoretical models of depression assume that interpretation biases are triggered by self-relevant information, specifically information linked to individuals' negative schemas (Clark et al., 1999). Experimental studies of interpretation bias in depression often utilize standardized self-referent stimuli in lieu of idiographic stimuli. Self-referential stimuli refer to the respondent's own character and/or their experience. Indeed, in a meta-analysis of interpretation bias in depression (Everaert et al., 2017), self-relevant (vs. non-self-relevant) stimuli were associated with a larger effect size. Although both types of stimuli were associated with interpretation bias in depression, authors warn that the use of non-self-relevant stimuli may cause an underestimation of interpretation biases (Everaert et al., 2017). The importance of the stimuli's self-relevance extends also to anxiety disorders. For example, in a study comparing individuals with panic disorders to those suffering from social anxiety and to healthy controls, Rosmarin et al. (2009) found that individuals with panic disorder (vs. those with social anxiety or controls) misinterpreted panic-related body sensations more strongly. Importantly, by comparing self-relevant vs. global scenarios, the authors found that the interpretation bias displayed by individuals with panic disorder was limited to the self and did not extend to beliefs about others. However, future studies assessing interpretation bias using idiographic self-relevant stimuli (e.g., scenarios based on participants' memories; viewing facial expressions of close others) are needed.

Another interesting comparison is looking at biases regarding self vs. close others. Wisco and Nolen-Hoeksema (2010) investigated whether the effect of interpretation bias was different when it was self-relevant or other-focused. In a cross-sectional study of an undergraduate sample ($N = 98$), Wisco and Nolen-Hoeksema (2010) asked participants to complete the interpretation bias questionnaire (IBQ; Wisco & Nolen-Hoeksema, 2010). In this version of the questionnaire, participants were asked to generate interpretations for themselves, a close friend, or a hypothetical other, thus examining self-relevance effects. Results of this study showed that regardless of depression levels, all participants generated and selected significantly more positive interpretations for friends than for themselves, but generated significantly more negative interpretations for hypothetical others than for themselves. Further, participants who met the clinical cut-off on the Beck Depression Inventory (BDI-II; Beck et al., 1996a) generated and selected significantly more negative interpretations of the scenarios compared to those below the clinical cut-off.

4.4.2.3 Content Specificity of the Stimuli

The degree to which the content of the stimuli is specifically related to the emotional disorder may also influence interpretation bias. The cognitive specificity hypothesis (Beck, 1976) argues that disorder-specific schemas are activated more strongly when triggered by disorder-relevant content. Research on different disorders lends support to the content-specificity theory. For example, the content-specificity hypothesis would posit that if the content of the stimuli is related to OCD, like contamination (e.g., "You smell something foul"; Kuckertz et al., 2013) it would impact individuals with OCD more than stimuli with content related to social situations, which are less relevant to OCD. Indeed, in a set of two studies using a variation of the Word Sentence Association Test (WSAP; Beard & Amir, 2009) that were adapted to examine OCD-relevant interpretation biases, Kuckertz et al. (2013) compared 38 individuals high in OCD symptoms, 34 individuals high in anxiety and dysphoric symptoms, and 31 asymptomatic individuals. They found that interpretation bias related to OCD content was stronger in the OCD group compared to the two control groups. Moreover, interpretation bias assessed using the WSAP with OCD-related content predicted avoidance in individuals with OCD. Further support for the importance of content specificity comes from a study regarding the risk for panic disorder (Woud et al., 2014). In this study, women were examined at two time points, approximately 17 months apart. At baseline, participants completed questionnaires examining interpretation bias of ambiguous scenarios, some were panic-related and some were general threat-related. Results showed that a panic-related but not threat-related interpretation bias predicted the onset of panic disorder. Finally, in a meta-analysis of anxiety disorders in youth (Stuijfzand et al., 2018), it was found that there was a larger association between bias and anxiety when anxiety subtype and scenario content matched (vs. when they did not match). Notably, because most of the studies included in the meta-analysis were based on social anxiety, this finding was mostly based on comparing interpretation bias to social vs. non-social stimuli in social anxiety.

4.4.2.4 Stimuli Modality

Most of the studies reviewed in this chapter were based on text-based stimuli that participants were asked to read. However, this is not the only modality in which one can examine interpretation biases. Notably, a significant portion of the literature examines individuals' interpretational styles by examining interpretations of facial expressions (for a more detailed overview of studies using emotional faces as stimuli, see also Chap. 10 by Martens & Harmer) or videos of, for example, recorded social situations. Thus, the stimuli modality (e.g., visual, textual.) can also act as a moderator and attenuate the interpretation bias-emotional disorders link. In a meta-analysis of interpretation bias in social anxiety, Chen et al. (2020) found that the effect size for textual stimuli is larger than when the stimuli were visual. Moreover, facial photographs showed the smallest effect size, whereas video and text-based scenarios produced the largest effect size. Relatedly, in a study that directly compared the two modalities, Chen et al. (2019) found that negative interpretation bias mediated the relationship between trait social anxiety and perceived negative evaluation only when written social scenarios, but not facial expressions, were used as stimuli. It is possible that using facial expressions without a context make them more difficult to interpret, therefore weakening their effect. Indeed, a recent study compared pictures that depict complex social scenarios (vs. emotional expressions) to traditional verbal scenarios in a group of adolescents (Henricks et al., 2022). Results of Henricks et al. (2022) showed that the novel picture-based task was comparable to the text-based task. However, only the verbal task was linked to both fear of negative evaluation and to social anxiety symptoms, whereas the picture-based task was related only to fear of negative evaluation.

Another modality that can be used for ambiguous stimuli is hearing. For example, Dearing and Gotlib (2009) used two different modalities in two separate tasks. In the auditory task they presented ambiguous auditory stimuli that were constructed by blending word pairs that were different by only one phoneme (e.g., "joy-boy"). Participants were asked to listen to these word blends and to indicate which word they heard. In the text-based task, they had participants read ambiguous scenarios. Results of the study show that in response to both type of stimuli, daughters of depressed mothers (vs. daughters of mothers without depression) showed a negative interpretation bias, suggesting that modality did not moderate interpretation bias in this population. Additional studies using auditory stimuli and comparing stimuli modality directly are needed.

4.4.2.5 Measurement Method

Another central methodological aspect when assessing interpretation bias is the measurement method. Research in the field typically is distinguished into direct and indirect (Everaert et al., 2017), offline and online (Hirsch et al., 2016), or subjective and objective (Chen et al., 2020; and for an overview of measures to assess interpretation biases, see Chap. 3 by Würtz and Sanchez-Lopez). Direct (or offline/subjective) assessments often involve using questionnaires that require participants to rate the emotional tone of possible interpretation(s) to the stimuli presented. For example, interpretation bias questionnaires ask participants to rank-order interpretations according to their plausibility in solving the scenario's ambiguity (Butler & Mathews, 1983). Another type of direct measurement is the homograph task (e.g.,

Holmes et al., 2008), in which participants give their first interpretation of the presented homograph (e.g., "die"). The advantage of direct methods is that they are relatively easy to administer and interpret, and that they have higher face validity because they directly assess the subjective perception of emotional interpretations. However, direct methods are prone to response biases and demand characteristics (Blanchette & Richards, 2010).

Indirect (or online/objective) assessments were developed to minimize problems such as demand characteristics. Indirect assessments rely on differential behavioral or psychophysiological responses to ambiguous cues. For example, they use reaction times (Sears et al., 2011), startle responses (Lawson et al., 2002), or event-related potentials (Moser et al., 2012). Typically, these indirect measurements are taken during paradigms assessing interpretation bias (e.g., the WSAP; Cowden Hindash & Rottenberg, 2017). Similarly, Moser et al. (2012) examined behavioral and neural responses to ambiguous social scenarios using response time and even-related potentials (ERPs), in individuals with social anxiety, depression, both, or controls. Results showed that all clinical group had an ERP response suggestive of a lack of both positive and negative interpretation biases. Similarly, reaction times showed that all clinical groups showed a lack of positive interpretation bias. Indirect methods, however, have limited face validity and the degree to which results translate from indirect measurement to subjective experience or behavior is often a question.

In a meta-analysis examining interpretation biases in depression, Everaert et al. (2017) found that the measurement method significantly moderated the interpretation bias-depression link. Specifically, they found that the effect size of interpretation bias was larger when using direct methods. Similarly, in a meta-analysis of interpretation bias in anxiety disorders, Chen et al. (2020) found that the effect size was stronger for studies that use direct ("subjective" in her terms) vs. indirect ("objective") methods. As indirect methods (especially reaction-time based) often limit time of processing, it is possible that interpretation bias can only be detected once individuals had time to complete elaborate processing (Chen et al., 2020).

4.5   Summary and Outlook

Cognitive theories have long suggested that interpretation bias plays a central role in the development and maintenance of emotional disorders. This chapter sought to increase the understanding *how* interpretation biases impact emotional disorders (i.e., mediating variables), and to identify for *whom* or under what conditions (i.e., moderating variables) they influence it more (or less). The literature reviewed here suggests that emotion regulation, and particularly maladaptive strategies such as rumination and dampening, mediate the association between interpretation bias and emotional disorder symptoms. In addition, we also show that many factors moderate the association between interpretation bias and emotional disorders, some related to participant population characteristics (e.g., age), and some related to aspects of how interpretation bias was assessed (i.e., stimuli characteristic, measurement method).

Findings that emotion regulation mediates the interpretation bias-emotional disorders link may suggests that clinicians who encounter difficulties in challenging their clients' negative interpretations may instead consider focusing on their emotion regulation strategies as a focus for treatment. We also showed that interpretation bias may itself be considered as a mediating mechanism (e.g., between rejection sensitivity and depressive symptoms). Notably, the majority of the studies examining mediation did so in a cross-sectional research design, and none used an experimental manipulation, in direct contrast to recommendations (Kazdin, 2014). Indeed, one study that used a longitudinal design suggested that interpretation bias mediates the association between rumination and depressive symptoms, whereas rumination did not mediate the interpretation bias–depressive symptoms link (Wisco & Harp, 2021). Studies manipulating interpretation bias and longitudinal studies are thus needed.

The literature reviewed here also suggests there are many factors that moderate the association between interpretation bias and emotional disorder symptoms. Indeed, it appears that rather than claiming that interpretation biases are always maladaptive, we can say that their malevolent influence may be attenuated by the age of the perceiver, the type of psychopathology they suffer from, the type of stimuli, and the degree to which it is self-relevant. These moderators can be used to better design interventions that challenge interpretation biases. For example, guiding clients to use distancing when interpreting social situations can help reduce the self-relevance of the situation, thus attenuating the bias' effect on depression and anxiety symptoms. Notably, as most of the literature on moderators is cross-sectional, the direction of the association may be reverse, that is, it is possible that emotional disorder symptoms cause increased reliance on interpretation bias rather than the other way around.

This chapter highlights interesting directions for future research, beyond the need for longitudinal and experimental work. One important direction is examining how interpretation bias interacts with other biases (Hirsch et al., 2016; and for an overview of associated cognitive biases of interpretation biases, see Chap. 5 by Everaert et al.). Indeed, studies have shown that interpretation bias has a unique effect on emotional disorders, above and beyond other biases (e.g., Orchard & Reynolds, 2018). For example, one study has shown that interpretation bias mediates the effect of attention bias on memory biases (Everaert et al., 2013) in subclinical depression. Another avenue for future research is the developmental perspective. Learning about typical and atypical development of interpretation bias and its flexibility is crucial for understanding the role of interpretation bias in the etiology of emotional disorders. Work on older adults is also warranted, considering changes in cognitive and affective functioning that is evident later in life. Finally, research on the interpersonal context of interpretation bias is in its infancy, and mainly limited to the parent–child relationship. Understanding how close others impact our interpretation across the lifespan is a promising direction for future investigation considering the central role of close relationships in emotional disorders (Gadassi & Rafaeli, 2015).

References

Aktar, E., Nikolić, M., & Bögels, S. M. (2022). Environmental transmission of generalized anxiety disorder from parents to children: Worries, experiential avoidance, and intolerance of uncertainty. *Dialogues in Clinical Neuroscience, 19*(2), 137–147. https://doi.org/10.31887/DCNS.2017.19.2/eaktar

American Psychiatric Association, D. S., & American Psychiatric Association. (2013). *The diagnostic and statistical manual of mental disorders: DSM-5* (Vol. 5). American psychiatric association.

Badra, M., Schulze, L., Becker, E. S., Vrijsen, J. N., Renneberg, B., & Zetsche, U. (2017). The association between ruminative thinking and negative interpretation bias in social anxiety. *Cognition and Emotion, 31*(6), 1234–1242. https://doi.org/10.1080/02699931.2016.1193477

Beard, C., & Amir, N. (2009). Interpretation in social anxiety: When meaning precedes ambiguity. *Cognitive Therapy and Research, 33*(4), 406–415.

Beard, C., Weisberg, R. B., & Amir, N. (2011). Combined cognitive bias modification treatment for social anxiety disorder: A pilot trial. *Depression and Anxiety, 28*(11), 981–988. https://doi.org/10.1002/da.20873

Beck, A. T. (1976). *Cognitive therapy and the emotional disorders*. International Universities Press.

Beck, A. T., & Clark, D. A. (1988). Anxiety and depression: An information processing perspective. *Anxiety Research, 1*(1), 23–36. https://doi.org/10.1080/10615808808248218

Beck, A. T., Steer, R. A., Ball, R., & Ranieri, W. F. (1996a). Comparison of Beck depression inventories-IA and -II in psychiatric outpatients. *Journal of Personality Assessment, 67*, 588–597. https://doi.org/10.1207/s15327752jpa6703_13

Beck, A. T., Steer, R. A., & Brown, G. K. (1996b). *Beck depression inventory (BDI-II)* (Vol. 10). Pearson. https://doi.org/10.1037/t00742-000

Beauchaine, T. P., & Tackett, J. L. (2020). Irritability as a transdiagnostic vulnerability trait: Current issues and future directions. *Behavior Therapy, 51*(2), 350–364. https://doi.org/10.1016/j.beth.2019.10.009

Berna, C., Lang, T. J., Goodwin, G. M., & Holmes, E. A. (2011). Developing a measure of interpretation bias for depressed mood: An ambiguous scenarios test. *Personality and Individual Differences, 51*(3), 349–354. https://doi.org/10.1016/j.paid.2011.04.005

Bettencourt, B., Talley, A., Benjamin, A. J., & Valentine, J. (2006). Personality and aggressive behavior under provoking and neutral conditions: a meta-analytic review. *Psychological Bulletin, 132*(5), 751–777. https://doi.org/10.1037/0033-2909.132.5.751

Blanchette, I., & Richards, A. (2010). The influence of affect on higher level cognition: A review of research on interpretation, judgement, decision making, and reasoning. *Cognition and Emotion, 24*(4), 561–595. https://doi.org/10.1080/02699930903132496

Blanco, I., Boemo, T., & Sanchez-Lopez, A. (2021). An online assessment to evaluate the role of cognitive biases and emotion regulation strategies for mental health during the COVID-19 lockdown of 2020: Structural equation modeling study. *JMIR Mental Health, 8*(11), e30961. https://doi.org/10.2196/30961

Butler, G., & Mathews, A. (1983). Cognitive processes in anxiety. *Advances in Behaviour Research and Therapy, 5*(1), 51–62. https://doi.org/10.1016/0146-6402(83)90015-2

Cannon, M. F., & Weems, C. F. (2010). Cognitive biases in childhood anxiety disorders: Do interpretive and judgment biases distinguish anxious youth from their non-anxious peers? *Journal of Anxiety Disorders, 24*(7), 751–758. https://doi.org/10.1016/j.janxdis.2010.05.008

Chen, J., Milne, K., Dayman, J., & Kemps, E. (2019). Interpretation bias and social anxiety: Does interpretation bias mediate the relationship between trait social anxiety and state anxiety responses? *Cognition and Emotion, 33*(4), 630–645. https://doi.org/10.1080/0269993 1.2018.1476323

Chen, J., Short, M., & Kemps, E. (2020). Interpretation bias in social anxiety: A systematic review and meta-analysis. *Journal of Affective Disorders, 276*, 1119–1130. https://doi.org/10.1016/j. jad.2020.07.121

Cisler, J. M., & Olatunji, B. O. (2012). Emotion regulation and anxiety disorders. *Current Psychiatry Reports, 14*(3), 182–187. https://doi.org/10.1007/s11920-012-0262-2

Clark, D. M. (1999). Anxiety disorders: Why they persist and how to treat them. *Behaviour Research and Therapy, 37*(1), S5-27. https://doi.org/10.1016/s0005-7967(99)00048-0

Clark, D. A., Beck, A. T., & Alford, B. A. (1999). Scientific foundations of cognitive theory and-therapy of depression. New York: John Wiley & Sons.

Cowden Hindash, A. H., & Rottenberg, J. (2017). Turning quickly on myself: Automatic interpretation biases in dysphoria are self-referent. *Cognition and Emotion, 31*(2), 395–402. https://doi. org/10.1080/02699931.2015.1105792

Dearing, K. F., & Gotlib, I. H. (2009). Interpretation of ambiguous information in girls at risk for depression. *Journal of Abnormal Child Psychology, 37*(1), 79–91. https://doi.org/10.1007/ s10802-008-9259-z

Dillon, K. H., Allan, N. P., Cougle, J. R., & Fincham, F. D. (2016). Measuring hostile interpretation bias: The WSAP-hostility scale. *Assessment, 23*(6), 707–719. https://doi. org/10.1177/1073191115599052

Downey, G., & Feldman, S. I. (1996). Implications of rejection sensitivity for intimate relationships. *Journal of Personality and Social Psychology, 70*(6), 1327–1343. https://doi. org/10.1037/0022-3514.70.6.1327

Dumontheil, I. (2014). Development of abstract thinking during childhood and adolescence: The role of rostrolateral prefrontal cortex. *Developmental Cognitive Neuroscience, 10*, 57–76. https://doi.org/10.1016/j.dcn.2014.07.009

Elmadih, A., Wan, M. W., Downey, D., Elliott, R., Swain, J. E., & Abel, K. M. (2016). Natural variation in maternal sensitivity is reflected in maternal brain responses to infant stimuli. *Behavioral Neuroscience, 130*(5), 500–510. https://doi.org/10.1037/bne0000161

Everaert, J. (2021). Interpretation of ambiguity in depression. *Current Opinion in Psychology, 41*, 9–14. https://doi.org/10.1016/j.copsyc.2021.01.003

Everaert, J., Tierens, M., Uzieblo, K., & Koster, E. H. (2013). The indirect effect of attention bias on memory via interpretation bias: Evidence for the combined cognitive bias hypothesis in subclinical depression. *Cognition and Emotion, 27*(8), 1450–1459. https://doi.org/10.108 0/02699931.2013.787972

Everaert, J., Podina, I. R., & Koster, E. H. (2017). A comprehensive meta-analysis of interpretation biases in depression. *Clinical Psychology Review, 58*, 33–48. https://doi.org/10.1016/j. cpr.2017.09.005

Everaert, J., Bronstein, M. V., Cannon, T. D., & Joormann, J. (2018). Looking through tinted glasses: Depression and social anxiety are related to both interpretation biases and inflexible negative interpretations. *Clinical Psychological Science, 6*(4), 517–528. https://doi. org/10.1177/2167702617747968

Everaert, J., Bronstein, M. V., Castro, A. A., Cannon, T. D., & Joormann, J. (2020). When negative interpretations persist, positive emotions don't! Inflexible negative interpretations encourage depression and social anxiety by dampening positive emotions. *Behaviour Research and Therapy, 124*, 103510. https://doi.org/10.1016/j.brat.2019.103510

Feldman, G. C., Joormann, J., & Johnson, S. L. (2008). Responses to positive affect: A self-report measure of rumination and dampening. *Cognitive Therapy and Research, 32*(4), 507–525. https://doi.org/10.1007/s10608-006-9083-0

Fodor, L. A., Georgescu, R., Cuijpers, P., Szamoskozi, Ş., David, D., Furukawa, T. A., & Cristea, I. A. (2020). Efficacy of cognitive bias modification interventions in anxiety and depressive disorders: A systematic review and network meta-analysis. *The Lancet Psychiatry, 7*(6), 506–514. https://doi.org/10.1016/S2215-0366(20)30130-9

Ford, B. Q., Gross, J. J., & Gruber, J. (2019). Broadening our field of view: The role of emotion polyregulation. *Emotion Review, 11*(3), 197–208. https://doi.org/10.1177/1754073919850314

Gadassi Polack, R., Everaert, J., Uddenberg, C., Kober, H., & Joormann, J. (2021). Emotion regulation and self-criticism in children and adolescence: Longitudinal networks of transdiagnostic risk factors. *Emotion, 21*(7), 1438–1451. https://doi.org/10.1037/emo0001041

Gadassi, R., & Rafaeli, E. (2015). Interpersonal perception as a mediator of the depression–interpersonal difficulties link: A review. *Personality and Individual Differences, 87*, 1–7. https://doi.org/10.1016/j.paid.2015.07.023

Grob, A., & Smolenski, C. (2005). *Fragebogen zur Erhebung der Emotionsregulation bei Kindern und Jugendlichen – FEEL-KJ* (1st ed.). Hans Huber.

Gross, J. J. (2014). Emotion regulation: Conceptual and empirical foundations. In J. J. Gross (Ed.), *Handbook of emotion regulation* (pp. 3–20). Guilford Press.

Henricks, L. A., Lange, W. G., Luijten, M., & Becker, E. S. (2022). A new social picture task to assess interpretation bias related to social fears in adolescents. *Research on Child and Adolescent Psychopathology*, 1–14. https://doi.org/10.1007/s10802-022-00915-3

Hirsch, C. R., Meeten, F., Krahé, C., & Reeder, C. (2016). Resolving ambiguity in emotional disorders: The nature and role of interpretation biases. *Annual Review of Clinical Psychology, 12*, 281–305. https://doi.org/10.1146/annurev-clinpsy-021815-093436

Hofmann, S. G., Sawyer, A. T., Fang, A., & Asnaani, A. (2012). Emotion dysregulation model of mood and anxiety disorders. *Depression and Anxiety, 29*(5), 409–416. https://doi.org/10.1002/da.21888

Holmes, E. A., Lang, T. J., Moulds, M. L., & Steele, A. M. (2008). Prospective and positive mental imagery deficits in dysphoria. *Behaviour Research and Therapy, 46*(8), 976–981. https://doi.org/10.1016/j.brat.2008.04.009

Jamieson, J. P., Nock, M. K., & Mendes, W. B. (2012). Mind over matter: Reappraising arousal improves cardiovascular and cognitive responses to stress. *Journal of Experimental Psychology: General, 141*(3), 417–422. https://doi.org/10.1037/a0025719

Joormann, J., & Gotlib, I. H. (2010). Emotion regulation in depression: Relation to cognitive inhibition. *Cognition and Emotion, 24*(2), 281–298. https://doi.org/10.1080/02699930903407948

Kanai, Y., Sasagawa, S., Chen, J., Shimada, H., & Sakano, Y. (2010). Interpretation bias for ambiguous social behavior among individuals with high and low levels of social anxiety. *Cognitive Therapy and Research, 34*(3), 229–240. https://doi.org/10.1007/s10608-009-9273-7

Kazdin, A. E. (2014). Moderators, mediators and mechanisms of change in psychotherapy. In *Quantitative and qualitative methods in psychotherapy research* (pp. 87–101).

Kessler, R. C., Berglund, P., Demler, O., Jin, R., Merikangas, K. R., & Walters, E. E. (2005). Lifetime prevalence and age-of-onset distributions of DSM-IV disorders in the National Comorbidity Survey Replication. *Archives of General Psychiatry, 62*(6), 593–602. https://doi.org/10.1001/archpsyc.62.6.593

Kuckertz, J. M., Amir, N., Tobin, A. C., & Najmi, S. (2013). Interpretation of ambiguity in individuals with obsessive-compulsive symptoms. *Cognitive Therapy and Research, 37*(2), 232–241. https://doi.org/10.1007/s10608-012-9478-z

Lawson, C., MacLeod, C., & Hammond, G. (2002). Interpretation revealed in the blink of an eye: Depressive bias in the resolution of ambiguity. *Journal of Abnormal Psychology, 111*(2), 321–328. https://doi.org/10.1037//0021-843x.111.2.321

Lebowitz, E. R., Omer, H., Hermes, H., & Scahill, L. (2014). Parent training for childhood anxiety disorders: The SPACE program. *Cognitive and Behavioral Practice, 21*(4), 456–469. https://doi.org/10.1016/j.cbpra.2013.10.004

Leibenluft, E., & Stoddard, J. (2013). The developmental psychopathology of irritability. *Development and Psychopathology, 25*(4pt2), 1473–1487. https://doi.org/10.1017/S0954579413000722

Leitenberg, H., Yost, L. W., & Carroll-Wilson, M. (1986). Negative cognitive errors in children: Questionnaire development, normative data, and comparisons between children with and without self-reported symptoms of depression, low self-esteem, and evaluation anxiety.

Journal of Consulting and Clinical Psychology, 54(4), 528–536. https://doi.org/10.1037//
0022-006x.54.4.528

Marks, C. K., Kraft, J. D., Grant, D. M., & Wells, T. T. (2021). The relationship between hostile interpretation bias and symptoms of depression and social anxiety: A replication across two samples. *Journal of Psychopathology and Behavioral Assessment, 43*(2), 251–258. https://doi.org/10.1007/s10862-020-09839-y

Mathews, A., & MacLeod, C. (2005). Cognitive vulnerability to emotional disorders. *Annual Review of Clinical Psychology, 1*(1), 167–195.

Menne-Lothmann, C., Viechtbauer, W., Höhn, P., Kasanova, Z., Haller, S. P., Drukker, M., Van Os, J., Wichers, M., & Lau, J. Y. (2014). How to boost positive interpretations? A meta-analysis of the effectiveness of cognitive bias modification for interpretation. *PLoS One, 9*(6), e100925. https://doi.org/10.1371/journal.pone.0100925

Miers, A. C., Blöte, A. W., Bögels, S. M., & Westenberg, P. M. (2008). Interpretation bias and social anxiety in adolescents. *Journal of Anxiety Disorders, 22*(8), 1462–1471. https://doi.org/10.1016/j.janxdis.2008.02.010

Min, J.-A., Yu, J. J., Lee, C.-U., & Chae, J.-H. (2013). Cognitive emotion regulation strategies contributing to resilience in patients with depression and/or anxiety disorders. *Comprehensive Psychiatry, 54*(8), 1190–1197. https://doi.org/10.1016/j.comppsych.2013.05.008

Morris, A. S., Silk, J. S., Steinberg, L., Myers, S. S., & Robinson, L. R. (2007). The role of the family context in the development of emotion regulation. *Social Development, 16*(2), 361–388. https://doi.org/10.1111/j.1467-9507.2007.00389.x

Moser, J. S., Huppert, J. D., Foa, E. B., & Simons, R. F. (2012). Interpretation of ambiguous social scenarios in social phobia and depression: Evidence from event-related brain potentials. *Biological Psychology, 89*(2), 387–397. https://doi.org/10.1016/j.biopsycho.2011.12.001

Nieto, I., Robles, E., & Vazquez, C. (2020). Self-reported cognitive biases in depression: A meta-analysis. *Clinical Psychology Review, 82*, 101934. https://doi.org/10.1016/j.cpr.2020.101934

Nolen-Hoeksema, S. (2000). The role of rumination in depressive disorders and mixed anxiety/depressive symptoms. *Journal of Abnormal Psychology, 109*(3), 504–511. https://doi.org/10.1037/0021-843X.109.3.504

Nolen-Hoeksema, S., Wisco, B. E., & Lyubomirsky, S. (2008). Rethinking rumination. *Perspectives on Psychological Science, 3*(5), 400–424. https://doi.org/10.1111/j.1745-6924.2008.00088.x

Normansell, K. M., & Wisco, B. E. (2017). Negative interpretation bias as a mechanism of the relationship between rejection sensitivity and depressive symptoms. *Cognition and Emotion, 31*(5), 950–962. https://doi.org/10.1080/02699931.2016.1185395

Orchard, F., & Reynolds, S. (2018). The combined influence of cognitions in adolescent depression: Biases of interpretation, self-evaluation, and memory. *British Journal of Clinical Psychology, 57*(4), 420–435. https://doi.org/10.1111/bjc.12184

Raes, F., Smets, J., Nelis, S., & Schoofs, H. (2012). Dampening of positive affect prospectively predicts depressive symptoms in non-clinical samples. *Cognition and Emotion, 26*(1), 75–82. https://doi.org/10.1080/02699931.2011.555474

Rosmarin, D. H., Bourque, L. M., Antony, M. M., & McCabe, R. E. (2009). Interpretation bias in panic disorder: Self-referential or global? *Cognitive Therapy and Research, 33*(6), 624–632. https://doi.org/10.1007/s10608-009-9249-7

Schneider, S., Unnewehr, S., Florin, I., & Margraf, J. (2002). Priming panic interpretations in children of patients with panic disorder. *Journal of Anxiety Disorders, 16*(6), 605–624. https://doi.org/10.1016/S0887-6185(02)00126-3

Sears, C. R., Bisson, S., & Nielsen, K. E. (2011). Dysphoria and the immediate interpretation of ambiguity: Evidence for a negative interpretive bias in error rates but not response latencies. *Cognitive Therapy and Research, 35*(5), 469–476. https://doi.org/10.1007/s10608-010-9314-2

Sfärlea, A., Löchner, J., Neumüller, J., Asperud Thomsen, L., Starman, K., Salemink, E., Schulte-Körne, G., & Platt, B. (2019). Passing on the half-empty glass: A transgenerational study of interpretation biases in children at risk for depression and their parents with depression. *Journal of Abnormal Psychology, 128*(2), 151–161. https://doi.org/10.1037/abn0000401

Sfärlea, A., Takano, K., Buhl, C., Loechner, J., Greimel, E., Salemink, E., Schulte-Körne, G., & Platt, B. (2021). Emotion regulation as a mediator in the relationship between cognitive biases and depressive symptoms in depressed, at-risk and healthy children and adolescents. *Research on Child and Adolescent Psychopathology, 49*(10), 1345–1358. https://doi.org/10.1007/s10802-021-00814-z

Sroufe, L. A. (2009). The concept of development in developmental psychopathology. *Child Development Perspectives, 3*(3), 178–183. https://doi.org/10.1111/j.1750-8606.2009.00103.x

Stuijfzand, S., Creswell, C., Field, A. P., Pearcey, S., & Dodd, H. (2018). Is anxiety associated with negative interpretations of ambiguity in children and adolescents? A systematic review and meta-analysis. *Journal of Child Psychology and Psychiatry, 59*(11), 1127–1142. https://doi.org/10.1111/jcpp.12822

Tadic, D., MacLeod, C., Cabeleira, C. M., Wuthrich, V. M., Rapee, R. M., & Bucks, R. S. (2018). Age differences in negative and positive expectancy bias in comorbid depression and anxiety. *Cognition and Emotion, 32*(8), 1531–1544. https://doi.org/10.1080/02699931.2017.1414688

Treynor, W., Gonzalez, R., & Nolen-Hoeksema, S. (2003). Rumination reconsidered: A psychometric analysis. *Cognitive Therapy and Research, 27*(3), 247–259. https://doi.org/10.1023/A:1023910315561

Verhoeven, F. E., Booij, L., Van der Wee, N. J., Penninx, B. W., & Van der Does, A. J. (2011). Clinical and physiological correlates of irritability in depression: results from the Netherlands study of depression and anxiety. *Depression Research and Treatment, 2011*, 126895. https://doi.org/10.1155/2011/126895

Viana, A. G., Dixon, L. J., Stevens, E. N., & Ebesutani, C. (2016). Parental emotion socialization strategies and their interaction with child interpretation biases among children with anxiety disorders. *Cognitive Therapy and Research, 40*(5), 717–731. https://doi.org/10.1007/s10608-016-9783-z

Voncken, M. J., Bögels, S. M., & de Vries, K. (2003). Interpretation and judgmental biases in social phobia. *Behaviour Research and Therapy, 41*(12), 1481–1488. https://doi.org/10.1016/s0005-7967(03)00143-8

Weems, C. F., Berman, S. L., Silverman, W. K., & Saavedra, L. M. (2001). Cognitive errors in youth with anxiety disorders: The linkages between negative cognitive errors and anxious symptoms. *Cognitive Therapy and Research, 25*(5), 559–575.

Wenzlaff, R. M., & Bates, D. E. (1998). Unmasking a cognitive vulnerability to depression: How lapses in mental control reveal depressive thinking. *Journal of Personality and Social Psychology, 75*(6), 1559–1571. https://doi.org/10.1037/0022-3514.75.6.1559

Wilson, J. K., & Rapee, R. M. (2005). Interpretative biases in social phobia: Content specificity and the effects of depression. *Cognitive Therapy and Research, 29*(3), 315–331. https://doi.org/10.1007/s10608-005-2833-6

Wisco, B. E., & Harp, D. R. (2021). Rumination as a mechanism of the association between interpretation bias and depression symptoms: A longitudinal investigation. *Journal of Experimental Psychopathology, 12*(2), 20438087211015233. https://doi.org/10.1177/20438087211015233

Wisco, B. E., & Nolen-Hoeksema, S. (2010). Interpretation bias and depressive symptoms: The role of self-relevance. *Behaviour Research and Therapy, 48*(11), 1113–1122. https://doi.org/10.1016/j.brat.2010.08.004

Wisco, B. E., Gilbert, K. E., & Marroquín, B. (2014). Maladaptive processing of maladaptive content: Rumination as a mechanism linking cognitive biases to depressive symptoms. *Journal of Experimental Psychopathology, 5*(3), 329–350.

Woud, M. L., Zhang, X. C., Becker, E. S., McNally, R. J., & Margraf, J. (2014). Don't panic: Interpretation bias is predictive of new onsets of panic disorder. *Journal of Anxiety Disorders, 28*, 83–87. https://doi.org/10.1016/j.janxdis.2013.11.008

Woud, M. L., Zhang, X. C., Becker, E. S., Zlomuzica, A., & Margraf, J. (2016). Catastrophizing misinterpretations predict somatoform-related symptoms and new onsets of somatoform disorders. *Journal of Psychosomatic Research, 81*, 31–37. https://doi.org/10.1016/j.jpsychores.2015.12.005

Würtz, F., Zahler, L., Blackwell, S. E., Margraf, J., Bagheri, M., & Woud, M. L. (2022). Scrambled but valid? The scrambled sentences task as a measure of interpretation biases in psychopathology: A systematic review and meta-analysis. *Clinical Psychology Review, 93*, 102133. https://doi.org/10.1016/j.cpr.2022.102133

Yu, M., Westenberg, P. M., Li, W., Wang, J., & Miers, A. C. (2019). Cultural evidence for interpretation bias as a feature of social anxiety in Chinese adolescents. *Anxiety, Stress and Coping, 32*(4), 376–386. https://doi.org/10.1080/10615806.2019.1598556

Zahler, L., Sommer, K., Reinecke, A., Wilhelm, F. H., Margraf, J., & Woud, M. L. (2020). Cognitive vulnerability in the context of panic: Assessment of panic-related associations and interpretations in individuals with varying levels of anxiety sensitivity. *Cognitive Therapy and Research, 44*(4), 858–873. https://doi.org/10.1007/s10608-020-10103-6

Reuma Gadassi Polack is a postdoctoral fellow in the Departments of Psychology and Psychiatry at Yale University. After receiving her doctoral degree from Bar-Ilan University, she joined the Affect Regulation and Cognition Lab and the Cognitive & Affective Neuroscience Lab at Yale. Her research focuses on risk and protective factors in the development of depression. She focuses on the interpersonal context of depression and on the development of the neurocircuitry supporting emotion regulation and reward processing, and aims to characterize typical and atypical developmental trajectories. Her work integrates ecological momentary assessment, cognitive tasks, eye-tracking, hormonal measures, and brain imaging.

Anna Leah Davis is a Yale undergraduate, majoring in psychology at Yale University. While at Yale, she has been a research assistant in the Affect Regulation and Cognition Lab and at the Yale Center for Emotional Intelligence. Her research interests include understanding mechanisms in development that can inform early prevention and treatment of psychopathology.

Jutta Joormann is a Professor in the Department of Psychology at Yale University. She received her doctoral degree from the Free University of Berlin. Her main areas of interest include the identification of cognitive risk factors for depression and social anxiety disorder. Her current work examines attention and memory processes that are linked to rumination and emotion dysregulation. In her work, she integrates a multitude of measures, including cognitive tasks, psychophysiological measures of stress reactivity and regulation, eye tracking, neuroendocrine assessments, genotyping, and brain imaging. She is an Associate Editor of the *Journal of Psychopathology and Clinical Science* and of the *Annual Review of Clinical Psychology*.

Chapter 5
Biased Interpretation of Ambiguity in Depression and Anxiety: Interactions with Attention, Memory, and Cognitive Control Processes

Jonas Everaert, Sarah Struyf, and Ernst H. W. Koster

5.1 Introduction

Ambiguous situations are common in everyday life. Imagine that you notice a person in the audience frowning when you present your latest work or that you did not receive an invitation to a friend's wedding. People need to generate and select plausible interpretations to resolve the ambiguity of such situations to make sense of what is happening around them (Blanchette & Richards, 2010; Hirsch et al., 2016; Huppert et al., 2007). In the examples above, you might think that the person in the audience is in a bad mood because of a fight earlier that day and that the invitation for the wedding got lost at the post office. However, less benign interpretations are also possible. For instance, you might think that your presentation was poor and that you are not invited to the wedding because you are not a real friend of the couple. How people interpret ambiguity has major consequences for their mood state and emotional well-being (Everaert et al., 2017a; Hirsch et al., 2016).

Cognitive theories have postulated that biases in how ambiguous situations are interpreted contribute to the development and maintenance of anxiety and depressive disorders (Beck & Haigh, 2014; Clark & Wells, 1995; Clark et al., 1999; Ingram, 1984; Mathews & Macleod, 2005; Morrison & Heimberg, 2013; Ouimet et al., 2009; Rapee & Heimberg, 1997). Interpretation bias refers to a tendency to

J. Everaert (✉)
Department of Medical and Clinical Psychology, Tilburg School of Social and Behavioral Sciences, Tilburg University, Tilburg, The Netherlands
e-mail: j.everaert@tilburguniversity.edu

S. Struyf · E. H. W. Koster
Department of Experimental Clinical and Health Psychology, Faculty of Psychology and Educational Sciences, Ghent University, Ghent, Belgium
e-mail: sarah.struyf@ugent.be; Ernst.Koster@ugent.be

© The Author(s), under exclusive license to Springer Nature Switzerland AG 2023   79
M. L. Woud (ed.), *Interpretational Processing Biases in Emotional Psychopathology*,
CBT: Science Into Practice, https://doi.org/10.1007/978-3-031-23650-1_5

consistently resolve ambiguous situations in a characteristic direction such as inferring more negative or threatening and/or fewer positive or benign meanings. This hypothesis has generated a large body of empirical research using a variety of cognitive-experimental paradigms in various samples of individuals with depressive and anxiety symptoms (for an overview of measures to assess interpretation biases, see Chap. 3 by Würtz and Sanchez-Lopez; for an overview of mediators and moderators of interpretation biases, see Chap. 4 by Gadassi Polack et al.).

Extensive research has shown that clinical and subclinical forms of depression are characterized by a tendency to infer fewer positive and more negative interpretations to account for ambiguity (for a meta-analysis, see Everaert et al., 2017a). With respect to anxiety, research suggests that individuals with generalized anxiety disorder display an interpretation bias toward threats (Hirsch et al., 2016). Individuals with panic disorder display a tendency to draw more catastrophic self-referent interpretations of benign physical sensations (Clark et al., 1997; Hirsch et al., 2016; Rosmarin, et al., 2009). Finally, individuals with social anxiety infer more negative interpretations when elaborating on ambiguous social information and less positive online interpretations at the time of encountering ambiguous cues (Chen et al., 2020; Morrison & Heimberg, 2013).

Importantly, research indicates that interpretation biases predict future symptom levels (Hirsch et al., 2016; Rude et al., 2010). For example, Woud et al. (2014) observed that interpretation bias for panic-related scenarios predicted the onset of panic disorder 17 months later, even after controlling for anxiety sensitivity and fear of bodily sensations. In depression, a negative interpretation bias predicts symptom levels 4–6 weeks later (Rude et al., 2002) as well as diagnostic status 18–28 months later (Rude et al., 2003). In addition to its predictive utility, interpretation may causally influence depression and anxiety symptoms (Fodor et al., 2020; Hallion & Ruscio, 2011; Menne-Lothmann et al., 2014). Cognitive bias modification (CBM) studies that experimentally manipulate interpretation bias alter negative mood states (Menne-Lothmann et al., 2014) anxiety and depression symptoms following a stressful experience (Hallion & Ruscio, 2011; for an overview of how to manipulate interpretation biases, see Chap. 11 by Salemink et al.). Therefore, interpretation bias is often viewed as a transdiagnostic vulnerability mechanism that operates across anxiety and depressive disorders.

Although experimental research on interpretation biases has made important progress in elucidating its nature and role as a potential vulnerability factor for depression and anxiety disorders, the specific mechanisms driving the interpretation of ambiguity remain understudied and poorly understood. This is because interpretation processes have typically been studied in isolation as a distinct phenomenon (Everaert et al., 2012, 2020a, 2020b; Hirsch et al., 2006). Yet, knowledge of which factors contribute to the generation and selection of plausible interpretations seems important to advance scientific understanding of this purported vulnerability mechanism. This knowledge may not only be of theoretical importance but also clinical relevance in that it may inform potential approaches to ameliorate this cognitive bias and decrease the burden imposed by psychopathology.

Interpreting ambiguous situations represents a higher-level cognitive operation that involves integrating and weighing different aspects of a situation to construct new mental representations that resolve the ambiguity (Blanchette & Richards, 2010; Everaert et al., 2020a, 2020b). This process of ambiguity resolution is expected to rely on a set of basic attention and memory operations (Everaert et al., 2020a, 2020b; Everaert, 2021). Because depression and anxiety disorders are also characterized by mood-congruent biases in attention allocation and memory retrieval (Armstrong & Olatunji, 2012; Bar-Haim et al., 2007; Gaddy & Ingram, 2014; Herrera et al., 2017; Pergamin-Hight et al., 2015; Schweizer et al., 2019; Matt et al., 1992; Everaert et al., 2022), these information-processing biases in basic cognitive operations likely contribute to the skewed generation and selection of interpretations. These biases may shape how individuals with depression and anxiety resolve ambiguous situations. While research on interactions between cognitive biases in psychopathology is still at the early stages, some emerging work has started to illuminate potential interactions between interpretation biases and other cognitive operations. This chapter reviews theoretical frameworks and existing empirical research on potential interactions between interpretation bias and attention, memory, and cognitive control when processing emotional information. This chapter concludes by outlining directions for future research to advance research in this emerging area of interest.

5.2 Theoretical Frameworks on Interactions Between Cognitive Biases

Research on cognitive biases in psychopathology has been guided by cognitive theories of anxiety and depression. One of the earliest models that have attributed a critical role to cognitive biases is Beck's schema theory (Beck, 1967). In his cognitive model, three levels of cognition (i.e., dysfunctional schemas, biased information processing, and negative automatic thoughts) are proposed as vulnerability factors for the maintenance of anxiety and depressive symptoms (Beck, 1967; Clark & Beck, 2010). Dysfunctional schemas are generally described as negative attitudes and beliefs about the self, the world, and the future (i.e., *the cognitive triad*). These beliefs concern themes of loss and helplessness in depression (Beck, 1979) or threat and danger combined with low expectations of one's coping ability in anxiety (Beck, 1985; Beck et al., 2005). Stressful events or experiences are expected to activate dysfunctional schemas which then set the stage for biases in attention, interpretation, and memory that are congruent with the activated schema. Such negative biases in information-processing are expected to produce negative automatic thoughts, images, and memories that may elicit various emotional and/or behavioral problems. Beck's schema theory has been highly influential in guiding research characterizing the nature of information-processing biases in various emotional disorders with major implications for clinical practice (Woud, 2022). However, the model's predictions regarding specific interactions between different aspects of information processing are less specific. This limitation has been addressed by later cognitive theories described below.

One integrative multi-process model of anxiety has been proposed by Ouimet et al. (2009). Drawing on dual-system theories, the model assumes that two distinct systems of information processing, the associative and rule-based system, operate in tandem in guiding problem-solving, making judgments, and regulating emotions. In the associative system, the processing of information involves rapid activation of associated concepts via spreading activation (associative processing). In the rule-based system, information-processing is characterized by the rational analysis of factual relations between concepts (rule-based processing). The integrative model proposed by Ouimet et al. (2009) posits that individual differences in associative and rule-based processing are responsible for cognitive biases at different stages of processing threat-relevant stimuli, thereby contributing to the development and maintenance of anxiety disorders. It is proposed that encountering potentially threatening stimuli activates threat-related concepts in the associative system, which directly orients attention toward the threatening stimuli in the environment. The rule-based system is expected to use inputs from the associative system to interpret and appraise the stimuli. The resulting enhanced activation of threat-related associations sets the stage for interpretations that are biased toward the threat. In parallel to the process of interpreting the stimulus, threat-related associations in the associative system will enhance attentional engagement with the stimulus. This may further increase the activation of corresponding threat-related associations, instigating a dysfunctional feedback loop. To overcome this feedback loop, the rule-based system needs to override the effects of the associative system on attention and disengage from attending to the stimulus by deploying executive control (e.g., behavioral responses to avoid attending to the threatening stimulus). Reinterpreting the stimulus (i.e., rule-based process) may be an effective strategy in overcoming fear responses by deactivating threat-related associations and reducing attentional engagement with the stimulus. By specifying potential interactions between the activation of threat-related associations from memory, attentional orienting, and attentional engagement as well as interpretation, the model sheds light on how cognitive biases may operate together in various anxiety disorders.

With respect to depression, Wittenborn et al. (2016) proposed a causal loop diagram integrating cognitive, social, and environmental factors that may explain the etiology of depression. This model specifies a reinforcing feedback loop involving attention, interpretation, and memory biases in the consolidation of negative cognitions. The model proposes that negative cognitive representations that are stored in long-term memory direct attention toward relevant information. Specifically, negative memory representations are hypothesized to both orient and maintain attention on negative material in the environment that matches the content of the memory representations. The resulting negative bias of attention is expected to increase one's perceived stress level and produce negatively biased interpretations of the situation. This enhanced processing of negative material through biases of attention and interpretation is in turn expected to set the stage for increased negative affect and improved encoding of negative material into memory. This further consolidates the initial negative memory representations, which may in turn guide attention toward congruent information, etc. By defining a pathway with memory bias causing biases of attention and interpretation that in turn fuel memory bias, this model advocates the view that cognitive biases are highly interactive and interdependent processes that cannot be fully understood when studied in isolation.

In an attempt to understand how cognitive biases and their components interact and contribute to psychopathology, Everaert et al. (2020a) recently proposed a framework that is informed by recent advances in the fields of cognitive and affective science (see Fig. 5.1). The framework proposes several theoretical predictions about causal pathways between attention and memory biases at different stages of information-processing. Specifically, the framework proposes several mechanisms that may be important to understanding how attention biases, working memory difficulties, and long-term memory biases work together and, thereby, contribute to psychopathology. The framework proposes that attention bias improves memory for negative material by influencing both encoding and retrieval of emotional material. That is, attention bias may skew the processing of emotional material in favor of negative information, which increases the probability that negative material is encoded into memory and alters what is available for later recollection. In addition, attentional biases may also enhance memory biases after encoding by altering the retrieval of stored emotional items. In remembering emotional experiences, attention bias may influence which cues are used to guide memory search to retrieve

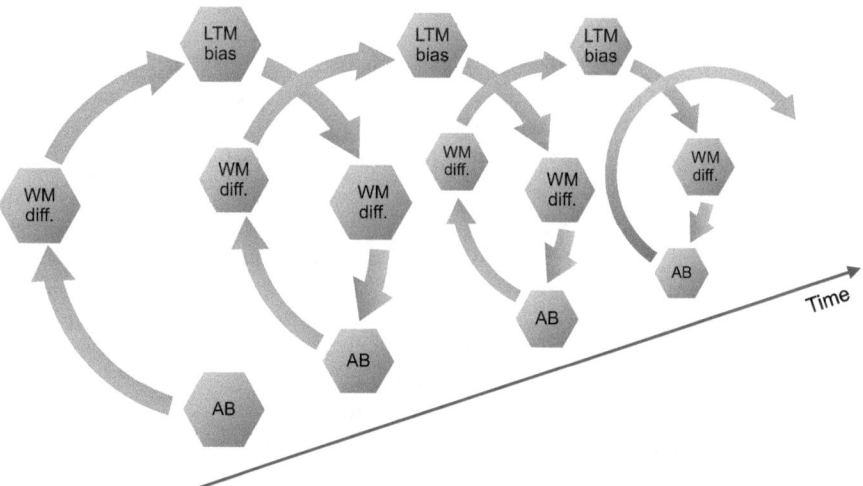

Fig. 5.1 Schematic overview of mechanisms and features of interactions among emotional biases in cognitive processes in psychopathology. *Note.* This figure illustrates five potential interactions: (1) attention bias (AB) during memory encoding modulates long-term memory (LTM) bias; (2) AB during memory retrieval modulates LTM bias; (3) LTM bias guides the allocation of attention; (4) working memory difficulties (WM diff.) modulate attention bias–LTM bias interactions; (5) interactions among biases of cognitive processes dynamically fluctuate across time and contexts

details of a past event. This attention bias during memory search is expected to increase the likelihood of remembering negative memories. In addition to the role of attention bias in influencing emotional memory, the framework proposes that memory biases may guide attention biases toward matching emotional material. Such a memory-guided attention bias may occur because someone's emotional learning history alters the attentional priority of certain cues in the environment. Alternatively, emotional memories can also be retrieved consciously when searching for relevant emotional information. Thus, the framework postulates that attention bias influences and is influenced by memory bias. It is expected that the interactions between these biased cognitive processes dynamically unfold over time. The framework suggests that such interactions between basic cognitive processes such as attention and memory are fundamental to many forms of higher-level cognition. Indeed, inferring interpretations to resolve ambiguity is a higher-level cognitive operation that is expected to rely on as set of basic attention and memory processes. The proposed attention–memory interactions may thus shape the (biased) outcome of interpretation processes. This framework is broadly applicable and may guide research on cognitive biases that operate within and across forms of psychopathology.

5.3 Empirical Research Examining Interactions Between Interpretation Bias and Basic Cognitive Processes

5.3.1 Attention Bias and Interpreting Ambiguity

Biased attention and interpretation processes are processes that have been proposed to be intimately related (Everaert et al., 2012; Everaert & Koster, 2020; Hirsch et al., 2006; Mathews & Mackintosh, 1998; Ouimet et al., 2009; Wittenborn et al., 2016). In the context of depression, empirical research yielded empirical support for an association between attention and interpretation biases. In one study (Everaert et al., 2014), participants with varying self-reported levels of depressive symptom severity were asked to complete a Scrambled Sentences Test (SST; Wenzlaff & Bates, 1998) that was developed for this study. In this test, participants unscramble emotional sentences in either a positive or negative manner (e.g., "born winner am loser a I" into either "I am a born loser" or "I am a born winner"; Everaert et al., 2014). When participants were unscrambling the sentences, biases in attention toward negative (e.g., "loser") versus positive (e.g., "winner") words were measured using eye-tracking. Results showed that a bias in fixation frequency favoring negative words was related to a higher proportion of SST sentences that were unscrambled in a negative manner (i.e., negative interpretations). This suggests that when attention is biased and prioritizes negative stimuli, more negative interpretations are derived. Of note, this relation between attention bias and subsequent biased interpretation of attended materials was also found by another study in a subclinical depressed sample using an exogenous cueing task in combination with a SST (Everaert et al., 2013). Moreover, a recent study on social anxiety provided further evidence in support of the association between attention and interpretation biases in the processing of emotional facial expressions (Leung et al., 2022). In this study, participants were asked to label various emotional expressions as quickly and accurately as possible (i.e., happy, angry, sad, disgust, fear). Facial stimuli displaying subtle expressions (i.e., low-intensity emotion) were then used to measure interpretation bias. Results showed that regardless of social anxiety levels, attention bias toward angry (but not disgusted) faces was associated with more negative interpretations of these angry expressions. This interpretation bias in turn predicted better recognition of the faces displaying anger.

While these cross-sectional studies optimized conditions to examine the effect of attention bias on interpretation bias (e.g., the temporal order of tasks, similar stimulus materials across tasks), third variables (for instance, elevated negative affect) could account for the observed relations. Direct proof of causality requires experimental manipulation of attention bias to track effects on interpretation processes.

Going beyond cross-sectional data, some studies have explicitly tested the causal role of attention bias in shaping interpretations of ambiguous information. These studies experimentally manipulate the acquisition or attenuation of a cognitive bias through cognitive bias modification procedures (e.g., inducing a negative or positive attention bias) to track effects on subsequent cognitive processes (e.g., interpretation of ambiguous stimuli). In samples of individuals reporting varying depressive symptom levels, two recent experiments have trained participants to orient attention toward either positive or negative words using a dot-probe training task (Everaert et al., 2015). Transfer of attention bias training to interpretation bias was examined by the Scrambled Sentences Test (SST) following the training procedure. Across both studies, it was observed that individual differences in attention bias acquisition were not related to the performance on the interpretation task. This work did not provide evidence for a causal influence of attention bias on interpretation bias in the context of depression. However, in this study, there was little evidence of successful manipulation of attention bias (measured before and after training), which precludes strong statements about the absence of influences of attention on interpretation. Similarly, a multi-session attention bias training using a visual search paradigm could not find transfer effects to interpretation processes in a sample of adolescents with heightened symptoms of anxiety and/or depression (Voogd et al., 2017). This finding is remarkable because, in contrast to earlier work (Everaert et al., 2015), the results of this study revealed that training successfully reduced attentional bias. Hence, the results of the study by Voogd and colleagues provide stronger evidence against the idea of a causal impact of attentional bias on interpretation bias.

However, a different pattern of results emerged in a study examining how an induced attention bias to threat affects how subsequent ambiguous information is interpreted (White et al., 2011). Participants were randomly assigned to the attention training group or the control group. In the attention training group, an attention bias to threat was induced using a dot-probe training procedure. In the control condition, no experimental manipulation of attention occurred. Next, participants completed a sentence completion task to measure interpretation bias. The task presented sentences describing ambiguous situations with the last word or phrase omitted. Participants needed to complete each sentence to disambiguate each situation by generating one word or short phrases that came to mind, and then selecting the response that they felt completed the sentence best. Results showed that participants who were trained to allocate attention toward threat displayed an increase in anxiety-related interpretations of ambiguous events when controlling for their initial interpretations of the ambiguous scenarios. Thus, attention bias may alter initial anxiety-related negative interpretations (White et al., 2011).

In addition to the potential influence of attention bias on interpretation bias, biased interpretations may, in turn, guide the allocation of attention to matching emotional information. To the best of our knowledge, in research on depression, there is only one study examining whether interpretation bias affects attention bias (LeMoult et al., 2017). In this study, adolescents with major depression received either six sessions of positive interpretation bias training or neutral training, followed by an interpretation and attention bias task. The training was effective in that adolescents receiving positive training also interpreted ambiguous scenarios more positively than did participants who received the neutral training. However, there was no transfer of the training to the dot-probe task as a measure of attention bias. This finding suggests that interpretation bias may not alter biased attention allocation in depression. However, a study on social anxiety did provide evidence for a causal effect of interpretation bias training on attention bias to threat (Amir et al., 2010). In this study, socially anxious individuals were randomly assigned to either a control condition or an interpretation bias modification program to make benign interpretations of ambiguous social scenarios. Results showed that only individuals who were trained to draw benign meanings of ambiguous situations showed a greater ability to disengage attention from threatening information.

Taken together, current research has not been able to provide unequivocal empirical support for mutual causal influences between attention and interpretation biases related to depression, but such reciprocal relationships may occur in anxiety. One potential explanation is that interpretation processes and *visual* attention are more closely connected in situations involving anxiety-eliciting threatening stimuli as compared to situations involving emotions such as sadness. This differential reliance on external stimuli (i.e., external attention) versus internal mental representations (i.e. internal attention) in anxiety versus sadness may (in part) explain observed differences between anxiety and depression with respect to performance on cognitive tasks using visual stimuli. Nevertheless, with unsuccessful manipulations of attentional bias and the problematic psychometric properties of commonly used cognitive paradigms to measure cognitive biases (Carlson & Herdman, 2012; Hirsch et al., 2016; O'Connor et al., 2021), there remain major challenges in this field of research.

5.3.2   Cognitive Control Difficulties and Interpreting Ambiguity

When someone generates an interpretation from ambiguous information, different options must be held online in working memory (WM), and the most plausible interpretation must be selected from its competitors. Difficulties in executive control likely influence this selection process. In particular, difficulties in inhibiting negative representations, shifting between negative and positive representations, and updating WM by removing irrelevant negative material may result in a disproportionate representation of negative versus positive interpretations in working memory (Everaert et al., 2020a, 2020b). In line with this notion, current research suggests that working memory difficulties when processing emotional information modulate how people with depressive symptoms interpret ambiguous information (Everaert et al., 2017a). This recent work indicates that both difficulties in shifting between negative working memory representations and difficulties in updating working memory to discard negative representations are uniquely related to depression-linked interpretation biases.

To date, similar work on anxiety-related difficulties in cognitive control when processing threatening information and interpretation bias is lacking. However, some studies have examined how working memory capacity may modulate the interpretation of ambiguity. One study tested whether working memory capacity for neutral information modulates the relation between social anxiety and threat-related interpretation bias in a nonclinical sample (Salemink et al., 2013). Participants' implicit social anxiety was measured using the Implicit Association Test (implicit social anxiety; Westberg et al., 2007). Interpretation bias was measured with the Word Sentence Association Paradigm (Beard & Amir, 2008) and working memory capacity was measured with the Complex Operation Span Task (Unsworth et al., 2005). Results indicated that working memory capacity moderated the relation between implicit social anxiety and threat-related interpretation bias. That is, social anxiety was positively related to interpretation bias for individuals with low but not high working memory capacity. Another study provided further evidence for the role of working memory in interpretation bias in high trait anxious individuals (Booth et al., 2017). In this study, participants were asked to read various ambiguous vignettes regarding physical or social threats under high and low working memory load. Participants' interpretations of the ambiguous vignettes were assessed via a recognition test. Results showed that trait anxiety was predictive of negative interpretation biases of social threat vignettes under high (but not low) working memory load. These findings provide some support for the hypothesis that the severity of biased interpretations of ambiguous stimuli is modulated by difficulties in executive control. However, it has yet to be investigated how cognitive control difficulties when processing emotional information are linked to interpretation biases for threat in anxiety.

5.3.3 Memory Bias and Interpreting Ambiguity

Inferring more biased interpretations may increase the probability that these mental representations are encoded into memory, as such setting the stage for a bias in memory retrieval. The potential impact of interpretation bias on memory seems particularly important because encoding of negative interpretations in memory may fuel negative beliefs about the self, others, and the future. Findings from studies examining associations between interpretation and memory in nonclinical samples suggest that memory recall is affected by interpretation biases operating during the encoding of emotional material as well as by interpretation biases acquired after emotional material has been encoded (Leung et al., 2022; Salemink et al., 2010; Tran et al., 2011). Some evidence from cross-sectional studies in samples of individuals reporting a variety of depressive symptom levels suggests that inferring more interpretations in a biased manner increases the likelihood of subsequent biased retrieval of those interpretations (Everaert et al., 2013, 2014). In these studies, participants completed a Scrambled Sentences Test (SST) to measure interpretation bias, and, following a short break, they were asked to recall their previously constructed sentences during the SST as accurately as possible. In support of the notion that interpretation bias modulates free recall, a negative bias in interpretive choices during the SST was related to enhanced retrieval of negative sentences from memory. These findings suggest that emotional biases in interpretation regulate what is subsequently remembered (Everaert et al., 2013, 2014).

Furthermore, a study sought to extend this work by recruiting a sample of clinically depressed individuals (Joormann et al., 2015). In this study, participants completed an interpretation bias training inducing either a positive or negative interpretation bias. Next, participants read a series of ambiguous stories during an interpretation task, followed by a recognition test to measure interpretation bias and a recall task measuring memory for the ambiguous stories. The results showed that the training was successful at inducing a positive and negative interpretation bias and that there were training training-congruent effects on the recall for endings (i.e., interpretations) of the ambiguous scenarios. Providing further support for the role of interpretation bias in regulating memory, a recent study showed that changes in interpretation bias, as a result of a cognitive bias modification procedure, also resulted in congruent changes in negative memory bias (Nieto & Vazquez, 2021).

Unfortunately, research examining the impact of interpretation bias on memory is still at the early stages in research on anxiety disorders. In one study by Hertel et al. (2008), participants with social anxiety disorder and healthy control group were instructed to interpret ambiguous social scenarios and formulate an ending for each scenario. During the subsequent memory task, participants were asked to recall the details from the presented scenarios and their endings. Compared to individuals in the healthy control group, participants with social anxiety disorder endorsed more negative interpretations of these scenarios and showed better memory. In other studies (Hertel et al., 2008; Hirsch et al., 2006, 2016), non-clinical participants were asked to read ambiguous scenarios with socially threatening endings. They were instructed to either imagine themselves as the central character of the scenario as vivid as possible or use no mental imagery. Next, they completed a memory task testing their memory of the scenarios. Results suggested that negative interpretations contributed to memory biases when participants used imagery and not when they processed the scenarios in a more verbal way (Hertel et al., 2008; Hirsch et al., 2006, 2016). These results suggest that memory in social anxiety may be influenced by interpretation processes (Hirsch et al., 2006). Though these studies used experimental manipulations of cognitive processes via instructions, future work should extend these findings by using cognitive bias modification procedures. This work could draw on previous studies examining how interpretation bias impacts memory in healthy individuals (Salemink et al., 2010; Tran et al., 2011).

While interpretation bias may impact memory, it is also plausible that the generation of interpretations is guided by prior knowledge and/or experiences in similar situations. Thus, memory bias is likely to influence interpretation bias. Because research on interactions between cognitive biases when processing emotional information is at the early stages, investigators have yet to examine the potential role of memory bias in shaping the generation and selection of interpretations in depression and anxiety.

5.4 Future Research Directions

Though research has made considerable progress in the past several years, important limitations remain and represent directions for future research. First, various aspects of interactions between interpretation bias and other cognitive processes have received only limited empirical attention or have yet to be investigated. To date, most studies have examined the role of attention bias in accounting for individual differences in interpretation bias toward negative or threatening material. As repeatedly noted in earlier sections of this chapter, various potential interactions between interpretation bias and other cognitive biases have received far less attention. Indeed, much has yet to be discovered about whether interpretation bias is also able to guide attention allocation as well as whether interpretation bias can both influence and be influenced by memory bias and emotional working memory difficulties in depression and anxiety. Research in this area may draw on comprehensive theoretical frameworks (e.g., Everaert et al., 2020a) to systematically explore how interpretation bias interacts with attention bias, cognitive control, and working memory difficulties. Also, though not discussed in this chapter, other cognitive processes such as mental imagery (Hirsch et al., 2006; Holmes et al., 2009; for an overview of the role of imagery in biased interpretational processing, see Chap. 6 by Blackwell) and expectations (Aue & Okon-Singer, 2015; Kube et al., 2020) may further help to understand emotional biases in interpretation processes in psychopathology.

Advances with respect to these issues require targeted research that can be guided by theoretical frameworks. Recent transdiagnostic research frameworks (Everaert et al., 2020a, 2020b) may provide specific directions for studying how attention biases, working memory difficulties, and long-term memory biases work together when interpreting ambiguous information in various forms of psychopathology. Future research could employ experimental procedures from basic cognitive and affective science to study how attention biases during memory encoding modulate long-term memory biases, how attention biases during memory retrieval modulate long-term memory biases, how long-term memory biases guide the allocation of attention, as well as how working memory difficulties modulate the interactions between biases of attention and long-term memory. As in many basic science studies, experimental psychopathology research in this area could employ multiple experimental tasks of cognitive biases in a fixed temporal order with the same ambiguous stimulus materials in a single study to investigate how stimuli are processed throughout different stages. This experimental setup may help to elucidate specific interactions during the process of interpretation.

While biases in cognitive processes may have transdiagnostic properties, research has yet to discover the extent to which mechanisms of attention–memory bias interactions during the interpretation of ambiguity generalize across different forms of psychopathology. Indeed, differences between mental disorders may arise depending on the nature of biased cognitive processes that are characteristic of a particular disorder. For example, whereas depression involves biases in both implicit and explicit long-term memory (LTM) processes (Gaddy & Ingram, 2014; Matt et al., 1992; Everaert et al., 2022), anxiety is related to the enhanced recall of threat-related information but not to biases in explicit recognition or implicit memory tasks (Mitte, 2008). Such distinctive features regarding the nature of cognitive biases may determine which mechanisms of attention–memory bias interactions during interpretation processes can be plausibly expected (Everaert et al., 2020a, 2020b).

Second, future research on interpretation bias and its underlying mechanisms could adopt more dynamic or context-sensitive perspectives on cognitive biases. Traditional clinical theories consider interpretation bias as an inherently maladaptive process. Yet, emerging *flexibility perspectives* on mental health challenge such static views (Mehu & Scherer, 2015; Stange et al., 2017) and emphasize that an interpretation bias may not always be (mal)adaptive (Everaert et al., 2018). Indeed, negative interpretations may motivate people to adjust their behavior (e.g., tactfully voicing your opinion at work), and overly positive interpretations may lead people to ignore negative or threatening situations (e.g., physical symptoms that could signal a serious disease). Whether interpretations promote (mal)adaptation depends on the fluctuating demands of the context in which these interpretations are made (Everaert et al., 2018; Mehu & Scherer, 2015). Independent of the content of interpretations, the inflexibility with which emotional interpretations are formed and maintained may determine the misfit with situational demands, thereby increasing the risk for psychological complaints. Consistent with this notion, three independent studies have shown that greater severity of depression and social anxiety is not only associated with elevated negative interpretations but also with reduced revision of negative interpretations in the face of disconfirmatory positive information (Everaert et al., 2020a, 2020b; Everaert et al., 2018). Recent work also showed that not interpretation bias, but reduced revision of negative interpretations based on positive information prospectively predicts changes in suicidal ideation (Everaert et al., 2021). These findings suggest that depression and social anxiety feature both biased and inflexible negative interpretations of ambiguity. Understanding how inflexible revision of interpretation recruits attention, cognitive control, and memory processes provides an important direction for future work to gain a better understanding of processes that are involved in toxic features of interpretation processes.

Finally, prior research has generally studied cognitive biases at the disorder level and ignored the heterogeneous nature of depression and anxiety. The dominant focus on the disorder level may be problematic because it overlooks critical differences in the importance of individual symptoms, differential relations between symptoms, as well as differential relations between symptoms, and risk factors such as cognitive biases (Fried, 2017; Fried & Nesse, 2015). From both a theoretical and clinical stance, knowledge of whether (clusters of) symptoms are more closely related to interpretation bias/inflexibility and its underlying cognitive processes is urgently required (Beevers et al., 2019; Marchetti et al., 2018). Therefore, future research could adopt a symptom-level approach to gain insight into how cognitive biases connect to (clusters of) depression and anxiety symptoms.

5.5 Conclusion

The past several years witnessed important methodological and empirical advances in discovering the nature and role of interpretation processes as well as its interactions with other cognitive mechanisms in depression and anxiety. This review provides an overview of theoretical models and recent research examining interactions between interpretation bias and attention, cognitive control, and memory operations. Though research is at an early stage, accumulated research findings provide some evidence for interrelations between interpretation bias and cognitive biases in attention and memory in depression and anxiety. Yet, there is much that remains to be understood about their complex interplay to gain a better understanding of the higher-level cognitive process of interpretation of ambiguous situations.

References

Amir, N., Bomyea, J., & Beard, C. (2010). The effect of single-session interpretation modification on attention bias in socially anxious individuals. *Journal of Anxiety Disorders, 24*(2), 178–182. https://doi.org/10.1016/j.janxdis.2009.10.005

Armstrong, T., & Olatunji, B. O. (2012). Eye tracking of attention in the affective disorders: A meta-analytic review and synthesis. *Clinical Psychology Review, 32*(8), 704–723. https://doi.org/10.1016/j.cpr.2012.09.004

Aue, T., & Okon-Singer, H. (2015). Expectancy biases in fear and anxiety and their link to biases in attention. *Clinical Psychology Review, 42*, 83–95. https://doi.org/10.1016/j.cpr.2015.08.005

Bar-Haim, Y., Lamy, D., Pergamin, L., Bakermans-Kranenburg, M. J., & van IJzendoorn, M. H. (2007). Threat-related attentional bias in anxious and nonanxious individuals: A meta-analytic study. *Psychological Bulletin, 133*(1), 1–24. https://doi.org/10.1037/0033-2909.133.1.1

Beard, C., & Amir, N. (2008). A multi-session interpretation modification program: Changes in interpretation and social anxiety symptoms. *Behaviour Research and Therapy, 46*(10), 1135–1141. https://doi.org/10.1016/j.brat.2008.05.012

Beck, A.T. (1967). Depression. Harper and Row: New York.

Beck, A. T. (1979). *Cognitive therapy and the emotional disorders*. Penguin.

Beck, A. T. (1985). Theoretical perspectives on clinical anxiety. In A. H. Tuma & J. D. Maser (Eds.), Anxiety and the anxiety disorders (pp. 183–196). Lawrence Erlbaum Associates, Inc.

Beck, A. T., & Haigh, E. A. P. (2014). Advances in cognitive theory and therapy: The generic cognitive model. *Annual Review of Clinical Psychology, 10*(1), 1–24. https://doi.org/10.1146/annurev-clinpsy-032813-153734

Beck, A. T., Emery, G., & Greenberg, R. L. (2005). Anxiety disorders and phobias: A cognitive perspective. Basic Books/Hachette Book Group.

Beevers, C. G., Mullarkey, M. C., Dainer-Best, J., Stewart, R. A., Labrada, J., Allen, J. J. B., McGeary, J. E., & Shumake, J. (2019). Association between negative cognitive bias and depression: A symptom-level approach. *Journal of Abnormal Psychology, 8*(3). https://doi.org/10.1037/abn0000405

Blanchette, I., & Richards, A. (2010). The influence of affect on higher level cognition: A review of research on interpretation, judgement, decision making and reasoning. *Cognition & Emotion, 24*(4), 561–595. https://doi.org/10.1080/02699930903132496

Booth, R. W., Mackintosh, B., & Sharma, D. (2017). Working memory regulates trait anxiety-related threat processing biases. *Emotion (Washington, D.C.), 17*(4), 616–627. https://doi.org/10.1037/emo0000264

Carlson, K. D., & Herdman, A. O. (2012). Understanding the impact of convergent validity on research results. *Organizational Research Methods, 15*(1), 17–32. https://doi.org/10.1177/1094428110392383

Chen, J., Short, M., & Kemps, E. (2020). Interpretation bias in social anxiety: A systematic review and meta-analysis. *Journal of Affective Disorders, 276*, 1119–1130. https://doi.org/10.1016/j.jad.2020.07.121

Clark, D. A., & Beck, A. T. (2010). Cognitive theory and therapy of anxiety and depression: Convergence with neurobiological findings. *Trends in Cognitive Sciences, 14*(9), 418–424. https://doi.org/10.1016/j.tics.2010.06.007

Clark, D. M., & Wells, A. A. (1995). A cognitive model of social phobia. In R. G. Heimberg, M. R. Liebowitz, D. A. Hope, & F. R. Schneier (Eds.), *Social Phobia: Diagnosis, assessment and treatment* (pp. 69–93). Guilford Press.

Clark, D. M., Salkovskis, P. M., Ost, L. G., Breitholtz, E., Koehler, K. A., Westling, B. E., Jeavons, A., & Gelder, M. (1997). Misinterpretation of body sensations in panic disorder. *Journal of Consulting and Clinical Psychology, 65*(2), 203–213. https://doi.org/10.1037//0022-006x.65.2.203

Clark, D. A., Beck, A. T., & Alford, B. A. (1999). *Scientific foundations of cognitive theory and therapy of depression*. Wiley.

Everaert, J. (2021). Interpretation of ambiguity in depression. *Current Opinion in Psychology, 41*, 9–14. https://doi.org/10.1016/j.copsyc.2021.01.003

Everaert, J., & Koster, E. H. W. (2020). Chapter 9 - The interplay among attention, interpretation, and memory biases in depression: Revisiting the combined cognitive bias hypothesis. In T. Aue & H. Okon-Singer (Eds.), *Cognitive biases in health and psychiatric disorders* (pp. 193–213). Academic Press. https://doi.org/10.1016/B978-0-12-816660-4.00009-X

Everaert, J., Koster, E. H. W., & Derakshan, N. (2012). The combined cognitive bias hypothesis in depression. *Clinical Psychology Review, 32*(5), 413–424. https://doi.org/10.1016/j.cpr.2012.04.003

Everaert, J., Tierens, M., Uzieblo, K., & Koster, E. H. W. (2013). The indirect effect of attention bias on memory via interpretation bias: Evidence for the combined cognitive bias hypothesis in subclinical depression. *Cognition & Emotion, 27*(8), 1450–1459. https://doi.org/10.108 0/02699931.2013.787972

Everaert, J., Duyck, W., & Koster, E. H. W. (2014). Attention, interpretation, and memory biases in subclinical depression: A proof-of-principle test of the combined cognitive biases hypothesis. *Emotion, 14*(2), 331–340. https://doi.org/10.1037/a0035250

Everaert, J., Mogoaşe, C., David, D., & Koster, E. H. W. (2015). Attention bias modification via single-session dot-probe training: Failures to replicate. *Journal of Behavior Therapy and Experimental Psychiatry, 49*, 5–12. https://doi.org/10.1016/j.jbtep.2014.10.011

Everaert, J., Podina, I. R., & Koster, E. H. W. (2017a). A comprehensive meta-analysis of interpretation biases in depression. *Clinical Psychology Review, 58*, 33–48. https://doi.org/10.1016/j. cpr.2017.09.005

Everaert, J., Grahek, I., & Koster, E. H. W. (2017b). Individual differences in cognitive control over emotional material modulate cognitive biases linked to depressive symptoms. *Cognition and Emotion, 31*(4), 736–746. https://doi.org/10.1080/02699931.2016.1144562

Everaert, J., Bronstein, M. V., Cannon, T. D., & Joormann, J. (2018). Looking through tinted glasses: Depression and social anxiety are related to both interpretation biases and inflexible negative interpretations. *Clinical Psychological Science, 6*(4), 517–528. https://doi. org/10.1177/2167702617747968

Everaert, J., Bernstein, A., Joormann, J., & Koster, E. H. W. (2020a). Mapping dynamic interactions among cognitive biases in depression. *Emotion Review, 12*(2), 93–110. https://doi. org/10.1177/1754073919892069

Everaert, J., Bronstein, M. V., Castro, A., Cannon, T. D., & Joormann, J. (2020b). When negative interpretations persist, positive emotions don't! Inflexible negative interpretations encourage depression and social anxiety by dampening positive emotions. *Behaviour Research and Therapy, 124*, 103510. https://doi.org/10.1016/j.brat.2019.103510

Everaert, J., Bronstein, M. V., Cannon, T. D., Klonsky, E. D., & Joormann, J. (2021). Inflexible interpretations of ambiguous social situations: A novel predictor of suicidal ideation and the beliefs that inspire it. *Clinical Psychological Science, 9*(5), 879–899. https://doi. org/10.1177/2167702621993867

Everaert, J., Vrijsen, J. N., Martin-Willett, R., van de Kraats, L., & Joormann, J. (2022). A meta-analytic review of the relationship between explicit memory bias and depression: Depression features an explicit memory bias that persists beyond a depressive episode. *Psychological Bulletin, 148*(5–6), 435–463. https://doi.org/10.1037/bul0000367

Fodor, L. A., Georgescu, R., Cuijpers, P., Szamoskozi, Ş., David, D., Furukawa, T. A., & Cristea, I. A. (2020). Efficacy of cognitive bias modification interventions in anxiety and depressive disorders: A systematic review and network meta-analysis. *The Lancet Psychiatry, 7*(6), 506–514. https://doi.org/10.1016/S2215-0366(20)30130-9

Fried, E. I. (2017). The 52 symptoms of major depression: Lack of content overlap among seven common depression scales. *Journal of Affective Disorders, 208*, 191–197. https://doi. org/10.1016/j.jad.2016.10.019

Fried, E. I., & Nesse, R. M. (2015). Depression sum-scores don't add up: Why analyzing specific depression symptoms is essential. *BMC Medicine, 13*(1), 72. https://doi.org/10.1186/ s12916-015-0325-4

Gaddy, M. A., & Ingram, R. E. (2014). A meta-analytic review of mood-congruent implicit memory in depressed mood. *Clinical Psychology Review, 34*(5), 402–416. https://doi.org/10.1016/j. cpr.2014.06.001

Hallion, L. S. S., & Ruscio, A. M. M. (2011). A meta-analysis of the effect of cognitive bias modification on anxiety and depression. *Psychological Bulletin, 137*(6), 940–958. https://doi. org/10.1037/a00243552011-13412-001

Herrera, S., Montorio, I., Cabrera, I., & Botella, J. (2017). Memory bias for threatening information related to anxiety: An updated meta-analytic review. *Journal of Cognitive Psychology, 29*(7), 832–854. https://doi.org/10.1080/20445911.2017.1319374

Hertel, P. T., Brozovich, F., Joormann, J., & Gotlib, I. H. (2008). Biases in interpretation and memory in generalized social phobia. *Journal of Abnormal Psychology, 117*(2), 278–288. https://doi.org/10.1037/0021-843X.117.2.278

Hirsch, C. R., Clark, D. M., & Mathews, A. (2006). Imagery and interpretations in social phobia: Support for the combined cognitive biases hypothesis. *Behavior Therapy, 37*(3), 223–236. https://doi.org/10.1016/j.beth.2006.02.001

Hirsch, C. R., Meeten, F., Krahé, C., & Reeder, C. (2016). Resolving ambiguity in emotional disorders: The nature and role of interpretation biases. *Annual Review of Clinical Psychology, 12*(1), 281–305. https://doi.org/10.1146/annurev-clinpsy-021815-093436

Holmes, E. A., Lang, T. J., & Deeprose, C. (2009). Mental imagery and emotion in treatment across disorders: Using the example of depression. *Cognitive Behaviour Therapy, 38*, 21–28. https://doi.org/10.1080/16506070902980729

Huppert, J. D., Pasupuleti, R. V., Foa, E. B., & Mathews, A. (2007). Interpretation biases in social anxiety: Response generation, response selection, and self-appraisals. *Behaviour Research and Therapy, 45*(7), 1505–1515. https://doi.org/10.1016/j.brat.2007.01.006

Ingram, R. E. (1984). Toward an information-processing analysis of depression. *Cognitive Therapy and Research, 8*(5), 443–477. https://doi.org/10.1007/BF01173284

Joormann, J., Waugh, C. E., & Gotlib, I. H. (2015). Cognitive bias modification for interpretation in major depression. *Clinical Psychological Science, 3*(1), 126–139. https://doi.org/10.1177/2167702614560748

Kube, T., Schwarting, R., Rozenkrantz, L., Glombiewski, J. A., & Rief, W. (2020). Distorted cognitive processes in major depression: A predictive processing perspective. *Biological Psychiatry, 87*(5), 388–398. https://doi.org/10.1016/j.biopsych.2019.07.017

LeMoult, J., Colich, N., Joormann, J., Singh, M. K., Eggleston, C., & Gotlib, I. H. (2017). Interpretation bias training in depressed adolescents: Near- and far-transfer effects. *Journal of Abnormal Child Psychology*, 1–9. https://doi.org/10.1007/s10802-017-0285-6

Leung, C. J., Yiend, J., & Lee, T. M. C. (2022). The relationship between attention, interpretation and memory bias during facial perception in social anxiety. *Behavior Therapy*. https://doi.org/10.1016/j.beth.2022.01.011

Marchetti, I., Everaert, J., Dainer-Best, J., Loeys, T., Beevers, C. G., & Koster, E. H. W. (2018). Specificity and overlap of attention and memory biases in depression. *Journal of Affective Disorders, 225*, 404–412. https://doi.org/10.1016/j.jad.2017.08.037

Mathews, A., & Mackintosh, B. (1998). A cognitive model of selective processing in anxiety. *Cognitive Therapy and Research, 22*(6), 539–560. https://doi.org/10.1023/A:1018738019346

Mathews, A., & Macleod, C. M. (2005). Cognitive vulnerability to emotional disorders. *Annual Review of Clinical Psychology, 1*(1), 167–195. https://doi.org/10.1146/annurev.clinpsy.1.102803.143916

Matt, G. E., Vázquez, C., & Campbell, W. K. (1992). Mood-congruent recall of affectively toned stimuli: A meta-analytic review. *Clinical Psychology Review, 12*(2), 227–255. https://doi.org/10.1016/0272-7358(92)90116-P

Mehu, M., & Scherer, K. R. (2015). The appraisal bias model of cognitive vulnerability to depression. *Emotion Review, 7*(3), 272–279. https://doi.org/10.1177/1754073915575406

Menne-Lothmann, C., Viechtbauer, W., Höhn, P., Kasanova, Z., Haller, S. P., Drukker, M., van Os, J., Wichers, M., & Lau, J. Y. F. (2014). How to boost positive interpretations? A meta-analysis of the effectiveness of cognitive bias modification for interpretation. *PLoS One, 9*(6), e100925. https://doi.org/10.1371/journal.pone.0100925

Mitte K. (2008). Memory bias for threatening information in anxiety and anxiety disorders: a meta-analytic review. *Psychological Bulletin, 134*(6), 886–911. https://doi.org/10.1037/a0013343

Morrison, A. S., & Heimberg, R. G. (2013). Social anxiety and social anxiety disorder. *Annual Review of Clinical Psychology, 9*(1), 249–274. https://doi.org/10.1146/annurev-clinpsy-050212-185631

Nieto, I., & Vazquez, C. (2021). Disentangling the mediating role of modifying interpretation bias on emotional distress using a novel cognitive bias modification program. *Journal of Anxiety Disorders, 83*, 102459. https://doi.org/10.1016/j.janxdis.2021.102459

O'Connor, C. E., Everaert, J., & Fitzgerald, A. (2021). Interpreting ambiguous emotional information: Convergence among interpretation bias measures and unique relations with depression severity. *Journal of Clinical Psychology, 77*(11), 2529–2544. https://doi.org/10.1002/jclp.23186

Ouimet, A. J., Gawronski, B., & Dozois, D. J. A. (2009). Cognitive vulnerability to anxiety: A review and an integrative model. *Clinical Psychology Review, 29*(6), 459–470. https://doi.org/10.1016/j.cpr.2009.05.004

Pergamin-Hight, L., Naim, R., Bakermans-Kranenburg, M. J., van IJzendoorn, M. H., & Bar-Haim, Y. (2015). Content specificity of attention bias to threat in anxiety disorders: A meta-analysis. *Clinical Psychology Review, 35*, 10–18. https://doi.org/10.1016/j.cpr.2014.10.005

Rapee, R. M., & Heimberg, R. G. (1997). A cognitive-behavioral model of anxiety in social phobia. *Behaviour Research and Therapy, 35*(8), 741–756. https://doi.org/10.1016/S0005-7967(97)00022-3

Rosmarin, D. H., Bourque, L. M., Antony, M. M., & McCabe, R. E. (2009). Interpretation bias in panic disorder: Self-referential or global? *Cognitive Therapy and Research, 33*(6), 624–632. https://doi.org/10.1007/s10608-009-9249-7

Rude, S. S., Wenzlaff, R. M., Gibbs, B., Vane, J., & Whitney, T. (2002). Negative processing biases predict subsequent depressive symptoms. *Cognition and Emotion, 16*(3), 423–440. https://doi.org/10.1080/02699930143000554

Rude, S. S., Valdez, C. R., Odom, S., & Ebrahimi, A. (2003). Negative cognitive biases predict subsequent depression. *Cognitive Therapy and Research, 27*(4), 415–429. https://doi.org/10.1023/A:1025472413805

Rude, S. S., Durham-Fowler, J. A., Baum, E. S., Rooney, S. B., & Maestas, K. L. (2010). Self-report and cognitive processing measures of depressive thinking predict subsequent major depressive disorder. *Cognitive Therapy and Research, 34*(2), 107–115. https://doi.org/10.1007/s10608-009-9237-y

Salemink, E., Hertel, P. T., & Mackintosh, B. (2010). Interpretation training influences memory for prior interpretations. *Emotion, 10*(6), 903–907. https://doi.org/10.1037/a0020232

Salemink, E., Friese, M., Drake, E., Mackintosh, B., & Hoppitt, L. (2013). Indicators of implicit and explicit social anxiety influence threat-related interpretive bias as a function of working memory capacity. *Frontiers in Human Neuroscience, 7*, 22. https://doi.org/10.3389/fnhum.2013.00220

Schweizer, S., Satpute, A. B., Atzil, S., Field, A. P., Hitchcock, C., Black, M., Barrett, L. F., & Dalgleish, T. (2019). The impact of affective information on working memory: A pair of meta-analytic reviews of behavioral and neuroimaging evidence. *Psychological Bulletin, 145*(6), 566–609. https://doi.org/10.1037/bul0000193

Stange, J. P., Alloy, L. B., & Fresco, D. M. (2017). Inflexibility as a vulnerability to depression: A systematic qualitative review. *Clinical Psychology: Science and Practice, 24*(3), 245–276. https://doi.org/10.1111/cpsp.12201

Tran, T. B., Hertel, P. T., & Joormann, J. (2011). Cognitive bias modification: Induced interpretive biases affect memory. *Emotion, 11*(1), 145–152. https://doi.org/10.1037/a0021754

Unsworth, N., Heitz, R. P., Schrock, J. C., & Engle, R. W. (2005). An automated version of the operation span task. *Behavior Research Methods, 37*(3), 498–505. https://doi.org/10.3758/BF03192720

Voogd, E. L. D., Wiers, R. W., & Salemink, E. (2017). Online visual search attentional bias modification for adolescents with heightened anxiety and depressive symptoms: A randomized controlled trial. *Behaviour Research and Therapy, 92*, 57–67. https://doi.org/10.1016/j.brat.2017.02.006

Wenzlaff, R. M., & Bates, D. E. (1998). Unmasking a cognitive vulnerability to depression: How lapses in mental control reveal depressive thinking. *Journal of Personality and Social Psychology, 75*, 1559–1571. https://doi.org/10.1037/0022-3514.75.6.1559

Westberg, P., Lundh, L.-G., & Jönsson, P. (2007). Implicit associations and social anxiety. *Cognitive Behaviour Therapy, 36*(1), 43–51. https://doi.org/10.1080/08037060601020401

White, L. K., Suway, J. G., Pine, D. S., Bar-Haim, Y., & Fox, N. A. (2011). Cascading effects: The influence of attention bias to threat on the interpretation of ambiguous information. *Behaviour Research and Therapy, 49*(4), 244–251. https://doi.org/10.1016/j.brat.2011.01.004

Wittenborn, A. K., Rahmandad, H., Rick, J., & Hosseinichimeh, N. (2016). Depression as a systemic syndrome: Mapping the feedback loops of major depressive disorder. *Psychological Medicine, 46*(3), 551–562. https://doi.org/10.1017/S0033291715002044

Woud, M. L. (2022). Interpretational biases in emotional psychopathology. *Cognitive and Behavioral Practice, 29*(3), 520–523.

Woud, M. L., Zhang, X. C., Becker, E. S., McNally, R. J., & Margraf, J. (2014). Don't panic: Interpretation bias is predictive of new onsets of panic disorder. *Journal of Anxiety Disorders, 28*(1), 83–87. https://doi.org/10.1016/j.janxdis.2013.11.008

Jonas Everaert is an Assistant Professor at the Department of Medical and Clinical Psychology at Tilburg University. His research bridges cognitive, affective, and social science approaches to uncover the nature, causes, and effects of biased interpretations and inflexible belief revision to develop transdiagnostic and transtherapeutic models of psychopathology. To this end, Jonas combines diverse methods and statistical techniques to capture toxic features of interpretation and socio-affective processes in the lab and in real life.

Sarah Struyf is a clinical psychologist and doctoral student at the department of experimental clinical and health psychology at Ghent University. From a perspective of risk and resilience factors for affective disorders, her research mainly focuses on individual differences in information-processing flexibility and emotion regulation. In her clinical work, she mainly has experience in the field of anxiety, depression, and developmental disorders such as ADHD and autism spectrum disorder in adolescents and adults.

Ernst H. W. Koster is full professor of clinical psychology at Ghent University at the department of experimental clinical and health psychology. He is co-PI of the Psychopathology and Affective Neuroscience Lab. His research examines cognitive risk factors for depression and anxiety and their modification through cognitive training.

Chapter 6
Mental Imagery and Interpretational Processing Biases

Simon E. Blackwell

6.1 Introduction

The term "mental imagery" refers to "representations and the accompanying experience of sensory information without a direct external stimulus" (Pearson et al., 2015, p.590), or in less formal terms "'seeing with the mind's eye,' 'hearing with the mind's ear,' and so on" (Kosslyn et al., 2001, p. 635). People may experience mental imagery in many different circumstances in the course of their daily lives, for example when recalling events from the past, imagining possible events in the future, or simply daydreaming, and this everyday mental imagery is thought to play a number of important roles (Blackwell, 2020a). Dysfunctions in mental imagery may therefore have wide-ranging impacts and in fact are found across many psychological disorders (e.g. Ji et al., 2019b).

The use of mental imagery in cognitive behaviour therapy (CBT) and psychological therapies more generally has a long history (e.g. Singer, 2006; Edwards, 2007). The development of mental imagery approaches within CBT mirrors the broader development of CBT itself, with techniques arising from both the more cognitively focused and the more behaviourally focused traditions (Blackwell, 2021). This chapter starts by considering the relationship between mental imagery and interpretation biases. This then forms a basis for the second part of this chapter, which reviews the use of mental imagery as a means or tool to change interpretation biases.

S. E. Blackwell (✉)
Mental Health Research and Treatment Center, Faculty of Psychology,
Ruhr-University Bochum, Bochum, Germany

© The Author(s), under exclusive license to Springer Nature Switzerland AG 2023   97
M. L. Woud (ed.), *Interpretational Processing Biases in Emotional Psychopathology*,
CBT: Science Into Practice, https://doi.org/10.1007/978-3-031-23650-1_6

6.2 The Relationship Between Mental Imagery and Interpretation Biases

Mental imagery and interpretation biases are closely interconnected and can serve to reinforce each other. To fully understand this interconnection, it is necessary to consider the nature of mental imagery and its basic properties, as well as the functional roles mental imagery is thought to play in daily life.

The neural representation of mental imagery is very similar to that of actual perception in sensory areas of the cortex (Pearson et al., 2015). This has been most intensively investigated in relation to visual imagery, where research has indicated the involvement of even very early levels of the visual cortex such as V1 (Pearson, 2019). Retrieval or generation of mental imagery, for example when recalling a past event or imagining one in the future, involves a distributed network of activation including frontal areas and early sensory pathways. This leads to an experience that is sensory, but has an internal rather than an external source. The neural "as if perception" representation of imagery means that imagining a situation or scene provides us with an experience "as if reality" (Ji et al., 2016). This in turn means that imagery can have a particularly strong impact on emotion (e.g. Holmes & Mathews, 2005), cognition (e.g. Holmes & Mathews, 2005), and behaviour (e.g. Renner et al., 2019).

As mentioned earlier, mental imagery appears to be involved in many different functions in daily life. For example, we often experience mental imagery when we recall events from the past or imagine possible events in the future. This allows us not only to "picture", but also to replay and re-experience events from the past, and to "pre-play" and pre-experience future possibilities, including our emotional reactions. Imagery-rich recall of past events can have a significant impact on how we feel in the present, in terms of not just mood, but also our sense of self (D'Argembeau, 2021; Stopa, 2009; Rathbone et al., 2012), and our past experiences are also often drawn on to predict what might happen in the present or future. In relation to future-oriented imagery, this can be particularly helpful in planning, decision-making, and making predictions. For example, it can help us "test out" future possibilities in our imagination and thus inform our decisions, enhance our motivation, or protect us from potentially dangerous courses of action. There is also evidence that people's experience of future-oriented mental imagery is connected to their perception of the future. For example, optimism is associated with particularly vivid positive future-oriented imagery, depression with positive future imagery that is not very vivid, and anxiety with particularly vivid negative future imagery (Ji et al., 2017). Further, if someone finds it difficult to imagine an event occurring, they may evaluate it as unlikely to occur (Kahneman & Tversky, 1982; Szpunar & Schacter, 2013).

Most people experience past- and future-oriented episodic imagery, often termed "mental time travel", frequently throughout the day, and much of this imagery occurs spontaneously, triggered via external or internal cues (e.g. Berntsen & Jacobsen, 2008; Barsics et al., 2016). Importantly, the retrieval of such imagery is part of the reconstructive process of memory (Schacter & Addis, 2007). That is, when we recall an event or imagine something in the future, we do not just "read off" an exact copy of a stored perception from memory, but rather reconstruct the perceptual experience. This means that this process is open to influence from our own emotional and motivational state at the time of retrieval or imagining, which may affect the relative accessibility of different kinds of information, and from other cognitive biases.

When it comes to the interconnection between mental imagery and interpretation bias, some aspects of this interconnection have in fact already been spelt out explicitly in the context of certain disorders. For example, in the context of social phobia, Hirsch et al. (2006) proposed a *combined cognitive biases hypothesis* to describe the interplay between the imagery dysfunctions and interpretation biases associated with this disorder (for an overview of associated cognitive biases of interpretation biases, see Chap. 5 by Everaert et al.). Drawing on both previous experimental studies and theoretical considerations, they suggest that negative interpretations (e.g. of one's behaviour or appearance in a social situation) can be incorporated into the content of imagery experienced (e.g. seeing oneself blushing bright red, shaking, and sweating). Such distorted imagery may not only increase anxiety directly, but also contribute to and reinforce negative interpretations, as well as blocking benign interpretations that could arise from observation of external reality. Given that people with social anxiety often tend to have an internal rather than external attentional focus in social situations, they may be particularly likely to use such imagery as a source of information to monitor their performance. Further, negative interpretations made during or in the aftermath of social situations may be incorporated into imagery and thus the episodic memory of these events, meaning that these memories may serve to reinforce negative interpretations or provide a source for negative social imagery in future situations.

In the context of depression, Holmes et al. (2009a) explored some potential relationships between imagery and interpretation bias. Depression is characterized not only by a negative interpretation bias (Everaert et al., 2017), but by frequent experience of negative imagery and a relative lack of positive imagery (Holmes et al., 2016). Holmes et al. (2009a) suggest that the emotional meanings of negative interpretations may be enhanced via their representation in imagery form, therefore reinforcing depressed mood and thus a negative bias. Further, when positive or benign interpretations do occur, these may not be represented via imagery, but rather processed verbally, contributing to self-comparisons that may in fact further reinforce depressed mood (e.g. Joormann et al., 2007; Holmes et al., 2009b).

Beyond these disorder-specific accounts, drawing on our knowledge of the nature of mental imagery and its basic properties also provides an opportunity to consider more broadly how we might best understand the relevance of mental imagery for interpretation biases. A first possibility to consider is that the mental imagery experienced in daily life may reflect distorted perceptions or memories, and this could influence someone's interpretation or even perception of an event (see Fig. 6.1). In fact, there is evidence from laboratory studies that mental imagery can distort not only interpretation of situations (e.g. Hirsch et al., 2003), but also interpretation of simple ambiguous visual scenes (e.g. perceiving a neutral face as angry; Diekhof

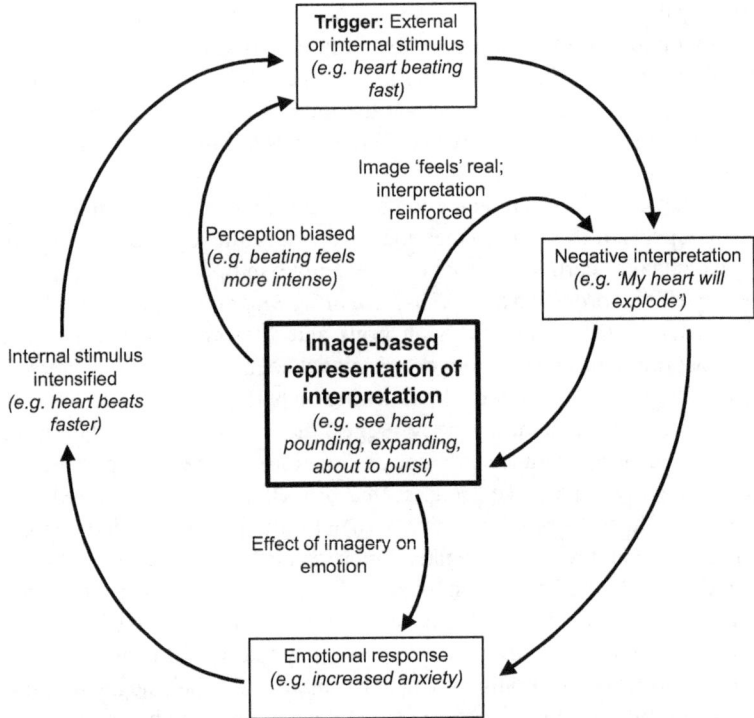

Fig. 6.1 Illustration of one interconnection between imagery and interpretation biases: Biases in interpretation may be represented by or incorporated into imagery, which then reinforces the biased interpretation and its downstream effects. The interconnection is illustrated here using the example of a panic attack, for which the initial triggering stimulus (the target of interpretation) is internal (e.g. heart beating fast); in other disorder contexts the initial triggering stimulus may be external (e.g. a social situation)

et al., 2011), and even simple perceptual information (e.g. Pearson, 2014). To illustrate, when someone who is afraid of spiders thinks of a spider, they may "see" it in their mind's eye as larger, faster, and more aggressive than it is in reality (Pratt et al., 2004). On encountering a spider they may "see" the feared event of a spider running up onto them and under their clothes in their mind. The realness of such imagery may reinforce their perceptions of spiders, and also feel like a premonition of what is about to happen, leading to a sense of danger. As another example, someone with panic disorder may "see" their heart pumping harder and harder, expanding as if about to explode, reinforcing their interpretation of their physical sensations as dangerous (e.g. Day et al., 2004; see also Fig. 6.1). As a final example, someone with social phobia may misinterpret their image of themselves looking foolish, blushing, and shaking, as reality, reinforcing their interpretation of how others see them (Hirsch et al., 2006).

A second possible basis for the relationship between imagery and interpretation bias is that the relative accessibility of positive versus negative imagery in memory

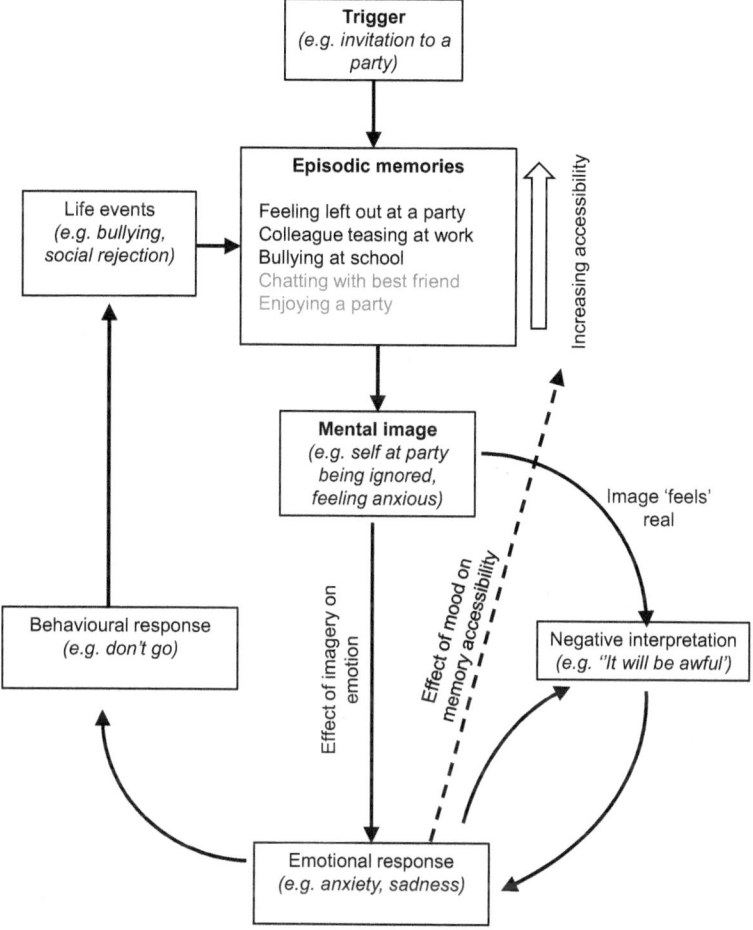

Fig. 6.2 Illustration of one interconnection between imagery and interpretation biases. Retrieval from episodic memory, the contents of which stem from life events or imagined scenes, can lead to experience of a mental image that is then taken as a prediction or explanation of an event, that is, an interpretation. The relative accessibility of positive versus negative material in memory, which can be influenced by current mood, can therefore be reflected in a bias to interpret events relatively positively or negatively. The interconnection is illustrated here using social anxiety as an example

might lead to biased evaluations of situations (Fig. 6.2). For example, if when someone thinks about the future only negative, but no positive, possibilities come to mind, and further if the negative imagery is much more vivid than the positive imagery, this may lead them to interpret the future pessimistically. At an extreme, if someone is only able to retrieve negative memories or imagine negative outcomes, it would be very difficult for them to interpret an ambiguous situation in a positive way. Additionally, following Kahneman and Tversky (1982), even when someone is able to imagine positive interpretations, if imagining these is difficult the interpretations may be seen as less plausible than easily imagined negative possibilities.

As a third, and broader, perspective, much of the time what manifests as an interpretation bias may be a reflection of dysfunctional imagery. That is, cognitive biases can be conceptualized as the product of memory-based representations (Arntz, 2020), and these representations, or the schemas that provide the building blocks for interpretation biases, may be stored and retrieved in the form of key episodic memories rather than verbal propositions (Brewin, 2006). Or, to put it another way, if across many situations what is retrieved from memory (or what pops to mind) are negative images that reinforce negative beliefs about a situation or its outcomes, this will manifest as a bias in interpretation (also represented in Fig. 6.2). Although there is most likely an important role for non-episodic, semantic memory in interpretive processes and interpretation biases (Hirsch et al., 2006), to some extent dysfunctional imagery and dysfunctional interpretations could potentially be seen as mutually reinforcing components of a common underlying processes (see also Nanay, 2021).

6.3   Using Mental Imagery to Change Interpretation Biases

This section will first consider the use of mental imagery within standard CBT approaches. It will then discuss cognitive training approaches that use mental imagery to target interpretations biases directly.

6.3.1   Using Mental Imagery in CBT

There are many ways in which mental imagery may be used to change interpretation biases within standard CBT (for an overview of therapeutic techniques to change interpretation biases, see also Chap. 12 by Woud & Hofmann). To some extent, any CBT therapeutic procedure that might be used to change interpretation biases could potentially be enhanced via the use of imagery, given imagery's properties such as its effect on emotion and realness (Blackwell, 2019). Interestingly, imagery occurs recurrently throughout Beck's writings and descriptions of cognitive therapy (e.g. Beck, 1976; Beck et al., 1979). For example, when introducing cognitive techniques in the context of depression, Beck et al. (1979) suggests that therapists define the term *cognition* to patients; the definition he then provides explicitly mentions both thoughts and images. Further, in order to demonstrate the relationship between cognition and emotion to patients – the cornerstone of the cognitive model – Beck suggests an imagery-based behavioural experiment. When it comes to therapeutic interventions, Beck's (1979) suggestions include using replay of positive memories or imagery of positive future events to improve mood in depression (albeit with the caveat that with severely depressed patients this runs the risk of turning negative), and manipulating the content of anxiety-inducing imagery to reduce its impact (similar to imagery rescripting, described later in this chapter). Mental imagery therefore clearly played a central role in cognitive therapy as he envisioned it. However, until relatively recently the possibilities offered by using mental imagery within CBT have often been neglected (Blackwell, 2021).

Josefowitz (2017) provides a detailed description of how imagery can be used to enhance one common CBT tool for changing interpretation biases, the thought record. Within CBT, keeping a record of negative automatic thoughts can help to identify a patient's interpretation biases (e.g. a tendency to interpret social ambiguity as rejection) and the beliefs hypothesized to underpin them (e.g. "I am unlikeable"). The process of collecting evidence against and challenging negative thoughts, and the underlying beliefs, can then help in correcting these biases when they occur in the moment and in starting to change the beliefs that are theoretically their underlying source. As outlined by Josefowitz (2017; see also Greenberger & Padesky, 2015), imagery can be used to evoke and better understand the meaning of negative automatic thoughts, via identifying images or memories associated with the thought and examining their meaning. Generation of imagery can be used to increase the believability of evidence against negative thoughts, for example, via detailed recall and re-experiencing of events that contradict the belief. Imagery can then be used to increase emotional engagement with and believability of alternative thoughts or beliefs, helping to increase how real they "feel" and not just how logically they can be understood, and further to improve their accessibility in memory. For example, in the context of social anxiety, a key technique to counteract negative beliefs about how the patient appears to others during social interactions is video feedback; observing video footage of themselves in a social interaction provides a powerful way to show that in fact how they look in reality is very different to how they think and imagine they appear. The patient can then later mentally rehearse the image of how they really looked to reinforce this benign (and accurate) interpretation (Warnock-Parkes et al., 2017).

Other standard CBT techniques used to change interpretations can also be enhanced or carried out via imagery. To the extent that exposure-based approaches can be conceptualized as a way of changing interpretations – for example of a feared stimulus or situation as threatening – these can also be conducted entirely in imagery, that is, imaginal exposure (for an overview of how stimuli may be interpreted in fear conditioning paradigms and exposure, see Chap. 7 by Scheveneels and Boddez). However, in vivo exposure can potentially also be enhanced by drawing on imagery, for example, via imaginal rehearsal of the exposure between sessions (McGlade & Craske, 2021), or reactivation of a past mastery experience to increase self-efficacy prior to exposure (Raeder et al., 2019). When exposure involves an element of cognitive restructuring, for example, in enhanced reliving for post-traumatic stress disorder (Ehlers et al., 2005), the cognitive restructuring may also be incorporated into the memory via imagery to enhance emotional integration, as with imagery rescripting (discussed below). Behavioural experiments, which offer an efficient and direct way of changing interpretations via testing beliefs and predictions directly, can also be enhanced via imagery in a similar way (e.g. use of imagery in preparation,

making predictions, or in replaying and reinforcing learning) or in the ways suggested by Josefowitz (2017) for thought records. Imagery can also be used to effect
change in meta-cognitive appraisals, that is, interpretations of thoughts, such as the
belief that they are dangerous and uncontrollable. For example, via visualizing
thought processes in a concrete manner (e.g. as a river flowing past, or as memories
on a cinema or TV screen), the patient can learn to re-interpret them as controllable
and non-threatening mental events rather than overwhelming and compelling (e.g.
Wells, 2005; Holmes et al., 2019).

Perhaps the most direct and imagery-intensive technique for changing interpretations in standard CBT is imagery rescripting; a major aim of imagery rescripting is
to modify or update dysfunctional or distressing appraisals of events, thoughts, or
memories, and this is carried out primarily via imagery (Arntz, 2012). There are
many different forms of imagery rescripting, but in general they involve some form
of imaginal reliving of a distressing memory (or future projection), and then with
the help of the therapist constructing an alternative ending, which is then incorporated into the memory via imagery. For example, in one kind of protocol often
applied in the context of childhood trauma (e.g. Arntz & Weertman, 1999), a patient
might first relive (via imagery) the traumatic event through their own eyes, as they
perceived it at the time. They then relive the scene again, but take the perspective of
their adult self, coming in to intervene in the situation. In the final step, they relive
the scene again from their child perspective and witness the adult's intervention;
after this they can request further interventions (often providing comfort to the
child). While such an imagery rescripting procedure undoubtedly contains an element of simple exposure to the distressing memory, it also provides a powerful way
to update the beliefs, for example, that the child was responsible or that the danger
felt by the child is still present. In another form of imagery rescripting (Holmes
et al., 2019), the thoughts, beliefs, and emotions encapsulated in the image are
explicitly elicited and "antidote" thoughts and emotions identified; these antidotes
are then built into an image that is used as an alternative ending for the scene.

Imagery rescripting can be applied not only to memories, but also to future pro-
jections or "flashforwards" (e.g. Taylor et al., 2020), nightmares (e.g. Kunze et al.,
2017), and even metaphorical images generated purely for the purpose of being
rescripted (Butler et al., 2010): Essentially it can be applied to anything image-
based with a problematic meaning that causes distress or impairment. Imagery
rescripting is not generally conceptualized as directly trying to change interpretation biases. Nevertheless, from the perspective that such biases are in part the output
of the representations targeted in rescripting (Arntz, 2020), via imagery rescripting
we would expect such biases to also change. However, while there is now much
evidence accumulated for the effectiveness of imagery rescripting in changing
beliefs and reducing symptoms (e.g. Morina et al., 2017), whether it does in fact
change interpretation biases themselves is unexplored.

6.3.2 Mental Imagery and Cognitive Training

In the past 20 years there has been increasing interest in changing interpretation biases via simple cognitive training procedures. While these do not form part of the standard CBT repertoire, they build on the same scientific foundations and are increasingly being investigated as adjuncts to CBT and other treatments (e.g. Williams et al., 2013; Woud et al., 2021). These kind of cognitive training approaches are generally described as *cognitive bias modification* (CBM) procedures (Koster et al., 2009). Of relevance for this chapter, in several forms of CBM mental imagery plays a central role.

The most commonly investigated form of CBM for changing interpretation biases (CBM-I) is based on repeated presentation of ambiguous scenarios that are consistently resolved in a specific manner. For example, to train a negative bias (for experimental purposes), the scenarios would be consistently resolved negatively, whereas for to train a positive bias (e.g. for therapeutic purposes) they would be consistently resolved positively. In the original version (Mathews & Mackintosh, 2000), ambiguous scenarios were presented as written text of a few lines, followed by a word fragment of a final word that would resolve the ambiguity, which participants would have to resolve. For example, "You get out of bed at the start of a busy day. You think about the day ahead and everything you need to do. As you do so you start to feel full of ...", "_ n _ r g _ " (*energy* for a positive resolution), or a "d _ e _ d" (*dread* as negative resolution). Comprehension questions requiring yes/no responses would also be used to reinforce the interpretations (e.g. "Does your energy increase as you think about the day ahead?"). Because this original CBM-I training paradigm is covered in detail in another chapter it will not be further discussed here (for an overview of how to manipulate interpretation biases, see Chap. 11 by Salemink et al.). However, it is important to note that participants were instructed to imagine themselves in the situations and anticipate the ending, with the rationale that this would help resolve the word fragment; that is, learning to imagine more positive resolutions would help complete the task more efficiently. As this imagery was seen as a central mechanism for how the training could change interpretation biases, versions of the training intended to enhance this imagery component were then developed, and these will now be discussed further.

In these more imagery-focussed versions of the scenario-based CBM-I, the paradigm was adjusted to facilitate generation of vivid imagery (e.g. Holmes & Mathews, 2005; Holmes et al., 2006). This "imagery CBM" paradigm used the same kinds of ambiguous scenarios as the original paradigm, but they were presented as audio descriptions, rather than written text, and participants listened to them via headphones. This meant that participants could close their eyes and focus on generating and being absorbed in imagery. Further there was no requirement to solve word fragments, and the comprehension questions were removed. Instead, after each scenario participants were simply asked to report how vividly they had imagined it. Finally, the training itself was preceded by an introduction to mental imagery led by the researcher, in which participants were guided through various mental imagery exercises and practice scenarios in order to increase the likelihood that they would be able to engage in the imagery in the required way during the training.

Early experimental studies focussed on the potential of imagery CBM to change interpretation biases and state affect, and in particular the role of the imagery component. Several such studies demonstrated the importance of participants being instructed to imagine themselves in the training scenarios to have these effects, contrasting this against instructions to focus on the words and meanings (e.g. Holmes et al., 2008a, 2009b; Nelis et al., 2012).

Subsequent clinical studies using imagery CBM have mostly been conducted in the context of depression. As mentioned earlier, depression is characterized not only by a negative interpretation bias (Everaert et al., 2017), but also by deficits in positive imagery, and positive *future*-oriented imagery in particular (Holmes et al., 2016). Compared to people who are not depressed, people with depression or depressed mood are not only less likely to experience spontaneous positive future-oriented imagery (Ji et al., 2019a), but when they deliberately try to imagine positive events in their future the imagery they generate is less vivid (Morina et al., 2011). It was proposed that positive imagery-based CBM might therefore be particularly beneficial in the context of depression, by training these two processes in conjunction (Holmes et al., 2009a). That is, via repeatedly imagining positive outcomes for ambiguous situations in the training, depressed individuals may acquire a more positive bias to automatically imagine positive outcomes for ambiguous situations in daily life.

The first clinical study used a single-case series design to make the transition from experimental paradigm to potential clinical intervention (Blackwell & Holmes, 2010). In this study, seven adults with current major depression completed a 1-week training schedule. This comprised a first training session in the lab, and then six subsequent training sessions completed at home, one each day. Each training session included 64 scenarios, with no scenario repeated, so over the course of the week participants imagined themselves in 448 different scenarios. Following promising results in this study, further initial translational studies also found promising results in reducing negative interpretation biases and symptoms of depression over 1 week of training, this time compared to a sham training control condition (Lang et al., 2012; Torkan et al., 2014), including when added to Internet-delivered CBT (Williams et al., 2013, 2015, albeit for the second study only amongst people who completed the training and not in an "intention to treat" sample). However, a larger randomized controlled trial (CBT) examining a 4-week training schedule (Blackwell et al., 2015) found no difference between the imagery CBM and a sham training control condition in reductions in depression. Interestingly, post-hoc and secondary analyses of data from this trial found that the imagery CBM was superior to the control condition in reducing anhedonic symptoms of depression (Blackwell et al., 2015) and increasing behavioural activation (Renner et al., 2017). Anhedonia is the loss of interest and pleasure in previously enjoyed activities, and together these results suggest that repeatedly imagining ambiguous situations resolving positively may help increase the anticipation of situations being rewarding and increase motivation to engage in goal-directed behaviour. Through the lens of interpretation biases, this could be expressed as interpreting ambiguous situations as being potentially rewarding and worth investing effort in. Several lines of research have now followed up on the idea of imagery CBM as a potential means to reduce anhedonia, with encouraging results (Pictet et al., 2016; Bibi et al., 2020; Westermann et al., 2021).

A parallel line of research has examined the use of an imagery CBM paradigm to reduce negative interpretation biases and thus reduce worry and rumination amongst people with depression and generalized anxiety disorder. This follows work indicating a role for interpretation biases in contributing to these kinds of perseverative negative thinking (e.g. Hayes et al., 2010). Hirsch and colleagues used a training procedure similar to that described above (i.e. aural presentation of scenarios and no word fragments), but also including comprehension questions. After initial experimental work (Hirsch et al., 2009; Hayes et al., 2010), clinical studies also found promising results for reducing negative interpretation biases, repetitive negative thinking, and symptoms of depression and anxiety compared to sham training (e.g. Hirsch et al., 2018, 2020, 2021), and these effects could be enhanced by additional imagery instructions (Feng et al., 2020; Hirsch et al., 2020). Generalized anxiety is an area where imagery deficits and dysfunctions are also apparent, and hence such an imagery-focussed training may be particularly helpful (Koerner & Blackwell, 2021).

Another line of research using scenario-based CBM-I has investigated using imagery to enhance the effects of a training specifically focussed on modifying the kinds of "cognitive errors" identified by Beck as characterizing depression (Lester et al., 2011). This training is text-based as in the original Mathews and Mackintosh (2000) paradigm but uses scenarios specifically tailored to tackle "cognitive errors" such as selective abstraction, dichotomization (black and white thinking), and catastrophization (Beck et al., 1979). An experimental study with non-depressed participants found that adding an instruction to generate future-oriented imagery related to the scenario after completing the comprehension question led to greater immediate reductions in negative interpretation biases compared to a version of the training without this additional instruction (Lee et al., 2015). A clinical study in which participants were diagnosed with current major depression found superiority of this training to a sham training control in terms of immediate effects on interpretation biases, but not in stress reactivity or depression symptoms 1 month later (Yiend et al., 2014). However, only one training session was used and it seems likely that more training sessions would be needed to have effects on symptom outcomes.

Moving away from scenario-based training, another imagery-based CBM-I paradigm uses ambiguous picture cues as the basis for modifying interpretation biases. In this "picture–word" training, ambiguous photos of everyday scenes are paired with a caption of one or a few words that can be used to resolve the valence of the scene in a particular direction. For example, a photo of a clifftop could be paired with the word "view" for a positive resolution, or with the word "slip" for a negative resolution. Participants are asked to combine the picture and word to form a mental image of a scene in which they are actively involved (e.g. standing on the clifftop and admiring the view vs. standing on the clifftop and slipping down). An initial experimental study found that combining the picture and word via imagery, as opposed to forming a sentence, led to greater training-congruent changes in state mood and interpretation bias (Holmes et al., 2008b). A subsequent study with dysphoric individuals found that a single session of positive training (i.e. the pictures were always paired with positive captions) led to more positive mood, interpretation bias, and better performance on a behavioural task than a single session of negative or mixed valence (50% positive, 50% negative captions) training (Pictet et al., 2011). This picture–word training has been combined with scenario-based training in some clinical studies (Lang et al., 2012; Blackwell et al., 2015), but its effects in clinical applications have not been tested in isolation amongst adults. In adolescent samples, one study has investigated the effects of repeated sessions of Internet-based training using the picture–word paradigm on its own (De Voogd et al., 2017). In this study, adolescents with elevated symptoms of depression or anxiety were recruited and they completed the training at home. The results did not suggest that the training was effective in changing interpretation biases and symptoms of depression and anxiety relative to a sham training control, and participant feedback suggested that they found the task difficult to understand and engage with. In contrast, in an experimental study carried out in schools with adolescent male participants (Burnett Heyes et al., 2017), a single session of picture–word training appeared effective in changing state mood and interpretation biases, and participants apparently found the training easy and in fact enjoyable to engage with. The difference between these two studies' results could plausibly be due the fact that participants in the study by De Voogd et al. (2017) were required to complete the training from home after school in their own time with only written instructions, whereas in the study by Burnett Heyes et al. (2017) they completed the training during school hours with instructions and initial guidance from a researcher. A third study has used a picture–word training paradigm as part of a package of training methods to try to reduce hostile attributions amongst school children (Schmidt & Vereenooghe, 2021). The combined training package appeared effective and also acceptable to the participants, but it is not possible to disentangle the contribution of the picture–word paradigm itself from the combined package. Overall, although the picture–word paradigm has been used in some clinical studies there is not yet compelling evidence for its potential as a stand-alone training paradigm for reducing negative interpretation biases and symptoms in this context.

When it comes to evaluating the clinical effectiveness of imagery-based CBM-I methods, this is complicated by the fact that most meta-analyses tend to group them together with other CBM-I approaches. As an exception to this, Hitchcock et al. (2017) included a meta-analysis of purely imagery-focussed CBM-I training in their broader review of episodic memory training-based interventions and found that these were superior to no training or waiting list but not to sham training conditions. However, this meta-analysis only includes a small number of studies as the majority were published after the date of their literature review. The most recent meta-analysis including all CBM approaches targeting interpretation biases (Fodor et al., 2020) found that in terms of reducing symptoms of anxiety, CBM-I (all kinds combined) was superior to both a waitlist ($d = 0.55$, 95% CIs: 0.19–0.91) and sham training ($d = 0.30$, 95% CIs: 0.10–0.50), but when it came to reducing symptoms of depression, CBM-I was superior only to waitlist ($d = 0.63$, 95% CIs: 0.23–1.04), but not sham training ($d = 0.26$, 95% CIs: −0.06–0.57). However, in the context of depression, the results were unstable due to a poorly connected network and should be treated with caution. Further, since the literature review of this more recent meta-analysis was completed several more studies using imagery-based CBM-I in the context of depression or depressed mood with positive results have been published (Bibi et al., 2020; Hirsch et al., 2020, 2021; Sit et al., 2020). Overall, studies so far indicate the potential for imagery-based CBM-I methods to reduce negative interpretation biases and symptoms of depression and anxiety in clinical applications. However, the clinical trials conducted so far are all relatively early-phase translational studies and larger trials and replications would be needed to make confident recommendations about clinical applications.

6.4 Conclusions and Future Directions

As outlined in this chapter, mental imagery and interpretation biases appear closely interconnected, with a number of potential mechanisms via which they could influence and reinforce each other. Further, mental imagery can be used in many ways within a CBT framework to change negative interpretation biases, whether via doing so directly or via changing the underlying beliefs that may give rise to such biases. Building on the basic properties of mental imagery, such as its realness and effect on emotion, allows its incorporation into many standard CBT techniques that can be used to change interpretation biases. Additionally, there are some imagery-specific techniques used within CBT such as imagery rescripting that are powerful methods for changing such biases, albeit not conceptualized as such. Finally, more recently targeted cognitive training procedures have been developed that focus on changing interpretation biases directly and include mental imagery as a central element.

A number of questions remain to be explored in relation to the ideas presented in this chapter. For example, as noted earlier, many of the techniques presented here are not normally conceptualized as changing interpretation biases, and although from a conceptual perspective they may be expected to change such biases, whether they in fact do so is not known. Greater investigation of the effect of such techniques in isolation on cognitive processes such as interpretation biases would help clarify this. Second, the extent to which imagery may enhance such techniques is also largely based on theoretical considerations and clinical intuition, and has not been investigated systematically (with a few exceptions, e.g. McEvoy et al., 2015; van Teffelen et al., 2021). Third, in relation to cognitive training techniques, while approaches such as imagery-based CBM-I show promise in reducing negative interpretation biases and symptoms of psychopathology, most of the clinical studies are at relatively early phases of translational research, and larger pragmatic trials would be needed to make confident claims about their effectiveness or clinical utility (for an overview of the stepwise process in the context of translational research, see Chap. 2 by Cludius and Ehring). Further, exactly how they might be most clinically useful is not yet clear (e.g. Blackwell, 2020b). For example, it may be that imagery CBM is best seen as a potential adjunctive intervention to other treatments, or it could possibly have a useful role to play as stand-alone low-intensity self-help intervention.

A somewhat bigger question, that goes beyond the remit of this chapter, is a more fundamental one about the relationship between imagery and interpretation biases, or rather episodic memory and interpretation biases. As noted earlier, interpretation biases may simply be the output of representations commonly described as beliefs or schemas (Arntz, 2020), in line with Beck's cognitive model (Beck, 1976). These in turn may in part be contributed to by, or even represented as, episodic memories (Brewin, 2006). Thus imagery-based representations may be fundamental to at least some manifestations of interpretation biases. For example, an interpretation of a friend's lack of contact as meaning that they do not like you could be the result of an involuntary memory popping to mind that makes this idea "feel" true. From this perspective, creating positive representations in memory that may be easily accessed may be a more effective method of changing such biases than targeting the apparent biased cognitive processing itself. In fact, this has been speculated to be a potential mechanism of imagery CBM (Blackwell & Holmes, 2017) and is the direct aim of other cognitive training procedures such as competitive memory training (COMET; Korrelboom et al., 2009). To elaborate, if we are intending to directly change biased processing we might aim to instil processing rules such as "in the context of ambiguity, retrieve/generate a positive interpretation" or "accept positive interpretations that occur, reject negative ones"; conversely, if we are intending to change the underlying representations we might not aim to change this level of processing, but rather aim to make it more likely that positive interpretations will be retrieved or generated – and then accepted – by changing the source material from which these interpretations arise (see Arntz, 2020, for more detailed consideration). However, this question of how interpretation biases are best conceptualized and most effectively changed goes beyond the scope of a single chapter in this volume.

Regardless of how this more fundamental question is resolved, and when, both the basic science underlying mental imagery and the research conducted so far indicate great potential in using it to change interpretation biases. In fact, in the face of any approach to change interpretation biases one could usefully ask "could mental imagery be used to enhance this technique" (Blackwell, 2021). This of course cannot be assumed and requires systematic testing, but is a question with potential to open many fruitful avenues for research and clinical practice.

References

Arntz, A. (2012). Imagery rescripting as a therapeutic technique: Review of clinical trials, basic studies, and research agenda. *Journal of Experimental Psychopathology*, 189–208. https://doi.org/10.5127/jep.024211

Arntz, A. (2020). A plea for more attention to mental representations. *Journal of Behavior Therapy and Experimental Psychiatry, 67*, 101510. https://doi.org/10.1016/j.jbtep.2019.101510

Arntz, A., & Weertman, A. (1999). Treatment of childhood memories: Theory and practice. *Behaviour Research and Therapy, 37*(8), 715–740. https://doi.org/10.1016/s0005-7967(98)00173-9

Barsics C., Van der Linden M., & D'Argembeau A. (2016). Frequency, characteristics, and perceived functions of emotional future thinking in daily life. *Quarterly Journal of Experimental Psychology, 69*, 217–233. https://doi.org/10.1080/17470218.2015.1051560

Beck, A. T. (1976). *Cognitive therapy and the emotional disorders.* International Universities Press.

Beck, A. T., Rush, J. A., Shaw, F. B., & Emery, G. (1979). *Cognitive therapy of depression.* Guilford Press.

Berntsen, D., & Jacobsen, A. S. (2008). Involuntary (spontaneous) mental time travel into the past and future. *Consciousness and Cognition, 17*(4), 1093–1104. https://doi.org/10.1016/j.concog.2008.03.001

Bibi, A., Margraf, J., & Blackwell, S. E. (2020). Positive imagery cognitive bias modification for symptoms of depression among university students in Pakistan: A pilot study. *Journal of Experimental Psychopathology.* https://doi.org/10.1177/2043808720918030

Blackwell, S. E. (2019). Mental imagery: From basic research to clinical practice. *Journal of Psychotherapy Integration, 29*(3), 235–247. https://doi.org/10.1037/int0000108

Blackwell, S. E. (2020a). Emotional mental imagery. In A. Abraham (Ed.), *The Cambridge handbook of the imagination (Cambridge handbooks in psychology)* (pp. 241–257). Cambridge University Press. https://doi.org/10.1017/9781108580298.016

Blackwell, S. E. (2020b). Clinical efficacy of cognitive bias modification interventions. *The Lancet. Psychiatry, 7*(6), 465–467. https://doi.org/10.1016/S2215-0366(20)30170-X

Blackwell, S. E. (2021). Mental imagery in the science and practice of cognitive behaviour therapy: Past, present, and future perspectives. *International Journal of Cognitive Therapy, 14*, 160–181. https://doi.org/10.1007/s41811-021-00102-0

Blackwell, S. E., & Holmes, E. A. (2010). Modifying interpretation and imagination in clinical depression: A single case series using cognitive bias modification. *Applied Cognitive Psychology, 24*, 338–350. https://doi.org/10.1002/acp.1680

Blackwell, S. E., & Holmes, E. A. (2017). Brightening the day with flashes of positive mental imagery: A case study of an individual with depression. *Journal of Clinical Psychology, 73*(5), 579–589. https://doi.org/10.1002/jclp.22455

Blackwell, S. E., Browning, M., Mathews, A., Pictet, A., Welch, J., Davies, J., Watson, P., Geddes, J. R., & Holmes, E. A. (2015). Positive imagery-based cognitive bias modification as a web-based treatment tool for depressed adults: A randomized controlled trial. *Clinical Psychological Science: A Journal of the Association for Psychological Science, 3*(1), 91–111. https://doi.org/10.1177/2167702614560746

Brewin, C. R. (2006). Understanding cognitive behaviour therapy: A retrieval competition account. *Behaviour Research and Therapy, 44*(6), 765–784. https://doi.org/10.1016/j.brat.2006.02.005

Burnett Heyes, S., Pictet, A., Mitchell, H., Raeder, S. M., Lau, J., Holmes, E. A., & Blackwell, S. E. (2017). Mental imagery-based training to modify mood and cognitive bias in adolescents: Effects of valence and perspective. *Cognitive Therapy and Research, 41*(1), 73–88. https://doi.org/10.1007/s10608-016-97958

Butler, G., Fennell, M. J. V., & Hackmann, A. (2010). *Cognitive-behavioral therapy for anxiety disorders: Mastering clinical challenges.* Guilford Press.

D'Argembeau, A. (2021). Memory, future thinking, and the self. In honour of Martial Van Der Linden. *Psychologica Belgica, 61*(1), 274–283. https://doi.org/10.5334/pb.1074

Day, S. J., Holmes, E. A., & Hackmann, A. (2004). Occurrence of imagery and its link with early memories in agoraphobia. *Memory, 12*(4), 416–427. https://doi.org/10.1080/09658210444000034

de Voogd, E. L., de Hullu, E., Burnett Heyes, S., Blackwell, S. E., Wiers, R. W., & Salemink, E. (2017). Imagine the bright side of life: A randomized controlled trial of two types of interpretation bias modification procedure targeting adolescent anxiety and depression. *PLoS One, 12*(7), e0181147. https://doi.org/10.1371/journal.pone.0181147

Diekhof, E. K., Kipshagen, H. E., Falkai, P., Dechent, P., Baudewig, J., & Gruber, O. (2011). The power of imagination--How anticipatory mental imagery alters perceptual processing of fearful facial expressions. *NeuroImage, 54*(2), 1703–1714. https://doi.org/10.1016/j.neuroimage.2010.08.034

Edwards, D. (2007). Restructuring implicational meaning through memory-based imagery: Some historical notes. *Journal of Behavior Therapy and Experimental Psychiatry, 38*(4), 306–316. https://doi.org/10.1016/j.jbtep.2007.10.001

Ehlers, A., Clark, D. M., Hackmann, A., McManus, F., & Fennell, M. (2005). Cognitive therapy for post-traumatic stress disorder: Development and evaluation. *Behaviour Research and Therapy, 43*(4), 413–431. https://doi.org/10.1016/j.brat.2004.03.006

Everaert, J., Podina, I. R., & Koster, E. (2017). A comprehensive meta-analysis of interpretation biases in depression. *Clinical Psychology Review, 58*, 33–48. https://doi.org/10.1016/j.cpr.2017.09.005

Feng, Y. C., Krahé, C., Meeten, F., Sumich, A., Mok, C., & Hirsch, C. R. (2020). Impact of imagery-enhanced interpretation training on offline and online interpretations in worry. *Behaviour Research and Therapy, 124*, 103497. https://doi.org/10.1016/j.brat.2019.103497

Fodor, L. A., Georgescu, R., Cuijpers, P., Szamoskozi, Ş., David, D., Furukawa, T. A., & Cristea, I. A. (2020). Efficacy of cognitive bias modification interventions in anxiety and depressive disorders: A systematic review and network meta-analysis. *The Lancet. Psychiatry, 7*(6), 506–514. https://doi.org/10.1016/S2215-0366(20)30130-9

Greenberger, D., & Padesky, C. A. (2015). *Mind over mood: Change how you feel by changing the way you think* (2nd ed.). Guilford Publications.

Hayes, S., Hirsch, C. R., Krebs, G., & Mathews, A. (2010). The effects of modifying interpretation bias on worry in generalized anxiety disorder. *Behaviour Research and Therapy, 48*(3), 171–178. https://doi.org/10.1016/j.brat.2009.10.006

Hirsch, C. R., Mathews, A., Clark, D. M., Williams, R., & Morrison, J. (2003). Negative self-imagery blocks inferences. *Behaviour Research and Therapy, 41*(12), 1383–1396. https://doi.org/10.1016/s0005-7967(03)00057-3

Hirsch, C. R., Clark, D. M., & Mathews, A. (2006). Imagery and interpretations in social phobia: Support for the combined cognitive biases hypothesis. *Behavior Therapy, 37*(3), 223–236. https://doi.org/10.1016/j.beth.2006.02.001

Hirsch, C. R., Hayes, S., & Mathews, A. (2009). Looking on the bright side: Accessing benign meanings reduces worry. *Journal of Abnormal Psychology, 118*(1), 44–54. https://doi.org/10.1037/a0013473

Hirsch, C. R., Krahé, C., Whyte, J., Loizou, S., Bridge, L., Norton, S., & Mathews, A. (2018). Interpretation training to target repetitive negative thinking in generalized anxiety disorder and depression. *Journal of Consulting and Clinical Psychology, 86*(12), 1017–1030. https://doi.org/10.1037/ccp0000310

Hirsch, C. R., Krahé, C., Whyte, J., Bridge, L., Loizou, S., Norton, S., & Mathews, A. (2020). Effects of modifying interpretation bias on transdiagnostic repetitive negative thinking. *Journal of Consulting and Clinical Psychology, 88*(3), 226–239. https://doi.org/10.1037/ccp0000455

Hirsch, C. R., Krahé, C., Whyte, J., Krzyzanowski, H., Meeten, F., Norton, S., & Mathews, A. (2021). Internet-delivered interpretation training reduces worry and anxiety in individuals with generalized anxiety disorder: A randomized controlled experiment. *Journal of Consulting and Clinical Psychology, 89*(7), 575–589. https://doi.org/10.1037/ccp0000660

Hitchcock, C., Werner-Seidler, A., Blackwell, S. E., & Dalgleish, T. (2017). Autobiographical epi-sodic memory-based training for the treatment of mood, anxiety and stress-related disorders: A systematic review and meta-analysis. *Clinical Psychology Review, 52*, 92–107. https://doi.org/10.1016/j.cpr.2016.12.003

Holmes, E. A., & Mathews, A. (2005). Mental imagery and emotion: A special relationship? *Emotion, 5*(4), 489–497. https://doi.org/10.1037/1528-3542.5.4.489

Holmes, E. A., Mathews, A., Dalgleish, T., & Mackintosh, B. (2006). Positive interpretation train-ing: Effects of mental imagery versus verbal training on positive mood. *Behavior Therapy, 37*(3), 237–247. https://doi.org/10.1016/j.beth.2006.02.002

Holmes, E. A., Coughtrey, A. E., & Connor, A. (2008a). Looking at or through rose-tinted glasses? Imagery perspective and positive mood. *Emotion (Washington, D.C.), 8*(6), 875–879. https://doi.org/10.1037/a0013617

Holmes, E. A., Mathews, A., Mackintosh, B., & Dalgleish, T. (2008b). The causal effect of mental imagery on emotion assessed using picture-word cues. *Emotion, 8*(3), 395–409. https://doi.org/10.1037/1528-3542.8.3.395

Holmes, E. A., Lang, T. J., & Deeprose, C. (2009a). Mental imagery and emotion in treatment across disorders: Using the example of depression. *Cognitive Behaviour Therapy, 38*(Suppl 1), 21–28. https://doi.org/10.1080/16506070902980729

Holmes, E. A., Lang, T. J., & Shah, D. M. (2009b). Developing interpretation bias modification as a "cognitive vaccine" for depressed mood: Imagining positive events makes you feel better than thinking about them verbally. *Journal of Abnormal Psychology, 118*(1), 76–88. https://doi.org/10.1037/a0012590

Holmes, E. A., Blackwell, S. E., Burnett Heyes, S., Renner, F., & Raes, F. (2016). Mental imagery in depression: Phenomenology, potential mechanisms, and treatment implications. *Annual Review of Clinical Psychology, 12*, 249–280. https://doi.org/10.1146/annurev-clinpsy-021815-092925

Holmes, E. A., Hales, S. A., Young, K., & Simplicio, M. D. (2019). *Imagery-based cognitive therapy for bipolar disorder and mood instability.* Guilford Publications.

Ji, J. L., Heyes, S. B., MacLeod, C., & Holmes, E. A. (2016). Emotional mental imagery as simu-lation of reality: Fear and beyond-a tribute to Peter Lang. *Behavior Therapy, 47*(5), 702–719. https://doi.org/10.1016/j.beth.2015.11.004

Ji, J. L., Holmes, E. A., & Blackwell, S. E. (2017). Seeing light at the end of the tunnel: Positive prospective mental imagery and optimism in depression. *Psychiatry Research, 247*, 155–162. https://doi.org/10.1016/j.psychres.2016.11.025

Ji, J. L., Holmes, E. A., MacLeod, C., & Murphy, F. C. (2019a). Spontaneous cognition in dyspho-ria: Reduced positive bias in imagining the future. *Psychological Research, 83*(4), 817–831. https://doi.org/10.1007/s00426-018-1071-y

Ji, J. L., Kavanagh, D. J., Holmes, E. A., MacLeod, C., & Di Simplicio, M. (2019b). Mental imag-ery in psychiatry: Conceptual & clinical implications. *CNS Spectrums, 24*(1), 114–126. https://doi.org/10.1017/S1092852918001487

Joormann, J., Siemer, M., & Gotlib, I. H. (2007). Mood regulation in depression: Differential effects of distraction and recall of happy memories on sad mood. *Journal of Abnormal Psychology, 116*(3), 484–490. https://doi.org/10.1037/0021-843X.116.3.484

Josefowitz, N. (2017). Incorporating imagery into thought records: Increasing engagement in bal-anced thoughts. *Cognitive and Behavioral Practice, 24*(1), 90–100. https://doi.org/10.1016/j.cbpra.2016.03.005

Kahneman, D., & Tversky, A. (1982). The simulation heuristic. In D. Kahneman, P. Slovic, & A. Tversky (Eds.), *Judgement under uncertainty: Heuristics and biases* (pp. 201–208). Cambridge University Press. https://doi.org/10.1017/CBO9780511809477.015

Koerner, N., & Blackwell, S. E. (2021). Mental imagery in chronic worry and generalized anxiety disorder: Shining a spotlight on a key research and clinical target. *Behaviour Research and Therapy, 137*, 103785. https://doi.org/10.1016/j.brat.2020.103785

Korrelboom, K., de Jong, M., Huijbrechts, I., & Daansen, P. (2009). Competitive memory training (COMET) for treating low self-esteem in patients with eating disorders: A randomized clinical trial. *Journal of Consulting and Clinical Psychology, 77*(5), 974–980. https://doi.org/10.1037/a0016742

Kosslyn, S. M., Ganis, G., & Thompson, W. L. (2001). Neural foundations of imagery. *Nature Reviews. Neuroscience, 2*(9), 635–642. https://doi.org/10.1038/35090055

Koster, E. H., Fox, E., & MacLeod, C. (2009). Introduction to the special section on cognitive bias modification in emotional disorders. *Journal of Abnormal Psychology, 118*(1), 1–4. https://doi.org/10.1037/a0014379

Kunze, A. E., Arntz, A., Morina, N., Kindt, M., & Lancee, J. (2017). Efficacy of imagery rescripting and imaginal exposure for nightmares: A randomized wait-list controlled trial. *Behaviour Research and Therapy, 97*, 14–25. https://doi.org/10.1016/j.brat.2017.06.005

Lang, T. J., Blackwell, S. E., Harmer, C. J., Davison, P., & Holmes, E. A. (2012). Cognitive bias modification using mental imagery for depression: Developing a novel computerized intervention to change negative thinking styles. *European Journal of Personality, 26*(2), 145–157. https://doi.org/10.1002/per.855

Lee, J. S., Mathews, A., Shergill, S., Chan, D. K., Majeed, N., & Yiend, J. (2015). How can we enhance cognitive bias modification techniques? The effects of prospective cognition. *Journal of Behavior Therapy and Experimental Psychiatry, 49*(Pt A), 120–127. https://doi.org/10.1016/j.jbtep.2015.03.007

Lester, K. J., Mathews, A., Davison, P. S., Burgess, J. L., & Yiend, J. (2011). Modifying cognitive errors promotes cognitive well being: A new approach to bias modification. *Journal of Behavior Therapy and Experimental Psychiatry, 42*(3), 298–308. https://doi.org/10.1016/j.jbtep.2011.01.001

Mathews, A., & Mackintosh, B. (2000). Induced emotional interpretation bias and anxiety. *Journal of Abnormal Psychology, 109*(4), 602–615. https://doi.org/10.1037/0021-843X.109.4.602

McEvoy, P. M., Erceg-Hurn, D. M., Saulsman, L. M., & Thibodeau, M. A. (2015). Imagery enhancements increase the effectiveness of cognitive behavioural group therapy for social anxiety disorder: A benchmarking study. *Behaviour Research and Therapy, 65*, 42–51. https://doi.org/10.1016/j.brat.2014.12.011

McGlade, A. L., & Craske, M. G. (2021). Optimizing exposure: Between-session mental rehearsal as an augmentation strategy. *Behaviour Research and Therapy, 139*, 103827. https://doi.org/10.1016/j.brat.2021.103827

Morina, N., Deeprose, C., Pusowski, C., Schmid, M., & Holmes, E. A. (2011). Prospective mental imagery in patients with major depressive disorder or anxiety disorders. *Journal of Anxiety Disorders, 25*(8), 1032–1037. https://doi.org/10.1016/j.janxdis.2011.06.012

Morina, N., Lancee, J., & Arntz, A. (2017). Imagery rescripting as a clinical intervention for aversive memories: A meta-analysis. *Journal of Behavior Therapy and Experimental Psychiatry, 55*, 6–15. https://doi.org/10.1016/j.jbtep.2016.11.003

Nanay, B. (2021). Implicit bias as mental imagery. *Journal of the American Philosophical Association, 7*(3), 329–347. https://doi.org/10.1017/apa.2020.29

Nelis, S., Vanbrabant, K., Holmes, E. A., & Raes, F. (2012). Greater positive affect change after mental imagery than verbal thinking in a student sample. *Journal of Experimental Psychopathology, 3*(2), 178–188. https://doi.org/10.5127/jep.021111

Pearson, J. (2014). New directions in mental-imagery research: The binocular-rivalry technique and decoding fMRI patterns. *Current Directions in Psychological Science, 23*(3), 178–183. https://doi.org/10.1177/0963721414532287

Pearson, J. (2019). The human imagination: The cognitive neuroscience of visual mental imagery. *Nature Reviews. Neuroscience, 20*(10), 624–634. https://doi.org/10.1038/s41583-019-0202-9

Pearson, J., Naselaris, T., Holmes, E. A., & Kosslyn, S. M. (2015). Mental imagery: Functional mechanisms and clinical applications. *Trends in Cognitive Sciences, 19*(10), 590–602. https://doi.org/10.1016/j.tics.2015.08.003

Pictet, A., Coughtrey, A. E., Mathews, A., & Holmes, E. A. (2011). Fishing for happiness: The effects of generating positive imagery on mood and behaviour. *Behaviour Research and Therapy, 49*(12), 885–891. https://doi.org/10.1016/j.brat.2011.10.003

Pictet, A., Jermann, F., & Ceschi, G. (2016). When less could be more: Investigating the effects of a brief internet-based imagery cognitive bias modification intervention in depression. *Behaviour Research and Therapy, 84*, 45–51. https://doi.org/10.1016/j.brat.2016.07.008

Pratt, D., Cooper, M. J., & Hackmann, A. (2004). Imagery and its characteristics in people who are anxious about spiders. *Behavioural and Cognitive Psychotherapy, 32*, 165–176. https://doi.org/10.1017/S1352465804001158

Raeder, F., Woud, M. L., Schneider, S., et al. (2019). Reactivation and evaluation of mastery experiences promotes exposure benefit in height phobia. *Cognitive Therapy and Research, 43*, 948–958. https://doi.org/10.1007/s10608-019-10018-x

Rathbone, C. J., Moulin, C. J. A., Conway, M. A., & Holmes, E. A. (2012). Autobiographical memory and the self. In N. Braisby & A. Gellatly (Eds.), *Cognitive psychology* (2nd ed., pp. 546–577). Oxford University Press.

Renner, F., Ji, J. L., Pictet, A., Holmes, E. A., & Blackwell, S. E. (2017). Effects of engaging in repeated mental imagery of future positive events on behavioural activation in individuals with major depressive disorder. *Cognitive Therapy and Research, 41*(3), 369–380. https://doi.org/10.1007/s10608-016-9776-y

Renner, F., Murphy, F. C., Ji, J. L., Manly, T., & Holmes, E. A. (2019). Mental imagery as a "motivational amplifier" to promote activities. *Behaviour Research and Therapy, 114*, 51–59. https://doi.org/10.1016/j.brat.2019.02.002

Schacter, D. L., & Addis, D. R. (2007). Constructive memory: The ghosts of past and future. *Nature, 445*(7123), 27. https://doi.org/10.1038/445027a

Schmidt, N. B., & Vereenooghe, L. (2021). Targeting hostile attributions in inclusive schools through online cognitive bias modification: A randomised experiment. *Behaviour Research and Therapy, 146*, 103949. https://doi.org/10.1016/j.brat.2021.103949

Singer, J. L. (2006). *Imagery in psychotherapy*. American Psychological Association.

Sit, H. F., Hall, B. J., Wang, Y., Zhang, Y., Ju, Q., & Gan, Y. (2020). The effect of positive mental imagery training on Chinese university students with depression: A pilot study. *Current Psychology: A Journal for Diverse Perspectives on Diverse Psychological Issues*. https://doi.org/10.1007/s12144-020-00867-1. Advance online publication.

Stopa, L. (Ed.). (2009). *Imagery and the threatened self: Perspectives on mental imagery and the self in cognitive therapy*. Routledge/Taylor & Francis Group.

Szpunar, K. K., & Schacter, D. L. (2013). Get real: Effects of repeated simulation and emotion on the perceived plausibility of future experiences. *Journal of Experimental Psychology: General, 142*(2), 323–327. https://doi.org/10.1037/a0028877

Taylor, C., Bee, P. E., Kelly, J., Emsley, R., & Haddock, G. (2020). iMAgery focused psychological therapy for persecutory delusions in PSychosis (iMAPS): A multiple baseline experimental case series. *Behavioural and Cognitive Psychotherapy, 48*(5), 530–545. https://doi.org/10.1017/S1352465820000168

Torkan, H., Blackwell, S. E., Holmes, E. A., Kalantari, M., Neshat-Doost, H. T., Maroufi, M., & Talebi, H. (2014). Positive imagery cognitive bias modification in treatment-seeking patients with major depression in Iran: A pilot study. *Cognitive Therapy and Research, 38*(2), 132–145. https://doi.org/10.1007/s10608-014-9598-8

van Teffelen, M. W., Voncken, M. J., Peeters, F., Mollema, E. D., & Lobbestael, J. (2021). The efficacy of incorporating mental imagery in cognitive restructuring techniques on reducing hostility: A randomized controlled trial. *Journal of Behavior Therapy and Experimental Psychiatry, 73*, 101677. https://doi.org/10.1016/j.jbtep.2021.101677

Warnock-Parkes, E., Wild, J., Stott, R., Grey, N., Ehlers, A., & Clark, D. M. (2017). Seeing is believing: Using video feedback in cognitive therapy for social anxiety disorder. *Cognitive and Behavioral Practice, 24*(2), 245–255. https://doi.org/10.1016/j.cbpra.2016.03.007

Wells, A. (2005). Detached mindfulness in cognitive therapy: A metacognitive analysis and ten techniques. *Journal of Rational – Emotive and Cognitive – Behavior Therapy, 23*(4), 337–355. https://doi.org/10.1007/s10942-005-0018-6

Westermann, K., Woud, M. L., Cwik, J. C., Graz, C., Nyhuis, P. W., Margraf, J., & Blackwell, S. E. (2021). Feasibility of computerised positive mental imagery training as a treatment adjunct in in-patient mental health settings: Randomised controlled trial. *BJPsych Open, 7*(6), e203. https://doi.org/10.1192/bjo.2021.1042

Williams, A. D., Blackwell, S. E., Mackenzie, A., Holmes, E. A., & Andrews, G. (2013). Combining imagination and reason in the treatment of depression: A randomized controlled trial of internet-based cognitive-bias modification and internet-CBT for depression. *Journal of Consulting and Clinical Psychology, 81*(5), 793–799. https://doi.org/10.1037/a0033247

Williams, A. D., O'Moore, K., Blackwell, S. E., Smith, J., Holmes, E. A., & Andrews, G. (2015). Positive imagery cognitive bias modification (CBM) and internet-based cognitive behavioral therapy (iCBT): A randomized controlled trial. *Journal of Affective Disorders, 178*, 131–141. https://doi.org/10.1016/j.jad.2015.02.026

Woud, M. L., Blackwell, S. E., Shkreli, L., Würtz, F., Cwik, J. C., Margraf, J., Holmes, E. A., Steudte-Schmiedgen, S., Herpertz, S., & Kessler, H. (2021). The effects of modifying dysfunctional appraisals in posttraumatic stress disorder using a form of cognitive bias modification: Results of a randomized controlled trial in an inpatient setting. *Psychotherapy and Psychosomatics, 90*(6), 386–402. https://doi.org/10.1159/000514166

Yiend, J., Lee, J.-S., Tekes, S., Atkins, L., Mathews, A., Vrinten, M., Ferragamo, C., & Shergill, S. (2014). Modifying interpretation in a clinically depressed sample using 'cognitive bias modification-errors': A double blind randomised controlled trial. *Cognitive Therapy and Research, 38*(2), 146–159. https://doi.org/10.1007/s10608-013-9571-y

Simon E. Blackwell is a postdoctoral researcher at the Mental Health Research and Treatment Center, Faculty of Psychology, Ruhr-University Bochum. His research focuses on mental imagery, in particular positive mental imagery, its role in both psychopathology and healthy functioning, and how it can be used in psychological interventions. In addition, he has an interest in the process by which we go about developing and testing psychological interventions and how we can make this more efficient.

Chapter 7
Fear Conditioning Biases in Anxiety Disorders: A Matter of Interpretation?

Sara Scheveneels and Yannick Boddez

With a lifetime prevalence between 25% and 30%, anxiety disorders are a prevalent and debilitating condition, associated with significant individual and societal burden (Kessler et al., 2005). Research about factors involved in the onset, maintenance, and exacerbation of anxiety disorders has focused on the role of information selection and processing (Beck & Clark, 1997; Lau & Waters, 2017). For example, relative to non-anxious controls, patients diagnosed with an anxiety disorder show an attentional bias toward threat, including facilitated threat detection, difficulties in disengagement from threat, and attentional avoidance (Bar-Haim et al., 2007; Cisler & Koster, 2010). Moreover, patients diagnosed with an anxiety disorder exhibit a tendency to consistently resolve ambiguous cues and situations in a specific direction by selecting threatening instead of benign meanings (Hirsch et al., 2016; and for an overview of the role of interpretation biases in emotional psychopathology, see Chap. 12 by Woud and Hofmann). Another example concerns research that focuses on biases in fear conditioning. In this chapter, we will start by providing an overview of such fear conditioning biases in anxiety and discuss how these can be linked to interpretation biases. Subsequently, we will discuss different ways of defining biases. We will conclude this chapter by discussing how (fear conditioning) biases play a role in interventions directed at reducing anxiety.

S. Scheveneels (✉)
Center for the Psychology of Learning and Experimental Psychopathology, KU Leuven, Leuven, Belgium
e-mail: sara.scheveneels@kuleuven.be

Y. Boddez
Department of Experimental Clinical and Health Psychology, Ghent University, Ghent, Belgium
e-mail: Yannick.Boddez@ugent.be

© The Author(s), under exclusive license to Springer Nature Switzerland AG 2023
M. L. Woud (ed.), *Interpretational Processing Biases in Emotional Psychopathology*,
CBT: Science Into Practice, https://doi.org/10.1007/978-3-031-23650-1_7

7.1 Biases of Anxiety Patients in the Context of Fear Conditioning and Links to Interpretational Processing

Learning mechanisms play a crucial role in the etiology and maintenance of anxiety (Mineka & Zinbarg, 2006; Scheveneels et al., 2019). These learning mechanisms are often studied under highly controlled conditions using (fear) conditioning procedures (Beckers et al., 2013; Lonsdorf et al., 2017). In a standard fear conditioning paradigm, a neutral stimulus (e.g., a geometrical figure) is paired with another stimulus that is aversive in nature (e.g., an electric shock). As a result of these stimulus pairings, responding indicative of fear and anxiety is elicited by the first (initially neutral) stimulus. This stimulus – to which responding changes conditional upon being paired with the aversive stimulus – is called a *conditional stimulus* or CS. The (aversive) stimulus that is paired with the CS and changes responding to it is called the *unconditional stimulus* (US). The response to the CS that changes due to CS–US pairings is termed the *conditional response* (CR). In the context of anxiety, among the responses of interest are US expectancies (Boddez et al., 2013), subjective fear, physiological indices of anxiety (e.g., skin conductance, fear-potentiated startle), and avoidance.

Interestingly, empirical evidence indicates that patients diagnosed with an anxiety disorder behave differently in fear conditioning procedures as compared to non-anxious controls. In particular, patients show a tendency or bias to respond fearfully to ambiguous or in fact safe stimuli in the context of fear conditioning. Interestingly, these observable differences in fear conditioning can be linked to interpretation biases. In this chapter, we will describe how a tendency to interpret ambiguous or safe stimuli as threatening might (partially) mediate responding in a fear conditioning procedure.[1] We will start with providing a summary of the evidence for differences between anxiety patients and controls in different fear conditioning procedures (Fig. 7.1) and then describe the relevance of biased interpretational processes during these conditioning procedures.

When adding a second stimulus that is never paired with the US (i.e., a CS−) to a standard fear conditioning procedure, it is observed that individuals diagnosed with an anxiety disorder tend to respond with increased anxiety or fear to this stimulus – a stimulus that in fact can be considered as safe – as compared to control participants (Duits et al., 2015; Dvir et al., 2019). Related to this, anxiety patients tend to show *reduced CS+/CS− discrimination* in fear conditioning procedures (Cooper et al., 2018). These observations (i.e., increased CS− responding and reduced discrimination) can be (partially) mediated by interpretation biases, namely, the tendency of patients to misinterpret the safe CS− as threatening. A real-life translation

---

[1] Notably, as we will discuss below, when defining biases, this is one possible view on interpretation biases, namely, as a mediating latent (mental) process. Alternatively, fear conditioning biases can be seen as one specific instance of interpretation bias, with both biases then situated at the level of behavior (also see De Houwer, 2019). In this chapter we will elaborate on interpretation bias as a mediating mental process that (partially) drives behavior in fear conditioning procedures.

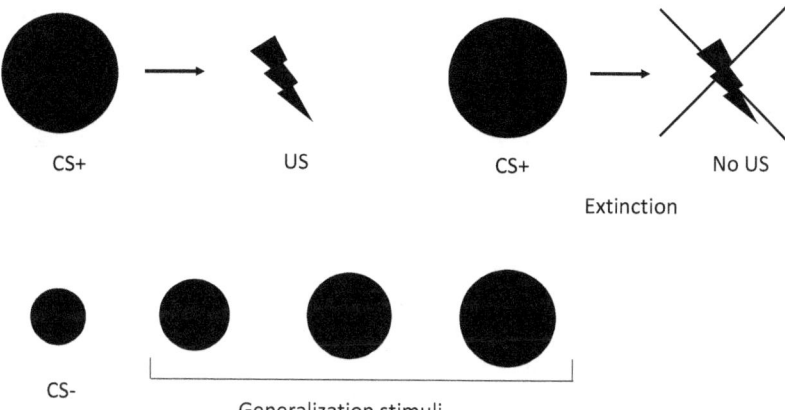

Fig. 7.1 Overview of some fear condition procedures

of such reduced discrimination between danger and safety situations can, for example, be observed in the context of panic disorder, when innocuous physiological symptoms are misinterpreted and treated as a sign of having a heart attack (Haddad et al., 2012). Strongly related to this possible bias in responding fearfully to *safe* situations, individuals diagnosed with an anxiety disorder tend to react fearfully to *ambiguous* stimuli. We now discuss two fear conditioning procedures that induce an ambiguous situation.

First, individuals diagnosed with an anxiety disorder, as compared to non-anxious controls, are slower to learn that a threatening stimulus has become safe. This has been demonstrated using extinction procedures, in which a CS+ that was previously paired with a US is presented without the US (Hermans et al., 2006). In particular, *reduced and/or delayed extinction* is observed (i.e., stronger responding to the CS+ and/or slower reduction in responding) in patients compared to controls (Duits et al., 2015, 2017; Dvir et al., 2019).[2] These results suggest that individuals diagnosed with an anxiety disorder need more learning experiences to acquire a sense of safety. Again, this can (partially) be driven by an interpretation bias in patients. Namely, the extinguished CS+ might still be interpreted as threatening despite experiences in which the US was absent. Possibly, patients may need more correcting experiences to change their interpretation of the CS+ from dangerous to safe, resulting in sustained CS+ responding during extinction. Translated to real life, after a car accident, fear will decrease with a slower rate in the case of new safe experiences with driving in individuals at risk of developing pathological anxiety. Linked to interpretation biases, these at risk individuals may continue to interpret driving a car as dangerous, despite experiences with driving without accidents. Put

---

[2] Notably, these differences in acquisition and extinction between anxiety and controls have not always been replicated (Pöhlchen et al., 2020).

differently, interpretation biases may hamper the expression of new learning experiences.

These extinction trials can be considered as instances of ambiguous situations. It has been argued that during extinction, the CS acquires an ambiguous meaning by not being paired with the US anymore. This is supported by extensive evidence on reinstatement and renewal of fear, showing that fear responding to the CS after extinction is modulated by context (Bouton, 1988, 2002). When an extinguished CS is presented in a threatening context again, fear can be "reinstated," and when the CS is presented in another context than the extinction context, renewal of fear occurs. In order to explain this, it has been suggested that a CS that underwent extinction training has two meanings: a threatening and a safe one (due to acquisition training and the subsequent extinction training, respectively). Individuals diagnosed with anxiety disorders seem to have a tendency to still select the threatening meaning, which might be (partially) driven by a biased interpretation of the ambiguous CS as being dangerous (but see: McLaughlin et al., 2015).

A second observation is that anxiety patients tend to respond fearfully to (generalization) stimuli that are situated on the continuum between safe and threat signals. In fear conditioning procedures, a generalization test phase can be added after an acquisition phase with CS–US pairings. In this test phase, generalization stimuli are presented that are conceptually or perceptually related to the CS, and thus can be considered as (partly) ambiguous cues. Compared to controls, individuals diagnosed with anxiety disorders have shown more shallow generalization gradients, exhibiting stronger anxiety responding to stimuli that are dissimilar from the CS+ (El-Bar et al., 2017; Kaczkurkin et al., 2017; Lissek et al., 2010, 2014). This pattern is often referred to as overgeneralization. Overgeneralization can be affected by interpretational processes as well, namely, the (ambiguous) generalization stimuli are misinterpreted as threatening, and as a result elicit elevated fear responding. Overgeneralization of fear responding can, for instance, occur when after being bitten by a dog, fear is not confined to this particular dog but spreads to other dogs that look similar or even to other animals that can bite, such as cats or rabbits. It is, however, important to note that patient–control differences regarding overgeneralization are not always unequivocally replicated (Ahrens et al., 2016; Morey et al., 2020; Tinoco-González et al., 2015).

In extension to this, a *covariation or expectancy bias* is observed in patients in the context of fear conditioning (Tomarken et al., 1989; Wiemer & Pauli, 2016). In ambiguous situations, anxiety patients tend to overestimate the contingency between fear-relevant stimuli (CSs) and aversive consequences (USs) despite the actual absence of a correlation (i.e., illusory correlation). Evidence for this covariation bias has been found in a variety of fears and anxiety disorders, including social anxiety (De Jong et al., 1998), specific fears (de Jong et al., 1992, 1995a; Pauli et al., 1998), and panic disorder (Pauli et al., 2001). For example, in an experimental context, it has been demonstrated that individuals with spider phobia overestimate the covariation between a spider picture and an electric shock (de Jong et al., 1992), and individuals retaining this bias after treatment are more vulnerable to relapse (De Jong et al., 1995b). These exaggerated expectations of an aversive outcome (US) after a fear-relevant stimulus (CS) can even occur prior to any actual conditioning experience or stimulus pairings, also termed a priori *expectancy bias* (Van Overveld et al., 2010; Wiedemann et al., 2001). Notably, this a priori expectancy bias can still be due to real-life, naturalistic learning experiences outside the experimental context. For example, a spider phobic who had a panic attack during a confrontation with a spider (outside the laboratory) might infer from this experience that the chances that the picture of the spider in the experiment will also be paired with something unpleasant are rather high, despite the lack of an actual contingency between the picture of the spider and the shock in the experimental task.

In conclusion, anxiety patients tend to exhibit biases in fear responding in conditioning tasks, and such biases may be partly linked to biases in interpretational processing, for example, in how someone is interpreting a stimulus in a conditioning procedure. Regarding biases in fear responding, it has been claimed that these biases are not merely epiphenomena, consequences of anxiety disorders, or just a diagnostic marker. Impaired discrimination, reduced extinction, and overgeneralization have also been argued to be involved in the onset of anxiety symptoms (Scheveneels et al., 2021). Prospective studies have been particularly influential in this regard. For example, Lommen et al. (2013) found in a sample of soldiers that reduced extinction learning pre-trauma (i.e., before deployment in Afghanistan) predicted post-traumatic stress disorder (PTSD) symptom severity after deployment. The effect remained while controlling for pre-trauma PTSD symptoms and other risk factors, such as neuroticism.[3] Based on the results of this and other prospective studies (Lenaert et al., 2014; Lommen et al., 2013; Orr et al., 2012; Guthrie & Bryant, 2006; Scheveneels et al., 2021), it has been argued that fear conditioning biases can constitute a predisposing factor that make individuals more vulnerable for developing an anxiety disorder (Britton et al., 2011). In addition, fear conditioning biases may contribute to the *persistence* of anxiety. For example, Sijbrandij et al. (2013) showed that reduced safety learning in a fear conditioning procedure in soldiers approximately 2 months after their deployment to Afghanistan predicted the persistence of post-traumatic stress symptoms at 9 months after deployment. To the extent that the fear conditioning biases are driven by skewed interpretations at the mental level, this suggests the important role that interpretational processes may play in the onset of pathological anxiety.

In this section, we provided a summary of differential behavioral outcomes in fear conditioning procedures (i.e., termed fear conditioning biases) in individuals diagnosed with an anxiety disorder and linked these to biases in interpretational processing (as a latent mental process). In the next section, we further elaborate on how these biases can be defined and theoretically linked to each other.

---

[3] Notably, in a conceptual replication study in a sample of firefighters, Lommen and Boddez (2022) failed to replicate these results.

7.2   Defining Biases: Bias as (Observable) Behavior and Bias as a (Cognitive) Deficit

In this section, we consider different perspectives on biases, namely, biases as an effect (observable behavior) and biases as a(n) (underlying) mental process or deficit. We apply this perspective to both fear conditioning and interpretation biases. However, it should be noted that this perspective is not confined to these specific biases and can also be extended to other types of bias (De Houwer, 2019). We discuss how etiological factors, including genetic and temperamental factors, in interaction with learning history, could give rise to biased behaviors (in fear conditioning tasks). This relation can be fully or partially mediated by unobservable latent mental processes (i.e., a cognitive deficit). A visual representation of this model is displayed in Fig. 7.2.

7.2.1   Bias as (Observable) Behavior

In line with how we described fear conditioning biases in the previous section, biases can be primarily defined in terms of *behavior* that is *observed in individuals diagnosed with an anxiety disorder* (in fear conditioning tasks) and more specifically, how this behavior deviates from what healthy controls would do (Scherer, 2021). In particular, in the context of fear conditioning, patients tend to exhibit stronger fear responding to safe or ambiguous stimuli or situations than controls. Biases are then defined in terms of *observable behavior*, in this case in a fear conditioning task. This definition can be extended to other biases as well, such as differences in performance of patients as compared to non-anxious controls in a dot-probe task or in a visual search task in the case of attention bias (Cisler et al., 2009). Similarly, with regard to interpretation bias, lexical decision tasks, sentence completion tasks, or scrambled sentences tasks have been used (among other tasks) to demonstrate differences between anxiety patients and controls (Schoth & Liossi,

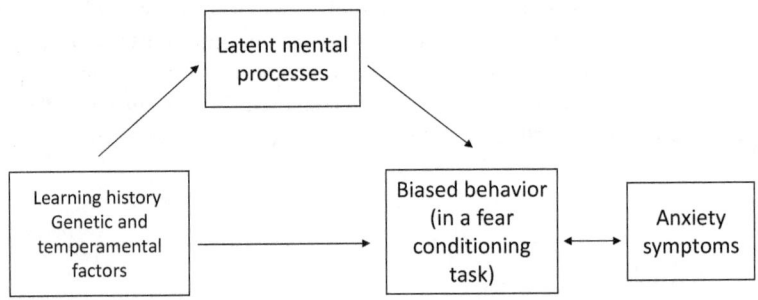

Fig. 7.2 Mediational model of biases in behavior and its impact on anxiety, mediated by latent mental processes

2017; Würtz et al., 2022; and for an overview of measures to assess interpretation biases, see Chap. 3 by Würtz and Sanchez-Lopez). It can be noted that this definition of interpretation bias as observable behavior (or effect) differs from how we described interpretation bias previously (cf. Sect. 7.1) as a latent mental process that (partially) explains the observable behavior in fear conditioning tasks (see later).

7.2.2 The Etiology of (Fear Conditioning) Biases

In going one step further than merely inspecting observable behavior, we can try to explain these observable differences between patients and controls. This concerns the *etiology* of biases or the question: "Why do some people show biased behavior whereas others do not?" This is a relevant question since it has been argued that biased behavior (observed in fear conditioning) is not just a consequence of anxiety disorders, but that it is also observed in healthy individuals with an increased vulnerability to develop an anxiety disorder (Scheveneels et al., 2021).

7.2.2.1 Temperamental and Genetic Factors

A first possibility is that some individuals are born with a bias. In line with this view, temperamental factors and genetic variations have been linked to biased responding in fear conditioning procedures (Lonsdorf & Kalisch, 2011; Lonsdorf & Merz, 2017). With regard to temperamental factors, individual differences in *neuroticism* (i.e., the tendency to express negative affect) and *trait anxiety* have been examined among others temperamental factors. Studies on the association between individual differences in fear conditioning, on the one hand, and neuroticism and trait anxiety, on the other hand, provide a heterogeneous picture (Lonsdorf & Merz, 2017). The majority of studies report null findings regarding the association with (differential) acquisition learning for neuroticism (e.g., Arnaudova et al., 2017; Lommen et al., 2010; Tzschoppe et al., 2014; Torrents-Rodas et al., 2013), and a large number of studies finds null results for trait anxiety as well (e.g., Arnaudova et al., 2013; Sehlmeyer et al., 2011). Regarding generalization, results are mixed (e.g., Arnaudova et al., 2017; Lommen et al., 2010; Torrents-Rodas et al., 2013), with a recent meta-analysis revealing a small, positive relationship between anxious personality (including neuroticism and trait anxiety) and fear generalization (Sep et al., 2019). For fear extinction, many studies fail to find an association with neuroticism (e.g., Pineles et al., 2009; Rattel et al., 2020; Tzschoppe et al., 2014) and for trait anxiety findings are inconsistent with some studies showing deficient extinction learning in high trait anxious individuals but only in some of the outcome measures (Barrett & Armony, 2009; Gazendam et al., 2013; Sehlmeyer et al., 2011). Regarding the link with interpretation bias, one possibility is that individuals high on neuroticism/trait anxiety exhibit a stronger tendency to select a threatening meaning, which might give rise to stronger fear responding in a fear conditioning task (Lommen et al., 2010; Salemink & van den Hout, 2010).

Studies uncovering genetic risk factors have revealed that variation in the serotonin transporter (5HTT) and the catechol-o-methyltransferase (COMT) genes are associated with reduced CS+/CS− discrimination, CS− responding (i.e., less CS− inhibition), and impaired extinction (i.e., less CS− inhibition and stronger CS+ responding) (Garpenstrand et al., 2001; Lonsdorf et al., 2009). At the same time, these genetic polymorphisms explain a relatively small proportion of the total variance in fear conditioning behavior, suggesting that this at best does not tell the whole story (for an overview of genetic factors underlying interpretation biases, see Chap. 8 by Vincent and Fox).

7.2.2.2 Environmental Factors and Learning History

Additionally and/or alternatively, environmental factors, such as learning experiences, might explain why some individuals develop a bias and others do not. Anxiety patients and individuals vulnerable to develop an anxiety disorder might show a bias in fear conditioning tasks due to a *different learning history* than non-anxious controls. This can include, for instance, dysfunctional interpersonal experiences (e.g., family dynamics, attachment) or stressful life events (e.g., trauma). For example, an individual growing up in an unpredictable environment (e.g., with an emotionally volatile father) may have learned that safety on one or even several occasions (e.g., father behaving friendly and sweet) does not imply that the situation is always safe (e.g., as the father could suddenly and unpredictably behave aggressively). Such individuals may have learned to be on guard even in seemingly safe situations and therefore remain on guard when confronted with an apparently safe stimulus in a fear conditioning task (CS− or extinguished CS). This would result in maintained fear responding toward such stimuli despite "safe experiences" (Spix et al., 2021; Vervliet & Boddez, 2020). Moreover, if also other, similar individuals (e.g., a male teacher of a similar age as father, an uncle) behaved in an unpredictable, volatile manner, the individual may infer that similar people or situations pose similar risks. That is, one may have learned to generalize. As a consequence, anxiety responding might generalize strongly in a generalization test in a fear conditioning procedure (Boddez et al., 2017). These learning experiences and environmental factors may then interact with biological and predisposing factors in explaining biases in current behavior (Lonsdorf & Merz, 2017). Whereas research consistently revealed associations between learning history, such as dysfunctional interpersonal experiences and stressful life events, on the one hand, and an increased risk for developing pathological anxiety, on the other hand (e.g., Jinyao et al., 2012; Lindert et al., 2014; Yap et al., 2014), the amount of studies that directly links learning history and fear conditioning biases is scarce. Linking this to interpretation bias, it can be hypothesized that the behavior of individuals with a particular learning history (cf. above) in a fear conditioning task is (partially) driven by interpretational processes, for instance, as a result of these learning experiences these individuals might show a tendency to misinterpret safe situations as threatening.

7.2.3   Bias as a Latent Mental Process

So far we discussed biases as observable behavior resulting from the interaction between predispositional biological factors and learning history.[4] Additionally, it is often assumed that this relation is mediated by particular *latent mental processes* (Fig. 7.2; also see De Houwer, 2011). In particular, learning history in interaction with an inborn vulnerability could generate a particular internal model of the world, which can take the form of cognitive schemata, processing styles, trust issues, expectancy bias, and so on. On their turn, these mental processes would drive the behavior in experimental tasks, such as fear conditioning tasks, dot-probe tasks, and lexical decision tasks.

Some researchers do not put the mental processes in this merely mediational role, but see them as a unique and independent source of variance in (biased) behavior. From this perspective, individuals diagnosed with an anxiety disorder do not (only) differ in their learning history and inborn vulnerability, but also in the way in which they cognitively process information. In line with this, biases have been ascribed as deficits or as "flaws in the design of the mind" (Haselton et al., 2005). This deficit view readily aligns with terminology suggesting that the patient *is* *biased* or *has a bias* (De Houwer, 2019). In contrast, perspectives that put more emphasis on environmental determinants, including some learning perspectives, align more readily with terminology suggesting that prior events *bias the behavior* of the patient. Relying on the examples introduced above, one could then say that prior exposure to an emotionally volatile father biases (i.e., systematically impacts) fear extinction or that exposure to a CS+ *biases responding* to a CS− or to a GS. That is, the biasing factors are (also) situated in the environment rather than (only) in the mind of the patient (see De Houwer, 2019).

We now describe one influential mental process that accounts for biases in fear conditioning, suggesting that patients would mentally rely on a *better safe than sorry processing strategy* (Lommen et al., 2010; Van den Bergh et al., 2021). Recently, Van den Bergh et al. (2021) further elaborated on this account by applying a predictive processing approach. This approach states that individuals have prior beliefs or expectancies about the world (e.g., one might expect to get a shock, to be socially rejected, to be bitten by a dog). Learning experiences, combined with biological factors, may trigger such prior beliefs (cf. above). These prior beliefs or expectancies, however, may differ from the actual outcome in a given situation (e.g., getting no shock, being accepted by others, not being bitten). In case of such a

---

[4] Note that in discussing the link with interpretation bias, interpretation bias was defined already as a mental process.

mismatch between the expected and real outcome, a prediction error occurs. The brain supposedly functions as a prediction machine that aims to minimize these prediction errors. If, however, such mismatch occurs, this can be handled in several ways. The most straightforward way is to update prior beliefs and expectancies in a way that they better fit with reality (Rescorla & Wagner, 1972). Another way of dealing with the mismatch is by responding in a perceptual, behavioral, and physiological way that generates input that is consistent with the prior expectancies. This then results in discarding the information from the environment (e.g., offered during the experiment or experiences), that is, information that does not match. Transferring this to the context of anxiety, individuals vulnerable for anxiety disorders (and broader psychopathology) might rely on information processing that tends to be low in sensory–perceptual detail (i.e., oversimplifying input from the environment) and heavily relies on categorical threat-related priors or beliefs (i.e., *jumping to conclusions*). In fact, such processing styles can also be related to biased interpretational processing, for example, in the context of *jumping to conclusions*, whereby unwarranted assumptions are made based on limited information (e.g., a threatening interpretation is generated very quickly). As a consequence, processing is then primarily informed by threat-related priors or beliefs (e.g., others do not like me and reject me) at the cost of actual (disconfirming) input (e.g., others might be interested in me). The benefit of such processing strategy is that it allows for greater speed in categorizing input and may reduce uncertainty in the short term. At the same time, this processing heuristic is believed to result in poor updating of prior threat-related beliefs and thus allow these beliefs to remain dominant (stagnated error reduction process). This way, prior threat-related beliefs can be maintained despite their mismatch with reality. In the context of fear conditioning, this could explain the link between fear conditioning and interpretation biases, that is, prior threat-related beliefs may be associated with a biased interpretational processing style, which, in turn, can explain the observation that anxiety patients tend to interpret in fact safe stimuli or contexts as being threating, despite having safe experiences with the stimulus/context (e.g., a CS– or extinguished CS). It would be predicted that patients experience fewer prediction errors and are less sensitive to corrective experiences.

The mediational model that we introduced earlier (Fig. 7.2) can also be useful to understand the potential link between interpretation bias (as a mental process) and biases in a fear conditioning task as observable behavior (see Fig. 7.3).[5] Earlier we described how differences in behavior in fear conditioning between patients and controls might (partially) be driven by interpretation bias. Interpretation bias can be seen as an inborn and learned processing style or underlying cognitive tendency that reflects a tendency to interpret unclear or ambiguous situations or stimuli as threatening. In fear conditioning tasks, participants are typically presented with ambiguous situations, for example, stimuli that show some resemblance to the threatening stimulus or CS (i.e., generalization test) or stimuli that have acquired both a

---

[5] Note that interpretation bias can be defined as (1) observable behavior in experimental tasks, such as a lexical decision task or (2) a latent mental processing style. In the mediation model that we propose here, interpretation bias is seen as a latent mental process.

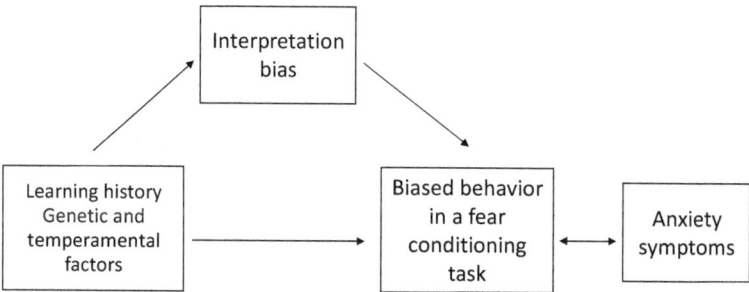

Fig. 7.3 Mediational model of the link between interpretation bias as a mental process and biased behavior in fear conditioning tasks

threatening and a safe meaning (i.e., extinction procedure). In line with this, it has been argued that the more ambiguous and unclear the situation (also referred to as "weak situations"), the more sensitive the procedure is to pick up differences between individuals vulnerable for anxiety and controls (Beckers et al., 2013; Lissek et al., 2006). Hence, in these weak or ambiguous situations, there might be more room for interpretation biases (as a mental process) to exert an influence on fear responding in the conditioning task (i.e., the observable behavior). For example, a generalization or extinction stimulus that is ambiguous and is interpreted as threatening will then elicit stronger fear responding.

In conclusion, we discussed different perspectives on biases and integrated these in a mediational model (Figs. 7.2 and 7.3). We started with defining a bias in terms of observable behavior (for instance, in experimental tasks, such as a fear conditioning task). It was then discussed how an interaction between biological (e.g., genetic and temperamental) factors and learning history could lie at the basis of biased behavior. Latent mental information processing strategies, such as a *better safe than sorry processing strategy* or interpretation biases, if defined as a mental process, could then mediate the relation between etiological factors and observable biased behavior (in this case in fear condition tasks).

7.3 The Role of (Fear Conditioning) Biases in Reducing Anxiety

In this section, we discuss how fear conditioning biases might play a role in the treatment of anxiety and how knowledge about fear conditioning biases, including the potential role of interpretation biases, may inform and enhance treatment strategies.

Exposure therapy is the treatment of choice for anxiety disorders and has proven highly effective for, for example, social anxiety disorder (Mayo-Wilson et al., 2014; Scaini et al., 2016), specific phobias (Wolitzky-Taylor et al., 2008), PTSD (Cusack et al., 2016), and panic disorder (Pompoli et al., 2018). During exposure therapy, the patient is confronted with fear-eliciting stimuli that they would normally avoid. One of the currently prevailing models of exposure therapy is the inhibitory learning theory (ILT; Craske et al., 2008, 2014, 2022). Based on associative learning models and extinction research, this theory prescribes that expectancy violation or prediction error violation are crucial in driving the effects of exposure through the formation of an inhibitory association that counteracts the original fear association (Boddez et al., 2020; Bouton, 1988, 2002; Rescorla & Wagner, 1972). More specifically, if a patient experiences during exposure that the fear-eliciting stimulus (or CS) is not paired with the expected aversive outcome (or US), their fearful expectancy would be violated and the inhibitory association would gain strength. A stronger inhibitory association, supposedly, would be reflected in less feared expectancies (but see Boddez et al., 2020), representing a reduction in fearful cognitions after exposure therapy.

Based on these theoretical premises, it can be predicted that individuals who show poor inhibitory or safety learning would show a reduced outcome of exposure treatment. This has (at least partially) been confirmed in several studies on predicting exposure therapy outcome by laboratory-based extinction learning (Forcadell et al., 2017; Lange et al., 2020; Raeder et al., 2020; Scheveneels et al., 2021). However, significant results are typically found in only a subset of the dependent variables and are not always replicated by other studies, with some studies finding no association (Wannemueller et al., 2018) and others showing different associations than what would be expected (Geller et al., 2019). An association between reduced safety learning and worse exposure therapy outcome would also be in line with the predictive processing account and *better safe than sorry processing* strategy. Due to stagnated error reduction processes, some individuals might be less sensitive for corrective experiences and would be impaired in updating their fearful expectancies or prior beliefs.

Impairments in safety learning could have several implications for the treatment of anxiety. First, individuals with poor safety learning might need more corrective experiences to adjust both their fearful expectancies and their biased interpretation of the (previously) feared stimulus. In addition, a stronger mismatch between their fearful expectancies and the actual outcome might be required to counteract impairments in inhibitory or safety learning. In line with this, several strategies have been proposed to maximize expectancy violation and inhibitory learning during exposure therapy (Craske et al., 2014; Pittig et al., 2018; Weisman & Rodebaugh, 2018). Some evidence has been found for the prediction that expectancy violation is related to better exposure treatment outcome (Deacon et al., 2013). However, more research is needed to further test the effects of these strategies (Craske et al., 2022).

Departing from a predictive processing framework, it has been emphasized that treatment interventions should (additionally) target the way threat-relevant information is processed at all levels, including defensive action tendencies that are part of the fearful prior beliefs or expectancies (Van den Bergh et al., 2021). This implies encouraging openness to process threat-relevant information in a more detailed and less biased way and disengage from defensive action tendencies during processing. It has been claimed that more detailed sensory processing will then promote updating the fearful prior expectancies. In other words, not only learning that the aversive stimulus or US is not coming will be a target in effective intervention but also encouraging information processing that is no longer inspired by a *better safe than sorry strategy* but by a *wait-and-see attitude* (Van den Bergh et al., 2021).

In line with the above, it can be predicted that individuals with a stronger interpretation bias might also be less sensitive to the corrective experiences in exposure therapy and cognitive behavioral therapy (CBT) because they are expected to interpret unclear or ambiguous outcomes as threatening (but see Baumgardner et al., 2022, in which baseline interpretation bias did not predict anxiety levels after CBT, or Mobach et al., 2021, in which stronger baseline interpretation bias predicted better CBT outcome). Moreover, changing interpretation bias (e.g., by cognitive bias modification techniques) could potentially enhance the sensitivity to corrective experiences and the efficacy of exposure treatment or CBT (Butler et al., 2015). However, a study by Steinman and Teachman (2014) found no evidence for an added effect of cognitive bias modification on exposure therapy. Some research suggests that interpretation bias decreases after cognitive behavioral therapy CBT (Baumgardner et al., 2022) and that this decrease in interpretation bias might be a mechanism of therapeutic change in CBT for anxiety (Mobach et al., 2021; Pereira et al., 2018; Steinman & Teachman, 2014; Waters et al., 2008) and mediate long-term outcomes of anxiety interventions (Makover et al., 2020).

Above, we focused on how poor safety learning relates to treatment outcome. Additionally, we argued that the tendency to *overgeneralize* based on prior learning experiences might constitute a vulnerability factor for developing anxiety (Lenaert et al., 2014). We illustrated this with the example of having a learning history with a volatile father, which could give rise to continuingly being on guard despite safe experiences and in the presence of, for instance, other men. In line with this view, promoting the discrimination between the CS+ (e.g., volatile father) and generalization stimuli (e.g., other men) could be a promising target in anxiety interventions. In other words, in a discrimination training individuals could learn that other men are different from the volatile father. Lommen et al. (2017) demonstrated in a fear conditioning study that such discrimination training could effectively reduce avoidance toward generalization stimuli. Similarly, in another fear conditioning study, promoting perceptual discrimination has found to result in decreased generalization of fear responding (Ginat-Frolich et al., 2017). In a first attempt to test the effects of discrimination training in a high-anxious sample (fear of spiders), Ginat-Frolich et al. (2019) demonstrated that the group receiving discrimination training showed less avoidance toward spiders with increased similarity to a live spider.

7.4   Conclusion

This chapter discussed how fear conditioning biases are related to pathological anxiety by providing a summary of patient–control differences in fear responding during conditioning procedures. In addition, we linked these biases in fear conditioning (as observable behavior) to interpretation biases (as a latent mental process). For example, in certain fear conditioning procedures (i.e., "weak" situations), such as generalization tests and extinction trials, individuals vulnerable for anxiety might have a tendency to interpret ambiguous stimuli as threatening and as a consequence (still) respond fearfully to these (in fact safe) stimuli. Further empirical testing of whether and how interpretational processes impact fear conditioning is, however, needed to verify these predictions.

In providing different perspectives on biases, we explicitly distinguished biases as observable behavior (i.e., measured with experimental tasks) and biases as an underlying cognitive processes that could (partially) drive or mediate this observable behavior (also see De Houwer, 2019). We discussed the link between fear conditioning and interpretation biases in the light of a mediation model in which interpretation biases are an inborn and learned cognitive marker and processing style that could (partially) drive the observable differences in responding in fear conditioning procedures between individuals vulnerable for anxiety and controls.

Finally, we discussed how these biases might impact the treatment of anxiety. In particular, we suggest that both biases might negatively impact treatment outcome. However, current evidence for this claim is mixed. Building further on this, techniques to remediate biases might enhance the efficacy of anxiety-focused interventions.

Acknowledgments The authors would like to thank the editor, Marcella Woud, for her thought-provoking suggestions. Funding: S.S. is employed on KU Leuven C1 project C16/19/02. Y.B. is employed on Methusalem Grant BOF16/MET_V/002.

References

Ahrens, L. M., Pauli, P., Reif, A., Mühlberger, A., Langs, G., Aalderink, T., & Wieser, M. J. (2016). Fear conditioning and stimulus generalization in patients with social anxiety disorder. *Journal of Anxiety Disorders, 44*, 36–46. https://doi.org/10.1016/j.janxdis.2016.10.003

Arnaudova, I., Krypotos, A. M., Effting, M., Boddez, Y., Kindt, M., & Beckers, T. (2013). Individual differences in discriminatory fear learning under conditions of ambiguity: A vulnerability factor for anxiety disorders? *Frontiers in Psychology, 4*, 298. https://doi.org/10.3389/fpsyg.2013.00298

Arnaudova, I., Krypotos, A.-M., Effting, M., Kindt, M., & Beckers, T. (2017). Fearing shades of grey: Individual differences in fear responding towards generalisation stimuli. *Cognition and Emotion, 31*(6), 1181–1196. https://doi.org/10.1080/02699931.2016.1204990

Bar-Haim, Y., Lamy, D., Pergamin, L., Bakermans-Kranenburg, M. J., & van IJzendoorn, M. H. (2007). Threat-related attentional bias in anxious and nonanxious individuals: A meta-analytic study. *Psychological Bulletin, 133*(1), 1–24. https://doi.org/10.1037/0033-2909.133.1.1

Barrett, J., & Armony, J. L. (2009). Influence of trait anxiety on brain activity during the acquisition and extinction of aversive conditioning. *Psychological Medicine, 39*(2), 255–265. https://doi.org/10.1017/S0033291708003516

Baumgardner, M., Silk, J. S., & Allen, K. B. (2022). Interpretation bias and anticipated distress in the face of ambiguity: Predictors of change in cognitive behavioral therapy for youth anxiety. *Child Psychiatry and Human Development, 53*, 479–488. https://doi.org/10.1007/s10578-021-01147-0

Beck, A. T., & Clark, D. A. (1997). An information processing model of anxiety: Automatic and strategic processes. *Behaviour Research and Therapy, 35*(1), 49–58. https://doi.org/10.1016/s0005-7967(96)00069-1

Beckers, T., Krypotos, A. M., Boddez, Y., Effting, M., & Kindt, M. (2013). What's wrong with fear conditioning? *Biological Psychology, 92*(1), 90–96. https://doi.org/10.1016/j.biopsycho.2011.12.015

Boddez, Y., Baeyens, F., Luyten, L., Vansteenwegen, D., Hermans, D., & Beckers, T. (2013). Rating data are underrated: Validity of US expectancy in human fear conditioning. *Journal of Behavior Therapy and Experimental Psychiatry, 44*(2), 201–206. https://doi.org/10.1016/j.jbtep.2012.08.003

Boddez, Y., Bennett, M. P., van Esch, S., & Beckers, T. (2017). Bending rules: The shape of the perceptual generalisation gradient is sensitive to inference rules. *Cognition & Emotion, 31*(7), 1444–1452. https://doi.org/10.1080/02699931.2016.1230541

Boddez, Y., Moors, A., Mertens, G., & De Houwer, J. (2020). Tackling fear: Beyond associative memory activation as the only determinant of fear responding. *Neuroscience and Biobehavioral Reviews, 112*, 410–419. https://doi.org/10.1016/j.neubiorev.2020.02.009

Bouton, M. E. (1988). Context and ambiguity in the extinction of emotional learning: Implications for exposure therapy. *Behaviour Research and Therapy, 26*(2), 137–149. https://doi.org/10.1016/0005-7967(88)90113-1

Bouton, M. E. (2002). Context, ambiguity, and unlearning: Sources of relapse after behavioral extinction. *Biological Psychiatry, 52*(10), 976–986. https://doi.org/10.1016/s0006-3223(02)01546-9

Britton, J. C., Lissek, S., Grillon, C., Norcross, M. A., & Pine, D. S. (2011). Development of anxiety: The role of threat appraisal and fear learning. *Depression and Anxiety, 28*(1), 5–17. https://doi.org/10.1002/da.20733

Butler, E., Mobini, S., Rapee, R. M., Mackintosh, B., & Reynolds, S. A. (2015). Enhanced effects of combined cognitive bias modification and computerised cognitive behaviour therapy on social anxiety. *Cogent Psychology, 2*(1), 1011905. https://doi.org/10.1080/23311908.2015.1011905

Cisler, J. M., & Koster, E. H. (2010). Mechanisms of attentional biases towards threat in anxiety disorders: An integrative review. *Clinical Psychology Review, 30*(2), 203–216. https://doi.org/10.1016/j.cpr.2009.11.003

Cisler, J. M., Bacon, A. K., & Williams, N. L. (2009). Phenomenological characteristics of attentional biases towards threat: A critical review. *Cognitive Therapy and Research, 33*(2), 221–234. https://doi.org/10.1007/s10608-007-9161-y

Cooper, S. E., Grillon, C., & Lissek, S. (2018). Impaired discriminative fear conditioning during later training trials differentiates generalized anxiety disorder, but not panic disorder, from healthy control participants. *Comprehensive Psychiatry, 85*, 84–93. https://doi.org/10.1016/j.comppsych.2018.07.001

Craske, M. G., Kircanski, K., Zelikowsky, M., Mystkowski, J., Chowdhury, N., & Baker, A. (2008). Optimizing inhibitory learning during exposure therapy. *Behaviour Research and Therapy, 46*(1), 5–27. https://doi.org/10.1016/j.brat.2007.10.003

Craske, M. G., Treanor, M., Conway, C. C., Zbozinek, T., & Vervliet, B. (2014). Maximizing exposure therapy: An inhibitory learning approach. *Behaviour Research and Therapy, 58*, 10–23. https://doi.org/10.1016/j.brat.2014.04.006

Craske, M. G., Treanor, M., Zbozinek, T. D., & Vervliet, B. (2022). Optimizing exposure therapy with an inhibitory retrieval approach and the OptEx Nexus. *Behaviour Research and Therapy, 152*, 104069. https://doi.org/10.1016/j.brat.2022.104069

Cusack, K., Jonas, D. E., Forneris, C. A., Wines, C., Sonis, J., Middleton, J. C., Feltner, C., Brownley, K. A., Olmsted, K. R., Greenblatt, A., Weil, A., & Gaynes, B. N. (2016). Psychological treatments for adults with posttraumatic stress disorder: A systematic review and meta-analysis. *Clinical Psychology Review, 43*, 128–141. https://doi.org/10.1016/j.cpr.2015.10.003

De Houwer, J. D. (2011). Why the cognitive approach in psychology would profit from a functional approach and vice versa. *Perspectives on Psychological Science, 6*(2), 202–209. https://doi.org/10.1177/1745691611400238

De Houwer, J. (2019). Implicit bias is behavior: A functional-cognitive perspective on implicit bias. *Perspectives on Psychological Science, 14*(5), 835–840. https://doi.org/10.1177/1745691619855638

de Jong, P. J., Merckelbach, H., Arntz, A., & Nijmam, H. (1992). Covariation detection in treated and untreated spider phobics. *Journal of Abnormal Psychology, 101*(4), 724–727. https://doi.org/10.1037/0021-843X.101.4.724

de Jong, P. J., Merckelbach, H., & Arntz, A. (1995a). Covariation bias in phobic women: The relationship between a priori expectancy, on-line expectancy, autonomic responding, and a posteriori contingency judgment. *Journal of Abnormal Psychology, 104*(1), 55–62. https://doi.org/10.1037/0021-843X.104.1.55

de Jong, P. J., van den Hout, M. A., & Merckelbach, H. (1995b). Covariation bias and the return of fear. *Behaviour Research and Therapy, 33*(2), 211–213. https://doi.org/10.1016/0005-7967(94)e0024-d

de Jong, P. J., Merckelbach, H., Bögels, S., & Kindt, M. (1998). Illusory correlation and social anxiety. *Behaviour Research and Therapy, 36*(11), 1063–1073. https://doi.org/10.1016/S0005-7967(98)00099-0

Deacon, B., Kemp, J. J., Dixon, L. J., Sy, J. T., Farrell, N. R., & Zhang, A. R. (2013). Maximizing the efficacy of interoceptive exposure by optimizing inhibitory learning: A randomized controlled trial. *Behaviour Research and Therapy, 51*(9), 588–596. https://doi.org/10.1016/j.brat.2013.06.006

Duits, P., Cath, D. C., Lissek, S., Hox, J. J., Hamm, A. O., Engelhard, I. M., van den Hout, M. A., & Baas, J. M. (2015). Updated meta-analysis of classical fear conditioning in the anxiety disorders. *Depression and Anxiety, 32*(4), 239–253. https://doi.org/10.1002/da.22353

Duits, P., Richter, J., Baas, J. M. P., Engelhard, I. M., Limberg-Thiesen, A., Heitland, I., Hamm, A. O., & Cath, D. C. (2017). Enhancing effects of contingency instructions on fear acquisition and extinction in anxiety disorders. *Journal of Abnormal Psychology, 126*(4), 378–391. https://doi.org/10.1037/abn0000266

Dvir, M., Horovitz, O., Aderka, I. M., & Shechner, T. (2019). Fear conditioning and extinction in anxious and non-anxious youth: A meta-analysis. *Behaviour Research and Therapy, 120*, 103431. https://doi.org/10.1016/j.brat.2019.103431

El-Bar, N., Laufer, O., Yoran-Hegesh, R., & Paz, R. (2017). Over-generalization in youth with anxiety disorders. *Social Neuroscience, 12*(1), 76–85. https://doi.org/10.1080/1747091 9.2016.1167123

Forcadell, E., Torrents-Rodas, D., Vervliet, B., Leiva, D., Tortella-Feliu, M., & Fullana, M. A. (2017). Does fear extinction in the laboratory predict outcomes of exposure therapy? A treatment analog study. *International Journal of Psychophysiology, 121*, 63–71. https://doi.org/10.1016/j.ijpsycho.2017.09.001

Garpenstrand, H., Annas, P., Ekblom, J., Oreland, L., & Fredrikson, M. (2001). Human fear conditioning is related to dopaminergic and serotonergic biological markers. *Behavioral Neuroscience, 115*(2), 358–364. https://doi.org/10.1037/0735-7044.115.2.358

Gazendam, F. J., Kamphuis, J. H., & Kindt, M. (2013). Deficient safety learning characterizes high trait anxious individuals. *Biological Psychology, 92*(2), 342–352. https://doi.org/10.1016/j.biopsycho.2012.11.006

Geller, D. A., McGuire, J. F., Orr, S. P., Small, B. J., Murphy, T. K., Trainor, K., Porth, R., Wilhelm, S., & Storch, E. A. (2019). Fear extinction learning as a predictor of response to cognitive behavioral therapy for pediatric obsessive compulsive disorder. *Journal of Anxiety Disorders, 64*, 1–8. https://doi.org/10.1016/j.janxdis.2019.02.005

Ginat-Frolich, R., Klein, Z., Katz, O., & Shechner, T. (2017). A novel perceptual discrimination training task: Reducing fear overgeneralization in the context of fear learning. *Behaviour Research and Therapy, 93*, 29–37. https://doi.org/10.1016/j.brat.2017.03.010

Ginat-Frolich, R., Klein, Z., Aderka, I. M., & Shechner, T. (2019). Reducing avoidance in adults with high spider fear using perceptual discrimination training. *Depression and Anxiety, 36*(9), 859–865. https://doi.org/10.1002/da.22930

Guthrie, R. M., & Bryant, R. A. (2006). Extinction learning before trauma and subsequent posttraumatic stress. *Psychosomatic Medicine, 68*(2), 307–311. https://doi.org/10.1097/01. psy.0000208629.67653.cc

Haddad, A. D. M., Pritchett, D., Lissek, S., & Lau, J. Y. F. (2012). Trait anxiety and fear responses to safety cues: Stimulus generalization or sensitization? *Journal of Psychopathology and Behavioral Assessment, 34*(3), 323–331. https://doi.org/10.1007/s10862-012-9284-7

Haselton, M. G., Nettle, D., & Andrews, P. W. (2005). The evolution of cognitive bias. In D. M. Buss (Ed.), *The handbook of evolutionary psychology* (pp. 724–746). John Wiley & Sons, Inc..

Hermans, D., Craske, M. G., Mineka, S., & Lovibond, P. F. (2006). Extinction in human fear conditioning. *Biological Psychiatry, 60*(4), 361–368. https://doi.org/10.1016/j.biopsych.2005.10.006

Hirsch, C. R., Meeten, F., Krahé, C., & Reeder, C. (2016). Resolving ambiguity in emotional disorders: The nature and role of interpretation biases. *Annual Review of Clinical Psychology, 12*, 281–305. https://doi.org/10.1146/annurev-clinpsy-021815-093436

Jinyao, Y., Xiongzhao, Z., Auerbach, R. P., Gardiner, C. K., Lin, C., Yuping, W., & Shuqiao, Y. (2012). Insecure attachment as a predictor of depressive and anxious symptomology. *Depression and Anxiety, 29*(9), 789–796. https://doi.org/10.1002/da.21953

Kaczkurkin, A. N., Burton, P. C., Chazin, S. M., Manbeck, A. B., Espensen-Sturges, T., Cooper, S. E., Sponheim, S. R., & Lissek, S. (2017). Neural substrates of overgeneralized conditioned fear in PTSD. *The American Journal of Psychiatry, 174*(2), 125–134. https://doi.org/10.1176/appi.ajp.2016.15121549

Kessler, R. C., Berglund, P., Demler, O., Jin, R., Merikangas, K. R., & Walters, E. E. (2005). Lifetime prevalence and age-of-onset distributions of DSM-IV disorders in the national comorbidity survey replication. *Archives of General Psychiatry, 62*(6), 593–602. https://doi.org/10.1001/archpsyc.62.6.593

Lange, I., Goossens, L., Michielse, S., Bakker, J., Vervliet, B., Marcelis, M., Wichers, M., van Os, J., van Amelsvoort, T., & Schruers, K. (2020). Neural responses during extinction learning predict exposure therapy outcome in phobia: Results from a randomized-controlled trial. *Neuropsychopharmacology, 45*(3), 534–541. https://doi.org/10.1038/s41386-019-0467-8

Lau, J. Y., & Waters, A. M. (2017). Annual research review: An expanded account of information-processing mechanisms in risk for child and adolescent anxiety and depression. *Journal of Child Psychology and Psychiatry, 58*(4), 387–407. https://doi.org/10.1111/jcpp.12653

Lenaert, B., Boddez, Y., Griffith, J. W., Vervliet, B., Schruers, K., & Hermans, D. (2014). Aversive learning and generalization predict subclinical levels of anxiety: A six-month longitudinal study. *Journal of Anxiety Disorders, 28*(8), 747–753. https://doi.org/10.1016/j.janxdis.2014.09.006

Lindert, J., von Ehrenstein, O. S., Grashow, R., Gal, G., Braehler, E., & Weisskopf, M. G. (2014). Sexual and physical abuse in childhood is associated with depression and anxiety over the life course: Systematic review and meta-analysis. *International Journal of Public Health, 59*(2), 359–372. https://doi.org/10.1007/s00038-013-0519-5

Lissek, S., Pine, D. S., & Grillon, C. (2006). The strong situation: A potential impediment to studying the psychobiology and pharmacology of anxiety disorders. *Biological Psychology, 72*(3), 265–270. https://doi.org/10.1016/j.biopsycho.2005.11.004

Lissek, S., Rabin, S., Heller, R. E., Lukenbaugh, D., Geraci, M., Pine, D. S., & Grillon, C. (2010). Overgeneralization of conditioned fear as a pathogenic marker of panic disorder. *The American Journal of Psychiatry, 167*(1), 47–55. https://doi.org/10.1176/appi.ajp.2009.09030410

Lissek, S., Kaczkurkin, A. N., Rabin, S., Geraci, M., Pine, D. S., & Grillon, C. (2014). Generalized anxiety disorder is associated with overgeneralization of classically conditioned fear. *Biological Psychiatry, 75*(11), 909–915. https://doi.org/10.1016/j.biopsych.2013.07.025

Lommen, M., & Boddez, Y. (2022). Extinction learning as pretrauma vulnerability factor of posttraumatic stress: A replication study. *European Journal of Psychotraumatology, 13*(1), 2051334. https://doi.org/10.1080/20008198.2022.2051334

Lommen, M. J. J., Engelhard, I. M., & van den Hout, M. A. (2010). Neuroticism and avoidance of ambiguous stimuli: Better safe than sorry? *Personality and Individual Differences, 49*(8), 1001–1006. https://doi.org/10.1016/j.paid.2010.08.012

Lommen, M. J., Engelhard, I. M., Sijbrandij, M., van den Hout, M. A., & Hermans, D. (2013). Pre-trauma individual differences in extinction learning predict posttraumatic stress. *Behaviour Research and Therapy, 51*(2), 63–67. https://doi.org/10.1016/j.brat.2012.11.004

Lommen, M., Duta, M., Vanbrabant, K., de Jong, R., Juechems, K., & Ehlers, A. (2017). Training discrimination diminishes maladaptive avoidance of innocuous stimuli in a fear conditioning paradigm. *PLoS One, 12*(10), e0184485. https://doi.org/10.1371/journal.pone.0184485

Lonsdorf, T. B., & Kalisch, R. (2011). A review on experimental and clinical genetic associations studies on fear conditioning, extinction and cognitive-behavioral treatment. *Translational Psychiatry, 1*(9), e41. https://doi.org/10.1038/tp.2011.36

Lonsdorf, T. B., & Merz, C. J. (2017). More than just noise: Inter-individual differences in fear acquisition, extinction and return of fear in humans – Biological, experiential, temperamental factors, and methodological pitfalls. *Neuroscience and Biobehavioral Reviews, 80*, 703–728. https://doi.org/10.1016/j.neubiorev.2017.07.007

Lonsdorf, T. B., Weike, A. I., Nikamo, P., Schalling, M., Hamm, A. O., & Ohman, A. (2009). Genetic gating of human fear learning and extinction: Possible implications for gene-environment interaction in anxiety disorder. *Psychological Science, 20*(2), 198–206. https://doi.org/10.1111/j.1467-9280.2009.02280.x

Lonsdorf, T. B., Menz, M. M., Andreatta, M., Fullana, M. A., Golkar, A., Haaker, J., Heitland, I., Hermann, A., Kuhn, M., Kruse, O., Meir Drexler, S., Meulders, A., Nees, F., Pittig, A., Richter, J., Römer, S., Shiban, Y., Schmitz, A., Straube, B., et al. (2017). Don't fear 'fear conditioning': Methodological considerations for the design and analysis of studies on human fear acquisition, extinction, and return of fear. *Neuroscience and Biobehavioral Reviews, 77*, 247–285. https://doi.org/10.1016/j.neubiorev.2017.02.026

Makover, H. B., Kendall, P. C., Olino, T., Carper, M. M., Albano, A. M., Piacentini, J., Peris, T., Langley, A. K., Gonzalez, A., Ginsburg, G. S., Compton, S., Birmaher, B., Sakolsky, D., Keeton, C., & Walkup, J. (2020). Mediators of youth anxiety outcomes 3 to 12 years after treatment. *Journal of Anxiety Disorders, 70*, 102188. https://doi.org/10.1016/j.janxdis.2020.102188

Mayo-Wilson, E., Dias, S., Mavranezouli, I., Kew, K., Clark, D. M., Ades, A. E., & Pilling, S. (2014). Psychological and pharmacological interventions for social anxiety disorder in adults: A systematic review and network meta-analysis. *The Lancet Psychiatry, 1*(5), 368–376. https://doi.org/10.1016/S2215-0366(14)70329-3

McLaughlin, N. C., Strong, D., Abrantes, A., Garnaat, S., Cerny, A., O'Connell, C., Fadok, R., Spofford, C., Rasmussen, S. A., Milad, M. R., & Greenberg, B. D. (2015). Extinction retention and fear renewal in a lifetime obsessive-compulsive disorder sample. *Behavioural Brain Research, 280*, 72–77. https://doi.org/10.1016/j.bbr.2014.11.011

Mineka, S., & Zinbarg, R. (2006). A contemporary learning theory perspective on the etiology of anxiety disorders: It's not what you thought it was. *The American Psychologist, 61*(1), 10–26. https://doi.org/10.1037/0003-066X.61.1.10

Mobach, L., Rapee, R. M., & Klein, A. M. (2021). The role of distorted cognitions in mediating treatment outcome in children with social anxiety disorder: A preliminary study. *Child Psychiatry and Human Development*. https://doi.org/10.1007/s10578-021-01268-6. Advance online publication.

Morey, R. A., Haswell, C. C., Stjepanović, D., Brancu, M., Beckham, J. C., Calhoun, P. S., Dedert, E., Elbogen, E. B., Fairbank, J. A., Tupler, L. A., Van Voorhees, E. E., Wagner, H. R., Kimbrel, N. A., Kirby, A., Marx, C. E., Kilts, J. D., Moore, S. D., Naylor, J. C., Swinkels, C., et al. (2020). Neural correlates of conceptual-level fear generalization in posttraumatic stress disorder. *Neuropsychopharmacology, 45*(8), 1380–1389. https://doi.org/10.1038/s41386-020-0661-8

Orr, S. P., Lasko, N. B., Macklin, M. L., Pineles, S. L., Chang, Y., & Pitman, R. K. (2012). Predicting post-trauma stress symptoms from pre-trauma psychophysiologic reactivity, personality traits and measures of psychopathology. *Biology of Mood & Anxiety Disorders, 2*(1). https://doi.org/10.1186/2045-5380-2-8

Pauli, P., Wiedemann, G., & Montoya, P. (1998). Covariation bias in flight phobics. *Journal of Anxiety Disorders, 12*(6), 555–565. https://doi.org/10.1016/S0887-6185(98)00033-4

Pauli, P., Montoya, P., & Martz, G. E. (2001). On-line and a posteriori covariation estimates in panic-prone individuals: Effects of a high contingency of shocks following fear-irrelevant stimuli. *Cognitive Therapy and Research, 25*(1), 23–36. https://doi.org/10.1023/A:1026470514475

Pereira, A. I., Muris, P., Roberto, M. S., Marques, T., Goes, R., & Barros, L. (2018). Examining the mechanisms of therapeutic change in a cognitive-behavioral intervention for anxious children: The role of interpretation bias, perceived control, and coping strategies. *Child Psychiatry & Human Development, 49*, 73–85. https://doi.org/10.1007/s10578-017-0731-2

Pineles, S. L., Vogt, D. S., & Orr, S. P. (2009). Personality and fear responses during conditioning: Beyond extraversion. *Personality and Individual Differences, 46*(1), 48–53. https://doi.org/10.1016/J.PAID.2008.09.003

Pittig, A., Treanor, M., LeBeau, R. T., & Craske, M. G. (2018). The role of associative fear and avoidance learning in anxiety disorders: Gaps and directions for future research. *Neuroscience & Biobehavioral Reviews, 88*, 117–140. https://doi.org/10.1016/J.NEUBIOREV.2018.03.015

Pöhlchen, D., Leuchs, L., Binder, F. P., Blaskovich, B., Nantawisarakul, T., Topalidis, P., Brückl, T. M., Norrholm, S. D., Jovanovic, T., Spoormaker, V. I., Binder, E. B., Czisch, M., Erhardt, A., Grandi, N. C., Ilic-Cocic, S., Lucae, S., Sämann, P., & Tontsch, A. (2020). No robust differences in fear conditioning between patients with fear-related disorders and healthy controls. *Behaviour Research and Therapy, 129*, 103610. https://doi.org/10.1016/j.brat.2020.103610

Pompoli, A., Furukawa, T. A., Efthimiou, O., Imai, H., Tajika, A., & Salanti, G. (2018). Dismantling cognitive-behaviour therapy for panic disorder: A systematic review and component network meta-analysis. *Psychological Medicine, 48*(12), 1945–1953. https://doi.org/10.1017/S0033291717003919

Raeder, F., Merz, C. J., Margraf, J., & Zlomuzica, A. (2020). The association between fear extinction, the ability to accomplish exposure and exposure therapy outcome in specific phobia. *Scientific Reports, 10*(1), 4288. https://doi.org/10.1038/s41598-020-61004-3

Rattel, J. A., Miedl, S. F., Liedlgruber, M., Blechert, J., Seidl, E., & Wilhelm, F. H. (2020). Sensation seeking and neuroticism in fear conditioning and extinction: The role of avoidance behaviour. *Behaviour Research and Therapy, 135*, 103761. https://doi.org/10.1016/J.BRAT.2020.103761

Rescorla, R. A., & Wagner, A. R. (1972). A theory of Pavlovian conditioning: Variations on the effectiveness of reinforcement and non-reinforcement. In A. H. Black & W. F. Prokasy (Eds.), *Classical conditioning II: Current research and theory* (pp. 64–99). Appleton-Century-Crofts.

Salemink, E., & van den Hout, M. (2010). Validation of the "recognition task" used in the training of interpretation biases. *Journal of Behavior Therapy and Experimental Psychiatry, 41*, 140–144. https://doi.org/10.1016/j.jbtep.2009.11.006

Scaini, S., Belotti, R., Ogliari, A., & Battaglia, M. (2016). A comprehensive meta-analysis of cognitive-behavioral interventions for social anxiety disorder in children and adolescents. *Journal of Anxiety Disorders, 42*, 105–112. https://doi.org/10.1016/J.JANXDIS.2016.05.008

Scherer, K. R. (2021). Evidence for the existence of emotion dispositions and the effects of appraisal bias. *Emotion, 21*(6), 1224–1238. https://doi.org/10.1037/emo0000861

Scheveneels, S., Boddez, Y., & Hermans, D. (2019). Learning mechanisms in fear and anxiety. In *The Cambridge handbook of anxiety and related disorders* (pp. 13–40). Cambridge University Press. https://doi.org/10.1017/9781108140416.002

Scheveneels, S., Boddez, Y., & Hermans, D. (2021). Predicting clinical outcomes via human fear conditioning: A narrative review. *Behaviour Research and Therapy, 142*, 103870. https://doi.org/10.1016/J.BRAT.2021.103870

Schoth, D. E., & Liossi, C. (2017). A systematic review of experimental paradigms for exploring biased interpretation of ambiguous information with emotional and neutral associations. *Frontiers in Psychology, 8*, 171. https://doi.org/10.3389/fpsyg.2017.00171

Sehlmeyer, C., Dannlowski, U., Schöning, S., Kugel, H., Pyka, M., Pfleiderer, B., Zwitserlood, P., Schiffbauer, H., Heindel, W., Arolt, V., & Konrad, C. (2011). Neural correlates of trait anxiety in fear extinction. *Psychological Medicine, 41*(4), 789–798. https://doi.org/10.1017/S0033291710001248

Sep, M. S. C., Steenmeijer, A., & Kennis, M. (2019). The relation between anxious personality traits and fear generalization in healthy subjects: A systematic review and meta-analysis. *Neuroscience & Biobehavioral Reviews, 107*, 320–328. https://doi.org/10.1016/J.NEUBIOREV.2019.09.029

Sijbrandij, M., Engelhard, I. M., Lommen, M. J. J., Leer, A., & Baas, J. M. P. (2013). Impaired fear inhibition learning predicts the persistence of symptoms of posttraumatic stress disorder (PTSD). *Journal of Psychiatric Research, 47*(12), 1991–1997. https://doi.org/10.1016/J.JPSYCHIRES.2013.09.008

Spix, M., Lommen, M. J. J., & Boddez, Y. (2021). Deleting "fear" from "fear extinction": Estimating the individual extinction rate via non-aversive conditioning. *Behaviour Research and Therapy, 142*, 103869. https://doi.org/10.1016/J.BRAT.2021.103869

Steinman, S. A., & Teachman, B. A. (2014). Reaching new heights: Comparing interpretation bias modification to exposure therapy for extreme height fear. *Journal of Consulting and Clinical Psychology, 83*(3), 404–417. https://doi.org/10.1037/a0036023

Tinoco-González, D., Fullana, M. A., Torrents-Rodas, D., Bonillo, A., Vervliet, B., Blasco, M. J., Farré, M., & Torrubia, R. (2015). Conditioned fear acquisition and generalization in generalized anxiety disorder. *Behavior Therapy, 46*(5), 627–639. https://doi.org/10.1016/J.BETH.2014.12.004

Tomarken, A. J., Mineka, S., & Cook, M. (1989). Fear-relevant selective associations and covariation bias. *Journal of Abnormal Psychology, 98*(4), 381–394. https://doi.org/10.1037//0021-843x.98.4.381

Torrents-Rodas, D., Fullana, M. A., Bonillo, A., Caseras, X., Andión, O., & Torrubia, R. (2013). No effect of trait anxiety on differential fear conditioning or fear generalization. *Biological Psychology, 92*, 185–190. https://doi.org/10.1016/j.biopsycho.2012.10.006

Tzschoppe, J., Nees, F., Banaschewski, T., Barker, G. J., Büchel, C., Conrod, P. J., Garavan, H., Heinz, A., Loth, E., Mann, K., Martinot, J. L., Smolka, M. N., Gallinat, J., Ströhle, A., Struve, M., Rietschel, M., Schumann, G., & Flor, H. (2014). Aversive learning in adolescents: Modulation by amygdala-prefrontal and amygdala-hippocampal connectivity and neuroticism. *Neuropsychopharmacology, 39*(4), 875–884. https://doi.org/10.1038/npp.2013.287

Van den Bergh, O., Brosschot, J., Critchley, H., Thayer, J. F., & Ottaviani, C. (2021). Better safe than sorry: A common signature of general vulnerability for psychopathology. *Perspectives on Psychological Science, 16*(2), 225–246. https://doi.org/10.1177/1745691620950690

Van Overveld, M., De Jong, P. J., & Peters, M. L. (2010). Disgust and fear-related UCS-expectancy bias in blood-fearful individuals. *Clinical Psychology and Psychotherapy, 17*(2), 100–109. https://doi.org/10.1002/cpp.639

Vervliet, B., & Boddez, Y. (2020). Aversive stimulus pairings are an unnecessary and insufficient cause of pathological anxiety. *Biological Psychiatry, 87*(10), 870–871. https://doi.org/10.1016/j.biopsych.2020.03.006

Wannemueller, A., Moser, D., Kumsta, R., Jöhren, H. P., Adolph, D., & Margraf, J. (2018). Mechanisms, genes and treatment: Experimental fear conditioning, the serotonin transporter gene, and the outcome of a highly standardized exposure-based fear treatment. *Behaviour Research and Therapy, 107*, 117–126. https://doi.org/10.1016/J.BRAT.2018.06.003

Waters, A. M., Wharton, T. A., Zimmer-Gembeck, M. J., & Craske, M. G. (2008). Threat-based cognitive biases in anxious children: Comparison with non-anxious children before and after cognitive behavioural treatment. *Behaviour Research and Therapy, 46*(3), 358–374. https://doi.org/10.1016/J.BRAT.2008.01.002

Weisman, J. S., & Rodebaugh, T. L. (2018). Exposure therapy augmentation: A review and extension of techniques informed by an inhibitory learning approach. *Clinical Psychology Review, 59*, 41–51. https://doi.org/10.1016/J.CPR.2017.10.010

Wiedemann, G., Pauli, P., & Dengler, W. (2001). A priori expectancy bias in patients with panic disorder. *Journal of Anxiety Disorders, 15*(5), 401–412. https://doi.org/10.1016/S0887-6185(01)00072-X

Wiemer, J., & Pauli, P. (2016). Fear-relevant illusory correlations in different fears and anxiety disorders: A review of the literature. *Journal of Anxiety Disorders, 42*, 113–128. https://doi.org/10.1016/J.JANXDIS.2016.07.003

Wolitzky-Taylor, K. B., Horowitz, J. D., Powers, M. B., & Telch, M. J. (2008). Psychological approaches in the treatment of specific phobias: A meta-analysis. *Clinical Psychology Review, 28*(6), 1021–1037. https://doi.org/10.1016/j.cpr.2008.02.007

Würtz, F., Zahler, L., Blackwell, S. E., Margraf, J., Bagheri, M., & Woud, M. L. (2022). Scrambled but valid? The scrambled sentences task as a measure of interpretation biases in psychopathology: A systematic review and meta-analysis. *Clinical Psychology Review, 93*, 102133. https://doi.org/10.1016/J.CPR.2022.102133

Yap, M. B. H., Pilkington, P. D., Ryan, S. M., & Jorm, A. F. (2014). Parental factors associated with depression and anxiety in young people: A systematic review and meta-analysis. *Journal of Affective Disorders, 156*, 8–23. https://doi.org/10.1016/J.JAD.2013.11.007

Sara Scheveneels is a postdoctoral researcher at KU Leuven and an assistant professor at Open University of the Netherlands. Her research centers around the question how (learning) processes contribute to the onset and treatment of anxiety-related disorders and psychopathology.

Yannick Boddez is a postdoctoral researcher and an assistant professor at Ghent University. He uses conditioning models to optimize the understanding and treatment of psychological suffering.

Chapter 8
Interpretational Bias in Psychopathology and Psychological Well-Being: What Role Does Genetics Play?

John Vincent and Elaine Fox

Cognitive theories have placed fundamental biases in information processing at the heart of psychopathology. For example, the pioneering work of Aaron Beck and his colleagues (Beck, 1967, 1983; Beck et al., 1985; and for a recent commentary, see Woud, 2022) proposed that the way in which information is acquired and processed has a profound influence on the aetiology of depression and anxiety (for an overview of the role of interpretation biases in the aetiology of emotional psychopathology, see Chap. 12 by Woud and Hofmann). A large body of evidence subsequent to this early work led to suggestions that depressive and anxious mood states may be associated with distinct patterns of cognitive processes (Mathews & MacLeod, 1994; Williams et al., 1988), with biases in attention and the interpretation of ambiguity being considered central to anxiety while memory biases may be more pertinent in depression. While the jury is still out as to whether specific biases are linked with specific forms of psychopathology, recent studies emphasize the importance of taking a range of co-occurring biases into account as they are likely to impact on each other (Songco et al., 2020).

Interpretation bias, which is the tendency to interpret ambiguous situations as either positive or negative, is associated with both anxiety and depression (Beck & Clark, 1997), and there are some suggestions that it may play a causal role in the onset and maintenance of emotional disorders (Hirsch et al., 2016; Mathews &

J. Vincent
Institute of Psychiatry, Psychology and Neuroscience, Kings College London, London, UK
e-mail: john.p.vincent@kcl.ac.uk

E. Fox (✉)
Faculty of Health and Medical Sciences, The University of Adelaide, Adelaide, SA, Australia
e-mail: elaine.fox@adelaide.edu.au

© The Author(s), under exclusive license to Springer Nature Switzerland AG 2023   139
M. L. Woud (ed.), *Interpretational Processing Biases in Emotional Psychopathology*,
CBT: Science Into Practice, https://doi.org/10.1007/978-3-031-23650-1_8

MacLeod, 2005). Further, interpretation biases are core transdiagnostic processes associated with a range of psychopathologies (Krahé et al., 2019).

8.1 The Aetiology of Interpretational Processing Biases

Only a few studies have explored how and why interpretation biases emerge. Theoretical perspectives, such as Beck's original theory (Beck, 1967), make little mention of their heritability, suggesting that they develop chiefly as a result of early childhood adverse experiences (for a related discussion, see also Chap. 7 by Scheveneels and Boddez). However, in an update to Beck's original theory, a more comprehensive model of depression has been proposed integrating clinical, cognitive, biological, as well as evolutionary perspectives (Beck & Bredemeier, 2016). Here, the authors considered biological factors, including genetic variation and physiological stress reactivity, as well as environmental factors such as early adversity and trauma in the development of negative information processing biases, and in turn emotional disorders such as depression and anxiety.

8.2 Twin Studies

Quantitative genetic studies or twin studies represent an important first step to understanding the aetiology of intermediate phenotypes as they allow for the exploration of variance explained by genes (the heritability) as well as shared and non-shared environments. These studies compare within-pair concordance or correlations in identical (monozygotic – MZ) twins, who share 100% of their DNA, and non-identical (dizygotic – DZ) twins, who on an average share 50% of their DNA. A greater within-pair correlation in MZ twins, compared to DZ twins, indicates a genetic influence on a phenotype, while a within-pair correlation that is similar for MZ and DZ twins implicates the role of a shared environment. Twin studies also allow for the estimated effect of the non-shared environment, which refers environmental factors unique to each member of the pair and are indexed by the degree of discordance within MZ twin pairs.

In support of Beck and Bredemeier's (2016) theory, findings from quantitative genetic studies have demonstrated that several cognitive biases, including interpretational processing biases are, at least partly heritable. For example, a twin study assessing interpretation bias in children measured using both a homophone task and ambiguous scenarios task found heritability estimates of 30% for the homophone ambiguous words task, with shared environmental effects accounting for 2%, and the remaining 68% accounted for by non-shared environmental factors (Eley et al., 2008). As testament to the validity of the measures, the estimates for the ambiguous scenarios task were very similar to that of the homophone task, with a heritability estimate of 24%, shared environment estimated at 7%, and non-shared environmental effects accounting for the remaining 69%.

Another risk factor that is characterized by interpretation biases is anxiety sensitivity (Teachman, 2005; Zahler et al., 2020). Anxiety sensitivity can be reliability measured in children using The Child Anxiety Sensitivity Index (CASI; Silverman et al., 1999). In a study by Eley and colleagues (2007), using the CASI in a sample of 300 eight-year-old twin pairs, a heritability estimate of 37% was reported for anxiety sensitivity, with non-shared environmental estimates responsible for the remaining 63%, while the heritability estimate was found to be 50% with non-shared environments accounting for the remaining variance in an adult sample (Stein et al., 1999). This increase in heritability may be due to slight measurement variations between the CASI, which uses a 3-point Likert scale, and the Anxiety Sensitivity Index (Reiss et al., 1986) used for adults, which uses a 5-point Likert scale. It is possible that allowing for greater variations in the adult measures of anxiety sensitivity may have increased heritability estimates. However, evidence from other studies suggests that genetic effects on traits, including cognitive biases, do increase from childhood into adulthood as new genetic influences become active. For example, a twin study examining attributional style (the explanation to one's self regarding why an event was experienced as either positive or negative) found heritability estimates of 35% in a large sample of 15-year-olds (Lau et al., 2006). At a 2-year follow-up involving the same sample, the heritability estimate for attributional style had increased to 44% (Lau & Eley, 2008).

Quantitative genetic studies have also provided insight regarding the interplay between both genetic and cognitive factors in the aetiology of emotional psychopathology. For instance, applying a bivariate extension of the classic twin model researchers have also investigated the aetiological overlap of interpretational processing biases and depression in a sample of 8-year-old children (Eley et al., 2008). A genetic correlation of 0.65 was reported suggesting a substantial overlap regarding the genes that cause interpretation biases and those that cause symptoms of depression.

The research presented above provides support for the involvement of both genetic and environmental factors in the aetiology and development of interpretational processing biases, whilst also providing evidence for a shared genetic architecture with depression. Research of this kind is of great importance when it comes to understanding genetic and environmental influences on both psychiatric disorders as well as behavioural phenotypes. However, a significant drawback of the approach is that it does not provide any information on the specific environments or genetic variants that are involved.

8.3 Molecular Genetic Studies

To date, there have been very few molecular genetic studies, and most of them focussed on assessing attentional biases. Nevertheless, the few studies that have been conducted suggest that the same genetic variants that have been shown to moderate the effects of adversity on the development of depression and anxiety, also influence interpretational processing biases. For example, the much assessed serotonin transporter polymorphism 5-HTTLPR, originally demonstrated as moderating the effects of stressful life events and childhood maltreatment on depression in those with the short (S)-allele (Caspi et al., 2003; Pergamin-Hight et al., 2012) has also been associated with the interpretation biases for emotionally ambiguous information (Fox & Standage, 2012). This study used a verbally presented list of 56-word consisting of 28 unambiguous neutral words, 14 unambiguous threat-related words, and 14 homophones with both neutral and threat-related meaning (e.g. 'die'/'dye') (Mathews et al., 1989). It was found that those with low expression genotypes of the LPR (S/S, LG/LG, or S/LG) interpreted homophones as more threatening significantly than those with the high expression (LA/LA) of the same variant. This provides some evidence that those with the low expression form of this gene might be predisposed to developing a negative interpretational bias for emotionally ambiguous information. However, this finding has not been replicated yet and additional research is clearly needed.

However, unpublished research has assessed associations between several candidate genetic variants and interpretational processing biases in an adolescent longitudinal sample (Booth et al., 2017). This research, which assessed 28 systematically selected candidate genetic variants previously implicated to increase sensitivity to environmental effects in GxE studies of depression and anxiety, highlighted several significant associations with interpretational processing biases. To illustrate, the A-allele of rs110402 in the corticotropin-releasing hormone receptor 1 (CRHR1) gene was significantly associated with social interpretation bias over a 4-year period within the adolescent sample, with the direction of effect consistent with previous research. That is, the A-allele of rs110402, which has previously been shown to have an association with depression (Ishitobi et al., 2012), was found to be associated with an increased negative social interpretation bias as assessed using the Adolescent Interpretation and Belief Questionnaire (AIBQ; Miers et al., 2008). These findings suggest that negative social interpretation biases may explain why the effects of maltreatment appear to be greater for A-allele carriers in GxE studies of depression and anxiety (Nugent et al., 2011). While this was the first time this variant had been explored in the context of interpretation biases, a previous study investigated the role of rs110402 in the cognitive symptoms of depression (Davis et al., 2018), showing that a haplotype containing the A-allele of rs110402 was associated with, for example, difficulty with decision-making, higher rumination, and poorer learning and memory.

Previous research reported that the G-allele of rs1049353 in the Cannabinoid receptor 1 (CNR1) gene moderates the association between childhood physical abuse on anhedonic depression in a sample of young American women and an independent Australian sample (Agrawal et al., 2012). In both samples, carriers of the minor A-allele exhibited less anhedonic depression following childhood physical abuse, than those homozygous for the major G-allele. Anhedonia, which refers to the inability to experience pleasure from stimuli or activities that would normally be considered joyful, has been positively correlated with a negative interpretation bias (Pictet et al., 2016). In the CogBIAS sample, rs1049353 was also significantly

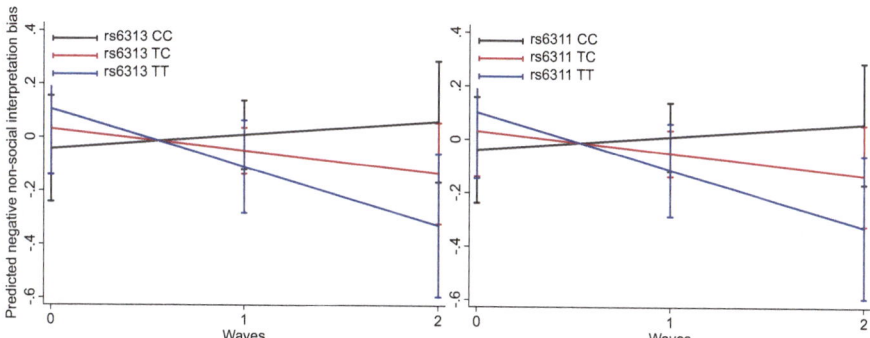

Fig. 8.1 Margin plot displaying the predicted effects for genotypes of rs6313 in HTR2A (left), and rs6311 in HTR2A (right) by time interaction over three-time points. *Note.* In both cases, three genotypic groups are represented by each of the three lines. The black lines represent GG genotypes in 6313 (left) and CC genotypes 6311 (right), the red lines represent AG genotypes in 6313 (left) and TC genotypes 6311 (right), and the blue lines represent AA genotypes in 6313 (left) and TT genotypes 6311 (right). The wave, or time points are shown on the X-axis

associated with social interpretation bias over the same 4-year period but not in the expected direction. Instead, the major G-allele of rs1049353, which has been shown to confer increased sensitivity to the environment, was associated with a more positive bias for social interpretation rather than a more negative social interpretation bias. Results also provided evidence for variant-by-time interactions on negative non-social interpretation biases with regards to variants rs6313 and rs6311, both in the 5-hydroxytryptamine receptor 2A (HTR2A) gene (see Fig. 8.1).

As illustrated in Fig. 8.1, results demonstrated that for homozygote T-allele carriers of both rs6313 and of 6311, levels of *negative* non-social interpretation bias reduced over three different time points at ages 12, 14 and 16 (Booth et al., 2017), whilst the other genotypes of the same variants showed no significant change. Also worth noting, is the near-identical effect of genotypes in rs6313 (CC, TC and TT) when compared to those in rs6311 (CC, TC and TT). This is due to both variants existing very close together on the same gene. This effect is more often described in terms of variants having high linkage disequilibrium (LD), meaning that they are highly correlated with one another. These results suggest that having a TT genotype at these respective loci has a protective effect over time by significantly reducing a negative non-social interpretation bias. Whilst these effects were somewhat unexpected, it is important to remember that they also represent the only time that this association has been assessed and therefore require replication to further validate the findings.

Previous research examining associations between various gene variants and major depression, including rs6313 and rs6311, has produced very mixed results. While it may be the case that variations in age and ethnicity between studies are the cause of contradictory findings, a hypothesis arising from our results in the CogBIAS study is that past conflicting results may be due to individual differences in latent cognitive biases within the samples. As such, more research is required to better understand the potential interplay between these variants and phenotypes.

Whilst there are very few molecular genetic studies that assess interpretational processing biases, the findings discussed above, along with those from quantitative genetic studies, serve to demonstrate the importance of such phenotypes in terms of better understanding the aetiological underpinnings of emotional psychopathology. Our results also highlight the need for more investigation into genetic effects, as well as potential GxE effects, on interpretational processing biases.

8.4   The Importance of Genome-Wide Approaches

Despite the contribution of candidate gene studies to the understanding of behavioural traits and disorders it is important to note that the approach carries several limitations (see Munafo, 2006). First, a strong biological hypothesis is required for the selection of appropriate candidate genetic variants. Second, findings from candidate gene studies have been notoriously difficult to replicate with few candidates showing the same effect across separate samples and with several meta and mega-analyses contradicting initial results. Third, recent research in psychiatric genetics has provided robust evidence suggesting that the genetic effect for complex traits and disorders is made up of thousands of genetic variants of small effect rather than individual variants of large effect (e.g. Munafo et al., 2014). This is the case for emotional psychopathologies such as depression and anxiety as well as cognitive phenotypes including interpretational processing biases.

The relatively recent introduction of genome-wide association studies (GWAS) has made it possible to assess the whole genome for associations with psychiatric disorders by assaying upwards of 500,000 variants simultaneously. As such, GWAS are able to take a hypothesis-free approach which does not require any a priori assumptions regarding the role of specific genes on a specific phenotype, which brings with it a substantial multiple-testing burden resulting in a stringent genome-wide significance threshold of $p < 5 \times 10^{-8}$ in order to protect against false positives. However, the formation of consortia and the pooling of data have made mega-analysis and meta-analysis possible, resulting in the potential to identify replicable variants associated with specific behavioural traits and disorders. For instance, GWAS have made progress in identifying specific genetic variants associated with depression (e.g. Wray et al., 2018; Howard et al., 2019) and anxiety (Purves et al., 2017). However, even the collective effects of these variants tend to explain only a minimal proportion of the heritability observed in studies using quantitative genetic methods.

8.5 Polygenic Approaches

New polygenic approaches, such as the use of polygenic risk scores (PRS), offer an exciting new approach to help in closing the gap between heritability estimates from quantitative genetic studies and those from molecular genetic studies. This approach simultaneously takes into account the effect of all genotyped variants, including those that do not reach genome-wide significance, to make a single PRS, the effect of which, on a given phenotype, is determined through linear or logistic regression which also includes a proportion of variance explained (Wray et al., 2014). It is similar to using a questionnaire in which each individual question is equivalent to each individual genetic variant. Each specific question may have little predictive value on its own, but taken together a full-scale questionnaire, or full PRS, may provide a more reliable predictor of psychopathology. Studies using such polygenic approaches have demonstrated that the aggregate effect of common variants explains considerably more of the proportion of heritability found in twin studies in comparison with GWAS (Okbay et al., 2016; Wray et al., 2018). They have also confirmed findings from previous bivariate twin studies highlighting the considerable genetic overlap between phenotypes such as depression, anxiety and subjective well-being showing correlations ranging from $r = .33$ to $r = .88$ (Okbay et al., 2016).

Furthermore, research has shown how a previously defined PRS for depression can predict variance in both depression *and* anxiety in independent samples (Demirkan et al., 2011), lending further support to a shared genetic architecture between the two psychopathologies. This relatively novel approach of using a PRS for one specific phenotype to predict variance in others has also highlighted several cross-phenotype associations. For example, a systematic review, that included 25 studies, has shown how both a major depressive disorder (MDD) and bipolar disorder (BD) PRS can predict a range of psychiatric disorders including depression, bipolar, schizophrenia, as well as other phenotypic outcomes such as creative professions and higher educational attainment (Mistry et al., 2018). Across most of the phenotypes assessed, both PRSs explained a small, but significant amount of the variance (<2%). These studies demonstrate the potential of the polygenic approach. However, thus far this approach is yet to be implemented to assess the developmental trajectory of common complex disorders such as depression and anxiety and examine possible phenotypic precursors, such as interpretational processing biases, that may represent mechanisms through which genetic risk becomes psychopathology.

There is a need for research to develop our understanding of associations between genetics, interpretational processing biases, and emotional psychopathology. There is also the need to move away from the assessment of individuals candidate genes, and instead focus on assessing these relationships using whole genome polygenic approaches. Integrating cognitive experimental research with the broad range of genetic and environmental theory provides a unique and novel insight into the development, maintenance, and potential treatment of highly prevalent and debilitating emotional psychopathology (for a related discussion about the interplay of scientific research and clinical practice, see Chap. 1 by Holmes).

8.6   The CogBIAS Hypothesis: An Integrated Model for Well-Being and Emotional Disorders

Research presented throughout this chapter has demonstrated that interpretational processing biases are heritable, with research also highlighting a shared genetic architecture between interpretation processing biases and emotional psychopathology. Additionally, traditional cognitive theory and research have suggested that in the presence of stressful or negative life events, interpretational processing biases can lead to the development, maintenance, and recurrence of psychopathologies such as depression and anxiety. This in turn suggests that cognitive biases, including interpretational processing biases, are not state dependent, meaning that a diagnosis of emotional psychopathology, or being in a depressive or anxious state, is not required to exhibit such a bias. As such, cognitive biases may indeed represent potential mechanisms mediating genetic risk for emotional psychopathology. Such biases could therefore help explain the differential interpretation, experience, and effects of environmental factors across individuals and improve our understanding of how emotional psychopathologies such as depression and anxiety develop and are maintained. It may well be that genetic risk for depression and anxiety manifests as biases in cognitive processing, which in time can lead to symptoms of psychopathology, affectively mediating the genetic risk.

The CogBIAS hypothesis (Fox & Beevers, 2016; Fox & Keers, 2019) presents a theoretical framework describing how specific genetic factors in tandem with either negative ("toxic") or positive ("enhancing") cognitive biases might together lead to the development of later psychopathology or well-being (see Fig. 8.2).

Central to the CogBIAS hypothesis is the suggestion that cognitive biases, including interpretation biases, may potentially lie on a causal pathway between the effects of genetic factors and psychopathology or well-being. In keeping with the findings of both quantitative and molecular genetic research, genetic effects on emotional psychopathology involve genetic influences that are both overlapping and distinct. Such influences include genetic variants with a direct main effect on emotional disorders or well-being, *stress-sensitivity* variants that influence an individual's sensitivity to stress, *vantage sensitivity* variants that influence an individual's sensitivity to positive environmental effects, and *differential susceptibility* variants that increase an individuals' general sensitivity in response to the effects of both positive and negative environmental effects (Belsky & Pluess, 2009; Pluess & Belsky, 2013).

The context of early environment, displayed along an axis of neutral to negative and neutral to positive, is proposed to delineate the effect of each of these variant types. Genetic variants that are said to have a direct main effect on emotional

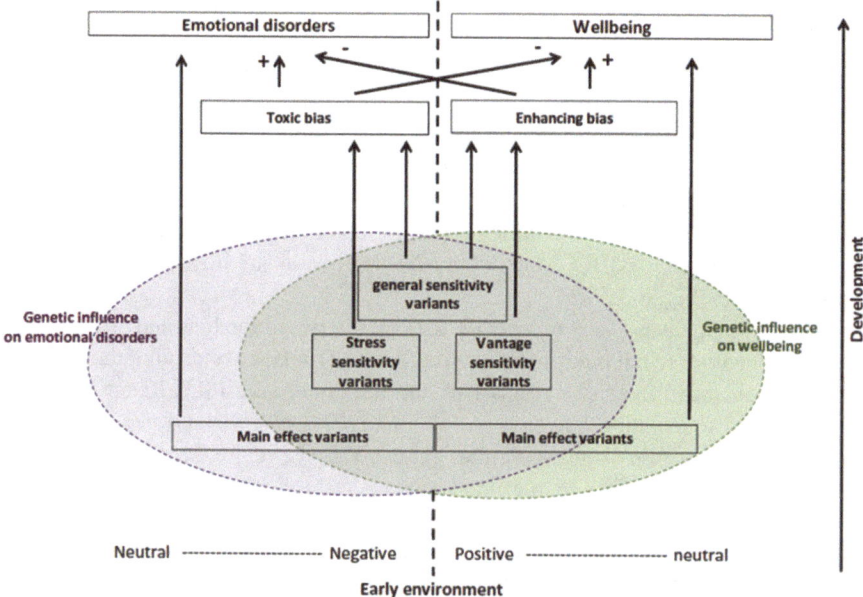

Fig. 8.2 The extended CogBIAS model. A developmental model regarding how the combination of common genetic variants and biases in cognitive processing might influence both psychological well-being and emotional psychopathology

disorders and well-being are represented through a direct pathway from genetic risk to the specific outcome being assessed. The model hypothesizes that these factors are not influenced by early environmental effects and are not mediated by cognitive biases. *Stress–sensitivity* variants, that increase sensitivity to negative environmental effects, lead to the development of negative ("toxic") cognitive biases, but only when early adverse environmental effects are present. Conversely, *vantage sensitivity* variants, that increase sensitivity to positive environmental effects, lead to the development of positive ("enhancing") cognitive biases, but only when early positive environmental effects are present. Finally, *differential susceptibility* variants that increase sensitivity to both positive and negative environmental effects may lead to either negative ("toxic") or positive ("enhancing") biases, depending on the context of the early environment (i.e. positive vs. negative). The development of negative or positive cognitive biases by the time of adolescence will therefore leave an individual more sensitive to the effects of either negative or positive environments and lead to emotional disorders or well-being, respectively.

Research aiming to empirically test specific elements of the CogBIAS hypothesis by bringing together cognitive as well as genetic and environmental theory and approaches have recently been conducted. Whilst this research is currently in preparation, we will outline some of the key findings, before discussing to what extent they support the hypothesis, some of their potential implications and what future directions may need to be taken.

The CogBIAS project is the first study of its kind designed to assess the development of cognitive biases, in conjunction with the assumptions of the CogBIAS hypothesis. A clinically defined adult PRS for major depression (Wray et al., 2018) was assessed for associations with both positive and negative cognitive biases, including interpretational processing biases, in the adolescent CogBIAS longitudinal study (CogBIAS-L-S) sample (Booth et al., 2017). Preliminary results showed that the major depression PRS was significantly associated with a negative social interpretation bias which was assessed using the Adolescent Interpretation and Belief Questionnaire (AIBQ; Miers et al., 2008). Results are illustrated in the heatmap below (see Fig. 8.3).

Interestingly, it was a lack of a positive social interpretation bias and not the presence of a negative social interpretation bias that was found to be driving the association between social interpretation biases and the depression PRS. Results showed no significant association between the major depression PRS and negative social interpretation bias, thus suggesting that genetic risk for major depression is likely associated with an inability to interpret social events as positive, and not a tendency to interpret social events as negative. Cross-sectional analysis revealed that the variance of social interpretation bias explained by the major depression PRS at age 12, 14 and 16 ranged from approximately 1–4%, which is comparable to that of previous studies of adults both within and across disorders (Cross-Disorder Group of the Psychiatric Genomics Consortium, 2013; Demirkan et al., 2011). Here, it was also found that whilst the association between the major depression PRS and positive social interpretation bias was relatively consistent at each timepoint, there was a spike in association with negative social interpretation bias at the second timepoint, which also aligned with an increase in depression symptoms. This suggests that a

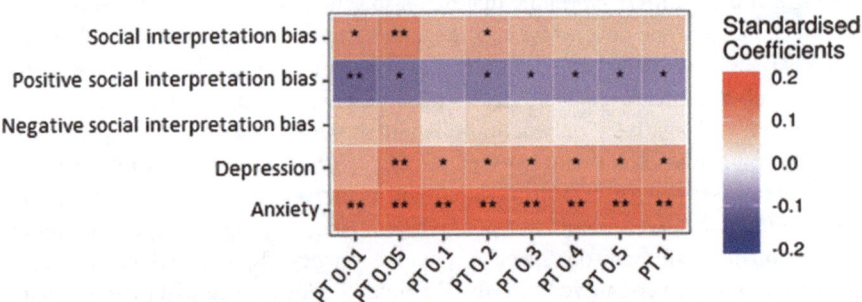

Fig. 8.3 Heatmap displaying the associations between a major depression PRS and both positive and negative social interpretational processing biases, as well as depression and anxiety measures across all three timepoints collectively within the CogBIAS longitudinal study. *Note.* The heatmap displays eight *p*-value thresholds (PT) ranging from 0.01 to 1 for social interpretational processing biases, and both positive and negative components, as well as depression and anxiety scores. The colours within the heatmap represent the direction of effect as defined by the standardised beta coefficients. A single asterisk ('*') indicates a *p*-value that was significant prior to multiple testing corrections, whilst a double asterisk ('**') indicates those significant following correction for multiple testing

negative interpretation bias may be a result of depression symptoms whilst a lack of a positive interpretation bias may be more indicative of genetic risk for depression, preceding and potentially leading to depression symptoms and a negative social interpretation. However, this finding which is yet to be published in full detail will require replication to confirm this hypothesis.

The above-summarized findings suggest that the positive components of social interpretation bias may have a stronger genetic basis whilst the negative components maybe more environmentally driven. Furthermore, associations between genetic risks for depression and the positive components were shown to drop from timepoint one to timepoint two, as associations with depression scores increased. This could suggest that the genetic effects on the positive components of social interpretation bias are somewhat dynamic, behaving in a transdiagnostic fashion and moving, in this case, from an absence of a positive bias to an increase in depressive symptoms, and in turn triggering a more negative interpretational processing bias in certain environmental circumstances. Taken together, the absence of a positive bias may be far more important to the development of both psychopathology and negative cognitive biases when compared to the presence of a negative bias. The CogBIAS hypothesis does not make the possibility of this effect clear in the current model, suggesting only that in combination with other factors, negative ("toxic") biases increase the risk of psychopathology, and positive ("enhancing") biases increase the likelihood of psychological well-being. In light of these findings, and if replicated, this would suggest that the current CogBIAS model would need to be fine-tuned to reflect positive and negative biases as not simply the opposing ends of the same scale but instead representing separate phenotypes with distinct dimensions and effects.

The same study also examined GxE interaction effects regarding the major depression PRS and both positive and negative life events on interpretation biases. It was demonstrated that having a high PRS for major depression moderated the

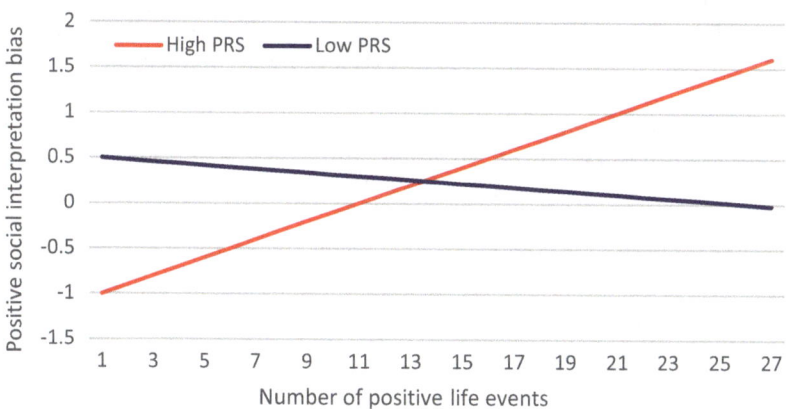

Fig. 8.4 Line graph illustrating the effects of positive life events for those with high (red line) and those with low (blue line) polygenic risk for major depression

effect of positive life events to significantly increase a positive social interpretation bias, whilst those with a low PRS showed no significant change. This finding is illustrated in the figure below (see Fig. 8.4).

Whilst the low PRS group show little change in bias score as the number of positive life events increases, those in the high PRS group show a clear increase in positive social interpretation bias as they experience more positive life events. Whilst this effect was shown to be independent of current psychopathology, all GxE effects regarding negative life events were found to be driven by existing depression and anxiety symptoms. Since these life events were self-reported as either positive or negative it is possible that those experiencing symptoms of depression, and anxiety, were perceiving and reporting life events as more negative than those without such symptoms.

This is a particularly important finding as it suggests that the association between experiencing life events as negative and the development of a negative social interpretation bias may depend on current depression and anxiety symptoms. In contrast, life events experienced as positive were shown to be independent of depression and anxiety symptoms. Furthermore, and of particular interest is that this finding is in keeping with a *vantage sensitivity* pattern of GxE interaction. This potentially suggests that those with a higher genetic risk for depression have increased sensitivity to both the absence and presence of positive life events, independent of current depression and anxiety symptoms. However, as all GxE interactions regarding negative life events were driven by the presence of depression and anxiety symptoms, there is no evidence to support a *stress-sensitivity* or *differential susceptibility* pattern of interaction regarding the major depression PRS.

The CogBIAS hypothesis also suggests that cognitive biases, including interpretational processing biases, mediate the relationship between genetic variance that increase sensitivity to environmental effects and later emotional psychopathology. Studies examining the effect of any cognitive processing biases as mediators between genetic risk and an outcome of psychopathology are few. However, research has examined anxiety sensitivity (containing elements of both attention and interpretational biases) in relation to panic/somatic ratings (Eley et al., 2007) and depression and anxiety (Zavos et al., 2012) in samples of 300 twin pairs and 1300 twins and siblings respectively. In the former study, researchers found a substantial genetic correlation between anxiety sensitivity and panic/somatic ratings, whilst in the latter study, it was noted that the relationship between depression and anxiety may be influenced by anxiety sensitivity over time. Whilst neither study had sufficient data to examine whether anxiety sensitivity mediated these relationships the authors both called for further research to examine whether the genetic risk for panic disorder (an anxiety subtype) and the relationship between depression and anxiety, might be mediated by anxiety sensitivity.

A more recent study by Navrady et al. (2018) has attempted to test mediators of polygenic risk using genome-wide data. In their study, the relationship between genetic risk for depression and both self-reported and clinical depression was found to be independently mediated by both neuroticism (43–57%) and in the opposing direction by resilience (37–40%), in a population-based cohort of 4166 individuals. However, no study to date using this approach has considered interpretational processing biases as a mediator, despite evidence from research suggesting this as a potential likelihood. In an attempt to address this gap in the literature, and test the assumption of the CogBIAS hypothesis, we assessed whether the effects of the same major depression PRS on depression and anxiety symptoms at 16 years of age were mediated by interpretational processing biases at age 14 within the same adolescent CogBIAS-L-S sample. Whilst social interpretation bias was found to mediate the relationship between genetic risk for depression and later depression symptoms, the mediation was not robust to reverse causality, as evidence for reciprocal mediation was also found. That is, earlier depression symptoms also mediated genetic risk for depression on later social interpretation bias. To disentangle this effect and to determine which develops first, it is thought that earlier measurements of both social interpretation bias and depression symptoms would have been required to assess the emergence of each, and their corresponding effect on one another. Despite this issue, however, the reciprocal relationship does suggest that social interpretation bias may be a potential driving force for the maintenance of depression and, although speculative, measurements at earlier timepoints may also highlight its involvement in the development of depression symptoms.

The CogBIAS dataset indicated that the major depression PRS had a more consistent association with anxiety symptoms than it did with depression symptoms. Whilst the PRS only became consistently associated with depression symptoms from timepoint two onwards, it showed very strong consistent associations with anxiety across all timepoints. This finding is in keeping with previous twin studies (Eley & Stevenson, 1999; Silberg et al., 2001) and molecular genetic research (Demirkan et al., 2011; Okbay et al., 2016) that found strong genetic correlations between these two psychopathologies in both children and adolescents. Furthermore, as the MDD PRS was more associated with anxiety than depression the current findings can also be seen as in keeping with the notion that anxiety may act as a precursor to depression onset (Avenevoli et al., 2001). When we examined the trajectory of phenotypes within the CogBIAS-L-S sample we found that whilst anxiety symptoms showed no increase across the three timepoints, there were a significant increase in depression symptoms from age 12 to 16 years, suggesting that anxiety onset had already peaked by age 12 (Booth et al., 2017). It is therefore likely that despite the shared genetic architectures between the two psychopathologies, the limited association between the MDD PRS and depression scores compared to anxiety scores was simply because symptoms of depression had not yet settled in.

The research findings presented above are preliminary and there is a distinct need for further research to assess the possible mediating effects of social interpretation bias in the relationship between genetic risk and psychopathologies such as depression and anxiety. It is important that any future research incorporates earlier timepoints and significantly increased sample size in order to examine the genetic effects on social interpretation bias, and depression and anxiety, as they develop through early childhood.

8.7 Implications

The preliminary analysis of the CogBIAS results demonstrated that a major depression PRS derived from GWAS studies of clinical depression was consistently associated with a lack of the positive components of social interpretation biases and drove associations with negative social interpretation biases in an adolescent sample. The positive components of cognitive biases, associated with genetic variants for major depression, and driving the development and maintenance of a negative social interpretation bias, may therefore be an important factor in the development of emotional psychopathology. Such associations between a lack of positive biases and depression may also have wider implications, potentially going some way to explaining the development of anhedonia, which is often present in, and a core symptom of depression. This has important implications for both the prevention and treatment of such disorders, as trainings to increase positive biases rather than reducing negative biases could result in far better treatment efficacy (for an overview of how to manipulate interpretation biases, see Chap. 11 by Salemink et al.). Furthermore, if it is only the positive components of cognitive biases that share their genetic architecture with affective disorders, such positive bias training may have important protective effects. For example, interpretation bias modification techniques (CBM-I) have shown that an increase in positive interpretation bias can increase levels of positive affect and reduce levels of negative affect in healthy adolescents (Lothmann et al., 2011), with similar findings also reported in healthy adults and those suffering from emotional psychopathologies (e.g. Joorman et al., 2015; LeMoult et al., 2018). Building on this, the findings presented through this chapter could suggest that such trainings could also buffer against potential genetic susceptibility for low positive bias and an increased risk of developing a more severe disorder in the future, and further highlights the importance of better understanding the potential preventative effect of cognitive trainings. Finally, given that an adult PRS for major depression was associated with the development of cognitive biases at early adolescence (e.g. 11–12 years of age), and likely during childhood, these preliminary results from the CogBIAS study (Booth et al., 2017) also highlight that this developmentally sensitive period may represent an important time period for such targeted trainings. However, there is still a need for further assessment and replication before such findings can be effectively used in intervention and treatment programs. Despite this, given such findings, and past research demonstrating associations between selective cognitive processing and emotional well-being (Mathews & MacLeod, 2005), as well as differential effects of cognitive intervention (Fox et al., 2011), there is ample evidence to suggest that such investigation represents an important area for future study.

Whilst findings presented from the CogBIAS study also demonstrated that the mediation of genetic risk for depression on later depression symptoms by social interpretation biases was not robust to reverse causality, the result was somewhat inconclusive as the developmental chronicity of these associated phenotypes remains unclear. Despite this issue, this result did highlight a reciprocal relationship between social interpretation bias and depression symptoms. This potentially implicates social interpretational processing biases as an important phenotype in terms of the maintenance and triggering of depression. Therefore, it may also represent a potential target for the treatment of depression as both bias and psychopathology were shown to drive the maintenance of one another.

8.8 Future Directions

There is still much to be done to test the assumptions proposed by the CogBIAS hypothesis (Fox & Beevers, 2016; Fox & Keers, 2019), which requires replication in an independent sample to validate and build on the findings. The use of whole genome polygenic approaches, in particular, is essential for future evaluation of genetic and GxE effects on the development of interpretational and other processing biases, and their role in the development and maintenance of emotional psychopathology. Further longitudinal research is needed, with a greater focus on the differential effects of positive and negative biases and whether they represent opposite ends of the same spectrum, or separate co-existing cognitive behavioural traits. Categories such as 'social' or 'physical' threats used in cognitive bias research are of course broad and it would be useful for future research to evaluate associations with specific items. For instance, social withdrawal items may be related to depression while social evaluation items might be more linked to anxiety. It is also important to assess interpretational and other cognitive biases well before adolescence (e.g. Stuijfzand et al., 2020) in order to evaluate genetic effects and depression and anxiety as they develop through early childhood. This would allow for the associations between biases and emotional psychopathology to be disentangled further, capturing the developmental trajectory and chronicity of both and allowing assessment of whether the genetic risk associated with psychopathology is mediated by cognitive biases.

Another factor is the presence of multiple cognitive biases – so far research has tended to assess cognitive biases in attention, memory, and interpretation separately, and it remains unclear how these biases collectively impact on the development and maintenance of emotional psychopathology. The combined cognitive bias hypothesis proposes that the collective influence of such cognitive biases may have a greater impact on the maintenance of psychopathology when compared to these biases acting in isolation (Hirsch et al., 2006; Songco et al., 2020). This interrelationship of cognitive biases may function in a simultaneous and/or successive manner influencing each other in several ways. For instance, an attentional bias during the initial encoding phase of information processing may impact on subsequent memory bias (Russo et al., 2001). Alternatively, it may be that biases function simultaneously whilst remaining independent of each other (Everaert et al., 2012; Hirsch et al., 2006). A further causal pathway expressed in the combined cognitive bias hypothesis and incorporated in the current CogBIAS hypothesis is that there may also be bidirectional or reciprocal relationships between separate biases

(Songco et al., 2020). For example, attentional biases may impact on later interpretational biases which in turn, could lead to further biases in attentional processing, and so on (for an overview of associated cognitive biases of interpretation biases, see Chap. 5 by Everaert et al.).

Assessing the combined effect of such cognitive biases would likely lead to valuable insight and more comprehensive understanding of the cognitive processes that underlie emotional psychopathologies (Everaert et al., 2012; Hertel et al., 2008; Hirsch et al., 2006; Klein et al., 2018; Songco et al., 2020). For instance, such approaches are being implemented in the CogBIAS study by creating a single 'polybias score' longitudinally and assessing genetic associations with the inclusion of various polygenic score (Booth et al., 2017; Songco et al., 2020). Approaches such as this represent an important direction for future research since a deeper understanding of the components and determinants of vulnerability to emotional psychopathology and psychological well-being need to be reached.

Demonstrating robust causal relationships between genes, information processing biases, and both emotional psychopathology and well-being remains a highly important future research direction. We have highlighted growing evidence for genetic correlations between cognitive biases and indices of mental health. Whilst this could suggest, in line with the CogBIAS hypothesis, that biases in cognitive processing lie on a causal pathway between genes and emotional psychopathology, there are also other potential explanations for such correlations. For example, it is possible that biases in cognitive processing are a consequence of emotional psychopathology. The findings discussed above lead to the possibility that this may be the case for negative biases, but not necessarily for the absence of positive biases. Both cognitive processing biases and emotional psychopathology may of course be the result of a higher-order trait such as negative affectivity. To establish whether there are causal pathways from genes to biases in cognitive processing and subsequent emotional psychopathology and well-being, large-scale longitudinal study designs with good measures of cognitive biases, psychopathology and psychological well-being measured at multiple timepoints are required. This will also require measurements at early childhood and continuing through adolescents to capture the development and chronicity of cognitive biases and psychopathology. The application of cross-lagged mediation models could then be used to assess the extent to which the genetic effects on emotional psychopathology and psychological well-being are mediated by cognitive biases, or conversely, whether the effects of genes on cognitive biases are mediated by emotional psychopathology and psychological well-being. An additional approach for establishing such causal relationships would be to assess symptoms of emotional psychopathology following the manipulation of cognitive biases using cognitive bias modification (CBM) techniques whilst taking genetic variation into account. Some research has reported the successful manipulation of cognitive biases among different single-candidate gene groups, based on the serotonin transporter, using such CBM techniques (Fox et al., 2011). However, future research needs to move beyond the candidate gene approach to use PRS approaches. If genetic factors were to explain a reduced degree of variance in both psychopathology and psychological well-being following CBM aimed at inducing a healthy pattern of biases, it would support the idea that cognitive biases play a mediating role in the relationship between genetic risk and emotional psychopathology.

8.9 Conclusion

To conclude, the CogBIAS hypothesis and the genetic correlates of interpretational processing biases provide an exciting and potentially fruitful future research agenda. It has been demonstrated throughout this chapter that interpretation biases are the result of both genetic and environmental factors, and likely play a significant role in the development and maintenance of emotional psychopathologies such as depression and anxiety. However, the limited amount of genetic and GxE research using genome-wide and polygenic approaches needs to be addressed. Furthermore, the preliminary findings and their potential implications presented above specifically highlight the need for more longitudinal research with repeat measures of multiple biases and psychopathology from early childhood onwards, as well as a greater focus on the absence and presence of both positive and negative biases respectively. Disentangling the pathways to resilience or psychopathology is an important focus for future research and will potentially provide novel targets for prevention and treatment interventions.

Acknowledgements The authors are grateful to the European Research Council who funded the CogBIAS research project by means of an Advanced Investigator Award to Elaine Fox (grant agreement number: 324176) when she was at the University of Oxford, and to the CogBIAS team who helped collect data for the longitudinal study – Charlotte Booth, Annabel Songco, Lauren Heathcote, and Sam Parsons. We would also like to acknowledge our dear friend and colleague, Rob Keers, who guided us both in the complexities of combining genetic approaches with cognitive studies and sadly passed away in 2020. His influence remains strong as we continue to analyze data from the CogBIAS project.

References

Agrawal, A., Nelson, E. C., Littlefield, A. K., Bucholz, K. K., Degenhardt, L., Henders, A. K., Madden, P. A. F., Martin, N. G., Montgomery, G. W., Pergadia, M. L., Sher, K. J., Heath, A. C., & Lynskey, M. T. (2012). Cannabinoid receptor genotype moderation of the effects of childhood physical abuse on anhedonia and depression. *Archives of General Psychiatry, 69*(7), 732–740. https://doi.org/10.1001/archgenpsychiatry.2011.2273

Avenevoli, S., Stolar, M., Li, J., Dierker, L., & Merikangas, K. R. (2001). Comorbidity of depression in children and adolescents: Models and evidence from a prospective high-risk family study. *Biological Psychiatry, 49*(12), 1071–1081. https://doi.org/10.1016/s0006-3223(01)01142-8

Beck, A. T. (1967). *Depression. Clinical, experimental and theoretical aspects.* Hoeber Medical Division, Harper & Row.

Beck, A. T. (1983). Cognitive therapy of depression: New perspectives. In P. J. Clayton & J. E. Barett (Eds.), *Treatment of depression. Old controversies and new approaches* (pp. 265–284). Raven Press.

Beck, A. T., & Bredemeier, K. (2016). A unified model of depression: Integrating clinical, cognitive, biological, and evolutionary perspectives. *Clinical Psychological Science, 4*(4), 596–619. https://doi.org/10.1177/2167702616628523

Beck, A. T., & Clark, D. A. (1997). An information processing model of anxiety: Automatic and strategic processes. *Behaviour Research and Therapy, 35*(1), 49–58. https://doi.org/10.1016/s0005-7967(96)00069-1

Beck, A. T., Emery, G., & Greenberg, R. (1985). *Anxiety disorders and phobias: A cognitive perspective*. Basic Books.

Belsky, J., & Pluess, M. (2009). Beyond diathesis stress: Differential susceptibility to environmental influences. *Psychological Bulletin, 135*(6), 885–908. https://doi.org/10.1037/a0017376

Booth, C., Songco, A., Parsons, S., Heathcote, L., Vincent, J., Keers, R., & Fox, E. (2017). The CogBIAS longitudinal study protocol: Cognitive and genetic factors influencing psychological functioning in adolescence. *BMC Psychology, 5*(1), 41. https://doi.org/10.1186/s40359-017-0210-3

Caspi, A., Sugden, K., Moffitt, T. E., Taylor, A., Craig, I. W., Harrington, H., MyClay, J., Mill, J., Martin, J., Braithwaite, A., & Poulton, R. (2003). Influence of life stress on depression: Moderation by a polymorphism in the 5-HTT gene. *Science, 301*(5631), 386–389. https://doi.org/10.1126/science.1083968

Cross-Disorder Group of the Psychiatric Genomics Consortium. (2013). Identification of risk loci with shared effects on five major psychiatric disorders: A genome-wide analysis. *The Lancet, 381*(9875), 1371–1379. https://doi.org/10.1016/s0140-6736(12)62129-1

Davis, E. G., Keller, J., Hallmayer, J., Pankow, H. R., Murphy, G. M., Gotlib, I. H., & Schatzberg, A. F. (2018). Corticotropin-releasing factor 1 receptor haplotype and cognitive features of major depression. *Translational Psychiatry, 8*(1), 5. https://doi.org/10.1038/s41398-017-0051-0

Demirkan, A., Penninx, B. W. J. H., Hek, K., Wray, N. R., Amin, N., Aulchenko, Y. S., van Dyck, R., de Geus, E. J. C., Hofman, A., Uitterlinden, A. G., Hottenga, J.-J., Nolen, W. A., Oostra, B. A., Sullivan, P. F., Willemsen, G., Zitman, F. G., Tiemeier, H., Janssens, A. C. J. W., Boomsma, D. I., et al. (2011). Genetic risk profiles for depression and anxiety in adult and elderly cohorts. *Molecular Psychiatry, 16*(7), 773–783. https://doi.org/10.1038/mp.2010.65

Eley, T. C., & Stevenson, J. (1999). Exploring the covariation between anxiety and depression symptoms: A genetic analysis of the effects of age and sex. *Journal of Child Psychology and Psychiatry, 40*(8), 1273–1282. https://doi.org/10.1111/1469-7610.00543

Eley, T. C., Gregory, A. M., Clark, D. M., & Ehlers, A. (2007). Feeling anxious: A twin study of panic/somatic ratings, anxiety sensitivity and heartbeat perception in children. *Journal of Child Psychology and Psychiatry, 48*(12), 1184–1191. https://doi.org/10.1111/j.1469-7610.2007.01838.x

Eley, T. C., Gregory, A. M., Lau, J. Y., McGuffin, P., Napolitano, M., Rijsdijk, F. V., & Clark, D. M. (2008). In the face of uncertainty: A twin study of ambiguous information, anxiety and depression in children. *Journal of Abnormal Child Psychology, 36*(1), 55–65. https://doi.org/10.1007/s10802-007-9159-7

Everaert, J., Koster, E. H., & Derakshan, N. (2012). The combined cognitive bias hypothesis in depression. *Clinical Psychology Review, 32*(5), 413–424. https://doi.org/10.1016/j.cpr.2012.04.003

Fox, E., & Beevers, C. G. (2016). Differential sensitivity to the environment: Contribution of cognitive biases and genes to psychological wellbeing. *Molecular Psychiatry, 21*(12), 1657–1662. https://doi.org/10.1038/mp.2016.114

Fox, E., & Keers, R. (2019). Bringing together cognitive and genetic approaches to the understanding of stress vulnerability and psychological wellbeing. In M. Neta & I. J. Haas (Eds.), *Emotion in the mind and body*. Springer. https://doi.org/10.1007/978-3-030-27473-3_4

Fox, E., & Standage, H. (2012). Variation on the serotonin transporter gene and bias in the interpretation of ambiguity. *Journal of Cognitive Psychology, 24*(1), 106–114. https://doi.org/10.108 0/20445911.2011.613821

Fox, E., Zougkou, K., Ridgewell, A., & Garner, K. (2011). The serotonin transporter gene alters sensitivity to attention bias modification: Evidence for a plasticity gene. *Biological Psychiatry, 70*(11), 1049–1054. https://doi.org/10.1016/j.biopsych.2011.07.004

Hertel, P. T., Brozovich, F., Joorman, J., & Gotlib, I. H. (2008). Biases in interpretation and memory in generalized social phobia. *Journal of Abnormal Psychology, 117*(2), 278–288. https://doi.org/10.1037/0021-843X.117.2.278

Hirsch, C. R., Clark, D. M., & Mathews, A. (2006). Imagery and interpretations in social phobia: Support for the combined cognitive biases hypothesis. *Behavior Therapy, 37*(3), 223–236. https://doi.org/10.1016/j.beth.2006.02.001

Hirsch, C. R., Meeten, F., Krahé, C., & Reeder, C. (2016). Resolving ambiguity in emotional disorders: The nature and role of interpretation biases. *Annual Review of Clinical Psychology, 12,* 281–305. https://doi.org/10.1146/annurev-clinpsy-021815-093436

Howard, D. M., Adams, M. J., Clarke, T.-K., Hafferty, J. D., Gibson, J., Shirali, M., Coleman, J. R. I., Hagenaars, S. P., Ward, J., Wigmore, E. M., Alloza, C., Shen, X., Barbu, M. B., Xu, E. Y., Whalley, H. C., Marioni, R. E., Porteous, D. J., Davies, G., Deary, I. J., et al. (2019). Genome-wide meta-analysis of depression identifies 102 independent variants and highlights the importance of the prefrontal brain regions. *Nature Neuroscience, 22*(3), 343–352. https://doi.org/10.1038/s41593-018-0326-7

Ishitobi, Y., Nakayama, S., Yamaguchi, K., Kanehisa, M., Higuma, H., Maruyama, Y., Ninomiya, T., Okamoto, S., Tanaka, Y., Tsuru, J., Hanada, H., Isogawa, K., & Akiyoshi, J. (2012). Association of CRHR1 and CRHR2 with major depressive disorder and panic disorder in a Japanese population. *American Journal of Medical Genetics Part B: Neuropsychiatric Genetics, 159*(4), 429–436. https://doi.org/10.1002/ajmg.b.32046

Joorman, J., Waugh, C. E., & Gotlib, I. H. (2015). Cognitive bias modification for interpretation in major depression: Effects on memory and stress reactivity. *Clinical Psychological Science, 3*(1), 126–139.

Klein, A. M., de Voogd, L., Wiers, R. W., & Salemink, E. (2018). Biases in attention and interpretation in adolescents with varying levels of anxiety and depression. *Cognition and Emotion, 32*(7), 1478–1486. https://doi.org/10.1080/02699931.2017.1304359

Krahé, C., Whyte, J., Bridge, L., Loizou, S., & Hirsch, C. R. (2019). Are different forms of repetitive negative thinking associated with interpretation bias in generalized anxiety disorder and depression? *Clinical Psychological Science, 7*(5), 969–981. https://doi.org/10.1177/2167702619851808

Lau, J. Y., & Eley, T. C. (2008). Attributional style as a risk marker of genetic effects for adolescent depressive symptoms. *Journal of Abnormal Psychology, 117*(4), 849–859. https://doi.org/10.1037/a0013943

Lau, J. Y., Rijsdijk, F., & Eley, T. C. (2006). I think, therefore I am: A twin study of attributional style in adolescents. *Journal of Child Psychology and Psychiatry, 47*(7), 696–703. https://doi.org/10.1111/j.1469-7610.2005.01532.x

LeMoult, J., Colick, N., Joorman, J., Singh, M. K., Eggleston, C., & Gotlib, I. H. (2018). Interpretation bias training in depressed adolescents: near and far-transfer effects. *Journal of Abnormal Child Psychology, 46*(1), 159–167.

Lothmann, C., Holmes, E. A., Chan, S. W., & Lau, J. Y. (2011). Cognitive bias modification training in adolescents: Effects on interpretation biases and mood. *Journal of Child Psychology and Psychiatry, 52*(1), 24–32. https://doi.org/10.1111/j.1469-7610.2010.02286.x

Mathews, A., & MacLeod, C. (1994). Cognitive approaches to emotion and emotional disorders. *Annual Review of Psychology, 45*(1), 25–50. https://doi.org/10.1146/annurev.ps.45.020194.000325

Mathews, A., & MacLeod, C. (2005). Cognitive vulnerability to emotional disorders. *Annual Review of Clinical Psychology, 1,* 167–195. https://doi.org/10.1146/annurev.clinpsy.1.102803.143916

Mathews, A., Richards, A., & Eysenck, M. (1989). Interpretation of homophones related to threat in anxiety states. *Journal of Abnormal Psychology, 98*(1), 31–34. https://doi.org/10.1037//0021-843x.98.1.31

Miers, A. C., Blöte, A. W., Bögels, S. M., & Westenberg, P. M. (2008). Interpretation bias and social anxiety in adolescents. *Journal of Anxiety Disorders, 22*(8), 1462–1471. https://doi.org/10.1016/j.janxdis.2008.02.010

Mistry, S., Harrison, J. R., Smith, D. J., Escott-Price, V., & Zammit, S. (2018). The use of polygenic risk scores to identify phenotypes associated with genetic risk of bipolar disorder and depression: A systematic review. *Journal of Affective Disorders, 234*, 148–155. https://doi.org/10.1016/j.jad.2018.02.005

Munafo, M. R. (2006). Candidate gene studies in the 21st century: Meta-analysis, mediation, moderation. *Genes, Brain & Behavior, 5*(S1), 3–8. https://doi.org/10.1111/j.1601-183X.2006.00188.x

Munafo, M. R., Zammit, S., & Flint, J. (2014). Practitioner review: A critical perspective on gene-environment interaction models. What impact should they have on clinical perceptions and practice? *Journal of Child Psychology and Psychiatry, 55*(10), 1092–1101. https://doi.org/10.1111/jcpp.12261

Navrady, L., Adams, M., Chan, S., Ritchie, S., & McIntosh, A. (2018). Genetic risk of major depressive disorder: The moderating and mediating effects of neuroticism and psychological resilience on clinical and self-reported depression. *Psychological Medicine, 48*(11), 1890–1899. https://doi.org/10.1017/S0033291717003415

Nugent, N. R., Tyrka, A. R., Carpenter, L. L., & Price, L. H. (2011). Gene–environment interactions: Early life stress and risk for depressive and anxiety disorders. *Psychopharmacology, 214*(1), 175–196. https://doi.org/10.1007/s00213-010-2151-x

Okbay, A., Baselmans, B. M., De Neve, J.-E., Turley, P., Nivard, M. G., Fontana, M. A., Meddens, S. F. W., Linnér, R. K., Rietveld, C. A., Derringer, J., Gratten, J., Lee, J. J., Liu, J. Z., de Vlaming, R., Ahluwalia, T. S., Buchwald, J., Cavadino, A., Frazier-Wood, A. C., Furlotte, N. A., et al. (2016). Genetic variants associated with subjective well-being, depressive symptoms, and neuroticism identified through genome-wide analyses. *Nature Genetics, 48*(6), 624–633. https://doi.org/10.1038/ng.3552

Pergamin-Hight, L., Bakermans-Kranenburg, M. J., van IJzendoorn, M. H., & Bar-Haim, Y. (2012). Variations in the promoter region of the serotonin transporter gene and biased attention for emotional information: A meta-analysis. *Biological Psychiatry, 71*(4), 373–379. https://doi.org/10.1016/j.biopsych.2011.10.030

Pictet, A., Jermann, F., & Ceschi, G. (2016). When less could be more: Investigating the effects of a brief internet-based imagery cognitive bias modification intervention in depression. *Behaviour Research and Therapy, 84*, 45–51. https://doi.org/10.1016/j.brat.2016.07.008

Pluess, M., & Belsky, J. (2013). Vantage sensitivity: Individual differences in response to positive experiences. *Psychological Bulletin, 139*(4), 901–916. https://doi.org/10.1037/a0030196

Purves, K. L., Coleman, J. R., Rayner, C., Hettema, J. M., Deckert, J., McIntosh, A. M., Nicodemus, K., Breen, G., & Eley, T. C. (2017). The common genetic architecture of anxiety disorders. *BioRxiv*, 203844. https://doi.org/10.1101/203844

Reiss, S., Peterson, R. A., Gursky, D. M., & McNally, R. J. (1986). Anxiety sensitivity, anxiety frequency and the prediction of fearfulness. *Behaviour Research and Therapy, 24*(1), 1–8. https://doi.org/10.1016/0005-7967(86)90143-9

Russo, R., Fox, E., Bellinger, L., & Nguyen-Van-Tam, D. P. (2001). Mood-congruent free recall bias in anxiety. *Cognition and Emotion, 15*(4), 419–433. https://doi.org/10.1080/0269993004200259

Silberg, J. L., Rutter, M., & Eaves, L. (2001). Genetic and environmental influences on the temporal association between earlier anxiety and later depression in girls. *Biological Psychiatry, 49*(12), 1040–1049. https://doi.org/10.1016/s0006-3223(01)01161-1

Silverman, W. K., Ginsburg, G. S., & Goedhart, A. W. (1999). Factor structure of the childhood anxiety sensitivity index. *Behaviour Research and Therapy, 37*(9), 903–917. https://doi.org/10.1016/s0005-7967(98)00189-2

Songco, A., Booth, C., Spiegler, O., Parsons, S., & Fox, E. (2020). Anxiety and depressive symptom trajectories in adolescence and the co-occurring development of cognitive biases: Evidence from the CogBIAS longitudinal study. *Journal of Abnormal Child Psychology, 48*(12), 1617–1633. https://doi.org/10.1007/s10802-020-00694-9

Stein, M. B., Jang, K. L., & Livesley, W. J. (1999). Heritability of anxiety sensitivity: A twin study. *American Journal of Psychiatry, 156*(2), 246–251. https://doi.org/10.1176/ajp.156.2.246

Stuijfzand, S., Stuijfzand, B., Reynolds, S., & Dodd, H. (2020). Anxiety-related attention bias in four to eight year olds: An eye-tracking study. *Behavioral Sciences, 10*(12), 194. https://doi.org/10.3390/bs10120194

Teachman, B. A. (2005). Information processing and anxiety sensitivity: Cognitive vulnerability to panic reflected in interpretation and memory biases. *Cognitive Therapy and Research, 29*(4), 479–499. https://doi.org/10.1007/s10608-005-0627-5

Williams, J. M., Watts, F. N., MacLeod, C., & Mathews, A. (1988). *Cognitive psychology and emotional disorders*. John Wiley & Sons.

Woud, M. L. (2022). Interpretational biases in emotional psychopathology. *Cognitive and Behavioral Practice, 29*(3), 520–523.

Wray, N. R., Lee, S. H., Mehta, D., Vinkhuyzen, A. A., Dudbridge, F., & Middeldorp, C. M. (2014). Research review: Polygenic methods and their application to psychiatric traits. *Journal of Child Psychology and Psychiatry, 55*(10), 1068–1087. https://doi.org/10.1111/jcpp.12295

Wray, N. R., Ripke, S., Mattheisen, M., Trzaskowski, M., Byrne, E. M., Abdellaoui, A., Adams, M. J., Agerbo, E., Air, T. M., Andlauer, T. M. F., Bacanu, S.-A., Bækvad-Hansen, M., Beekman, A. F. T., Bigdeli, T. B., Binder, E. B., Blackwood, D. R. H., Bryois, J., Buttenschøn, H. N., Bybjerg-Grauholm, J., et al. (2018). Genome-wide association analyses identify 44 risk variants and refine the genetic architecture of major depression. *Nature Genetics, 50*(5), 668–681. https://doi.org/10.1038/s41588-018-0090-3

Zahler, L., Sommer, K., Reinecke, A., Wilhelm, F. H., Margraf, J., & Woud, M. L. (2020). Cognitive vulnerability in the context of panic: Assessment of panic-related associations and interpretations in individuals with varying levels of anxiety sensitivity. *Cognitive Therapy and Research, 44*(4), 858–873. https://doi.org/10.1007/s10608-020-10103-6

Zavos, H. M., Rijsdijk, F. V., & Eley, T. C. (2012). A longitudinal, genetically informative, study of associations between anxiety sensitivity, anxiety and depression. *Behavior Genetics, 42*(4), 592–602. https://doi.org/10.1007/s10519-012-9535-0

Dr. John Vincent received his PhD in behavioural genetics from Queen Mary University of London (UK), focusing on the developmental trajectory of multiple positive and negative cognitive biases, their impact on psychopathology/well-being, and the influence of genetic and environmental factors on these relationships. He is interested and highly committed to interdisciplinary approaches to research, and the benefits that come from collaborating with researchers from other disciplines, using multiple approaches and techniques to address research questions. Dr. Vincent is currently a Research Associate at Kings College London assessing the impact of genetic and environmental factors on several developmental and neurodevelopmental disorders.

Elaine Fox is Professor of Psychology and Head of the School of Psychology at the University of Adelaide (Australia). In her research, she examines the role of cognitive-emotional processes in mental health across the lifespan. She aims to advance our understanding of individual differences in responding to stressful life events. She has received various research grants, including an ERC Advanced Investigator Award when at the University of Oxford. Professor Fox has published over 120 academic papers in peer-reviewed journals/edited volumes and two popular science books, 'Rainy Brain Sunny Brain' (2012) and 'Switchcraft: How Mental Agility Can Transform Your Life' (2022).

Chapter 9
Neural Correlates of Interpretation Processing Biases

Ya-Chun Feng and Colette R. Hirsch

Life is full of ambiguity, and people interpret ambiguous situations in different ways. A smile can be interpreted as friendliness, but it can also be interpreted as derision. The consistent tendency of generating negative interpretations, that is, negative interpretation bias, for ambiguous situations may play a role in developing and maintaining psychological dysfunction (see review Hirsch et al., 2016). Therefore, it is important to understand how people interpret situations, and whether there are consistent interpretation biases that are associated with emotional symptoms. Negative interpretation biases are associated with higher levels of anxiety, worry, and depression (e.g., Anderson et al., 2012; Krahé et al., 2019; Everaert et al., 2017). Studies also showed the causal roles between interpretation biases and emotional symptoms (anxiety: Grey & Mathews, 2000; Mathews & Mackintosh, 2000; Beard & Amir, 2008; worry: Feng et al., 2020; Hirsch et al., 2018, 2020, 2021; depression: Lang et al., 2012).

The field investigating interpretation biases has been established via the use of behavioral measures. Traditionally, interpretation biases are assessed by methods requiring ranking or rating potential interpretations, self-generation of interpretations, or reaction times to categorize target words in keeping with positive or negative interpretations, respectively (for an overview of measures to assess interpretation biases, see Chap. 3 by Würtz and Sanchez-Lopez). These measures provide rich information on how people process ambiguity when it is first encountered, that is, online interpretations, or when they have time to reflect on the presented material,

Y.-C. Feng
Institute of Education, National Sun Yat-sen University, Kaohsiung City, Taiwan
e-mail: ycfeng@g-mail.nsysu.edu.tw

C. R. Hirsch (✉)
Institute of Psychiatry, Psychology & Neuroscience, King's College London, London, UK
e-mail: colette.hirsch@kcl.ac.uk

© The Author(s), under exclusive license to Springer Nature Switzerland AG 2023
M. L. Woud (ed.), *Interpretational Processing Biases in Emotional Psychopathology*,
CBT: Science Into Practice, https://doi.org/10.1007/978-3-031-23650-1_9

that is, offline interpretations. However, studies have rarely focused on the underlying neural mechanisms of interpretation processing biases. Behavioral responses (e.g., reaction times, rating) to target words in keeping with positive or negative interpretations may not be the most immediate and direct indices for online interpretations. Multiple cognitive processes can be involved in such behavioral indices, for example, selecting a response and executing a button press. In contrast, neural indices may reflect more specific cognitive processes, thereby index interpretation biases more directly and can detect the very early interpretation biases that occur before a behavioral response is actually executed. Hence, understanding the underlying neural mechanisms of interpretation processing when assessing interpretations by behavioral measures will help us understand the psychopathology of emotional disorders more fully, and may guide treatment to target specific interpretation processes. Therefore, there is a need to explore what neural activities are responsible for specific interpretation processes when assessing interpretations, and how the neural system functions during interpretation assessments. Establishing a neural index for interpretation biases will help identify whether interpretation biases are neural-evident in the target populations, and whether interventions also change interpretation biases at a neurological level. These findings will enable us to understand the fundamental interpretation mechanisms of psychological disorders and the key mechanisms of change during treatment.

In order to identify interpretation biases, the neural index needs to identify the time-specific moment when interpretations are generated, be specific to the interpretation-related processing, and be capable of differentiating potential interpretations. Two neural measures may meet these requirements. Functional magnetic resonance imaging (fMRI) is one and is widely used to detect changes in blood oxygenation and flow that occur in response to neural activities at different brain regions. If a specific brain region is more active, it consumes more oxygen and needs higher blood flow. This blood-oxygen-level dependent (BOLD) signal can help identify what brain regions are activated during given events (e.g., perceiving stimuli and making decision). However, the BOLD response takes several seconds in total after the onset of a brief neural activation (Glover, 2011). This is slower than the actual interpretation processes that researchers would want to assess, since interpretations are likely to occur within milliseconds or less after encountering ambiguous information. The few seconds required for BOLD may also involve multiple cognitive processes. Therefore, it is not possible to be time-specific to the moment of interpretation processing using BOLD. As a consequence, it may be difficult to develop methods to identify online interpretation biases using fMRI.

Another option is electroencephalography (EEG), a neurophysiological measure that may be a suitable marker to assess interpretation processing and related cognitive processes. EEG is a way of recording the electrical activity from the neurons in the brain. For example, the real-time neural activities when reading or listening to lingual information can be recorded continually on a millisecond basis. The neural activities when individuals read a specific word can be isolated to explore cognitive processes (e.g., comprehension) at a specific time point (e.g., between 100 and 200 ms). Indeed, isolated neural activities that are based on a given stimulus or event have consistently been shown to be associated with specific sensory, cognitive, or motor activities, and are called *event-related potential* (ERP). In order to understand how people process information (e.g., extract meaning and interpret information), linguistic research uses ERPs to reveal the real-time comprehension of written and spoken language. For example, by comparing established ERPs elicited during reading different words, different levels of comprehension when reading the different words can be examined. These established language-related ERPs could help explore the fundamental mechanisms of interpretation biases in relation to emotional disorders. In the interpretation assessment, people could read or listen to, for example, ambiguous scenarios, followed by a target word that is congruent with either a positive or negative interpretation of the scenario. The established language-related ERPs can then detect whether or not the target words are congruent with the interpretations the individuals generated when reading or listening to the scenarios. In this case, EEG meets the requirements of detecting interpretations at a specific time frame, specified to the investigated cognitive process, and distinguishing reactions to different interpretations as a neural marker for interpretation biases. Moreover, EEG can capture the dynamics of neural responses to the given stimuli, which could be the process researchers are most interested in (e.g., the immediate reaction to the presented interpretations). EEG also reflects the information processing at the moment when encountering information, so EEG recordings are not affected by demand effects or response biases or in fact any process that occurs prior to executing a behavioral response (e.g., button press or self-reported responses). Therefore, EEG combined with behavioral tasks can provide further evidence of the direct interpretation processing (see Fig. 9.1 for the EEG cap and experiment setting example).

Fig. 9.1 A participant wearing an EEG cap and electrodes in front of a monitor

In this chapter, we aim for elucidating how ERPs can contribute to our understanding of interpretation processing. We hope to (1) provide a brief review of the language-related ERP components that can be used to investigate interpretation biases in psychopathology, and (2) illustrate the current examples of how ERPs have been applied in psychopathology research. We will also discuss (3) relevant methodological and technical issues when assessing interpretation processing using ERPs.

9.1 Language-Related ERPs

In the language-related research field, one of the ERPs – N400 – has been investigated in numerous studies and is particularly useful when investigating how language is processed. The N400 is a negative shift waveform that peaks around 400 ms after presenting language stimuli (e.g., words). It can reflect the level of associations between words, for example, when using word pairs. If the presented words are associated, that is, the words presented second are expected to follow the words presented first, a smaller N400 amplitude will be elicited. However, if the words are not associated with each other, there will be a greater N400 amplitude, indicating the words presented second are not expected to appear in that specific context. In a priming task, where one word is presented first, the prime, which is then followed by a target word, increased N400 amplitudes were found for unrelated (e.g., doctor – chair) compared to related word pairs (e.g., doctor – nurse) (Holcomb, 1993). This indicates that the N400 indexes the expectancy of the presented information. This N400 semantic priming effect (i.e., different amplitudes between related and unrelated target words to the prime) is observed because the prime has already activated some of the target's features (e.g., meaning, category), which, in turn, makes the target more predictable (Kutas & Federmeier, 2009). Priming effects have been used to explore the semantic network differences between clinical and non-clinical samples. Reduced N400 priming effects (i.e., less differences between related and unrelated word pairs) were found in patients suffering from schizophrenia compared to healthy controls (Sharma et al., 2017). This finding may indicate that the N400 could be a potential marker of differential functional connectivity in semantic networks, which may be a disease-specific process in schizophrenia and could be a potential marker of the psychopathological mechanisms in schizophrenia.

Besides word pairs, the N400 is also used to investigate lingual processing with more context. When more context is provided, such as background information, sentences, or pictures prior to presenting the target word, the N400 can reflect whether the target word is congruent or incongruent with the former semantic context. If a target word is harder to be integrated into the preceding context or out of expectation, then a greater N400 amplitude is evident than if a target word matches the context or expectation (Kutas & Hillyard, 1980; Van Berkum et al., 1999). By comparing critical target words in sentences, studies have shown reduced N400 amplitude to these critical words when the words' meanings were consistent with the preceding context (e.g., Sitnikova et al., 2002; Thornhill & Van Petten, 2012). For example, the sentence "He was afraid that doing drugs would damage his ..." can be completed best with the word "brain" (i.e., best completion word), or the word "mind" that is a synonym of the best completion word, or the unrelated word "reputation" (Thornhill & Van Petten, 2012). The word that completes the sentence best usually has a high cloze probability, which means a high proportion of people completing the sentence with this word. Results of Thornhill and Van Petten (2012) showed that the synonyms elicited a smaller N400 amplitude than the best completion words. This can be attributed to the lower predictability of the synonyms. Despite having equal cloze probability with the unrelated words, synonyms still elicited a smaller N400 amplitude than the unrelated words, indicating synonyms are easier to integrate into the preceding context. This shows that cloze probability is one important factor that influences the N400. The higher the semantic similarity of the words to the best completion words, the smaller the amplitudes of the N400.

The sensitivity of the N400 to the congruity of semantic meaning has been applied to other research fields. Stereotypes were detected by a word priming task, where a gender-stereotype prime word (men or women) was followed by a gender-stereotype target word (e.g., caring, aggressive, secretary, or engineer) (White et al., 2009). As expected, the enhanced N400 amplitude was found in the gender-stereotype incongruent word pairs (e.g., women – engineer) compared to gender-stereotype congruent word pairs (e.g., men – aggressive). This showed that stereotype incongruent words were less expected. The N400 index was also used to detect responses to social rejection (Zayas et al., 2009). When romantic contexts were presented, for example, "If I need help from my partner, my partner will be...," rejection-related words (e.g., dismissing) elicited greater N400 amplitudes than acceptance-related words (e.g., supporting), which means rejection-related words were less expected among these participants. This result was found especially in individuals with higher levels of anxiety and lower levels of avoidant attachment. This indicated that individual differences in anxiety and attachment style were associated with early-stage neurophysiological responses to social rejection indexed by the N400. Together, the results show that unexpected outcomes yield greater N400 than expected ones. The predictability of these outcomes is based on participants' world or factual knowledge, and personal semantic memories based on experiences (Kutas & Federmeier, 2000). Given that the individual semantic memory varies from person to person, it also varies how a given word integrates into the preceding context, that is, based on whether or not the association between the context and the given word has already existed in the individual's semantic memory. Therefore, the N400 may index how people interpret the presented stimuli (e.g., situations) by reflecting on whether or not the interpretations were already existing in their semantic memory and therefore match their expectations.

It should be noted that while the N400 has been the main ERP component investigated in the context of semantic integration, another ERP component – P600 – has also been used to indicate semantic integration, in fact in a similar way to the N400. However, the P600 is more sensitive to language-based characteristics like linguistic structures and semantic anomaly, and it reflects effortful syntactic processing

(Hoeks et al., 2004; Brouwer et al., 2012; Swaab et al., 2012) that the N400 is less sensitive to. For example, although the target word "plant" yielded a greater N400 amplitude than the target word "eat" in the sentence "Every morning at breakfast the boys would *plant/eat…*," the target word "eat" in another semantically violated sentence "Every morning at breakfast the eggs would *eat*" did not elicit a greater N400 but a greater P600 (Kuperberg et al., 2003). This indicates that the later P600 captures the plausibility of the target words ("eggs would *eat*" is less plausible than "boys would *plant/eat*") that do not activate the earlier N400 effect in time (Kutas & Federmeier, 2011; Kuperberg et al., 2003). Given that the N400 is sensitive to the predictability of words; plus, neither violations in linguistic structure nor plausibility are relevant when assessing interpretation biases, we focus on the N400 in the later section when discussing interpretation biases and ERPs.

9.2 Applying ERPs to Understand Interpretations in Relation to Psychopathology

The N400 can be used to investigate interpretations in conjunction with behavioral measures that target online interpretation biases. Online interpretation biases are best assessed by reaction time tasks that present ambiguous scenarios and then require participants to respond as soon as possible to a final target word resolving the scenario's ambiguity. One frequently used paradigm in this context is lexical decision tasks (e.g., Hirsch & Mathews, 1997, 2000), where participants indicate whether a letter string (i.e., the target) is a real word or non-word. The original task was adapted in the context of emotional psychopathology with shorter sentences as ambiguous scenarios (e.g., Feng et al., 2019). For example, the ambiguity of the sentence "Your new job has changed your life for the…" can be resolved by the final target word "better" or "worse," which corresponds to a benign or negative interpretation, respectively, or by a non-word (e.g., "kdjlsnw"). Participants need to indicate as quickly as possible whether the final targets are real words. A faster reaction time to existing target words designed to match a given interpretation can then be taken as an index that the participant indeed generated that interpretation. This is because the ambiguous scenario is supposed to activate a certain concept (or interpretation) in participants' mind and then, when presenting a target representing that concept, participants should be quick to respond to it, given the activated semantic match between the generated and presented interpretation (i.e., the target). In contrast, a slower reaction time suggests that there is no sematic match between participants' generated and experimentally presented interpretation. Therefore, during lexical decision tasks, the assessed reaction times are indicative of the overall sematic match between the presented target words (i.e., the presented interpretation) and participants' self-generated interpretations following the ambiguous scenarios. Similar to the rationale of using reaction time as an interpretation index, the N400 amplitude also reflects whether the presented target word matches participants' interpretation of the ambiguous scenario: If the presented target fits with the concept which participants generated in response to the ambiguous scenario, then there will be no conflict between the target word and participants' interpretation, thus yielding a smaller N400 amplitude. However, if the presented target word violates participants' interpretation, a greater N400 amplitude will be elicited. Therefore, the N400 amplitude in response to the presented target words in online interpretation measures can serve as an index of participants' interpretational styles, by signaling whether or not the target words resolve the scenarios' ambiguity in a manner that semantically matches individuals' expectations (i.e., their interpretations).

Combining online interpretation measures such as lexical decision tasks while simultaneously assessing the N400 is helpful in terms of understanding whether interpretation biases occur at a very early processing stage, that is, when people encounter ambiguity, and whether the N400 can be considered as a neural basis for interpretation biases. Studies have used different online interpretation assessments with the N400, in clinical and sub-clinical populations, to explore whether this very early interpretation bias, captured by the N400, is indeed associated with psychopathological symptoms or psychological dysfunction.

Moser and colleagues (2008, 2012), for example, investigated online interpretations using the N400 in individuals with emotional disorders (2012) and sub-clinical groups (2008). They used a grammar decision task during which participants listened to incomplete, ambiguous sentences that described social situations, for example, "As you give a speech, you see a person in the crowd, smiling, which means that your speech is…" The sentences' ambiguity could be resolved in a negative, for example, "stupid," or positive manner, for example, "funny," represented by a final target word presented on the screen. Non-grammatical endings, for example, "You've just started reading a new book that you bought, and you find it to be… *bore*," were also included. Participants were instructed to decide whether or not the final target word was a grammatically correct ending of the ambiguous sentence. The N400 elicited by the target was then supposed to reveal whether the target (i.e., the presented interpretation) matched participants' interpretations. Results demonstrated that the healthy comparison group showed a benign interpretation bias (Moser et al., 2012), evidenced by greater N400 amplitudes for target words representing negative interpretations than target words representing benign interpretations. In contrast, individuals with emotional disorders showed the reverse pattern: Their N400 amplitudes were greater for benign than for negative target words, pointing to both a more negative and a lack of a benign interpretation bias. Behavioral results were consistent with the N400 results in that the healthy comparison group reacted faster and made the grammatical decisions more accurately in response to benign than negative target words, compared to the clinically anxious populations.

Moser et al. (2008), however, did not find the interpretation bias effect on either the N400 or the reaction time indices across both sub-clinical socially anxious participants and low socially anxious participants. Instead, a later P600 effect was found in the low social anxiety group such that the P600 was larger for negative than benign target words, indicating a positive interpretation bias, while such an effect was absent in the high social anxiety group. The difference in results between the two studies may be due to the differences in the studied population – clinical samples were used in the 2012 study and a non-clinical sample was used in the 2008 study, rendering it likely that the used materials were more relevant to the clinical populations (i.e., Moser et al., 2012). Further, in the 2012 but not in the 2008 study, symptom questionnaires were applied prior to the biases' assessment. This could have served as an emotional trigger, activating the concepts of interest (i.e., interpretation biases). To summarize, the 2012 set-up may have enhanced the chances to find the expected biases indexed by the early N400 amplitudes, that is, clinical populations were used for whom the material was more salient, in combination with a procedure that could have been a bias activation in the first place. Given that the materials were the same in the two studies, it is less likely that the differences in results were due to the linguistic characteristics of the materials.

The N400, in conjunction with online interpretation biases measures, was also used to explore the early and automatic interpretations in individuals with posttraumatic stress disorder (PTSD, Kimble et al., 2012). In a sentence reading task, ambiguous sentences (e.g., "The field was littered with ….") were presented word by word. The sentences' final words were either congruent with benign (e.g., "trash") or negative interpretations (e.g., "bodies"), or were unrelated words (e.g., "traffic"). Generally, all final words made sense, grammatically and syntactically; however, the unrelated final words were always semantically incorrect. Throughout the task, participants were instructed to decide whether the sentences made sense by pressing buttons. Results showed that individuals with PTSD accepted negative final words more often than individuals who experienced a traumatic incident but did not meet the criteria for PTSD. This indicated that individuals with PTSD had a negative interpretation bias. This negative interpretation bias was also evident in direct neural activities where smaller N400 amplitudes were found for negative words in the PTSD compared to the non-PTSD group. These results replicate findings from other areas of emotional psychopathology and also show that patients suffering from PTSD may have automatically expected negative outcomes when being confronted with trauma-relevant, ambiguous scenarios.

More recently, Feng et al. (2019) examined the N400 index in online interpretation bias tasks to investigate online interpretation biases in relation to worry. Two tasks were used to examine whether the N400 can capture interpretation biases in these tasks. One of the tasks, the lexical decision task, described earlier in this chapter, presented ambiguous sentences that were resolved by a final word, which was presented as a lexical decision (i.e., word or non-word). Another task, the sentence word association task (adapted from Beard & Amir, 2009), presented sentence fragments, for example, "Your friend opens your gift. You can tell how he feels by his face," and required participants to decide whether or not a word, for example, "happy" or "disappointed," was related to the preceding sentence. Across both tasks, all sentences were ambiguous and related to topics of worry, and the target words were the interpretations of those ambiguous scenarios. Before both tasks were administered, worry was activated via a worry induction. The reaction time findings across the two tasks showed that low worriers reacted faster to benign than negative interpretations on the lexical decision task, and they were faster to endorse benign than negative interpretations in the sentence word association task. Low worriers also endorsed more benign than negative interpretations in the sentence word association task. The evidence of benign interpretation biases in low worriers was also found using an ERP index, showing greater N400 amplitudes for negative than benign interpretations, while such a benign interpretation bias was lacking in high worriers (Fig. 9.2). However, the effect on the N400 amplitude was only found for the lexical decision task, not the sentence word association task. This may be explained by the fact that the target words (i.e., the interpretations) were not part of the sentences in the latter task but presented separately, so both the negative and the positive target words were harder to be integrated into the preceding context, thus yielding similar N400 amplitudes here.

A later study (Feng et al., 2022) also used the sentence word association task with EEG to investigate interpretation biases, this time in relation to social anxiety.

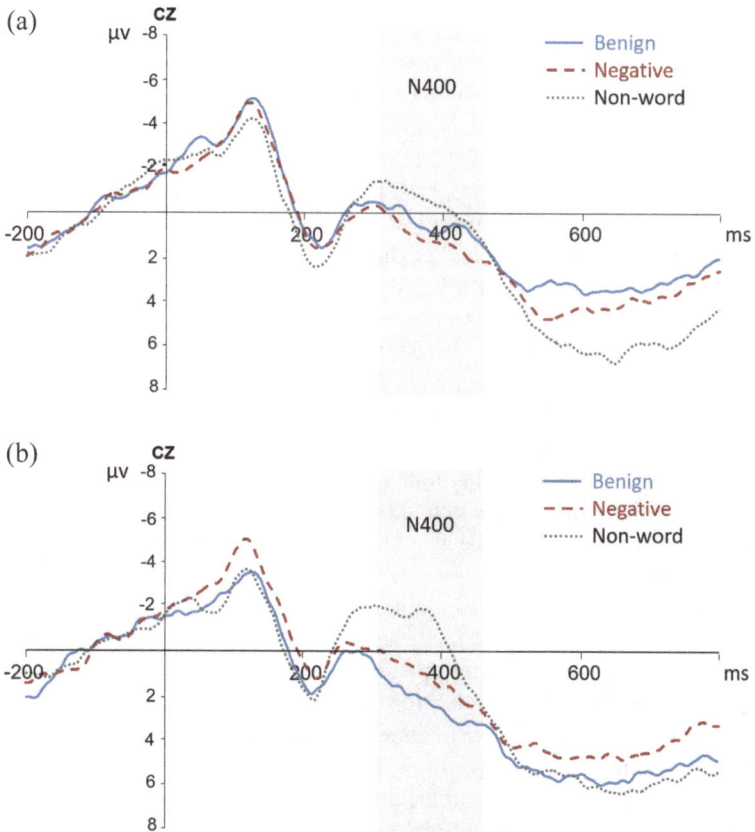

Fig. 9.2 *N400 amplitudes during lexical decision task. Note.* N400 at Cz electrode time-locked to the benign (blue), negative (red dash) target words, and non-words (grey dot) in the lexical decision task from the high worry group (**a**) and the low worry group (**b**). (The figures were redrawn from Feng et al. (2019). Negative voltage plotted up)

Ambiguous social-related or social-unrelated sentences were presented, prior to negative or benign target words. Again, participants were instructed to indicate whether the sentence and target word were related or not. Greater N400 amplitudes for benign target words following ambiguous social-related sentences were found in the high social anxiety group, compared to the low social anxiety group, indicating that socially anxious individuals had a weaker benign interpretation bias than non-socially anxious individuals. This is consistent with the behavioral results on trials including social-related sentences, such that the high social anxiety group endorsed fewer benign target words than the low social anxiety group. However, there were no group differences in N400 amplitudes for negative target words, neither for the social-related nor social-unrelated trials. In contrast to the null findings on the N400 amplitude in the previous study (Feng et al., 2019) using the same sentence word association task, the significant N400 result in Feng et al. (2022) may be due to population differences. Individuals with social anxiety may have more focal concerns than people who worry, since worriers worry about a range of different topics. Therefore, the social-related scenarios included in the Feng et al. (2022) study may have been more salient to socially anxious individuals, compared to the heterogonous worry-related scenarios included in the Feng et al. (2019) study. This, in turn, could explain why the expectancy effects, represented by the N400 amplitudes, could be shown in the context of social anxiety but not in worry.

Given the finding that worries lack a benign interpretation bias (Feng et al., 2019), Feng et al. (2020) investigated whether interpretation biases, indexed by the N400, can be modified by using cognitive bias modification for interpretation (CBM-I). During a single session CBM-I training, the generation of benign interpretations in relation to ambiguous scenarios was trained, and it was investigated to what extent such training would transfer to online interpretation processes, indexed via reaction times and N400 amplitudes (both assessed via a lexical decision task). Although positive interpretations increased and levels of worry reduced pre-post CBM-I training, no differences in N400 amplitudes were found. This may be due to a single session of CBM-I training not being sufficient to change the semantic neural network. Hence, future research should investigate whether a longer training including more sessions would be able to do so, that is, change biases at a very early stage of interpretation processing such as captured by the N400. It may be also worth exploring whether CBM-I training in combination with other treatments (e.g., cognitive behavior therapy, medication) is a more powerful combination when aiming at changing immediate interpretations as indexed by the N400, since such change may be an important marker for more sustained changes in symptoms and/ or changes associated with better treatment outcomes.

The studies summarized above show the potential of assessing neural correlates, especially the N400, to understand the underlying processes involved in interpretation processing biases in clinical and subclinical populations, and provide good examples of combining behavioral measures with ERP measures. In addition, these studies show that the N400 emerged in different populations and in different online interpretation tasks, in which scenarios were presented visually and verbally, with different response requirements per task. Further, the N400 index may have the potential to become a marker of change, that is, a marker for change in interpretation biases following an intervention. However, this and many other exciting follow-up issues now need to be addressed in future (clinical) research.

9.3 Methodological Issues

Developing adequate materials for both behavioral and neural interpretation bias measures is one of the most important elements when investigating interpretation biases. This section will discuss the essential issues in developing such materials, including the following issues: levels of constraint and cloze probability, content specificity and relevance, and self-reference. During these sections, difficulties and limitations relevant to material development as well as issues relevant to EEG testing will be discussed. We will also provide brief guidelines for developing materials for EEG studies.

9.3.1 Issues in Developing Materials for Assessing Online Interpretation Biases

9.3.1.1 Levels of Constraint and Cloze Probability

Two critical issues when developing materials for online interpretation tasks that include an EEG or behavioral assessment are the levels of constraint of the ambiguous scenarios and the cloze probability of target words - both influence whether interpretation biases can be assessed accurately and the N400 effect can be detected. Constraint of the ambiguous scenarios refers to the consistency of people generating the same completion for the same scenario. For example, a high-constraint sentence "On his vacation, he got some much needed…" can be completed with a very limited number of words, for example, "rest," which is the word the majority of people would use to complete the sentence. In contrast, a low-constraint sentence, for example, "Everyone on the scene gathered around to look at the…" activates a broad range of concepts and words, and people will provide a wide range of completions (e.g., "accident," "crash," "celebrity") for this sentence (examples are from Thornhill & Van Petten, 2012). Cloze probability is the proportion of people who provide a particular word to complete the sentence. It is one of the most important factors influencing N400 amplitudes (Kutas & Federmeier, 2009, Kutas & Hillyard, 1984). If the cloze probability of the most expected word is high, then the sentence is highly constrained.

The range of concepts that the scenarios can activate is important when generating materials for online interpretation tasks. Online interpretations can be indexed by behavioral responses such as reaction times and the N400 index; both signaling whether the presented target words resolve the ambiguity in line with participants' interpretation. During interpretation tasks, participants encounter ambiguity and generate their own interpretations to that ambiguity. If the target words are in line with participants' interpretation, participants will respond faster and/or have smaller N400 amplitudes. If the target words, however, do not match participants' interpretations, participants will react slower and/or have greater N400 amplitudes. By comparing both the behavioral responses and N400 amplitudes to positive and negative target words, we can determine whether participants have generated positive or negative interpretations, so the target words in combination with the respective ambiguous scenario are of crucial importance.

Relatedly, if the materials (i.e., the ambiguous scenarios) are not specific enough, a wide range of positive (or negative) concepts may be activated when different participants encounter the materials. In this case, the activated concepts may not be congruent with the target words, even if the concepts and the target words are either positive or negative, thereby failing interpretation biases to be detected due to the constraint of materials rather than the absence of a bias. For example, an ambiguous sentence: "Your father is losing his hair recently, you think that it is due to his ..." can be completed with, for example, the target words "illness" or "age." There are, however, various reasons for losing hair. If participants have a negative interpretation bias and automatically generate the concept "stress," they will expect to see "stress" and will be slow when they see the word "illness." As a consequence, a negative interpretation bias cannot be shown. This indicates a slower reaction time or greater N400 would be found even if the participant's interpretation was of the same valence (e.g., benign or negative) as the one matching the target. As a result, an existing interpretation bias cannot be detected, neither by reaction time nor N400 indices – only if the materials are very specific and only activate a narrow range of concepts, both indices are able to reflect interpretation biases.

A further issue is that, if the constraint of a sentence is very high, everyone will generate the same concept, implying that there will be only one high cloze probability word for the given scenario. For example, most of the people generated "expensive" to complete the sentence "Your friend suggests going to a restaurant you haven't been to before. Looking at the prices on the menu, you realise the dishes are quite ..." In this case, there is no room to generate both positive and negative interpretations, such very high-constraint scenarios should not be used when assessing interpretation biases. Accordingly, it is necessary to develop scenarios that allow for both positive and negative solutions, and both solutions should have similar probabilities to be generated. In addition, scenarios should include a narrow range of concepts (high-constraint sentence) related to the scenarios' ambiguity, such that participants generate either positive or negative interpretations of the same concept. People who generate a positive/negative interpretation should think of the same positive/negative word to complete the sentence, so the positive and negative words have similar cloze probability. For example, the ambiguous scenario "You overhear someone saying that a child in the nursery has meningitis. That night, you go to check on your toddler and find they are ..." has already been narrowed down to a specific concept (health), thus only allows a limited option of target words that can reflect the negative and positive interpretations of this situation (e.g., "sick" or "fine"). In this way, both target words have equal chances to be selected by the participants, and, as a consequence, they have similar cloze probability.

However, it may be hard to achieve similar cloze probability for target words. Due to the requirement of having both positive and negative interpretations for the scenarios, the constraint of the scenario would not be very high. Even when people have generated the same concept, they may not generate the exact same target words. People often generate synonyms within the same concept of the best completion word for each type of interpretation, so the cloze probability for target words may not be high. For example, target words for completing the scenario "You hear that your supervisor is looking for you. You think about your recent work and expect to be ..." could be "praised," "congratulated," and "complimented" as benign interpretations. Negative interpretation words could be "reprimanded," "scolded," and "punished." The targets are in fact synonyms for each other (e.g., praised and complimented, reprimanded and scolded), or represent the same meaning (e.g., praised and congratulated, reprimanded and punished). This indicates that the scenario is narrowed down to a specific concept (outcome of performance), with most participants who make a positive (or negative) interpretation responding with synonyms of that particular concept. However, multiple synonyms can complete the scenarios for each valence around the concept; hence, the cloze probability for each word is deemed not high. However, the low cloze probability of the target words here will not be an issue when assessing interpretation biases if the positive and negative interpretation words have a similar degree of cloze probability. The reaction time will still be fast when the presented target words are in line with the interpretations generated by the individuals. In addition, although the best completion words elicit a smaller N400 than the synonyms, the synonyms still yield a smaller N400 than unrelated words even if the cloze probabilities are the same (Thornhill & Van Petten, 2012). Synonyms remain likely to detect whether the target words are consistent with the generated interpretations. As a result, interpretation biases can still be distinguished using synonyms of the best completion words, and these materials are appropriate to select for the interpretation bias measures.

9.3.1.2 Content Specificity and Relevance

Interpretation biases are content-specific to the central concerns for a given disorder (Beck et al., 1985), and Hirsch et al. (2016) suggest that materials for assessing interpretation biases should be developed based on these central clinical issues. For example, it is more likely that socially anxious participants show a negative interpretation bias, particularly when processing information related to social interactions. Indeed, Stopa and Clark (2000) found that socially anxious participants showed stronger negative interpretation biases than anxious controls, specifically in relation to social interaction scenarios. Given that the main concerns are different across different clinical (and non-clinical) populations, the materials to assess or to modify interpretation biases should thus be matched to the key concern of the tested populations (for a similar argument, see also Hughes et al., 2016). Everaert et al.

(2017) also point out that materials need to be self-relevant - this personal relevance is also crucial to identify interpretation biases. For example, academic-related topics are relevant to students but are not likely to be relevant to older adults who may not be concerned about academic performance. Hence, the topics of scenarios should be carefully chosen and generated in line with both the corresponding clinical issues and the individuals' characteristics.

Another relevant issue that should be noted is that the materials developed for clinical populations may not elicit similar N400 results in sub-clinical populations (e.g., Moser et al., 2008 vs. 2012). This may be because the semantic linkage between ambiguous situations and negative interpretations is weaker in sub-clinical than in clinical populations. Sub-clinical socially anxious individuals, for example, may not expect negative outcomes for such a broad range of social situations as frequently as clinically anxious individuals do. Therefore, in sub-clinical versus clinical populations, the expectancy for negative interpretations, represented by, for example, a negative target word following an ambiguous, social-relevant scenario, is lower, which is then further indexed by weaker N400 amplitudes. Accordingly, it is likely that the materials for sub-clinical populations need to be tailored more specifically and idiosyncratically – to capture individual differences in interpretations (e.g., select different materials by topics for different individuals), which can then be captured by reaction time and/or the N400 index.

9.3.1.3 Self-Referent

Another important issue to consider when developing materials lies in a self-referent manner. It is important to ensure that the materials are phrased in a self-referent manner (e.g., "You applied for a loan"), instead of in relation to others (e.g., "Your brother applied for a loan"). Hirsch et al. (2016) suggest that self-referential processing should be encouraged when assessing interpretation biases. Pertinent interpretations that drive clinical issues tend to occur most likely when patients process information in relation to themselves and their own perspective, rather than in relation to another protagonist. To illustrate, Hirsch et al. (2005) demonstrated that when socially anxious individuals process information from the perspective of someone else, that is, someone who is socially confident, socially anxious individuals in fact had a positive online interpretation (and for similar results in the context of social anxiety, see, e.g., Amir et al., 1998). The role of self-reference has also been supported by studies in other contexts of emotional psychopathology, for example, in dysphoric participants (e.g., Cowden Hindash & Rottenberg, 2017) or individuals with panic disorder (Clark et al., 1997). Given that individuals may demonstrate clinically relevant interpretation biases only for self-referent and personally self-relevant ambiguous materials, we suggest using both self-referent and self-relevant materials in order to design a sufficiently sensitive task that allows triggering interpretation biases adequately.

When summarizing the issues discussed in the earlier sections, the scenarios' ambiguity should be constructed so that very specific interpretations of different valences can be generated. This, in turn, makes it possible to test whether the activated concept in participants' mind matches the benign or negative targets, that is, the presented interpretation, which is then indicative of participants' interpretation biases. Further, individuals with different clinical problems have different main concerns and may only demonstrate interpretation biases if the presented materials are relevant to these concerns and participants themselves (i.e., self-relevant), and are encouraging for self-referential processing. Therefore, materials should be content-specific to the characteristics of the investigated disorders and presented in a self-relevant and self-referential way.

9.3.2   Issues Relevant to EEG Testing and Measurement

Given the requirements for developing materials for interpretation tasks, the range of materials and target words are limited. In addition, in online interpretation bias measures like the lexical decision task, participants make lexical decisions for the target words. Hence, each target word can only be presented once. This is another limitation that constrains the number of trials in the task. The issue of limited number of trials is more profound in EEG than, for example, behavioral-cognitive research, since EEG research needs a lot of trials. In order to have a good signal-to-noise ratio (i.e., levels of a signal against noise, more trials lead to a better quality of data) for the ERPs, there is a need for sufficient trials for each condition to even out the random noise. One challenge with EEG is that the data are sometimes contaminated by artifacts, such as muscular activation, electrodes artefacts, sweat artifacts, or equipment failures (see Britton et al., 2016, Appendix 4. *Common Artefacts During EEG Recording* for artifacts' examples). Trials including such artifacts need to be excluded from the analysis manually or automatically. Hence, it should be ensured that artifacts are reduced as much as possible in order to avoid losing many trials. To illustrate, muscular activation can be reduced by explaining to the participants what such muscular activation includes, for example, chewing, blinking, and head and body movements. They all influence EEG recoding. Thus, participants should be encouraged to sit still during critical points of the experiment. Other methods are also helpful, such as programming the task in small blocks with many breaks, letting participants know when they can move or blink their eyes or move their body, or letting participants decide when to start another trial/block. All these 'tiny' methods will help participants to complete the task as optimal as possible, leading to a better EEG recording and thus better data quality.

Attention is also an important factor influencing N400 amplitudes (McCarthy & Nobre, 1993). It is crucial to consider the best way to engage participants in the task when designing it, in order to record good quality data. There are a few strategies that are helpful in this context. For example, we suggest presenting sentences in segments (i.e., in a few words at a time) instead of a complete sentence at a time. By doing so, participants cannot predict when the sentence ends since the numbers of segments for each sentence are different. We also suggest letting participants use self-paced reading since it is more similar to an active reading process. Further, comprehension questions after some trials (e.g., a third of all trials) will also help participants to remain engaged in reading the material. Once the materials and specific task have been constantly shown the association with the N400 effect, indicating the task is sensitive to detect interpretation biases, researchers could consider dropping the lexical decision component of the task (i.e., categorizing the final target word as a word vs. non-word). This will reduce the number of trials by half since non-word trials would no longer be required. However, at this stage, this is a suggestion that requires future research studies.

Word frequency is another factor that needs consideration when using N400 amplitudes as indices of interpretation biases. Words with low-frequency elicit larger N400 amplitudes than ones with high-frequency (Rugg, 1990). Ideally, positive and negative target words included in interpretation bias measures should thus score similarly in terms of frequency. However, this may be hard to accomplish. And in the end, a task may include targets of unequal frequencies due to the requirements discussed above, such as levels of constraint and cloze probability (see Sect. 9.3.1.1). Further, it is also likely that certain benign words are more commonly used than certain negative words in written and oral language (e.g., the frequency for "good" is 1,130,353, for "bad" it is 286,866, based on the Corpus of Contemporary American English). That said, Kretzschmar et al. (2015) investigated the effects of word frequency and cloze probability on the N400. They found that word frequency did not influence the N400 when the target words were posited around the tenth in the sentences. These results indicate that the later position of the target words potentially minimized the word frequency issue in relation to the tasks used for assessing interpretation biases. Consistently, another study found that word frequency influenced the N400 only when the target words were presented early in the sentence (Van Petten & Kutas, 1990). Therefore, the consideration of word frequency in assessing interpretation biases may depend on the specific task design. If the target words are presented at the end of the sentences (e.g., like lexical decision tasks do), word frequency may not be a major issue when developing the task's materials. Given that cloze probability represents the predictability of the concept within the corresponding ambiguous scenario, it instead seems more important to select final target words that best represent the corresponding concept (i.e., interpretation). It ensures adequate cloze probability while accepting that the benign versus negative target word frequencies may not be exactly the same. Nevertheless, researchers should be aware of the effect of frequency influencing the N400 in the task design.

In order to decide whether the materials have the potential to elicit a valid N400 effect (i.e., distinguish the expectancy of target words), it may be also useful to use lower expectancy words that supposedly elicit a greater N400 than the target words, as comparisons in the task. Thus, the differences in N400 amplitudes can be attributed to the expectancy levels that reflect interpretations. For example, the unexpected words in the sentence word association task (Feng et al., 2019) and in the sentence reading task (Kimble et al., 2012) are the comparison ones for expected words. These unexpected words were included in the tasks because the participants were to decide whether the target words were related to the sentence, or whether the sentences made sense with the final target words. It is also beneficial to include these unexpected words. They can serve as comparisons to the target words to confirm the N400 effect before conducting the main analysis. In both studies that included the step of checking the N400 effect (Feng et al., 2019, Kimble et al., 2012), they showed that the unexpected words elicited greater N400 amplitudes than the expected words, confirming that the N400 indexed the expectancy levels of the target words in the tasks. The step of checking whether the N400 effect can be detected by a task may be necessary, especially when developing measures with different materials and task designs. The N400 may also be used to help validate the appropriateness of materials even for a behavioral study.

9.3.3   Guidelines for Material Development Procedures for Assessing Online Interpretation Biases

Step 1 Pooling materials and developing specific materials for target population.

Before developing materials, it is helpful to search for existing material sets for the target population the researcher is interested in. Then, examine whether the materials:

1. Are content-specific to the disorder-specific concerns or interpretations under investigation, involve self-relevant topics related to the populations, and are presented in a self-referential way (Hirsch et al., 2016; Hughes et al., 2016).
2. Are ambiguous but narrowed down to a specific concept (constrain issue).
3. Allow for both positive and negative interpretations, whereby both interpretations have similar possibilities to be generated, and most of the people would think of the same target word representing the corresponding valence (cloze probability issue).

If there are no suitable or sufficient materials, new materials can be developed based on the same rules. We suggest developing the materials two times more than the actual use.

Step 2 Pilot materials

A pilot study is needed to ensure the suitability of the materials and obtain the cloze probabilities of the target words. Piloting can be done by asking people to generate potential final words for the incomplete scenarios, that is, administer the task as a sentence completion task during the pilot phase. In a sentence completion task, participants are asked to think of a word to complete the sentence (scenario) best. These final words can then form target words for the lexical decision or other similar tasks. For the sentence word association task (or other similar ones using complete sentences and isolating the related target words), the sentences can be modified to fit the designs of the tasks. For example, during piloting, the materials can be presented as a sentence completion task like: "Your friend opens your gift.

You can tell how he feels by his face that he is …" Participants are then supposed to generate an ending that is likely to be "happy" or "disappointed." Then the scenario can be changed to a complete sentence: "Your friend opens your gift. You can tell how he feels by his face" and the word "happy" can be presented following the scenario for the word association decision.

After piloting, all endings participants generated should be coded, for example, as negative, benign (which includes positive or neural), or other categories, based on the interpretations represented by the words for the corresponding ambiguous scenario, rather than by the "isolated" meaning of the word. The cloze probabilities of each word are the number of participants generating a specific target word, divided by the number of total participants who generated a valid word in response to the scenario. After coding, researchers can then examine whether the scenarios produce a narrow range of responses that match a specific concept, by checking the amount of different target words generated that represent different concepts, and that there is thus one main benign and one main negative interpretation (represented by the targets). Researchers can review the cloze probabilities for the final words to see whether the low cloze probabilities are caused by participants generating more synonym endings or low constraints of the scenarios. If a scenario has too many potential interpretations representing different concepts, or most people generate only positive (or negative) interpretations, these scenarios are not suitable for assessing interpretation biases. If multiple potential final words are generated but are synonyms (within a given valence), then the scenario is still suitable (see synonyms example in earlier Sect. 9.3.1.1). After developing the first set, one has to check for repeated target words since a given target should be presented only once during the task. Hence, some sentences may have to end with the second-highest cloze probability word (usually synonyms). The cloze probabilities between positive and negative target words (i.e., interpretation) can then be examined; optimally they should be equal across both target sets. If the materials do not meet the criteria described above, further modifications (and potentially piloting) are required.

9.4 Other Potential Neural and Biological Correlates for Interpretation Biases

As mentioned earlier, the P600 may also index interpretation biases, but with limited findings to date. Moser et al. (2008) is the only study that demonstrated a P600 effect when assessing interpretation biases. That is, in the low social anxiety group, negative target words elicited greater P600 amplitudes than positive target words, indicating a positive interpretation bias. Other studies (e.g., Feng et al., 2019; Kimble et al., 2012) did not assess the P600 amplitude when assessing online interpretation bias. But the data shown in the figures seem to indicate that there was no enhanced P600 for the unrelated words (Feng et al., 2019) or the unexpected word (Kimble et al., 2012), compared with the related and expected words. In addition, as mentioned earlier, the P600 is also sensitive to more lingual characteristics such as plausibility and other properties (Kuperberg et al., 2003, see Swaab et al., 2012, for review of the N400 and P600). Therefore, it remains unclear whether the P600 can also index interpretation bias, and under which tasks the P600 can be used to index interpretation. The P600 may potentially be useful in detecting interpretations using certain interpretation bias measures, but this needs further exploration. This could be explored by examining whether the comparison words (e.g., unexpected words) elicit a greater P600 than the target words in the interpretation bias measures (as mentioned in the Sect. 9.3.2 above).

Studies have also investigated other biological markers of biased interpretation processing. Heart rate, eye-blink reflexes, and pupillary reactivity have been linked to interpretation biases. Howard et al. (2018), for example, found that individuals with high negative affectivity and social inhibition showed higher levels of heart rate when reading negative scenarios (compared to neutral social scenarios) and when reading social scenarios that remained ambiguous compared with the ones that started ambiguously but included some negatively oriented indications. The heart-rate findings indicate that social situations with higher ambiguity were more threatening than those with more indications towards the outcomes. The findings also reveal that heart rate has the potential to index interpretation biases when reading scenarios, but this needs further investigation. In Lawson et al.'s (2002) first study, participants' eye-blink reflexes were assessed while they were listening to words and imagined a situation evoked by the last word (negative or neutral) they heard. Results showed that startle eye-blink reflexes magnitudes were greater when participants imagined a situation evoked by the negative than the neutral words. Therefore, eye-blink reflexes magnitude may also reflect the valence of how individuals interpret ambiguous words. Their second study investigated whether depression is associated with interpretations of ambiguous words, specifically words with missing phonemes. In this case, the words can be interpreted in neutral or negative ways, such as "*loom" can be interpreted as "gloom" (negative) or "bloom" (neutral). The findings showed that only individuals with higher depression scores had larger blink reflex magnitudes when engaging in imagery evoked by ambiguous words than the neutral words. This indicated that participants with more depression symptoms interpreted ambiguity more negatively. However, more studies are needed to determine if eye-blink reflexes can index interpretation biases or just indicate, for example, an emotional state (Grillon & Baas, 2003). Cowden Hindash et al. (2021) investigated pupillary reactivity during the presentation of the target words in the sentence word association task. Individuals with depression endorsed more negative target words (interpretation) as being associated with the ambiguous sentence than the control group. They also showed increased pupil size relative to baseline when endorsing negative target words than the controls. However, the result did not support the original hypothesis that greater pupillary reactivity would be observed when benign interpretation target words would be presented. Benign interpretations are supposed to be inconsistent with the negative processing style of depressed individuals and therefore should have elicited greater pupillary reactivity.

As such, more studies are needed to better understand whether pupillary reactivity may be an index of interpretation biases.

The benefit of having neural and biological interpretation bias indices is that they are the direct responses to the presented stimuli and may therefore reveal fundamental mechanisms of cognitive processing. Furthermore, they are free from, for example, response biases, demand effects, positive self-representation, or other processes influencing participants' responses during self-report or behavioral interpretation measures. Future studies are needed to verify the neural and biological interpretation bias approaches and see whether they can indeed represent interpretation biases independently (for an overview of additional neural mechanisms underlying interpretation biases, see Chap. 10 by Martens and Harmer).

9.5   Conclusion

Interpretation processes in relation to psychopathology have been investigated using a wide range of self-report and behavioral measures. Only limited research has focused on the neural basis of interpretation biases. ERPs are promising tools to investigate interpretation processing directly, and they are less likely to be affected by confounding variables such as response biases or demand effects. One of the language-related ERPs, N400, indexes participants' expectancy of a certain target word within a given context. Indeed, the N400 has been shown to index interpretation biases in emotional psychopathological research, targeting social anxiety, PTSD, and worry, using various task operationalizations. Several important issues should be kept in mind when developing materials for this kind of interpretation bias measure. For example, the scenarios should be narrowed down to a specific context (high-constraint scenario) and allow both benign and negative interpretations to be generated. At the same time, they should be content-specific to the key aspects of the clinical concern that is investigated. Therefore, piloting is an important step and should include several consecutive procedures. Enhancing data quality during recording is another important issue. This can be done by, for example, implementing a task design that encourages engagement and reduces fatigue, and by making participants aware of the effects of their muscular activities during testing. Other potential neural and biological correlates for interpretation biases, such as the P600, heart rate, startle eye-blink reflex, and pupillary reactivity, may be additional interesting future markers. With our chapter, we hope that we have shown the usefulness of ERPs in understanding interpretation processing biases, and we also hope that the practical information we provided will help to optimally design future studies to assess them.

References

Amir, N., Foa, E. B., & Coles, M. E. (1998). Negative interpretation bias in social phobia. *Behaviour Research and Therapy, 36*, 945–957. https://doi.org/10.1016/s0005-7967(98)00060-6

Anderson, K. G., Dugas, M. J., Koerner, N., Radomsky, A. S., Savard, P., & Turcotte, J. (2012). Interpretive style and intolerance of uncertainty in individuals with anxiety disorders: A focus on generalized anxiety disorder. *Journal of Anxiety Disorders, 26*(8), 823–832. https://doi.org/10.1016/j.janxdis.2012.08.003

Beard, C., & Amir, N. (2008). A multi–session interpretation modification program: Changes in interpretation and social anxiety symptoms. *Behaviour Research and Therapy, 46*, 1135–1141. https://doi.org/10.1016/j.brat.2008.05.012

Beard, C., & Amir, N. (2009). Interpretation in social anxiety: When meaning precedes ambiguity. *Cognitive Therapy and Research, 33*, 406–415.

Beck, A. T., Emery, G., & Greenberg, R. L. (1985). *Anxiety disorders and phobias. A cognitive perspective* (pp. 300–368). Basic Books.

Britton, J. W., Frey, L. C., Hopp, J. L., Korb, P., Koubeissi, M. Z., Lievens, W. E., Pestana-Knight, E. M., & St. Louis, E. K. (2016). In E. K. St. Louis, & L. C. Frey (Eds.), *Electroencephalography (EEG): An introductory text and atlas of normal and abnormal findings in adults, children, and infants*. American Epilepsy Society. https://doi.org/10.5698/978-0-9979756-0-4

Brouwer, H., Fitz, H., & Hoeks, J. (2012). Getting real about semantic illusions: Rethinking the functional role of the P600 in language comprehension. *Brain Research, 1446*, 127–143. https://doi.org/10.1016/j.brainres.2012.01.055

Clark, D. M., Salkovskis, P. M., Ost, L. G., Breitholtz, E., Koehler, K. A., Westling, B. E., Jeavons, A., & Gelder, M. (1997). Misinterpretation of body sensations in panic disorder. *Journal of Consulting and Clinical Psychology, 65*(2), 203–213. https://doi.org/10.1037//0022-006x.65.2.203

Cowden Hindash, A. H., & Rottenberg, J. (2017). Turning quickly on myself: Automatic interpretation biases in dysphoria are self-referent. *Cognition and Emotion, 31*(2), 395–402. https://doi.org/10.1080/02699931.2015.1105792

Cowden Hindash, A. H. C., Siegle, G. J., Kelley, A., Christopher, R., McLean, J., & Rottenberg, J. A. (2021). Eyeing ambiguity: Pupillary reactivity during early automatic interpretations in major depressive disorder. *International Journal of Psychophysiology, 164*, 41–51. https://doi.org/10.1016/j.ijpsycho.2021.02.014

Everaert, J., Podina, I. R., & Koster, E. H. (2017). A comprehensive meta-analysis of interpretation biases in depression. *Clinical Psychology Review, 58*, 33–48. https://doi.org/10.1016/j.cpr.2017.09.005

Feng, Y.-C., Krahé, C., Sumich, A., Meeten, F., Lau, J., & Hirsch, C. R. (2019). Using event-related potential and behavioural evidence to understand interpretation bias in relation to worry. *Biological Psychology, 148*, 107746. https://doi.org/10.1016/j.biopsycho.2019.107746

Feng, Y. C., Krahé, C., Meeten, F., Sumich, A., Mok, C., & Hirsch, C. R. (2020). Impact of imagery-enhanced interpretation training on offline and online interpretations in worry. *Behaviour Research and Therapy, 124*, 103497. https://doi.org/10.1016/j.brat.2019.103497

Feng, Y. -C., Huang, M. -H., Hsu, W. -Y., Lai, Y. -J., Krahé, C., Meeten, F., Sumich, A., Mok, C. M., & Hirsch, C. R. (2022). *Assessing interpretation bias using the N400 language-related event-related potential (ERP)*. 2022 Inaugural Conference of the Association for Cognitive Bias Modification (ACBM), Tel Aviv-Yafo, Israel.

Glover, G. H. (2011). Overview of functional magnetic resonance imaging. *Neurosurgery Clinics of North America, 22*(2), 133–139. https://doi.org/10.1016/j.nec.2010.11.001

Grey, S., & Mathews, A. (2000). Effects of training on interpretation of emotional ambiguity. *The Quarterly Journal of Experimental Psychology, 53*(4), 1143–1162. https://doi.org/10.1080/713755937

Grillon, C., & Baas, J. (2003). A review of the modulation of the startle reflex by affective states and its application in psychiatry. *Clinical Neurophysiology, 114*(9), 1557–1579. https://doi.org/10.1016/s1388-2457(03)00202-5

Hirsch, C. R., & Mathews, A. (1997). Interpretative inferences when reading about emotional events. *Behaviour Research and Therapy, 35*(12), 1123–1132. https://doi.org/10.1016/S0005-7967(97)80006-X

Hirsch, C. R., & Mathews, A. (2000). Impaired positive inferential bias in social phobia. *Journal of Abnormal Psychology, 109*(4), 705–712. https://doi.org/10.1037/0021-843X.109.4.705

Hirsch, C. R., Clark, D. M., Williams, R., Morrison, J., & Mathews, A. (2005). Interview anxiety: Taking the perspective of a confident other changes inferential processing. *Behavioural and Cognitive Psychotherapy, 33*(1), 1–12. https://doi.org/10.1017/S1352465804001729

Hirsch, C. R., Meeten, F., Krahé, C., & Reeder, C. (2016). Resolving ambiguity in emotional disorders: The nature and role of interpretation biases. *Annual Review of Clinical Psychology, 12*, 281–305. https://doi.org/10.1146/annurev-clinpsy-021815-093436

Hirsch, C. R., Krahé, C., Whyte, J., Loizou, S., Bridge, L., Norton, S., & Mathews, A. (2018). Interpretation training to target repetitive negative thinking in generalized anxiety disorder and depression. *Journal of Consulting and Clinical Psychology, 86*(12), 1017–1030. https://doi.org/10.1037/ccp0000310

Hirsch, C. R., Krahé, C., Whyte, J., Bridge, L., Loizou, S., Norton, S., & Mathews, A. (2020). Effects of modifying interpretation bias on transdiagnostic repetitive negative thinking. *Journal of Consulting and Clinical Psychology, 88*(3), 226–239. https://doi.org/10.1037/ccp0000455

Hirsch, C. R., Krahé, C., Whyte, J., Krzyzanowski, H., Meeten, F., Norton, S., & Mathews, A. (2021). Internet-delivered interpretation training reduces worry and anxiety in individuals with generalized anxiety disorder: A randomized controlled experiment. *Journal of Consulting and Clinical Psychology, 89*(7), 575–589. https://doi.org/10.1037/ccp0000660

Hoeks, J. C., Stowe, L. A., & Doedens, G. (2004). Seeing words in context: The interaction of lexical and sentence level information during reading. *Cognitive Brain Research, 19*(1), 59–73. https://doi.org/10.1016/j.cogbrainres.2003.10.022

Holcomb, P. J. (1993). Semantic priming and stimulus degradation: Implications for the role of the N400 in language processing. *Psychophysiology, 30*(1), 47–61. https://doi.org/10.1111/j.1469-8986.1993.tb03204.x

Howard, S., O'Riordan, A., & Nolan, M. (2018). Cognitive bias of interpretation in Type D personality: Associations with physiological indices of arousal. *Applied Psychophysiology and Biofeedback, 43*(3), 193–201. https://doi.org/10.1007/s10484-018-9397-1

Hughes, A. M., Gordon, R., Chalder, T., Hirsch, C. R., & Moss-Morris, R. (2016). Maximizing potential impact of experimental research into cognitive processes in health psychology: A systematic approach to material development. *British Journal of Health Psychology, 21*(4), 764–780. https://doi.org/10.1111/bjhp.12214

Kimble, M., Batterink, L., Marks, E., Ross, C., & Fleming, K. (2012). Negative expectancies in posttraumatic stress disorder: Neurophysiological (N400) and behavioral evidence. *Journal of Psychiatric Research, 46*(7), 849–855. https://doi.org/10.1016/j.jpsychires.2012.03.023

Krahé, C., Whyte, J., Bridge, L., Loizou, S., & Hirsch, C. R. (2019). Are different forms of repetitive negative thinking associated with interpretation bias in generalized anxiety disorder and depression? *Clinical Psychological Science, 7*(5), 969–981. https://doi.org/10.1177/2167702619851808

Kretzschmar, F., Schlesewsky, M., & Staub, A. (2015). Dissociating word frequency and predictability effects in reading: Evidence from coregistration of eye movements and EEG. *Journal of Experimental Psychology: Learning, Memory, and Cognition, 41*(6), 1648–1662. https://doi.org/10.1037/xlm0000128

Kuperberg, G. R., Sitnikova, T., Caplan, D., & Holcomb, P. J. (2003). Electrophysiological distinctions in processing conceptual relationships within simple sentences. *Cognitive Brain Research, 17*(1), 117–129. https://doi.org/10.1016/s0926-6410(03)00086-7

Kutas, M., & Federmeier, K. D. (2000). Electrophysiology reveals semantic memory use in language comprehension. *Trends in Cognitive Sciences, 4*(12), 463–470. https://doi.org/10.1016/s1364-6613(00)01560-6

Kutas, M., & Federmeier, K. D. (2009). N400. *Scholarpedia, 4*(10), 7790. https://doi.org/10.4249/scholarpedia.7790

Kutas, M., & Federmeier, K. D. (2011). Thirty years and counting: Finding meaning in the N400 component of the event-related brain potential (ERP). *Annual Review of Psychology, 62*, 621–647. https://doi.org/10.1146/annurev.psych.093008.131123

Kutas, M., & Hillyard, S. A. (1980). Reading senseless sentences: Brain potentials reflect semantic incongruity. *Science, 207*(4427), 203–205. https://doi.org/10.1126/science.7350657

Kutas, M., & Hillyard, S. A. (1984). Brain potentials during reading reflect word expectancy and semantic association. *Nature, 307*(5947), 161–163. https://doi.org/10.1038/307161a0

Lang, T. J., Blackwell, S. E., Harmer, C. J., Davison, P., & Holmes, E. A. (2012). Cognitive bias modification using mental imagery for depression: Developing a novel computerized intervention to change negative thinking styles. *European Journal of Personality, 26*(2), 145–157. https://doi.org/10.1002/per.855

Lawson, C., MacLeod, C., & Hammond, G. (2002). Interpretation revealed in the blink of an eye: Depressive bias in the resolution of ambiguity. *Journal of Abnormal Psychology, 111*(2), 321–328. https://doi.org/10.1037//0021-843x.111.2.321

Mathews, A., & Mackintosh, B. (2000). Induced emotional interpretation bias and anxiety. *Journal of Abnormal Psychology, 109*, 602–615. https://doi.org/10.1037/0021-843X.109.4.602

McCarthy, G., & Nobre, A. C. (1993). Modulation of semantic processing by spatial selective attention. *Electroencephalography and Clinical Neurophysiology/Evoked Potentials Section, 88*(3), 210–219. https://doi.org/10.1016/0168-5597(93)90005-A

Moser, J. S., Hajcak, G., Huppert, J. D., Foa, E. B., & Simons, R. F. (2008). Interpretation bias in social anxiety as detected by event-related brain potentials. *Emotion, 8*(5), 693–700. https://doi.org/10.1037/a0013173

Moser, J. S., Huppert, J. D., Foa, E. B., & Simons, R. F. (2012). Interpretation of ambiguous social scenarios in social phobia and depression: Evidence from event-related brain potentials. *Biological Psychology, 89*(2), 387–397. https://doi.org/10.1016/j.biopsycho.2011.12.001

Rugg, M. D. (1990). Event-related brain potentials dissociate repetition effects of high-and low-frequency words. *Memory and Cognition, 18*(4), 367–379. https://doi.org/10.3758/BF03197126

Sharma, A., Sauer, H., Hill, H., Kaufmann, C., Bender, S., & Weisbrod, M. (2017). Abnormal N400 semantic priming effect may reflect psychopathological processes in schizophrenia: A twin study. *Schizophrenia Research and Treatment, 2017*, 7163198. https://doi.org/10.1155/2017/7163198

Sitnikova, T., Salisbury, D. F., Kuperberg, G., & Holcomb, P. J. (2002). Electrophysiological insights into language processing in schizophrenia. *Psychophysiology, 39*(6), 851–860. https://doi.org/10.1111/1469-8986.3960851

Stopa, L., & Clark, D. M. (2000). Social phobia and interpretation of social events. *Behaviour Research and Therapy, 38*(3), 273–283. https://doi.org/10.1016/S0005-7967(99)00043-1

Swaab, T. Y., Ledoux, K., Camblin, C. C., & Boudewyn, M. A. (2012). Language-related ERP components. In S. J. Luck & E. S. Kappenman (Eds.), *The Oxford handbook of event-related potential components* (pp. 397–440). Oxford University Press. https://doi.org/10.1093/oxfordhb/9780195374148.013.0197

Thornhill, D. E., & Van Petten, C. (2012). Lexical versus conceptual anticipation during sentence processing: Frontal positivity and N400 ERP components. *International Journal of Psychophysiology, 83*(3), 382–392. https://doi.org/10.1016/j.ijpsycho.2011.12.007

Van Berkum, J. J. V., Hagoort, P., & Brown, C. M. (1999). Semantic integration in sentences and discourse: Evidence from the N400. *Journal of Cognitive Neuroscience, 11*(6), 657–671. https://doi.org/10.1162/089892999563724

Van Petten, C., & Kutas, M. (1990). Interactions between sentence context and word frequencyinevent-related brainpotentials. *Memory and Cognition, 18*(4), 380–393. https://doi.org/10.3758/BF03197127

White, K. R., Crites, S. L., Jr., Taylor, J. H., & Corral, G. (2009). Wait, what? Assessing stereotype incongruities using the N400 ERP component. *Social Cognitive and Affective Neuroscience, 4*(2), 191–198. https://doi.org/10.1093/scan/nsp004

Zayas, V., Shoda, Y., Mischel, W., Osterhout, L., & Takahashi, M. (2009). Neural responses to partner rejection cues. *Psychological Science, 20*(7), 813–821. https://doi.org/10.1111/j.1467-9280.2009.02373.x

Ya-Chun Feng is a clinical psychologist and assistant professor at National Sun Yat-sen University, Taiwan. She is interested in the cognitive mechanism of emotional disorders and has investigated cognitive biases in relation to worry, anxiety, and social anxiety using behavioral and neurophysiological methods. She is also interested in exploring how cognitive processes interact with each other, such as how memory is influenced by previous interpretations. Her current research aims to understand how attention control and attention bias are interactively related to emotional symptoms and develop new interventions targeting cognitive deficits.

Colette R. Hirsch is a Professor in Cognitive Clinical Psychology at King's College London (UK). She is also a Consultant Clinical Psychologist and leads the Generalised Anxiety Disorder Service at the Centre for Anxiety Disorders and Trauma, South London, and Maudsley NHS Foundation Trust. In her research, she examines the role of cognitive processes in emotional psychopathology, for example, generalized anxiety disorder, social anxiety, and depression, including clinical and sub-clinical samples. Prof. Hirsch's work is also characterized by a translational research approach, focusing on developing new interventions to prevent and treat emotional disorders.

Chapter 10
Pharmacological Manipulations of Emotional Processing Biases: From Bench to Bedside

Marieke A. G. Martens and Catherine J. Harmer

10.1 Introduction

How we think is influenced by our emotions, affecting what we attend to, how we interpret information, the decisions we make, and the memories we form. Biases in how emotional information is processed has been reported across many psychiatric disorders, including anxiety disorder (Davey & Meeten, 2016), bipolar disorder (Miskowiak et al., 2019), and schizophrenia (Potvin et al., 2016). This chapter will however focus on patients with major depressive disorder (MDD), where negative biases in attention, interpretation, and memory have consistently been reported (Godlewska & Harmer, 2021; Mathews & MacLeod, 2005; Robinson & Roiser, 2016).

Patients with MDD have a tendency to perceive social cues as more negative (interpretation bias), to preferentially attend to aversive information (attentional bias), and to recall more negative than positive information concerning themselves (memory bias). According to Beck's cognitive model of depression (Beck, 1979; Disner et al., 2011) these biases are believed to play a fundamental role in the development and maintenance of MDD (for a recent commentary, see Woud, 2022). Moreover, these biases have been suggested as a mechanism underpinning vulnerability as they can precede depression and depressive relapse (Disner et al., 2011; Harmer et al., 2017; Roiser et al., 2012).

Beck (1979) hypothesised that negative interpretation biases are the result of negative early life experiences that colour the processing of external sensory inputs (for a related discussion about the role of negative early life experiences in the

M. A. G. Martens · C. J. Harmer (✉)
Wellcome Centre for Integrative Neuroimaging, Department of Psychiatry,
University of Oxford, Oxford, UK
e-mail: marieke.martens@psych.ox.ac.uk; catherine.harmer@psych.ox.ac.uk

© The Author(s), under exclusive license to Springer Nature Switzerland AG 2023
M. L. Woud (ed.), *Interpretational Processing Biases in Emotional Psychopathology*,
CBT: Science Into Practice, https://doi.org/10.1007/978-3-031-23650-1_10

context of interpretation biases, see Chap. 7 by Scheveneels and Boddez, and Chap. 8 by Vincent and Fox). This could be seen as a 'top-down' bias whereby individuals interpret stimuli as more negative because these accord with their expectations. However, more recent cognitive models of depression also acknowledge that the reverse is possible, whereby perceptual systems themselves are set to receive negative over positive information; in other words, a 'bottom-up' bias. These negative biases could be distally caused by either genetic or environmental influences (like cortisol release due to stressful events) that alter transmission in the brain (Godlewska & Harmer, 2021; Robinson & Roiser, 2016).

Even today, more than 30 years later, Beck's model is still useful to explain the persistence of MDD. Based on his early work it has been suggested that prolonged and consistent exposure to negatively biased inputs ('bottom-up' processing biases) causes the brain to develop negatively biased expectations and a depressive world-view ('top-down' processing biases). Since negative inputs accord with negative expectations, this state of combined 'top-down' and 'bottom-up' bias can become extremely stable and self-reinforcing. When this is experienced over a long period, these dysfunctional negative beliefs will become ingrained, eliciting high-level negative cognitions, low mood, and increased responses to negative or stressful events, and therefore increasing vulnerability to the development of depression (Beck, 1979; Disner et al., 2011; Harmer et al., 2017; Robinson & Roiser, 2016; Roiser et al., 2012).

Over the years these theoretical constructs about emotional processing have focussed their attention on targeting cognitive biases using psychological treatments for MDD, including, for example, cognitive restructuring to modify dysfunctional beliefs in cognitive behavioural therapy (CBT) (Holmes et al., 2018). However, there is growing evidence that pharmacological treatments also have a direct effect on emotional biases, and that changes in such biases may be involved in their mechanism of action.

10.2   How Do Antidepressants Affect Emotional Processing and Interpretation Bias?

Most currently licensed antidepressants are believed to act by increasing the availability of the neurotransmitters serotonin (serotonin reuptake inhibitor (SSRI)) or norepinephrine (norepinephrine reuptake inhibitors (SNRIs)), or both (SNRIs), across cortico-limbic brain circuits (Godlewska & Harmer, 2021; Harmer et al., 2017). Even though these molecular, cellular, and chemical effects can be detected within hours after drug administration, the therapeutic effect of antidepressant treatment requires a number of weeks to become clinically important. The cognitive neuropsychological model of antidepressant drug action hypothesises that antidepressants target emotional processing rather than mood directly (Harmer et al., 2009a, 2017). Thus, antidepressants are believed to have fast effects on how emotional information is processed, including changes in interpretation biases, which could then lead to gradual changes in social reinforcement, behaviour, and mood over time and experience. Therefore, for improvement in the mood to take place, the new more positive emotional processing bias needs to be reinforced by positive interactions with the social environment, which lead to the development of new positive associations. This process would be expected to take time and practice and thereby could explain the delay in symptomatic improvement (Harmer et al., 2009a, 2017). The predictions made by this model have been tested in a number of different experimental studies in the lab, and more recently also in a clinical context. Most of this work used faces as stimuli, that is, requiring the fast interpretation of ambiguous facial expressions, rather than, for example, interpretation of homophones or of ambiguous scenarios (for an overview of measures to assess interpretation biases, see Chap. 3 by Würtz and Sanchez-Lopez). This has perhaps evolved out of the different techniques commonly used in different fields and perhaps also a different focus on capturing bottom-up versus top-down influences in interpretation tasks.

10.3   Evaluation of the Cognitive Neuropsychological Model

10.3.1   Antidepressants and Emotional Processing Bias: Evidence from Behavioural Studies

The first studies that provided direct support for this model were performed in the early 2000s (Harmer et al., 2003a, b). Initially, healthy volunteers were studied to control for the effects of depression and symptom improvement in patients with depression following antidepressant administration, which would also be expected to affect negative emotional processing bias. Excluding the impact of mood, memory and executive function deficits on emotional processing is crucial to test for direct actions of the drug on emotional processing rather than indirect change via mood improvement. In these early studies, changes in emotional processing were measured by tasks which tap into attention, interpretation, and memory for emotionally charged stimuli, such as the interpretation of facial expressions displaying emotions (see Fig. 10.1).

In one of the first studies (Harmer et al., 2003a), twenty-four healthy volunteers were given a single dose of the noradrenergic antidepressant reboxetine or placebo, in a double-blind, randomised, between-groups design. Effects on emotional processing were assessed through a battery of tasks including facial expression recognition (see Fig. 10.1), which is sensitive to negative interpretation bias in depression. In this study, participants showed greater recognition of happy facial expressions after reboxetine than after placebo, in the absence of more general changes in facial expression recognition of other emotions. In contrast to the processing of emotional information, the processing of non-emotional information was not affected by

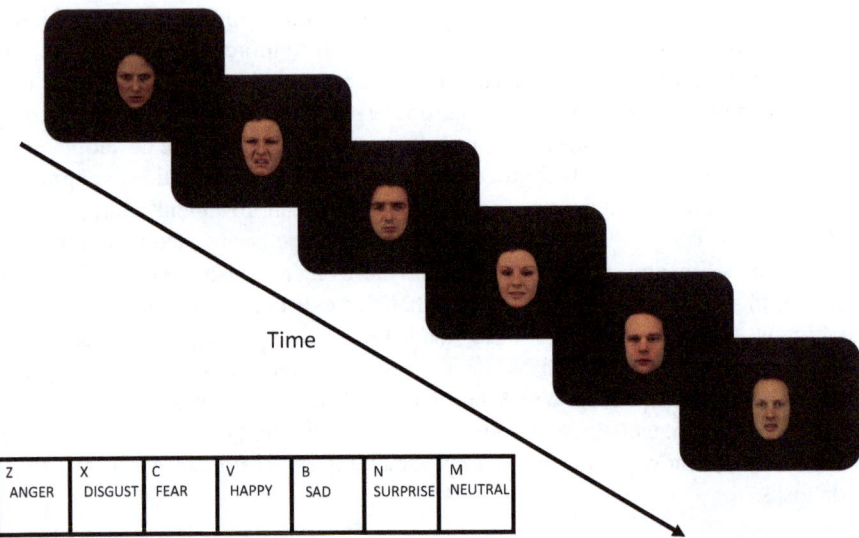

Z	X	C	V	B	N	M
ANGER	DISGUST	FEAR	HAPPY	SAD	SURPRISE	NEUTRAL

Fig. 10.1 Illustration of the FERT. *Note*. In the facial expression task (FERT) participants are presented with pictures of human facial expressions of six basic emotions (anger, disgust, fear, happiness, sadness, and surprise), at different intensity levels to increase ambiguity. Participants are then instructed to correctly classify each facial expression as quickly and as accurately as possible. The main outcomes of interest are accuracy, reaction time for correct classifications, and misclassifications (e.g. classifying a surprised face as a fearful face)

reboxetine, suggesting that the better performance found in the emotional tasks did not represent more global actions on speed, memory, or attention. There was also no effect of reboxetine on ratings of subjective mood, and inclusion of these mood ratings as covariates did not abolish the effects, suggesting that the observed changes following drug administration represent direct effects of the drug on emotional processing bias rather than a secondary consequence on mood. Therefore, the authors concluded that processing of positively valenced information in healthy volunteers could be facilitated by antidepressant treatment within hours of administration, in the absence of improved cognitive performance and effects on subjective mood. In a follow-up study, 7 days of treatment with reboxetine, compared to placebo, moreover reduced the recognition of the negative emotions like fear and anger (Harmer et al., 2004). These shifts in information processing were suggested to represent an early effect of antidepressant medication that potentially could act to reverse the negative biases in interpretation seen in depressed patients, that is, a shift from negative to more positive processing (Harmer et al., 2003a, b, 2004).

A logical next step therefore was to also investigate whether these antidepressant effects on emotional processing seen in healthy volunteers would be also apparent in depressed patients early in treatment, prior to changes in mood and symptoms. This was indeed the case, first shown by Harmer et al., in 2009. In this study, depressed patients and healthy controls were randomised to receive either reboxetine or placebo in a double-blind design. Depressed patients recognised fewer happy facial expressions compared to healthy volunteers under placebo conditions, but this was reversed by a single dose of reboxetine treatment, again prior to any mood changes. Moreover, reboxetine also facilitated the recognition of happy facial expressions in healthy volunteers (Harmer et al., 2009b).

In addition to facial stimuli, researchers have also used classical assessment tasks to investigate the effects of antidepressants on negative interpretation bias. For example, Mogg et al. (2004) used the homophone interpretation task, whereby participants listen to a series of homophones and are asked to write them down. Homophones are words that share the same sound but have different meanings (e.g. 'die/dye', 'weak/week'). Patients with generalised anxiety disorder produced significantly fewer threat-related spellings of homophones following a 4-week treatment with an SSRI compared to before treatment. Furthermore, this reduction in interpretation bias was positively correlated with clinical improvement, suggesting that it was relevant to the therapeutic action of the drug (Mogg et al., 2004).

To be able to again distinguish the direct action of the drug from the non-specific effects of symptom change produced by the SSRI treatment, Murphy et al. (2009b) assessed the effects of a 7-day treatment with the SSRI citalopram compared to placebo (in a double-blind design) on the same homophone task in healthy volunteers. In addition to the homophone task, the authors also included an emotional dot probe task. Citalopram reduced attentional vigilance towards fearful faces but did not affect the interpretation of ambiguous homographs as threatening. The authors suggested that the difference in treatment duration (4 weeks vs. 7 days) could potentially explain the lack of effect on the homophone task in this particular study. Whilst the early effects of SSRIs may relate specifically to selective attention to threat, over time it is possible that they may generalise to influence a broader spectrum of emotional and social processing (Murphy et al., 2009b).

The improvement of positive versus negative processing seen early in treatment has been suggested to contribute to later clinical response. Consistent with this, depressed patients receiving citalopram or reboxetine in an open-label study showed enhanced processing of happy facial expressions after 2 weeks of drug treatment, and this was predictive of therapeutic response after a further 4 weeks of treatment (Tranter et al., 2009). Furthermore, in a study by Browning et al. (2019), seventy-four primary care patients diagnosed with depression completed the facial expression recognition task (FERT, see Fig. 10.1) and two emotional memory tasks (word-based memory encoding and recall) both before drug treatment was started and after a week, with response to treatment assessed after 4–6 weeks. By using machine learning methods, the authors were able to create classifiers that would predict treatment response based on these measures of emotional processing bias. The classifier that was able to predict treatment response best (with 77% accuracy) was a combination of subjective symptoms and performance on the FERT. This classifier was then tested in another sample of 239 patients, resulting in 60% accuracy (Browning et al., 2019). These data support the hypothesis that emotional processing changes may be involved in the therapeutic actions of antidepressants. However, it should be noted that early change in emotional processing bias is not always seen across studies. For example, Ahmed et al. (2021) found no effect of antidepressant treatment with sertraline on emotional memory bias in a large prag-matic trial in primary care, which included patients with and without diagnoses of depression and general anxiety disorder, for whom there was uncertainty from both the general practitioner (GP) and patient about the possible benefit of an antidepres-sant (Ahmed et al., 2021). The authors suggested that based on their finding and the observation that adding word categorisation or recall did not improve the prediction of treatment response in the study by Browning et al. (2021), facial emotion recog-nition tasks may be more sensitive to changes in emotional processing by antide-pressants than word recall tasks. More work is needed to understand the specific mechanisms underpinning emotional processing bias change and the most sensitive and reliable markers and tasks to capture these effects.

In sum, these valence-dependent effects on emotional processing after different types of antidepressant administration can be observed both in patients with depres-sion as well as in healthy volunteers, suggesting that they may be an inherent effect of antidepressant treatment and not simply an epiphenomenon of improvements in psychopathology. Moreover, these studies suggest that an early shift in emotional processing bias precedes mood improvement and is predictive of clinical response (Harmer et al., 2009b). Further work is nonetheless needed to improve the sensitiv-ity and reliability of emotional processing measures.

10.3.2   How Do We Measure the Neural Correlates of Depression and the Effects of Antidepressants on the Brain?

In the above studies, the biological processes underlying depression were only indi-rectly studied by a behavioural outcome measure of emotional processing. Developments in functional magnetic resonance imaging (fMRI), however, made it possible to advance our understanding of the functional neural underpinnings of affective processing in depression and its treatment. fMRI therefore allowed bio-logical and psychological processes underlying depression and clinical response to treatments to be studied together. This resulted in a better understanding of the biological underpinnings of the phenomena traditionally considered at a psycho-logical level (Godlewska & Harmer, 2021; Holmes et al., 2018).

10.3.3   What Are the Neural Correlates of Negative Emotional Processing Bias?

Emotional processing bias has been associated with changes in activity across cor-ticolimbic circuitry including subcortical areas such as the amygdala, anterior cin-gulate cortex (ACC), and prefrontal regulatory responses (Benoit et al., 2014; Blair et al., 2013; Disner et al., 2011; Erthal et al., 2021). Evidence for this association comes from both healthy participants as well from patients with MDD. For example, the amygdala is more active when more optimistic people, who tend to expect better outcomes, imagined future positive, compared to negative events (Sharot et al., 2007). Furthermore, Ito et al. (2017) used the two-alternative forced choice task involving a series of graded facial stimuli that morphed from happy to sad during event-related fMRI, to try to better understand the neural correlates of negative emotional processing bias. Negativity bias was associated with hyperactivity in the bilateral pregenual ACC (pgACC) when ambiguous faces were perceived as sad versus happy. Additionally, the strength of the functional connectivity between components of the salience network such as the bilateral pgACC and the right dorsal ACC/right thalamus was positively correlated with a measure of hopelessness, suggesting a negative over a positive perception of ambiguous facial expressions in individuals with higher levels of hopelessness. These regional associations may contribute to the negativity bias in depression, which may influence both symptom formation and social dysfunction (Ito et al., 2017).

Depression is seen as a network disorder, with meaningful aberrations related to the networks of brain structures rather than individual regions (Li et al., 2018). When studying the brain during a fMRI task designed to elicit responses to emotional stimuli – such as viewing facial expressions of fear, sadness, or happiness – activity in the extended limbic system including the amygdala, pgACC, and hippocampus differ between healthy volunteers and patients with MDD (Godlewska et al., 2012; Godlewska & Harmer, 2021). The limbic system is a complex network of brain areas for controlling emotion. Together with the ventral striatum and insula, the amygdala is responsible for fast automatic processing of emotionally salient information (both environmental stimuli as well as emotional memories) (Davis & Whalen, 2001; Harmer et al. 2003a, b; Ito et al., 2017; Morris et al., 1996). Important to note is that amygdala activity increases even in healthy volunteers during processing of (especially negative) emotional information. But, when individuals with depression process negative emotional stimuli, they show amygdala reactivity that is more intense (by up to 70%) and longer lasting (up to three times as long) than healthy controls. This pattern of amygdala response, indicative of biased stimulus processing, appears to be automatic and exists even if the emotional valence of the stimulus is masked to the conscious mind through subliminal presentation (Disner et al., 2011). This, in turn, suggests that the amygdala plays an important role in the development and maintenance of negative emotional processing bias (Fu et al., 2004; Godlewska & Harmer, 2021; Leppänen, 2006; Mayberg, 2003; Surguladze et al., 2005).

Furthermore, the networks for increasing attention to salient and important stimuli are thought to be modulated by signals from the amygdala, together with frontoparietal circuitry (Vuilleumier & Driver, 2007). For instance, patients with depression show increased responses to sad facial expressions and decreased responses to happy facial expressions in frontoparietal areas including the precuneus and fusiform gyrus (Surguladze et al., 2005). The precuneus is an important hub between the frontal and parietal lobes and is thought to have a central role in a wide spectrum of highly integrated tasks, including visuo-spatial imagery, episodic memory retrieval, and self-processing operations (Cavanna & Trimble, 2006). Therefore, the coordinated responses by these brain areas to affective stimuli may provide a neural assay of emotional processing bias or the salience level of affective stimuli to an individual (Disner et al., 2011; Surguladze et al., 2005).

Limbic areas such as the amygdala are believed to rapidly respond to emotionally salient stimuli in the environment, to increase vigilance, and coordinate rapid behavioural responses. This reactivity is believed to be regulated by higher cortical areas such as the dorsal and ventral lateral prefrontal cortex (dl and vlPFC) and medial prefrontal cortex (PFC), which allows responses to be modulated by context and situation. Evidence for this hypothesis comes, for example, from studies showing that amygdala activity in healthy individuals is negatively correlated with dorsolateral PFC activation (e.g. Foland-Ross et al., 2010). This control of the PFC on the limbic system is thought to be the neural correlate of 'top-down' processing, whilst the effects of limbic and sensory networks reactivity contribute to 'bottom-up' processing. The pgACC acts as a crucial hub centrally located between the two (Disner et al., 2011; Godlewska & Harmer, 2021; Mayberg, 2003). The balance between the limbic system and the PFC is believed to be affected in depression, such that there is overactivity in limbic reactivity and/or reduced inhibitory or regulation within the PFC. Evidence for this comes from studies showing both limbic hyperactivation and prefrontal cortex hypoactivation in depression in response to emotional stimuli (Pizzagalli & Roberts, 2022; Zhong et al., 2011). Negative emotional processing biases may therefore be driven by enhanced negative evaluation within limbic areas coupled with deficient higher-order emotional modulation of cognitive processes within areas such as the dorsolateral and ventromedial PFC, or the pgACC which acts as a hub between these two systems.

10.3.4 Antidepressants and Emotional Processing Bias: Neural Mechanisms

Antidepressant treatment has been reported to modulate limbic and ACC response to negative versus positive information as well as increasing engagement of PFC areas such as the dorsolateral PFC (dlPFC) (Godlewska & Harmer, 2021; Ma, 2015). As mentioned in the previous section, more intense and longer-lasting amygdala reactivity to (especially negative) emotional information is indicative of biased emotional processing. When presenting healthy volunteers with pictures of fearful and happy faces, the antidepressant citalopram decreased amygdala, medial PFC, and hippocampal responses to fearful facial expressions of emotion after 7 days of administration and compared to a placebo control (Harmer et al., 2006). These neural differences were accompanied by decreased recognition of fearful facial expressions assessed after the scan. Such a reduction in amygdala reactivity to fearful faces was also seen with just a single dose of citalopram (Murphy et al., 2009a) and another antidepressant mirtazapine (Rawlings et al., 2010) compared to placebo.

Similar effects have been reported when studying patients with depression early in treatment for depression. Godlewska et al. (2012), for example, found increased amygdala responses to fearful facial expressions in depressed versus healthy participants, which was normalised after 7 days of escitalopram administration (Godlewska et al., 2012). These effects were seen prior to changes in mood and depression as there were no mood differences between the placebo and the escitalopram group at baseline and after 7 days of treatment. This suggests that normalisation of amygdala responsiveness was caused by medication and not by an improvement of mood.

In addition to these studies using facial stimuli, in a study by Young et al. (2020), 17 depressed individuals underwent fMRI during the performance of a task involving rating of self-relevance of emotionally positive and negative cue words before and after receiving 12 weeks of SSRI therapy. At post-treatment, SSRI responders ($n = 11$) had increased amygdala activity in response to positive stimuli, and decreased activity in response to negative stimuli, compared to non-responders ($n = 6$). The authors therefore suggested that normalising amygdala responses to salient information is a correlate of SSRI efficacy.

Similar to the results of the behavioural studies described in the previous section, normalisation of emotional processing on a neural level during antidepressant treatment was also shown to correlate with clinical improvement (Browning et al., 2019; Godlewska et al., 2016; Ruhé et al., 2011; Shiroma et al., 2014; Williams et al., 2015). For example, 35 unmedicated depressed patients who showed at least 50% symptom reduction after treatment with escitalopram by week six, had a greater reduction in neural activity to fearful compared to happy facial expressions (therefore not just a general reduction towards emotional stimuli) after just 7 days of escitalopram across a network of regions including the ACC, insula, amygdala, and thalamus (Godlewska et al., 2016). Mediation analysis confirmed that the direct effect of neural change on symptom reduction was not mediated by initial changes in depressive symptoms. Moreover, escitalopram responders showed increased neural amygdala activity to happy faces following treatment that was not seen in treatment non-responders.

In sum, accumulating evidence seem to indicate that early effects of antidepressants on amygdala reactivity to negative versus positive stimuli can be seen prior to changes in symptoms and are associated with later clinical response. This suggests that antidepressants may not directly target mechanisms directly underpinning mood but rather work by changing the balance of positive versus negative emotional processing which, over time and in interaction with social and emotional experiences, leads to their antidepressant effects. These neural effects may contribute to differences in interpretation biases measured behaviourally but more work is needed to understand this link.

10.3.5   Do These Neural Findings Concur with the 'Top-Down' and 'Bottom-Up' Hypothesis of Psychological Treatment Versus Antidepressant Action?

An understanding of the psychological effects of antidepressants provides a common mechanism of action for both pharmacological and psychological treatments, and is thus likely to be of value given that these types of treatment are often used in combination (Nord et al., 2021). While some evidence suggests that psychological treatments also influence negative emotional processing bias, there is also evidence not supporting such an effect (Porter et al., 2016; Ruzickova et al., 2021; Yılmaz et al., 2019). For example, Porter et al. (2016) found no change in performance on the facial expression recognition task (FERT) after 16 weeks of psychotherapy. However, Yılmaz et al. (2019) did find such an improvement in the FERT, for both cognitive behavioral therapy (CBT) and psychotherapy (ExP). That is, ExP improved the patients' ability to recognise almost all emotions except anger, whilst CBT improved only the recognition of happy emotions. Both treatments also significantly reduced depression scores on the Hamilton Depression Rating Scale (HAM-D, Hamilton, 1960). However, the authors did not test whether there was a correlation between the depression ratings and the improvement in emotional processing bias by CBT or ExP.

In a recent study by Ruzickova et al. (2021), remote behavioural activation (BA) was shown to improve emotional processing bias on several components of the Facial Emotion Recognition Task (FERT). Behavioural activation shifted the identification of negative faces towards more positive or neutral interpretations by week four of treatment. Furthermore, in comparison to the control group, the BA group showed a significant decrease in depression, anxiety, and anhedonia after the intervention, as well as an increase in self-reported activation and social support. Benefits persisted at 1-month follow-up. Moreover, early changes in biases were associated with later therapeutic gain. These findings suggest bidirectional effects to occur between cognition and behaviour. As discussed earlier in this chapter, such effects have previously been shown mainly for antidepressant treatments for depression.

The cognitive neuropsychological model suggests that psychotherapy targets emotional/affect circuitry in the brain via top-down mechanisms (i.e. enhancing PFC signalling), whilst antidepressants alter emotional processing via bottom-up mechanisms (i.e. targeting subcortical structures such as the amygdala). As a result, psychotherapy may change cognitive control of affect processing, or attention and awareness of affective state, whereas antidepressants may alter generation of affective and visceral sensations directly (Roiser et al., 2012; Satpute & Lindquist, 2019).

This idea might, however, be an over-simplification. For example, studies have shown that antidepressants influence prefrontal cortex-related activity like the medial PFC during emotional processing (Godlewska & Harmer, 2021; Ma, 2015), while changes in amygdala response have also been found after successful CBT (Kalsi et al., 2017; Sankar et al., 2018). Moreover, the neural response between top-down and bottom-up areas is highly interconnected and can be difficult to tease apart (Ochsner et al., 2009). Therefore, several neuroimaging studies suggest that changes due to both types of therapy (i.e. drug vs. psychotherapy) occur at the network level rather than in a single structure (Comte et al., 2016; Ochsner et al., 2009).

Further discrepancies between the studies' results may occur because individual trials of neuroimaging measures can suffer from relatively low statistical power, and few studies have directly compared the two treatments in a randomised design. An alternative way of comparing both treatment avenues is therefore by first summarising the two different treatments separately in a meta-analysis, and then having a quantitative comparison between the two. Nord and colleagues (Nord et al., 2021) did exactly that by using the primary data from two meta-analyses (Ma, 2015; Marwood et al., 2018), testing whether treatment with antidepressants versus psychotherapy evoked overlapping and/or distinct neural changes. By using data from a third meta-analysis of emotional processing in the brain, they then separately tested whether neural changes from antidepressant medication versus psychotherapy overlapped with known affect circuitry. This allowed them to directly test whether or not the proximal mechanisms of treatment were overlapping or distinct (or both). Irrespective of whether or not patients responded to the psychotherapy or antidepressant they received, Nord et al. (2021) demonstrated treatment-specific brain effects following antidepressant treatment versus psychotherapy, consistent with theories of different proximal mechanisms of action. Namely, changes in amygdala reactivity were most consistently associated with antidepressant drug treatment whereas changes in mPFC were seen most reliably with psychotherapy, both assessed during negative versus positive affective processing. Nevertheless, the effects of both interventions overlapped with a network involved in representing affective states. This overlap might explain the enhanced efficacy of combined pharmacological and psychological treatment (DeRubeis et al., 2008; Hollon et al., 2005, 2019). Important to note is that not only patients with depression were compared in this paper by Nord et al. (2021), but also other affective disorders like anxiety disorders, posttraumatic stress disorder (PTSD), and obsessive-compulsive disorder (OCD). Also, inherent to the type of intervention, different treatment durations were compared. Antidepressants were delivered daily and assessed after less time, whilst psychotherapy was delivered less frequently and assessed after a longer time. Future work should address the question of what a comparable 'dose' between the two treatment approaches would be, and to measure pre- and post-treatment neural activation at a comparable interval.

10.3.6 Interaction with the Environment

Differences in the processing of external cues (e.g. positive social stimuli) and internal cues (e.g. positive memories) may occur early in the course of antidepressant treatment, but interaction with the environment over time is required before these changes in processing biases lead to clinically improved mood. For example, an increased tendency to interpret social signals (e.g. facial expressions) more positively may not immediately lead to improved mood states, but could reinforce social participation and social functioning, which, over repeated experience, then improves mood and other symptoms of depression, like anhedonia. Therefore, it has been suggested that everyday life stressors and events need to be experienced with this new more positive context before antidepressant effects are seen (Godlewska & Harmer, 2021).

Although more research is necessary to test this prediction of the model, recent studies have provided some support. For example, in depressed individuals with late-life depression, an early bias shift as measured with the FERT was predictive of treatment response, however, only in patients with good levels of social support (Shiroma et al., 2014). Moreover, social and environmental factors may moderate the effects of antidepressants. In a study by Chiarotti et al. (2017), citalopram amplified the positive influence that positive living conditions have (like employment status) on mood in a dose-dependent manner.

The idea that emotional bias affects mood through interactions with the environment – for example, a stressful situation – was also shown by Browning et al. (2011). In this study, citalopram was found to reduce the negative effects of a mood induction, and the magnitude of this effect was associated with individuals' reduction in negative bias consistent with a bias by stress interaction. The converse has also been exemplified by a study conducted by MacLeod et al. (2002) in which it was demonstrated that an experimentally induced negative bias did not affect mood until participants were later exposed to a stressful situation (for a schematic presentation of how antidepressants (SSRIs) may improve mood and interact with the environment, see Fig. 10.2).

The cognitive neuropsychological model therefore provides a potential explanation for treatment non-response in depression: if a patient is socially isolated or in a particularly toxic environment, then increased positive versus negative processing would be expected to have only limited effects. Adding psychological and/or behavioural interventions to pharmacological treatments may thus help patients engage with their environment and experience stimuli necessary for creating and stabilising new positive interpretations. Therefore, the early stages of anti-depressant treatment may be really important for a successful clinical outcome. It will be interesting to test whether early improvements in negative interpretation biases with antidepressants could be potentiated with behavioural interventions (like behavioural activation, psychotherapy, or activities with friends) to assess whether synergistic effects can be attained.

An additional reason why the therapeutic effect of antidepressant treatment requires a number of weeks to become clinically apparent may be that a certain level of cognitive flexibility is required for expectations about negative and positive events to be corrected. Next to low mood and motivation, cognitive inflexibility is a key component of depression (Rock et al., 2014). Cognitive flexibility is commonly defined as the ability to switch between different types of tasks or concepts (Diamond, 2013), but this definition can be expanded to also include a broader ability to adjust to new situations or to change and update ingrained beliefs. Therefore another reason why traditional antidepressants may take multiple weeks to have

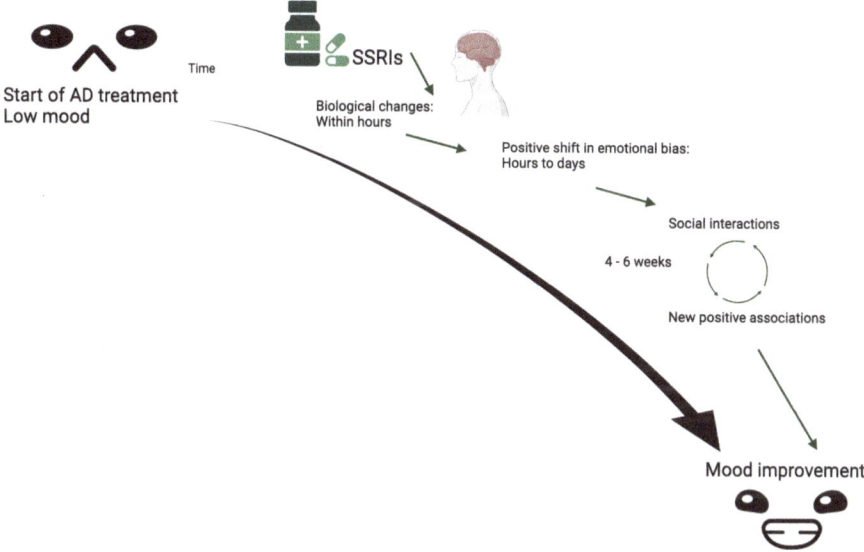

Fig. 10.2 Hypothetical schematic presentation of how antidepressants (SSRIs) improve mood and interact with the environment

their effect could be that they only affect cognitive inflexibility indirectly, and because of that need more time to correct this (Haarsma et al., 2021). For that reason, potential drug treatments which can more directly target flexibility and plasticity, like novel potential antidepressants like ketamine, may therefore have the potential for faster onset of action in depression.

10.4 Can Measuring Emotional Processing Biases Help the Future Treatment of MDD?

10.4.1 Providing an Early Marker of Treatment Response to Antidepressants

As described in this chapter, changes in emotional processing bias can provide a sensitive, early measure of antidepressant efficacy for individual patients. Therefore, early treatment-induced changes in emotional processing may be used to guide antidepressant therapy and reduce the time taken for depressed patients to return to good mental health.

The ease of assessing emotional processing biases allows it to be used in the clinical setting. If, for example, after a week of antidepressant treatment no improvement in negative interpretation bias occurred, it may benefit the patient to move over to a different form of treatment, for example, a treatment that would usually only be prescribed after other treatments have failed. Currently, outcome of treatment can be assessed only after a lengthy period of time (but for an alternative approach to make psychotherapy research more efficient, see Blackwell et al., 2019). A recent study by Browning et al. (2021) assessed whether it was clinically effective to guide and personalise antidepressant treatment based on the facial expression recognition test (FERT) and subjective symptoms. This study was a follow-up from Browning et al. (2019) where the authors predicted treatment response post-treatment only. In a recent study, however, Browning and colleagues conducted an open-label randomised controlled trial in 913 medication-free depressed primary-care patients with symptoms of depression and anxiety (Browning et al., 2021). Patients were either randomly assigned to have their antidepressant treatment guided by the predictive algorithm or receive treatment as usual. Patient follow-up took place 1 year after randomisation. The authors found that use of the predictive algorithm did not increase the rate of response to antidepressant treatment, estimated by depressive symptoms, but did improve symptoms of anxiety at week eight and functional outcome at week 24. Therefore, this study provides initial support for the use of personalised medicine approaches based on emotional processing in the clinic. However, further work is needed to increase the accuracy with which the shift in emotional processing bias can predict the outcome and to fit the model to differentiate between specific groups of drugs or individual medications (Browning et al., 2019, 2021; Godlewska & Harmer, 2021).

10.4.2   Providing an Experimental Medicine Model for Treatment Development

Current screens of novel antidepressant treatments for potential efficacy are largely based on pre-clinical animal models which have relatively low predictive validity for what happens in the human brain. The cognitive neuropsychological hypothesis of antidepressant drug action was developed into a human-based emotion model to screen and understand novel treatments in development (e.g. as used in the study by Post et al. (2016) with a candidate treatment for depression). This approach can furthermore be used to repurpose older drugs and/or eliminate medications without potential earlier in clinical development. It is also of interest whether this model could be applied in the development of psychological treatments and/or their combination with antidepressants. This would speed up decision-making during novel treatment development and facilitate successful translation into patient care. It allows novel treatments to be understood in more detail, in humans, before large-scale and costly randomised controlled trials (RCTs) are conducted.

10.5   Overall Perspective

In recent years, considerable progress has been made in understanding mechanisms of antidepressant drug action to remedy low mood and anhedonia in MDD. Although the role of cognitive biases, such as interpretation biases, in producing and maintaining depression has long been acknowledged, it is only in the past two decades that we have really begun to recognise their role in the action of antidepressant treatment. This perspective revolves that even though conventional antidepressants can swiftly change the balance of positive versus negative emotional processing in the brain, it is only with time and in interaction with social and emotional experiences that effects on mood and subjective experience can be seen. It is hoped that this perspective might not only explain how antidepressants work, but could also become a tool for improving the future treatment of depression. In particular, preliminary evidence highlights a role in treatment response prediction and refining treatment strategies for individual patients as well as in the development of new treatments. It also provides a framework by which to consider the effects of different pharmacological and psychological treatment combinations. As such, combining multidisciplinary expertise across disciplines from cognitive and clinical psychology to pharmacology may be beneficial to our field (Holmes et al., 2014; and for a related discussion about the interplay of scientific research and clinical practice, see Chap. 1 by Holmes), in order to stimulate innovation that indeed moves the field forward.

References

Figure 10.2 was created with BioRender.com https://biorender.com

Ahmed, N., Bone, J. K., Lewis, G., Freemantle, N., Harmer, C. J., Duffy, L., & Lewis, G. (2021). The effect of sertraline on emotional processing: Secondary analyses of the PANDA randomised controlled trial. *Psychological Medicine*, 1–8. https://doi.org/10.1017/S0033291720004985

Beck, A. T. (1979). *Cognitive therapy of depression*. Guilford press.

Benoit, R. G., Szpunar, K. K., & Schacter, D. L. (2014). Ventromedial prefrontal cortex supports affective future simulation by integrating distributed knowledge. *Proceedings of the National Academy of Sciences, 111*(46), 16550–16555. https://doi.org/10.1073/pnas.1419274111

Blackwell, S. E., Woud, M. L., Margraf, J., & Schönbrodt, F. D. (2019). Introducing the leapfrog design: A simple Bayesian adaptive rolling trial design for accelerated treatment development and optimization. *Clinical Psychological Science, 7*(6), 1222–1243. https://doi.org/10.1177/2167702619858071

Blair, K. S., Otero, M., Teng, C., Jacobs, M., Odenheimer, S., Pine, D. S., & Blair, R. J. R. (2013). Dissociable roles of ventromedial prefrontal cortex (vmPFC) and rostral anterior cingulate cortex (rACC) in value representation and optimistic bias. *NeuroImage, 78*, 103–110. https://doi.org/10.1016/j.neuroimage.2013.03.063

Browning, M., Grol, M., Ly, V., Goodwin, G. M., Holmes, E. A., & Harmer, C. J. (2011). Using an experimental medicine model to explore combination effects of pharmacological and cognitive interventions for depression and anxiety. *Neuropsychopharmacology, 36*(13), 2689–2697. https://doi.org/10.1038/npp.2011.159

Browning, M., Kingslake, J., Dourish, C. T., Goodwin, G. M., Harmer, C. J., & Dawson, G. R. (2019). Predicting treatment response to antidepressant medication using early changes in emotional processing. *European Neuropsychopharmacology, 29*(1), 66–75. https://doi.org/10.1016/j.euroneuro.2018.11.1102

Browning, M., Bilderbeck, A. C., Dias, R., Dourish, C. T., Kingslake, J., Deckert, J., Goodwin, G. M., Gorwood, P., Guo, B., Harmer, C. J., Morriss, R., Reif, A., Ruhe, H. G., van Schaik, A., Simon, J., Sola, V. P., Veltman, D. J., Elices, M., Lever, A. G., et al. (2021). The clinical effectiveness of using a predictive algorithm to guide antidepressant treatment in primary care (PReDicT): An open-label, randomised controlled trial. *Neuropsychopharmacology, 46*(7), 1307–1314. https://doi.org/10.1038/s41386-021-00981-z

Cavanna, A. E., & Trimble, M. R. (2006). The precuneus: A review of its functional anatomy and behavioural correlates. *Brain, 129*(3), 564–583. https://doi.org/10.1093/brain/awl004

Chiarotti, F., Viglione, A., Giuliani, A., & Branchi, I. (2017). Citalopram amplifies the influence of living conditions on mood in depressed patients enrolled in the STAR*D study. *Translational Psychiatry, 7*(3), e1066. https://doi.org/10.1038/tp.2017.35

Comte, M., Schön, D., Coull, J. T., Reynaud, E., Khalfa, S., Belzeaux, R., Ibrahim, E. C., Guedj, E., Blin, O., Weinberger, D. R., & Fakra, E. (2016). Dissociating bottom-up and top-down mechanisms in the cortico-limbic system during emotion processing. *Cerebral Cortex, 26*(1), 144–155. https://doi.org/10.1093/cercor/bhu185

Davey, G. C. L., & Meeten, F. (2016). The perseverative worry bout: A review of cognitive, affective and motivational factors that contribute to worry perseveration. *Biological Psychology, 121*(Pt B), 233–243. https://doi.org/10.1016/j.biopsycho.2016.04.003

Davis, M., & Whalen, P. J. (2001). The amygdala: Vigilance and emotion. *Molecular Psychiatry, 6*(1), 13–34. https://doi.org/10.1038/sj.mp.4000812

DeRubeis, R. J., Siegle, G. J., & Hollon, S. D. (2008). Cognitive therapy versus medication for depression: Treatment outcomes and neural mechanisms. *Nature Reviews Neuroscience, 9*(10), 788–796. https://doi.org/10.1038/nrn2345

Diamond, A. (2013). Executive functions. *Annual Review of Psychology, 64*(1), 135–168. https://doi.org/10.1146/annurev-psych-113011-143750

Disner, S. G., Beevers, C. G., Haigh, E. A. P., & Beck, A. T. (2011). Neural mechanisms of the cognitive model of depression. *Nature Reviews Neuroscience, 12*(8), 467–477. https://doi.org/10.1038/nrn3027

Erthal, F., Bastos, A., Vilete, L., Oliveira, L., Pereira, M., Mendlowicz, M., Volchan, E., & Figueira, I. (2021). Unveiling the neural underpinnings of optimism: A systematic review. *Cognitive, Affective, & Behavioral Neuroscience, 21*(5), 895–916. https://doi.org/10.3758/s13415-021-00931-8

Foland-Ross, L. C., Altshuler, L. L., Bookheimer, S. Y., Lieberman, M. D., Townsend, J., Penfold, C., Moody, T., Ahlf, K., Shen, J. K., Madsen, S. K., Rasser, P. E., Toga, A. W., & Thompson, P. M. (2010). Amygdala reactivity in healthy adults is correlated with prefrontal cortical thickness. *Journal of Neuroscience, 30*(49), 16673–16678. https://doi.org/10.1523/JNEUROSCI.4578-09.2010

Fu, C. H. Y., Williams, S. C. R., Cleare, A. J., Brammer, M. J., Walsh, N. D., Kim, J., Andrew, C. M., Pich, E. M., Williams, P. M., Reed, L. J., Mitterschiffthaler, M. T., Suckling, J., & Bullmore, E. T. (2004). Attenuation of the neural response to sad faces in major depression by antidepressant treatment: A prospective, event-related functional magnetic resonance imaging study. *Archives of General Psychiatry, 61*(9), 877–889. https://doi.org/10.1001/archpsyc.61.9.877

Godlewska, B. R., & Harmer, C. J. (2021). Cognitive neuropsychological theory of antidepressant action: A modern-day approach to depression and its treatment. *Psychopharmacology, 238*(5), 1265–1278. https://doi.org/10.1007/s00213-019-05448-0

Godlewska, B. R., Norbury, R., Selvaraj, S., Cowen, P. J., & Harmer, C. J. (2012). Short-term SSRI treatment normalises amygdala hyperactivity in depressed patients. *Psychological Medicine, 42*(12), 2609–2617. https://doi.org/10.1017/S0033291712000591

Godlewska, B. R., Browning, M., Norbury, R., Cowen, P. J., & Harmer, C. J. (2016). Early changes in emotional processing as a marker of clinical response to SSRI treatment in depression. *Translational Psychiatry, 6*(11), e957. https://doi.org/10.1038/tp.2016.130

Haarsma, J., Harmer, C. J., & Tamm, S. (2021). A continuum hypothesis of psychotomimetic rapid antidepressants. *Brain and Neuroscience Advances, 5*, 1–11. https://doi.org/10.1177/23982128211007772

Hamilton, M. (1960). A rating scale for depression. *Journal of Neurology, Neurosurgery and Psychiatry, 23*(1), 56–62. https://doi.org/10.1136/jnnp.23.1.56

Harmer, C. J., Bhagwagar, Z., Perrett, D. I., Völlm, B. A., Cowen, P. J., & Goodwin, G. M. (2003a). Acute SSRI administration affects the processing of social cues in healthy volunteers. *Neuropsychopharmacology, 28*(1), 148–152. https://doi.org/10.1038/sj.npp.1300004

Harmer, C. J., Hill, S. A., Taylor, M. J., Cowen, P. J., & Goodwin, G. M. (2003b). Toward a neuropsychological theory of antidepressant drug action: Increase in positive emotional bias after potentiation of norepinephrine activity. *American Journal of Psychiatry, 160*(5), 990–992. https://doi.org/10.1176/appi.ajp.160.5.990

Harmer, C. J., Shelley, N. C., Cowen, P. J., & Goodwin, G. M. (2004). Increased positive versus negative affective perception and memory in healthy volunteers following selective serotonin and norepinephrine reuptake inhibition. *American Journal of Psychiatry, 161*(7), 1256–1263. https://doi.org/10.1176/appi.ajp.161.7.1256

Harmer, C. J., Mackay, C. E., Reid, C. B., Cowen, P. J., & Goodwin, G. M. (2006). Antidepressant drug treatment modifies the neural processing of nonconscious threat cues. *Biological Psychiatry, 59*(9), 816–820. https://doi.org/10.1016/j.biopsych.2005.10.015

Harmer, C. J., Goodwin, G. M., & Cowen, P. J. (2009a). Why do antidepressants take so long to work? A cognitive neuropsychological model of antidepressant drug action. *The British Journal of Psychiatry, 195*(2), 102–108. https://doi.org/10.1192/bjp.bp.108.051193

Harmer, C. J., O'Sullivan, U., Favaron, E., Massey-Chase, R., Ayres, R., Reinecke, A., Goodwin, G. M., & Cowen, P. J. (2009b). Effect of acute antidepressant administration on negative affective bias in depressed patients. *American Journal of Psychiatry, 166*(10), 1178–1184. https://doi.org/10.1176/appi.ajp.2009.09020149

Harmer, C. J., Duman, R. S., & Cowen, P. J. (2017). How do antidepressants work? New perspectives for refining future treatment approaches. *The Lancet Psychiatry, 4*(5), 409–418. https://doi.org/10.1016/S2215-0366(17)30015-9

Hollon, S. D., DeRubeis, R. J., Shelton, R. C., Amsterdam, J. D., Salomon, R. M., O'Reardon, J. P., Lovett, M. L., Young, P. R., Haman, K. L., Freeman, B. B., & Gallop, R. (2005). Prevention of relapse following cognitive therapy vs medications in moderate to severe depression. *Archives of General Psychiatry, 62*(4), 417–422. https://doi.org/10.1001/archpsyc.62.4.417

Hollon, S. D., Cohen, Z. D., Singla, D. R., & Andrews, P. W. (2019). Recent developments in the treatment of depression. *Behavior Therapy, 50*(2), 257–269. https://doi.org/10.1016/j.beth.2019.01.002

Holmes, E. A., Craske, M. G., & Graybiel, A. M. (2014). Psychological treatments: A call for mental-health science. *Nature, 511*, 287–289. https://doi.org/10.1038/511287a

Holmes, E. A., Ghaderi, A., Harmer, C. J., Ramchandani, P. G., Cuijpers, P., Morrison, A. P., Roiser, J. P., Bockting, C. L. H., O'Connor, R. C., Shafran, R., Moulds, M. L., & Craske, M. G. (2018). The Lancet Psychiatry Commission on psychological treatments research in tomorrow's science. *The Lancet Psychiatry, 5*(3), 237–286. https://doi.org/10.1016/S2215-0366(17)30513-8

Ito, T., Yokokawa, K., Yahata, N., Isato, A., Suhara, T., & Yamada, M. (2017). Neural basis of negativity bias in the perception of ambiguous facial expression. *Scientific Reports, 7*(1), 420. https://doi.org/10.1038/s41598-017-00502-3

Kalsi, N., Altavilla, D., Tambelli, R., Aceto, P., Trentini, C., Di Giorgio, C., & Lai, C. (2017). Neural correlates of outcome of the psychotherapy compared to antidepressant therapy in anxiety and depression disorders: Meta-analysis. *Frontiers in Psychology, 8*, 927. https://doi.org/10.3389/fpsyg.2017.00927

Leppänen, J. M. (2006). Emotional information processing in mood disorders: A review of behavioral and neuroimaging findings. *Current Opinion in Psychiatry, 19*(1), 34–39. https://doi.org/10.1097/01.yco.0000191500.46411.00

Li, B.-J., Friston, K., Mody, M., Wang, H.-N., Lu, H.-B., & Hu, D.-W. (2018). A brain network model for depression: From symptom understanding to disease intervention. *CNS Neuroscience and Therapeutics, 24*(11), 1004–1019. https://doi.org/10.1111/cns.12998

Ma, Y. (2015). Neuropsychological mechanism underlying antidepressant effect: A systematic meta-analysis. *Molecular Psychiatry, 20*(3), 311–319. https://doi.org/10.1038/mp.2014.24

MacLeod, C., Rutherford, E., Campbell, L., Ebsworthy, G., & Holker, L. (2002). Selective attention and emotional vulnerability: Assessing the causal basis of their association through the experimental manipulation of attentional bias. *Journal of Abnormal Psychology, 111*(1), 107–123. https://doi.org/10.1037/0021-843X.111.1.107

Marwood, L., Wise, T., Perkins, A. M., & Cleare, A. J. (2018). Meta-analyses of the neural mechanisms and predictors of response to psychotherapy in depression and anxiety. *Neuroscience and Biobehavioral Reviews, 95*, 61–72. https://doi.org/10.1016/j.neubiorev.2018.09.022

Mathews, A., & MacLeod, C. (2005). Cognitive vulnerability to emotional disorders. *Annual Review of Clinical Psychology, 1*, 167–195. https://doi.org/10.1146/annurev.clinpsy.1.102803.143916

Mayberg, H. S. (2003). Modulating dysfunctional limbic-cortical circuits in depression: Towards development of brain-based algorithms for diagnosis and optimised treatment. *British Medical Bulletin, 65*(1), 193–207. https://doi.org/10.1093/bmb/65.1.193

Miskowiak, K. W., Seeberg, I., Kjaerstad, H. L., Burdick, K. E., Martinez-Aran, A., del Mar Bonnin, C., Bowie, C. R., Carvalho, A. F., Gallagher, P., Hasler, G., Lafer, B., López-Jaramillo, C., Sumiyoshi, T., McIntyre, R. S., Schaffer, A., Porter, R. J., Purdon, S., Torres, I. J., Yatham, L. N., et al. (2019). Affective cognition in bipolar disorder: A systematic review by the ISBD targeting cognition task force. *Bipolar Disorders, 21*(8), 686–719. https://doi.org/10.1111/bdi.12834

Mogg, K., Baldwin, D. S., Brodrick, P., & Bradley, B. P. (2004). Effect of short-term SSRI treatment on cognitive bias in generalised anxiety disorder. *Psychopharmacology, 176*(3), 466–470. https://doi.org/10.1007/s00213-004-1902-y

Morris, J. S., Frith, C. D., Perrett, D. I., Rowland, D., Young, A. W., Calder, A. J., & Dolan, R. J. (1996). A differential neural response in the human amygdala to fearful and happy facial expressions. *Nature, 383*(6603), 812–815. https://doi.org/10.1038/383812a0

Murphy, S. E., Norbury, R., O'Sullivan, U., Cowen, P. J., & Harmer, C. J. (2009a). Effect of a single dose of citalopram on amygdala response to emotional faces. *The British Journal of Psychiatry, 194*(6), 535–540. https://doi.org/10.1192/bjp.bp.108.056093

Murphy, S. E., Yiend, J., Lester, K. J., Cowen, P. J., & Harmer, C. J. (2009b). Short-term serotonergic but not noradrenergic antidepressant administration reduces attentional vigilance to threat in healthy volunteers. *International Journal of Neuropsychopharmacology, 12*(2), 169–179. https://doi.org/10.1017/S1461145708009164

Nord, C. L., Barrett, L. F., Lindquist, K. A., Ma, Y., Marwood, L., Satpute, A. B., & Dalgleish, T. (2021). Neural effects of antidepressant medication and psychological treatments: A quantitative synthesis across three meta-analyses. *The British Journal of Psychiatry, 219*(4), 546–550. https://doi.org/10.1192/bjp.2021.16

Ochsner, K. N., Ray, R. R., Hughes, B., McRae, K., Cooper, J. C., Weber, J., Gabrieli, J. D. E., & Gross, J. J. (2009). Bottom-up and top-down processes in emotion generation: Common and distinct neural mechanisms. *Psychological Science, 20*(11), 1322–1331. https://doi.org/10.1111/j.1467-9280.2009.02459.x

Pizzagalli, D. A., & Roberts, A. C. (2022). Prefrontal cortex and depression. *Neuropsychopharmacology, 47*(1), 225–246. https://doi.org/10.1038/s41386-021-01101-7

Porter, R. J., Bourke, C., Carter, J. D., Douglas, K. M., McIntosh, V. V. W., Jordan, J., Joyce, P. R., & Frampton, C. M. A. (2016). No change in neuropsychological dysfunction or emotional processing during treatment of major depression with cognitive–behaviour therapy or schema therapy. *Psychological Medicine, 46*(2), 393–404. https://doi.org/10.1017/S0033291715001907

Post, A., Smart, T. S., Krikke-Workel, J., Dawson, G. R., Harmer, C. J., Browning, M., Jackson, K., Kakar, R., Mohs, R., Statnick, M., Wafford, K., McCarthy, A., Barth, V., & Witkin, J. M. (2016). A selective nociceptin receptor antagonist to treat depression: Evidence from preclinical and clinical studies. *Neuropsychopharmacology, 41*(7), 1803–1812. https://doi.org/10.1038/npp.2015.348

Potvin, S., Tikàsz, A., & Mendrek, A. (2016). Emotionally neutral stimuli are not neutral in schizophrenia: A mini review of functional neuroimaging studies. *Frontiers in Psychiatry, 7*, 115. https://doi.org/10.3389/fpsyt.2016.00115

Rawlings, N. B., Norbury, R., Cowen, P. J., & Harmer, C. J. (2010). A single dose of mirtazapine modulates neural responses to emotional faces in healthy people. *Psychopharmacology, 212*(4), 625–634. https://doi.org/10.1007/s00213-010-1983-8

Robinson, E. S. J., & Roiser, J. P. (2016). Affective biases in humans and animals. In T. W. Robbins & B. J. Sahakian (Eds.), *Translational neuropsychopharmacology* (pp. 263–286). Springer International Publishing. https://doi.org/10.1007/7854_2015_5011

Rock, P. L., Roiser, J. P., Riedel, W. J., & Blackwell, A. D. (2014). Cognitive impairment in depression: A systematic review and meta-analysis. *Psychological Medicine, 44*(10), 2029–2040. https://doi.org/10.1017/S0033291713002535

Roiser, J. P., Elliott, R., & Sahakian, B. J. (2012). Cognitive mechanisms of treatment in depression. *Neuropsychopharmacology, 37*(1), 117–136. https://doi.org/10.1038/npp.2011.183

Ruhé, H. G., Booij, J., Veltman, D. J., Michel, M. C., & Schene, A. H. (2011). Successful pharmacologic treatment of major depressive disorder attenuates amygdala activation to negative facial expressions: A functional magnetic resonance imaging study. *The Journal of Clinical Psychiatry, 72*(4), 20218. https://doi.org/10.4088/JCP.10m06584

Ruzickova, T., Carson, J., Argabright, S., Gillespie, A., Guinea, C., Pearse, A., Barwick, R., Murphy, S. E., & Harmer, C. J. (2021). Online behavioural activation during the COVID-19 pandemic decreases depression and negative affective bias. *Psychological Medicine*, 1–10. https://doi.org/10.1017/S0033291721002142

Sankar, A., Melin, A., Lorenzetti, V., Horton, P., Costafreda, S. G., & Fu, C. H. Y. (2018). A systematic review and meta-analysis of the neural correlates of psychological therapies in major depression. *Psychiatry Research: Neuroimaging, 279*, 31–39. https://doi.org/10.1016/j.pscychresns.2018.07.002

Satpute, A. B., & Lindquist, K. A. (2019). The default mode network's role in discrete emotion. *Trends in Cognitive Sciences, 23*(10), 851–864. https://doi.org/10.1016/j.tics.2019.07.003

Sharot, T., Riccardi, A. M., Raio, C. M., & Phelps, E. A. (2007). Neural mechanisms mediating optimism bias. *Nature, 450*(7166), 102–105. https://doi.org/10.1038/nature06280

Shiroma, P. R., Thuras, P., Johns, B., & Lim, K. O. (2014). Emotion recognition processing as early predictor of response to 8-week citalopram treatment in late-life depression. *International Journal of Geriatric Psychiatry, 29*(11), 1132–1139. https://doi.org/10.1002/gps.4104

Surguladze, S., Brammer, M. J., Keedwell, P., Giampietro, V., Young, A. W., Travis, M. J., Williams, S. C., & Phillips, M. L. (2005). A differential pattern of neural response toward sad versus happy facial expressions in major depressive disorder. *Biological Psychiatry, 57*(3), 201–209. https://doi.org/10.1016/j.biopsych.2004.10.028

Tranter, R., Bell, D., Gutting, P., Harmer, C., Healy, D., & Anderson, I. M. (2009). The effect of serotonergic and noradrenergic antidepressants on face emotion processing in depressed patients. *Journal of Affective Disorders, 118*(1), 87–93. https://doi.org/10.1016/j.jad.2009.01.028

Vuilleumier, P., & Driver, J. (2007). Modulation of visual processing by attention and emotion: Windows on causal interactions between human brain regions. *Philosophical Transactions of the Royal Society B: Biological Sciences, 362*(1481), 837–855.

Williams, L. M., Korgaonkar, M. S., Song, Y. C., Paton, R., Eagles, S., Goldstein-Piekarski, A., Grieve, S. M., Harris, A. W., Usherwood, T., & Etkin, A. (2015). Amygdala reactivity to emotional faces in the prediction of general and medication-specific responses to antidepressant treatment in the randomized iSPOT-D trial. *Neuropsychopharmacology, 40*(10), 2398–2408.

Woud, M. L. (2022). Interpretational biases in emotional psychopathology. *Cognitive and Behavioral Practice, 29*(3), 520–523.

Yılmaz, O., Mırçık, A. B., Kunduz, M., Çombaş, M., Öztürk, A., Deveci, E., & Kırpınar, İ. (2019). Effects of cognitive behavioral therapy, existential psychotherapy and supportive counselling on facial emotion recognition among patients with mild or moderate depression. *Psychiatry Investigation, 16*(7), 491–503. https://doi.org/10.30773/pi.2019.03.14

Young, K. D., Friedman, E. S., Collier, A., Berman, S. R., Feldmiller, J., Haggerty, A. E., Thase, M. E., & Siegle, G. J. (2020). Response to SSRI intervention and amygdala activity during self-referential processing in major depressive disorder. *NeuroImage: Clinical, 28*, 102388. https://doi.org/10.1016/j.nicl.2020.102388

Zhong, M., Wang, X., Xiao, J., Yi, J., Zhu, X., Liao, J., Wang, W., & Yao, S. (2011). Amygdala hyper-activation and prefrontal hypoactivation in subjects with cognitive vulnerability to depression. *Biological Psychology, 88*(2–3), 233–242. https://doi.org/10.1016/j.biopsycho.2011.08.007

Marieke A. G. Martens is currently a post-doctoral researcher within the Psychopharmacology and Emotion Research Laboratory (PERL), in the Department of Psychiatry at the University of Oxford (UK). The main focus of her role is providing supervision and support for projects within the NIHR Oxford Health BRC's Depression Therapeutics Theme, aimed at investigating the mechanisms of established and novel treatments for mood disorders. Her academic qualifications include two bachelor's degrees (Biomedical Sciences and Psychology), as well as two master's degrees (Neuroscience and Neuropsychology) from the University of Utrecht (The Netherlands), and a DPhil (PhD) in Psychiatry from the University of Oxford (UK).

Catherine J. Harmer is a Professor of Cognitive Neuroscience in the Department of Psychiatry at the University of Oxford in the UK. Her work focuses on the psychological mechanisms of antidepressant treatments in depression. She explores how current treatments work using neuro-cognitive models of depression in humans and applies this knowledge to help predict, personalise and develop novel treatments for depression. Catherine Harmer trained in experimental psychology at the University of York (BSc) and completed a PhD in Psychopharmacology also at the University of York before moving to Oxford in 1998, where she has been based since.

Chapter 11
Cognitive Bias Modification Training to Change Interpretation Biases

Elske Salemink, Marcella L. Woud, Vera Bouwman, and Lynn Mobach

11.1 Cognitive Bias Modification – Interpretation (CBM-I) Training

According to cognitive models of psychopathology, many psychological disorders are characterized by interpretation biases and a great body of research has provided empirical support for this claim (Harvey et al., 2004; Schoth & Liossi, 2017). This assumption has been especially influential with respect to emotional disorders (Hirsch et al., 2016; Mathews & Macleod, 2005). To illustrate, depressed or anxious individuals are, compared to non-anxious individuals, more likely to interpret disorder-relevant ambiguity in a negative or threatening manner (Hirsch et al., 2016); individuals suffering from Posttraumatic Stress Disorder (PTSD) will appraise the experienced traumatic event and its consequences in a dysfunctional manner (Brown et al., 2019; McNally & Woud, 2019), and interpreting normal intrusive thoughts (e.g., "I will jump in front of the train") as threatening is a core problem in Obsessive Compulsive Disorder (OCD) (Salkovskis, 1985).

Cognitive models not only argue that psychopathology is associated with biased interpretations, but that these biases play a critical role in the etiology and maintenance of emotional psychopathology (Beck, 1976; Beck et al., 1985; Williams et al., 1997; (for an overview of the role of interpretation biases in the etiology of

E. Salemink (✉) · V. Bouwman · L. Mobach
Department of Clinical Psychology, Faculty of Social and Behavioural Sciences,
Utrecht University, Utrecht, The Netherlands
e-mail: e.salemink@uu.nl; v.bouwman@uu.nl; l.mobach@uu.nl

M. L. Woud
Mental Health Research and Treatment Center, Faculty of Psychology,
Ruhr-University Bochum, Bochum, Germany
e-mail: marcella.woud@rub.de

© The Author(s), under exclusive license to Springer Nature Switzerland AG 2023
M. L. Woud (ed.), *Interpretational Processing Biases in Emotional Psychopathology*,
CBT: Science Into Practice, https://doi.org/10.1007/978-3-031-23650-1_11

emotional psychopathology, see Chap. 12 by Woud and Hofmann). Put differently, they argue that biased interpretations play a *causal* role in pathological emotions and behaviors. Despite the great body of research emphasizing the strong and robust association between interpretation biases and symptoms of emotional psychopathology, up to 2000, the causal role of biases remained largely unstudied. To examine whether a factor (i.e., interpretation bias) is a causal risk factor, it should not only be shown that the factor is a correlate of and precedes psychopathology, but, importantly, it should also be demonstrated that the factor can be manipulated (variable risk factor) and that such a manipulation results in an increase or decrease in levels of psychopathology (framework by Kraemer et al., 1997). Applied to the present context of interpretation biases, this implies that if the biases' manipulation is indeed followed by a congruent change in levels of psychopathology, the variable risk factor should then be regarded as a causal risk factor. A similar line of argumentation has been adopted by Grafton et al. (2017). To test the hypothesized causal role of interpretation biases on psychopathology symptoms, researchers started to design computerized procedures manipulating interpretation biases from about 2000 onwards to examine whether this manipulation has an effect on symptoms of emotional psychopathology. This approach is called Cognitive Bias Modification (CBM) (Koster et al., 2009; MacLeod & Mathews, 2012) and the specific training procedure central for the present chapter is called Cognitive Bias Modification-Interpretation[1] (CBM-I).

The past two decades have witnessed a surge of interest in CBM-I. Originally, CBM-I was applied primarily with a theoretical aim to probe the potential causal role of interpretation biases in psychopathology. As those initial studies provided evidence consistent with a causal role of interpretation biases (see, for example, Mathews & Mackintosh, 2000; Salemink et al., 2007), a subsequent more clinically oriented line of research investigated the potential clinical utility of CBM-I, aiming to reduce symptoms of emotional psychopathology. Based on the rationale that if there is a training that can systematically reduce interpretation biases, such a training might have therapeutic effects given the expected impact upon emotions and behaviors.

In this chapter, we will provide an overview of (a) CBM-I paradigms that are often used to modify emotional interpretation biases; (b) results from recent meta-analyses regarding the effects of CBM-I training; and (c) mediators and moderators of CBM-I training effects. This summary will include studies in which CBM-I has been applied in both an experimental and clinical research context. We will round off the chapter with some concluding remarks and a discussion of future directions.

---

[1] This term will be used as an umbrella term for all procedures that target interpretive biases and related processes, i.e., procedures that all target the manipulation of interpretive, evaluative, and appraisal-related processes.

11.2 Overview CBM-I Training Paradigms

During the past two decades, different CBM-I training paradigms have been developed. However, all of them have a common aim, that is, modifying interpretation biases and by doing so affecting symptoms of emotional psychopathology. Generally, existing interpretation bias *assessment* tasks were adapted to training tasks to modify the biases. Specifically, these *training* tasks include an experimentally established contingency between the presented cue and a certain response, expecting that participants' biases can be manipulated via learning the contingency (cf. Koster et al., 2009). So how does this work in the context of CBM-I? A commonality across CBM-I paradigms is that participants are presented with ambiguous materials and repeatedly trained to interpret this material in a certain way (e.g., positively or negatively, depending on the training's conditions). Across many training trials, participants therefore learn to anticipate positive/negative outcomes for the ambiguous information, and, in turn, acquire a bias to interpret ambiguous information accordingly. The types of ambiguous stimuli vary across training paradigms, and can include for example words, short stories, and images. Trainings also vary in *content* given the disorder-specificity in interpretations. Thus, the stimuli presented in the training need to capture the salient cognitions of the respective psychological disorder (e.g., anxious- vs. depression-related cognitions). In the next paragraphs, we will present a chronological overview of training approaches in the context of CBM-I. We will provide examples of CBM-I training for different types of symptoms and psychopathology, to illustrate the match between training stimuli/content and salient cognitions of psychological disorders.

11.2.1 Scenario-Based CBM-I

The scenario-based CBM-I training procedure was one of the first developed paradigms and has been used most in subsequent research. In this scenario-based training developed by Mathews and Mackintosh (2000), participants are presented with ambiguous, open-ended scenarios. Participants are instructed to imagine themselves in the scenario, as if they are part of the described situation. Each scenario ends with a word fragment (i.e., a word with missing letters) such that the meaning of the scenario remains ambiguous until the word fragment is completed. It is the participants' task to finish each scenario by completing the word fragment. The word fragments are designed such that only one possible solution completes the scenarios' meaning. Completing the word fragment then produces a valenced outcome consistent with the training condition (e.g., a positive or negative interpretation of the ambiguous scenario). An example for a scenario in the context of social anxiety is as follows (see Mathews & Mackintosh, 2000, p. 604): "Your partner asks you to go to an anniversary dinner that their company is holding. You have not met any of their work colleagues before. Getting ready to go, you think that the new people you will

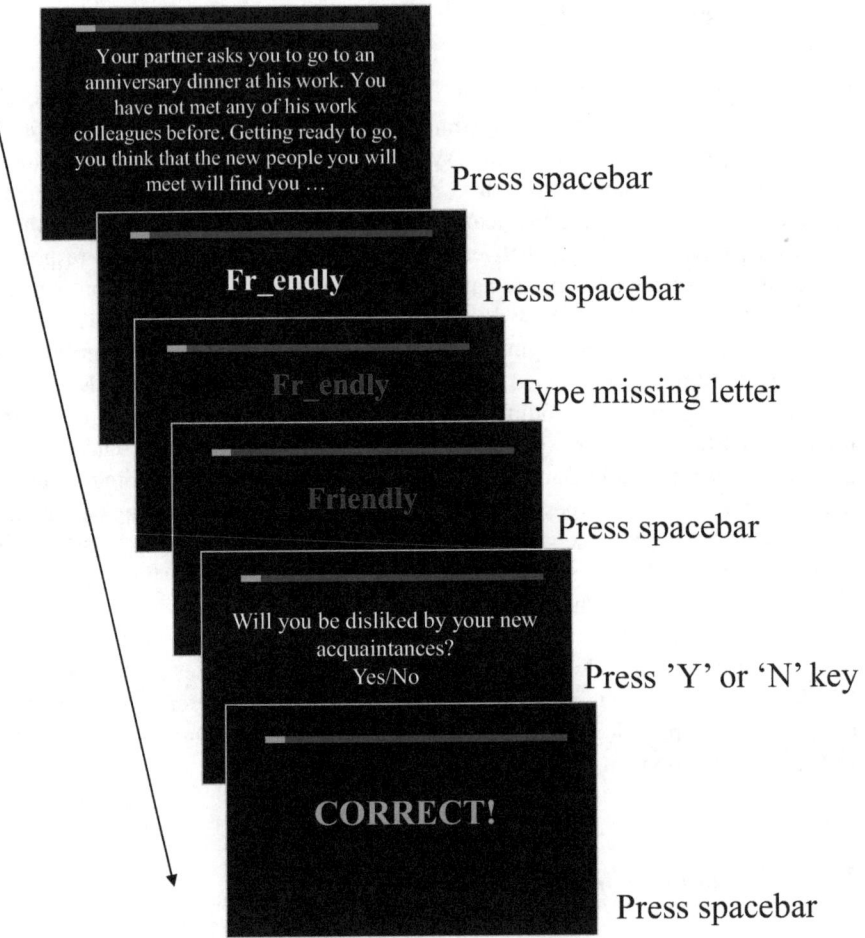

Fig. 11.1 Example of a positive scenario-based CBM-I training for social anxiety

meet will find you ...", "fri-ndly" (*friendly* in the positive training condition) or "b-ring" (*boring* in the negative training condition). To encourage participants to thoroughly process the scenario's meaning, scenarios are followed by a yes/no comprehension question. For the previous example this might be: "Will you be disliked by your new acquaintances?", and participants receive feedback for (in)correct responses (see Fig. 11.1 for an illustration).

The scenarios in Mathews and Mackintosh's (2000) experiments described ambiguous social situations as they aimed to modify interpretations in the context of social anxiety. In the following paragraphs, we will provide some examples of this scenario-based training applied to other emotional disorders (anxiety, depression, PTSD, and OCD), to illustrate how this paradigm can be tailored to modify disorder-specific interpretations. Teachman and Addison (2008), for example, trained positive interpretations of spiders in individuals high in spider fear using the scenario-based training. An example trial in the positive condition is: "You wake up in the middle of the night and see something on your alarm clock. You realize it is a spider. You think that it is …", "h-rmless" (*harmless* in the positive training condition) (p. 451). Post-training, while the positive training group interpreted novel spider-relevant scenarios more positively and less negatively, there were no group differences on spider fear. This scenario-based training has also been applied in other areas of anxiety, for example to height phobia (see, for example, Steinman & Teachman, 2014) or anxiety sensitivity (Steinman & Teachman, 2010). In the context of anxiety sensitivity, the training aimed to reduce negative interpretations in individuals with high anxiety sensitivity using scenarios such as: "You are jogging. Your heart starts to beat quickly. This is …", "in-igorating" (*invigorating* in the positive training condition) (p. 73). Compared to two control conditions (neutral vs. no training), the positive training group had lower scores on a self-report measure of anxiety sensitivity symptoms post-training.

The scenario-based CBM-I training has also been frequently applied to depression. For example, Lang et al. (2009) designed a scenario-based CBM-I training to target maladaptive appraisals of intrusive memories that are associated with depression. Stimuli in the positive condition utilized adaptive appraisals/interpretations such as "Having an intrusive memory means nothing is wrong with me" (p. 141). Healthy participants who underwent the positive CBM-I training (compared to the negative training) showed a more positive appraisal bias and reported fewer intrusions of a depressive film 1 week later. Joormann et al. (2015) showed that two sessions of this type of positive training in individuals diagnosed with major depressive disorder resulted in participants reporting more positive interpretations, more positive memory intrusions, and showed a smaller increase in heart rate in response to a stressor. Another example in the context of depression is the CBM-I training by Yiend et al. (2014). This training targets the full range of depression-related cognitive errors including interpretation biases, thus broadening the scope of the training.

In the context of PTSD, an appraisal-based CBM-I training was designed to train both functional and dysfunctional trauma-related reappraisals or interpretations of self-efficacy and secondary emotions (e.g., De Kleine et al., 2019; Woud et al., 2012, 2013, 2018c). For example, "In a crisis, I predict my responses will be …", "h-lpf-l" (*helpful* in the positive training condition) or "u-el-ss" (*useless* in the negative training condition) (Woud et al., 2012, p. 780). Compared to the negative training, the positive training induced more functional appraisals and resulted in fewer intrusions and lower levels of posttraumatic stress symptoms post-training, and these results were replicated in a clinical sample of PTSD (Woud et al., 2021). In OCD, CBM-I training targets the misinterpretations (as threatening) of (normal) intrusive thoughts/obsessions (Clerkin & Teachman, 2011; Williams & Grisham, 2013; Wolters et al., 2021). In adolescents with OCD, a CBM-I scenario could be the following: "You bought some roses for your mum and accidently got pricked by a thorn. You are bleeding and ask your mum to put a band-aid on it. It is … unli-ely (*unlikely* in the positive training condition) that this would make your mother sick. If you are bleeding, is there a great risk of making somebody else sick?" (Salemink et al., 2015, p. 114). Results indicated that the positive CBM-I training, compared to a placebo version of the training, resulted in lower levels of self-reported and clinician-rated OCD symptoms.

Application of this scenario-based CBM-I training has also been applied beyond the emotional domain. For example, it has been applied to the field of alcohol consumption. In an alcohol-related CBM-I training (Salemink et al., 2019) that focused on alcohol consumption in negative affective situations, an example scenario is the following: "I am worrying about the presentation I gave. To relax, I'll take a ...", "n-p" versus "b-er" (respectively *nap* or *beer*) (Salemink et al., 2019, p. 108, see also Woud et al., 2015). The training has also been applied to aggression. In that domain, CBM-I training tends to target hostile attribution/interpretation biases (the tendency to interpret others' motives and intentions in ambiguous situations as hostile) (Van Bockstaele et al., 2020b). An example of such a CBM-I-scenario in the context of hostile attributions is the following: "You're at the tennis court. A player hits the ball hard against your head. It hurts a lot. The player is ...", "inexp-rienc-d" (*inexperienced*) (p. 4).

11.2.2   Homograph CBM-I Training

In the homograph training developed by Grey and Mathews (2000), participants are presented with a cue word, followed by a word fragment. Participants are told that the cue word helps them to resolve the word fragment, and they are instructed to complete the word fragment by pressing its first missing letter. Unbeknown to the participants, the cue words are homographs (i.e., words with multiple meanings), and the word fragments are constructed in such a way that they either represent a neutral/positive or negative interpretation of the previously presented homograph, depending on the participant's training condition. Some examples of homographs with a negative and neutral/positive meaning in the context of anxiety: "choke": "throat" versus "engine"; "patient": "sick" versus "kind"; "parting": "leaving" versus "center". In a series of proof of principle experiments, Grey and Mathews (2000) showed that this homograph CBM-I training was indeed capable of changing interpretation biases. In a later study, it was examined whether the homograph CBM-I training would also impact on anxiety reactivity to a stressor (Wilson et al., 2006). Participants were randomly allocated to either a positive or a negative training condition using Grey and Mathews' (2000) homograph paradigm. After the training, participants watched stressful videos (i.e., a stress task) with state anxiety measurements before and after. Results indicated that interpretation biases were changed and that they affected stress reactivity accordingly. That is, only participants who were trained to interpret the homographs in a negative manner (compared to the

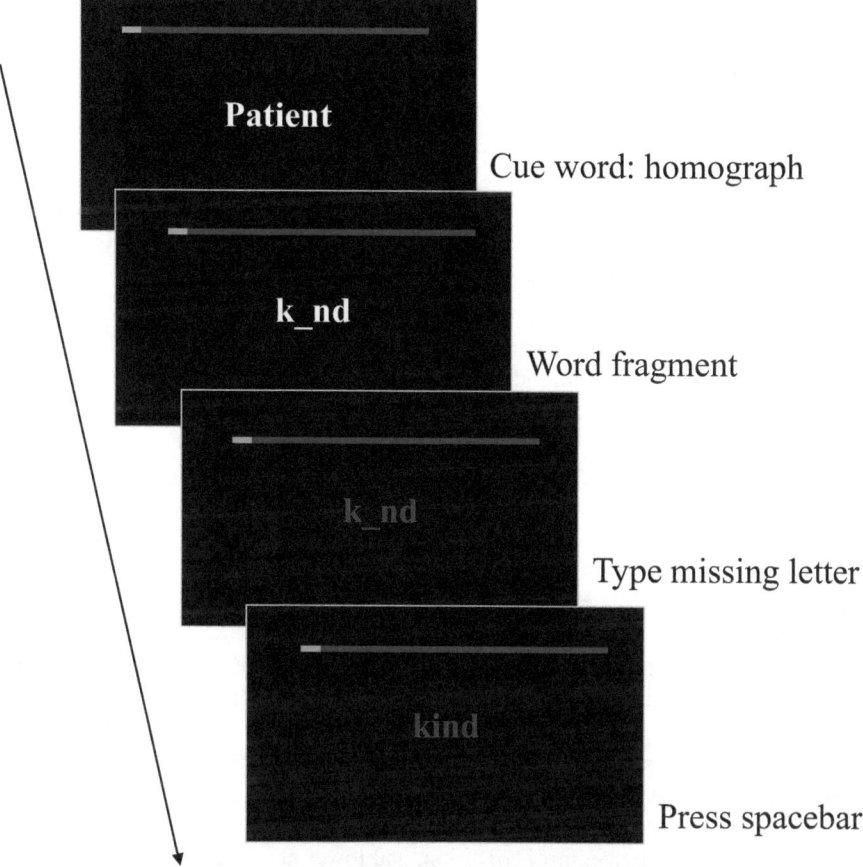

Fig. 11.2 Example of a positive homograph-based CBM-I training for anxiety

positive training) experienced an increase in state anxiety in response to the stressful videos. See Fig. 11.2 for an illustration.

There have only been a limited number of studies that have used this homograph CBM-I training. This low number is especially apparent when comparing it to the large number of studies that have used the scenario-based CBM-I training as both paradigms were introduced in a publication in the year 2000. The requirement of having enough homographs with two meanings of opposing valence or content might have hindered the application to use in multi-session training and to other domains of psychopathology. Also, translation from the English homographs (Grey & Mathews, 2000) to other languages has been difficult as there is no 1-to-1 translation.

11.2.3   Interpretation Modification Program (IMP): Word Sentence Association Paradigm (WSAP)

During the Interpretation Modification Program: Word Sentence Association Paradigm (IMP-WSAP) developed by Beard and Amir (2008), participants are presented with ambiguous disorder-relevant sentences. Every sentence is presented twice; once with a word prime that corresponds to a disorder-relevant interpretation, and once with a word prime that corresponds to a disorder-irrelevant interpretation. An example in the context of social anxiety: "criticize" versus "praise" – "Your boss wants to meet with you". It is the participants' task to decide as quickly as possible whether the word prime is related to the ambiguous sentence. This is followed by feedback, depending on the participants' training condition: Participants in the positive condition receive reinforcing feedback during trials where they accept word-sentence combinations with a positive word prime and reject word-sentence combinations with a negative word prime. Participants in the negative condition receive the opposite feedback. An eight-session training completed over 2 weeks by socially anxious individuals revealed that the IMP-WSAP successfully decreased threat interpretations, increased benign interpretations, and decreased social anxiety symptoms compared to a control condition (Beard & Amir, 2008). See Fig. 11.3 for an illustration.

Steinman and Teachman (2014) adapted the IMP-WSAP for the context of fear of heights by associating positive words with ambiguous, height-relevant sentences. For example, the presented word "risky" or "stable" was followed by the sentence "As you stand on a stepladder, you feel it rock slightly beneath you" (Steinman & Teachman, 2014, p. 408). This training was combined with the scenario-based CBM-I training. Extremely height-fearful individuals completed two training sessions and compared to a control condition, had lower negative interpretation biases and less fear of heights. These IMP-WSAP results were comparable to the effects of an exposure condition. Möbius et al. (2015) adapted the IMP-WSAP to allow for modifying depression-related interpretations. In their training, the following sentence "Your supervisor is surprised by your work" was for example presented with a benign word (e.g., "competent") or a negative word (e.g., "incompetent") (Möbius et al., 2015, p. 39). In a sample of healthy participants, the IMP-WSAP training enhanced a healthy bias favoring benign interpretations, however, it did not attenuate emotional vulnerability during a stressful task. Also, Conley and Wu (2018) examined the effectiveness of the IMP-WSAP training in the context of OCD by combining, for example, the word "disease" with "You visit someone who is ill" (Conley & Wu, 2018, p. 58). Participants with elevated contamination concerns who completed the training, compared to a control condition, showed a decrease in interpretation biases for threat cues and when ceiling effects were accounted for, completed more steps when approaching contaminants in a behavioral approach task. Additionally, beyond the emotional psychopathology domain, this IMP-WSAP training has, for example, also been applied to body dissatisfaction where appearance-related interpretations were re-trained (Dietel et al., 2020).

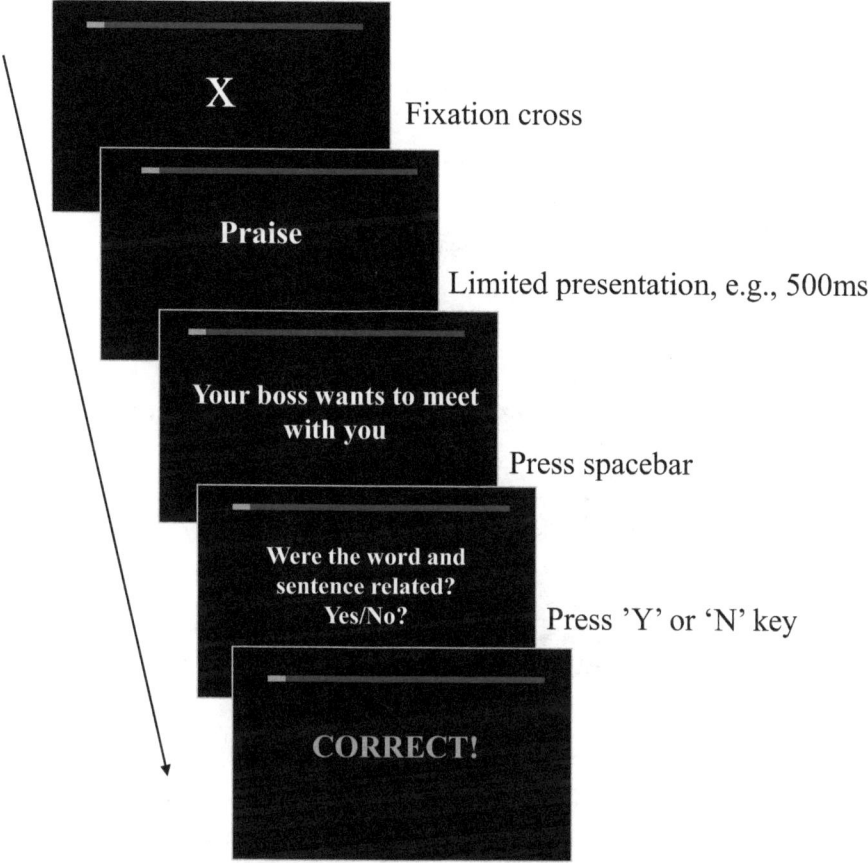

Fig. 11.3 Example of a positive Word-Sentence Association Paradigm CBM-I training for anxiety

11.2.4 CBM-I Training Paradigms with Images or Imagery

Given the importance of mental images in emotions and affect (Holmes & Mathews, 2005; Holmes et al., 2016), CBM-I training paradigms have been developed that use images and pictures instead of words and sentences as stimuli (with the latter used as the comparison training condition). These training paradigms focus more on visual/imagery processing given the hypothesized stronger link to emotions (for an overview of imagery-based training paradigms to reduce interpretation biases, see Chap. 6 by Blackwell). One such paradigm is the picture-word training (Holmes et al., 2008). During this training, participants are presented with colored, ambiguous photographs of mostly neutral, ambiguous, everyday scenes: e.g., people sitting in a park, a bus, or a classroom (Holmes et al., 2008). Each picture is combined with a word or short phrase, providing potential positive or negative interpretations of the

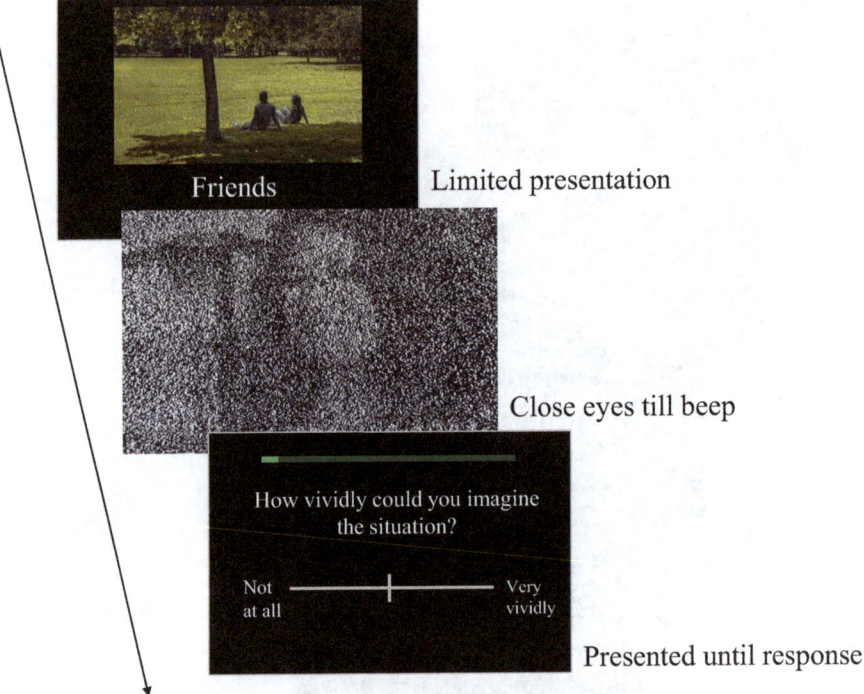

Fig. 11.4 Example of a positive picture-word CBM-I training for anxiety

picture. An example in a social context is a picture of a person sitting in the park accompanied by the word "friends" for a positive interpretation, or by the word "excluded" for a negative interpretation. Participants are instructed to form a mental image of the picture-word combination. Participants in both the positive and negative training conditions receive the same pictures. However, during the positive training, participants are repeatedly presented with positive interpretations, whereas participants of the negative condition are repeatedly presented with negative interpretations. Using this picture-word training, Holmes et al. (2008) compared an imagery task instruction (i.e., imagine the combination of the picture and word) with a verbal task instruction (i.e., create a grammatically correct sentence using the picture and word) (see Fig. 11.4 for an illustration). It was shown that the imagery training condition had a greater impact on state anxiety than the verbal training condition, which is consistent with the hypothesis that imagery, compared to verbal processing, evokes stronger affective responses.

Another approach has been to present the scenario-based training auditorily via headphones with participants being instructed to imagine the situation and presented interpretation (see, for example, Hirsch et al., 2009, for an application in worry). In the context of depression, Blackwell and Holmes (2010) examined the effectiveness of this imagery version with scenarios such as: "You ask a friend to look over some work you have done. They come back with some comments, which are *all very positive*" (resolution in italics) (Blackwell & Holmes, 2010, p. 341). In a case-series design, seven individuals experiencing a major depressive episode completed daily CBM-I training sessions for a week and four of them demonstrated improvements in mood, bias, and/or mental health. In 2015, Blackwell and colleagues examined the effectiveness of the picture-word training (six sessions) combined with the auditory scenario-based training (six sessions) as a treatment for individuals with a major depression. Unexpectedly, there was no significant advantage for the combined CBM-I trainings compared with a control condition on depression symptoms. However, when exploring subgroups, imagery CBM-I training significantly improved anhedonia and improved depression symptoms (compared with the control condition) for those participants with fewer than five episodes of depression and those who imagined the scenarios more vividly.

In the context of aggression, a different type of pictorial training has been developed (Penton-Voak et al., 2013). Aggressive individuals tend to interpret ambiguous social cues as hostile and angry (Nasby et al., 1980). In the training, images of ambiguous faces are used to encourage the perception of happiness over anger (Penton-Voak et al., 2013). Stimuli consisted of a morphed continuum of images ranging from an unambiguously happy face to an unambiguously angry face with emotionally ambiguous images in the middle. During the training, participants indicate whether the face is happy or angry. The subsequently provided feedback (correct versus incorrect) aims to shift the decision towards happier interpretations. Youth being at risk for committing a crime completed four of these training sessions (Penton-Voak et al., 2013; Experiment 2). Results indicated that, compared to a control condition, participants in the training condition shifted their interpretations which resulted in a decrease in self-reported aggression and clinician-rated aggressive behavior.

11.2.5 Assessing Effects on Interpretation Bias

The aim of all described CBM-I paradigms is to change interpretation biases and an important step is to test whether a CBM-I training was successful in modifying those biases. Various tasks have been used to measure interpretation biases and two will be described as an illustration (for an overview of measures to assess interpretation biases, see Chap. 3 by Würtz and Sanchez-Lopez). A recognition test (Mathews & Mackintosh, 2000; Salemink & van den Hout, 2010) is often used. It consists of an encoding phase where participants are presented with novel ambiguous scenarios that have an identifying title. In the subsequent recognition phase, the titles are presented again, each followed by a set of four related sentences. Participants have to rate how close in meaning each new sentence seems to the original scenario the title belongs to on a 4-point Likert scale. Two sentences represent a possible positive and a negative interpretation of the original scenario (target items). The other two sentences have a general positive/negative meaning, but do not provide an actual resolution of the scenario's ambiguity (foil items). Generally, it is expected that those participants that were trained positively give higher similarity ratings for positive compared to negative target items, and vice versa for those trained negatively. This recognition task is often used to evaluate the scenario-based CBM-I training effects on interpretation biases.

Another task to assess interpretation biases is the Word Sentence Association Paradigm-assessment task (Beard & Amir, 2008). Sentences are presented two times: once with a word prime that corresponds to a disorder-relevant interpretation, and once with a word prime that corresponds to a disorder-irrelevant interpretation. Contrary to the set-up in the IMP-WSAP training, in the assessment task, there is no feedback provided after participants indicated whether a word and sentence are related. The decision time and the endorsement rates of the relatedness between word and sentence are recorded. Here, one would expect that those trained positively, compared to those trained negatively, are faster to accept than to reject positive interpretations and endorse more positive than negative interpretations.

11.3   Overview Empirical Findings CBM-I Effects

From 2000 onwards, there have been an increasing number of studies examining the effects of CBM-I training. Here we would like to provide a summary of the main findings using results from various reviews and meta-analyses. Remarkably, the conclusions drawn by authors from such reviews and meta-analyses have been quite different. For example, the conclusions drawn by the first meta-analyses (Hallion & Ruscio, 2011; Menne-Lothmann et al., 2014) were quite positive, while a later meta-analysis by Cristea et al. (2015) was more critical. Differences between these meta-analyses could be related to inclusion of combinations of other types of cognitive bias modification training, experimental and more clinically oriented studies and outcomes, different disorders, and including assessment of mechanisms of change (see below Sect. 11.4). Here we will try to focus exclusively on CBM-I and effects on anxiety and depressive symptoms. We will discuss findings from the more recent meta-analyses, as these publications contain the largest number of individual studies.

In a review of multiple meta-analyses, Jones and Sharpe (2017) showed that CBM-I training has a significant effect on changes in interpretation biases, and thus conclude that CBM-I training can reliably modify interpretation biases. With respect to transfer effects on anxiety symptoms, Jones and Sharpe (2017) concluded that CBM training (combining the findings for CBM-I training with the findings for Attentional Bias Modification, -ABM-, trainings designed to change attentional biases) consistently reduced anxiety symptoms. Also, with respect to differences between attention and interpretation training, they concluded that "CBM-I training may have more power as a paradigm in symptom reduction compared with ABM" (Jones & Sharpe, 2017, p. 179). These effects on anxiety are consistent with the conclusions drawn in a recent network meta-analysis (Fodor et al., 2020) where CBM-I training outperformed both waitlist and sham-training control conditions in reducing anxiety symptoms. While there is variability in the effects of CBM-I training on anxiety in individual studies, across all studies, there seems to be a promising effect on anxiety. The CBM-I effects on depressive symptoms seem less compelling as Fodor et al. (2020) concluded that CBM-I only outperformed waitlist control conditions (and not sham-training) in reducing depressive symptoms. Similarly, Jones and Sharpe (2017) indicated that CBM effects (again ABM and CBM-I combined) on depressive symptoms are less robust and smaller than the effects on anxiety. When taking together the recent meta-analyses, the findings for CBM-I have been quite positive and underscore the conclusion formulated by Fodor et al. (2020): "CBM-I emerged as a promising treatment" (p. 507).

11.4 Mediators and Moderators of CBM-I Training Effects

Various studies have examined mediators and moderators of CBM-I training effects and those will be discussed here.

11.4.1 Mediators of CBM-I Training Effects

With respect to mediators, based on theoretical models and the designed CBM-I paradigms, change in interpretation biases is a clear hypothesized mediator of CBM-I training. As summarized above, Jones and Sharpe (2017) concluded in their review of multiple meta-analyses, that CBM-I training can indeed reliably modify interpretation biases. As a crucial next step, there are empirical studies that have shown that symptom change was indeed *mediated by* the change in interpretation biases. For example, Steinman and Teachman (2014) demonstrated that change in interpretation biases was a mediator of CBM-I's effects on fear of heights. Further, Woud et al. (2021) showed that reductions in PTSD-related appraisals were correlated with reductions in PTSD symptoms from pre- to post-training, and that the differential impact of CBM-I versus sham training on PTSD symptoms was mediated by reductions in dysfunctional appraisals.

In the past, there has been some debate about the effectiveness of CBM-I training as not all CBM-I studies resulted in the intended symptom change. Some meta-analyses (e.g., Cristea et al., 2015) have exclusively focused on symptom change while not taking into account whether the CBM-I studies actually changed the hypothesized mechanism/mediator, i.e., interpretation biases. Theoretically, one would only expect change in symptoms, when the CBM-I training was capable of changing the targeted bias. If the training was not successful in changing interpretation biases (the mediator), then effects on symptoms are not to be expected. The implication is that when using CBM-I training to examine the causal role of interpretation biases in for example anxiety, and the training did not impact interpretation biases, the study cannot be used to evaluate the causal impact of those biases on anxiety (cf. Grafton et al., 2017; Kraemer et al., 1997). Similarly, when evaluating the clinical utility of CBM-I training for reducing symptoms, a differentiation should be made between studies that did and did not successfully modify the bias. Grafton et al. (2017) not only provided an eloquent description of this issue, but also re-analyzed a previous meta-analysis (Cristea et al., 2015). Grafton et al.'s results indicated that not all CBM training paradigms successfully elicited a cognitive bias change, but that when the bias was successfully changed, reliable influences on emotional vulnerability were observed.

Various mechanisms have been proposed to explain how CBM-I works. While it has been shown that priming effects, demand effects, and response bias effects are unlikely mechanisms (e.g., Clarke et al., 2014; Hoppitt et al., 2010a, b; Macleod & Mathews, 2012; Mathews & Mackintosh, 2000), the *production rule* mechanism seem more likely. It has been proposed that CBM-I training could be understood as a procedure that modifies an implicit production rule concerning the resolution of ambiguity (Clarke et al., 2014; Hoppitt et al., 2010a, b; Wilson et al., 2006). In CBM-I training, participants are repeatedly exposed to ambiguous material that activates competing alternative meanings (Richards, 2004). As already described, the training guides the participant in resolving the ambiguity by consistently providing a positive interpretation of that ambiguity. With repeated practice, this could result in an implicit production rule on how to resolve ambiguity and to generate and select positive meanings. Consequently, after training, participants, unintentionally continue to do so when later encountering new and potentially threatening events (see Hoppitt et al., 2010a, b). The development of a production rule has been put forward as a mechanism of CBM-I effects, however, it remains unclear what exactly a production rule is (association between ambiguity and a positive resolution, or a proposition that if I encounter ambiguity, I can interpret it positively), and how it is acquired (which learning mechanisms play a role).

In sum, the findings with respect to mediators are promising. Across studies, CBM-I paradigms tend to be capable of modifying interpretation biases (Jones and Sharpe, 2017) and generally, changes in such biases tend to translate to effects on symptoms (Grafton et al., 2017). With respect to the underlying mechanism, a production rule explanation has been put forward, though there are many remaining questions to be answered.

11.4.1.1 Moderators of CBM-I Training Effects

Different moderators of CBM-I training effects have been investigated, with some inconsistency in the findings. With respect to moderators related to the sample characteristics, there is generally no strong evidence for demographic variables such as age and gender moderating training effects (Jones & Sharpe, 2017). There is some evidence suggesting that sample type and associated baseline symptom level play a role in the effectiveness of CBM-I training effects on cognitive bias. That is, sample type was a significant moderator in two out of six meta-analyses with larger effect sizes in high symptomatology samples compared to healthy samples (Jones &

Sharpe, 2017). This is a promising finding when considering the potential application of CBM-I training as a psychological treatment in clinical samples. Whether CBM-I training might also be a preventative intervention in relatively healthy samples is less clear. CBM-I training may, for example, provide a *cognitive vaccine* against low mood (Holmes et al., 2009) or the development of symptoms of post-traumatic stress (Woud et al., 2013).

With respect to the number of training sessions; a meta-analysis that exclusively focused on CBM-I training (Menne-Lothmann et al., 2014) concluded that more CBM-I training sessions were related to stronger effects on interpretation biases and mood. However, more recently, Jones and Sharpe (2017) concluded that the evidence for a moderating role of a number of sessions is inconsistent, and it was not significant in Fodor et al.'s (2020) meta-analysis.

There is variability in the setting where CBM-I training is delivered; some studies provided the training in the laboratory, while others have provided it online with participants often completing the training at home. While in Fodor et al. (2020) delivery setting (lab versus others) was not related to outcome, delivery setting was related to outcome in Jones and Sharpe (2017), where CBM-I training was most effective when delivered in the laboratory. It is an open question of why training might work better in the lab. Many CBM-I studies have been conducted in the context of social anxiety and performing a lab-based CBM-I training requires participants to travel to the lab and interact with others. This might actually be an exposure exercise for individuals with social anxiety and the CBM-I training might inadvertently been combined with an element from Cognitive Behavior Therapy (see also Sect. 11.5 below). The social nature of the lab-based training might also have increased state anxiety and arousal, which might have played a role in the effectiveness of CBM-I training (for their role in Attentional Bias Modification, see Kuckertz et al., 2014; Nuijs et al., 2020). Finally, there is some evidence that imagining the CBM-I training materials increased the effectiveness of the training (Jones & Sharpe, 2017; Menne-Lothmann et al., 2014). In the next section, some other, novel moderators are described as part of more recent studies that were designed to improve CBM-I training.

11.5 Concluding Comments and Avenues for Future Directions

CBM-I training was initially developed to examine the causal role of interpretation biases in emotional psychopathology. Given the evidence consistent with such a role, more recent studies have examined the curative and preventative possibilities of the training. In this chapter, we have described the many different types of CBM-I paradigms that have been designed to modify interpretation biases. Based on meta-analyses, we described that, in general, those paradigms are capable of changing the targeted interpretation biases and subsequent anxiety. The effects of depression are less consistent. As such, CBM-I training is a valuable and promising approach, though there is also room for improvement and there is still uncertainty about how training paradigms exactly work. Here we will highlight a few areas that could be improved and offer novel approaches that seem successful in achieving the desired improvement. As such, they represent encouraging avenues for future directions.

At the moment, some basic, mechanistic questions regarding CBM-I training have received minimal attention. For example, it is not yet clear what the optimal dose of the training is; with respect to number of training trials per session, total number of sessions, and the distribution of sessions across days (is it better to space out training across days?). In addition, most outcome measures have been self-report measures and the field would benefit from studies including measures that are less susceptible to demand characteristic. Some promising steps have been taken though with, for example, examining effects on clinician-rated symptoms (e.g., Wolters et al., 2021) and on heart rate responses (Joormann et al., 2015; Van Bockstaele et al., 2020a).

Across studies, the CBM-I effects on interpretations biases seem more robust than its effects on symptoms. This might suggest that the transfer from the successfully changed interpretations to emotional symptoms is sub-optimal. Given that symptom change tends to be the goal when considering clinical application of the training, the observation that changed interpretations do not always result in changes in emotions poses a challenge for such clinical applications. Future research might need to focus on improving the transfer from changed interpretations to changes in emotions. There have been some recent studies that aimed to improve CBM-I training, for example by adding d-cycloserine (Woud et al., 2018a), cognitive load (Van Bockstaele et al., 2020a), or napping (Woud et al., 2018b), or by developing a fMRI-based neurofeedback training to boost cognitive reappraisal ability (Lisk et al., 2020). Another approach has been to increase engagement with the training. Participants often consider the training monotonous and boring (Beard et al., 2012; de Voogd et al., 2017) and this might have a negative impact on training engagement and learning of new interpretations. It might also result in drop-out during multi-session training. To increase engagement, there have been attempts to gamify CBM-I training. Recently, the scenario-based CBM-I training was changed into a shooting game with sound effects, visual feedback, and adaptive speed (Salemink et al., 2022). Another approach has been to use Virtual Reality (VR) technology. Otkhmezuri et al. (2019), for example, developed a mobile VR-based CBM-I training that contained simulated real-life environments that matched the scenarios and where individuals could fully immerse themselves and explore the environment by head movements. The promising finding was that this VR-based training not only resulted in higher enjoyment compared to the standard scenario-based training, but also in stronger reductions in state anxiety. To conclude, there is some inconsistency in CBM-I training effects on symptoms and future research should be dedicated to improving such effects. Recently, different approaches have been examined with some having promising effects.

A final point concerns translation from experimental studies to clinical trials (for a guide, see Blackwell & Woud, 2022). Given the causal role of interpretation biases in emotional psychopathology and the advantages of computerized CBM-I training that can be easily offered online with 24/7 access, there seems great potential for CBM-I training as a treatment possibility for anxiety and depressive symptomatology. There have been some studies investigating the effectiveness of CBM-I training as a stand-alone treatment with inconsistent findings across studies (e.g., Bowler et al., 2012; Salemink et al., 2014). The question is whether the training is potent enough to change psychopathology in patients. Psychological disorders tend to be multifactorial; many factors and processes play a role in the etiology and maintenance of a disorder. As CBM-I training targets one specific process (interpretation biases), it remains an open question whether it is powerful enough as a curative intervention and/or might be better suited as a prevention program. Another approach has been to combine CBM-I training with evidence-based psychological treatments such as Cognitive Behavioral Therapy (CBT) and some promising findings have been obtained (e.g., Butler et al., 2015; Williams et al., 2015; Wolters et al., 2021; Woud et al., 2021). There are several ways to combine CBM-I with CBT; CBM-I might be used as a pre-treatment training completed for example during the time an individual is on a waitlist for treatment, or training could be offered in parallel to CBT treatment as an adjunct or be offered after treatment to prevent the return of fear and depression (for a related discussion about the interplay of scientific research and clinical practice, see Chap. 1 by Holmes). There is clearly room and need for exciting CBM-I studies that examine mechanistic questions in experimental, lab-based studies as well as examine the applied value of CBM-I for patients with various types of psychopathology.

References

Beard, C., & Amir, N. (2008). A multi-session interpretation modification program: Changes in interpretation and social anxiety symptoms. *Behaviour Research and Therapy, 46*(10), 1135–1141. https://doi.org/10.1016/j.brat.2008.05.012

Beard, C., Weisberg, R. B., & Primack, J. (2012). Socially anxious primary care patients' attitudes toward cognitive bias modification (CBM): A qualitative study. *Behavioural and Cognitive Psychotherapy, 40*, 618–633. https://doi.org/10.1017/S1352465811000671

Beck, A. T. (1976). *Cognitive therapy and emotional disorders*. International Universities Press.

Beck, A. T., Emery, G., & Greenberg, R. L. (1985). *Anxiety disorders and phobias: A cognitive perspective*. Basic Books.

Blackwell, S. E., & Holmes, E. A. (2010). Modifying interpretation and imagination in clinical depression: A single case series using cognitive bias modification. *Applied Cognitive Psychology: The Official Journal of the Society for Applied Research in Memory and Cognition, 24*(3), 338–350. https://doi.org/10.1002/acp.1680

Blackwell, S. E., & Woud, M. L. (2022). Making the leap: From experimental psychopathology to clinical trials. *Journal of Experimental Psychopathology, 13*(1), 20438087221080076. https://doi.org/10.31234/osf.io/et6f4

Blackwell, S. E., Browning, M., Mathews, A., Pictet, A., Welch, J., Davies, J., & Holmes, E. A. (2015). Positive imagery-based cognitive bias modification as a web-based treatment tool for depressed adults: A randomized controlled trial. *Clinical Psychological Science, 3*(1), 91–111. https://doi.org/10.1177/2167702614560746

Bowler, J. O., Mackintosh, B., Dunn, B. D., Mathews, A., Dalgleish, T., & Hoppitt, L. (2012). A comparison of cognitive bias modification for interpretation and computerized cognitive behavior therapy: Effects on anxiety, depression, attentional control, and interpretive bias. *Journal of Consulting and Clinical Psychology, 80*(6), 1021–1033. https://doi.org/10.1037/a0029932

Brown, L. A., Belli, G. M., Asnaani, A., & Foa, E. B. (2019). A review of the role of negative cognitions about oneself, others, and the world in the treatment of PTSD. *Cognitive Therapy and Research, 43*(1), 143–173. https://doi.org/10.1007/s10608-018-9938-1

Butler, E., Mobini, S., Rapee, R. M., Mackintosh, B., & Reynolds, S. A. (2015). Enhanced effects of combined cognitive bias modification and computerised cognitive behaviour therapy on social anxiety. *Cogent Psychology, 2*(1), 1011905. https://doi.org/10.1080/23311908.2015.1011905

Clarke, P. J., Nanthakumar, S., Notebaert, L., Holmes, E. A., Blackwell, S. E., & MacLeod, C. (2014). Simply imagining sunshine, lollipops and rainbows will not budge the bias: The role of ambiguity in interpretive bias modification. *Cognitive Therapy and Research, 38*(2), 120–131. https://doi.org/10.1007/s10608-013-9564-x

Clerkin, E. M., & Teachman, B. A. (2011). Training interpretation biases among individuals with symptoms of obsessive compulsive disorder. *Journal of Behavior Therapy and Experimental Psychiatry, 42*(3), 337–343. https://doi.org/10.1016/j.jbtep.2011.01.003

Conley, S. L., & Wu, K. D. (2018). Experimental modification of dysfunctional interpretations in individuals with contamination concerns. *Journal of Behavior Therapy and Experimental Psychiatry, 59*, 56–64. https://doi.org/10.1016/j.jbtep.2017.11.005

Cristea, I. A., Kok, R. N., & Cuijpers, P. (2015). Efficacy of cognitive bias modification interventions in anxiety and depression: Meta-analysis. *The British Journal of Psychiatry, 206*(1), 7–16. https://doi.org/10.1192/bjp.bp.114.146761

De Kleine, R. A., Woud, M. L., Ferentzi, H., Hendriks, G. J., Broekman, T., Becker, E. S., & Van Minnen, A. (2019). Appraisal-based cognitive bias modification in patients with posttraumatic stress disorder: A randomised clinical trial. *European Journal of Psychotraumatology, 10*(1), 1625690. https://doi.org/10.1080/20008198.2019.1625690

de Voogd, E. L., De Hullu, E., Burnett Heyes, S., Blackwell, S. E., Wiers, R. W., & Salemink, E. (2017). Imagine the bright side of life: A randomized controlled trial of two types of interpretation bias modification procedure targeting adolescent anxiety and depression. *PLoS One, 12*, e0181147. https://doi.org/10.1371/journal.pone.0181147

Dietel, F. A., Zache, C., Bürkner, P. C., Schulte, J., Möbius, M., Bischof, A., et al. (2020). Internet-based interpretation bias modification for body dissatisfaction: A three-armed randomized controlled trial. *International Journal of Eating Disorders, 53*(6), 972–986. https://doi.org/10.1002/eat.23280

Fodor, L. A., Georgescu, R., Cuijpers, P., Szamoskozi, Ş., David, D., Furukawa, T. A., & Cristea, I. A. (2020). Efficacy of cognitive bias modification interventions in anxiety and depressive disorders: A systematic review and network meta-analysis. *The Lancet Psychiatry, 7*(6), 506–514. https://doi.org/10.1016/S2215-0366(20)30130-9

Grafton, B., MacLeod, C., Rudaizky, D., Holmes, E. A., Salemink, E., Fox, E., & Notebaert, L. (2017). Confusing procedures with process when appraising the impact of cognitive bias modification on emotional vulnerability. *The British Journal of Psychiatry, 211*(5), 266–271. https://doi.org/10.1192/bjp.bp.115.176123

Grey, S., & Mathews, A. (2000). Effects of training on interpretation of emotional ambiguity. *The Quarterly Journal of Experimental Psychology Section A, 53*(4), 1143–1162. https://doi.org/10.1080/713755937

Hallion, L. S., & Ruscio, A. M. (2011). A meta-analysis of the effect of cognitive bias modification on anxiety and depression. *Psychological Bulletin, 137*(6), 940–958. https://doi.org/10.1037/a0024355

Harvey, A. G., Watkins, E., & Mansell, W. (2004). *Cognitive behavioural processes across psychological disorders: A transdiagnostic approach to research and treatment.* Oxford University Press.

Hirsch, C. R., Hayes, S., & Mathews, A. (2009). Looking on the bright side: Accessing benign meanings reduces worry. *Journal of Abnormal Psychology, 118*(1), 44–54. https://doi.org/10.1037/a0013473

Hirsch, C. R., Meeten, F., Krahé, C., & Reeder, C. (2016). Resolving ambiguity in emotional disorders: The nature and role of interpretation biases. *Annual Review of Clinical Psychology, 12*, 281–305. https://doi.org/10.1146/annurev-clinpsy-021815-093436

Holmes, E. A., & Mathews, A. (2005). Mental imagery and emotion: A special relationship? *Emotion, 5*(4), 489–497. https://doi.org/10.1037/1528-3542.5.4.489

Holmes, E. A., Mathews, A., Mackintosh, B., & Dalgleish, T. (2008). The causal effect of mental imagery on emotion assessed using picture-word cues. *Emotion, 8*(3), 395–409. https://doi.org/10.1037/1528-3542.8.3.395

Holmes, E. A., Lang, T. J., & Shah, D. M. (2009). Developing interpretation bias modification as a "cognitive vaccine" for depressed mood: Imagining positive events makes you feel better than thinking about them verbally. *Journal of Abnormal Psychology, 118*(1), 76–88. https://doi.org/10.1037/a0012590

Holmes, E. A., Blackwell, S. E., Burnett Heyes, S., Renner, F., & Raes, F. (2016). Mental imagery in depression: Phenomenology, potential mechanisms, and treatment implications. *Annual Review of Clinical Psychology, 12*, 249–280. https://doi.org/10.1146/annurev-clinpsy-021815-092925

Hoppitt, L., Mathews, A., Yiend, J., & Mackintosh, B. (2010a). Cognitive bias modification: The critical role of active training in modifying emotional responses. *Behavior Therapy, 41*(1), 73–81. https://doi.org/10.1016/j.beth.2009.01.002

Hoppitt, L., Mathews, A., Yiend, J., & Mackintosh, B. (2010b). Cognitive mechanisms underlying the emotional effects of bias modification. *Applied Cognitive Psychology, 24*(3), 312–325. https://doi.org/10.1002/acp.1678

Jones, E. B., & Sharpe, L. (2017). Cognitive bias modification: A review of meta-analyses. *Journal of Affective Disorders, 223*, 175–183. https://doi.org/10.1016/j.jad.2017.07.034

Joormann, J., Waugh, C. E., & Gotlib, I. H. (2015). Cognitive bias modification for interpretation in major depression: Effects on memory and stress reactivity. *Clinical Psychological Science, 3*(1), 126–139. https://doi.org/10.1177/2167702614560748

Koster, E. H., Fox, E., & MacLeod, C. (2009). Introduction to the special section on cognitive bias modification in emotional disorders. *Journal of Abnormal Psychology, 118*(1), 1–4. https://doi.org/10.1037/a0014379

Kraemer, H. C., Kazdin, A. E., Offord, D. R., Kessler, R. C., Jensen, P. S., & Kupfer, D. J. (1997). Coming to terms with the terms of risk. *Archives of General Psychiatry, 54*(4), 337–343. https://doi.org/10.1001/archpsyc.1997.01830160065009

Kuckertz, J. M., Gildebrant, E., Liliequist, B., Karström, P., Väppling, C., Bodlund, O., Stenlund, T., Hofmann, S. G., Andersson, G., Amir, N., & Carlbring, P. (2014). Moderation and mediation of the effect of attention training in social anxiety disorder. *Behaviour Research and Therapy, 53*, 30–40. https://doi.org/10.1016/j.brat.2013.12.003

Lang, T. J., Moulds, M. L., & Holmes, E. A. (2009). Reducing depressive intrusions via a computerized cognitive bias modification of appraisals task: Developing a cognitive vaccine. *Behaviour Research and Therapy, 47*, 139–145. https://doi.org/10.1016/j.brat.2008.11.002

Lisk, S., Kadosh, K. C., Zich, C., Haller, S. P., & Lau, J. Y. (2020). Training negative connectivity patterns between the dorsolateral prefrontal cortex and amygdala through fMRI-based neurofeedback to target adolescent socially-avoidant behaviour. *Behaviour Research and Therapy, 135*, 103760. https://doi.org/10.1016/j.brat.2013.03.008

MacLeod, C., & Mathews, A. (2012). Cognitive bias modification approaches to anxiety. *Annual Review of Clinical Psychology, 8*, 189–217. https://doi.org/10.1146/annurev-clinpsy-032511-143052

Mathews, A., & Mackintosh, B. (2000). Induced emotional interpretation bias and anxiety. *Journal of Abnormal Psychology, 109*(4), 602–615. https://doi.org/10.1037/0021-843X.109.4.602

Mathews, A., & MacLeod, C. (2005). Cognitive vulnerability to emotional disorders. *Annual Review of Clinical Psychology, 1*, 167–195. https://doi.org/10.1146/annurev.clinpsy.1.102803.143916

McNally, R. J., & Woud, M. L. (2019). Innovations in the study of appraisals and PTSD. A commentary. *Cognitive Therapy and Research, 43*, 295–302. https://doi.org/10.1007/s10608-018-09995-2

Menne-Lothmann, C., Viechtbauer, W., Höhn, P., Kasanova, Z., Haller, S. P., Drukker, M., van Os, J., Wichers, M., & Lau, J. Y. (2014). How to boost positive interpretations? A meta-analysis of the effectiveness of cognitive bias modification for interpretation. *PLoS One, 9*(6), e100925. https://doi.org/10.1371/journal.pone.0100925

Möbius, M., Tendolkar, I., Lohner, V., Baltussen, M., & Becker, E. S. (2015). Refilling the half-empty glass–investigating the potential role of the Interpretation Modification Paradigm for Depression (IMP-D). *Journal of Behavior Therapy and Experimental Psychiatry, 49*, 37–43. https://doi.org/10.1016/j.jbtep.2015.03.002

Nasby, W., Hayden, B., & Depaulo, B. M. (1980). Attributional bias among aggressive boys to interpret unambiguous social-stimuli as displays of hostility. *Journal of Abnormal Psychology, 89*(3), 459–468. https://doi.org/10.1037//0021-843x.89.3.459

Nuijs, M. D., Larsen, H., Bögels, S. M., Wiers, R. W., & Salemink, E. (2020). Context matters: The role of subjective arousal during attentional bias modification targeting socially anxious students. *Journal of Behavior Therapy and Experimental Psychiatry, 68*, 101545. https://doi.org/10.1016/j.jbtep.2019.101545

Otkhmezuri, B., Boffo, M., Siriaraya, P., Matsangidou, M., Wiers, R. W., Mackintosh, B., Ang, C. S., & Salemink, E. (2019). Believing is seeing: A proof-of-concept, semi-experimental study on using mobile virtual reality to boost the effects of interpretation bias modification for anxiety. *JMIR Mental Health, 6*, e11517. https://doi.org/10.2196/11517

Penton-Voak, I. S., Thomas, J., Gage, S. H., McMurran, M., McDonald, S., & Munafò, M. R. (2013). Increasing recognition of happiness in ambiguous facial expressions reduces anger and aggressive behavior. *Psychological Science, 24*(5), 688–697. https://doi.org/10.1177/0956797612459657

Richards, A. (2004). Anxiety and the resolution of ambiguity. In J. Yiend (Ed.), *Cognition, emotion and psychopathology: Theoretical, empirical and clinical directions* (pp. 130–148). Cambridge University Press. https://doi.org/10.1017/CBO9780511521263.008

Salemink, E., & van den Hout, M. A. (2010). Validation of the "recognition task" used in training of interpretation biases. *Journal of Behavior Therapy and Experimental Psychiatry, 41*, 140–144. https://doi.org/10.1016/j.jbtep.2009.11.006

Salemink, E., van den Hout, M., & Kindt, M. (2007). Trained interpretive bias: Validity and effects on anxiety. *Journal of Behavior Therapy and Experimental Psychiatry, 38*(2), 212–224. https://doi.org/10.1016/j.jbtep.2006.10.010

Salemink, E., Kindt, M., Rienties, H., & van den Hout, M. (2014). Internet-delivered cognitive bias modification of interpretations in patients with anxiety disorders: A randomised controlled trial. *Journal of Behavior Therapy and Experimental Psychiatry, 45*, 186–195. https://doi.org/10.1016/j.jbtep.2013.10.005

Salemink, E., Wolters, L., & de Haan, E. (2015). Augmentation of treatment as usual with online cognitive bias modification of interpretation training in adolescents with obsessive compulsive disorder: A pilot study. *Journal of Behavior Therapy and Experimental Psychiatry, 49*, 112–119. https://doi.org/10.1016/j.jbtep.2015.02.003

Salemink, E., Woud, M. L., Roos, M., Wiers, R. W., & Lindgren, K. P. (2019). Reducing alcohol-related interpretive bias in negative affect situations: Using a scenario-based cognitive bias modification training paradigm. *Addictive Behaviors, 88*, 106–113. https://doi.org/10.1016/j.addbeh.2018.07.023

Salemink, E., de Jong, S. C., Notebaert, L., MacLeod, C., & Van Bockstaele, B. (2022). Gamification of cognitive bias modification for interpretations in anxiety increases training engagement and enjoyment. *Journal of Behavior Therapy and Experimental Psychiatry, 76*, 101727. https://doi.org/10.1016/j.jbtep.2022.101727

Salkovskis, P. M. (1985). Obsessional-compulsive problems: A cognitive-behavioural analysis. *Behaviour Research and Therapy, 23*, 571–583. https://doi.org/10.1016/0005-7967(85)90105-6

Schoth, D. E., & Liossi, C. (2017). A systematic review of experimental paradigms for exploring biased interpretation of ambiguous information with emotional and neutral associations. *Frontiers in Psychology, 8*, 171. https://doi.org/10.3389/fpsyg.2017.00171

Steinman, S. A., & Teachman, B. A. (2010). Modifying interpretations among individuals high in anxiety sensitivity. *Journal of Anxiety Disorders, 24*, 71–78. https://doi.org/10.1016/j.janxdis.200

Steinman, S. A., & Teachman, B. A. (2014). Reaching new heights: Comparing interpretation bias modification to exposure therapy for extreme height fear. *Journal of Consulting and Clinical Psychology, 82*(3), 404–417. https://doi.org/10.1037/a0036023

Teachman, B. A., & Addison, L. M. (2008). Training non-threatening interpretations in spider fear. *Cognitive Therapy and Research, 32*(3), 448–459. https://doi.org/10.1007/s10608-006-9084-z

Van Bockstaele, B., Clarke, P., Notebaert, L., MacLeod, C., & Salemink, E. (2020a). Effects of cognitive load during interpretation bias modification on interpretation bias and stress reactivity. *Journal of Behavior Therapy and Experimental Psychiatry, 68*, 101561. https://doi.org/10.1016/j.jbtep.2020.101561

Van Bockstaele, B., Van der Molen, M., van Nieuwenhuijzen, M., & Salemink, E. (2020b). Modification of hostile attribution bias reduces self-reported reactive aggressive behaviour in adolescents. *Journal of Experimental Child Psychology, 194*, 104811. https://doi.org/10.1016/j.jecp.2020.104811

Williams, A. D., & Grisham, J. R. (2013). Cognitive bias modification (CBM) of obsessive compulsive beliefs. *BMC Psychiatry, 13*(1), 1–9. https://doi.org/10.1186/1471-244X-13-256

Williams, J. M. G., Watts, F. N., Macleod, C., & Mathews, A. (1997). *Cognitive psychology and emotional disorders*. John Wiley and Sons.

Williams, A. D., O'Moore, K., Blackwell, S. E., Smith, J., Holmes, E. A., & Andrews, G. (2015). Positive imagery cognitive bias modification (CBM) and internet-based cognitive behavioral therapy (iCBT): A randomized controlled trial. *Journal of Affective Disorders, 178*, 131–141. https://doi.org/10.1016/j.jad.2015.02.026

Wilson, E. J., MacLeod, C., Mathews, A., & Rutherford, E. M. (2006). The causal role of interpretive bias in anxiety reactivity. *Journal of Abnormal Psychology, 115*(1), 103–111. https://doi.org/10.1037/0021-843X.115.1.103

Wolters, L., Hagen, A., Op de Beek, V., Dol, P., de Haan, E., & Salemink, E. (2021). Effectiveness of an online interpretation training as a pre-treatment for cognitive behavioral therapy for obsessive-compulsive disorder in youth: A randomized controlled trial. *Journal of Obsessive-Compulsive and Related Disorders, 29*, 100636. https://doi.org/10.1016/j.jocrd.2021.100636

Woud, M. L., Holmes, E. A., Postma, P., Dalgleish, T., & Mackintosh, B. (2012). Ameliorating intrusive memories of distressing experiences using computerized reappraisal training. *Emotion, 12*(4), 778–784. https://doi.org/10.1037/a0024992

Woud, M. L., Postma, P., Holmes, E. A., & Mackintosh, B. (2013). Reducing analogue trauma symptoms by computerized cognitive reappraisal training – Considering a cognitive prophylaxis? *Journal of Behavior Therapy and Experimental Psychiatry, 44*, 312–315. https://doi.org/10.1016/j.jbtep.2013.01.003

Woud, M. L., Hutschemaekers, M. M. H., Rinck, M., & Becker, E. S. (2015). The manipulation of alcohol-related interpretation biases by means of Cognitive Bias Modification – Interpretation (CBM-I). *Journal of Behavior Therapy and Experimental Psychiatry, 49*, 61–68. https://doi.org/10.1016/j.jbtep.2015.03.001

Woud, M. L., Blackwell, S. E., Steudte-Schmiedgen, S., Browning, M., Holmes, E. A., Harmer, C. J., Margraf, J., & Reinecke, A. (2018a). Investigating d-cycloserine as a potential pharmacological enhancer of an emotional bias learning procedure. *Journal of Psychopharmacology, 32*(5), 569–577. https://doi.org/10.1177/0269881118754679

Woud, M. L., Cwik, J. C., Blackwell, S. E., Kleim, B., Holmes, E. A., Adolph, D., Zhang, H., & Margraf, J. (2018b). Does napping enhance the effects of cognitive bias modification-appraisal training? An experimental study. *PLoS One, 13*(2), e0192837. https://doi.org/10.1371/journal.pone.0192837

Woud, M. L., Zlomuzica, A., Cwik, J. C., Margraf, J., Shkreli, L., Blackwell, S. E., Gladwin, T. E., & Ehring, T. (2018c). Effects of appraisal training on responses to a distressing autobiographical event. *Journal of Anxiety Disorders, 56*, 26–34. https://doi.org/10.1016/j.janxdis.2018.03.010

Woud, M. L., Blackwell, S. E., Shkreli, L., Würtz, F., Cwik, J. C., Margraf, J., Holmes, E. A., Steudte-Schmiedgen, S., Herpertz, S., & Kessler, H. (2021). The effects of modifying dysfunctional appraisals in post-traumatic stress disorder using a form of cognitive bias modification: Results of a randomized controlled trial in an inpatient setting. *Psychotherapy and Psychosomatics, 90*(6), 386–402. https://doi.org/10.1159/000514166

Yiend, J., Lee, J. S., Tekes, S., Atkins, L., Mathews, A., Vrinten, M., Ferragamo, C., & Shergill, S. (2014). Modifying interpretation in a clinically depressed sample using "cognitive bias modification-errors": A double blind randomised controlled trial. *Cognitive Therapy and Research, 38*(2), 146–159. https://doi.org/10.1007/s10608-013-9571-y

Dr. Elske Salemink is an Associate Professor in Clinical Psychology at Utrecht University. Her research consists of an experimental approach to understand the development and treatment of anxiety and related disorders with a focus on information processing biases. Dr. Salemink received several grants for her research (including personal grants from the Netherlands Organization for Scientific Research (NWO)). Dr. Salemink is also a registered cognitive behavior therapist (member of the Association of Behavioral and Cognitive Therapy (VGCt)).

Marcella L. Woud is a Junior-Professor of Clinical Psychology and Experimental Psychopathology at Ruhr-University Bochum. Via her research, she aims to better understand how cognitive biases contribute to the development and maintenance of emotional psychopathology, including assessing their neural, physiological, and behavioral underpinnings, using both rigorous experimental and clinical studies. This research has been funded by several (personal) grants, including grants from the German Research Foundation (Deutsche Forschungsgemeinschaft, DFG). Prof. Woud also works a licensed therapist, with a specialization in Cognitive Behavioral Therapy (CBT).

Vera Bouwman is a PhD candidate at the Department of Clinical Psychology at Utrecht University in the Netherlands. Her research focuses on dynamic predictors of treatment response for individuals with anxiety disorders and is part of a NWO VIDI grant awarded to Dr. Salemink. Vera is supervised by Dr. Elske Salemink and Prof. Iris Engelhard and Dr. Lynn Mobach.

Dr. Lynn Mobach completed her PhD on cognitive distortions in childhood social anxiety and their relation to treatment outcome in 2021 at Radboud University and Macquarie University, supervised by Prof. Mike Rinck, Prof. Jennie Hudson, Prof. Eni Becker, Prof. Ron Rapee, and Dr. Anke Klein. Since 2020, Lynn is working as a postdoctoral researcher at the Department of Clinical Psychology at Utrecht University with Dr. Elske Salemink on dynamic predictors of treatment response for individuals with anxiety disorders. Lynn also works as a psychologist at Pro Persona Overwaal where she treats patients suffering from anxiety disorders.

Part II
Clinical Guidance for Interpretational Bias Modification Across Different Emotional Disorders

Chapter 12
Changing Biased Interpretations in CBT: A Brief History and Overview

Marcella L. Woud and Stefan G. Hofmann

Cogito, ergo sum – I think, therefore I am – is probably one of the most famous statements in philosophy (René Descartes; cf. Burns, 2001). Put simply, that we are thinking is evidence for the existence of the self. As psychologists, we might add that not only does thinking provide evidence for a self, but in fact thinking is one of the driving ingredients in *creating and shaping* the self, for example via processes such as attention, interpretation, and encoding into as well as retrieval from memory. This brings us firmly into the realm of clinical psychology, as these processes provide the fundamental targets for many cognitive-behavioral interventions. Given the focus of the present chapter and book, however, the "interpreting self" is of primary relevance.

In the following sections we would like to take the reader on a brief journey back in time, not quite so far back as Descartes, but far enough to provide a brief summary of the historical background of the development of cognitive-behavioral interventions. We will then provide an overview of how such cognitive-behavioral interventions may modify the process of interpreting the world – even if this was not always their original rationale – and thus set the scene for the case studies presented next in this book, targeting biased interpretational processes via techniques derived from Cognitive Behavior Therapy (CBT).

M. L. Woud (✉)
Mental Health Research and Treatment Center, Faculty of Psychology,
Ruhr-University Bochum, Bochum, Germany
e-mail: marcella.woud@rub.de

S. G. Hofmann
Department of Clinical Translational Psychology, Faculty of Psychology,
Philipps-University Marburg, Marburg, Germany
e-mail: shofmann@bu.edu

© The Author(s), under exclusive license to Springer Nature Switzerland AG 2023
M. L. Woud (ed.), *Interpretational Processing Biases in Emotional Psychopathology*,
CBT: Science Into Practice, https://doi.org/10.1007/978-3-031-23650-1_12

12.1   A Brief Historical Background

It is difficult to pin down what exactly we should consider as "the" starting point of
CBT, or even if there is any such thing; rather, where we stand today reflects a
moment in a dynamic and ongoing developmental process that likely emerged
organically from the scientific investigations and theories of the early twentieth century. However, a plausible proxy for a starting point is provided by the publications
of the first theoretical and practical pioneers behind our current CBT techniques.
Strictly chronologically, this should start with the "B" for behavior, for example
from the works of Pavlov (1927), and later Skinner (1953), with both formulating
important theoretical principles such as classical and operant conditioning, that is,
the associative learning principles that are still highly relevant for today's interventions. Those who developed these ideas further and also transformed the theoretical
B into more practical methods for changing psychopathology-relevant behaviors
(i.e., Behavioral Therapy, BT) include Cover Jones (1924), Mowrer (1939), Watson
and Rayner (1920), and Wolpe (1952). For example, via her "Little Peter" experiments, Mary Cover Jones provided an early example of behavioral treatment of a
simple phobia (Cover Jones, 1924), and in a landmark theoretical paper, Mowrer
provided a theory of the onset and maintenance of anxiety disorders such as phobias
via classical and operant learning principles (Mowrer, 1939). The "C" of CBT, i.e.,
the cognitive component, arose from the "cognitive revolution" that took root in the
60s but further flourished during the 70s. The bringing in and integration of the
cognitive component was in part fueled by the increasingly apparent shortcomings
of BT: Despite its clear success in many cases, particularly in the context of anxiety
disorders, BT was also characterized by a number of limitations. These limitations
were not just restricted to treatment efficacy, but also more fundamental considerations that in fact relate back to the statement at the beginning of this chapter. That
is, human beings think, interpret, believe, and imagine, but neither these cognitive
processes themselves nor their interaction with behaviors seemed to be satisfacto-
rily accounted for or targeted in BT. Hence, cognitive phenomena and processes
entered psychotherapy. The publication of Beck's Cognitive Therapy and the
Emotional Disorders (1976) and his Cognitive Therapy of Depression (Beck et al.,
1979) were important milestones here (Woud, 2022; and for a recent special issue
on Beck's contributions to the science and practice of CBT, see editorial Kazantzis,
2022) and laid the basic foundations for Cognitive Therapy (CT) (for an update and
specification of Beck's model, see Beck & Haigh, 2014). Importantly, these seminal
publications were very soon followed by clinical research trials, e.g., in the context
of depression, indicating that CT was as effective as anti-depressants (Rush et al.,
2005). At the same, several others were carrying out important and influential work
on targeting the "C", such as Ellis (Rational-Emotive Therapy, 1962) and
Meichenbaum (Cognitive-Behavioral-Modification, 1977). In the 80s, the "C" and
"B" became fully fused into CBT, which then became firmly established. Both the
effectiveness and the durability of CBT continued to receive growing support from
randomized controlled trials, as did evidence also grew for its applicability across a

number of disorders (for reviews and meta-analyses, see e.g., Butler et al., 2006; Carpenter et al., 2018; Cuijpers et al., 2010; Gould et al., 1995; Hofmann et al., 2012; Hofmann & Smits, 2008; Kazantzis et al., 2018). Alongside this evidence of treatment efficacy, and in line with CBT's commitment to empiricism, an increasing number of studies also investigated the mechanisms underlying CBT's effects, resulting in the ongoing interplay between basic science and clinical implementation that we associate with CBT today (e.g., Blackwell & Heidenreich, 2021; Hofmann et al., 2013; Ingram, 2007).

12.2 CBT – The Basic Principles in a Nutshell

Cognition and behavior provide the core of CBT. In relation to cognitions, the main assumption is that an individual's response towards a certain situation is influenced by how the individual thinks about, appraises, and interprets the situation. The cognitive processing of the situation, not the situation itself, is the key determinant of the individual's behavioral response. Put differently, what the individual "does", their behavior, is (mostly) in line with the way the situation has been cognitively processed. To illustrate, if someone goes to a party and interprets the guests' faces as "smiling and welcoming", this will most likely result in the person staying at the party. In contrast, if they interpreted the same facial expressions as "smirking and patronizing" they may very well leave. However, there are of course more than cognitions and behavioral responses involved here, and CBT also emphasizes how these are tightly related to emotional and physiological states. With the present example, interpreting the faces in a negative and threatening manner may trigger e.g., anxiety, whereas a positive interpretation may trigger e.g., joy. In fact, the physiological response could be similar for either interpretations, e.g., in terms of arousal-related responses. However, in the end the situation's idiosyncratic processing determines the interpretation of these physiological phenomena. To illustrate, interpreting the faces positively and deciding to stay at the party may result in positive arousal such as increased heartbeat and sweating, reflecting the excitement and the expectation of having a great night out. Conversely, interpreting the faces negatively may result in a similar physiological reaction, but resulting from anxiety, and the individual themselves may then interpret this further negatively. Within CBT the interactions between cognitions, behavior, emotion, and physiology (see Fig. 12.1) are therefore given a central role in many disorder and treatment models, and it is assumed that these four components influence each other via ongoing and complex feedback loops. Further, individuals do not exist in isolation but rather within a broader environment and social context, and thus there are important interactions and feedback loops between, e.g., an individual's behavior and the response to their social environment.

Alongside this core role given to the interactions between internal and external processes, CBT has a few other notable key principles. Another principle is that psychological problems and disorders are not defined as categorically distinct

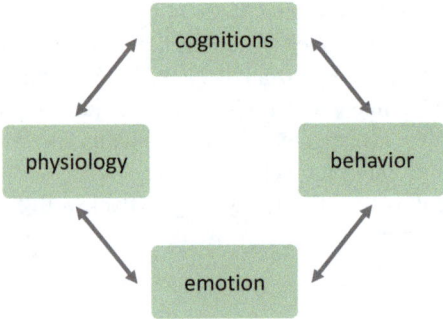

Fig. 12.1 The interaction between cognitions, behavior, emotion, and physiology

phenomena; instead, they are defined as phenomena on a continuum with normal functioning, that result from extreme or dysfunctional outputs of the systems outlined above. Whether or not the balance shifts towards and is maintained in a dysfunctional state depends on various factors, such as the individual itself, their vulnerabilities versus resources, and their present situation (see also "stress vulnerability models", e.g., Ingram & Luxton, 2005). The third principle in CBT is a focus on the here and now, which can be mostly attributed to the roots of BT and the idea that what should be tackled via therapeutic interventions are the observable symptoms. Consequently, CBT focuses on the individual's present, targeting processes that currently maintain rather than those thought to have originally caused the reported psychological problems. A final principle, which has been touched in an earlier section of this chapter already, is the idea that both therapy and theory should be the subject of an ongoing evaluation process, via systematic and rigorous research, optimally via a fusion of experimental, clinical, and multimodal approaches.

We would also like to present a few therapeutic principles of CBT. Some of the presented principles will be also shared by other therapeutic approaches, while some others are a logical consequence of the above-presented principles. To start with, a good working relationship needs to be established and should be regarded as an essential condition to make CBT successful. In this context, the term *collaborative empiricism* has been coined and implies that patients and therapists work as a scientific team: The patients are experts for their own problems, the therapists are experts for the adequate techniques to work on these problems. Together they e.g., test whether the patients' biased belief is correct and whether a certain technique is helpful to reduce that belief. To do so, therapists apply a way of "Socratic questioning" (for more detailed information, see e.g., Beck, 2020) that helps patients to reflect on and challenge their dysfunctional way of thinking. This, in turn, should widen the patients' perspective and trigger new insights, followed by more functional ways of thinking. These techniques, as well the therapists' attitude when applying these techniques, are often summarized via the umbrella term *guided discovery*, which represents another important principle of CBT. Further, CBT is problem-oriented, i.e., specific problems are identified, followed by goals of how to target these problems. Finally, CBT is time-limited and, in case severe comorbidities or co-exiting personality disorders are absent, rather brief.

This last section will include an overview of the key principles regarding the conceptualization of CBT and its underlying theory. In line with the *here and now principle*, CBTs' therapeutic models have a stronger focus on hypotheses regarding maintenance than etiology. One of the most highly influential therapeutic models is the cognitive model by Beck (1976), which proposes three levels of cognitions to be relevant during information processing: core beliefs, dysfunctional assumptions, and negative automatic thoughts. Core beliefs, or schemas, are acquired early in life and influenced by childhood experiences. As such, they are deep and fundamental beliefs about oneself, other people, and the world, and serve as a first filter through which information is processed. They manifest themselves via absolute statements (e.g., "Others cannot be trusted"). Dysfunctional assumptions are described as conditional and rigid rules for living, and thus more specific than core beliefs. Typically, they take the form of "must" or "should" statements and can be culturally reinforced (e.g., "I must perform well when starting my new job otherwise the others will not respect me."). Like core beliefs, they are not always obvious and may be difficult to verbalize, and need to be inferred from e.g., behavioral patterns. Negative automatic thoughts refer to the ongoing stream of interpretations and appraisals of what is happening in the environment, noticeable once attention is paid to them. As their definition implies, negative automatic thoughts are activated involuntarily, especially if they are very habitual. However, they can become conscious and people can learn to become aware of them. Specific situations automatically trigger specific thoughts (e.g., "The new task my boss allocated to me is to make my life even harder at work."). Negative automatic thoughts are said to have a direct influence on emotional states and are generally experienced as not only plausible but statements of truth. This Beckian model therefore outlines three different levels at which biased interpretations may be identified or targeted. Not all CBT models make these distinctions, but they share a common premise: that cognitions play a key role in the maintenance of disorders, and thus changing these cognitions should lead to reductions in distress and impairment.

12.3 Techniques

CBT-based interventions share a common basic premise that psychological disorders reflect a dysfunctional, associative structure between cognitions, behaviors, emotions, and psychophysiology, maintained by dysfunctional cognitive (e.g., attention, interpretation, memory) and behavioral responses (e.g., avoidance, reinforcement). Most CBT-based interventions aim to identify and modify these interacting processes, i.e., intervene at the level of a disorder's maintaining factors, guided via the aforementioned key principles. In the following section, we will present a brief overview of some of the core techniques of CBT, focusing in particular on how they may modify biased cognitions. Interestingly, for many of these techniques' identification and modification of dysfunctional cognitions may not be the core aim. However, by highlighting this aspect, we hope to focus on the central role of modifying such cognitions in CBT, and put the reader in a suitable frame of mind for the rest of this book.

12.4   Cognitive Restructuring

CBT aims to change how patients think. As such, cognitive restructuring can be considered one of classical CBT's most essential techniques, targeting core mechanisms that lie at the heart of its theoretical foundations. Cognitive restructuring is typically carried out as a stepwise process, which starts with the therapist helping patients to observe and note down the dysfunctional thoughts that occur in their daily lives. For example, during a therapy session, a patient might be invited to think back to a situation that elicited strong, negative emotions, and then report the thoughts that came to mind. The aim is to identify the "hot" cognitions, which according to Beck et al. (1979) are those most directly linked to the patients' most significant emotions and which play a critical causal role in the subsequent emotional and behavioral responses. Next, these hot cognitions are evaluated, for example, via the therapist asking a series of Socratic questions that help the patient evaluate their empirical and logical basis. The overarching goal of this phase is to widen and shift the patient's focus, and by doing so to help them start to re-evaluate their negative thoughts. As a result, the patient is guided to come up with more adaptive, for example more accurate, cognitions, which, in turn should have the potential to decrease the patient's negative emotional response during the described situation.

Within this general framework (i.e., first identification then modification of negative thoughts), there are many variations in how exactly the two steps are carried out. In a classical CBT-based approach, patients would be asked to keep a diary in which they record their feelings and cognitions in certain situations, rating the strength of their emotional responses and strength of their belief in each thought. These diary entries are then discussed during therapy, and may also be used to identify reoccurring themes or to identify specific cognitive biases, i.e., exaggerated thinking errors that trigger intensive negative emotional responses. Thought records such as the seven-column-thought-record (Greenberger & Padesky, 1995) or the dysfunctional thought record (Beck, 2020) can be used to help structure this process and initiate the modification. Patients will be asked to provide evidence for their negative thoughts, to develop alternative thoughts, and by doing so test whether the new way of thinking changes the original negative thoughts and feelings. To train and foster this new and more adaptive way of thinking patients are asked to continue completing these records at home or keep a positive data log, recoding all observations that are consistent with the new and functional way of thinking (Padesky, 1994). A huge variety of techniques have been developed to evaluate and challenge dysfunctional thoughts, for example, weighing pros and cons in combination with their long- and short-term outcomes, identifying the worst outcome and potential coping strategies, trying to take the perspective of someone else in that situation, or using more experimental techniques such as role-play or imagery. In fact, the described procedures can be applied to all levels of cognitions, i.e., for negative automatic thoughts, dysfunctional assumptions, and core beliefs. At the beginning of the therapy, however, the focus will most likely be on working on specific thoughts and emotions in specific situations, i.e., mainly on negative automatic thoughts. But, in an advanced stage of therapy and in order to establish more long-lasting changes, both the patients' dysfunctional assumptions and core beliefs should be targeted as well. It is important to note that the purpose of cognitive restructuring is not just identifying specific cognitions and modifying them, but also to change patients' relationships with their automatic thoughts and socialize them into the cognitive model (see e.g., Beck et al., 1979). Via the process, they learn that their intense negative feelings are often the result of thoughts popping automatically into their mind, and that in fact these thoughts are often not statements of fact but rather reflections of their own beliefs and personal histories. This increased meta-cognitive understanding can be liberating for many patients and may enable them to start simply ignoring or dismissing their negative cognitions, as well as paving the way for more direct methods of testing them, such as the behavioral experiments to be discussed next.

12.5   Behavioral Experiments

As with cognitive restructuring, behavioral experiments aim to identify and modify biased cognitions. However, behavioral experiments go one step further – first, they directly test the biased cognitions rather than evaluating them verbally; second, they are also used to actively generate evidence to further corroborate the patients' new and more functional way of thinking. Behavioral experiments therefore have the potential to be a more powerful tool, especially in situations in which a patient reports a mismatch between cognitions and emotions: Patients may be aware of the partly irrational nature of their cognitions and theoretically able to endorse a more functional way of thinking (in fact, the diagnostic criteria for several disorders include the patient being aware of the irrational nature of their fears). However, patients may also report that their emotions do not develop in accordance with their new way of thinking, and the old, biased way of thinking "feels more true". Directly testing the cognitions via a behavioral experiment, which will often also involve experiencing new and functional emotions while executing a new behavior, can help to initiate emotional change and bridge the "logical" vs. "emotional" divide. Although behavioral experiments are not new, for example with Beck (e.g., Beck et al., 1979) mentioning the use of experiments to test out patients' beliefs, they have played an increasingly important role from the 80s and 90s onwards, such that they can now be seen as the core driver for cognitive change in most modern CBT.

According to Bennett-Levy et al. (2004), behavioral experiments can be observational versus active, and hypothesis-testing versus discovery-oriented. This leads to four types of behavioral experiments. In the first, patients observe and test a hypothesis, such as, via a survey, investigating other people's opinion about a certain topic (e.g., how they would react if they saw someone walking through town with large sweat patches under their arms). A second option is that patients observe a situation in a discovery-oriented way, i.e., to simply collect information rather than test a hypothesis. For example, the therapist could wet their armpits to pretend they are sweating a lot, and then walk through the city center. Here, the patients' task would be simply to observe what is happening and not happening. This could then be adapted for a third option, in which the patient could play the active role instead of the therapist and observe people's reactions. The fourth and final option is that the patients are active and test a specific hypothesis, for example their prediction of what will happen in a certain situation, e.g., that if they walk through the town with large sweat patches under their armpits, people will point and laugh, and they will be unable to cope. In anxiety disorders, behavioral experiments are also used to collect evidence for and test hypotheses about the role of patient's safety behaviors (Salkovskis, 1996). In accordance with CBT's empirical foundation, each phase of a behavioral experiment (i.e., planning, execution, and reflection) is often accompanied by record-keeping and ratings, for example noting what the patient's initial prediction is, how plausible this prediction is before and after the behavioral experiment, what the outcome is and what the patient learned from it, and so on.

Behavioral experiments are sometimes combined with cognitive restructuring, e.g., beforehand to bring the patient to the point where they can see the logic of conducting an experiment, or afterwards to consolidate the learning. However, behavioral experiments can also sometimes happen spontaneously, for example when something happens in a session that can be easily translated into a behavioral experiment, and it makes sense to seize the moment. However, regardless of how the behavioral experiment is conducted, it is generally thought to be as very important that the prediction to be tested is clear and appropriately operationalized, and that, independent of the experiment's outcome, the patient will learn something when testing their predictions. As with cognitive restructuring, behavioral experiments are something that patients should ideally continue with outside of the therapy sessions.

12.6 Exposure

Behavioral experiments often include an element of exposure: To test a prediction about an anxiety-inducing situation, the patient must enter the situation and thus be "exposed" to it. However, we think it is useful to consider exposure separately in this chapter, and in fact, when viewed as a "behavior therapy" technique, the reader might wonder why it is relevant to a chapter about cognitions. With behavioral experiments – even if the crucial part involves exposure to a feared situation or object – the main aim is explicitly to help patients to initiate a cognitive change. In contrast, from a traditional behaviorist view, the main aim of exposure was to help patients to endure and habituate to their fears, via repeated and systematic exposure to exactly those cues they fear and avoid (Craske et al., 2014). Within this behaviorist viewpoint, cognitions play no mechanistic role. However, this conceptualization of exposure has since changed, developing from a "fear habituation" approach to a "belief disconfirmation" approach as more evidence as to its mechanisms have been gathered (see Craske et al., 2014, p. 10). According to this more recent conceptualization, exposure should be tailored to the patient's most important idiosyncratic feared outcome, and expectation and operationalized such that the patients' biased expectation is maximally violated. Thus, while termed "exposure", the technique is closely aligned to behavioral experiments and cognitive restructuring as described above, in that a major aim is initiating cognitive change.

In CBT exposure can be carried out either in-vivo or via imagery (imaginal exposure). Generally, in-vivo exposure – that is, to the actual feared situation – would be preferred, but sometimes this is not possible (e.g., the object of exposure is a traumatic experience that happened in the past) and thus imaginal exposure is used. In recent years, exposure conducted via virtual reality has also become a possibility, expanding the scope of what is possible (see e.g., Lindner, 2021, for an overview). Virtual reality enables immersive computer simulations of the feared object or situation, rendering it possible to also expose patients to situations that are difficult to encounter or re-build in real life (e.g., when thinking of a PTSD patient who was traumatized during combat). Regardless of how exactly the exposure is implemented, in vivo, via imagery, or virtual reality, there are also different ways in which it can be conducted, for example with or without a stepwise fear hierarchy (graded exposure vs. flooding) or can be combined with relaxation exercises (systematic desensitization).

Based on recent developments in research on exposure and its underlying effects, there are various recommendations of how to foster and consolidate the intended cognitive change (see e.g., Craske et al., 2018; Pittig et al., 2016, 2019). For example, exposure sessions are continued for the duration needed to most effectively violate the patients' expectations – put differently, the session's length is not determined by the level of fear reduction. Further, any type of (evaluating) cognitive technique is applied after the actual exposure has been completed. Typical questions include asking the patients what they learned regarding the non-occurrence of the feared expectation, and identify discrepancies between what was expected and what actually happened.

12.7 Mental Imagery-Based Techniques

The use of mental imagery has a long history in CBT, with techniques emerging from both the cognitive and behavioral strands of its development (e.g., Blackwell, 2021), and there are several ways in which mental imagery can be used to change cognitions (for an overview of the role of imagery in biased interpretational processing, see Chap. 6 by Blackwell). In his early works, Beck (e.g., Beck, 1976) already emphasized the role of mental images in psychopathology. For example, he suggested that mental images, memories, or dreams may contain important information on how patients interpret themselves, others, and the world, and also suggested manipulations of mental imagery as a method to change beliefs. Importantly, from the perspective of this chapter, mental images do not occur in isolation and are often accompanied by other cognitive responses – such as interpretations (see e.g., Blackwell, 2020). In fact, for some disorders the interpretation of mental imagery is seen as highly important, for example in PTSD, where maladaptive interpretations of recurring intrusive memories (e.g., "The fact that I have these memories means I am going mad") are given a central role in some cognitive models (e.g., Ehlers & Clark, 2000), fueling dysfunctional coping strategies that contribute to maintaining distress.

In terms of imagery-based techniques, Holmes et al. (2007) differentiate between two broad categories: Techniques that involve directly working on the mental image versus those that are indirect. In turn, both kinds of techniques can be used either to reduce negative imagery or enhance positive imagery. Of direct techniques, the one with the clearest relevance to changing cognitions is imagery rescripting (Arntz, 2012). Imagery rescripting, which can be applied to memories, future-oriented imagery, or even deliberately generated metaphorical imagery (Butler et al., 2010), aims to integrate new information into a distressing image and thus change the meaning at an emotional level. As mentioned above, imagery can also be used to conduct exposure (e.g., to memories of a traumatic event in PTSD, see e.g., Foa et al., 2007). During imaginal exposure, patients are asked to deliberately evoke a highly distressing image or to listen to imagined, highly distressing situations, and by doing so expose themselves to all negative emotions and cognitions that come along. As with exposure more generally, as discussed above, imaginal exposure can be explained (as it was originally) without any mention of cognitions or cognitive change. However, most modern conceptualizations would understand imaginal exposure as leading to changes in processes such as how a memory or situation is interpreted. In contrast, indirect techniques do not engage with the imagery but instead target aspects of its properties, such as e.g., the dysfunctional emotional and cognitive responses to it. In the context of reducing negative mental imagery, meta-cognitive imagery-based interventions often aim to change how patients relate to the mental image by learning to appraise the mental image as "being just an image" – an image that comes and goes, just like other images. This image thus does not need special attention and is not representative of reality (e.g., Holmes et al., 2019).

12.8   Behavioral Activation and Activity Scheduling

Activity scheduling and behavioral activation, whether carried out as treatments in their own right or as sub-parts of broader CBT packages, are core "behavioral" approaches in the context of depression, and thus, as with exposure, may seem odd inclusions in a chapter on changing cognitions. And as with exposure, behavioral activation can be conceptualized from a purely behaviorist perspective without invoking cognitions: By increasing how much they engage in activities that are positively reinforced, the patient receives more positive reinforcement in daily life, improving their mood and also strengthening the link between the behavior and reinforcement. However, behavioral activation can also be viewed from a more cognitive perspective (e.g., Beck et al., 1979; Bennett-Levy et al., 2004). From this angle, there may be biased cognitions that contribute to and maintain a patient's inactivity. In the context of depression, for example, a patient's inactivity may be fueled by a cognition such as "I don't enjoy anything anyway so there's no point". Keeping an activity record in which they also record enjoyment and mastery can thus be used as an experiment to test out this cognition, for example highlighting how their enjoyment fluctuates and is not at a constant "zero", or to test the idea that lack of enjoyment means that an activity was therefore not worthwhile (see e.g., Beck et al., 1979). Initiating and fostering a cognitive change can therefore become a central aim of behavioral activation.

A common technique in the context of behavioral activation is monitoring daily activities via a weekly activity schedule. Using such a 7-day schedule, patients are asked to complete for each day and every hour of that day what they did, and the patients' entries are then reviewed during the session. Initially, monitoring is an important aim here, i.e., obtaining a better understanding of what the patients' activities are, and to identify activities that give the patients at least some experience of mastery and pleasure or relief from their negative thoughts. Importantly, however, such a weekly schedule can be also used to plan changes in the patients' future activities, which, in turn, should also initiate cognitive changes. That is, enhancing the patients' level of activity will also lead a to change in the patients' negative cognitions, and via pleasure and achievement ratings, such changes can be monitored and evaluated.

12.9   Cognitive Training Approaches

A number of more recent developments include the use of simple training approaches to change cognitions. For example, several methods involving repeated practice of memory retrieval have been developed and tested (Hitchcock et al., 2017). To illustrate, during Competitive Memory Training (COMET; Korrelboom et al., 2009) patients train to generate vivid, personal memories of themselves in which they are the central figure, and by doing so train to construct more positive, stronger mental representations of themselves. Although not conceptualized as a method to change interpretations, it could be hypothesized that COMET would have such an effect by increasing the accessibility of positive memories that might be drawn on when patients encounter ambiguous self-relevant situations.

The area of cognitive training most relevant for changing interpretations comes from the Cognitive Bias Modification (CBM) literature (cf. Koster et al., 2009; Woud & Becker, 2014). CBM involves repeated and systematic computer training targeting cognitive processing biases in e.g., attention, appraisal, or interpretation, and within a treatment context, the aim is to reduce such biases (e.g., Lazarov et al., 2018; Salemink et al., 2015; Vrijsen et al., 2019; Woud et al., 2021; and for an overview of how to manipulate interpretation biases, see Chap. 11 by Salemink et al.). The most commonly used CBM paradigms used to modify interpretations biases involve the presentation of ambiguous scenarios that are then resolved positively. Being repeatedly constrained to resolve the ambiguous scenarios positively during the training is thought to lead to a more positive interpretation style that patients will then apply to ambiguous situations encountered in daily life. In most forms of CBM-I participants are encouraged to imagine themselves in the training scenarios to enhance emotional processing (e.g., Mathews & Mackintosh, 2000), and in some clinical applications, this imagery component has been particularly emphasized and expanded upon (e.g., Blackwell et al., 2015; Hirsch et al., 2021).

12.10 "Third Wave" Approaches

The past 20 years have seen an increase in what has been termed a "third wave" of CBT approaches (Hayes, 2004), for example including mindfulness-based cognitive therapy, acceptance and commitment therapy (ACT), and compassion-focused approaches. Some of these explicitly target cognitions, for example, compassion-focused approaches that include imagery and other experiential techniques to foster more compassionate beliefs about oneself. Others, such as mindfulness-based approaches and ACT, may not have changes in interpretations as their primary focus, or even part of their conceptualization, but can be viewed within a cognitive framework as changing meta-cognitive interpretations. For example, via the act of observing their thoughts mindfully and not being "sucked in" to unhelpful patterns of responding, patients learn to interpret their thoughts as passing events rather than statements of truth that must be acted upon. Hence, techniques developed within the context of third-wave CBT can also be incorporated into more classical cognitively focused approaches. The most recent developments in this field emphasize the processes of change using an idiographic and network-analytic, functional, and contextual approach. This stands in contrast to a syndromal, disease-entity focused, nomothetic, and linear approach (Hayes & Hofmann, 2021; Hofmann & Hayes, 2019). This movement introduces a fundamental shift in clinical science and is likely to introduce new and improved methods for studying treatment change (Hofmann, Curtiss, & Hayes, 2020).

12.11 Summary and Outlook

In this chapter we presented a brief overview of CBT-based techniques that are commonly used, or can be used, to identify and modify biased interpretational processes. Given CBT's empirical nature and evidence-based perspective, these techniques are under continuous scientific evaluation using both rigorous experimental and clinical studies (for a related discussion about the interplay of scientific research and clinical practice, see Chap. 1 by Holmes). For example, the section on exposure, with its shift from habituation to cognitions, noted how scientific progress can affect clinical techniques, and this in turn offers new input for research on exposure. To illustrate, in the context of fear conditioning and extinction learning, researchers have started to explore the role of cognitive processes such as the effects of verbal instruction on CS-US contingencies (cf. Mertens et al., 2018) or by adding imagery-based techniques (e.g., Hendrikx et al., 2021; Krypotos et al., 2020; and see for review Mertens et al., 2020). Further, during fear conditioning, stimuli may in fact become ambiguous stimuli, resulting in increased fear in anxiety-prone individuals, and this may have consequences for exposure-based techniques (for a related discussion about the role of interpretational processing during fear conditioning, see Chap. 7 by Scheveneels and Boddez). As another example, taken from the section on cognitive training approaches, CBM techniques, which were developed from experimental psychopathology research, may offer promising new therapeutic add-ons. For example, CBM training targeting biased interpretations and appraisals (e.g., de Kleine et al., 2019; Salemink et al., 2015; Woud et al., 2021) may offer fruitful treatment adjuncts that could facilitate or further reinforce the cognitive change established during therapy. Specifically, "take home trainings" could be developed that patients do as computerized homework, helping to foster a generalization and transfer of the learning into the patient's everyday life.

To conclude, there is an ongoing drive for continued improvements of CBT and CBT-based techniques to ease the suffering of our patients more efficiently, both in the short and long term (for a recent special issue on future directions in CBT, see editorial Hofmann, 2021). Interventions involving initiating and maintaining cognitive change, via systematically modifying patients' biased way of thinking, provide a promising and robust route to do so. In the next section, you will find five case studies using various techniques applied to modify biased cognitive processing, namely in the context of posttraumatic stress disorder (Chap. 13 by Schnyder), depression (Chap. 14 by Moulds), obsessive-compulsive disorder (Chap. 15 by Purdon), social anxiety disorder (Chap. 16 by Daniel and Teachman), and panic disorder (Chap. 17 by Becker), and we hope that the present chapter provided you with a good starting point for reading them.

References

Arntz, A. (2012). Imagery rescripting as a therapeutic technique: Review of clinical trials, basic studies, and research agenda. *Journal of Experimental Psychopathology, 3*(2), 189–208. https://doi.org/10.5127/jep.024211

Beck, A. T. (1976). *Cognitive therapy and the emotional disorders.* New American Library.

Beck, J. S. (2020). *Cognitive therapy: Basics and beyond.* Guilford Publications.

Beck, A. T., & Haigh, E. A. (2014). Advances in cognitive theory and therapy: The generic cognitive model. *Annual Review of Clinical Psychology, 10*, 1–24. https://doi.org/10.1146/annurev-clinpsy-032813-153734

Beck, A. T., Rush, A. J., & Shaw, B. F. (1979). *Cognitive therapy of depression.* Guilford Press.

Bennett-Levy, J., Butler, G., Fennell, M., Hackmann, A., Mueller, M., Westbrook, D., & Rouf, K. (2004). *Oxford guide to behavioural experiments in cognitive therapy.* Oxford University Press. https://doi.org/10.1093/med:psych/9780198529163.001.0001

Blackwell, S. E. (2020). Emotional mental imagery. In A. Abraham (Ed.), *The Cambridge handbook of the imagination* (pp. 241–257). Cambridge University Press. https://doi.org/10.1017/9781108580298.016

Blackwell, S. E. (2021). Mental imagery in the science and practice of cognitive behaviour therapy: Past, present, and future perspectives. *International Journal of Cognitive Therapy, 14*(1), 160–181. https://doi.org/10.1007/s41811-021-00102-0

Blackwell, S. E., & Heidenreich, T. (2021). Cognitive behavior therapy at the crossroads. *International Journal of Cognitive Therapy, 14*(1), 1–22. https://doi.org/10.1007/s41811-021-00104-y

Blackwell, S. E., Browning, M., Mathews, A., Pictet, A., Welch, J., Davies, J., Watson, P., Geddes, J. R., & Holmes, E. A. (2015). Positive imagery-based Cognitive Bias Modification as a web-based treatment tool for depressed adults: A randomized controlled trial. *Clinical Psychological Science, 3*(1), 91–111. https://doi.org/10.1177/2167702614560746

Burns, W. E. (2001). *The scientific revolution: An encyclopedia.* ABC-CLIO.

Butler, A. C., Chapman, J. E., Forman, E. M., & Beck, A. T. (2006). The empirical status of cognitive-behavioral therapy: A review of meta-analyses. *Clinical Psychology Review, 26*(1), 17–31. https://doi.org/10.1016/j.cpr.2005.07.003

Butler, G., Fennell, M., & Hackmann, A. (2010). *Cognitive-behavioral therapy for anxiety disorders: Mastering clinical challenges.* Guilford Press.

Carpenter, J. K., Andrews, L. A., Witcraft, S. M., Powers, M. B., Smits, J., & Hofmann, S. G. (2018). Cognitive behavioral therapy for anxiety and related disorders: A meta-analysis of randomized placebo-controlled trials. *Depression and Anxiety, 35*(6), 502–514. https://doi.org/10.1002/da.22728

Craske, M. G., Treanor, M., Conway, C. C., Zbozinek, T., & Vervliet, B. (2014). Maximizing exposure therapy: An inhibitory learning approach. *Behaviour Research and Therapy, 58*, 10–23. https://doi.org/10.1016/j.brat.2014.04.006

Craske, M. G., Hermans, D., & Vervliet, B. (2018). State-of-the-art and future directions for extinction as a translational model for fear and anxiety. *Philosophical Transactions of the Royal Society of London. Series B, Biological Sciences, 373*(1742), 20170025. https://doi.org/10.1098/rstb.2017.0025

Cuijpers, P., Smit, F., Bohlmeijer, E., Hollon, S. D., & Andersson, G. (2010). Efficacy of cognitive-behavioural therapy and other psychological treatments for adult depression: Meta-analytic study of publication bias. *The British Journal of Psychiatry: the Journal of Mental Science, 196*(3), 173–178. https://doi.org/10.1192/bjp.bp.109.066001

de Kleine, R. A., Woud, M. L., Ferentzi, H., Hendriks, G. J., Broekman, T. G., Becker, E. S., & Van Minnen, A. (2019). Appraisal-based cognitive bias modification in patients with posttraumatic stress disorder: A randomised clinical trial. *European Journal of Psychotraumatology, 10*(1), 1625690. https://doi.org/10.1080/20008198.2019.1625690

Ehlers, A., & Clark, D. M. (2000). A cognitive model of posttraumatic stress disorder. *Behaviour Research and Therapy, 38*(4), 319–345. https://doi.org/10.1016/s0005-7967(99)00123-0

Ellis, A. (1962). *Reason and emotion in psychotherapy*. Lyle Stuart.

Foa, E. B., Hembree, E. A., & Rothbaum, B. (2007). *Prolonged exposure therapy for PTSD*. Oxford University. https://doi.org/10.1093/med:psych/9780195308501.001.0001

Gould, R. A., Ott, M. W., & Pollack, M. H. (1995). A meta-analysis of treatment outcome for panic disorder. *Clinical Psychology Review, 15*(8), 819–844. https://doi.org/10.1016/0272-7358(95)00048-8

Greenberger, D., & Padesky, C. A. (1995). *Mind over mood: A cognitive therapy treatment manual for clients*. Guilford Press.

Hayes, S. C. (2004). Acceptance and commitment therapy, relational frame theory, and the third wave of behavioral and cognitive therapies. *Behavior Therapy, 35*(4), 639–665. https://doi.org/10.1016/S0005-7894(04)80013-3

Hayes, S. C., & Hofmann, S. G. (2021). "Third-wave" cognitive and behavioral therapies and the emergence of a process-based approach to intervention in psychiatry. *World Psychiatry, 20*, 363–375. https://doi.org/10.1002/wps.20884

Hendrikx, L. J., Krypotos, A. M., & Engelhard, I. M. (2021). Enhancing extinction with response prevention via imagery-based counterconditioning: Results on conditioned avoidance and distress. *Journal of Behavior Therapy and Experimental Psychiatry, 70*, 101601. https://doi.org/10.1016/j.jbtep.2020.101601

Hirsch, C. R., Krahé, C., Whyte, J., Krzyzanowski, H., Meeten, F., Norton, S., & Mathews, A. (2021). Internet-delivered interpretation training reduces worry and anxiety in individuals with generalized anxiety disorder: A randomized controlled experiment. *Journal of Consulting and Clinical Psychology, 89*(7), 575–589. https://doi.org/10.1037/ccp0000660

Hitchcock, C., Werner-Seidler, A., Blackwell, S. E., & Dalgleish, T. (2017). Autobiographical episodic memory-based training for the treatment of mood, anxiety and stress-related disorders: A systematic review and meta-analysis. *Clinical Psychology Review, 52*, 92–107. https://doi.org/10.1016/j.cpr.2016.12.003

Hofmann, S. G. (2021). The future of cognitive behavioral therapy. *Cognitive Therapy and Research, 45*, 383–384. https://doi.org/10.1007/s10608-021-10232-6

Hofmann, S. G., & Smits, J. A. (2008). Cognitive-behavioral therapy for adult anxiety disorders: A meta-analysis of randomized placebo-controlled trials. *The Journal of Clinical Psychiatry, 69*(4), 621–632. https://doi.org/10.4088/jcp.v69n0415

Hofmann, S. G., & Hayes, S. C. (2019). The future of intervention science: Process-based therapy. *Clinical Psychological Science, 7*, 37–50. https://doi.org/10.1177/2167702618772296

Hofmann, S. G., Curtiss, J. E., & Hayes, S. C. (2020). Beyond linear mediation: Toward a dynamic network approach to study treatment processes. *Clinical Psychology Review, 76*, https://doi.org/10.1016/j.cpr.2020.101824

Hofmann, S. G., Asnaani, A., Vonk, I. J., Sawyer, A. T., & Fang, A. (2012). The efficacy of cognitive behavioral therapy: A review of meta-analyses. *Cognitive Therapy and Research, 36*(5), 427–440. https://doi.org/10.1007/s10608-012-9476-1

Hofmann, S. G., Asmundson, G. J., & Beck, A. T. (2013). The science of cognitive therapy. *Behavior Therapy, 44*(2), 199–212. https://doi.org/10.1016/j.beth.2009.01.007

Holmes, E. A., Arntz, A., & Smucker, M. R. (2007). Imagery rescripting in cognitiv behaviour therapy: Images, treatment techniques and outcomes. *Journal of Behavior Therapy and Experimental Psychiatry, 38*(4), 297–305. https://doi.org/10.1016/j.jbtep.2007.10.007

Holmes, E. A., Hales, S. A., Young, K., & Di Simplicio, M. (2019). *Imagery-based cognitive therapy for bipolar disorder and mood instability*. Guilford Press.

Ingram, R. E. (2007). Introduction to the special section on cognitive processes and psychotherapy. *Journal of Consulting and Clinical Psychology, 75*(3), 359–362. https://doi.org/10.1037/0022-006X.75.3.359

Ingram, R. E., & Luxton, D. D. (2005). Vulnerability-stress models. In B. L. Hankin & J. R. Abela (Eds.), *Development of psychopathology: A vulnerability-stress perspective* (pp. 32–46). Sage. https://doi.org/10.4135/9781452231655.n2

Jones, M. C. (1924). A laboratory study of fear: The case of Peter. *The Journal of Genetic Psychology, 31*(4), 308–315. https://doi.org/10.1080/08856559.1924.9944851

Kazantzis, N. (2022). A special feature in commemoration of Aaron T. Beck's contributions to the science and practice of CBT. *Cognitive and Behavioral Practice, 29*, 501.

Kazantzis, N., Luong, H. K., Usatoff, A. S., Impala, T., Yew, R. Y., & Hofmann, S. G. (2018). The processes of cognitive behavioral therapy: A review of meta-analyses. *Cognitive Therapy and Research, 42*(4), 349–357. https://doi.org/10.1007/s10608-018-9920-y

Korrelboom, K., de Jong, M., Huijbrechts, I., & Daansen, P. (2009). Competitive memory training (COMET) for treating low self-esteem in patients with eating disorders: A randomized clinical trial. *Journal of Consulting and Clinical Psychology, 77*(5), 974–980. https://doi.org/10.1037/a0016742

Koster, E. H., Fox, E., & MacLeod, C. (2009). Introduction to the special section on cognitive bias modification in emotional disorders. *Journal of Abnormal Psychology, 118*(1), 1–4. https://doi.org/10.1037/a0014379

Krypotos, A. M., Mertens, G., Leer, A., & Engelhard, I. M. (2020). Induction of conditioned avoidance via mental imagery. *Behaviour Research and Therapy, 132*, 103652. Advance online publication. https://doi.org/10.1016/j.brat.2020.103652

Lazarov, A., Marom, S., Yahalom, N., Pine, D. S., Hermesh, H., & Bar-Haim, Y. (2018). Attention bias modification augments cognitive-behavioral group therapy for social anxiety disorder: A randomized controlled trial. *Psychological Medicine, 48*(13), 2177–2185. https://doi.org/10.1017/S003329171700366X

Lindner, P. (2021). Better, virtually: The past, present, and future of virtual reality cognitive behavior therapy. *International Journal of Cognitive Therapy, 14*, 23–46. https://doi.org/10.1007/s41811-020-00090-7

Mathews, A., & Mackintosh, B. (2000). Induced emotional interpretation bias and anxiety. *Journal of Abnormal Psychology, 109*(4), 602. https://doi.org/10.1037/0021-843X.109.4.602

Meichenbaum, D. (1977). *Cognitive-behavior modification: An integrative approach.* Plenum. https://doi.org/10.1007/978-1-4757-9739-8

Mertens, G., Boddez, Y., Sevenster, D., Engelhard, I. M., & De Houwer, J. (2018). A review on the effects of verbal instructions in human fear conditioning: Empirical findings, theoretical considerations, and future directions. *Biological Psychology, 137*, 49–64. https://doi.org/10.1016/j.biopsycho.2018.07.002

Mertens, G., Krypotos, A. M., & Engelhard, I. M. (2020). A review on mental imagery in fear conditioning research 100 years since the "Little Albert" study. *Behaviour Research and Therapy, 126*, 103556. https://doi.org/10.1016/j.brat.2020.103556

Mowrer, O. H. (1939). A stimulus-response analysis of anxiety and its role as a reinforcing agent. *Psychological Review, 46*(6), 553–565. https://doi.org/10.1037/h0054288

Padesky, C. A. (1994). Schema change processes in cognitive therapy. *Clinical Psychology and Psychotherapy, 1*, 267–278. https://doi.org/10.1002/cpp.5640010502

Pavlov, I. P. (1927). *Conditioned reflexes.* Oxford University Press.

Pittig, A., van den Berg, L., & Vervliet, B. (2016). The key role of extinction learning in anxiety disorders: Behavioral strategies to enhance exposure-based treatments. *Current Opinion in Psychiatry, 29*(1), 39–47. https://doi.org/10.1097/YCO.0000000000000220

Pittig, A., Kotter, R., & Hoyer, J. (2019). The struggle of behavioral therapists with exposure: Self-reported practicability, negative beliefs, and therapist distress about exposure-based interventions. *Behavior Therapy, 50*(2), 353–366. https://doi.org/10.1016/j.beth.2018.07.003

Rush, A. J., Beck, A., Kovács, M. J., & Hollon, S. D. (2005). Comparative efficacy of cognitive therapy and pharmacotherapy in the treatment of depressed outpatients. *Cognitive Therapy and Research, 1*, 17–37. https://doi.org/10.1007/BF01173502Salemi

Salemink, E., Wolters, L., & de Haan, E. (2015). Augmentation of treatment as usual with online Cognitive Bias Modification of Interpretation training in adolescents with obsessive compulsive disorder: A pilot study. *Journal of Behavior Therapy and Experimental Psychiatry, 49*(Pt A), 112–119. https://doi.org/10.1016/j.jbtep.2015.02.003

Salkovskis, P. (1996). *Trends in cognitive and behavioural therapies*. Wiley.

Skinner, B. (1953). *Science and human behavior*. Macmillan Pub Co.

Vrijsen, J. N., Dainer-Best, J., Witcraft, S. M., Papini, S., Hertel, P., Beevers, C. G., Becker, E. S., & Smits, J. (2019). Effect of cognitive bias modification-memory on depressive symptoms and autobiographical memory bias: Two independent studies in high-ruminating and dysphoric samples. *Cognition & Emotion, 33*(2), 288–304. https://doi.org/10.1080/0269993 1.2018.1450225

Watson, J. B., & Rayner, R. (1920). Conditioned emotional reactions. *Journal of Experimental Psychology, 3*(1), 1–14. https://doi.org/10.1037/h0069608

Wolpe, J. (1952). Experimental neuroses as learned behavior. *British Journal of Psychology, 43*, 243–268.

Woud, M. L. (2022). Interpretational biases in emotional psychopathology. *Cognitive and Behavioral Practice, 29*(3), 520–523.

Woud, M. L., & Becker, E. S. (2014). Editorial for the special issue on Cognitive Bias Modification techniques: An introduction to a time traveller's tale. *Cognitive Therapy and Research, 38*, 83–88. https://doi.org/10.1007/s10608-014-9605-0

Woud, M. L., Blackwell, S. E., Shkreli, L., Würtz, F., Cwik, J. C., Margraf, J., Holmes, E. A., Steudte-Schmiedgen, S., Herpertz, S., & Kessler, H. (2021). The effects of modifying dysfunctional appraisals in posttraumatic stress disorder using a form of Cognitive Bias Modification: Results of a randomized controlled trial in an inpatient setting. *Psychotherapy and Psychosomatics, 90*(6), 386–402. https://doi.org/10.1159/000514166

Marcella L. Woud is a Junior-Professor of Clinical Psychology and Experimental Psychopathology and the head of the Translational Research in Anxiety, Cognition & Emotion (TRACE) lab at Ruhr-University Bochum (Germany). Via her research she aims to better understand how cognitive biases contribute to the development and maintenance of emotional psychopathology, including assessing their neural, physiological, and behavioral underpinnings, using both rigorous experimental and clinical studies. This research has been funded by several (personal) grants, including grants from the German Research Foundation (Deutsche Forschungsgemeinschaft, DFG). Prof. Woud also works a licensed therapist, with a specialization in Cognitive Behavioral Therapy (CBT).

Stefan G. Hofmann is the Alexander von Humboldt Professor at Philipps University of Marburg (Germany). In addition, he received the LOEWE Spitzenprofessur for Translational Clinical Psychology (Germany) and holds a position as Professor of Psychology at the Department of Psychological and Brain Sciences at Boston University (USA). Prof. Hofmann is a leading expert in researching and treating anxiety disorders, with a focus in Cognitive Behavioral Therapy. Since 2012, he is editor in chief of the journal Cognitive Therapy and Research. Prof. Hofmann has published more than 400 peer-reviewed scientific articles and 20 books.

Chapter 13
"If Only I Was a Doctor! The Burger Bite" – A Case Study in Posttraumatic Stress Disorder

Ulrich Schnyder

13.1 The Case

A man in his early 50s (let's call him John) comes home from a rather stressful day at work. He feels tired, exhausted, and a bit tense due to some minor stressors he had been struggling with in the office. On his way home, John buys two cheeseburgers for dinner. It is planned that his fiancée (let's call her Anna) who lives in her own flat will visit and join him for dinner. When opening the front door of his apartment, the door key gets stuck so that he has to struggle a bit until he manages to release the key from the lock, which increases his nervousness and bad temper. Anna is there already, and he gives her a mouthful, accusing her of having created the problem with the door key. He drops the bag with the burgers on the kitchen table and tells her he is going to take a shower before dinner. When John is in the shower, he suddenly sees Anna entering the bathroom, gagging, looking at him with a strange expression, then collapsing. He jumps out from under the shower, naked and wet, Anna lying on the ground motionless, lifeless. He shakes her, screams at her, to no avail. He runs to find his phone and calls the ambulance. In the kitchen, he sees that his fiancée has obviously taken a big bite from one of the cheeseburgers. She still lies lifeless in the bathroom. He calls the ambulance a second time, asking them angrily why it takes them so long to come. After a felt eternity, the paramedics arrive, only to testify Anna's death.

John is devastated. He cannot sleep. He cannot concentrate on anything. He senses an unbearable restlessness, both physically and psychologically. He consults his family doctor who puts him on sick leave. Yet John barely makes it through the first days in the immediate aftermath of his fiancée's tragic passing away due to

U. Schnyder (✉)
University of Zurich, Zurich, Switzerland
e-mail: ulrich.schnyder@access.uzh.ch

© The Author(s), under exclusive license to Springer Nature Switzerland AG 2023   247
M. L. Woud (ed.), *Interpretational Processing Biases in Emotional Psychopathology*,
CBT: Science Into Practice, https://doi.org/10.1007/978-3-031-23650-1_13

what is called *bolus death* in medicine: the burger bite she had taken had gotten stuck in her throat, causing a vagal reflex, which had led to sudden cardiovascular arrest.

Eight days after the event, John visits the emergency department of the university hospital, and asks for the psychiatrist on duty. The resident psychiatrist makes a clinical diagnosis of acute stress disorder, and refers the patient to a psychiatrist and psychotherapist experienced in treating patients suffering from trauma-related psychological disorders. Two days later the psychotherapist sees John for the first time. The patient complains about sleeplessness and an extreme inner tension and restlessness. He suffers from strong guilt feelings, thinking he should have been able to rescue his fiancée. He also reports frequent flashbacks and nightmares in which he re-experiences Anna's gagging, collapsing, and ultimately passing away. John fulfills the diagnostic criteria for acute stress disorder (ASD). The therapist provides him with psychoeducation about typical acute stress responses in the aftermath of potentially traumatic events (Schnyder et al., 2012, 2015; Wessely et al., 2008), and tells him what he can expect with regard to the course and development of his symptoms. Furthermore, the therapist tries to convey a confident, optimistic attitude, and suggests "watchful waiting": given that John has no major risk factors for the development of PTSD such as pre-traumatic psychiatric morbidity or lack of post-traumatic social support, the therapist expects John's ASD symptoms to decrease gradually over the following days and weeks. They agree on weekly appointments over the next couple of weeks.

13.1.1 Assessment

Six weeks after Anna's tragic death, John has developed full-blown posttraumatic stress disorder (PTSD). His total score on the German version of the Clinician-administered PTSD Scale for DSM-5 (CAPS-5) (Mueller-Engelmann et al., 2020; Weathers et al., 2018) is 60, suggesting pronounced symptom severity. In addition, John fulfills the diagnostic criteria for major depression. He is still extremely nervous and restless, and has difficulties concentrating which had led his family doctor to put him on sick leave in the first place. He also has great difficulties falling asleep as well as staying asleep. He continues experiencing flashbacks on a daily basis, and frequent nightmares related to the traumatic event. He avoids going to the cemetery and visiting Anna's grave. He is also extremely hypervigilant and experiences exaggerated startle responses, for instance, to sudden loud tones. On top of his PTSD symptoms, John is in a depressed mood, and suffers from what he describes as "crying fits" during which he cannot help but crying loudly and uncontrollably for several minutes. He spends hours ruminating about his responsibility for Anna's death: "If only I was a doctor, I could have applied the Heimlich maneuver,[1] thus rescuing

---

[1] The Heimlich maneuver is a medical emergency procedure which can relieve foreign body airway obstruction if applied timely and properly.

her"; or "If we had not argued over the problem with the door keys, she wouldn't have been so stressed out, and thus would not have gagged on the burger bite!".

13.2 Main Cognitions Targeted

John's predominant dysfunctional cognitions were mostly related to the extent to which he was responsible for Anna's death. He was constantly haunted by his guilt feelings. Whenever he was reminded of the incident, instead of actually mourning her, he immediately jumped to the idea of being guilty of her death. For instance, when he woke up in the morning, he instantly became aware that Anna was dead, and started ruminating about what he should have done to save her life. During the first weeks following her passing away, he almost never felt sadness about having lost her, about her no longer being around. Rather, he tortured himself ruminating about why he had been unable to do the right thing immediately after she had collapsed ("If only I was a doctor, I could have saved her life"). He spoke about this to everybody who was willing to listen: to his family doctor, to Anna's parents, to his boss, to some of his friends: they all tried to assure him that they don't blame him for not having realized that Anna had been dying, and that only by immediately applying the Heimlich maneuver, helping her to get rid of the burger bite, he would have had a chance to rescue her (see Fig. 13.1).

When he spoke about his belief of having failed, the therapist did not try to talk him out of his guilt feelings but rather "normalized" his questions of whether or not he could have, and accordingly should have done something to assist his fiancée prior to the paramedics' arrival on site (more about this in the next section on treatment).

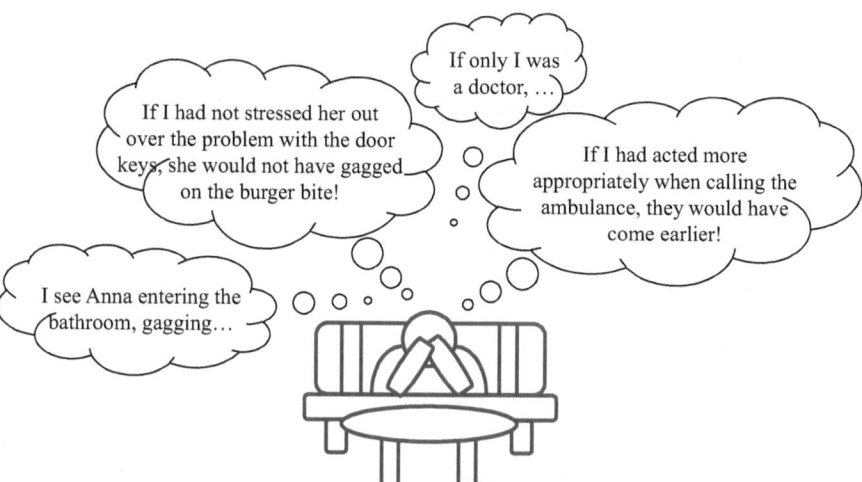

Fig. 13.1 John's dysfunctional cognitions

John's guilt feelings were additionally fueled by the little argument the couple had had over the problem with the front door keys. He was painfully aware that the "key problem" and his being stressed out about it had nothing to do with Anna but was primarily related to the stressful day he himself had experienced in the office. Later on, he learned from the pathologist's report on Anna's postmortem examination that she had been on a heavy dosage of psychotropic medication, plus a fair amount of alcohol, when the fatal incident had happened. However, he was unable to perceive this information as helpful or exonerating: He thought that, given he was her fiancé, he should have known better, i.e., he should have been aware about her vulnerability and her being on psychotropic medication. Therefore, he should have been more careful to not pick a fight over such a minor issue. Had they not had that dispute, she would not have become upset, and would not have hastily taken an inappropriately large bite of the cheeseburger which then got stuck as a bolus in her throat, causing her sudden death.

In the immediate aftermath of Anna's death, John's bouts of dysfunctional cognitions were triggered very easily. Using the front door keys, having a shower, eating dinner, the siren of an ambulance, the death notices in the newspapers, you name it: most of his daily activities had the capacity to trigger traumatic memories and, almost automatically, dysfunctional interpretational processes. Apart from external triggers, he also responded to all sorts of internal triggers: memories of past activities with Anna, breathing heavily when climbing a flight of stairs, coughing, but also making plans for the future precipitated ruminations about his not having prevented Anna's death. When engaged in his dysfunctional interpretations, John got extremely upset. He experienced great inner tension and restlessness, felt his heart racing, and started sweating profusely. When in such a state, he couldn't tolerate staying at home. He left his apartment and walked the streets, which eventually calmed him down a bit. Sometimes, however, when he didn't succeed in regaining his composure, he had one of his "crying fits," screaming and crying loudly and uncontrollably.

Clearly, John suffered greatly from his dysfunctional cognitions and guilt feelings as well as from his intrusive memories. Accordingly, his main treatment goals in the beginning were to gain more clarity about his responsibility. He hoped that once he would have sorted out the question of guilt, he would become more able to find peace, mourn Anna's passing away, and let go of his fiancée.

13.3   Treatment

13.3.1   Introduction to Trauma-Focused Treatment and Crisis Intervention

The first four sessions of John's treatment were challenging: John was extremely upset, his restlessness being almost unbearable. His ASD symptomatology fluctuated over the course of his days. He did have short moments when he felt some more stability, especially when he had a chance to talk to Anna's parents. However, most of the time he felt distressed and had great difficulties concentrating. His therapist tried to apply elements of trauma-focused cognitive-behavior treatment (tf-CBT) (O'Donnell et al., 2020) in combination with the principles of psychological first aid and crisis intervention, with questionable success. At least, John was interested in the therapist's attempts at providing psychoeducation: he saw him as the expert in traumatic stress-related issues, so he was very keen in learning about the therapist's views on the psychological, physical, and social impact of potentially traumatic events on an individual. More specifically, he wanted to discuss in which way a "psychological trauma" such as the one he had gone through could generate the typical symptoms of PTSD, such as flashbacks, nightmares, and hyperarousal. Moreover, John was eager to learn and understand the principles of both psychotherapeutic approaches and psychotropic medication for treating trauma-related psychological problems. He clearly idealized the therapist to some extent in these early sessions. However, this was not addressed since John's positive transference appeared to help building a trusting therapeutic relationship.

Six weeks had passed since Anna's death. John felt somewhat stabilized. His "crying fits" had decreased in both frequency and intensity. He had acquired a set of emotion regulation skills such as going for a walk, or taking a shower, when he was distressed, so his initially almost uncontrollable emotional instability had subsided to some degree. However, he still suffered from re-experiencing symptoms (flashbacks and nightmares related to the traumatic event) on a daily basis. He persistently avoided external reminders of Anna's death that aroused distressing memories. For instance, he still had a hard time visiting her grave at the cemetery. He also could not muster the courage to dispose of the rest of "her" cheeseburger which he had put in the deep freezer after her dead body had been taken to the pathology department for a post-mortem. Most prominently, John suffered massive negative alterations in cognitions and mood: he had persistent, distorted cognitions about his role in the course and development of the events that had led to Anna's bolus death. He blamed himself for not having been able to save her life, and felt extremely guilty about it. Furthermore, he had lost all interest in activities he had previously enjoyed, such as visiting friends, hiking, or going to work. As mentioned before, he showed marked alterations in arousal and reactivity: he was hypervigilant, experienced exaggerated startle responses, had debilitating difficulties concentrating, and kept suffering from massive sleep disturbance. In other words, John fulfilled the diagnostic criteria for PTSD according to the Diagnostic and Statistical Manual of Mental Disorders DSM-5 (APA, 2013). In addition, John suffered from comorbid moderate major depressive disorder. He was in a depressed mood most of the time, and apart from his diminished interest, insomnia and difficulties concentrating, he experienced great loss of energy, and felt completely worthless.

13.3.2 Trauma-Focused CBT

Now it seemed to be the right time to start trauma-focused CBT. The therapist told John that the core elements of evidence-based psychotherapy for PTSD included psychoeducation (which they had done extensively already), emotion regulation training (which they had discussed in the first sessions as well), imaginal exposure to the traumatic event, and cognitive work, i.e., cognitive processing, restructuring, and meaning-making (Schnyder & Cloitre, 2022; Schnyder et al., 2015). However, although he strongly believed in science, and was asking for empirically supported treatment, John was scared to death to engage in exposure treatment. He simply could not imagine going back in guided imagination to the day when his fiancée had passed away. He feared he would "go crazy" if he were to confront the dreadful moments of that day. As much as the therapist tried to inform him (or, rather, to convince him…) that getting rid of his intrusions would probably require a number of exposure sessions, John categorically refused to even give it a try. Given his persistent difficulties falling asleep, and staying asleep, the therapist suggested prescribing Mirtazapine 30 mg before going to bed, which John accepted.

In the following session, John reported that his sleep had improved with the new medication. He had thought about exposure sessions, and had also performed some more internet research. He acknowledged that the therapist was probably right to suggest exposure, but still he was too scared to confront his traumatic memories. He would rather be willing to tolerate his intrusions for the time being. In the meantime, the therapist himself had also done some thinking, and accepted John's refusal. He decided to follow the patient's preference, and changed plans accordingly, no longer urging him to undergo exposure therapy. Instead, they agreed to focus on the patient's guilt feelings. John agreed to discuss this, although he emphasized that he actually was guilty of Anna's death, and that he would not expect to change his mind about this fact.

13.3.3 Cognitive Work: Socratic Dialogue and Cognitive Restructuring

Over the following 3 months, about ten sessions took place that were almost exclusively focused on cognitive work. In the beginning, the therapist emphasized that it seemed legitimate and appropriate for John to ask himself whether he could (and should) have done something to prevent Anna's death. After all, he had been the only person present when she collapsed in the bathroom! Had he done something wrong? Had he failed doing something that he should have done? Had he acted too slowly when calling the ambulance? In short, had he committed any acts or omissions that had caused, or partially caused Anna's death? John responded very positively to his therapist's attitude: He thanked him for being willing to talk about these issues. All others had symbolically or literally given him a pat on the back, trying in vain to talk him out of his guilt feelings and self-contempt. He was convinced that he had made the biggest mistake of his life, and he was grateful that his therapist understood his wish to talk about it.

> **Therapist:** I think these are important questions. So tell me, do you think you did something unlawful, something you will be prosecuted for?
>
> **John:** No, I know very well I didn't break the law. I will not be sent to prison. But still, ...
>
> **Therapist:** Still?
>
> **John:** Still, I have this strong sense of being guilty. If I was a doctor, I would have immediately realized that Anna was about to die. I would have applied the Heimlich maneuver, and would thus have been able to relieve her from the burger bite that had obstructed her airways!
>
> **Therapist:** True. However, as a matter of fact, you are not a doctor.
>
> **John:** Yes, but I read in the internet that the Heimlich maneuver can also be performed by lay people, if instructed appropriately, e.g., in a first-aid course.
>
> **Therapist:** Agreed. Did you recently complete a first-aid course? And do first-aid courses in Switzerland routinely teach and train the Heimlich maneuver?
>
> **John:** No. It's just, ... I felt so helpless when I saw her lying on the floor, lifeless.
>
> **Therapist:** I understand. This must have been terrible.
>
> **John (crying):** I am her fiancé. Sorry: I was her fiancé. I should have done something!

Over several sessions, they kept discussing the issue of responsibility, using the principles of Socratic dialogue. John at first kept obsessing about his guilt, that he should have done something to rescue Anna. Slowly but steadily, over time, he started getting in touch with his underlying emotions of sadness and loneliness that seemed even more difficult to tolerate. Anna and John had been a couple for 17 years. Their relationship had seen many ups and downs. Anna had suffered from severe mental disorder for a long time, and had been on psychotropic medication on a regular basis. John had been looking after her and had supported her when she went through one of her psychological crises; however, he had also often been impatient with her, and grumpy when he himself was distressed.

His grumpiness was another thing he tortured himself about: He deeply regretted having raised the "front door keys" issue with her at all. In retrospect, he felt he had simply brought home tension from his work. He had been grumpy. While she had been looking forward to a joint dinner at his place, he had snapped at her about something that had nothing to do with her.

John: If we had not argued over the problem with the door keys, she wouldn't have been so stressed out, would not have started eating the cheeseburger before I had finished taking a shower, and thus would not have gagged on the burger bite!

Therapist: I understand: You think your argument about the front door keys must have distressed Anna, which caused her starting to eat by taking a (too) big bite of the cheeseburger, which then got stuck in her throat and killed her: right?

John: Precisely!

Therapist: Do you think this fully explains Anna's death?

John: Well, … maybe not to 100%.

Therapist: Are you telling me there were other, additional causes?

John: Well, she was on psychotropic medication, and according to the post--mortem, she was drunk…

Therapist: … meaning the "front door keys" issue might only partially explain her death?

John: Yes, possibly.

Therapist: Which percentage of the total causality would you attribute to Anna's medication and being drunk?

John: I don't know. Maybe 75%?

Therapist: So, that leaves us with 25% for the "front door keys" issue. Plus, since it always takes two to tango, Anna probably shares part of the responsibility for the "front door keys" issue as well, right?

John: Hmm…

Over time, John started getting "sadder but wiser" (Gersons & Schnyder, 2013): He realized that although his relationship with Anna had been complicated and sometimes really difficult and burdensome, he had loved her. Losing her saddened him deeply, and left him with a strong feeling of abandonment, of having been left alone in this world. He also realized that his obsessing about being responsible for her death not only generated enormous guilt feelings: it also offered him at least a certain illusion of having been in control of the situation. Gradually, he started facing, and eventually accepting, the fact that he had been completely out of control, that given the circumstances there was nothing he could have done, that the terrible sequence of events that had led to Anna's death had just simply been happening, a cruel twist of fate.

After ten sessions of Socratic dialogue and cognitive restructuring, John had achieved a more realistic view of his role in his fiancée's passing away 3 months previously. He still entertained some guilt feelings from time to time, but he was much more able to put them into perspective and relativize them. Compared to the first month, he spent much less time ruminating about what he could and should have done to prevent Anna's death. He now no longer fulfilled the PTSD symptom cluster of negative alterations in cognition and mood. He was also much less depressed, his hyperarousal symptoms were much less pronounced, and his sleep had considerably improved. However, the intrusive memories of the day of Anna's death still persisted, almost as vividly as in the immediate aftermath of the tragic event. John was still haunted by nightmares, and suffered intense flashbacks on a daily basis.

13.3.4 Exposure

It was at this point in time during his therapeutic process that John came up with an interesting idea: One of his dysfunctional beliefs had consistently been that when he had called the ambulance, he was so distressed that he behaved in an inappropriately aggressive way towards the receptionist on the other end of the line. He recalled that the receptionist had asked him "lots of irrelevant questions," for instance, whether Anna had diabetes or any pre-existing cardiac problems, which she didn't. John got angry at the receptionist, and yelled at him, demanding that he should send the ambulance immediately, rather than "asking silly questions." In retrospect, John thought that by picking a fight with the receptionist he had caused an unnecessary delay in the rescue operation. Now he was wondering if he could somehow get hold of the audio recordings of the two phone calls he had made: He felt that by listening to the original recording of his phone calls, he could maybe get objective information on how inappropriately he actually had behaved. He also felt that when calling the rescue service, he could apologize for his misbehavior. Not knowing where this would lead them, the therapist encouraged John to give it a try.

Interestingly, this turned out much easier than expected: The following week, John brought two electronic audio files to the therapy session. However, similarly to their discussions 3 months previously when the therapist had suggested to start exposure sessions, John was too scared to listen to the recordings. He asked if the recordings could be transcribed, to which the therapist agreed.

The following week, when the therapist handed the transcription over to John, he found himself unable to read it. Even when merely looking at the transcript from the distance, he started trembling and sweating. He said he felt like being the culprit in a court trial, shortly before the final judgment was being delivered. The evidence of the recordings would finally convince himself as well as the therapist that he was guilty of Anna's death. He thought he would not be able to live with the final verdict. The two of them discussed this, and it turned out that John was in fact ambivalent: while expecting his "death sentence," he was also hoping for acquittal, or at least for a mild verdict. After some negotiations, he agreed that the therapist should read the transcript to him. The therapist instructed him to listen carefully, maybe even closing his eyes while listening. At the same time, he should allow any thoughts and feelings to emerge, with no censorship whatsoever. The therapist encouraged John to assume a non-judgmental attitude, to simply observe and be mindful of his own inner response, including bodily reactions as well as visual imagery and other sensory perceptions such as sounds or smells. The therapist also asked John to raise his hand should the experience become too stressful or frightening. The transcript contained the two phone calls, the first one of about 90 seconds duration, the second one much shorter, maybe 40 seconds. When the therapist started reading, John was extremely distressed. He could hardly sit still, was moaning, breathing heavily, his heart pounding. John asked to continue, and the therapist kept reading. John listened intently. The therapist again asked him to be mindful of his bodily reactions, and he sensed an intense pain in his chest. When they approached the end of the first phone call, John started crying. It took him quite a while to regain his composure.

The recording provided clear evidence that John had been very agitated when he had made the call. The receptionist had in fact asked a number of actually less than "irrelevant" questions about Anna's health condition. Towards the end of the call, John had shouted at the receptionist, who had kept his professional composure. By no means at all had John's perceived "inappropriate behavior" caused any delay in the whole procedure. At the time of the second call, the paramedics had already been on their way to John's apartment. According to the rescue service's files, they had arrived 8 minutes after John's first call. John realized that he himself had been his merciless judge, that he had sentenced himself to maximum penalty without taking into account the evidence.

John left this therapy session relieved and relaxed. It had been a self-invented or self-designed exposure session which had taken him directly back into the core scene of the traumatic event. Thanks to the original recording, this exposure had a much more realistic touch than what is usually done in imaginal exposure, while at the same time John was able to experience his going back to the worst moment in his life in the safe surroundings of the therapy setting. It was agreed to repeat the procedure in a similar way during the next two sessions: first, John managed to read the transcript himself, and finally, he listened to the audio recording. Again, he was very much emotionally involved, and cried towards the end of the recording. At the end of the third "exposure" session, John declared himself "only partially guilty": He was now able to recognize that he had actually upset his fiancée in the first place when coming home and arguing with her over the problem with the front door keys which had raised her stress level. However, once she had collapsed in the bathroom, he had done all he had been able to do to save her life, given the fact that he actually wasn't a doctor but an IT specialist. Sadly, this had not been enough to rescue Anna. It was only now that John was able to see that his guilt feelings had been fueled by his pronounced cognitive schema of being in control as a means of ensuring that nothing bad would happen to him and his loved ones. He started understanding that life cannot be entirely controlled, and that he would have to learn to distinguish between things one can control and things that are beyond our control, and thus need to be accepted and dealt with accordingly.

Shortly after these three "exposure" sessions, John reported he no longer suffered from any significant intrusions. He had no flashbacks anymore, and hardly any nightmares. Moreover, his hyperarousal symptoms had decreased significantly, and he also said he was in a better mood, and much better able to let go of his ruminations and repetitive, obsessive thinking about him being responsible for Anna's death. The exposure sessions not only significantly reduced John's re-experiencing symptoms. They also yielded substantial cognitive change which in turn helped him to better understand the biographical origins and impact of his cognitive schema of having control as a guarantee for success in life. He was able to link his cognitive setup to experiences in childhood and adolescence, particularly to his father's frequent and unpredictable outbursts of anger which John had been extremely scared of at the time.

John was sad. He visited Anna's grave, spending time there, crying, mourning, engaging in an imaginal mutual conversation with her. He started putting his apartment in order, and he got feedback from his boss that his performance at work was much better now, "almost back to normal." He also joined a self-help group for people who had lost a partner. There, he found people with whom he could share his feelings and have in-depth conversations about how to cope and to find new meaning in life.

13.3.5   Follow-Up Sessions

When the therapist saw him for a follow-up assessment 1 year after Anna's death, John was no longer a "patient": He had almost fully recovered from his psychopathological symptoms, and no longer fulfilled the diagnostic criteria for PTSD and depression. His CAPS-5 total score had dropped from 60 to 23. He had stopped psychotropic medication. He had resumed work. He went out seeing friends, and even making new friends. He was still very sad about having lost Anna, though. In retrospect, he felt that he had initially been thinking "In a wrong, unhealthy way" about his role in the course and development that had led to Anna's death. He said he had found it helpful that the therapist had not tried to talk him out of his exaggerated guilt feelings. He felt that the cognitive work had been very helpful for two reasons: First, it had helped him putting his thinking into perspective, and relativize his sense of responsibility; and second, according to his view, the cognitive work paved the way for his self-invented "exposure therapy" that in turn had relieved him from his intrusive re-experiencing symptoms.

John kept asking for an appointment with his therapist once or twice a year. He seemed doing well, although he also explicitly stated that he had become a different person from prior to Anna's passing away. It was only when the therapist saw him last time, 7 years after Anna's death that John reported he had finally been able to dispose of the rest of Anna's cheeseburger which he had been keeping in his freezer for so many years.

13.4   Special Challenges and Problems

John was an academically trained, and intellectually interested patient. Even before seeing him for the first time, he had googled his therapist, and realized that his main focus of interest in research, clinical work, and teaching, was traumatic stress. So, from the very beginning, he addressed the therapist as an MD, and an expert in psychotraumatology. He was not only highly motivated to learn about the patho-physiology of bolus death, and the medical emergency procedure called *Heimlich maneuver* which can relieve foreign body airway obstruction if applied timely and properly. Even more so, he wanted to know everything about the pathogenesis, epi-demiology, and treatment of PTSD. He read books and research articles, and spent hours searching the internet for information about the best possible treatment for his condition. The therapist usually encourages patients to do so, since obviously shared decision-making is more constructive and efficient when the patient has sufficient informational background to engage in a discussion about the next diagnostic and therapeutic steps to be taken (Cloitre et al., 2020; Courtois et al., 2020). However, in this case, he was worried at times that John might overdo it in his futile attempt at gaining control over a tragic moment in his life, including its repercussions, which he had been unable to control, and thus avoid mourning his loss. While at the beginning of treatment, his intellectual approach, and the positive transference he had developed, had made it rather easy for the therapist to relate to him, the therapist occasionally felt "trapped" by John's urge to engage in an intellectual discussion with the therapist. Especially in the beginning, engaging John in a Socratic dialogue and discussing his basic assumptions and cognitive schemas was a challenge because he showed a great tendency to constantly sidestep the dialogue with all sorts of objections ("True, but…"). Also, when the therapist tried to gently move their conversation away from some recent research findings John had discovered, towards exploring his emotions connected to recently having been bereaved, the patient was much less responsive. Although he frequently spoke about his "crying fits," and about how devastated he was about Anna's death, and even more so because of his perceived failure, it was only towards the end of treatment that he started allowing himself to feel the pain of his loss, and to confront the full range of emotions from sadness that Anna had passed away to anger at her for having aban-doned him.

However, the greatest challenge the therapist encountered with John was his reluctance to engage in exposure sessions. Although the therapist did recognize his marked negative alterations in cognitions and mood, particularly his persistent, dis-torted cognitions and dysfunctional interpretations of the cause-and-effect chain that had led to Anna's death, he felt that John's flashbacks and nightmares were so prominent that they deserved immediate therapeutic attention, using exposure tech-niques. Initially, he was confident that John would follow his advice, based on the trusting therapeutic relationship they had developed. However, to the therapist's surprise, John "stubbornly" refused. He was just simply too scared. He was afraid

This is a therapeutic principle - doing exposure is the right thing now…

I am too afraid that I will go crazy if I have to do exposure…

Fig. 13.2 Thoughts of John versus therapist when discussing exposure

of "going crazy" if he were to go back in imagination to the worst moment of his life, seeing himself failing to save Anna's life. It took a couple of sessions to realize and acknowledge that the therapist had "stubbornly" held on to the idea that in the presence of pronounced re-experiencing symptoms, he should start addressing the intrusive memories prior to cognitive restructuring (see Fig. 13.2). Once the therapist was able to recognize the impasse he (rather than John!) had unnecessarily created by holding on to his therapeutic principles, they were able to jointly overcome the obstacle, and start trauma-focused cognitive work.

In retrospect, the therapist could see clearly that John had been right: regardless of whether or not John's fear of "going crazy" was justified, the therapist might have lost him by insisting on what the therapist had felt was best for his patient, and John might have dropped out of treatment. He was in fact scared, and he intuitively felt that he was emotionally too unstable at the time to engage in a confrontative approach that always requires quite some courage on the side of the patient.

A couple of months later, once he had worked through his distorted cognitions, John mustered the courage to devise his own "exposure therapy," namely listening to the audio recording of his phone calls to the rescue service's receptionist. One more time, the therapist was challenged: Should he agree to this suggestion, or rather insist on evidence-based exposure techniques, e.g., according to Edna Foa's Prolonged Exposure Therapy (Foa et al., 2007)? Initially, he found John's idea of retrieving the audio recording of his phone calls rather unconventional, even a bit outlandish. He also doubted that the rescue service would be willing to provide John with the audio recordings. However, John somehow convinced the therapist that it would be worth trying, and surprisingly, it turned out much easier than expected. Sure enough, as described above, his intrusions abated after three sessions of listening to the recordings.

13.5 Summary, Conclusions, and Learning Points

Twenty-five years ago, van der Kolk, McFarlane, and Weisæth (van der Kolk et al., 1996, preface, pp. XV–XVI) stated that "The overall aim of therapy with traumatized patients is to help them move from being haunted by the past and interpreting subsequent emotionally arousing stimuli as a return of the trauma, to being present in the here and now, capable of responding to current exigencies to their fullest potential. In order to do that, *people need to regain control over their emotional responses* (my italics) and place the trauma in the larger perspective of their lives – as a historical event (or series of events), that occurred at a particular time and in a particular place, and that can be expected not to recur if the traumatized individuals take charge of their lives. The key element in the psychotherapy of people with PTSD is the integration of the alien, the unacceptable, the terrifying, and the incomprehensible; the trauma must come to be 'personalized' as an integrated aspect of one's personal history".

Over many years now, trauma-focused therapy has been concerned to a large extent with helping trauma survivors "to regain control over their emotional responses" (van der Kolk et al., 1996). Exposure-focused approaches such as Prolonged Exposure Therapy (Foa et al., 2007) or Eye Movement Desensitization and Reprocessing Therapy (Shapiro, 2001) emphasize the issue of control particularly strongly, however, more cognitively oriented tf-CBT such as Cognitive Processing Therapy (Galovski et al., 2022; Resick et al., 2007) or Cognitive Therapy for PTSD (Ehlers et al., 2005; Ehlers & Wild, 2022) also do so to a large extent. The idea is that once patients have learned to control their intrusions, they can start taking charge of their lives, meaning in turn that healing in a broader sense can take place. This is understandable, given the general nature of traumatic experiences: the core of a traumatic event is something unpleasant and (life-)threatening happening to me, often unexpectedly, that I have little or no control over. In that regard, the initial traumatic experience is very similar to the experience of intrusions once PTSD has developed: flashbacks and nightmares are equally unpleasant and distressing, albeit no longer actually threatening in real life. They frequently occur unexpectedly, and I cannot control them.

So far, so good. However, such an attitude implicitly conveys a potentially problematic message, namely that everything in life can be controlled. As a matter of fact, like it or not, bad things do happen, and they happen not only to other people but to us as well: we fall ill, we lose a loved one, we have an accident, a natural or industrial disaster happens and we are directly or indirectly affected. In many such instances, there is little or nothing we can do about it. These events can happen just like that, as mere coincidences, and we are affected just by chance. Thus, in John's case, I think it was crucial for him to understand that he had experienced a cruel twist of fate. Anna had died from bolus death, and he had been unable to save her life. While towards the end of therapy he was happy to gain control over his intrusions, it was probably even more important to him to learn to accept that he had had no control over the unfolding of events on the day when Anna passed away.

Moreover, he learned to distinguish between things on the one hand that were potentially controllable, and were thus worth the effort of trying to control, and things on the other hand that are beyond his control, and that have to be accepted and coped with, along with the pain and suffering they bring about. This way, John had successfully transitioned, at least in part, from "fighting fate" to "accepting fate."

Talking about acceptance, John's therapist had to learn his lesson as well: he had a hard time initially to accept that John refused to follow his advice and collaborate with the sequence of treatment he had suggested. It was crucially beneficial for the course and development of John's treatment that at some point he stopped insisting but rather listened to John's concerns, and also to his "outlandish," creative idea to retrieve the audio files of his phone calls to the rescue service's receptionist, have them transcribed, and listen to them as a form of exposure treatment. In retrospect, the therapist was most grateful to John to have taught him this lesson.

References

American Psychiatric Association. (2013). *Diagnostic and statistical manual of mental disorders: DSM-5* (5th ed.). APA.

Cloitre, M., Cohen, Z., & Schnyder, U. (2020). Building a science of personalized interventions for PTSD. In D. Forbes, J. I. Bisson, C. M. Monson, & J. Berliner (Eds.), *Effective treatments for PTSD. Practice guidelines from the International Society for Traumatic Stress Studies* (3rd ed., pp. 451–468). Guilford Press.

Courtois, C. A., Ford, J. D., Cloitre, M., & Schnyder, U. (2020). Best practices in psychotherapy for adults. In J. D. Ford & C. A. Courtois (Eds.), *Treating complex traumatic stress disorders in adults* (2nd ed., pp. 62–98). Guilford Press.

Ehlers, A., & Wild, J. (2022). Cognitive therapy for PTSD: Updating memories and meanings of trauma. In U. Schnyder & M. Cloitre (Eds.), *Evidence based treatments for trauma-related psychological disorders: A practical guide for clinicians* (2nd ed., pp. 181–210). Springer International Publishing.

Ehlers, A., Clark, D. M., Hackman, A., McManus, F., & Fennell, M. J. V. (2005). Cognitive therapy for post-traumatic stress disorder: Development and evaluation. *Behaviour Research and Therapy, 43*, 413–431. https://doi.org/10.1016/j.brat.2004.03.006

Foa, E. B., Hembree, E. A., & Rothbaum, B. O. (2007). *Prolonged exposure therapy for PTSD. Emotional processing of traumatic experiences. Therapist guide.* Oxford University Press.

Galovski, T. E., Schuster Wachen, J., Chard, K. M., & Monson, C. M. (2022). Cognitive processing therapy. In U. Schnyder & M. Cloitre (Eds.), *Evidence based treatments for trauma-related psychological disorders: A practical guide for clinicians* (2nd ed., pp. 211–226). Springer International Publishing.

Gersons, B. P. R., & Schnyder, U. (2013). Learning from traumatic experiences with brief eclectic psychotherapy for PTSD. *European Journal of Psychotraumatology, 4*, 21369. https://doi.org/10.3402/ejpt.v4i0.21369

Mueller-Engelmann, M., Schnyder, U., Dittmann, C., Priebe, K., Bohus, M., Thome, J., Fydrich, T., Pfaltz, M. C., & Steil, R. (2020). Psychometric properties and factor structure of the German version of the Clinician-Administered PTSD Scale for DSM-5. *Assessment, 27*(6), 1128–1138. https://doi.org/10.1177/1073191118774840

O'Donnell, M. L., Pacella, B. J., Bryant, R. A., Olff, M., & Forbes, D. (2020). Early intervention for trauma-related psychopathology. In D. Forbes, J. I. Bisson, C. M. Monson, & L. Berliner

(Eds.), *Effective treatments for PTSD. Practice guidelines from the International Society for Traumatic Stress Studies* (3rd ed., pp. 117–136). Guilford Press.

Resick, P. A., Monson, C. M., & Chard, K. M. (2007). *Cognitive processing therapy: Veteran/ military version*. Department of Veterans' Affairs.

Schnyder, U., & Cloitre, M. (Eds.). (2022). *Evidence based treatments for trauma-related psychological disorders: A practical guide for clinicians* (2nd ed.). Springer International Publishing.

Schnyder, U., Pedretti, S., & Müller, J. (2012). Trauma education. In C. R. Figley (Ed.), *Encyclopedia of trauma: An interdisciplinary guide* (pp. 709–714). SAGE Publications.

Schnyder, U., Ehlers, A., Elbert, T., Foa, E. B., Gersons, B. P. R., Resick, P. A., Shapiro, F., & Cloitre, M. (2015). Psychotherapies for PTSD: What do they have in common? *European Journal of Psychotraumatology, 6*, 28186. https://doi.org/10.3402/ejpt.v6.28186

Shapiro, F. (2001). *Eye movement desensitization and reprocessing: Basic principles, protocols, and procedures* (2nd ed.). Guilford Press.

van der Kolk, B. A., McFarlane, A. C., & Weisæth, L. (Eds.). (1996). *Traumatic stress: The effects of overwhelming experience on mind, body, and society*. Guilford Press.

Weathers, F. W., Bovin, M. J., Lee, D. J., Sloan, D. M., Schnurr, P. P., Kaloupek, D. G., Keane, T. M., & Marx, B. P. (2018). The Clinician-Administered PTSD Scale for DSM-5 (CAPS-5): Development and initial psychometric evaluation in military veterans. *Psychological Assessment, 30*(3), 383–395. https://doi.org/10.1037/pas0000486

Wessely, S., Bryant, R. A., Greenberg, N., Earnshaw, M., Sharpley, J., & Hughes, J. H. (2008). Does psychoeducation help prevent post traumatic psychological distress? *Psychiatry, 71*(4), 287–302.

Ulrich Schnyder, MD, is a psychiatrist and licensed psychotherapist. He is an Emeritus professor of psychiatry and psychotherapy at the University of Zurich, Switzerland. His scientific activities are focused on various aspects of traumatic stress research, including epidemiology, neurobiology, psychotherapy and pharmacotherapy for PTSD, resilience to stress, refugee mental health, and the emotional, psychosocial, and physical consequences of child maltreatment. He is a past president of the European Society for Traumatic Stress Studies (ESTSS), the International Federation for Psychotherapy (IFP), and the International Society for Traumatic Stress Studies (ISTSS).

Chapter 14
"I am Incompetent – I Just Can't Cope" – A Case Study in Depression

Michelle L. Moulds

14.1 The Case

Naomi was a 41-year-old female who presented for psychological assessment following a series of stressful events in the workplace. She was employed as a nurse at a large, inner-city hospital in Australia. Naomi was married with two sons, aged 6 and 12 years old. Naomi was referred by her GP for "work-related stress". She reported a history of depression and anxiety symptoms that appeared to have been precipitated by periods of stress elicited by work-related events. She first experienced these symptoms ten years ago, following a major workplace incident. She sought psychological support (6 sessions with a psychologist), which she described as beneficial. Following therapy, and after a change in her role, Naomi's symptoms remitted ("I got my confidence back"), and she described a period of several years without psychological symptoms. However, over time the symptoms returned, and she noticed feeling increasingly anxious, worried and sad. Her symptoms fluctuated in frequency and intensity, and culminated in another period of significant stress which commenced approximately two years before Naomi presented for assessment.

At the time of assessment, Naomi was still employed in her role as a nurse. However, her symptoms made it difficult for her to carry out her job. When challenging situations arose, she initially described feeling in control, and being able to respond to tasks she faced appropriately and 'automatically', which she attributed to her extensive training and years of experience. However, once underway, Naomi reported that she would begin to doubt herself (e.g., ask "Do I have the ability to do this?"). Once this chain of thought commenced, Naomi described it as overwhelming

M. L. Moulds (✉)
School of Psychology, UNSW Sydney, The University of New South Wales,
Sydney, NSW, Australia
e-mail: m.moulds@unsw.edu.au

© The Author(s), under exclusive license to Springer Nature Switzerland AG 2023
M. L. Woud (ed.), *Interpretational Processing Biases in Emotional Psychopathology*,
CBT: Science Into Practice, https://doi.org/10.1007/978-3-031-23650-1_14

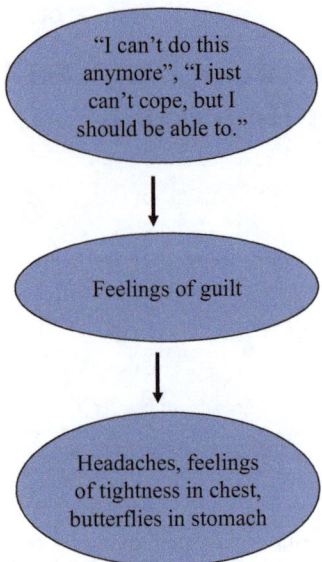

Fig. 14.1 Naomi's chain of thoughts

and 'cascading' – and a stream of persistent thoughts of self-doubt (e.g., "I can't do this anymore", "I just can't cope, but I should be able to") and feelings of guilt would ensue. These thoughts triggered a range of physical symptoms, including headaches, feelings of tightness in the chest and butterflies in the stomach (see Fig. 14.1).

This pattern typically continued in the evening, after Naomi had left work. She reported often thinking back to these situations and dwelling on her actions, and being highly self-critical about the way she responded. She reported that the feelings and rumination typically persisted until she was distracted – either by purposefully putting the thoughts out of her mind or by being distracted by a conversation or change of scenery.

14.1.1 Assessment

Naomi's symptoms were consistent with a diagnosis of major depressive disorder. She reported low mood and irritability, and described herself as 'moody', particularly with her husband and junior colleagues. She reported a lack of interest in activities she typically enjoyed, including reading and socialising, and described herself as withdrawn and disengaged (particularly from her husband and children). She also described disrupted sleep (waking at 3 am and having difficulty returning to sleep), poor concentration (e.g., when completing administrative tasks, work documents), and fatigue. Naomi experienced significant guilt about her work performance, frequent rumination about her competence and worry about her ability to cope with future stressors ("What if I can't cope?", "What if I fail?"). She denied suicidal ideation, plans or intent, either current or past. Despite having witnessed traumatic situations in the course of her work (e.g., dying patients), Naomi denied any PTSD symptoms (e.g., intrusive memories, avoidance of reminders). However, she described replaying previous situations and evaluating how she responded to them, as well as ruminating about what she should have done differently. Naomi's symptoms were having a negative impact on her work and family relationships. At the time of presentation, when asked to rate the severity of her symptoms (on a scale from 1 = *not at all severe* to 10 = *extremely severe*), Naomi rated them as 7.5/10; at their worst, she rated her symptoms as 10/10 in severity. In addition to the clinical interview, Naomi completed self-report measures indexing the presence and severity of symptoms of depression, anxiety and stress (i.e., Depression Anxiety Stress Scales, DASS: Lovibond & Lovibond, 1995), and the tendency to engage in depressive rumination (i.e., Ruminative Response Scale, RRS: Nolen-Hoeksema & Morrow, 1991).

In summary, Naomi presented with depressed mood and a range of anxiety/stress symptoms which impaired her occupational, emotional and social functioning. She described a history of similar symptoms that appeared to have been precipitated by stressful work-related events. Naomi was receptive to the idea of psychological intervention and described being motivated to engage in treatment, although was not optimistic about her prognosis. She reported that she didn't understand why she was experiencing these symptoms and wanted someone to tell her why they were happening and acknowledged the need to seek help ("I can't do this on my own").

14.2 Main Cognitions Targeted

A number of key cognitive themes emerged in Naomi's initial assessment, and the extent to which they influenced her emotions and behaviour became more apparent as treatment progressed. A prevailing theme was Naomi's belief that her psychological symptoms and distress reflected that she was incompetent and unable to cope – primarily in her role as a nurse, but also as a wife and a mother. Prior to the first period of significant stress she experienced ten years earlier, Naomi described viewing herself as capable and confident, and able to deal with any challenging situation or pressures she encountered, particularly in her role as a nurse. However, over the past two years, as her symptoms worsened, Naomi was increasingly plagued by self-doubt, and had become more and more self-critical. She interpreted her depression and anxiety symptoms as signs that she could not cope at work or in her family life – that is, as evidence that she was no longer 'competent' in either domain. She also worried about being perceived as incompetent by her colleagues.

Another theme that repeatedly emerged in the context of treatment was Naomi's belief that she shouldn't disclose her difficulties to other people; for example, "I should be able to deal with this on my own". Naomi held the view that "Everyone has their own problems", and that she should have been able to deal with hers without burdening other people (including her husband, colleagues and friends). She also acknowledged that this belief applied to the therapist, too. That is, despite presenting for treatment and being open to engage in therapy, Naomi nonetheless endorsed the belief that she should have been equipped to deal with her symptoms on her own. This cognition appeared closely linked to the abovementioned theme of incompetence, reflecting a belief that seeking help from others rather than being able to manage her distress alone provided further evidence of her inability to cope. Naomi was also convinced that others (in particular her husband) also believed that she should be able to handle her difficulties on her own.

As treatment progressed it became evident that throughout her adult life Naomi had derived much of her sense of self and her identity from her professional role. She viewed herself as a carer and protector, and felt an overwhelming sense of responsibility for others' health and safety owing to her training and nursing skills. Cognitions such as "It's my responsibility" (e.g., to care for and protect others) frequently arose in therapy sessions and were captured in Naomi's daily monitoring, and were more frequent at times of stress. They also had a significant impact on Naomi in her daily life, outside work. For example, when she was in situations such as sporting events or a crowded local playground with her children, she described being on the alert to identify potential ways that a child could be hurt, and then to worry about whether she would be able to help if necessary. Such thoughts of responsibility made Naomi feel anxious, and resulted in otherwise potentially pleasant outings with her children becoming a source of stress – thus worsening rather than improving her mood. In addition, the absence of experiencing positive emotions in response to events that she previously enjoyed such as spending time with her children prompted a sense of hopelessness, and questions such as "Will I ever feel happy again?"

A key cognitive feature of Naomi's presentation was her tendency to engage in repetitive negative thinking: to dwell on (i.e., ruminate about) events that had happened at work, and also worry about hypothetical stressful situations that could arise in the future. Her rumination and worry typically focused on the cognitive themes described above, and appeared to strengthen these unhelpful beliefs, and exacerbate her depression and anxiety symptoms. For example, Naomi described often waking at 3 am and replaying recent events at work (e.g., situations with patients, conversations with the patients' relatives, interactions with colleagues) and thinking about how she could have handled them differently. Naomi's rumination in turn led her to imagine potential future scenarios, which typically prompted a cascade of thoughts such as "What if I can't handle it?", "What if I mess things up?", "Why can't I do my job the way I used to?", "Will I ever feel like the old me again?" Furthermore, Naomi's rumination appeared in part to be maintained by her unhelpful metacognitive beliefs about its potential benefits (e.g., "Analysing events in the past helps me to understand them and be ready if they happen again"). The impact of these beliefs was particularly evident regarding Naomi's tendency to replay and ruminate about past events in order to 'learn lessons' to help her to navigate future stressful situations, so that she could 'do better next time'.

14.3 Treatment

At the outset, the therapist's primary approach to targeting Naomi's dysfunctional cognitions was to adopt a standard cognitive therapy approach (e.g., Beck et al., 1979).

14.3.1 Introduction of the Cognitive Model and Monitoring

Accordingly, cognitive therapy commenced with an explanation of the cognitive model (ABC) – emphasising that the relationship between events in the world (e.g., stressors, A) and our emotional responses (e.g., sadness, anxiety, C) is mediated by our automatic thoughts and interpretations (B). Next, the therapist helped Naomi identify and monitor examples of her own unhelpful automatic thoughts, to illustrate the event-interpretations-emotion chain in her own life. Following this, the therapist introduced the idea of cognitive distortions (or thinking errors): unhelpful patterns of thinking that result in biased interpretations of events, and in turn, negative emotions. Finally, the therapist introduced the rationale for and process of cognitive challenging; specifically, questioning automatic thoughts and generating alternative, more balanced interpretations with which to replace them.

Naomi initially appeared to respond to and conceptually grasp the cognitive model well. With assistance from the therapist in-session, she was readily able to generate examples of A (events), B (interpretations) and C (emotions) from the past week, using a simple ABC monitoring form. However, when prompted to generate examples independently, it became evident that Naomi had difficulty making the distinction between thoughts and feelings. Furthermore, when she was able to provide examples of thoughts, they were often vague and abstract. One of Naomi's key dysfunctional cognitions was her interpretation of her psychological symptoms as evidence that she was no longer able to cope, particularly in her professional role. The following excerpt illustrates both of these difficulties (i.e., discriminating thoughts and feelings, lack of specificity) in the context of reviewing Naomi's between-session monitoring, and eliciting the cognition, "I just can't cope with anything anymore".

> **Therapist:** Last week we spoke about the relationship between events in our lives, and how we feel when they happen. We also discussed how the way we think about or interpret things is the critical link between events and our feelings.
> **Naomi:** Yes, that was interesting – so it's not what happens that makes you feel bad, but how you think about it.
> **Therapist:** Exactly. And we discussed how that's good news, because although in many instances we can't control or change the events we expe-

(continued)

rience, we can change how we interpret them. Now let's take a look at some of the ABC examples you recorded on your form (that is, events, interpretations, feelings).

Naomi: Ok. The first one was when I woke up worrying about everything I had to do at work, and felt overwhelmed about the day ahead.

Therapist: Great. So let's focus on some of the details. What happened? When did it happen? Where were you?

Naomi: It was on Monday morning, at about 7 am. I just woke up and started worrying. I was about to get up, but all of these feelings came over me.

Therapist: Great, those specifics really help to paint a picture of the event for me – let's write them down in the A column. Monday morning, 7 am, woke up worrying. Great.

Let's focus on your thoughts next. What thoughts did you notice going through your mind?

Naomi: I felt nervous and jittery. My heart was racing and I just started to cry. I just sat there and cried, and the heavy feelings got worse and worse. I just didn't know why I felt like I did, and why I can't just get back to my old self.

Therapist: Ok, so you've mentioned a number of things there. Let's unpack them a little. Why don't we start with the feelings first – both your emotions, your responses, as well as any sensations you noticed in your body. You've described them very well – you mentioned feeling nervous and jittery, that you were crying, your heart was heart-racing, and your feelings were 'heavy'. Let's put them in the C column.

Naomi: Ok. Although I feel embarrassed now. It sounds ridiculous seeing all of this written down. For goodness' sake, the day hadn't even started and I was already a wreck. What is wrong with me?

Therapist: Given all of the sensations and emotions you were experiencing, I'm not at all surprised you felt overwhelmed – it's hard to imagine you could feel anything else in that moment.

I'm interested now in the thoughts that were going thought your mind at the time. What were you saying to yourself? What thoughts popped in? You've given me a lot of detail about what was happening in your body, but I'd also like to know what you were thinking. If I was there and had been listening to the voice in your head as you woke up and were feeling anxious about the day ahead, what would I have heard it saying?

Naomi: It was asking questions over and over and worrying.

Therapist: That's getting closer to describing your thoughts, but it still sounds a bit more like a summary or description of what you were thinking about. I'm interested in each one of your specific thoughts. Can you tell me word for word what the voice in your head said?

Naomi: It said 'What is wrong with me? Why do I feel like this? I'll never be able to handle my job again. I can't cope with anything anymore'.

Therapist: Great job, they are very specific thoughts – just what I was looking for. Now let's add them to the B column.

With practice during sessions, Naomi became more specific in her monitoring, and better able to articulate her cognitions, and differentiate them from her emotional responses. Nonetheless, at the commencement of each session, the therapist conducted a detailed review of her between-session monitoring, and highlighted any examples of cognitions that were lacking in specificity (e.g., summarised the theme of her thoughts, rather than a specific cognition), or were in fact a description of her emotion/s. This process of identifying specific cognitions was a critical step in Naomi's cognitive therapy, and the therapist did not proceed with cognitive challenging until Naomi had developed and practiced this skill.

The excerpt above provided the therapist with insight into some of Naomi's primary dysfunctional cognitions, for example, "What is wrong with me?", "I'll never be able to handle my job again", "I can't cope with anything anymore". Naomi's language during this exchange also proved informative. For example, words such as 'wreck', 'ridiculous' and 'embarrassed' reflected Naomi's tendency to be highly self-critical. Not only did such examples illustrate the content of Naomi's thinking, but they also provided important information about the dysfunctional patterns of thinking she engaged in during times of distress.

14.3.2   Challenging Cognitive Distortions and Thinking Errors

The next step in cognitive therapy was to introduce the idea of cognitive distortions, or thinking errors. The therapist discussed and normalised the types of cognitive distortions that are common in depression, and drew Naomi's attention to a number of examples of black-and-white thinking recorded on her monitoring form. To illustrate, the therapist pointed out instances in which Naomi was highly self-critical. For example, whilst Naomi described herself as someone who used to be capable and able to cope with difficult situations, she currently perceived herself as incompetent and unable to cope with anything. Naomi responded well to this component of cognitive therapy. She was able to recognise examples of black-and-white thinking, particularly when they emerged in the context of her self-evaluations. She noticed how frequently her thinking was polarised in this way, and could see how her tendency to be black and white increased her feelings of anxiety and sadness.

Treatment then turned to cognitive challenging. The therapist reviewed the rationale for teaching Naomi strategies to question her negative automatic thoughts, generate and consider more helpful interpretations, and substitute her unhelpful thoughts with a more adaptive alternative. Again, Naomi evidenced good understanding of the rationale, and responded well to the suggestion of using questions such as "What is the evidence for this thought?", "Am I being black and white?" to begin the process of challenging her thoughts and generating more helpful alternative perspectives. The process of monitoring made her increasingly aware of how frequently her thoughts were self-deprecating. When she noticed self-critical thoughts, the therapist recommended that Naomi respond with "What would you say to a friend?" Naomi found this helpful in generating a more self-compassionate response in-session, and envisaged that this would be particularly helpful at times she felt anxious and distressed.

Whilst Naomi's response to the introduction to cognitive challenging was encouraging in-session, when she returned the following week, her monitoring was again lacking in specific detail. As per the initial cognitive therapy sessions, Naomi resumed recording vague, summary descriptions of her thought content, rather than specific cognitions. This tendency was particularly evident when she attempted to describe her new, alternative cognition. Despite being able to demonstrate understanding the process of questioning her thoughts and beginning to generate alternative cognitions when guided by the therapist during sessions, without support, the processes of monitoring her cognitions and attempting to challenge them proved extremely difficult. If anything, it appeared to serve as a catalyst for rumination, such that instead of generating an alternative, more helpful counter-cognition, Naomi instead recorded a thought (or more typically, a series of thoughts) that appeared more like a response to/analysis of her original cognition. For example, following a difficult conversation with her boss, Naomi reported the cognition: "She has always had it in for me". However, rather than proceed to question the evidence for this thought in order to arrive at a more balanced alternative, Naomi's monitoring included the following thought stream: "I have no idea why, for years I have been so reliable and worked hard and given everything to my job. And it's even worse now because she can see how stressed I am so she is even more convinced that I am incompetent. Although if I'm honest with myself maybe she is right because deep down I can't see how I will ever again be able to cope with work without feeling all of this tension and stress" (see Fig. 14.2).

The therapist persisted with a cognitive challenging approach, and a number of sessions were devoted to reviewing Naomi's monitoring, helping her to elicit

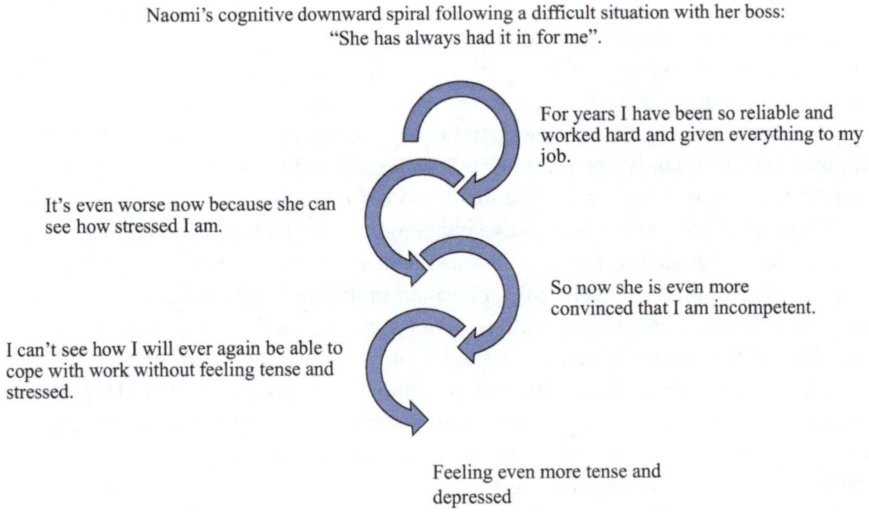

Naomi's cognitive downward spiral following a difficult situation with her boss:
"She has always had it in for me".

For years I have been so reliable and worked hard and given everything to my job.

It's even worse now because she can see how stressed I am.

So now she is even more convinced that I am incompetent.

I can't see how I will ever again be able to cope with work without feeling tense and stressed.

Feeling even more tense and depressed

Fig. 14.2 Naomi's ruminative downward spiral

specific examples of cognitions, specify the emotions associated with them, question the evidence for each cognition, generate more balanced, helpful alternative cognitions, and reflect on their emotional impact. That is, a significant amount of time in the early sessions was dedicated to Naomi and the therapist collaboratively stepping through each stage of the process of cognitive challenging. Although Naomi became more adept at each of these steps during treatment sessions, her between-session monitoring continued to demonstrate that rather than serving to generate alternative cognitions, the process of challenging remained extremely difficult. Her efforts to generate alternative cognitions were seemingly derailed by a tendency to analyse her thoughts; that is, to engage in rumination in response to them, fuelled by the initial thought. This was evident in her monitoring as well as in treatment sessions, as illustrated by the following exchange:

Therapist: Let's talk through this example from your monitoring form. So you woke in the middle of the night and started thinking about how you got upset at home yesterday, and how your husband thinks *"you should just be able to get over this"*.

Naomi: Yeh, I couldn't get the thought out of my head. I mean, everyone has problems. Why can't I just sort mine out?

Therapist: And you thought *"I know my husband thinks I should just pull myself together"*, and you felt embarrassed and also a bit annoyed.

Naomi: Yes.

Therapist: Ok, so let's take some time to look at this thought. First, what is the evidence for the thought?

Naomi: It was just the way he looks at me when I'm upset. I could tell. Well, maybe I couldn't tell, but I just sensed it.

Therapist: Can you tell me what you mean by "sensed" it? Was there something specific that he said or did that was evidence that he was thinking that?

Naomi: I just know him. And I could feel it. It just feels like everything has changed. I used to be the one he looked up to and who supported the whole family, and now he just thinks I can't manage anything and I really don't know why I feel so bad all the time and why I can't cope. Even the fact that this bothers me so much proves I can't cope.

Therapist: Ok, so you've mentioned a number of thoughts there. Let's go back to the thought you had in the middle of the night – *"I know he thinks I should just pull myself together"*. We've discussed a number of the patterns or traps of thinking that shape the way we interpret the world when we feel depressed or anxious. One of them was mind-reading. What do you remember about it? Do you think you could have been engaging in mind-reading here?

(continued)

Naomi: Yes. We spoke about how I sometimes assume I know what someone is thinking about me, and that it's never anything good. But I don't think I was doing that here. I know that's what he's always thinking.

Therapist: You sound very sure of that. I'm still wondering, how do you know he thinks that? What exactly did he say or do?

Naomi: I can't help thinking this and I just can't shake it.

Therapist: What would you say to a friend who was having a difficult time, and had that same thought after a conversation with her husband?

Naomi: I'd tell her that maybe he probably doesn't think that at all. But I can feel that my husband thinks that about me and I just don't see that ever changing.

Naomi's tendency to ruminate was clearly limiting the capacity of cognitive challenging to yield therapeutic benefit. Accordingly, the therapist opted to shift the focus and target her unhelpful cognitive processes with a more process-oriented (rather than content-oriented) approach. That is, rather than identifying and challenging the *content* of unhelpful thinking as per a traditional cognitive therapy approach, the therapist applied strategies drawn from interventions focused on the *process* of repetitive thought, grounded in behavioural approach and theory (e.g., Behavioural Activation: Addis & Martell, 2004; Martell et al., 2001; Rumination-focused CBT: Watkins, 2016).

14.3.3   Targeting the Ruminative Spiral

The therapist presented Naomi with a rationale for this shift in focus. They discussed Naomi's tendency to get 'stuck' in a ruminative spiral and jump from one ruminative thought to the next, and how this made the process of cognitive challenging more difficult. The therapist gave examples of rumination, and described some common qualities: thoughts that are abstract, hard to pin down (i.e., lacking in specific detail), commonly associated with 'big picture' themes (e.g., What kind of person am I?), and often characterised by 'why' questions (Why can't I cope? Why do I feel this way?). Naomi reported that she could relate to these features and to the sense of feeling 'stuck' in her rumination, and to having difficulty disengaging once it had started ("I can't get off the train once it's left the station"). As the first step, the therapist asked Naomi to monitor examples of 'why' thoughts during the following week, in order to draw her attention to the frequency of her rumination. The therapist emphasised that these needed be specific thoughts, rather than a summary of what she was thinking about – for example, questions starting with 'why'.

Naomi presented to the next session with a list of well over 50 different 'why' questions that she had noticed asking herself over the past week. She was surprised by the number (as was the therapist!). These questions revolved around the themes of her cognitions reported above, and included responses to her psychological symptoms (e.g., "Why do I feel like this?"), thoughts about her competence (e.g., as a nurse, wife and mother, e.g., "Why can't I be a better mother?"), her capacity to cope ("Why I am I unable to cope with my job?"). The extensive nature of the list highlighted to Naomi how frequently she engaged in ruminative thought. In addition, she noticed how asking one of these questions often prompted another question, rather than an answer to it – an observation that the therapist returned to later. In addition, this monitoring highlighted patterns of Naomi's rumination across the day, and drew her attention to cues (including specific times of day, places, people) which increased the frequency of her rumination.

The therapist then introduced strategies intended to interrupt or 'circuit break' Naomi's rumination. For example, Naomi was encouraged to apply the 'Two-Minute Rule for Recognizing Rumination' (Addis & Martell, 2004) when she noticed herself ruminating. Specifically, after two minutes, she was prompted to ask herself: (i) whether she had made progress toward solving the problem or resolving the situation she was thinking about, (ii) whether she understood her problem, her situation, or her feelings any better now, and (iii) whether she was feeling better (i.e., less depressed or anxious) than before she started thinking this way (see Fig. 14.3).

The therapist reminded Naomi that if the answer to these questions was no, it was very likely that she was ruminating. Naomi also came up with a simple prompt to remind herself to ask these questions when she noticed asking herself 'why' questions: "Is this why working for me?" If her answer was no, she was encouraged to think about how to shift her why question to a what or how question (e.g., "Why do I feel so bad? --> What could I do right now to make myself feel better?"). In addition to interrupting the spiral of rumination, this process served to shift Naomi from passive questioning into a specific action or behaviour (*rumination cues action*; Addis & Martell, 2004).

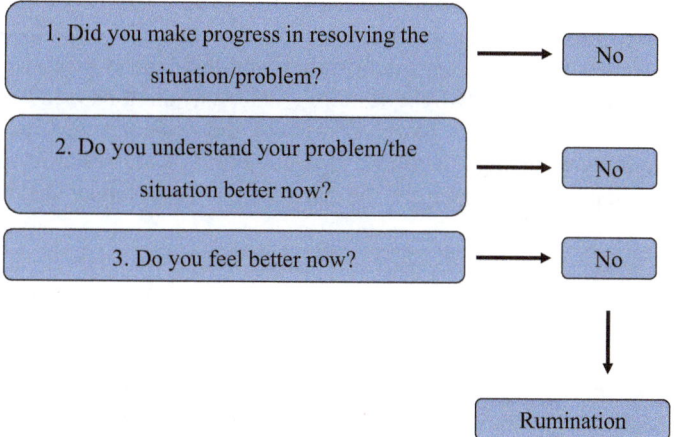

Fig. 14.3 The Two-Minute Rule for Recognizing Rumination. (See Addis & Martell, 2004)

Metacognitive beliefs about the utility of repetitive thinking are commonly held by people who frequently worry and ruminate (e.g., Papageorgiou & Wells, 2001; Watkins & Moulds, 2005). As treatment progressed it became apparent that Naomi held a number of metacognitive beliefs that encouraged her to persist in engaging in rumination; in particular, to dwell on events in the workplace. As described above, Naomi felt that thinking about and understanding why events unfolded the way they did helped her to 'learn lessons' from them. She reasoned that if she thought about why things happened, she would be better able to problem-solve and generate solutions for stressful events she encountered at work in the future – and that this would prepare her to handle them more effectively. When the therapist explored this, Naomi articulated the specific and strongly held belief: "Thinking about why things went wrong helps me to come up with a plan of action to prepare for next time". Given her previous difficulties with cognitive challenging, the therapist suggested that they try out an experiment to test the veracity of this belief.

14.3.4 Behavioural Experiment to Test the Benefit of Thinking About 'Why'

In order to keep Naomi focused and specific, the therapist worked collaboratively with her in-session to specify the belief she was testing, an alternative belief, the details of the experiment, her predictions about what would happen based on her belief, and finally, conduct a review of the experiment. Naomi's belief and alternative belief, and ratings of the extent to which she believed in both, were as follows, see Table 14.1:

The behavioural experiment was conducted in session. The therapist asked Naomi to recall a recent disagreement with a colleague that she was still upset about and felt she had handled badly, and then explained that they would conduct an experiment to test her belief about the usefulness of thinking about 'why' things went wrong to help her plan for future events. The therapist explained that she would ask Naomi to bring the event to mind, and then spend 5 minutes silently thinking about it and asking 'why' questions (e.g., "Why did it happen?", "Why did I say that?", "Why did I react like that?", "Why did my colleague disagree with me?"). Before commencing, Naomi rated the strength of her belief in her predictions about what would happen on the basis of her belief about the benefits of

Table 14.1 Challenging beliefs and testing alternative beliefs

Target belief	Strength of target belief (/100)	Alternative belief	Strength of alternative belief (/100)
Thinking about why things went wrong helps me to come up with a plan of action to prepare for next time	100	*Thinking about why things went wrong does not help me to come up with a plan of action to prepare for next time*	10

engaging in rumination; i.e., if it was true that "Thinking about why things went wrong helps me to come up with a plan of action for next time", after thinking this way how prepared do you think you will be for managing a similar event in the future? (0–100) (0 = not at all prepared, 100 = extremely prepared). As expected, Naomi rated her level of preparation as 100/100. Next, the therapist asked Naomi to spend 5 minutes asking herself 'why' questions about the event. Following this, she rated (on the same 0–100 scale) the item "How prepared do you feel right now to manage a similar event in the future?" Her rating was 40.

Naomi and the therapist then reviewed and discussed the process and outcomes of the experiment, including whether Naomi's predictions fit with her ratings of preparedness at the end of the 'why' exercise and what she learnt about her target belief. Naomi expressed surprise at the significant reduction in her ratings after a simple, brief experiment, as her target belief was long-standing. She commented that rather than helping her to generate plans as she predicted, asking 'why' questions merely prompted more such questions and further rumination, as opposed to answers or solutions. Thus, although her motivation for engaging in 'why' questions was to help her to generate active plans for dealing with future events, after the experiment Naomi recognised that this strategy was in fact passive. This insight prompted a conversation about the value of testing out an alternative way of reflecting on and recalling past events. Again, rather than focusing on 'why', the therapist suggested shifting to more active language, and thinking about 'what' happened and 'how' the event happened, as well as 'what' and 'how' she could do things differently in the future. Accordingly, the next behavioural experiment focused on comparing the relative outcomes of thinking about a past negative event by asking 'why' versus 'what/how'.

14.4   Special Challenges and Problems

As detailed above, one of the challenging aspects of treatment was Naomi's difficulty with some core aspects of cognitive therapy. This first emerged in the assessment and early treatment sessions, when the therapist described the cognitive model. Whilst she appeared to understand the ABC model (of events, thoughts, emotions), when prompted for examples from her own life, it was apparent that Naomi struggled to distinguish cognitions and emotions. Much of the first therapy session was therefore spent collaboratively generating examples of the ABC model, with an emphasis on helping Naomi to differentiate how she interpreted situations from her emotional responses to them. Naomi continued to struggle to make this distinction when completing monitoring between therapy sessions, and frequently described emotional responses when asked to record her cognitions. Accordingly, a significant portion of cognitive therapy early in treatment was devoted to reviewing Naomi's monitoring and differentiating thoughts and feelings. As treatment sessions progressed, it became apparent that drawing this distinction was the most difficult for Naomi at times of high emotion, particularly when she felt irritable, sad or under pressure.

Another aspect of cognitive therapy that proved challenging for Naomi was identifying specific, discrete examples of her cognitions. When she did record the content of her thinking between sessions, Naomi had a tendency to summarise and describe the topic/s of her stream of thoughts, as opposed to listing specific, discrete examples of her cognitions. Her descriptions of her thoughts tended to be long and detailed, reflecting the perseverative, ruminative cycle that often characterised her thinking. This lack of specificity is commonly observed in depressed individuals, consistent with the tendency to recall memories lacking in specificity (Williams et al., 2007) which is exacerbated by rumination (Watkins & Teasdale, 2001), as well as the abstract quality of depressive rumination (Watkins & Moulds, 2007). The abstract and non-specific nature of the entries in Naomi's thought record made cognitive challenging extremely difficult. It necessitated a large amount of discussion in order to help her draw out and articulate specific, 'online' examples of her automatic thoughts, rather than a summary of the broad theme of her thinking.

Both of these challenges meant that for Naomi, cognitive challenging was limited in its effectiveness, and did not lead to significant treatment gains. Even after a number of sessions focusing on helping Naomi to identify her negative thoughts and cognitive distortions (e.g., black-and-white thinking: I am competent versus I am incompetent), her unhelpful thoughts, bouts of rumination and low mood all persisted. This prompted the therapist to take a different approach to tackle her cognitions, and focus on the *process* of Naomi's unhelpful thinking, rather than address its *content*. As described above, therapy drew on behavioural principles, and was informed by approaches such as Behavioural Activation (Martell et al., 2001) as well as Rumination-focused Cognitive Behaviour Therapy (Watkins, 2016). These approaches proved more effective in addressing Naomi's unhelpful cognitions.

Why? First, the relative simplicity of strategies such as the Two-Minute Rule for Recognizing Rumination appeared to more effectively capture Naomi's attention and anchor it to the task at hand, and circumvent her tendency to summarise and analyse the themes and content of her thinking. In this way, having a clear set of questions to ask herself functioned as an effective circuit breaker, giving Naomi an immediate, concrete strategy to employ when needed. It is plausible that such an approach resonated with Naomi given the training and approach adopted in her professional life (e.g., having a clear protocol to follow in response to an incident). In addition, despite re-visiting the cognitive model and rationale for cognitive therapy on a number of occasions, the therapist was left unsure of whether Naomi truly grasped the principles of cognitive theory and therapy. It is also possible that the lack of any obvious benefit from cognitive therapy, as well as her difficulties with monitoring (described above) inadvertently served to provide Naomi with evidence of herself as incapable. By comparison, she reported finding implementing strategies such as the two-minute rumination rule useful, and was therefore motivated to continue to apply them. One hypothesis is that this may have given Naomi a sense of accomplishment and self-efficacy – and as such, some evidence counter to her belief that she was incapable. Regardless of the reason/s, the structured approach of responding to unhelpful cognitive streams with pre-specified questions proved more effective for Naomi than engaging with the content of her cognitions, with the latter often serving to further fuel her rumination.

A related challenge was the impact of Naomi's rumination on activity scheduling. At the beginning of treatment, Naomi was readily able to generate a detailed list of pleasant events that she frequently engaged in prior to the recent stressor, and that she derived pleasure from. She was motivated to re-introduce these activities into her daily life, as she could see a clear link between withdrawing from them (particularly social activities) and her reduced mood. Early sessions therefore involved detailed scheduling of specific behavioural activities, all of which Naomi carried out between sessions. However, a review of her monitoring forms in sessions revealed that these activities did not have the expected mood-bolstering effects. When the therapist probed for details about how the activities were implemented, it became apparent that when Naomi was completing them, she was often lost in thought – for example, replaying events at work and thinking critically about how she had handled them, and asking herself why she just couldn't get on with things the way she used to. This was particularly the case when she was exercising (e.g., walking alone). Also, as described above, Naomi often had a tendency to be on the lookout for potentially dangerous situations that could arise (e.g., a child falling from the climbing frame in the park), and to worry about whether she would be able to help.

To manage this, the therapist worked with Naomi to come up with strategies to help anchor herself to the present moment. The importance of attending to details during activity scheduling as a means by which to counter rumination is emphasised in a number of the treatment approaches utilised by the therapist in this case (see Martell et al., 2001; Watkins, 2016; see also Dunn et al., 2019). As a first step, Naomi was encouraged to attend to her surroundings by focusing on sensory information – what she could see, hear and smell. Whilst she applied this strategy of 'mindful walking' and found it beneficial initially, Naomi reported that it didn't hold her attention for long, and that her rumination would soon return. An alternative strategy that she proposed was to wear headphones and listen to material that she found engaging and interesting, including classical music or a podcast series. This strategy proved very helpful, enabling Naomi to maintain her focus on the present and for her mood to benefit from exercise, without drifting away into bouts of rumination and self-critical thinking.

14.5   Summary, Conclusions and Learning Points

In summary, cognitive distortions were a prominent feature of Naomi's clinical presentation and played a key role in maintaining her psychological distress. Engaging in cognitive challenging to address Naomi's cognitions did not prove to be effective for a number of reasons. First, she had a tendency to be vague and non-specific, in keeping with her tendency to engage in rumination. This difficulty in pinning down her thoughts made it difficult for Naomi both to identify specific cognitions, and in turn, engage in the process of challenging them and generating specific alternatives. Second, despite having a seemingly good understanding of the cognitive model and the process of cognitive challenging at the outset, Naomi persistently found it difficult to employ cognitive therapy alone, outside of the therapy room. Although she benefited from the therapist guiding her through this process (i.e., helping to keep her focused at each step of the challenging process) during treatment sessions, she struggled with each step when unsupported. Indeed, rather than help Naomi to question her thoughts and generate alternative, more helpful interpretations, cognitive therapy instead appeared to serve as a catalyst for further rumination.

What proved more helpful for Naomi was focusing on the process of her thinking; in particular, having a specified set of strategies to help her notice when she was ruminating, and prompt her to engage in alternative, more active responses. For example, Naomi benefited from asking herself very specific and clear questions (e.g., invoking the Two-Minute Rumination Rule), which appeared to be effective in cutting through the cycle of rumination and helping her to step back and disengage from its content. This approach is arguably more prescriptive than engaging in the process of cognitive challenging, and thus better suited to clients such as Naomi who tended to be overgeneral and struggle to be specific. With guidance, Naomi was also able to use behavioural experiments more effectively than cognitive restructuring as a means by which to challenge her cognitions. Nonetheless, given her tendency to be abstract and overgeneral, at the outset, it was important that Naomi worked collaboratively with the therapist to identify a specific cognition to target in experiments, and to articulate specific predictions to be tested.

For the therapist, the take-home message from this case was a reminder about the importance of keeping things simple. For Naomi, less was indeed more. She benefitted most when the therapeutic strategies were clear and easy to implement. The relative complexity of tasks such as cognitive challenging was compounded by Naomi's habit of analysing her thoughts. Indeed, key features of the cognitive profile of depressed individuals are a tendency to be analytical and evaluative: two of the defining qualities of rumination. Naomi's presentation and response to treatment highlighted the importance of therapists being vigilant to potential ways in which intervention strategies (particularly cognitive therapy) may be more challenging for highly ruminative clients owing to their tendency to be analytical.

Whilst cognitive therapy with Naomi was challenging owing to her tendency to describe and recount her thoughts in an analytical manner, it is also important to acknowledge that the therapist also struggled to deliver cognitive therapy in this case. On reflection, at times the therapist attempted to engage in cognitive challenging when the target cognition was not sufficiently specific. As a consequence, the therapeutic dialogue and challenging process proceeded at an abstract level of meaning, and as a consequence, inadvertently mimicked co-rumination. This is a critical possibility to monitor (and aim to avoid) throughout treatment with highly ruminative clients, particularly for therapists with less experience in delivering cognitive therapy. This case reminded the therapist of the importance of keeping things specific, and to focus therapy on dealing with cognitions at the grassroots, rather than at the level of meaning. In hindsight, it may have been preferential to either shift to a process-oriented approach to helping Naomi with her cognitions earlier in the course of treatment rather than persist with cognitive challenging, or to adopt such an approach at the outset.

References

Addis, M. E., & Martell, C. R. (2004). *Overcoming depression one step at a time*. New Harbinger Publications.

Beck, A. T., Rush, A. J., Shaw, B. F., & Emery, G. (1979). *Cognitive therapy of depression*. Guilford Press.

Dunn, B. D., Widnall, E., Reed, N., Owens, C., Campbell, J., & Kuyken, W. (2019). Bringing light into darkness: A multiple baseline mixed methods case series evaluation of Augmented Depression Therapy (ADepT). *Behaviour Research and Therapy, 120*, 103418. https://doi.org/10.1016/j.brat.2019.103418

Lovibond, S. H., & Lovibond, P. F. (1995). *Manual for the depression anxiety stress scales* (2nd ed.). Psychology Foundation.

Martell, C. R., Addis, M. E., & Jacobson, N. S. (2001). *Depression in context: Strategies for guided action*. WW Norton.

Nolen-Hoeksema, S., & Morrow, J. (1991). A prospective study of depression and posttraumatic stress symptoms after a natural disaster: The 1989 Loma Prieta earthquake. *Journal of Personality and Social Psychology, 61*, 115–121. https://doi.org/10.1037//0022-3514.61.1.115

Papageorgiou, C., & Wells, A. (2001). Metacognitive beliefs about rumination in recurrent major depression. *Cognitive and Behavioral Practice, 8*(2), 160–164. https://doi.org/10.1016/S1077-7229(01)80021-3

Watkins, E. R. (2016). *Rumination-focused cognitive-behavioral therapy for depression*. Guilford Press.

Watkins, E., & Moulds, M. L. (2005). Positive beliefs about rumination in depression – A replication and extension. *Personality and Individual Differences, 39*, 73–82. https://doi.org/10.1016/j.paid.2004.12.006

Watkins, E., & Moulds, M. L. (2007). Reduced concreteness of rumination in depression: A pilot study. *Personality and Individual Differences, 43*(6), 1386–1395. https://doi.org/10.1016/j.paid.2007.04.007

Watkins, E., & Teasdale, J. D. (2001). Rumination and overgeneral memory in depression: Effects of self-focus and analytic thinking. *Journal of Abnormal Psychology, 110*(2), 353–357. https://doi.org/10.1037/0021-843X.110.2.333

Williams, J. M. G., Barnhofer, T., Crane, C., Herman, D., Raes, F., Watkins, E., & Dalgleish, T. (2007). Autobiographical memory specificity and emotional disorder. *Psychological Bulletin, 133*(1), 122–148. https://doi.org/10.1037/0033-2909.133.1.122

Michelle L. Moulds is a Clinical Psychologist and Professor in the School of Psychology at UNSW Sydney, Australia. She was awarded her PhD at UNSW in 2003 and completed a Postdoctoral Fellowship at the Institute of Psychiatry, King's College London, before returning to UNSW to take up a lectureship. Her team's research primarily focuses on the nature and role of repetitive thinking (e.g., rumination) in depression and anxiety, and how repetitive thinking interacts with other cognitive deficits (e.g., autobiographical memory disturbances) to maintain psychological distress.

Chapter 15
"It Is Dangerous to Ignore This Thought" – A Case Study in Obsessive Compulsive Disorder

Christine Purdon

15.1 The Case

15.1.1 Background and Problem History

Sundeep was a 31-year-old pharmacist who lived with his wife and children, aged 4 and 2. At the time of assessment, he received a diagnosis of OCD (moderate to severe). Sundeep's symptoms included a near-constant preoccupation with making a mistake when dispensing medications and/or fears he had contaminated the medication. In addition, he feared he would transmit a virus to his children. Sundeep reported that these symptoms started in the final two years of his degree in pharmacy, when he was 21. At that time, he developed concerns about whether his hands were free of contagion and feared that the dispensing instruments and prescription bottles might be contaminated, and he would harm or kill someone. Upon assuming responsibility for filling prescriptions, he began doubting whether he had put the right medication and dose in the bottle, and whether his labels were correct. He began to wash his hands excessively and spent a good deal of time sanitizing prescription bottles, checking the written prescription and the prescription labels repeatedly, asking his supervisors to verify his work, and, at times, surreptitiously calling the prescribing physician to get verbal confirmation of the prescription details.

Sundeep's compulsions escalated when he began working as an independent pharmacist, which also coincided with the birth of his first child. His fears of

C. Purdon (✉)
Department of Psychology, University of Waterloo, Waterloo, ON, Canada
e-mail: christine.purdon@uwaterloo.ca

© The Author(s), under exclusive license to Springer Nature Switzerland AG 2023 281
M. L. Woud (ed.), *Interpretational Processing Biases in Emotional Psychopathology*,
CBT: Science Into Practice, https://doi.org/10.1007/978-3-031-23650-1_15

transmitting contamination to vulnerable people then took root in his home. He washed excessively before touching his son and he could not bring himself to prepare his son's bottles. Sundeep's contamination fears and cleaning, checking, and avoidance began to impair his ability to function as a pharmacist and as a parent. One day, Sundeep was exiting his doctor's office when he overheard the staff discussing the possibility that an earlier patient had symptoms of a rare, mildly contagious, and serious virus. Sundeep began to fear that he had come into contact with the virus and was now in danger of transmitting it to his children. Upon arrival at home, he took off his clothes, showered, and stowed the clothes in a bag in the shed. By the time of assessment, Sundeep was avoiding physical contact with his children, refusing to let them travel in his car, constantly monitoring his family for signs of illness, and spending a great deal of time researching the virus, at the expense of assisting his wife in caring for the children and managing the household. Sundeep called his doctor's office multiple times to establish whether a patient had had the virus, to the point that the doctor threatened to drop him as a patient. This, and his inability to be affectionate towards his children and participate in their hands-on care, led Sundeep to seek help for his obsessional preoccupations and compulsions.

15.1.2 Relevant Family History

Sundeep reported having had a relatively stable childhood and loving parents. He described his relationship with them as "close but strained". He described his father as distant, and both parents as perfectionists who could be very critical and judgmental. Sundeep has an older sister who is a physician, who is viewed as being more successful than him. Sundeep reported two pivotally distressing events involving his parents. When he was 13, he was required to care for his elderly grandmother, who had Alzheimer's, every day after school, on his own. One day Sundeep turned to take a boiling pot off the stove and while his back was turned, his grandmother bolted out of the house. The neighbours alerted his parents, who were furious with him and punished him for his "negligence" by taking away his allowance for a month. Sundeep also recalled an instance in his final year of high school when he proudly told his parents that his teacher planned to feature one of his drawings in the school yearbook. They dismissed the drawing as "amateurish" and questioned the teacher's acumen. Although he had a strong interest in art and was viewed by his teachers as talented his parents told him he hadn't the talent to succeed as an artist and insisted that he take science at university. Although Sundeep did well enough in his highly demanding pharmacy program his studies required all his time and effort. He enjoys many aspects of pharmacy but has never felt it is his true calling.

15.1.3 Assessment Results

Assessment was conducted to establish diagnoses, assess symptom severity, and develop a working case formulation. To this end, the therapist administered the Mini Neuropsychiatric Inventory (MINI; Sheehan et al., 1998) and the Yale Brown Obsessive Compulsive Scale, Second Edition (YBOCS-II; Storch et al., 2010). Sundeep met criteria for OCD and had a score of 32 on the YBOCS, which is in the moderate to severe range. Sundeep also completed the Interpretation of Intrusions Inventory (III; Obsessive Compulsive Cognitions Working Group [OCCWG], 1997, 2001) and the Obsessive Beliefs Questionnaire-44-item version (OBQ-44; OCCWG, 1997, 2001, 2003) to assess appraisal and beliefs about obsessions, respectively. Sundeep's scores on the OBQ and III were 149 and 52 respectively, well in the clinical range. He endorsed strong beliefs about responsibility (e.g., any responsibility for an outcome = full responsibility for an outcome), that thoughts would not occur unless they are meaningful, and that one cannot and should not proceed if one is uncertain. He appraised his obsessions as signaling harm for which he would be responsible (e.g., "If I don't do something about this intrusive thought, it will be my fault if something terrible happens"), that it would be immoral, dangerous, and irresponsible to ignore his obsessional concerns, and that the more he thought about getting a prescription wrong, transmitting contamination, etc., the more likely it was those things would happen.

As part of the assessment, Sundeep was asked to describe a recent obsessive-compulsive episode that was both typical and fraught. He described an incident the previous day when his wife was out, and his youngest child sneezed and then coughed. He immediately had the obsessional thought "He might have the virus!" He felt a wave of anxiety, feeling suddenly hot and trembly, with a racing heart and tight chest. He felt an overwhelming sense of dread and shame. He believed that his obsessional thought would not be occurring unless there was truth to it, and that it would thus be immoral or dangerous to ignore it. He had frightening "flash forwards" of having to take his ailing child to the hospital and explaining to his weeping wife that he had infected the child, and of his colleagues at the pharmacy shaking their heads in wonderment that someone who ought to know better could have been so careless. Sundeep also had a flashback to the day he returned from the doctor's and had entered the house without removing his shoes, thus recklessly spreading the virus, alongside the vivid memory of being chastized by his parents for allowing his grandmother to wander off. Finally, Sundeep had vivid memories of times he sought medical attention for his children for highly routine, non-urgent, manageable issues and was met with exasperation from the health care professionals, including one who told him that a pharmacist should have a better judgement.

Sundeep tried to assure himself that his son's symptoms were most likely due to allergies or a benign cold, but then had the thought "What if he has the virus and you don't take him, and he becomes very sick and dies?", and he thought "It's too risky to assume allergies, I have to completely rule out the possibility of virus". He took his son's temperature, which turned out to be normal. He was somewhat relieved, but to be sure, took it again, with the same result. However, he then thought "What if the batteries in the thermometer are low and it was giving me a faulty reading?" Once again, he took this doubt seriously ("I wouldn't be having this thought unless there was truth in it") and so inserted brand-new batteries, checked the temperature again (it was normal), and re-checked it several more times. Sundeep was about to move on to preparing dinner when he had the sudden thought that maybe he had misread the numbers, so he took the temperature again, and this time wrote down the number. He checked the thermometer and his recording of it multiple times, but now had no confidence that his eyes were perceiving things properly. He asked his older child to read the numbers aloud to him, but then doubted whether he had used the thermometer properly in the first place. When his wife returned, he asked her to take the child's temperature. She obliged and reported it was normal. He asked if she thought the son should go to the hospital, and she replied "Absolutely not! This is just allergies!", and only then did the obsessional concern and his concomitant distress abate.

15.2 Main Cognitions Targeted

15.2.1 Core Beliefs, Assumptions, and Rules for Living

Sundeep's core beliefs were that he was an irresponsible person whose judgement could not be trusted when it came to providing care for vulnerable and/or dependent others. As such, he assumed that he was in danger of causing harm, either by omission (failing to do something to prevent harm) or commission (doing something that causes harm). He also assumed that if he caused harm he would be rejected by his family and sanctioned by his coworkers. These ideas may have been formed when as a child he was held responsible for his grandmother's well-being, and by his parents' critical style, which implied there was a "right" way to do things that he was unable to discern. Sundeep had also entered a profession for which he believed himself to have little natural talent, and this contributed to his assumption that he was not as competent as other pharmacists. To compensate for his perceived shortcomings, Sundeep developed rules for living which included reliance on external information, societal/parental rules, and on the judgement of people he viewed as authoritative, rather than relying on his own judgement. Sundeep also took extensive steps to ensure he did not cause harm (that is, vigilance monitoring and compulsions).

Thus, Sundeep's compulsions were not simply done to meet a proximal goal, such as getting his hands clean, but to avoid being an irresponsible, bad person. It is important to note that Sundeep was not as concerned about the possibility of harm as he was being the one responsible for that harm; he accepted that mistakes happen in life but believed that because he was aware of his shortcomings, he had a special responsibility to mitigate the harm he could cause. However, Sundeep's core beliefs were not always active. For example, he trusted his judgement when it came to driving and could drive his children (in his wife's car) without undue anxiety about causing them harm. Like most people with OCD, his obsessive-compulsive cycles were triggered by situations relevant to perceived shortcomings in meaningful areas.

15.2.2   Appraisal of Obsessions

Thoughts relevant to being a source of harm to vulnerable others were internal threat stimuli for Sundeep, catching and holding his attention. When he experienced his obsessional concerns ("What if my children touched my contaminated clothing when they were in the shed?", "Did I give that patient the right prescription?") he implicitly rated them as credible and as warranting further consideration (e.g., "This thought wouldn't keep returning unless it was important", "It would be totally immoral and dangerous to ignore such a thought"). Sundeep would thus engage the obsessional doubts by thinking through ways they might be true, and could quickly develop fantastical narratives – e.g., "Maybe my eyes aren't working properly and I read the prescription wrong", "Maybe I touched my nose before opening this vial and contaminated the inside", "Maybe my children saw the bag with my clothes and jumped in it". These narratives were enough to convince Sundeep that the obsessional concern required immediate attention and that the threat of harm had to be completely neutralized, which evoked excessive checking and washing compulsions.

15.2.3   Appraisal of Compulsions

Sundeep believed that it was immoral and irresponsible to stop a compulsion before he felt certain that harm had been prevented. However, it is not possible to establish absence of harm; that is like trying to prove the null hypothesis, or to prove innocence. As such, there is no natural terminus for the behaviour. In deciding when it was okay to stop the compulsion, Sundeep instead relied on either arbitrary rules ("I wash my hands in hot water for five minutes") and/or an internal, felt sense that the threat had passed. Like many people with OCD, Sundeep's compulsions often "worked" in producing this felt sense, creating an intermittent reinforcement schedule for their use. However, equally often the "right" feeling was elusive, leading to repetition, prolongation, and/or inclusion of extraneous steps to achieve it. We know from research that repeating an action can undermine confidence in one's memory for the action, and in attention and sensory processes (see Purdon, 2018, for a review). When Sundeep repeated his compulsions, he would often start to doubt his memory ("Did I do that one right, or am I confusing this last one with a previous one?"), sensory ("Was that water truly hot?"), and attentional processes ("Maybe my mind wandered while reading the prescription and I missed a zero"), which made it increasingly difficult to achieve that felt sense. Furthermore, the more Sundeep repeated his compulsion the more responsible he felt for the outcome, and the greater his investment in ensuring harm had not yet occurred or was going to occur. Finally, Sundeep would often have other people check his prescriptions, or have his wife take over care of the children, which allowed him to transfer responsibility for any harm to other people, behaviour reinforced by the immediate relief he felt.

15.2.4   Compulsions and Values

Sundeep's compulsions were driven by his goal to be a responsible parent and pharmacist, and a good person. However, in his pursuit of being maximally responsible, Sundeep compromised another, equally important goal of being a loving parent and providing optimal care to his patients, which is what brought him to treatment. Furthermore, Sundeep judged his "success" in being a responsible person almost entirely by establishing with perfect certainty that he had mitigated the risks his shortcomings presented to his children and patients. He viewed himself as reckless and irresponsible if he moved on from an obsession or stopped a compulsion without being perfectly certain. As such, he never believed himself to be as responsible as he could or should be. The therapist used a two-dimensional plane to plot Sundeep's "success" in meeting his goals of being responsible and being loving/caring, each line anchored with 0 (0% responsible/caring) and 100 (100% responsible/caring) (see Fig. 15.1).

Sundeep rated himself at about 60% on responsibility and at 40% on being caring/loving. Successful therapy would put Sundeep's ratings in the upper right quadrant, meaning he could fulfill his goal of being responsible without doing compulsions, and this became our central treatment goal. A diagram representing the case formulation is presented in Fig. 15.2.

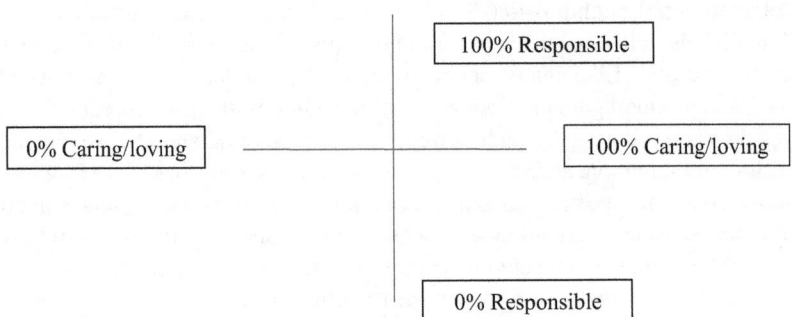

Fig. 15.1 Sundeep's two-dimensional plane

Fig. 15.2 Sundeep's case formulation

15.3   Treatment

Phases of treatment included sharing the formulation, psychoeducation and engagement, use of cognitive and behavioural strategies to help Sundeep change how he responded to his obsessional concerns, and core belief work.

15.3.1   Psychoeducation and Case Formulation

To help Sundeep to make sense of his OCD it was important to provide him with information on the anxiety response, on compulsion goals (i.e., unverifiable and impossible), the impact of repetition on memory, cognitive, and sensory confidence, and the role of core beliefs in driving the system. First, the therapist reviewed the purpose of the anxiety response (that is, to optimize our capacity to flee or fight danger), and how the infusion of adrenalin results in a wide range of physiological changes that people often do not recognize as being related. These include changes in blood flow, which produce tingling and coldness in the extremities and heat to the chest and face; increased heart rate and breathing, which can result in hyperventilation and a resulting sense of depersonalization; muscle tension, which can produce trembling and headaches; and changes in digestion. At the cognitive level, anxiety increases threat sensitivity, narrows attention to threat cues, and makes threat-relevant memories and images more accessible, at the expense of equally valid information and neutral and positive memories relevant to the threat and situation. Emotionally, the anxiety response can be mild, as in anxious anticipation; moderate, as in anxiety; strong, as in fear; and severe, as in panic, which comes with a sense of dread. Finally, in the absence of a clear and present danger, we tend to reason that there must be something to be anxious about, resulting in the generation of possible things that have occurred or will occur ("What if...?", "Maybe...").

The therapist then introduced Sundeep to the ironic effect of repetition on our confidence that the action has been done properly, and noted that as we repeat an action, we begin to process it conceptually, rather than perceptually; indeed, perceptual processing is inhibited. This explains why we can arrive at the end of a well-travelled drive to have very little memory of the trip. However, people with OCD, often demand of themselves a perceptually vivid memory for having done an action, particularly checking, but that is difficult to conjure if we have processed the action conceptually rather than perceptually. Finally, as we repeat an action our sense of responsibility for the outcome increases, thereby increasing investment in doing it properly. Sundeep found this very applicable to his experience. Sundeep and the therapist then reviewed the formulation using Fig. 15.2 as a guide and inserting examples of specific obsessions and compulsions. The therapist invited Sundeep to elaborate or edit as the session continued, and then highlighted the key "culprits" in the persistence of Sundeep's OCD and how treatment would address them. The goals of this were to help Sundeep make sense of his complex experience, identify the factors in the persistence of his compulsions, and instill hope that therapy could readily address these factors. Sundeep reported that he understood his symptoms for the first time, that he was highly motivated to get started, and believed that our work together was going to help him.

15.3.2   Initial Sessions of Treatment

Like many people with OCD Sundeep had a moral objection to taking the risk of ignoring his OCD doubts. Often people do not recognize all the steps that would have to occur for the obsessional concern to be realized, which elevates estimations of harm probability and severity, and Sundeep was no exception, assuming that failing to do a compulsion is akin to murder. Sundeep and the therapist first identified these steps and he assigned a general probability estimate of each: 1. Probability

Sundeep's clothing/hands had the virus on them: .02; 2. Probability that these traces of virus could transfer to his children: .10; 3. Probability that these traces of virus would result in infection: .05. The estimated probability of Sundeep's children being infected, then, is $.02 \times .10 \times .05 = .0001$, meaning there is a 99.9999% chance his obsessional fear will NOT be realized. The only things more certain are death and taxes. Yet, there was a 100% chance that Sundeep's attempts to prevent infection impaired his ability to function in his parental role and both saddened and confused his children. Of course, the exact probabilities of any of these events were unknown, but it was only necessary to identify Sundeep's anxiety-driven perceptions of the probabilities during the obsessive-compulsive cycle. Sundeep was taken aback by how low the probability likely was. Next, discussion focused on the fact that Sundeep drove his children to daycare without a second thought, which, he acknowledged, had a considerably higher probability of harm. He implicitly viewed this as an acceptable risk, provided the car was well maintained, the children had good quality car seats that were properly secured, and he drove sensibly. Thus, every day Sundeep took reasonable and acceptable risks without a second thought.

The goal of this exercise was not to provide reassurance or talk Sundeep out of being concerned about transmitting the virus. The goals were to illustrate how the OCD hijacks his perception of risk and harm, and to introduce the idea that being responsible involves due diligence and risk mitigation but does not require absolute certainty harm has been mitigated. It is both impossible to reduce risk to zero and to verify that one has done so (e.g., how can you get rid of all the germs, and how would you tell that you have done so?). Meanwhile, the search for certainty significantly interferes with daily functioning. Sundeep still needed to check his prescription labels as trained by his program and supervisors, and to respond reasonably if his children looked ill. The goal of therapy is to get rid of excessive efforts that are driven by negative appraisal of the obsessional thought's meaning and importance, and of the need for certainty, to develop people's trust in their own judgement, and to accept the risks that come with living one's life. This discussion helped set the moral ground for making changes in how Sundeep responded to his obsessions. He found this discussion very interesting, and it was agreed that over the next week, he would continue to reflect on the morality of accepting a risk.

15.3.3 Initial Sessions of CBT

Sundeep returned willing to start making changes in how he responded to his obsessional thoughts. The first goal was to help him become adept at identifying negative appraisal of the obsession. To this end, Sundeep and the therapist reviewed a recent obsessive-compulsive episode and together did a 4-column thought record of situation, feelings, thoughts, and actions. The focus was on identifying the appraisal that mediated Sundeep's emotional and behavioural response to his obsessional thoughts (see Purdon, 2021 for a review of cognitive restructuring). For the next two sessions, it was agreed that Sundeep would use the thought record at least once a day to catch his negative appraisal and start to consider it as a guess rather than a fact. Sundeep did reasonably well with this exercise. However, as is typical, the therapist had to work at helping him differentiate the appraisal of the obsession from the obsession itself. It was also useful to also break down the o-c cycle into pre-compulsion and compulsion phases, just as in social anxiety we might explore emotions and thoughts before, during, and after a social event separately. This allowed Sundeep to begin to identify his appraisal of obsessions and of compulsions. At the same time, the therapist asked Sundeep to keep an eye on his actions throughout the day to identify any sneaky compulsions and avoidance that he had not recognized as such, and reflect on which compulsions he wanted to tackle first in exposure.

In session 3, Sundeep and the therapist worked on the concept of the "hot thought"; that is, the thought that best explains the emotional and behavioural response, with the continued directive that he treats this as an idea rather than a fact, and consider how the anxiety response and his core beliefs might be directing that appraisal. Here is a thought record regarding a work situation, with the therapist prompts in the Appraisal column to help uncover the hot thought (see Table 15.1):

Sundeep found identification of the hot thought highly illuminating, but noted that he hadn't yet been asked to tackle the OCD directly, and was thus concerned he might not be able to face it down. This led to discussion of the ways this groundwork would serve him well when it came time to change how he responds to his obsessions, while building his capacity to override the automatic processing that puts the OCD system in motion.

15.3.4   Sessions 4–8 of CBT

The goal of the next phase of treatment was to help Sundeep override the automatic processes driving the OCD system, changing how he responded mentally and behaviourally to his obsessional thoughts. Each session included a cognitive and a

Table 15.1 Thought record for a work situation of Sundeep

Obsessional thought	Feelings	Actions	Appraisal
"Maybe I mixed up the last two prescriptions".	Dread – 85% Panic – 85% Shame – 95% Despair – 85%	Check each prescription, compare pills in bottle to dispensary bottle, compare pills from each to each other, check and re-check, phone client and say it's not ready yet	Why would I have this thought unless it was meaningful? [T: Why might the thought be meaningful? S: Because I filled them in a hurry so I could go to lunch T: What gets to you about that?] S: *I was being careless and selfish.

behavioural strategy, and between each session, Sundeep made changes in his cognitive and behavioural response to his obsessions, both at home and at work. Now that Sundeep was able to identify his hot thoughts as products of his anxiety/OCD system, it was time to bring to bear the range of relevant information on his appraisal, as opposed to just that which the anxiety makes accessible. For illustrative purposes, below is the information-weighing discussion of the situation above (see Table 15.2).

As is typical, Sundeep was readily able to list information that supports the hot thought. In the early stages, it took guided questions (not leading questions!) to help him identify information that does not support the hot thought. During this information-weighing stage, the therapist's attitude was of naïve curiosity, and the therapist simply collaborated with Sundeep to explore information, agnostic as to whether it would lead to a change in the hot thought. The therapist's purpose was not to sway Sundeep to a preconceived "truth" about the situation (see Purdon, 2021). Further, it was important to explore whether the information supporting the hot thought was a biased product of Sundeep's core beliefs and assumptions. Once Sundeep started reviewing information that did not support the hot thought his conviction in it began to visibly loosen. Sundeep then wrote a statement that best encapsulated all the reviewed information: "I am not careless, I take my work very seriously, and it is not selfish to take a lunch break". Sundeep rated his belief in the hot thought as 10% because he still thought he would benefit from improving his focus when filling prescriptions under time pressure. Therapy proceeded in this way for the next few sessions.

Table 15.2 Exploring Sundeep's hot thought

Appraisal of the obsession	Information that supports the hot thought	Information that does not support the hot thought
*I was being careless and selfish – initial level of conviction: 90%	I was rushing when I filled these two because I wanted to go for lunch so maybe I didn't pay enough attention to what I was doing. I am not a natural pharmacist The two types of pills look a bit the same. I almost killed my grandmother through my negligence. ***I was being careless and selfish – new level of conviction: 10%.**	I did them in sequence, so I didn't have both dispensary bottles out at same time. I always check the dispensary label against my label. I have never once mixed up a prescription, even when I haven't checked again and again. I have a very trained eye and notice the slightest differences in pills. Taking 15 minutes to fill two prescriptions is not 'rushed'. Taking a lunch break is not selfish, it's in fact mandatory. I had no training in working with people with dementia and I had turned my back to take a boiling pot off the stove so she wouldn't get hurt. **I am not careless, I take my work very seriously and it's not selfish to take a lunch break**

At the same time, the therapist introduced exposure with response prevention (ERP) and behavioural experiments. The traditional approach to ERP is to promote emotional habituation to the obsession by exposure to it while compulsions, safety strategies, and avoidance are prohibited. The goal is for the patient to achieve new learning about the obsession and the need to do the compulsion. Although it is conventional to develop an exposure hierarchy of increasingly challenging exercises early on and work through it, the therapist found merit in identifying a starting point and developing the next steps as the therapy proceeded. Whenever possible exposure sessions should be conducted during therapy sessions, and the client and therapist should process the client's experience and what that means about the negative automatic thoughts, assumptions, and core beliefs driving the system.

To start, Sundeep and the therapist established guidelines for handwash frequency and duration and standard practice guidelines for due diligence in managing prescriptions. They agreed that the ultimate goal of exposure was to get to the point that his washing and checking were within those parameters. They then identified what Sundeep wanted to target first, looking for an exposure that he could face, but which also truly tested his appraisal of obsessions and compulsions. He noted that the clothes he wore home from the doctor's office were still sitting in a bag in the shed. The therapist asked if he would be willing to bring them into the house and handle them. He visibly blanched and said he simply couldn't do that, but that he could handle them if he washed them first. The therapist then asked if the wash would eradicate his concern they were contaminated, and he said "No, the washing machine is not an autoclave". They agreed that in the next week, he would wash the clothes in a normal way, put them away with his other clothes, and then handle them daily, all without washing his hands afterwards, avoiding touching anything he would normally touch, nor avoiding any tasks he would normally do, such as meal preparation. They made sure to schedule exposure so it was not done just prior to any activity for which it is advised to wash hands, such as preparing food.

Sundeep also agreed to start exposure at work. He was very reluctant to start exposure at work due to his fear of harming someone and of the implications for his employment. To prepare Sundeep for exposure, the therapist reviewed all the steps in Sundeep's work compulsions and together they identified extraneous, repeated, and prolonged steps. The therapist asked Sundeep if he would be willing to begin by simply reducing the latter and cutting out the former, thereby reducing the impact of the compulsions on his work. Sundeep agreed to try this.

Meanwhile, Sundeep's tasks during exposure at home were to attend to what the OCD was telling him without giving in to the urge to self-reassure or otherwise engage it, and to record his distress level before, during, and after exposure. Sundeep was able to do the exposures, although confessed that after he unloaded the clothes, he ran the empty washer again to avoid contaminating future loads of laundry, something that would have been helpful to anticipate and discuss in advance. However, surprises are common when doing exposure, and the therapist told him that it was very helpful to share that information during therapy. Sundeep reported that it felt good to deal with the clothes and that over the week it had become easier and easier to handle them, much to his surprise. At work, Sundeep was able to reduce the steps in his compulsions except when preparing prescriptions that could seriously harm someone if taken in the wrong dose. He also reported that he had found it very gratifying to give up the 'weirder' parts of his compulsions and was starting to believe that striving for certainty made it more, rather than less, challenging to feel confident in his prescriptions.

Sundeep recounted what the OCD voice was saying to him during exposure and, with prompting, was able to identify its inaccuracies, which included the idea he was wholly irresponsible and incompetent for deliberately touching something "contaminated" without washing his hands, and that if he didn't wash his hands, it would bother him all day. The OCD also told him he was more likely to err when filling a "dangerous" prescription than a safer one, but while discussing this he realized that this was patently false. It was revelatory for him that the OCD voice was not correct, and he reported that his belief that he needed to listen and submit to it was now at 70%, down from 100%.

Sundeep said that next he would like to start driving his car, would like to stop sanitizing his hands and the prescription bottles at work, and stop asking people to review his work. Sundeep said he was not ready to get inside his car, so it was agreed that he would wipe the steering wheel with a cloth and then handle the cloth without washing his hands afterwards. If that met with early success, he could then move to handling the cloth and touching something in his children's rooms. For work, he agreed to follow standard workplace guidelines for handwashing, to put pills in bottles without sanitizing them first, and to refrain from asking others to check his work. The therapist reminded Sundeep that these were next-level exposures, so he should expect to feel pretty anxious, but to judge success by what he does (that is, not submit to the OCD) rather than how he feels.

At the next session, Sundeep reported that he had been able to start touching items in his children's rooms after handling the "contaminated" cloth, but it had been very tough. His OCD told him that the virus might have reactivated in the warmth of the house and so would be moral and right for him to not touch things in his children's rooms, and to sanitize whatever he touched already. He was able to do this exposure a few times but was exhausted after, and a couple of times he felt too tired and weak to do it. He admitted that he once went back and sanitized something he had touched in a previous exposure. At work, Sundeep was mostly able to keep handwashing within workplace guidelines and avoid sterilizing bottles. However, he still asked his co-workers to check his work. With respect to his work exposures, Sundeep acknowledged that he had "cheated" in his exposures by ensuring his co-workers shared responsibility for any harm. The therapist normalized Sundeep's challenges and noted that he would get stronger as therapy proceeded, but that the goal is to ensure he always has an opportunity for new learning, which "cheating" deprived him of. Despite these lapses, Sundeep said he was starting to view the OCD voice as misleading rather than authoritative, and his belief that he had to listen and submit to the OCD voice had weakened from 60% to 30%.

For next steps, Sundeep wanted to start driving his car, but not with his children yet. It was established that he would drive his car and then behave as he would have before the virus obsession started, without changing clothes, avoiding touching anything, etc. At work, he agreed to continue the same exposures, but with the recognition that asking co-workers to oversee his work made the OCD stronger, and completely obstructed his goal of being the pharmacist he wanted to be. They agreed that if, in the moment, he was overcome by the urge to ask a co-worker to check his prescription, he would put the prescription aside and come back to it later. If at home he was too tired to take on the OCD, they agreed that no matter what, he would do an exposure that he could manage, rather than doing no exposure. The following week Sundeep reported it was like "a log-jam had broken". He reported almost total success with the exposures, and he had started refusing to give into other compulsive urges. He was now able to hug his children at bedtime (although confessed he washed his hands first), and was no longer sanitizing bottles, washing his hands excessively, or asking his co-workers to review his work. He did say that he still found the idea of fully "taking the risk" of doing no compulsions when filling 'dangerous' prescriptions daunting.

15.3.5   Sessions 8–12

Sundeep now had had considerable experience recognizing that thoughts are not facts and that his OCD hijacked his perception of obsessions, compulsions, and threat estimations, and he was learning through exposure and behavioural experiments that the OCD was misleading. Next, deeper-level ideas were addressed. Initially, the therapist used Socratic dialogue in session to target key assumptions and core beliefs (see Purdon, 2021). In the example in which Sundeep's son sneezed and coughed, the primary source of distress was his appraisal that he could not trust his own judgement about what the sneeze and cough signified, resulting in panic, tortuous striving for perfect certainty as to whether it signalled the virus, and helpless indecision about what to do. Sundeep and the therapist agreed that a key culprit in the persistence of his OCD was his idea that perfect certainty was important and necessary, due to his perceived character flaws and shortcomings. Please note this presents a truncated version of the discussion, which took place over 45 minutes; it has been edited to highlight the key questions and key insights.

Therapist: So, the OCD is telling you that you must have perfect certainty the virus has not been transmitted before it is moral and safe to ignore the obsession.

Sundeep: Yes, exactly.

Therapist: You and I have often noted that in your pharmacy training the expectation is not certainty that you have not made errors, but rather following the guidelines and protocols designed to avoid errors. Yet you have applied a much higher standard to yourself, one that, as we have discussed, is impossible and unverifiable.

Sundeep: I just can't get past that the stakes are so high, and if what I'm worried about does happen, at least I will have tried to prevent it.

Therapist: This illustrates a key stuck point for you; you believe that people expect you to do everything you can to ensure you have prevented harm, at any cost. It seems that this is driving the certainty.

Sundeep: Yes, exactly. If I didn't do everything I could and if I stop without good reason, and harm comes and everyone will hate me.

Therapist: Does that apply to everyone or just you?

Sundeep: Well, just me. Which, I guess, goes back to that I am not a natural pharmacist, and I almost killed my grandmother, so I can't really trust myself, so if I don't compensate for all that people will rightly be mad at me.

Therapist: So first, let's look at your idea about being a natural pharmacist. Even if you don't think of yourself as a natural pharmacist, let's reflect on what level of knowledge and experience have you gained.

Sundeep: I have taken a lot of extra courses and seminars to help the particular clientele we have at our store. I have done a lot of work with people who struggle with addiction, and other pharmacists call me to consult about their patients. I also am asked to supervise practicum students (well, until this stupid OCD thing got so bad) and the students always gave me great evaluations.

Therapist: I wonder if it is possible to be competent even if it's not one's natural calling.

Sundeep: Yes, I actually know more than another pharmacist at the store who wanted to be a pharmacist since high school, and he's got more years of experience than me.

Therapist: So, your original idea was that because pharmacy is not your true calling, you are less competent at it. What do you think of that idea now?

Sundeep: That idea doesn't make a lot of sense. Just because it's not my true calling doesn't mean I don't know how to do it well.

Therapist: Let's turn to the event with your grandmother. I know it is upsetting not only because of the harm that might have befallen her but because it has always signified to you that you are careless and irresponsible. If you were to visit your former self after your parents expressed their anger, what would adult Sundeep say to 13-year old Sundeep?

Sundeep: I would say, you didn't have the training or authority to look after a person with dementia. I would also say the parents over-reacted because they were scared. And you didn't try to kill her, that's just wrong. You were trying to keep her safe when she left. And she wasn't even hurt! She could have just as easily fallen down the stairs inside the house as become hurt when she left the house.

Therapist: I am wondering, then, if we might want to reconsider 13-year old Sundeep's understanding of that event and update it with adult Sundeep's more informed perspective.

Sundeep: Okay, well, it was unfortunate, and I wish I had known she was in danger of bolting, but it could have happened to anyone – it could have happened to my parents! - and she wasn't harmed, and I can't control everything.

Therapist: That does seem like a better fit given our discussion. So, let's take this back to the need for certainty. That need is based on the idea you have character flaws and incompetencies, and you need to prove to others that you are aware of them and are always trying to overcome them.

Sundeep: Yes.

Therapist: I am wondering if it is the case that people will hold you responsible if something happens even if you did reasonable, due diligence? For example, does your wife become as exasperated with you if something happens despite due diligence as she does with your compulsions?

Sundeep: [laughs] Ha, you know, she doesn't blame me if something goes wrong, even if I didn't do it due diligence! She always says that stuff happens and you just deal. And neither does my sister. Or my children. My parents, that's another story.

Therapist: I am wondering what your thoughts are now about your compulsions and the need for certainty?

Sundeep: It's b-----t. Destructive b------t.

In the proceeding sessions, the therapist used the Socratic dialogue to address the meaning of the incident with his grandmother and that he is not a natural pharmacist, which paved the way to tackling the core belief that he was not trustworthy. To address core belief, the therapist used the continuum method. The therapist asked Sundeep to identify a person, dead or alive, fictional or nonfictional, who is the least trustworthy of all, and one who is the most trustworthy of all, and put their names on the left and right ends of a 100 mm horizontal line, respectively. On the left, Sundeep listed the captain of the Exxon Valdez, which leaked a massive amount of oil and destroyed a pristine coastline, and on the right, Winston Churchill. The therapist asked Sundeep to then identify the qualities that inform his sense of "trustworthiness". He listed reliability, conscientiousness, integrity, excellent training, strong knowledge, staying within your sphere of knowledge, being accountable, and being proactive.

Sundeep then identified someone he has known personally who would fall towards the untrustworthy end of the continuum, and one who would fall towards the other end. He identified two practicum supervisors, one who drank on the job and one who taught Sundeep a wide range of excellent skills, placing them about 15 mm from their respective ends. He then placed a close friend, then his wife, and finally himself on the line. Sundeep was surprised to realize that realistically he fell around where his wife fell, at about 70 mm on the line. He noted that when it came to himself, reliability and conscientiousness were the only qualities by which he judged trustworthiness, and he had always assumed he was neither. This discussion, combined with the discussion of the event with his grandmother was revelatory; for the first time in his adult life, Sundeep was able to view himself as normal, rather than tragically flawed. They agreed that Sundeep would spend the next week catching himself being trustworthy.

During this phase of treatment, Sundeep also did several behavioural experiments. The OCD voice told him that if he filled prescriptions without doing his checking compulsions, he was more likely to make errors. To explore this assumption, they agreed that for several days he would fill prescriptions that were to be picked up the following day without doing his compulsive checking. At the end of each day, he would check each once to see how many errors he made. However, when checking for errors he was to use his judgement as the well-trained, conscientious pharmacist he is, and checking them just as he would those of his trainees, rather than checking to assuage his obsessional concerns. After filling 30 prescriptions without doing his compulsions he found he had made no mistakes, noting only that he could have used a smaller bottle than he did for one prescription. He also realized that applying his own judgement was far less onerous and fraught than trying to get perfect certainty. They also discussed what happens if a pharmacist makes a mistake. Sundeep reported that there is a clear protocol to follow, which means that mistakes sometimes do happen. This led to a discussion of whether pharmacists are defined by their very rare errors, or by other factors. Sundeep had several "aha" moments in the course of this exposure, including the recognition that he had only judged himself by what he perceived to be errors, that he hadn't given himself the chance to learn whether he could trust himself, and that trusting his judgement was liberating.

At the end of treatment, Sundeep's YBOCS score had fallen to 13, which is in the "mild" range. He rated his success in being responsible at 80% and his success in being a caring, loving person at 85%. His belief that he couldn't trust his judgement declined from 85% to 20%. He still had obsessional thoughts about harm but was able to "hear" them without engaging them. At work, he was much more efficient and had increasingly more time for consultation. Sundeep reported that he was also beginning to stand up to his parents' criticisms. Most importantly, Sundeep was now enjoying a loving, affectionate relationship with his children.

15.4   Special Challenges and Problems

In the initial stages of treatment, Sundeep's OCD was active in the therapy room and would try to take over, particularly when he thought the goals facilitated by the compulsion (e.g., protecting his children) were under threat. It proved helpful to make a distinction between Sundeep himself and the anxiety-driven OCD system that hijacked his perceptions, which Sundeep and the therapist termed the "OCD voice". When the OCD voice was speaking, Sundeep would become intense, anxious, argumentative, and demanding, his discourse peppered with "Yes but…" and "What if…?" When this happened, the therapist would say "Your OCD is speaking right now and I don't want to hear from it, I want to hear from you, Sundeep. What do you, Sundeep think?" This strategy also helped Sundeep recognize for himself when his OCD was taking over in between the sessions, or, as he put it, he learned to recognize when "OCD is in the house".

The therapist also avoided challenging the obsessional thoughts themselves, and instead targeted the thoughts and behaviours that supported the OCD system. Sundeep's problem was not that he erroneously believed he was going to transmit a harmful virus to his children, or err with a prescription, but rather that he was unwilling to trust his own judgement, that he required a high degree of certainty that he had not erred or caused harm before he could move on, that if he bore any responsibility for harm others would reject/censure him, and that repeating his compulsions perpetuated them. The therapist did not want to desensitize Sundeep's feelings about his children being seriously ill or of poisoning a patient as this would have given the meta-message that to overcome his OCD Sundeep must forgo values of critical importance to him. Even if this approach helped de-toxify a particular obsession, the system would remain intact, and new obsessions would inevitably surface.

Finally, although it is a tradition in CBT to refer to between session work as "homework" the therapist avoided using this term because it can be experienced as infantilizing, it creates a teacher/pupil dynamic rather than a collaborative dynamic, and homework is something that is typically treated as optional rather than integral, depending on the mark the person wishes to get. Much can be gained from simply collaborating with the patient about what changes to make in their response to their obsessional thoughts over the next week rather than prescribing homework.

15.5   Summary, Conclusions, and Learning Points

Sundeep was a highly motivated patient with whom the therapist readily established a strong rapport and trust. Other keys to the success as a team were staying focused on the appraisal of the obsession rather than its content, refusing to engage the OCD voice in session, establishing the moral grounds for changing how he responded to his obsessions, recognizing that compulsions advance critically important goals, and proceeding at a pace that was manageable for him. Finally, it was necessary to address Sundeep's underlying core beliefs about his competence and ability/willingness to trust himself before he was willing to fully challenge his OCD voice. If we hadn't done so, his ability to tolerate uncertainty in "high stake" situations would have remained low and perceived the need to do his compulsions high.

References

Obsessive Compulsive Cognitions Working Group. (1997). Cognitive assessment of obsessive-compulsive disorder. *Behaviour Research and Therapy, 35*(7), 667–681.

Obsessive Compulsive Cognitions Working Group. (2001). Development and initial validation of the obsessive beliefs questionnaire and the interpretation of intrusions inventory. *Behaviour Research and Therapy, 39*(8), 987–1006.

Obsessive Compulsive Cognitions Working Group. (2003). Psychometric validation of the obsessive beliefs questionnaire and the interpretation of intrusions inventory: Part I. *Behaviour Research and Therapy, 41*(8), 863–878.

Purdon, C. (2018). There is a lot more to compulsions than meets the eye. *Clinical Neuropsychiatry, 15*(5), 291–298. https://doi.org/10.13140/RG.2.2.28139.18725

Purdon, C. (2021). Cognitive restructuring. Invited chapter for A. In Wenzel (Ed.), *Handbook of cognitive behavioral therapy* (Vol. 1, pp. 207–234). American Psychological Association.

Sheehan, D. V., Lecrubier, Y., Sheehan, K. H., Amorim, P., Janavs, J., Weiller, E., et al. (1998). The Mini-International Neuropsychiatric Interview (MINI): The development and validation of a structured diagnostic psychiatric interview for DSM-IV and ICD-10. *Journal of Clinical Psychiatry, 59*(20), 22–33.

Storch, E. A., Rasmussen, S. A., Price, L. H., Larson, M. J., Murphy, T. K., & Goodman, W. K. (2010). Development and psychometric evaluation of the Yale-Brown Obsessive-Compulsive Scale--second edition. *Psychological Assessment, 22*(2), 223–232. https://doi.org/10.1037/a0018492

Christine Purdon is a Professor of Psychology at the University of Waterloo (Canada) and the Director of the Clinical Training program for the university's PhD program in Clinical Psychology. Christine Purdon is an expert on OCD, anxiety, and CBT. In her research, she focusses on the persistence of anxiety and its cognitive (e.g., obsessions, worry) and behavioural manifestations (e.g., compulsions, avoidance). Further, she is a registered psychologist with the College of Psychologists of Ontario and has expertise in the assessment and treatment of mood and anxiety disorders in adults. She has taught and supervised CBT for over two decades.

Chapter 16
"I Don't Want to Bother You" – A Case Study in Social Anxiety Disorder

Katharine E. Daniel and Bethany A. Teachman

16.1 The Case

16.1.1 Presenting Problem

Gi, a 34-year-old second-generation Korean American man, lives with his wife, adolescent daughter, and biological parents. Gi is the full-time caretaker of his father, who has late-stage colon cancer, and Gi is responsible for running the majority of the family's errands. Gi and his wife recently sought treatment for their 14-year-old daughter, Hea, who has been experiencing depressed mood and anxiety in social situations over the past year. After a few family therapy sessions, Hea's therapist hypothesized that Gi's long-standing patterns of social avoidance and accommodation behaviors were interfering with Hea's treatment. Motivated to support his daughter more effectively, Gi presented to individual treatment.

16.1.2 History

Gi described that, during his adolescence, his parents only seemed to share happy, positive emotions with him and his younger brother. Negative emotions, on the other hand, were 'brushed under the rug.' Further, due to his parents' lack of English language proficiency, Gi was often expected to communicate on their behalf with doctors, car mechanics, and other service providers. Although Gi wanted to help and his parents were very appreciative, Gi noticed that these service providers

K. E. Daniel · B. A. Teachman (✉)
Department of Psychology, University of Virginia, Charlottesville, VA, USA
e-mail: ked4fd@virginia.edu; bteachman@virgina.edu

© The Author(s), under exclusive license to Springer Nature Switzerland AG 2023   301
M. L. Woud (ed.), *Interpretational Processing Biases in Emotional Psychopathology*,
CBT: Science Into Practice, https://doi.org/10.1007/978-3-031-23650-1_16

always seemed to be in a rush to end the conversation with him. He started to worry that this meant they were bothered by his 'stupid' questions. Finally, Gi experienced his classmates as critical and rejecting throughout his childhood. For example, he shared that they would make fun of him for being sweaty and smelly after recess. Likely due to these early formative experiences, Gi developed beliefs that sharing negative emotions with others is rude and burdensome, that he is incompetent and an annoyance, and that others are critical and rejecting. Gi's social anxiety is long-standing but had recently become more impairing and pressing due to his father's medical deterioration and Gi's subsequent need to communicate with many medical professionals. Also, Gi recognized that he needed to enter more social situations with his daughter as part of her treatment, which he is committed to supporting. Further, self-critical thoughts about jeopardizing his daughter's treatment and guilt around modeling socially avoidant tendencies throughout her childhood have contributed to Gi's worsened mood and low self-esteem, which in turn made him more certain that others will judge him harshly.

16.1.3   Chief Symptoms

Gi described a very limited social life outside of his family. When in public or while talking to service providers on the phone, he noted experiencing blurred vision, racing heart, shaking and sweaty hands, and a red face. He also reported trouble speaking loudly enough to be heard. Because of this, he shared that it is very distressing to run errands for his family, to communicate with Hea's teachers, or to go on family outings given he thinks that others will judge him for these 'weird' and 'rude' displays of anxiety. However, because duty to family and personal responsibility are very important to Gi, he would endure these everyday tasks with significant distress while going to extreme lengths to mitigate the perceived risk of being judged negatively during them. For example, Gi would only go to the grocery store when fewer than 15 cars were in the parking lot, and he never entered an aisle that had more than one other person in it. If 'too many' cars were in the parking lot, he would leave and come back later in the day. If the final item on his shopping list was in a crowded aisle, he would either walk around the store for as long as it took until the aisle cleared, or he would leave without buying what he needed. Gi shared that he found the amount of time and effort he put into this planning and avoidance pattern very restrictive and exhausting. At the time of intake, Gi met criteria for social anxiety disorder and comorbid major depressive disorder, single episode, mild. Social anxiety disorder was conceptualized as the primary diagnosis given Gi's depressive episode seemed to be driven by self-critical thinking tied to his persistent social avoidance.

16.2   Main Cognitions Targeted

Guided by the cognitive behavior therapy (CBT) (Beck, 2020) framework, the therapist approached Gi's case with special attention to the interpretations, assumptions, and beliefs that seemed to maintain his social anxiety. The way Gi saw himself and others' views of him seemed to be informed by a deeply held belief that "I am incompetent" and an expectation that others are critical and rejecting. This, coupled with dysfunctional assumptions that "I should never waste someone's time or get in someone's way," "Asking for help is annoying," and "It's rude to show negative emotions to others" contributed to Gi's experience of the world as a socially threatening place. From a CBT perspective, Gi's fear and avoidance of social situations was understandable given these beliefs and assumptions: he saw himself as both incompetent and unable to ask for help, he thought others were likely to be harsh and rejecting, and he thought showing signs of anxiety would give people more reason to reject him for "being rude."

To promote Gi and the therapist's shared treatment goal of reducing rigid avoidance and excessive planning around activities of daily life, in addition to exposure exercises (see below), the therapist identified the need to increase Gi's perceived competency, reduce Gi's fear of negative evaluation, and help Gi gain a more balanced perspective on help-seeking and emotional disclosure. Knowing that deeply held beliefs and dysfunctional assumptions like those expressed by Gi are challenging to shift directly (Beck, 2020), the therapist first worked with Gi to identify and shift situation-specific negative automatic thoughts throughout treatment. This process was expected to undermine the legitimacy of Gi's core beliefs and dysfunctional assumptions over time (Beck, 2020). For example, when imagining what it might be like to order food for his family from a drive-thru, Gi predicted, "I'll get so anxious that I won't be able to function and all the cars behind me will start honking and yelling at me for being too slow." This thought relied on the assumption that he was incapable of ordering food without making others angry with him. Believing in the accuracy of his worst-case scenario prediction, Gi anxiously avoided the drive-thru which, in turn, meant that his core belief was never questioned by disconfirming evidence.

Gi also tended to make assumptions about what others were thinking about him. Sometimes this happened as a statement that raced through his mind (e.g., "The store clerk thinks I'm rude"), and other times he pictured people laughing at him behind his back, like after he walked past them in the grocery store. Gi treated these thoughts and images as evidence that others do reject him. Even though they weren't reality-based, these thoughts maintained his fear of negative evaluation and avoidance of social situations. Relatedly, Gi also tended to think in extremes: "I forgot to change my dad's colostomy bag earlier today, I'm a terrible son." His incredibly high standards with no margin for error set him up to fall short, which he would then take as further evidence that he was in fact incapable.

The therapist's case conceptualization therefore focused on how these types of dysfunctional cognitions – predicting that the worst possible outcome would come true (*catastrophizing/fortune telling*), assuming that he knew what others were thinking about him (*mind reading*), and extreme thinking (*all-or-nothing thinking*) – maintained Gi's unhelpful behavioral responses and prolonged his emotional suffering. See Fig. 16.1 for a representation of the relationship between Gi's cognitions, physical sensations of anxiety, and behavioral responses.

16.3 Treatment

In this section, Gi's 17-session course of treatment is presented, focusing on collaborative efforts to identify and shift unhelpful cognitions. Gi's treatment was divided into three phases. The main treatment aims and interventions used during each phase will be outlined, and it will be discussed how collaborative empiricism,

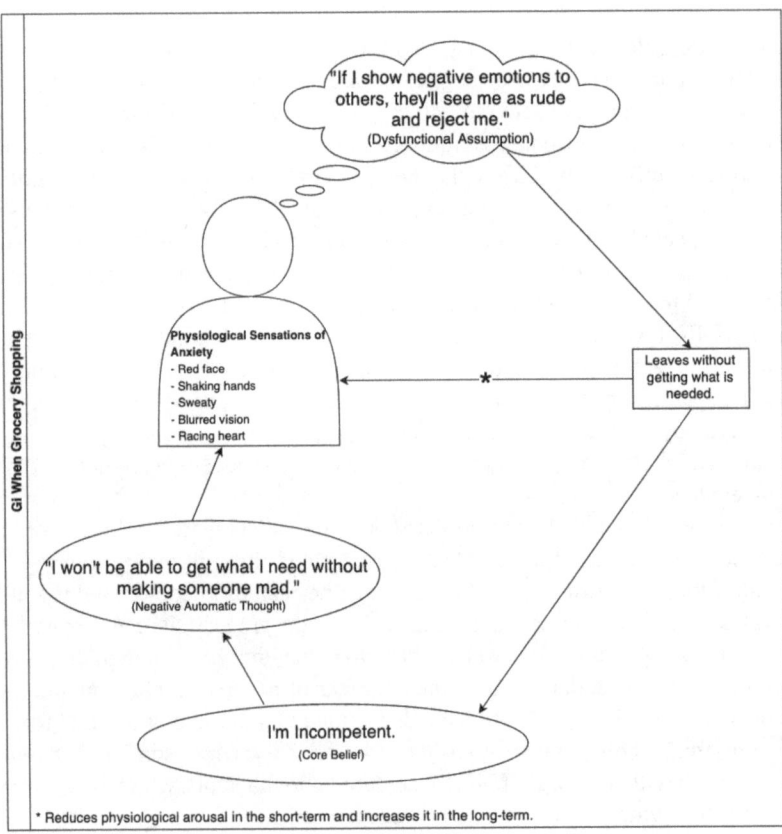

Fig. 16.1 Depiction of the relationship between Gi's thoughts, sensations, and behaviors while grocery shopping

including the use of routine outcome monitoring and being responsive to Gi's cultural context and preferences, informed treatment decisions throughout.

16.3.1   Phase 1 (Sessions 1–6)

Gi presented to his intake appointment via telehealth during the first year of the COVID-19 pandemic. At the beginning of his initial session, Gi's affect was anxious, and his face was so red and heated that his glasses became fogged. Based on his anxious presentation, the therapist created space to explore how Gi felt about the present meeting and normalized that many people feel uncomfortable when starting therapy.

> **Therapist:** It's really nice to meet you, Gi. You know, people feel all sorts of ways when they start therapy. Sometimes they're excited and hopeful. Other times they're terrified or anxious. Maybe even angry or embarrassed. Sometimes they have a mixture of feelings, even ones that don't seem like they should go together. How do you feel about being here today?
> **Gi:** Kind of embarrassed, I guess.
> **Therapist:** It can be really vulnerable to start this process. Being embarrassed usually makes people want to hide. I'm really impressed that you came today even though you're feeling embarrassed. That's a strength that I think will really help you pursue your treatment goals. Tell me more about why you're feeling embarrassed.
> **Gi:** I don't know… It's just…I've had a hard time with social things for a long time. It's really taken over. It seems silly that I've waited this long. Anyone else would have gotten help years ago…I guess I'm just a coward.

Already Gi and the therapist have uncovered an unhelpful cognition. The therapist took this opportunity to briefly comment on the power of thoughts like those to stir up emotions (embarrassment) and behaviors (delayed treatment seeking) that can keep people stuck. This demonstrated to Gi that the process he described as 'silly' is actually understandable and allowed the therapist to begin to familiarize Gi with the CBT model. The therapist also shared with Gi that over a third of people with social anxiety disorder do not seek treatment for 10 or more years (ADAA, 2022). Sharing this statistic conveyed the therapist's deep appreciation for how challenging it must have been for Gi to take a risk by showing up to therapy. It also normalized that many people experiencing similar fears wait just as long, if not longer, to ask for help, which gently offered evidence to counter the unhelpful thought Gi expressed. At this point, Gi's face became less red, and he was able to talk more openly about his experiences.

To guide case conceptualization and collaborative treatment planning, the therapist, who identified as a non-Hispanic white woman in her late 20 s, created space to explore how Gi saw aspects of his identity in relation to the treatment process.

Therapist: What do you see as the most important parts of your identity? Some people raise their gender, sexual orientation, ethnicity and culture, religion, or ability status. Some people raise multiple identities or ones beyond those I offered.
Gi: That I'm a second-generation Korean American.
Therapist: What are the most important aspects of this identity for you?
Gi: Being there for my family and supporting them any way I can.
Therapist: You really value your family. What aspects of this identity do you think make a difference for your mental health?
Gi: … It was hard to come in for this. We don't talk about mental health very openly.
Therapist: You're taking a risk here. How do you feel to be talking to someone about your mental health? Especially someone who is White, who doesn't share this important part of your identity?
Gi: I'd be uncomfortable talking to anyone about this stuff, to be honest. In some ways it might even feel a bit easier to talk to you because you aren't Korean. I don't know… but I guess it's important to me to make sure other people, even people I don't know, are not put out by me. I guess I worry that a therapist with Western values might try to get me to put myself over others. That wouldn't feel right to me.

The therapist non-defensively reflected his concern and positively reinforced him for raising it, and joined with him by sharing that the therapist's role is to help him find ways of living that are in line with his values and preferences, but that are more effective and sustainable for him in the long term than what he has been doing up to this point. Gi then shared that his primary goal for treatment was to be able to run errands when it's most convenient for him and to not have to schedule around how many other people were likely to be where he needed to go.

Therapist: It's exhausting to live your life on anxiety's terms. Anxiety is really good at protecting us from danger. If something is dangerous, it makes a lot of sense to avoid it. Back away from the cliff's edge on a rainy day! The trouble with anxiety starts when anxiety makes us think that we're in danger when it's not likely that we're facing an objective threat. Anxiety is acting as a false alarm. But our body doesn't really know the difference between anxiety due to a true threat and anxiety due to a false alarm. It feels the same and it's really uncomfortable. I'm curious, when you're in the store and you decide not to turn down the crowded aisle, what happens next?

Gi: I feel relieved. My hands stop shaking. No one said anything to me.
Therapist: Exactly…phew! The trouble is, now, without realizing it, you've learned that the reason nothing bad happened is *because* you avoided going down that crowded aisle. You never get to see what would have happened if you had walked down that aisle. Maybe no one would have even noticed you. Or, maybe if someone did say something kind of rude, you could have handled it okay. You have no idea. But, if you *think* the reason you stayed safe is *because* you avoided the aisle, what do you guess you're likely to do the next time you see that the bread aisle is crowded?
Gi: I'd avoid it.
Therapy: Totally! And avoiding it makes perfect sense given the contingency that you've set up. But it turns out that anxiety is really good at getting us to overestimate the likelihood that something bad will happen and underestimate our ability to manage bad things that do happen. So, if we only listen to our anxious thoughts, our life can get small. We never go down the bread aisle if someone else is there. In our work together we're going to find a bunch of different ways to reconsider anxious thoughts so that *you* get to decide when and how you do something, not anxiety. How does that sound?

The therapist then introduced the rationale for exposure therapy from an expectancy violation perspective. Whereas exposures were initially assumed to operate through habituation (Foa & Kozak, 1986), the expectancy violation theory of exposure assumes that exposures work by challenging long-standing beliefs through hypothesis testing (Craske et al., 2014): The patient articulates their feared expectancies ahead of time, carries out the exposure, and then makes sense of what did or did not happen *and why*. Oftentimes the patient is surprised to find that the terrible outcomes they expected to happen didn't happen, which promotes cognitive change. As such, exposures from this perspective are quite similar to behavioral experiments.

To increase Gi's buy-in to this treatment approach, the therapist used motivational interviewing techniques (Miller & Rollnick, 2012) to amplify Gi's reasons for choosing to tolerate his anxiety while 'testing out' his anxious predictions through exposures and behavioral experiments. He reported being motivated to engage in this treatment to support his daughter, spend less time planning errands, and spend more time with his ailing father. The therapist ensured that Gi understood why treatment would initially focus on approaching anxiety-provoking activities and shared that CBT is the gold-standard treatment approach for social anxiety disorder. The therapist also asked Gi what he thought about this treatment approach given his personal and cultural views. Because Gi reported that he thought the treatment approach was acceptable and in line with his goals, the remainder of the intake session involved identifying the social domains which bring up the most anxiety for Gi using the Social Anxiety Questionnaire (Leahy et al., 2012). He also completed the straight-forwardly worded factor of the Brief Fear of Negative Evaluation scale

Table 16.1 Testing it out

My Goal: *Go to the grocery store on Sunday at 3 pm and get something from the middle of an aisle with more than four other people in that aisle.*	
Why my goal is important to me: *I can get what I need when it makes the most sense for my schedule. I don't have to spend time wandering around the store until the aisle clears out or driving back and forth between the grocery store and home. I can use the time I save to be with my dad or do something else that interests me.*	
Before Exposure	
What I am most worried will happen:	*I'll get so anxious that I won't be able to function. I'll just stand there, frozen and in the way, until the people in the aisle get annoyed with me for taking too long. My hand will be shaking so much that when I do go to reach for something, I'll knock a bunch of things from the shelves on the ground. Then I'll just leave without getting anything.*
Expected SUDS:	*80*
Likelihood this will happen (0–100):	*70%*
How I will know if it happens:	*Someone will say "Get out of my way" and their tone of voice will be rude.*
After Exposure	
SUDS walking up:	*85*
Peak SUDS:	*90 – Going to reach for the jar of pasta sauce.*
What I was most worried about actually happened:	Yes/(No)
I knew this because:	*None of the other shoppers seemed to notice me. No one said anything to me, and I didn't see them make any gestures in my direction.*
What I learned:	*Even when I'm incredibly anxious I can still do what I need to do. I got the pasta sauce without making a scene even though my hands were shaking badly.*
If I did this again, I am _20%_ sure my feared outcome would happen.	

Note. SUDS Subjective Units of Distress Scale

(BFNE-S) (Norton & Weeks, 2019), which has good reliability for Asian samples (Harpole et al., 2015), and the Social Thoughts and Beliefs Scale (STABS) (Turner et al., 2003).

Gi's second session focused on collaboratively building an exposure hierarchy. The therapist then encouraged Gi to pick an activity on his hierarchy to try before the next session. The remainder of the session was spent filling out the 'Before Exposure' section of the *Testing It Out* worksheet (Table 16.1; adapted from Craske et al., 2014), which was designed to establish the expectancies that he would test through the exposure. Gi predicted that if he tried to grab an item from the middle of a crowded grocery aisle that he would get so anxious that his shaking hand would knock things over and the shoppers around him would become annoyed with him. For homework, Gi completed his first exposure activity. Counter to his prediction, Gi found that he was able to get a jar of pasta sauce without making a mess or getting into a confrontation with the other shoppers *even though* he was extremely anxious, and his hands were shaking uncontrollably. This experience violated his expectation and taught Gi that his ability to function does not totally disappear when he is anxious. As such, this experience began to undermine Gi's core belief that he was 'incapable' because he saw first-hand that he was able to perform a task that he otherwise predicted he would not be able to perform. It also challenged his biased probability estimation by showing him that his feared outcome did not happen as often as he expected. At the beginning of the next session, the therapist supported Gi in filling out the rest of the *Testing it Out* worksheet to consolidate the new learning offered by this disconfirming evidence.

Gi repeated this process over the next four sessions for a range of activities. To generalize his new learning, and to further undermine his core belief that he is 'incapable,' the therapist encouraged Gi to try activities in different domains that mattered to him (i.e., changing a doctor's appointment, asking a store clerk for help, ordering something from a drive-thru). After the first two exposure activities, the therapist discovered that Gi had been mentally rehearsing what he would do or say leading up to his exposures to reduce the perceived likelihood that he would 'mess up.' The therapist labeled this as a safety behavior (Piccirillo et al., 2016) that likely maintained his anxiety by teaching him that he can complete tasks *only* if he spends considerable time planning them out in his head. The therapist emphasized the importance of trying out his exposure tasks *without* mental rehearsal to facilitate more adaptive learning so that he can perform activities of daily life without excessive preparation. After labeling and then reducing this safety behavior in future exposures, the therapist noticed that Gi had begun to report spending less time planning and delaying errands and that he thought anxiety and avoidance were not getting in the way of his personal goals as often. Despite these positive behavioral changes, and higher levels of self-efficacy, his BFNE-S and STABS scores had not reduced. This suggested that the therapy had thus far not sufficiently helped Gi internalize desired new learning across all important areas of his thinking. Specifically, Gi remained convinced that if he did not perform a task 'correctly' and unobtrusively (e.g., if he did drop the jar of pasta sauce), then he would be seen as rude and be rejected. The therapist hypothesized that, although the exposure exercises had helped Gi begin to see himself as more capable, which had reduced his avoidance, his 'successful' completions of these exposure tasks did not challenge his expectancy that even minor missteps would result in ridicule, which kept his fear of negative evaluation and anxious thinking elevated.

To address the remaining high fear of negative evaluation and rigid anxious thinking, the therapist considered assigning exposures where Gi made mistakes in front of other people. However, hypothesizing that Gi would find those exposures less acceptable based on the cultural norms he described during an earlier conversation, the therapist decided to first offer additional cognitive strategies that might help Gi to develop more balanced thinking around the interpersonal significance of making mistakes. The therapist also thought it might be helpful to more closely explore if and how aspects of Gi's cultural identity relate to his fear of negative evaluation. With these considerations in mind, the therapist decided to shift towards directly exploring the thoughts and feelings Gi held about himself in interpersonal situations in a second phase of treatment (e.g., "Sharing negative emotions is burdensome to others and rude"). With this shift in therapy, the therapist hypothesized that promoting more flexible, values-aligned thinking would amplify the positive learning from exposures and behavioral experiments, and increase the likelihood that Gi would be willing to engage in future exposures where he intentionally made mistakes.

16.3.2 Phase 2 (Sessions 7–12)

To lay the foundation for flexible thinking skill development, the therapist provided psychoeducation around different styles of unhelpful thinking. As such, Gi was encouraged to log thoughts and images that occurred throughout the week that elicited strong emotions of anxiety, sadness, or shame. From the thought logs he brought to the session, Gi noticed that he tended to catastrophize, mind read, and fall into all-or-nothing thinking.

> **Therapist:** When the hospice nurse asked you when you had last changed your dad's colostomy bag, what went through your mind?
> **Gi:** I was mortified.
> **Therapist:** And what thought or image went through your mind?
> **Gi:** She thinks I'm neglectful.

The therapist then used Socratic questioning to help Gi label this thought as mind reading and explore the evidence for and against this negative automatic thought. For example, when Gi said evidence 'for' the thought was "She just looked disgusted in me," the therapist asked if that evidence would hold up in court. When he admitted it wouldn't, the therapist helped him identify concrete pieces of evidence by asking questions like "If someone else had been watching, what would they have noticed?" Throughout this exercise, Gi was able to construct a more balanced thought (i.e., "I'm not sure what she thought, but I think she was trying to help me find ways to take care of Dad more effectively and easily. She probably knows better than most people how much work it takes to look after someone who needs so much care, and it sounds like she's had these conversations with other caregivers before and she didn't seem to judge them."). He reported that his feeling of being mortified decreased from 90 to 40 (out of 100) after he restructured his initial "She thinks I'm neglectful" negative automatic thought to this more balanced interpretation. However, his feelings of guilt did not diminish after generating this restructured thought, which suggested to the therapist that another thought was driving his feeling of guilt. Gi's completed Though Record is reproduced in Table 16.2.

> **Therapist:** I notice that your guilty feeling is still at 95/100. That's a really powerful feeling. I wonder, what does it mean about you that you forgot to change his colostomy bag for about a half hour?
> **Gi:** That I'm a terrible son.

Table 16.2 Example thought record

Situation	Emotion or Feeling	Negative Automatic Thought	Evidence that supports the thought	Evidence that does not support the thought	Alternative Thought	Emotion or Feeling
Hospice nurse asked when the last time it was that I changed Dad's colostomy bag.	Mortified (90) Guilty (95)	"She thinks I'm neglectful." (mind reading)	~~She seemed disgusted in me.~~[a] She shook her head slightly. She gave a bunch of medical reasons to emphasize why it was important to change that bag regularly.	She did not report me to adult protective services. She offered a few suggestions for how to make it easier on me to remember to change his bag regularly. She said the ideas she gave me have also helped other caregivers keep track of all the things they have to remember. (Maybe this means other people forget sometimes, too?)	"I'm not sure what she thought, but I think she was trying to help me find ways to take care of Dad more effectively and easily. She probably knows better than most people how much work it takes to look after someone who needs so much care, and it sounds like she's had these conversations with other caregivers before and she didn't seem to judge them."	Mortified (40) Guilty (95)
Describe what was happening (who, what, when, where).	e.g., angry, sad, scared Rate 0–100	Identify core thought to work on. What thoughts, images, or memories were going through your mind?	What facts support the truthfulness of this thought or image?	What information supports the fact that this thought is not completely true all of the time? If my best friend had this thought, what would I tell them? Are there any small experiences that contradict this thought?	What's a new thought that considers the evidence for and against the original thought?	Rate 0–100

Note. [a]"She seemed disgusted in me" is crossed out to reflect Gi's realization that this statement was not evidence that would hold up in court

The therapist thought back to an earlier conversation when Gi shared that he deeply valued his family and their comfort, and reflected on how painful this situation must have been, given how at odds his interpretation of this event was with what he cares about most. The therapist then drew a line on a piece of paper and labeled one end with 'terrible son' and the other end with 'perfect son.' Gi was encouraged to write down examples of things that he thought a perfect son does and examples of things that he thought a terrible son does. The therapist also encouraged him to generate examples that weren't so extreme (e.g., "What would a son who is exactly in the middle of this continuum do?"; "What would a son who is 20 percent away from being terrible do?"). Finally, Gi was asked to place on the continuum where he thought that he fit. Gi was surprised to see that, even though he didn't see himself as perfect, his actions didn't seem to belong anywhere near the terrible son label. He reported that using the continuum method helped relieve him of some guilt.

The therapist was impressed by how quickly Gi learned these cognitive restructuring skills, but also suspected that Gi's value of prioritizing the comfort of others might still be at odds with how he was thinking about exposures. With this in mind, the therapist asked:

Therapist: We've talked before about how aspects of your identity as a Korean American sometimes impact your beliefs and what matters to you. I am curious if you think your different identities influence how you think about being anxious in front of others?

Gi: I learned from my parents not to bring up negative emotions, only happy ones. It wasn't that they were cold, it's just that they would switch the topic and bring up something happy the minute me or my brother said something wasn't going well. I guess that taught me that showing negative emotions makes people uncomfortable and it's rude to do that. I never want to make anyone uncomfortable. Like when my hands are shaking in the grocery store... I think it makes the other shoppers feel weird and I don't want to cause them to feel that way, so I stay away.

Therapist: What are the parts of that upbringing that you value and want to hang on to?

Gi: I want to make sure people feel comfortable. I don't want to be rude.

Therapist: Being polite is important to you. Are there any parts of that upbringing that you don't want Hea to hold onto in quite the same way as you?

Gi: I don't want her to feel like she is alone...that she's wrong for feeling how she's feeling. That she has to hide away.

The therapist used Socratic questioning to support Gi in exploring his values in this space. As part of this, the therapist circled back to better understand Gi's definition of what it means to be rude, and supported Gi in defining rude behavior from different perspectives: within his culture, within his family, within the majority culture in the Southeastern United States. The therapist asked how the various exposures he had done fit within his definitions of rudeness. Through this conversation, Gi began to think that being anxious in front of others might not be as rude as he originally thought, which signaled a shift in this previous dysfunctional assumption which the therapist hypothesized had been driving Gi's distress across a wide range of interpersonal events throughout his life. He also began to focus on how pushing himself to do things in public *even when he is anxious* is in line with his value of supporting Hea in her treatment. At this point, Gi started to spontaneously engage in exposures without pre-planning in addition to those that were set for therapy homework. He also started to design exposures where he intentionally did things that he thought might realistically irritate other people (e.g., he would take 'too' long to order in the restaurant, he would ask the store clerk for something and then change his mind about what he wanted).

Based on the CBT case conceptualization, it was believed that these exposures more directly targeted his expectancies that if he wasn't perfect, then others would be rejecting him. Because he directly obtained disconfirming evidence (e.g., when he stammered excessively when placing an order, the drive-thru worker was still able to place the order correctly and did so without raising her voice or yelling at him to 'spit it out already'), his thoughts began to shift. His STABS and BFNE-S scores decreased accordingly, and he reported feeling like he had met his functional goals. The therapist then began to engage Gi in termination planning. Gi reported that he thought he would be best positioned to continue improving after termination if he was able to be more emotionally vulnerable with his cousin and wife. With this new treatment aim in mind, the therapist and Gi moved to Phase 3.

16.3.3 Phase 3 (Sessions 13–15)

Gi had good insight into the cognitive barriers that made it anxiety-provoking and hard for him to share more openly with his wife and cousin. He worried that his wife would think he was weak (*mind reading*) if he told her that he sometimes struggles to do basic errands and that his cousin would stop counting on him if he knew that Gi went to therapy (*catastrophizing*). However, Gi strongly believed that it was important enough to strengthen his emotional connections with them that he was willing to tolerate the risk of sharing.

Gi was able to more independently apply the skills that he learned in Phases 1 and 2 to support this goal. The therapist positively reinforced Gi for using his skills effectively to arrive at more balanced thoughts, and also positively reinforced him for deciding to test out his feared predictions by initiating increasingly disclosing conversations with his cousin and wife, in line with his values. To help Gi have the most success in these conversations as possible, the therapist engaged Gi in role plays during session. This encouraged Gi to think through and practice what he wanted to communicate to them. During this phase of treatment, the therapist also encouraged Gi to use the 'Bull's Eye Exercise' (Hayes et al., 2012) to track how values-aligned his conversations were with his cousin and wife during each week. Having a plan and keeping in mind why it was important for him to take these risks made it easier for Gi to initiate these conversations and, in turn, test his unhelpful beliefs about how his family members would respond. After three sessions, his Bull's Eye responses showed greater values-action congruency and Gi described having connected emotionally with his cousin and wife in ways that felt very comforting and did not result in his feared outcomes. In fact, he noticed that his cousin seemed to come to him more often.

16.3.4 Termination and Booster Sessions

Throughout treatment, the therapist regularly presented termination as an opportunity to commit to independent use of the skills developed during treatment. During termination, the therapist and Gi celebrated treatment progress and explored Gi's thoughts and feelings about discontinuing regular meetings. As part of relapse prevention, the therapist supported Gi in proactive coping to plan for future situations when there may be high risk for increases in anxiety and talked through how Gi would know to pursue additional therapy in the future. Gi was encouraged to list out the therapy skills that he found most helpful, and was asked to teach back the principles of change underlying these skills on his list to ensure that he had accurately consolidated what was taught in therapy. The therapist emphasized that regular use of these skills is key to maintaining treatment gains and continuing to improve. They set a booster session for one month later to check in on progress and troubleshoot any unforeseen challenges since termination. At the end of the booster session, Gi said "I didn't know that treatment could help me as much as it did" and he described a confidence that "He can handle it" when anxiety spikes in the future. A summary of Gi's treatment aims, associated interventions, and measures of progress is provided in Table 16.3.

16.4 Special Challenges and Problems

Gi's motivation, engagement, and willingness to try things out were great strengths that positively influenced his course of treatment. Even still, there were several challenges that Gi and the therapist needed to address to make the treatment work for him. In this section, three of these challenges are highlighted and it is discussed how the therapist responded to each.

16.4.1 Difficulties Associated with the COVID-19 Pandemic

The entirety of Gi's treatment took place during the COVID-19 pandemic, prior to vaccinations being widely available to the public. This introduced two complications from a social anxiety treatment perspective. First, public health guidelines all recommended that adults wear face coverings when entering stores. Given that anxious avoidance was particularly impairing for Gi within stores, it was important for him to complete exposures in these locations. From an expectancy violation perspective, however, this raised the possibility that Gi might attribute the outcomes of his behavioral experiments to the fact that he was wearing a face covering rather than to his ability to effectively tolerate anxiety with or without a face covering.

Therapist: It sounds like you did some really good learning, there! Your ability to function doesn't go totally away even when you're super anxious. That's important to know. I wonder, what do you think would have happened in that grocery store aisle if you hadn't been wearing a face covering?

Gi: I would have been even more anxious…the mask keeps others from seeing how red my cheeks get. It helps me feel a little more invisible.

Therapist: Hmmm. I'm curious, would you still have been able to function if you were feeling more anxious and others could have seen your face?

Gi: …I'm not sure. Maybe? The mask definitely helps, though.

The therapist helped Gi recognize that although face coverings were a reasonable precaution given the current environment, they also functioned as a safety behavior (Piccirillo et al., 2016). Given that exposures and behavioral experiments are meant to promote cognitive shifts, it was important that Gi did not learn that he was only able to function while anxious *because* he was less visible to others. However, it would have been inappropriate for the therapist to instruct Gi to carry out his grocery store exposures without wearing a face covering. As such, the therapist and Gi did the following: they applied cognitive restructuring skills to reframe Gi's beliefs that wearing a face covering is necessary to function while anxious; they planned exposures that did not require Gi to wear a face covering (e.g., ordering from the drive-thru, calling to reschedule doctor appointments); they planned for how Gi would set up and re-do his grocery store exposures in the future when masks were no longer a public health recommendation.

Additionally, given that acts of racism against Asian individuals increased in the US during the COVID-19 pandemic (Gover et al., 2020), it was important for the therapist to differentiate between Gi's anxiety in public spaces due to social anxiety versus due to fear of racist abuse.

Therapist: There has been a sickening rise in acts of hate and racism against Asian individuals within our country and local community since the onset of this pandemic. Many Asian individuals are understandably feeling less safe in certain public settings because of this. I wonder, has your anxiety when going to places like the grocery store changed since the pandemic began?

Gi: I'm very angry about how Asian people are being treated and talked about by large groups of Americans… I don't know, though, for me… the anxiety that I'm feeling hasn't really changed because of this.

Table 16.3 Treatment aims, key cognitive distortions, and associated intervention strategies

	Primary Treatment Aim	Key Cognitive Distortions and Biases	Interventions Employed	Measures of Progress[a]
Phase 1 Session 1–6	*Reduce rigid avoidance of daily activities, especially those that have social components* (To increase ability to tolerate anxiety; to increase perceived ability to approach daily activities spontaneously and independently)	- Biased probability estimation - Catastrophizing (e.g., "If I order from the drive-thru I'll get so anxious that I won't be able to function and all the cars behind me with start honking and yelling at me for being too slow") - Dysfunctional assumptions (e.g., "I should never waste someone's time or get in someone's way")	- Psychoeducation and socialization to treatment - Functional analysis to explore the antecedents and consequences of avoiding his 'to-dos' unless very specific conditions are met (e.g., few cars in the store's parking lot, being with a family member, not wearing bright clothes, knowing exactly what he was going to order prior to entering the store/restaurant) - Expectancy violations through in vivo exposures	- Self-report of how much anxiety/ avoidance got in the way of personal goals that week ('a lot,' 'somewhat,' 'barely any') - Weekly - Time spent planning out errands - Weekly - BFNE-S - Monthly - STABS - Monthly
Phase 2 Sessions 7–12	*Increase ability to construct balanced thoughts and to engage in more flexible thinking* (To reduce fear of negative evaluation; to increase willingness to approach, remain, and return to anxiety-provoking social situations that are important to him)	- All-or-nothing thinking (e.g., "I forgot to change my dad's colostomy bag earlier today, I'm a terrible son."); mind reading (e.g., "The hospice nurse thinks I'm neglectful") - Dysfunctional assumptions (e.g., "Sharing negative emotions is burdensome to others and rude") - Core beliefs (e.g., "I'm incompetent")	- Thought records and other cognitive restructuring exercises to re-evaluate unhelpful thinking styles (e.g., all-or-nothing thinking, catastrophizing) tied to dysfunctional assumptions - Socratic questioning to explore values and to separate which cultural expectancies he wished to maintain in his nuclear family and which he wished to shift - Expectancy violations through in vivo exposures (*continued to maintain and improve treatment gains from Phase 1*)	- Shift in targeted core beliefs/ dysfunctional assumptions and associated feelings of shame and sadness (self-rated on a 0–100 scale) - Weekly

(continued)

Table 16.3 (continued)

	Primary Treatment Aim	Key Cognitive Distortions and Biases	Interventions Employed	Measures of Progress[a]
Phase 3 Sessions 13–15	*Reduce fear of negative evaluation* (To reduce rigid avoidance of self-disclosure with select family members; to increase relationship satisfaction; to promote maintenance and strengthening of treatment gains)	- Mind reading (e.g., "If I tell my wife that I've been sad, she will think that I'm weak") - Catastrophizing (e.g., "My cousin will never come to me for support if he knows that I also struggle sometimes") - Dysfunctional assumptions (e.g., "People who give support to others cannot ask to be supported back")	- Skills to openly express emotions and communicate expectations/needs within social relationships (e.g., role play, 'I' statements) - Thought records and other cognitive restructuring exercises to re-evaluate unhelpful thinking styles (e.g., mind-reading, fortune telling) tied to dysfunctional assumptions - Advantages-disadvantages analysis of (1) initiating open conversations with partner and cousin and (2) not initiating those conversations - Behavioral experiments to hypothesis test whether his partner or cousin would stop coming to him for support if he opened up to them about some of his emotional experiences	- Self-rated action in relationship domain using the 'Bull's Eye' (focusing on approaching desired, emotion focused conversations with partner and sister) - Weekly

Note. Gi completed 17 sessions total. Session 16 focused on consolidating skills gained throughout treatment and Session 17 was a planned booster session one month after Session 16

[a]Measures introduced in earlier phases were maintained throughout treatment. *BFNE-S* Brief Fear of Negative Evaluation Scale - Straightforwardly worded items, *STABS* Social Thoughts and Beliefs Scale

The therapist validated Gi's anger and created space for him to share and process additional thoughts and feelings tied to the social climate. Knowing that Gi's anxiety was not driven by fear of racist acts, the therapist decided that it was appropriate to continue with the plan to introduce the rationale of exposures and pursue them as part of treatment. However, had Gi endorsed fear of racist acts, the therapist would have needed to carefully consider which aspects of exposure therapy may have still been beneficial and which aspects may have been harmful (e.g., by dismissing or invalidating Gi's concerns about the likelihood of racism; by putting Gi in situations where he was likely to experience and re-experience racism).

16.4.2 Difficulties Associated with Inhibitory Learning

After around seven sessions, the therapist uncovered an unexpected cognitive barrier that seemed to partially explain why Gi's early exposures did not seem to meaningfully shift his fear of negative evaluation or socially anxious thoughts. Through Socratic questioning around what it meant to Gi that many of his expectations did not come true, he said that it meant "I have wasted my life and hurt my daughter for no reason." The therapist learned that this thought made Gi particularly sad and angry. While it is common for socially anxious people to mourn their years lost to anxious avoidance, this thought ironically led Gi to tell himself that the next time he entered an anxiety-provoking situation, his feared outcome *would* happen. This way, he could tell himself there was a reason for his years of avoidance and anxiety, thus (temporarily) reducing his anger and sadness. Of course, this pattern reinforced his exaggerated beliefs about the likelihood of negative outcomes, thereby maintaining his anxiety and fears of evaluation.

After uncovering this pattern, the therapist had Gi conduct a functional analysis of this thought. Gi was able to see that while it helped him feel a bit better in the short term, it also kept him stuck in the long term. After calling attention to this thought process, Gi was able to then effectively engage in cognitive restructuring to find a more adaptive way to respond to the thought "I have wasted my life and hurt my daughter for no reason." Had the therapist helped Gi better anticipate what it might feel like to have his expectancies disconfirmed, it is possible that Gi's defensive reaction to experiencing loss and regret could have been addressed sooner. Similarly, if the routine outcome monitoring schedule would have included measures of depressive symptoms and cognitions, the therapist may have picked up on this underlying self-critical thought process more quickly.

16.4.3 Difficulties Associated with Overly Positive Self-Talk

Gi had a long-standing history of trying to counter anxious thinking and post-event processing through overly positive self-talk. He also tended to berate himself for having 'irrational' thoughts.

Therapist: How do you feel when you tell yourself that your thoughts are irrational?

Gi: I feel bad…embarrassed.

Therapist: Does telling your thoughts that they're irrational seem to make them go away or change them somehow?

Gi: No! I wish. They're still there. I just try to crowd them out by thinking really positively…but….

Therapist: Do you believe those positive thoughts that you come up with?

Gi: Not really. But I keep trying to tell myself them over and over so my stupid irrational thoughts will go away. But they never do.

Therapist: That sounds really exhausting. You want to think positively, but telling yourself overly positive thoughts doesn't work…those positive thoughts aren't even close to being on the same page as the actual story that you're living. They aren't believable. The goal here isn't to trick yourself into thinking positively, or to criticize yourself for being 'irrational,' it's to figure out when a thought isn't helping you and to learn how to step back and figure out a thought that better captures the whole story, is believable, and supports you in doing what is effective for your goals.

In this conversation, when introducing cognitive restructuring and styles of unhelpful thinking, and when processing expectancy violations, the therapist took special care to avoid using potentially stigmatizing language. For example, although some patients like using the term 'cognitive distortions,' the therapist hypothesized that Gi might experience that as evidence that the therapist thought he was in fact irrational and silly. Instead, the therapist used the term 'unhelpful thinking styles.' Gi later said that he found it much easier to approach his anxious thoughts when he labeled them as unhelpful rather than as irrational. He also found it comforting to learn that his thoughts didn't need to be entirely positive for them to be helpful.

16.5 Summary, Conclusions, and Learning Points

Gi made great progress during treatment. A wide range of flexibly employed strategies designed to shift Gi's thinking helped him make significant changes within his life and family, which ultimately improved his quality of life and his relationships. After treatment, he reported reduced anticipatory anxiety, reduced post-event processing, greater willingness to tolerate anxiety to pursue his goals and to support Hea's treatment progress, greater acceptance of his emotions, increased ability to balance anxious and negative self-focused thinking, increased confidence, and greater engagement in emotional support-seeking behavior from his wife and cousin. Prior to treatment, he reported spending approximately 7 hours a week planning and delaying errands due to his anxiety and said that anxiety/avoidance got in the way of his goals 'a lot.' At his booster session, Gi said he was spending around 20 minutes a week on average planning and delaying errands and said that anxiety/avoidance got in the way of his goals 'barely any' each week. His BFNE-S and STABS scores also decreased from 36 and 72 to 21 and 49, respectively, from intake to booster. These individual progress markers positively impacted Hea's course of treatment given that Gi had begun to regularly model and support approach-oriented coping strategies.

Taken together, the therapist also took a great deal away from Gi's treatment. Most significantly, this case underscored the importance of continuously keeping aspects of a patient's identity in mind. Aspects of Gi's identity cut across all phases of the treatment. Had the therapist failed to create space to explore these aspects during different points in treatment, it's quite possible that Gi would have terminated treatment prematurely. As such, this case reinforced for the therapist the need to be continuously thinking about when and how to explore whether there are aspects of a patient's identity that influence how principles of change fit them and their values. Additionally, this case demonstrated that exposures going 'well' can also be threatening to patients for any number of reasons. This taught the therapist to create space for mixed reactions to exposures, not just enthusiasm.

References

Anxiety & Depression Association of America. (1.12.2022). Social anxiety disorder. https://adaa.org/understanding-anxiety/social-anxiety-disorder.

Beck, J. S. (2020). *Cognitive behavior therapy: Basics and beyond* (3rd ed.). Guilford Press.

Craske, M. G., Treanor, M., Conway, C. C., Zbozinek, T., & Vervliet, B. (2014). Maximizing exposure therapy: An inhibitory learning approach. *Behaviour Research and Therapy, 58*, 10–23. https://doi.org/10.1016/j.brat.2014.04.006

Foa, E. B., & Kozak, M. J. (1986). Emotional processing of fear: Exposure to corrective information. *Psychological Bulletin, 99*, 20–35. https://doi.org/10.1037/0033-2909.99.1.20

Gover, A. R., Harper, S. B., & Langton, L. (2020). Anti-Asian hate crime during the COVID-19 pandemic: Exploring the reproduction of inequality. *American Journal of Criminal Justice*, 1–21. https://doi.org/10.1007/s12103-020-09545-1

Harpole, J. K., Levinson, C. A., Woods, C. M., Rodebaugh, T. L., Weeks, J. W., Brown, P. J., Heimberg, R. G., Menatti, A. R., Blanco, C., Schneier, F., & Liebowitz, M. (2015). Assessing the straightforwardly-worded Brief Fear of Negative Evaluation scale for differential item functioning across gender and ethnicity. *Journal of Psychopathology and Behavioral Assessment, 37*(2), 306–317. https://doi.org/10.1007/s10862-014-9455-9

Hayes, S. C., Strosahl, K. D., & Wilson, K. G. (2012). *Acceptance and commitment therapy: The process and practice of mindful change* (2nd ed.). The Guilford Press.

Leahy, R. L., Holland, S. J. F., & McGinn, L. K. (2012). *Treatment plans and interventions for depression and anxiety disorders* (2nd ed.). Guilford Press.

Miller, W. R., & Rollnick, S. (2012). *Motivational interviewing: Helping patients change behavior* (3rd ed.). Guilford Press.

Norton, P. J., & Weeks, J. W. (2019). A multi-ethnic examination of social evaluative fears. *Journal of Anxiety Disorders, 23*, 904–908. https://doi.org/10.1016/j.janxdis.2009.05.008

Piccirillo, M. L., Taylor Dryman, M., & Heimberg, R. G. (2016). Safety behaviors in adults with social anxiety: Review and future directions. *Behavior Therapy, 47*(5), 675–687. https://doi. org/10.1016/j.beth.2015.11.00

Turner, S. M., Johnson, M. R., Beidel, D. C., Heiser, N. A., & Lydiard, R. B. (2003). The social thoughts and beliefs scale: A new inventory for assessing cognitions in social phobia. *Psychological Assessment, 15*(3), 384–391. https://doi.org/10.1037/1040-3590.15.3.384

Katharine E. Daniel, MA, is a PhD Candidate in Clinical Psychology at the University of Virginia. She studies emotion regulation and digital interventions in the daily lives of people with social anxiety disorder. Within her clinical work, Daniel aims to collaboratively employ evidence-based principles of change within a family systems approach to case conceptualization.

Bethany A. Teachman, PhD, is a Professor of Psychology and the Director of Clinical Training at the University of Virginia. Her lab studies cognitive biases and emotion dysregulation that contribute to anxiety disorders and uses digital assessments and interventions to help people in their daily lives. Dr. Teachman is Director of the public web site MindTrails (https://mindtrails.virginia. edu/), a web-based research infrastructure that has offered digital interventions to reduce anxious thinking to thousands of visitors around the world, and Project Implicit Health (www.projectimplicithealth.com), an educational site that allows visitors to assess implicit associations tied to mental and physical health topics.

Chapter 17
"There Is This Strange Feeling: Oh no, Another Panic Attack!" – A Case Study in Panic Disorder

Eni S. Becker

17.1 The Case

Susan is a 43 years old woman, a kindergarten teacher with three children of her own. Meeting her you are impressed by a tall and straight woman with short blonde hair, self-assured and poised. But once she starts talking some of this self-assuredness falls away. She is suffering panic attacks and does not find it easy to express her problems. And rather than talking about anxiety, she is talking about the struggle she is facing, how tired she is from keeping it all together, putting on a brave face and fighting against the panic. You can see the enormous tension she is under, and that her nerves are frayed.

Her troubles started 4 years ago. She took her then 2-year-old son to a medical check-up. It was flu season, and the waiting room was absolutely packed. She had to keep standing, against the wall, in the waiting room, when she realized that she was starting to feel nauseated and then dizzy. She really did not want to make a scene, especially not in front of her small son. He is a sensitive child, and she didn't want to scare him. But while she was considering to ask another mother to give up her seat, she actually did faint. Luckily, she was at the doctor's already. She came about, finding the paediatrician and the nurse looking at her. Susan was really shaken. She had never fainted before. The doctor asked questions, but she found it difficult to concentrate and to answer. Her attention divided, partly on what the doctor was saying, but mostly on her son. She needed to reassure him that everything was fine. At the same time, she really did not feel fine at all. She was shaky, nauseated, her vision was blurred, dark dots dancing in front of her eyes. She got something to drink and some time to rest. The nurse did some tests. Her blood pressure

E. S. Becker (✉)
Behavioural Science Institute, Radboud University Nijmegen, Nijmegen, The Netherlands
e-mail: eni.becker@ru.nl

© The Author(s), under exclusive license to Springer Nature Switzerland AG 2023
M. L. Woud (ed.), *Interpretational Processing Biases in Emotional Psychopathology*,
CBT: Science Into Practice, https://doi.org/10.1007/978-3-031-23650-1_17

was normal, her heart a bit fast, but nothing seemed to be amiss. She was sent home by the paediatrician and advised to see her GP to get thoroughly checked.

The whole episode shook her very much. What was going on? She was not the type to give in to illness. About a month before this incident, she had just recovered from a rather bad flu. During that flu, she had had some truly strange symptoms: her legs were feeling different, sluggish, almost a bit numb. She had never experienced something like this, and it made her nervous. She started to wonder if something more serious was going on and went to her GP to get herself checked. The GP had tested the legs, did some bloodwork and reassured her that all looked fine. But the worries had lingered. It took her way too long to recuperate. Susan was fit and saw herself as resilient. She had just started to work again, after having her youngest son, who had come as a bit of a surprise. Her other two boys were already teenagers. The logistics of family and work, getting back into a new routine, were really not helped by her getting ill.

After the fainting at the paediatrician she really started worrying. And a few days later, while doing the weekly shopping, all of a sudden, her legs felt very weak, there was a strange cold pressure at her temples, and then dizziness came on. Susan rushed to her car. Very shaken she drove directly to her doctor who started some serious diagnostics. Over the next weeks, all the tests came back negative, and Susan got a clean bill of health. At the same time, those strange spells of dizziness persisted. Susan was confused; on the one hand, the doctors kept on reassuring her, and on the other hand, she had never felt so bad in her life. She had more or less stopped driving, being afraid she might have one of those fainting spells behind the steering wheel. She tried to avoid shopping and going to church had become an ordeal. There were more and more things she did not dare to do. No place seemed to be safe, those spells could also come while she was at home. Worst were those moments when her little son was with her. When she felt the dizziness starting, she really did not want him to be around. She was afraid to spook him and did her very best to hide her fears in front of him.

Susan was told by her GP that the spells she had were most likely panic attacks. Now, 4 years later, she tells her therapist that she knows it is "nothing", just a "fluke", but somehow, although doing her very best to fight the attacks, they are persisting. By now, working has become exceedingly difficult. She is responsible for all those small children at work, she cannot leave them alone, cannot be weak in front of them. Susan is avoiding a lot of things but not very consistently. Some days she might still manage to drive her kids, although this is the most difficult situation for her. When asked when she last drove as a driver by herself, she admits it has been more than a year ago. She has never entered a plane again since the attacks started, and pretends that with her family of five, they cannot afford flying anyway. If possible, her husband does the shopping and takes the kids to their appointments. Susan is extremely bothered that she cannot take care of her boys. But she is afraid of actually endangering them when they are with her. Asked what she is hoping for in therapy, she says it is to learn to better cope with those attacks. She states that she is so tired and exhausted fighting them all the time. It is eating away all her energy and she is afraid that she cannot go on as it is.

17.2 Main Cognitions Targeted

Susan presents a typical case of someone with a panic disorder with agoraphobia. She has several attacks a week, some days several a day, and she is worrying to get another "spell". She shows agoraphobic avoidance in places she could not get out quickly or cannot get help, although she makes herself still do a lot of things risking an attack. She fulfils the criteria of panic disorder with agoraphobia and has no other comorbid disorder at the time she is looking for help. Although her mood has been impaired by the prolonged fight with her fears, she does not fulfil the criteria for a major depression.

Taking a closer look at her history, it all began with an actual flu that triggered dysfunctional interpretations that provided the fuel for the later panic disorder. As shown in Fig. 17.1, it started with some bodily symptoms that got a vicious circle going, namely her strange feelings in her legs.

These symptoms were interpreted as a sign of a serious illness; actually, Susan mentioned later she was thinking of Multiple Sclerosis (MS). The idea that she might have MS naturally led to anxiety and to behavioural changes. In Susan, and rather typical for patients with panic disorders (but also those with health anxiety), this made her check her body repeatedly for signs of such an illness, being hypervigilant for signs of bodily changes. She also visited the doctor and had herself checked. The doctor did reassure her, but it is very possible that doubts lingered, since the doctor could not provide a satisfactory explanation for her symptoms. The resulting hyper-vigilance was possibly the breeding ground for the following panic disorder.

The fainting episode at the paediatrician was the second important triggering situation. Since Susan actually fainted, we can assume that it was probably not a panic attack. A panic reaction is a fight-flight response that raises blood pressure and accelerates the heart rate. Fainting is not compatible with the activation. There is one possibility to faint during a panic attack, due to hyperventilation. Susan might have hyperventilated at the paediatrician's, or more likely she was still suffering from a residue of the flu, and standing for a prolonged time in a room with bad ventilation, without breakfast, actually led to a drop in the blood pressure and the

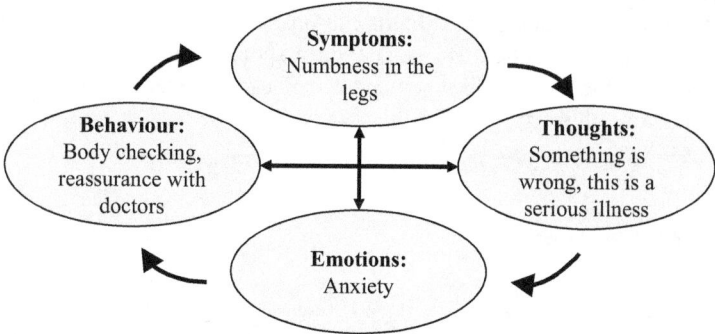

Fig. 17.1 Basic CBT-Model of the origin of the panic disorder for Susan

fainting. But Susan did not link the fainting to the aftermath of a "normal" flu. For Susan, the fainting was the confirmation of her fears that something was seriously wrong and that she better kept on finding the cause of the problems.

But when this cause was finally presented by her GP, telling her that she suffered from panic attacks, Susan was not convinced. Partly, because doctors are by no means infallible, but mostly because his explanation was contradicting a rather positive core belief of hers. Susan saw herself as a very strong person, self-sufficient, no whiner, responsible for her family. Such a person could not have an "anxiety problem", it truly did not fit her self-image. There was no other member in her family with mental problems (except for her brother who had a drinking problem). She came from working-class stock, resilient, used to hardship. Her parents had promoted that one "got things done" without a fuss, without talking about feelings or problems much at all. She had "made" something of herself, obtaining an education as a "kindergarten educator". Before the attacks, she was doing well in her job, probably on the way to becoming the head of the kindergarten, although the birth of her 3rd son had complicated matters. Thus, the explanation that those symptoms came from "nothing more" than anxiety went against her belief in herself. She was not an anxious person, and the symptoms were not really typical for anxiety either in her view. She reacted to the anxiety in a way consistent with her coping style, she tried to "fight" it, to wrestle it down. She mostly avoided situations where her "weakness" may be dangerous for others, but otherwise she tried to do her part. Nevertheless, the panic attacks were seriously undermining her self-esteem. For the treatment, this was also a challenge. A first step was thus to accept that it truly was a panic disorder, but this seemed to doom her as a "weak" person, a "loser". The therapist had to find a way to reconcile the rationale for a panic disorder with a self-image of a strong person.

17.3   Treatment

The treatment followed the manual for panic disorders and agoraphobia (Margraf & Schneider, 2013). The panic disorder manual is firmly based on the vicious circle of bodily symptoms and catastrophic interpretations. Those are mostly tackled directly by behavioural experiments. It is best suited for spontaneous uncued panic attacks. Susan's main problems were the spontaneous attacks, but she also did show agoraphobic behaviour, thus exposure for this was added, too.

17.3.1   Diagnostics

A structured interview (Margraf et al., 2013) was done to help with the diagnosis. Susan fulfilled the criteria for a panic disorder with agoraphobia. No other diagnosis passed the threshold, although there were subclinical depression symptoms. In the past, there had been problems concerning weight and eating, but also subthreshold. Susan had been extensively checked by her GP, all results being negative, so there were no indications of physical reasons for the panic attacks. Susan took no medication. She had tried benzodiazepines but they had enhanced the dizziness and "remoteness" she was feeling during the attacks, and thus she found them not helpful and was not using them anymore. Susan was also not drinking alcohol. She stopped her rather light use after the panic attacks had started, because alcohol also enhanced her feelings of dizziness. She did not smoke nor use any other recreational drugs.

Furthermore, questionnaires were used to monitor the panic symptoms, including three scales by Chambless and colleagues (Chambless et al., 1984, 1985, German version; Ehlers & Margraf, 1993), i.e., the Mobility Inventory (MI) to monitor the avoidance behaviour, the Agoraphobic Cognition's Questionnaire (ACQ), and the Body Sensation Questionnaire (BSQ). The Beck Depression Inventory (BDI II; Kühner et al., 2007) was administered to monitor depressive symptoms. Additionally, Susan was asked to fill in a panic diary every week. The diary had to be filled in daily and asked about panic attacks, their frequency and timing, and the maximum anxiety during the attack (on a scale from 0 to 100). The diary was a fixed part of the homework and could be adjusted, depending on the focus of the therapy. Table 17.1 gives an overview of the measures taken pre- and post-therapy and at 1-year follow-up.

17.3.2 Psychoeducation and the Treatment Rationale

17.3.2.1 Panic Disorder

The focus of the psychoeducational part is for the patient to get to an understanding of what a panic disorder is and how it developed. The results of the diagnostic phase are explained to the patient. Additionally, the treatment rational is being explained and the patient is motivated to do exposure treatment. Thus, in a first step, Susan was asked what she knew about panic disorder. Susan answered that she knew she had a panic disorder. Her GP had told her and had explained that it was "all in her

Table 17.1 Susan's questionnaire results pre- and post-treatment and 1-year follow-up

Questionnaire	Pre-treatment	Post-treatment	1-year follow-up
MI (alone)	.57	.21	.12
ACQ	1.2	.54	.46
BSQ	1.6	.9	.7
BDI II	8	5	4
Diary:			
Numbers of panic attacks per week	11	0	
Maximum anxiety	80	40	

E. S. Becker

head". In the beginning, this elicited rather mixed feeling, some relief, but also disbelief, because the symptoms were so very real. Also, a psychological disorder seemed a very unlikely diagnosis to her. No one in her family had been afflicted by anxiety so far, and Susan herself never thought she was an over-anxious person. But, her doubts had lessened over time. Susan said that by now she did accept the diagnosis. She had been extensively checked and always had gotten a clean bill of health. But, the panic attacks had not abated and every day was still a fight: A fight to get through the day, to get out of the house, to do her job, and she was just so very tired. Asked what she hoped to gain from treatment was not so much stopping the panic attacks, they seemed to be an affliction that she had to endure, but a better way to cope with the attacks.

The next step was to develop an individualized model of how the disorder developed in Susan's case. For this, the first panic attack was explored in more detail. Susan reported what had happened at the paediatrician. She was asked for possible triggers of the incident, and it was clear that she had not really linked the flu with the fainting. For her it came out of the blue. When questioned if there were possible connections Susan reported the "weird legs". Susan seemed to have lingering doubts, whether the doctors had not overlooked a crucial but rare medical problem. This explanation still fitted better with her idea of a "mentally sound" person. There was a conflict within her – if the panic was "all in her head", her head was not o.k., but she was bodily healthy. If she was not "mentally" ill, then it had to be a physical illness, and she was in danger of attacks. Susan was oscillating between these two possibilities.

As a next step, the therapist decided to give more information on what a panic attack is about, and to develop the model of the vicious circle. This was done with the example of the last bad panic attack, which Susan had experienced last week at church during mass. Susan was asked what the first symptom had been: "a strange feeling at her temples, some sort of pressure", this feeling is the usual sign for her that another attack is going to come on. And what was she thinking then: "Oh no! It is starting again". Then Susan was asked about the next symptoms she experienced. Well, her heart was going faster, she felt shortness of breath, dizzy and also a bit nauseated. Figure 17.2 shows the vicious circle the therapist drew with Susan's help. Once the description of the panic attack was more or less completed (depicted in black), the mechanisms of a panic attack were explained (depicted in red), starting with the enhanced attention for bodily symptoms. The therapist also explained that research shows that patients with panic disorder are much "better" in detecting bodily changes (McNally, 2002). In anxiety patients, attentional processes are changed, they are biased towards detecting threat, especially sensitive to signals of danger (Mogg & Bradley, 2016). Once the attention is directed at a potential threat, the patient's interpretation plays a major role (Austin & Richards, 2001). Those symptoms are interpreted as "danger signs", in Susan's case as an upcoming panic attack.

Next, the therapist explained how the interpretation as "Danger!" in fact does trigger a fear reaction, and thus functions as an avalanche of symptoms. With the help of a textbook diagram, the fear reaction was explained. It was stressed that the

In Church

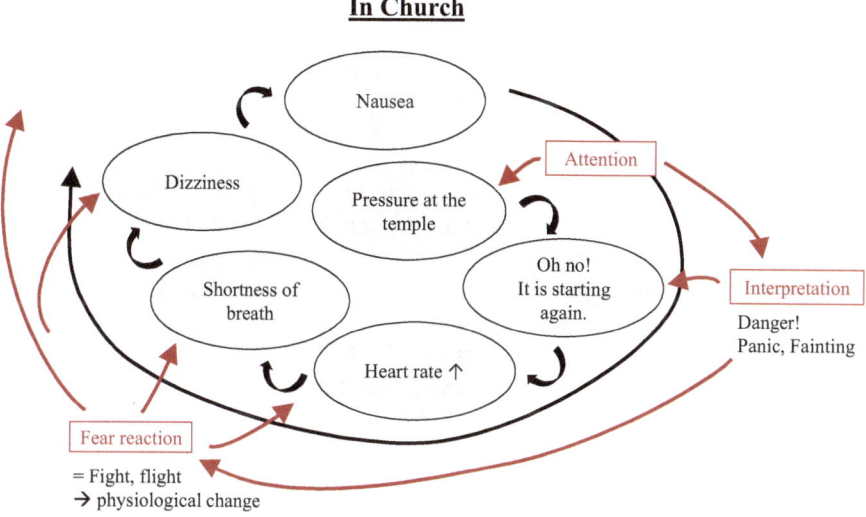

Fig. 17.2 Susan's vicious circle. *Note.* A model of her last major panic attack (in black is a description of the attack, in red the underlying mechanisms)

fight-flight response is highly automatic and triggered whenever danger is perceived. Every animal has this fight-flight reaction "hard-wired" in their brains to help survival. It is initiated whenever subjective danger is perceived; thus, it does also come into action when we merely "think" we are in danger. This is necessary otherwise we would not be able to react to unknown or "non-natural" dangers, like cars. But, this easy acquisition of fear and what to fear has its drawbacks. Panic patients interpret benign symptoms as a threat, and the following symptoms triggered by the fight-flight response as further signs of danger, resulting in the anxiety spiralling up. Susan was quite fascinated that many of her symptoms could be explained this way. On the one hand, this explanation did make a lot of sense. On the other hand, she also had her doubts, e.g., her first symptom, the pressure on the temple, did not seem to be entirely explained by the fight-flight response. Now, the therapist went back to the first "panic attack", the fainting situation at the paediatrician's, that started the panic disorder. She linked it to the flu and asked Susan if it is possible that she was still suffering from its aftermath. Susan admitted that she was not feeling fit the weeks after the illness. This flu had been strange and scary, those weaknesses in the legs, and it took forever to get better. For the longest time afterwards, she had been fatigued, had low energy and felt kind of foggy. Getting up the stairs to their apartment she had to stop several times. Thus, Susan conceded that at the paediatrician's, she may have still been affected by her flu. Standing there in the room with stale air had most likely led to a drop in her blood pressure and then to fainting. This meant that actually her first "panic attack" had neither been a panic attack nor a fight-flight reaction. But, it had constituted the trigger. Afterwards, she had been genuinely worried, she had no explanation of what had happened, and the reassurances of the paediatrician had little conviction. Thus, it was very natural that she started to watch her body much more closely, registering every change. It also made sense that she would interpret any changes as "danger signs", signs that something was indeed wrong, and thus triggering the "fight-flight" response. And the symptom triggered by this response had then been confirming her fear.

Susan thought this made a lot of sense but came back to her 'signalling symptom', the pressure on the temples, how could this be explained? First of all, the therapist said that actually when one feels anxious there can be many more symptoms. Textbook models explain the "typical" ones, but there is huge individual variance. Next, the therapist asked Susan if all symptoms had to be explained for her to accept that the symptoms experienced are part of a fight-flight reaction, and thus part of her panic disorder. The therapist went back to the model of the vicious circle while working on Susan's doubts. Doubting that the symptoms could be benign led to further attention to the body, fear that this might be dangerous, and thus upkeeping the circle. Although this made sense to Susan, doubts lingered. The therapist acknowledged that it takes time to adjust, and that part of the therapy was testing this model and exploring if the model was holding up.

The therapist asked for further questions and doubts. Susan said that since she "knows" the panic is not dangerous (her GP had explained this), but why is she still having those attacks? Should they not have gone away once she accepted the diagnosis? Well, for one thing, the panic attacks themselves had become a "danger". An attack is nothing one wants to suffer through. Second, the therapist asked Susan how much she did believe now, at this very moment, that she could die of an attack or faint. She said dying had a probability of 0% and fainting about 10–20%. Then she was asked if she could think back to the last attack. While experiencing the attack, did she think she might faint or die? If she should have estimated the probabilities while under the attack, what may they have been? Susan said, somewhat surprised by herself, that actually she had thought she may be fainting 70–80%, and that there may have been a fleeting thought of dying, but not more than 5%. Thus, the difference was made between "cold" and "hot" cognitions. While being outside of the situation, probabilities were down (cold ratio had a chance), but in the situation, emotions come in, and in the heat of the action, the probabilities shoot up. The body (and hot emotions) takes over the mind.

Susan also wondered how it could be that there seemed to be good times and then exceedingly bad times. If this was not linked to her physical condition, but to her interpretations, should it not be "all the same"? To explain this somewhat more, the therapist drew a picture, explaining the relationship of panic and stress. She described that we experience quite different stress levels, partly depending on our general stress in daily life. This can also be physical, like having had a bad night of sleep, or an infection coming, or psychological, e.g., demands of the job and family. There is a threshold that has to be passed for the symptoms of the panic attack to become apparent. If the general stress level is higher, this threshold is passed much more easily, and every small additional stressor can trigger an attack. Thus, there are fluctuations without necessarily a physical reason being present.

At the end of this session, the therapist summarized what had been talked about. It was stressed how important the interpretation of the symptoms was. The therapist laid out that there were now two alternative interpretations, that either something is wrong physiologically or that the fight-flight reaction might explain the attacks. A start was made to come up for a plausible explanation for Susan's problem, i.e., a fight-flight response triggering many symptoms, as well as a possible course for treatment, targeting the dysfunctional interpretation of the symptoms.

17.3.2.2 Agoraphobia

In the next session, the panic attacks were examined in context, and the role of avoidance was looked at more closely. The diaries were used, first focusing at the measurements Susan took to counter the panic. Susan said that mostly she was simply "fighting" the attack, and that this was also thoroughly draining her. The therapist asked what this fighting meant. Well, Susan said, she was trying to "hold it in", "keep it together", controlling her movements and trying to calm down. She was trying to take deep breaths. But mostly she was talking herself down, giving herself orders, not allowing the "panic thoughts". If she felt nausea coming up she was actually sitting down, because she was afraid that she might faint. The therapist asked Susan to take a closer look at how effective these strategies were and drew the first curve of one such panic attack Susan had while being at home, taking care of the washing. Looking at the height Susan's anxiety went up to in that context, it was around 70–80 and not 100. However, the attack lasted for 20–30 minutes before the anxiety went down slowly. This seemed to be true for most of the attacks at home or work that she tried her very best to control.

Next, the therapist was interested in full-blown attacks, in what way were they different? They occurred much more rarely and almost always outside home. The anxiety could go as high as a 100, but often went down quickly as soon as Susan could leave the situation. The therapist and Susan also drew 1–2 curves of those attacks (see Fig. 17.3, part a). Laying out the different graphs of panic attacks the role of avoidance was examined. In the short term, avoidance is very helpful, the anxiety goes down or is at least reduced, and this is what happened during those full-blown but shorter attacks. It was stressed that Susan was learning automatically that avoidance seemed to help. But if avoidance is not readily available, then the "safety behaviours" kick in, like talking herself down, drinking water, sitting down etc. In fact, they are also seen as avoidance because they try to get "away" from the symptoms. Thus, short-term avoidance and safety behaviour seem helpful, but looking at the long-term effects, they do nothing to reduce the panic attacks.

Next, the therapist wanted to know more about the catastrophic beliefs, that prevent staying in the threatening situation. For this, a thought experiment was conducted. Susan was asked about a situation she would be very afraid of, and then to imagine herself in that situation. For Susan, this was sitting in an airplane. Susan was asked to imagine herself on board of a plane, a plane that was in the air and would not land for a long time. She was asked to draw a curve of what would

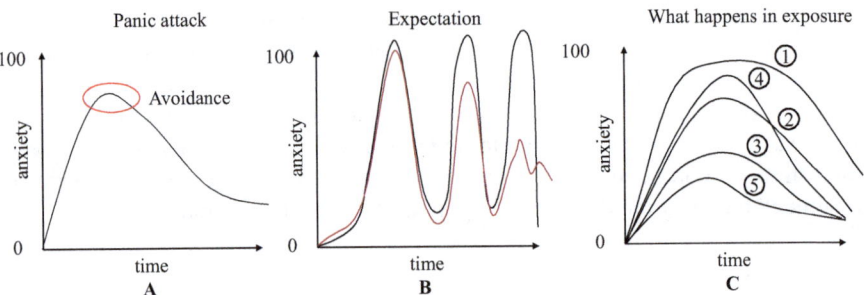

Fig. 17.3 Different steps in explaining the exposure rational. *Note.* (**a**) A "normal" panic attack and how avoidance helps to reduce the anxiety short term; (**b**) Expectations of what might happen if there would be no avoidance possible, black: repeated fainting spell resulting in death; red: repeated fainting spells, but ultimately the anxiety goes down; (**c**) The exposure rational including a setback

happen with her anxiety. At first, she drew a very, very steep line that in fact did go way beyond 100. When she was asked if this could go on forever, Susan found this unlikely. "So, what would happen after an hour?". She answered she would probably have fainted by then. "If you had fainted, would you wake up again?" "Well, yes!". "Imagine you wake up, the plane is still going, no way to land, what would happen?" "I would again be very much afraid!" "Ok, let's draw what would happen if you faint: the anxiety/arousal would go down to zero while you are unconscious. When you wake up, what would happen with the anxiety?" The therapist asked Susan again and again to imagine what would happen, over the next hours or, if necessary, days, thinking through all options very concretely. Since this was a thought experiment, time could be extended infinitely if necessary. By doing so, patients can be asked if it is possible to be afraid for several days. This is a good way to get to their beliefs and expectations. Susan's expectation was to faint repeatedly, and then either the anxiety would go down or she would die. Susan was asked how often she thinks she would faint and wake up again. Can one die from "fainting too much"? In the end, there were two possible outcomes: "fainting and dying" or "fainting and staying alive" (see Fig. 17.3, part b).

Making those expectations and the fears very explicit by drawing those curves and indeed thinking things through is an excellent way to find the central catastrophic beliefs that keep the panic going. The thought experiment, by detailing and visualizing the situation (in Susan's case being on a plane that is never going to land), gets to the beliefs' core. But, it is also very threatening. For many patients, this is the moment they realize what is in the making for them, that they will have to face the situations they fear. This part is therefore often very emotional. But not in Susan's case, because for her, trying to keep things "real and rational", she was rather reluctant to provide the catastrophic interpretations.

Susan was contemplating the information given. There was no sudden epiphany but some acknowledgement and some doubt. She needed time to process, and also time to talk about her innermost fears. Visualizing them with the graphs did help to process her fears and compelled her to talk about them. After the different outcomes were made explicit, Susan was asked for estimations of likelihoods, i.e., likelihoods related to the potential outcomes she feared. She thought that fainting was very likely, 80%; that dying was still very unlikely, about 10%; and that the anxiety would go down was quite likely, 70%. Since the numbers were very reasonable, the therapist did not go into a prolonged discussion of pros and cons for the different outcomes but proceeded to explain the exposure rational (Fig. 17.3, part c). The therapist explained that the anxiety goes down by itself after a time, if there is no avoidance and if the anxiety is allowed to come up. If the same situation is then encountered a second time, the anxiety might not get as high, or might decline faster. The therapist also made sure to predict setbacks. Doing exposure is in a way learning a new skill. And, as it is with all learning, it is not a straight line. Learning to drive a car or to play an instrument, we do get better with practice, but there are days when things do not go according to plan. This is also true for exposure learning. Thus, a panic attack might still occur surprisingly, but in general they will get less and less, until they are gone.

Susan followed this reasoning but brought up that she does not avoid that many situations, and even does them repeatedly, but the anxiety is not getting less. Again, the therapist explained how safety behaviour, more implicit forms of avoidance, do affect the course of the anxiety. To examine and better understand this, the curves of the anxiety attacks that came with less anxiety (up to 60–70 on a scale of 100) were inspected more closely. They usually had a less steep incline, but generally lasted much longer than the more intense attacks. They could last up to half an hour or, in the case of being in a traffic jam on the highway, even 2–3 hours. Susan was asked to reflect on her strategies she was using in such situations. It was a mixture of breathing deeply, drinking some water, sitting down, but mostly ordering herself to keep calm, trying with all her might to control her feelings. The therapist told Susan that all these strategies are considered as some kind of avoidance. They do help in the short term, at least somewhat, the anxiety is not going up to 100, but in the long run, they keep the vicious circle going. Paradoxically trying to control the anxiety is a way to keep it alive. To demonstrate this effect Susan was asked to NOT think of a white bear for the next 2 minutes. She was given a paper and pen and asked to always make a mark when she was thinking of a white bear. Not surprisingly, Susan did not succeed to "not think of a white bear". The little experiment was discussed and the mechanism of trying to control thoughts was explained (Wegner, 1994). Next, a second aspect of safety behaviours was discussed, namely that Susan cannot experience that anxiety will go down by itself if she continues to engage in safety behaviours. That is, her applied safety behaviours will not allow for testing out if those fears, namely fainting or possibly even dying of fear, could ever become true. Susan was asked to think about the proposed approach, i.e., exposure treatment, and if further questions or doubts came up, to note them, so they could be discussed in the next meeting.

Thus, the treatment rational for the exposure part was introduced and discussed. To summarize, first information was given regarding the role of avoidance and safety behaviours on short- and long-term outcomes. Next, Susan's expectations regarding the worst-case scenario were explored. Exposure therapy aims at testing those expectations and beliefs, and to change them by violating them (Craske et al., 2018), which, in turn, is supposed to lead to a reduction in anxiety (see Chap. 12 by Woud & Hofmann). In Susan's case, not fainting would be a violation of her expectation. Interestingly, so far, she had never fainted after the initial episode at the doctor's and still believed she would faint if the anxiety would get worse. Thus, the aim of the exposure was to trigger very intense levels of anxiety AND to not allow safety behaviour, because only then could Susan test if she would truly faint.

17.3.3   Exposure

17.3.3.1   Exposure of Internal Cues: Panic

The next session started with exposure to the panic attacks and was focusing on challenging Susan's beliefs regarding the attacks. The therapist came back to the vicious circle of panic attacks, again emphasizing that it is driven by misinterpretations of bodily symptoms. The therapist and Susan took a closer look at those automatic misinterpretations. To do so, they looked at the symptoms she usually suffered while having an attack (the diaries helped getting a good overview) and for each symptom, Susan was asked what thoughts came up when she experienced them, see Table 17.2.

It was quite obvious that Susan's immediate fear was to faint. She maintained that she was not really afraid of dying. Her initial symptom was the pressure to the temple that had become a sure sign for another attack. Palpitations were common but not that clearly linked to any catastrophic outcome. They were seen as a "by product". Then came "intermediate" symptoms, like hot flashes or shortness of breath. Then the groups of symptoms very clearly associated to fainting, i.e., the dizziness and trembling. Two symptoms only came when the attack was genuinely bad – the weakness in the legs and tunnel vision. The tunnel vision was linked to driving a car. The symptom she feared most was nausea – this was strongest associated to fainting.

Subsequently, the therapist asked Susan to do a test. Susan was asked to breathe deeply in and out (one cycle per second) for 2 minutes. The therapist modelled the breathing and breathed along with Susan. Susan did fine, although she certainly would have liked to stop after a minute when she was feeling very short of breath. After the test, Susan was asked to closely monitor her body and the symptoms. She was asked to get up and stand still to monitor how her legs were feeling. The therapist also asked Susan if she had any feelings of "detachment", things looking further away or not "real". Susan reported to have those feelings and that they actually were very familiar to her, they were also apparent when experiencing a panic attack, but so far, she had not been able to give these feelings a name.

Susan was asked to get back to the list and indicate if the symptoms were present right now and how "bad" they were during this test. Then, the present ratings and

Table 17.2 Susan's worksheet on interpretations of her symptoms during a panic attack, part I

Symptom	How bad (0–100)	Interpretation	Belief in interpretation (0–100)
Pressure on temple	70	Panic attack (dizziness will follow)	100
Palpitations	40	?? (heart might burst)	5
Feeling hot	60	Losing control	50
Shortness of breath	80	Fainting Losing control	70
Dizziness	100	Fainting	70
Trembling/weakness in legs	90–100	Fainting (illness)	70 (10)
Tunnel vision	100	Fainting	80
Nausea	100	Fainting	90

Table 17.3 Susan's worksheet on how typical/atrong her symptoms are during a panic attack and during the hyperventilation, part II

Symptom	Panic attack (0–100)	Hyperventilation test
Pressure on temple	70	0
Palpitations	40	70
Feeling hot	60	30
Shortness of breath	80	90
Dizziness	100	70
Trembling/weakness in legs	90–100	60
Tunnel vision	100	0
Nausea	100	20
Derealization	(80)	50

the ratings done to describe a usual panic attack (Table 17.2) were examined together. There was a very clear overlap, see Table 17.3.

Susan was asked what she thought looking at Table 17.3. Somewhat haltingly she said that she was puzzled. She had similar symptoms but actually had not felt "panicky", only very uncomfortable but no panic. The therapist explained that the test was a hyperventilation test. She went on explaining what happened when hyperventilating, and that it was entirely harmless. For some patients, hyperventilation is part of the panic reaction, getting as much oxygen in to be able to run or to fight as part of the natural fear response. Thus, it is possible that Susan is hyperventilating when having a panic attack, without being aware of it, and that this, in turn, could explain a lot of the overlap in symptoms. Susan countered that she breathed differently during the hyperventilation test than during an attack, but the therapist explained that the breathing can change much more subtly and still we hyperventilate. The fight-flight response goes along with breathing in more deeply, deep breaths are used to calm ourselves down. Taking deep breaths can lead to hyperventilation. Susan wondered if she thus should breathe differently while having an attack. But, the therapist stressed that this is not necessary, the hyperventilation, being a "natural" and benign process, is part of the fear reaction, and would go away by itself once the fear decreases. Initially, the therapist was a bit worried that Susan would use the new knowledge to start another safety behaviour, but since the therapist was planning to use the hyperventilation to enhance Susan's panic reaction during exposure, the therapist hoped this would further reinforce the insight that coping was not the goal.

After the hyperventilation exposure, the belief ratings regarding the panic attack symptoms were examined again, and Susan was asked if they had changed (see Table 17.4). For some of the beliefs, an alternative was added, namely that the symptoms may be due to the effect of hyperventilation. The ratings had gone down, for all the catastrophic interpretations related to the symptoms being a sign of fainting/losing control/or an underlying illness. But, there was certainly still room for improvement.

Thus, the first exposure for the panic attacks, the hyperventilation, was introduced as a behavioural experiment in a more classical Cognitive Therapy way, and less as an exposure exercise that should lead to "habituation". In the end, both exposure and behavioural experiments target changing dysfunctional beliefs, and cannot always clearly be "classified" as either or. Susan was asked to hyperventilate repeatedly as an exposure exercise as her homework, with the same aims as during therapy, i.e., not only getting used to the symptoms but also testing the belief those symptoms would be harmful.

In this session, there was time for one other panic exposure exercise: the therapist chose to ask Susan to stand in front of an entirely white wall and to stare at it for a

Table 17.4 Susan's worksheet on changes in her interpretations of her symptoms, part III

Symptom	Interpretation	Belief before test (0–100)	Belief after test (0–100)
Pressure on temple	Panic attack (dizziness will follow)	100	100
Palpitations	?? (heart might burst)	5	3
Feeling hot	Losing control	50	40
Shortness of breath	Fainting Losing control	70	40 (or – breathing differently)
Dizziness	Fainting	70	50 (hyperventilation?)
Trembling/weakness in legs	Fainting (illness)	70 (10)	50
Tunnel vision	Fainting	80	80
Nausea	Fainting	90	70
Derealization	Fainting	80	40 Hyperventilation!

while. This test produced symptoms of derealization that were quite strong as well as tunnel vision. The task was discussed in a similar way as the hyperventilation test. As homework, Susan was asked to "practice" hyperventilation and "staring at the wall", to get used to the panic symptoms. Susan was asked to reserve 3 days per week, and to do those exercises in a block of about 30 minutes. Additionally, Susan was asked to write down her levels of anxiety before, during, and after each exercise.

For the next session, a whole afternoon was planned for a different exposure, namely, to target the agoraphobic behaviour. As a preparation, Susan was asked to monitor the safety behaviours in her panic diary.

17.3.3.2 Exposure In Vivo: Agoraphobia

For the intensive agoraphobic-relevant exposure, several sessions were blocked and a long afternoon in a shopping centre was planned. This would allow for enough time to repeatedly practice different situations, allowing for variation in context (different shops, lifts, heights), making exposure more effective (Craske et al., 2008). Susan was very tense and nervous, and the anxiety was raising to about 60–70, but no major panic attack occurred. The therapist tried to raise the panic by using hyperventilation, but this did not lead to a raise in anxiety, although there was a bit more dizziness. The therapist wondered if she herself was a "safety signal" and thus gave Susan tasks to do by herself, e.g., doing some shopping, riding the underground by herself etc. She also stressed that Susan should allow the panic to come up. Susan did all these tasks, but neither did the anxiety go away nor did a full-blown panic attack occur. When the exposure session had finished, Susan and the therapist sat together, analysing the day and looking at the achievements. Susan was in no way elated, she was tired, stressed, and somewhat frustrated. She did not see what she had accomplished, but rather thought that for her not much had changed. She was still living under the cloud of the anxiety, and could not enjoy anything she

Therapist: It is really a pity that you worked so hard and did not manage to get into full blown panic!
Susan: What do you mean?
Therapist: Well, I mean: I understand you are frustrated not getting into the panic? Or did I misunderstand you?
Susan: I am more frustrated because the panic did not go away. It is always lingering in the background, ready to pounce! I so wish it would go away!
Therapist: Yes, I understand this. Let's have a closer look what might have happened today. Do you remember the curves we drew? If you think back on them, what was the goal of the exposure?
Susan: To reduce the panic by practicing – but as I said there was not much of a change yet, and I find it very exhausting.
Therapist: Yes, this is really tough going. Why do you think the anxiety did not go down?
Susan: Exposure might not be working in my case.

Therapist: Possible, but before we go there, let us review the rational and especially look closely at your behavior, for the short- and long-term consequences. Let's go back and draw some curves again of what happened today. After looking at one or two of the situations:

Therapist: So, the anxiety did not go up so very high, did you do something to regulate it down?

Susan: Well, not really....

Therapist: O.k.; what did you think in the moment when the anxiety was coming up?

Susan: I thought: See this is just hyperventilation! This is not dangerous!

Therapist: Ah o.k.! So, you were reassuring yourself, trying to calm yourself down.

Susan: Yes, sure!

Therapist: And it seemed to have worked somewhat, right? This is actually what we mean be safety behaviors, or by avoidance. This can also be thoughts or talking to yourself. It does not have to be a real action, like leaving the situation. Whatever you do or think to reduce the anxiety is kind of avoidance. And short term it has some effect. But, if I look at the curve, the anxiety did not really go down, right?

Susan: No, at this point I felt kind of wobbly and this is always a bad sign.

Therapist: I see. What do you think would have happened if you would not have talked yourself down, if you would have gone on concentration fully on the symptoms?

Susan: Well, I might have failed, lost control.

Therapist: That is an interesting choice of words, would anxiety be a failure?

Susan: It feels like one, like I should not be so weak, I should stop this stupid worrying, just get done with it.

Therapist: Thus, panic is a double threat? Panic attacks are really scaring and exhausting but additionally they mark you as a sissy, a failure?

Susan: I know it is stupid but yes, this is how it feels! Like a character flaw, marking me as weak!

Therapist: And you told me how important it is for you to be a strong person. And thus, if I go back to the exercise, you were fighting the panic all the time, right? To not be weak, not to give in!

Susan: Yes.

Therapist: Ok, and short term it helped somewhat, the panic was not going up to a hundred, but what happens long term?

Susan: Hm, it stayed the same, with the panic always being in the background.

Therapist: We have to test what happens if you allow yourself to give in to the panic. And in fact, I would say this is extremely courageous and strong, to surrender to the panic. To allow it to surface, and then to see what happens! What would we have to do for you to let this happen?

had done. She felt stuck. The therapist tried to find out what was "holding the panic back", and asked if Susan to share her frustration that they had not been able to elicit strong attacks.

Thus, this exposure session had not enabled Susan to test the hypothesis that a major panic attack will lead to fainting (or even dying), and change those beliefs. She had repeated her ingrained behaviour, to fight the anxiety. A way to allow her to actually get into a full-blown panic attack had to be found.

The therapist considered options, she had to find situations that would make it difficult for Susan to keep her safety behaviour going, and at the same time would trigger the symptoms she was fearing most, like dizziness or weakness. After some deliberation, she booked an afternoon at a women's gym, with a cardio-aerobics class. Susan had avoided exercise since the bout with the flu and the ensuing panic disorder. Thus, on the one hand, exercise should trigger the right sort of symptoms and fears. On the other hand, exercise would make it more difficult to engage in her typical safety behaviours. Susan and her therapist thus attended the cardio-aerobics class. The therapist's role was to keep Susan going beyond her fear and to sincerely go for it. Unfortunately, the therapist had a hard time to follow the class, too. Susan was fitter but also quite challenged. This exercise provided an excellent bonding opportunity. The therapist was setting a good example of being a "spectacle" and "weak", at least in a fitness-related way, and the willingness of the therapist to suffer for Susan, helped a lot. Susan did not mind being told to go on, getting into the fear, when the therapist was so obviously at her limit, too. The exercise indeed challenged a lot of Susan's fears, but on the one hand, it triggered a lot of symptoms, including the feeling that her legs were unstable, and on the other hand, it also made it impossible to always stay moderate and cool, to stay in charge. The symptoms that Susan feared most, the dizziness, derealization etc., however, were less prominent. But, after the aerobics class, the therapist took Susan to the sauna, and here the symptoms truly came up. The therapist asked Susan to focus on the symptoms and her body, and Susan managed to do it. And, this time, she endured it without avoidance, and the symptoms were fading, and Susan felt elated. She visited the sauna again, without the therapist, and essentially felt fine and relaxed for the first time in a long while.

This was the turning point in therapy. Susan had managed not to fight and to let go, and the anxiety had vanished, she had even enjoyed the sauna, hot and closed in, and surprisingly relaxed. Her surrender had brought freedom. Her surrender was probably only possible because she had really gone all out in the aerobics class, she had gone to her limits physically and had tested her body. And, although she had felt dizzy and exhausted, she had survived. This also showed her that she was healthy, her body could do the work out, the symptoms had not killed her. Furthermore, there was real trust now to the therapist who had been willing to go all the way with her. The sauna after the cardio work out was a perfect setting because it did allow to sit still and to really feel the symptoms. The biggest surprise for Susan was that once she focussed on them, they seemed to abate, even a bit elusive. Thus, her former idea that she needed to avoid feeling the symptoms, that she needed to somehow control and subdue them, was disproven. And something that was not expected by her (or the therapist) was that the sauna induced a pleasant exhaustion that was rewarding.

After this success, most of the remaining exposure exercises were done as homework assignments. An exception was a flight in a small airplane that was done together with the therapist. The plane was the worst situation on Susan's' list and thus the therapist thought Susan should confront herself with that specific situation while having some support. Although Susan was very apprehensive and anxious on the plane, the anxiety dropped while still being in the air, and Susan left the plane rather exhilarated and proud.

17.3.4 Relapse Prevention

To prevent relapse, the therapist now turned to some of the underlying beliefs that played a role in the development of Susan's panic. If maladaptive schemata that may have played a role in the development of the disorder would be kept untreated, they would pose a serious risk for relapse. Here, a more classical CT approach according to Beck was chosen. Susan had often mentioned that she was "not weak", "had to be strong" etc., these were automatic thoughts coming up when she was facing her anxiety or grappled with the fact that she had a disorder. These thoughts hinted at an underlying schema, the "need to be strong". Schemata are formed in childhood and accordingly, the possible beginning of Susan's beliefs was explored in more depth. In her family of origin, a lot of emphases were placed on being self-sufficient and strong. Her brother had not been able to keep "his end up", his drinking problems had been seen as a major weakness. It was her role to be the reliable one.

This was also true in some way in her own family now. Her husband was not as educated as she was, she took care of the finance administration, visited parent conferences, etc. Susan was asked what being a "strong person" means to her, and came up with reliable, responsible, a good person, a provider. She had been strongly reinforced by her family, showered with praise if she fit the role. But what was a weak person? Susan spontaneously said: the opposite, unreliably, irresponsible, a disappointment, well, shameful. The therapist used different techniques to question those statements, e.g., to promote less black and white thinking or overgeneralization, e.g., by asking Susan if she also judged friends as harshly as she judged herself. As homework, Susan had to interview a good friend what their ideas are of being "strong and weak". Susan was surprised by some of the answers, some friends found the concept of a "strong" person toxic.

Exploring further, Susan opened up about doubts regarding her marriage. She admitted that she admittedly found herself the "stronger" person, and that in a way, her being anxious might have kept a balance in her marriage, had allowed him to be the "stronger" one, by helping and supporting her. Now, that Susan had "conquered" her anxiety she was thinking about leaving her husband, having outgrown him. On the other hand, she started to realize that "strength" could be shown in many different ways, and that his steadfastness and willingness to support her was really a point in his favour. Susan understood that she needed to take more time to find out what she wanted from life, but also how their relationship could further develop now that she could act on her own again.

17.3.5 Outcome

Susan was seen for a booster session 2 months after the treatment had ended. She came into the meeting with lots of shopping bags and an entirely new outfit. She told her therapist that she enjoyed her new "freedom". She had told her husband that they should switch cars, she would drive his Mercedes for now, since she was using it much more, ferrying the kids. All in all, she was very positive and full of élan. She was asked what her plans were if the panic would come back, and she quite confidentially stated that she thought it to be unlikely but would start exposure right away. Susan called the therapist a year later and was still doing well. There had been no panic attacks (see Table 17.1 for outcomes at follow-up).

17.4 Special Challenges and Problems

In a way, Susan is a very typical case for a patient suffering from panic disorder, accompanied by a milder case of agoraphobia. At first sight, a mild form of agoraphobia seems to be an advantage, but in fact it often poses its own challenge. If patients with a panic disorder somehow manage to function and to hold on to a normal life as best as they can, they have developed some kind of ingrained safety behaviour. In exposure, it becomes then difficult to trigger panic because patients cannot let go of their strategies to battle the panic. These strategies are often cognitive routines that are indeed difficult to stop engaging in. As in Susan's case, these behaviours prevent new experiences that contradict the catastrophic beliefs. Additionally, therapists have to watch out that the patient does not feel blamed for the exposure not working, because they did not do it "right": They did their best, and it did not work. As such, the therapist has to find ways to help the patient to truly let go of the safety behaviours, and to test what will happen then.

Further, it is often worthwhile to explore if there are more central beliefs that may have played a role in the development of the disorder. In Susan's case this was her belief that she was and had to be a strong person. But it could also be linked to, for example, a strong sense of responsibility, perfectionism, or intolerance of uncertainty. Getting back to Susan, her belief strengthened her misconception that there had to be a medical reason, since a strong person does not get a psychological disorder. Second, if this was a psychological problem, it was her duty not to give in to it. This, in turn, made it truly difficult for her to actually "let go" while doing the exposure. As a result, her expectations could not have been challenged. The exercises with the therapist in the gym, where the therapist was a model of insufficient strength, of weakness (and was o.k. with being made fun of), were important to counter her ideas.

There was one other complicated matter, the marriage that had its problems. Susan was afraid that if the treatment was successful, she would have "to do something" about her marriage. She admitted feeling superior to her husband and thought she should leave him. Her anxiety had made her dependent. She needed him and the dependency had bred resentments. Now, she was free to get out of the relationship. On the other hand, in her time of need, he had been very supportive, and Susan was thankful. Leaving him felt like a betrayal. Susan was very torn. A situation like this is not unusual if one partner suffers from a psychological problem. A psychological problem can stabilize a relationship in some case because of creating dependencies. This also can threaten the treatment. Successful treatment changes the "power-balance". Some patients can get so afraid of those changes that they terminate treatment, because the success is seen as too big a threat to the family/the relationship. In Susan's case, she agreed that she would wait before she acts, to see what changes therapy would bring to her marriage. A year later the marriage seemed to have stabilized.

Besides challenges, there was also a bit of luck. When the agoraphobic exposure did not seem to work, Susan got very frustrated with the treatment and the therapist. She threatened to stop therapy. That the therapist was willing to show her own weaknesses (I am really not into sports!), was willing to be a laughingstock, tipped the scales, and truly strengthened the relationship between patient and therapist. Therapist and patient bonded over their "bad" fitness, could laugh while not getting any air anymore. Afterwards, Susan was trusting more and willing to risk more, and this is what was needed.

17.5   Summary and Conclusions

Misinterpretations lie at the heart of the panic disorder. They usually concern the misinterpretation of bodily symptoms as life-threatening, but as the disorder develops, these fears can change. Susan denied in the beginning that she was afraid of dying of a panic attack, she feared the attacks themselves. It is very important to take the time in the beginning of therapy, to find out what those dysfunctional beliefs might be. The psychoeducation, developing the individual models of the disorder, is thus of great importance. These models are the fundament on which therapy rests, helping to find the relevant misconceptions. However, they are also very important for the motivation and compliance of the patient.

Often the most efficient ways to change dysfunctional interpretations are behaviour experiments, and exposure therapy can be seen as a behavioural experiment. It is of great importance though that the behavioural experiments are indeed targeted to help change the patient's cognitions.

Still, in Susan's case, I think the therapy was also successful because a lot of the necessary "groundwork" was done. All the models and explanations were genuinely fitted to Susan, individualized, and Susan was given room to doubt the models and to test them. Exposure treatment needs a good preparation, and this is based on cognitive techniques.

References

Austin, D. W., & Richards, J. C. (2001). The catastrophic misinterpretation model of panic disorder. *Behavior Research and Therapy, 39*(11), 1277–1291.

Chambless, D. L., Caputo, G. C., Bright, P., & Gallagher, R. (1984). Assessment of fear of fear in agoraphobics: The body sensations questionnaire and the agoraphobic cognitions questionnaire. *Journal of Consulting and Clinical Psychology, 52*(6), 1090–1097. https://doi.apa.org/doi/10.1037/0022-006X.52.6.1090

Chambless, D. L., Caputo, G. C., Jasin, S. E., Gracely, E. J., & Williams, C. (1985). The mobility inventory for agoraphobia. *Behavior Research and Therapy, 23*(1), 35–44. https://doi.org/10.1016/0005-7967(85)90140-8

Craske, M. G., Kircanski, K., Zelikowsky, M., Mystkowski, J., Chowdhury, N., & Baker, A. (2008). Optimizing inhibitory learning during exposure therapy. *Behavior Research and Therapy, 46*(1), 5–27.

Craske, M. G., Hermans, D., & Vervliet, B. (2018). State-of-the-art and future directions for extinction as a translational model for fear and anxiety. *Philosophical Transactions of the Royal Society B: Biological Sciences, 373*(1742), 20170025. https://doi.org/10.1098/rstb.2017.0025

Ehlers, A., & Margraf, J. (1993). «Angst vor der Angst»: Ein neues Konzept in der Diagnostik der Angststörungen ["Fear of fear": A new concept in the assessment of anxiety disorders]. *Verhaltenstherapie, 3*(1), 14–24. https://doi.org/10.1159/000258732

Kühner, C., Bürger, C., Keller, F., & Hautzinger, M. (2007). Reliabilität und Validität des revidierten Beck-Depressionsinventars (BDI-II). Befunde aus deutschsprachigen Stichproben [Reliability and validity of the revised Beck Depression Inventory (BDI-II). Results from German samples]. *Der Nervenarzt, 78*(6), 651–656. https://doi.org/10.1007/s00115-006-2098-7

Margraf, J., & Schneider, S. (2013). *Panik: Angstanfälle und ihre Behandlung.* Springer.

Margraf, J., Schneider, S., Ehlers, A., DiNardo, P., & Barlow, D. (2013). *DIPS diagnostisches interview bei psychischen Störungen: Interviewleitfaden.* Springer.

McNally, R. J. (2002). Anxiety sensitivity and panic disorder. *Biological Psychiatry, 52*(10), 938–946. https://doi.org/10.1016/S0006-3223(02)01475-0

Mogg, K., & Bradley, B. P. (2016). Anxiety and attention to threat: Cognitive mechanisms and treatment with attention bias modification. *Behavior Research and Therapy, 87*, 76–108. https://doi.org/10.1016/j.brat.2016.08.001

Wegner, D. M. (1994). Ironic processes of mental control. *Psychological Review, 101*(1), 34. https://doi.org/10.1037/0033-295X.101.1.34

Eni S. Becker holds a position as chair of Clinical Psychology at Radboud University, The Netherlands. She is a trained psychotherapist, specializing in the treatment of anxiety disorders. She has published widely on the aetiology and treatment of anxiety disorders and affective disorders including several books on the treatment of Generalized Anxiety Disorder. Her research focuses on cognitive processes and their role in psychopathology. Recently, she has concentrated on how we can influence cognitive processes to benefit patients with the help of so-called Cognitive Bias Modification. Eni Becker is especially interested in bridging the gap between fundamental and applied research.

Index

© The Editor(s) (if applicable) and The Author(s), under exclusive license to
Springer Nature Switzerland AG 2023
M. L. Woud (ed.), *Interpretational Processing Biases in Emotional Psychopathology*,
CBT: Science Into Practice, https://doi.org/10.1007/978-3-031-23650-1